phonetics: the science of speech production

phonetics: the science of speech production

Second Edition

Ian R. A. MacKay, Ph.D.

Assistant Professor and Director of the Phonetics Laboratory,
Department of Linguistics, University of Ottawa, Ottawa, Ontario

A College-Hill Publication
Little, Brown and Company
Boston/Toronto/San Diego

Second Edition

Second Printing

Previous edition *Introducing Practical Phonetics*, copyright © 1978 by Little, Brown and Company (Inc.)

Library of Congress Catalog Card No. 86-45740

ISBN 0-316-54238-5

Printed in the United States of America

MV

Epigraphs are quoted from George Bernard Shaw, *On Language*. Abraham Tauber, editor. New York: Philosophical Library, 1963.

For

He was, I believe, not in the least an ill-natured man: very much the opposite, I should say; but he would not suffer fools gladly; and to him all scholars who were not rabid phoneticians were fools.

—George Bernard Shaw on Henry Sweet, the inspiration for the character Henry Higgins in his play *Pygmalion*, later the musical and movie *My Fair Lady*

But if the play makes the public aware that there are such people as phoneticians, and that they are among the most important people . . . , it will serve its turn.

—George Bernard Shaw on *Pygmalion*

Contents

Preface: to the phonetics instructor in communication disorders and linguistics programs

Phonetics: The Science of Speech Production is masquerading as the second edition of its predecessor, *Introducing Practical Phonetics*. In large measure, it is a new book, changed in content and format as well as title. I believe that I have retained those features that made the first edition popular while making comprehensive improvements to the text. All topics have been treated in greater depth. There are pedagogical innovations such as the boxed sections (see below) and the presentation of speech physiology as a function of the articulation of speech sounds. Certain topics are approached in a somewhat unorthodox manner where this will lead the student to insight and understanding, as in the section presenting certain aspects of speech in a nonsegmental way.

Numbered sections and boxed sections allow you to select and identify what you want your students to master, what you want them to read as background, and what you want to leave out of your course for reasons of time or your own theoretical orientation. As explained to the student in Chapter 1, the boxed sections contain somewhat more advanced material at the logical place in the text; the chapters may be read skipping these sections.

This new edition has also undergone a major restructuring. One point, perhaps, needs comment. Chapters 9 and 10 on physiology and acoustics have been included *after* the main part of the text rather than *before*, as in the first edition. These are topics that some instructors treat in great detail and others prefer to omit. Therefore, a brief introduction to the physiology of articulatory phonetics has been included at the appropriate place in Chapter 4. Placing Chapters 9 and 10 where they are has made possible an instructionally logical approach to these topics. However, these chapters are amenable to reordering if you wish.

I direct your attention to the following additional remarks applicable to your discipline.

A Note to Phonetics Instructors in Human Communication Disorders Programs

This book is an introduction to speech production with practical examples from clinical disorders and second language teaching. It comes from my experience teaching phonetics to speech pathology and audiology students and my dissatisfaction with the available textbooks. The wide adoption of the first edition in speech pathology programs and the encouragement and loyalty of many professors indicated that it filled a need.

The same general approach is maintained in the present volume. Indeed, additional practical examples have been included: for instance, a section on physical anomalies affecting speech production, mention of the Blom-Singer prosthesis for the laryngectomee, and the reference to Blissymbolics, to mention a few.

However, I have resisted suggestions that the book be turned into a therapy handbook. This is a book about *phonetics*, but one that will help the student of speech pathology see the relevance of the material he/she is studying. For example, in dealing with plosive articulation, I have mentioned the articulatory problems occasioned by cleft palate, velic deficiency, or poor velic control as in deaf speakers. Thus the student will understand the normal speech processes by reflecting on what happens when it goes wrong. It is hoped that the student thus recognizes, here as in other examples, that phonetic facts about normal speech processes are pregnant with implications for clinical applications.

A Note to Phonetics Instructors in Linguistics Programs

Many introductions to phonetics are written as if they were simply a pre-phonology course, selecting those details of articulatory and/or acoustic phonetics that support one particular approach to phonology. But the recent history of the discipline shows us that phonology is in a state of flux, with many cross-currents. One may cite not only various concrete versus abstract arguments, but a large number of different approaches: standard generative phonology, natural generative phonology, autosegmental phonology, metrical theory, lexical phonology, nonsegmental phonology, and so on. Even within the standard theory, the specifics of feature systems are often argued at length. This is not to trivialize the serious theoretical issues within phonology; to the contrary, it is to emphasize that the jury is still out with respect to the establishment of a definitive paradigm. For this reason, an introductory phonetics course ought to examine speech articulation and production beyond a simple rationalization of one set of distinctive features. Such a thorough approach supplies the student with sufficient phonetic knowledge to understand and evaluate current theory as well as other approaches that very well may gain currency in the near future. In short, it will produce better students of phonology.

Generally, phonetics is studied early in a linguistics program, and so the discussion of speech, language, and dialect (Chapter 2), written from a modern linguistic point of view, is a useful overview for the student. In fact, these sections are extensive enough that the book has been used in a number of "Linguistics 100" courses.

The treatment of writing systems, of non-English segments, of diachronic change, of phonetic phenomena (e.g., fundamental frequency, length, voice onset time, voice quality, etc.) whose phonological functioning is different in languages other than English, are all particularly useful to the student of linguistics, as are the many foreign-language examples.

As noted above, I have provided many examples at the appropriate points throughout the text of speech or language disorders and second language teaching. Such examples require no foreknowledge of communication disorders, and so, far from impeding the progress of the linguistics student, they render the text more interesting, alive, and relevant. Many of my undergraduate linguistics students express a fascination for these examples, a fascination which adds interest and immediacy to a subject some consider to be dry. These examples are not only pedagogically useful, but theoretically relevant as well: theoretical linguistics has recently become increasingly interested in such anomalous speech/language behavior as aphasia, reading disorders, spontaneous speech errors, and the like, as well as in first and second language acquisition, for what such processes can tell us about grammar and our models of it.

Examination Question Exchange

Phonetics instructors using this textbook and wishing to participate in an exchange of examination questions are invited to write on letterhead to the author: Ian MacKay, Ph.D., Phonetics Laboratory, Department of Linguistics, University of Ottawa, Ottawa, Ontario K1N 6N5 Canada.

I.M.

Acknowledgments

Many individuals have helped with this project. Some have provided inspiration, some information, some assistance of a concrete nature. All helped bring the project to fruition.

I would like to thank many individuals at Little, Brown for their support. Sarah Boardman originally took an interest in the book, and Joyce Connell and, before her, Barbara Ward have been most supportive as editors. Katherine Arnoldi, Senior Book Editor, shepherded the book through production with good sense and good humor. Thanks to Gretchen Dietz Denton for excellent copyediting (which means knowing better than the author when to fix the wording and when to leave well enough alone). Many others at Little, Brown, only some of whom I know by name, contributed to an excellent production.

I would like to thank Prof. Richard Kretschmer for the definition of language used in Chapter 2, though I should note that I have modified it for the pedagogical aims of the book. Dr. Paul Mercier provided the Chinese examples in Chapter 3 and elsewhere, and I would like to thank him and Szeto Yee-Kim for discussions of the examples of Chinese writing, which raised controversy far beyond their importance in the book.

Dr. Christine Futter and Prof. P.G. Patel furnished material on reading and writing disorders. Thanks to Patricia Balcom for bringing the citations from Shaw to my attention, and to Susan Wheeler for a number of Finnish examples. Thanks to Richard Green and Pamela Maser for furnishing information on a number of communicative disorders. Darlene LaCharité helped to assemble the exercises.

The graphics are primarily the work of Donald Desmarais, though there are illustrations by Lucie Gagnon and Gilles Morin as well. For struggling valiantly with the peculiarities of my handwriting and those of two different text editing programs, I would like to thank Susan Wheeler and Szeto Yee-Kim.

Régis Foré helped with the production of the spectrograms; Lori Schaefer provided a few of the speech samples.

The following individuals made constructive criticisms or contributions to the first edition: Prof. Joseph Agnello, Prof. Joseph Foster, Prof. Ernst Franke, Prof. Richard Kretschmer, Prof. Douglas Walker, and Prof. Louis Kelly. Prof. Agnello trusted me as his assistant to teach his introductory phonetics course, and thus it first came to my attention that a textbook with characteristics different from those available was needed. That led to the first edition of this book.

I would like to thank the many users and reviewers of the first edition who provided much encouragement. Equally, I would like to thank my own students, who have greatly influenced the final form of the book.

Naturally, none of those who gave me help or advice had any control over the final form of the text, and I am therefore responsible for any errors or omissions that may remain.

Preliminaries

Introduction

1

Objectives

To provide a very brief overview of phonetics.

To define special symbols and special uses of punctuation marks that appear in the book.

To discuss the format and philosophy of the book.

To give some advice and offer some cautionary remarks to the student wishing to master the material.

To indicate how the book relates to the educational objectives of students in communication disorders and in linguistics and to suggest how such students might approach the subject.

Phonetics is the study of speech sounds and their production. It is by its nature an interdisciplinary subject that involves principles and techniques from a number of independent areas of study.

The reason for its multifaceted character is to be found in the subject matter itself. Speech sounds are part of language, so some notions of language enter into phonetics. The act of speaking involves muscle movements of the various "organs of speech," so some notions of anatomy and physiology enter into its study. Principles of acoustics let us understand how the movements we make in speaking are translated into the particular sounds of language. Research into the phonetic aspects of speech uses experimental techniques from physiology, physics, and the social sciences. So it is easy to see that phoneticians rely on principles and methods from many fields, including linguistics, physiology, physics, the social sciences, and speech pathology.

However, the student of phonetics need know about only certain aspects of each of these disciplines, namely those that aid in an understanding of the processes involved in speech. So our explorations of physiology, linguistics, acoustics, etc., will be short side-trips that will lead back to our major theme, to introduce the reader to speech sounds and their production.

This first chapter has two objectives. First, it will present a very brief overview of phonetics. This will permit you, the reader, to approach the subsequent chapters with an overall perspective in mind. For organizational reasons a book must be divided into chapters, and it is sometimes easy in the middle of one chapter to lose sight of the forest for the trees. This is particularly true in phonetics, a field whose various subareas are so diverse. The survey given in this chapter should help you to keep sight of the forest and to see where what you are reading at a given moment fits into the general area of phonetics. The second objective of this chapter is to permit me, the author, to "editorialize,"—to give advice and to talk about the organization of the book and its pedagogic devices.

In reading the next section, keep in mind that each area mentioned will be examined in some detail later in the book. Your purpose at this point should be to gain a general overview rather than to understand the details.

1-1 Phonetics

What happens when a person talks?

There is, first of all, the step of **ideation,** the forming of an idea, the will to say something. The idea is transformed into a sentence or group of sentences (an **utterance**) in accordance with the speaker's knowledge of the rules of language. Vocabulary is selected, sentence structure is selected, grammatical adjustments are made (subject-verb agreement, etc.), and so on. The utterance is finally articulated.

The **articulation** of the utterance is a highly complex, minutely coordinated physical act. An airstream is created by the lungs, such that there is an airflow outward from the lungs, through the throat, and through the mouth and/or nose.

For many, but not all, speech sounds, the air passing through the **larynx** in the throat causes the vocal folds to vibrate. As they vibrate, they make a sound that is modified by the nose, throat, and mouth cavities.

Individual speech sounds are created by particular configurations of the vocal tract. That is, the "speech organs"—lips, tongue, velum, etc.—take up a particular posture or make a particular movement typical of a given speech sound. Speech sounds are classified and named for the type of movement that produces them and for their location in the vocal tract. The most basic classificatory distinction is between **vowels** and **consonants.**

Vowels are produced without obstruction in the vocal tract and almost always with the vocal folds vibrating. Consonants, on the other hand, are produced with some sort of obstruction to the airstream: it may be a total momentary blockage, as in the p-sound; it may involve a constriction through which the air must pass noisily, as in the f-sound; it may involve blocking the mouth but allowing air out through the nose, as in the m-sound; or it may involve some other sort of modification of the airstream. The vocal folds are vibrating for some consonants and not for others.

To recapitulate: Air moves out from the lungs, sometimes causing the vocal folds to vibrate, sometimes not. The speech organs in the oral area modify the airstream to create the various individual speech sounds.

The actual sound that is created by any given vocal tract configuration depends on any of several acoustic principles. In the case of the f-sound, for example, air is forced through a narrow opening, creating turbulence and noise, like steam escaping from a valve. All vowels and many consonants involve the acoustic principle of **resonance.** Resonance occurs when an air chamber like the vocal cavities emits a sound of a particular frequency or frequencies, depending on its size and shape, when supplied with acoustic energy. When the size and shape of the vocal cavities change—as happens when we talk—the particular frequencies change.

When we look closely at individual speech sounds in the context of an utterance, we find that they are modified by the sounds that surround them. For example, the l-sound in the word "lip" is different from the l-sound in "loop" or "full." So this "same" sound has in fact more than one pronunciation, depending on the surrounding sounds and its position in a word. Or to take an even more extreme case, What is the final sound of the word "phone"? An n-sound, of course. But in the expression "phone booth," many people, particularly in casual speech, pronounce the final sound of "phone" as an *m-sound:* They say "pho<u>m</u>e booth." Such modifications of sounds in context are the result of the dynamics of connected speech and will be the subject of a later chapter.

So far we have been examining individual speech sounds: the word "stop," for example, contains four individual sounds, or **segments.** But the entire word "stop" could be uttered as an order, barked out as a command, said meekly as a question, or given a neutral tone as simply a word in a list. These different utterances have *phonetic* differences, even though the word contains the same individual speech sounds in each. This kind of difference falls under the heading of **suprasegmental** aspects of speech, which we will examine in a later chapter, along with such things as **stress** (the difference between the verb "record" and the noun "record"). Grouped together, these phonetic features are called **suprasegmentals.**

We will also discuss the use of a special alphabet, the **phonetic alphabet,** to write down (or *transcribe*) speech sounds in an unambiguous way.

These, then, are the major areas of phonetics and the subjects of the rest of the book.

1-2 How to Use This Book

1-2.1 Symbols Used

Since this book is about phonetics, it deals with language. Since language is both the subject and the medium of the book, it is necessary to use special symbols and punctuation to clarify what is being discussed. For example, when reference is made to a word—say, *stop*—it may be the word's *spelling,* or its *meaning,* or its *sound* that is under scrutiny, and we must distinguish among these. Another reason for taking special care with symbols is that many letters of the phonetic alphabet look like ordinary letters of the Roman alphabet, so the interpretation of a written word can be open to misunderstanding. *Pot* as a regular spelling does not represent the same sound as /pot/ in the phonetic alphabet.

The following symbols are designed to clarify the text.

1. Slashes and square brackets: /kæt/, [pɑt]

Anything written between slashes or square brackets is written in the phonetic alphabet. Slashes and brackets are used differently—this difference will be discussed later—but for the moment let us say that between square brackets we find a very precise, detailed **phonetic transcription,** and between slashes we find a less detailed, broader transcription (called a **phonemic transcription**).

So you might see a sentence such as the following:

The words *phone booth* may be pronounced /fombuθ/ in casual speech.

By the way, the slash (/) is more correctly, but less commonly, called the *virgule.*

2. Double quotation marks: "cat", "pot"

Double quotation marks have been used to indicate *what a word sounds like.* The word has been written in its usual spelling instead of in the phonetic alphabet either to prevent distraction from the point at hand or because—in the early chapters—the phonetic alphabet has not yet been presented to the reader. Thus you might see a sentence like this:

The verb "record" is stressed on the second syllable, whereas the noun "record" is stressed on the first syllable.

3. Single quotation marks: 'cat', 'pot'

Single quotation marks indicate reference to the *meaning* of a word. They are generally used around the English meaning of a foreign word, or around a word from a dialect of English that many speakers are not familiar with. Thus you might see sentences like these:

The Scottish word "loch," meaning 'lake,' contains a velar fricative.

The anatomical term *trachea* comes from the Greek word for 'neck.'

4. Angle brackets: ⟨cat⟩, ⟨pot⟩

The angle brackets are used to specify a letter of the Roman alphabet (that is, our usual English alphabet, *not* the phonetic alphabet) or to specify a usual (*not* a phonetic) spelling. Many letters in these two alphabets have the same form, but not necessarily the same phonetic value, so we must be clear as to which way to interpret a letter. Thus you might see a sentence like this:

The ⟨t⟩ in "nation" represents the sound /š/, whereas the ⟨t⟩ in "fate" represents /t/.

5. The asterisk * :

The asterisk is used to indicate an incorrect, nonexistent, ungrammatical, or reconstructed form.

Thus you might see a sentence like this:

A sequence such as */sbɑt/ does not occur in English.

Other symbols should be familiar to you. *Italics* are used for foreign words, for emphasis, and to stress words as words (rather than their meaning or sound). When italics would not show up clearly, as when only a letter or two in a word are emphasized, underlining has been used instead (the vowel of "ski"). New terms are introduced with **bold type;** many of these terms are found in the glossary. Of course, quotation marks and square brackets are also used in the usual way as well as for the special purposes mentioned in this section.

1-3 Approaches to Phonetics

A student's success in and enjoyment of a particular course or subject depends in part upon his/her approach to the subject. In this section I would like to give a few words of advice and caution; the intent is to help you to get the most out of your study. Getting the most out of your study of phonetics means more than getting good marks. It also means learning about normal speech processes in enough depth to be useful in subsequent courses or in professional life (even though the relevance of the material is not always apparent at the time you are studying). And I would hope that getting the most out of phonetics means feeling some excitement about discovering the fascinating complexity of what happens when people talk.

1-3.1 About This Book

It is always hard for an author to know how much to put into a textbook. There is the necessity that the book be understandable to the student who is just beginning in a subject area. There is the hope that the book will remain a useful reference as the student progresses. There is the problem that the book will be used in different courses that do not all go into the subject in the same depth. And of course each instructor has his/her own idea about what is most important.

I have followed the "inclusion principle" in this book; that is, I have included material that I felt would be useful to at least some readers. It is likely that not all the information will be relevant to you in your first course. You will want to study in greatest depth those sections that your professor considers most central. The numbered sections make it easy for your professor to assign some sections and not others, or to assign a more superficial treatment of some than others.

Some of the information given is more advanced than a "bare-bones" basic phonetics course, but for the reasons just mentioned I felt it should be included. This material has been put in its logical place in the text but has been set apart by being enclosed by boxes. These sections can be skipped; in fact I recommend skipping them on your first reading.

A good deal of attention has been paid to making this book readable, interesting, and not too dry. I hope to share the sense of fun and excitement that I feel in studying speech processes. However, no textbook can be read like a novel; several readings and concentrated study will be necessary for mastery of the subject. I recommend that when you are assigned boxed sections to read, you ignore them on your first reading as you gain a broad understanding of the particular area. On the second and subsequent readings, you can then read these advanced sections (if they are assigned), integrating the new information into the general framework you have already assimilated. When using the book as a reference, after having completed a course, then the whole text, including the boxed sections, can be read as one continuous text.

Many of the footnotes found in the book contain information that can be treated like that found in the boxed sections. Other footnotes define terms or give the reader a cross-reference to another section of the book. Most give additional information or more detailed explanation than is felt necessary for the text.

1-4 A Few Words of Advice and Caution

1-4.1 Advice

This is a book about **phonetics**—speech sounds and their production. I recommend that you pronounce the examples *out loud*. Listen to yourself as you pronounce the examples, and train yourself to be a careful, analytical listener of your own and others' speech sounds. Concentrate not on what you think you *ought* to say but on what people really *do* say as they talk. The difference is often surprising. When we say words in isolation, when we are self-conscious about them, our pronunciation is often very different from actual, colloquial pronunciations. If asked how to pronounce the word "to," for example, you might say "too" (/tu/ in the phonetic alphabet). But in the context of the sentence "She went to the store," it would be most unnatural to pronounce "to" so fully; normally we would drop or reduce the vowel. We might represent this pronunciation as "t' " (/tə/ in the phonetic alphabet). Pay attention to real colloquial pronunciations, not idealized, artificial ones. Your first idea about how words are pronounced is very likely wrong. For example, if you pronounce "phone booth" in the way described earlier, you were probably unaware of it and inclined to deny the fact. More on this in Chapter 2.

Also pay attention to your own articulation of sounds when studying the pertinent sections of this book. Observe lip, jaw, and tongue movements, studying them with a mirror and a tongue depressor. Train yourself to pay attention to the sensory feedback you have from the inside of your mouth: Where is the tongue? Where is it touching the palate? You will learn a lot about articulatory phonetics this way; and, what is more, you will learn it not through rote memory, but because you feel it and understand it. I often notice my students during exams silently subvocalizing speech sounds to remind themselves of articulatory facts; understanding will be remembered long after memorized tables and charts are forgotten.

The chapter summaries, lists of objectives, and vocabulary lists accompanying each chapter are designed to help the serious student put the material into perspective, to verify his/her own understanding, and to test his/her memory of the important concepts introduced in the chapter. Of course, each individual student will find the way to use these features most productively in studying the material.

1-4.2 Caution

In the next chapter we will examine the question of dialect in some detail. For the moment, suffice it to say that English is pronounced differently in different places and by different people. As a result, no example words printed on a page can correctly represent the intended sounds for all speakers. The examples represent the most generalized type of North American speech and should be familiar to most Americans and Canadians from national television newscasters and other broadcasters. These examples will not be accurate reflections of speech in Britain, Australia, West Indian countries, or other English-speaking countries and will differ considerably from colloquial speech in many regions of the United States. Be aware of this fact as you read, and particularly so if your own speech differs considerably from the North American norm. Do not allow examples that differ from your speech to distract you from the principle being illustrated by the example.

It is also important to be wary of the technical terminology. There are three potential danger points here: inconsistent use of the terms by different persons, fine distinctions, and everyday words used in a specific sense. Unfortunately, phonetic terminology is not very well standardized; linguists, phoneticians, phonologists, speech scientists, and speech pathologists sometimes use different terms for the same thing or use the same term differently. For example, some speech pathology textbooks use the term *surd* for what is called *voiceless* in this book. The term *accent* is used by some where the term *stress* is used by others. This book will present a consistent set of terms, generally the ones most commonly used, although my own preferences show from time to time. Occasionally your professor may suggest a different term from the one used here.

Fine distinctions are sometimes made in phonetic terminology. The words *close* and *closed*, for example, are both technical terms, differing greatly in meaning.

And certain words are familiar ones given a specific precise meaning. Words like *vowel*, *intonation*, *grammar*, and others have special senses in phonetics, and their technical meaning should not be confused with their general everyday usage. Whenever a term is given in **bold type** or *italic*, pay attention to the specialized sense of the word, particularly if it is a common, everyday word you think you already know.

I have dealt with these problems of terminology by making consistent use of common terms and by giving explanatory notes where confusion is likely. You would benefit from paying careful attention to the terms and their meanings, particularly those that *seem* familiar, and by making use of the glossary when necessary.

Finally, be careful of the way you write the letters of the phonetic alphabet. The precise form of these letters is more important than in our everyday use of the alphabet. Personal modifications to the shape of letters are a way of showing our individuality as we write but may be just plain wrong in the phonetic alphabet.

1-4.3 Communication Disorders and Linguistics

This book is written as a *general introduction to the study of phonetics*, to be used by students of communication disorders (speech pathology, deaf education, etc.) as well as by students of linguistics and by anyone else taking a course in phonetics. I have chosen examples and have organized the material in such a way that it will be useful to students enrolled in **speech pathology** programs or interested in second language teaching. However, this is a *phonetics* book, not a book about clinical practice. It is my belief that readers intending to pursue clinical or pedagogical (second-language teaching) careers will benefit from a thorough grounding in phonetics, because it will give them an understanding of both normal and anomalous speech processes. Many pathological conditions of speech will therefore be mentioned where relevant, and their phonetic effects will be discussed, but principles of clinical practice will be left for other books.

Students of **linguistics** using this book in their phonetics course should not find allusions to abnormal speech processes distracting. Many linguists are studying such problems as aphasia, slips of the tongue, and second-language competence to see what they reveal about normal language processes, in order to contribute to the theory of language. (The ways in which a system—such as language—breaks down help us to understand how a system works normally.) In any case, the examples from speech pathology do not require prior knowledge of the subject and should serve to help you understand and remember the facts about general phonetics.

Finally, no one has solved the problem of the neutral third person pronoun, although most of us do not especially like the use of *he* in the sense of 'he or she.' I have used *he/she*, or, where that became too heavy, simply *he*. Not everyone will be satisfied with this solution, but I hope no one will take offense.

Language

2

Objectives

To stress the relatedness of phonetics to language in general.

To distinguish speech from language.

To discuss dialect, register, standards of correctness, and grammaticality.

To distinguish phonemics from phonetics.

To demonstrate that speaking a language often gives us misleading intuitions about the sounds of that language.

Phonetics, as we have said, is the study of speech sounds. Speech is a manifestation of language, and a study of speech sounds cannot be divorced entirely from language. So we will take a brief excursion into the realm of language.

2-1 Language

The word *language* has two main senses of interest to us here. First, it refers to specific, individual linguistic[1] systems: English is a language, as are Spanish, French, Quechua, Blackfoot, Igbo, and Basque. In this sense *language* is a count noun, having a plural: you have just read a list of seven language<u>s</u>. But there is a second, more abstract sense, which has no plural. Speakers of all the languages just named, and another 3000 or so besides, share a human ability called *language*.

"What is language like?" is a meaningful question, even when the answer says nothing specifically about English that would distinguish it from Spanish or Quechua. Many features are characteristic of language in general, even though many other features are highly variable from one language to another.

When we try to define language, we are led into pitfalls, but let us attempt a definition:

> Language is an arbitrary set of symbolic relationships, systematic in nature, mutually agreed upon by a speech community, to designate experience.

Let us take this definition piece by piece and see what it reveals about language.

This is a definition of *language*, not of speech nor of any individual language.

Language is *arbitrary*, at least initially. An English word such as *sun* has no iconic or absolute logical relationship to what it designates, and it could just as well be replaced with another word. This is a notion that we may easily overlook, since our native language is so strongly a part of our consciousness: Ask a child if you could call the sun the *moon* and the moon the *sun*, and he will probably reply, "No." "Why not?" "Because the sun shines in the day and the moon at night." The sun's qualities are, to the child, irrevocably tied up in the term. There is a story, probably apocryphal, of a hog farmer asked why pigs were called *pigs*. "Pigs is rightly named," he replied, "just look at 'em and see for yourself." The classical Greek philosophers believed that the Greek words were the perfect embodiment of what they represented, and that words of other languages were imperfect attempts at such embodiment. But we realize that the arbitrary selection of words and structures in English is no more or less logical than that of classical Greek or French or Russian.

Of course language is not arbitrary, in that we must take it as it is: we cannot do as Humpty Dumpty did in *Alice in Wonderland*, making words mean whatever he wanted. This brings us to the next part of the definition, namely that individual languages contain a *set* or prescribed number of items *mutually agreed upon by a speech community*. If a person were to write, "The woffer twarked the rimp," the reader would not understand the message, since most of the vocabulary items used are outside the set of English words. But while the set of items in one speech community at one time is finite, it changes with dialect and over time. Virtually all of this line from the Lord's Prayer in Old English is unrecognizable to us today:

> Ūrne gedæghwāmlīcan hlāf syle ūs tō dæg.

("Give us this day our daily bread.") And if an Australian announced that he was going to "syphon the python," most North Americans would not realize that he intended to urinate. The Australian belongs to a different speech community, which has agreed upon a somewhat different set of items from most other speakers of English. Likewise, the speakers of Old English formed a different speech community from those of Modern English.

Language is made up of *symbolic relationships*. Such symbolic relationships exist between words and things that we experience. The word *dog*, for example, *symbolizes* a certain class of quadruped, and the expression "I haven't got a red cent" *symbolizes* a certain financial state. Such symbols can be extended to represent new experiences. They are not situationally bound, and they can be used in creative ways. And they are culturally trans-

[1] **Linguistic** is used as the adjective of *language;* the structure of language is thus **linguistic structure;** human competence with language is **linguistic competence.**

mitted and learned; a cry of pain or gasp of surprise, by contrast, are at least partially reflexive.

Language is *systematic in nature.* This is perhaps the most characteristic aspect of human language, the one aspect to which the science of linguistics devotes most of its attention. The systematic nature of language can be seen in the "nonsense" sentence given above: "The woffer twarked the rimp." While the words are unfamiliar, the *structure* or *system* is familiar. (It is familiar in large measure because of the use of the English word *the* and the use of the English past tense ending *-ed.*) Clearly the woffer—whatever it is—did something to the rimp. The rimp did not do anything to the woffer, and we can tell that the action was in the past. We recognize the structural similarity between this sentence and, for example, "The dog attacked the cat" and "The paradox puzzled the philosopher." Our knowledge of the system is also shown by the fact that we can transform "The woffer twarked the rimp" into "The rimp was twarked by the woffer," and we know that the meaning of the sentence—whatever it is—is preserved despite the transformation from active to passive voice.

Finally, language *designates experience,* be it real or imagined: that is, *language has meaning.* But not necessarily truth, of course. "The ancients believed the earth to be the center of the universe" has a certain historical veracity. The cartoon stereotype of a schizophrenic who says, "I am Napoleon Bonaparte" is designating his experience; the utterance has meaning, despite the fact that to others the claim is demonstrably false.

2-1.1 Language Structure

A simple example will demonstrate that the number of English sentences is infinite. That is, no complete list of English sentences could ever be compiled. It is easy to disprove the completeness of any alleged "complete" list of English sentences: any sentence in such a list[2] could be transformed into another sentence by adding "Bertha says that . . ." at the beginning. While most sentences thus generated would be pretty silly, they would be grammatical English sentences, and so the point remains: No list of sentences could be complete, because I (or you) could always come up with another sentence not on the list.

This may seem an obvious point to make, but it has profound implications for a study of language. That is, you know English, not because you know a list of possible English sentences, but *because you know the systematic ways in which English structure works.* In other words, you know the code. Knowing the code permits you to produce and understand English sentences you have never heard or seen before. (By *produce* I mean 'convert ideas into understandable English sentences,' and by *understand* I mean 'convert sentences heard or read into ideas.') Indeed, when you think about it, almost every sentence you say or hear is a novel one—one that is new to you. (The obvious exceptions are common sentences used in social interaction: "Hello, how are you?" "Cold enough for you?" "How are the kids?" "Hope you're feeling better soon," and so on.)

Knowing a language, then, means knowing the "rules of the game": the rules that tell you how words go together to say what you mean to say, and what words mean when they're put together in a certain way. It also permits you to know when a sentence does not conform to those rules, that is, when a sentence is ungrammatical.

You know, for example, that—unless the copy-editor was asleep on the job—every sentence you have read so far in this book is grammatical. But you immediately know that the following group of words is not an English sentence, that it is ungrammatical:

*Went morning to this store the Mary.

This "sentence" just does not conform to the **rules** of English (although I have chosen words that could be rearranged to form a meaningful sentence).

The term **rule** as just used here has a special sense to linguists. They describe the structure of a language as being **rule-governed;** that is, the facts about language structure can be listed explicitly as a series of *rules.*

In elementary school you probably learned some so-called rules of grammar, such as "Don't say *ain't,*" "Don't use double negatives," "Don't split infinitives." These are really admonitions or

[2] In the indicative mood—i.e., not a question or command.

prescriptions about linguistic etiquette or "how to talk nicely." *They have little to do with grammar, and they are NOT the type of rule we are discussing here.*

The rules we are referring to are the internal, unconscious rules of grammar, most of which you knew before you ever went to school or saw a grammar teacher. For example, what is the negative of the sentence "I like cheese"? The answer, of course, is "I do not like cheese" (or, colloquially, "I don't like cheese"). Where did the verb *do* come from in the negative sentence? Well, there is a rule that tells you to construct the negative of *to like* that way. It is unlikely that—unless English is a foreign language to you—you ever were aware of the fact that you insert the verb *do* in most negative and interrogative sentences.

Or take the sentence "The little boy was playing with three big round red rubber balls." You will agree that this is a good sentence but that *"The little boy was playing with big red three rubber round balls" is not a good sentence. There are five words—*three, big, round, red,* and *rubber*—modifying *balls* in this sentence. There are 120 different orders that five words can be put into, *yet only one is correct.*[3] Adjective order is strictly rule-governed in English. In fact, the rules governing the order of adjectives are quite complex and involve categories of number, size, shape, color, and composition as well as a number of other categories that do not figure in our example. I doubt that the teacher who told you "Don't say *ain't*" ever mentioned the rules governing adjective order.[4] This is because you knew them before you went to school. That is true of most of the rules of grammar—you learned them from hearing English being used, not because someone taught them to you.

[3]Some speakers of English would accept more than one of these orders as correct. However, all would agree that far fewer than the 120 potential orders of these five words are acceptable. The point remains that English adjective order is strictly rule-governed, and that such rules do not usually find their way into "grammar" books.

[4]Essentially the "rules" of a grammar teacher are those expressions that are used "wrongly" (i.e., differently) by many speakers. Where the grammar teacher does not mention a rule, that is not because there are no rules, but rather because nearly everyone agrees on their use. Since most of us are in agreement over most rules of grammar—we understand each other, after all—most rules of grammar are never mentioned by anyone, *but they are used by everyone.*

Besides the use of the verb *do* in most negative and interrogative sentences, and the order of adjectives, we could mention the rules of tense selection, plural formation, word-building, and so on and so on. While no one has ever written a complete grammar of English, it is apparent that it would contain a very, very large number of rules. Of course that number is finite, as is the number of words in the vocabulary (the **lexicon,** as linguists call it). But this finite set of rules and finite lexicon produce an infinity of sentences.

The rules of a language, taken all together, form what is called the **grammar** of a language. The grammar could also be described as the *knowledge* of a language that a person has, or his/her **linguistic competence.**

When you studied "grammar" in school, the word probably had a different sense, as already noted: namely, adhering to a particular form of English that is socially acceptable. In other words, you were learning *linguistic etiquette.* But as we are using the term, there is no such thing as "bad" grammar; there is just grammar. Everyone has a grammar of his native language in his/her head, although each person's grammar is a little different. And some people's grammar is more socially acceptable than others' (more on this later in Section 2-3).

In this sense grammar is like gravity; it simply *exists.* Grammar exists in the head of all people who can speak any language, whether they have studied it formally or not. Grammar existed long before there were grammarians. The "rules" of grammar, as we are using the term, are like the "laws" of gravity discovered by physicists. Laws of physics simply state what gravity has always done (and what gravity will continue to do, whether or not anyone is interested in analyzing it). Thus these grammar rules are purely **descriptive.** But the term *grammar* often suggests another type of rule: the grammarian's edict or the schoolteacher's admonition ("Don't say *ain't*"). Such rules are termed **prescriptive,** since they tell people what they *should* do (of course, there is no analogue to the prescriptive rule in physics; no physicist presumes to tell gravity what it ought to do!). The prescriptive sense of the term *grammar rules* is not used in this book.

Any individual who speaks a language has a

grammar—that is, a set of rules—in his head that is infinitely more complex and detailed than the written grammar found in any book.[5]

A grammar is what permits the encoding of meanings or ideas into utterances as one speaks. It is what permits the decoding of utterances back into meanings as one listens to speech. Grammar is thus what *mediates* between *meaning* (thoughts in the brain) and *utterance* (speech or written language), as shown schematically below.

utterances ↔ grammar ↔ ideas/meanings.

In this section, I have tried to distinguish between two senses of the word *grammar:* (1) (the meaning you were probably familiar with) a list of admonitions about what is right or wrong in language, what linguists call *prescriptive grammar;* and (2) a set of statements explaining how a given language encodes meaning into utterances. We noted that the second sense is very important, since *all* forms of language have structure, even those forms that grammarians do not like. We noted that each statement in a grammar is called a *rule,* but that this is not to suggest what you *should* or *should not* do, but rather, how a given language is structured. The examples we looked at of adjective ordering and negative verb forms showed that language is highly structured, even in those areas where prescriptive grammarians have no axe to grind.

Let us take one more example to make this point clear. Consider the following English phrases:

1. a. That car has four *doors.*
   b. It is a four-*door* car.
2. a. That canoe holds up to three *men.*
   b. It is a three-*man* canoe.
3. a. That cake is made with *carrots.*
   b. It is a *carrot* cake.
4. a. That man is six *feet* tall.
   b. He is a six-*foot* man.

Notice that the italicized words in the *a* sentences are plural—*doors, men, carrots, feet*—whereas in the *b* sentences they are singular—*door, man, carrot, foot.* Why do we make these words, obviously plural in sense, singular in form? That is, if a car has four *doors,* why don't we call it a four-*doors* car? Indeed, many speakers to whom English is a second language make this very mistake. It is not logical or sensible to make *door* singular, but English happens to work that way. Slightly oversimplified, the rule can be stated this way: When a noun is used as an adjective, it is singular in form, whether or not it is plural in meaning.

The point to note is that *even speakers who have not the slightest idea what an adjective is, or what a noun is, follow this rule.* The rule was learned by each speaker of English as a child and does not depend on any explicit knowledge of "grammar" (in the traditional sense) or on any knowledge of prescriptive grammar, and certainly was not learned from a "grammar" teacher. Language is highly structured whether we notice it or not. And a grammar *rule* does not need to be in any book for us to follow it (in fact, the rules that we all follow often don't find their way into "grammar" books).

To find more examples of the wonderful complexity of English—thousands of things you know without knowing you know them—look in any book of English "grammar" written for the foreign learner.

2-2 Speech and Language

In the preceding section, the notion of *language* was introduced. Language can be described in a *grammar,* which is made up of many rules. Russian and English, for example, have different grammars, although there is much that is common between them. This is due in part to the fact that both Russian and English are natural human languages and thus share many characteristics; but they are also related languages, and thus have more features alike than, say, English and Quechua.[6]

When we think of language, or more particularly a specific language such as English, we are inclined to think of the written form. This is be-

[5] Probably the most complete written grammar of English is that written by Otto Jespersen [1949], a Dane. It fills seven volumes, yet it is far from complete.

[6] I should perhaps mention that Quechua is a South American Indian language spoken by those tribes formerly dominant in the Inca empire.

cause of the emphasis that our society places on literacy and the written word. However, writing is just one manifestation of linguistic ability, and not the most usual one at that. Language, as we noted, is a *knowledge* or *competence* possessed by an individual. That knowledge can be *realized* or *manifested* in writing or in speaking. (The hearing-impaired individual using sign language is realizing his linguistic ability through signing.)

This is a book about *phonetics*—speech sounds—and in this context it should be emphasized that *speech* is the most usual manifestation of language. While that may be obvious, we are an educated literate society, and we have a mind-set that leads us to think of language in terms of the written word rather than in terms of everyday, colloquial speech. To overcome this mind-set, let us take a few paragraphs to look at the importance of speech.

2-2.1 Speech

Human beings communicate with one another primarily by speech, and speech brings human beings closer together than one might imagine. Speech sounds travel through the air at the rate of about 1100 feet per second, whereas impulses travel along nerve pathways in the body at a rate of less than 200 feet per second. The time it takes for a spoken word to be heard and understood by a listener may be shorter than the time it takes for a neural message to travel from the toe to the brain. In this sense, speech brings a person closer to the mind of another than he is to parts of his own body!

For most of the time that humans have been on this earth, writing has been unknown. Only in very recent years have large populations been able to read and write. In many countries today there are relatively few literate people; even in "civilized" countries such as the United States and Canada illiteracy is rampant. Only one country in the world, Iceland, claims 100% literacy among its normal adult population. In the world today as many as 3000 languages are spoken, but only a few hundred of these have a standardized, commonly used writing system.

A casual examination of our own habits tells us a great deal about the relative roles of speech and writing. Most people find writing quite difficult, even a short term paper or a short letter. Few of us, though, are often at a loss for words. The letter home that did not get beyond the first paragraph easily turns into a long telephone conversation. Talking just comes naturally to us, and our thoughts are expressed more easily in speech than in writing.

Not only is speech a more natural way of expressing thoughts than writing, it is also the chief means by which most of us secure information from others. This truth may be obscured—particularly for students, academics, and professionals—by the fact that we tend to obtain information of a scholarly or learned nature from written sources, and these sources somehow seem more "important" than casual daily conversation. But it remains true that nearly everyone receives more information from hearing words than from reading words. For example, despite the proliferation of newspapers and newsmagazines, most of us know more about current events through television, radio, and conversation than through reading.

Speech is often easier to understand than the written word, and speech and writing may complement one another. In taking courses, you listen to lectures and read your textbooks. The lectures serve in part to help you to understand the texts. It is a common experience to discover that after you have heard an author speak on a topic, his books or articles are easier to read.

To take another example, the blind, paraplegics, and amputees generally socialize in a relatively normal way, while the severely hearing impaired tend not to socialize with the population at large.

In short, speech is our primary means of communication, whether for art or commerce, education or entertainment. The individual who is handicapped in speech is at a great disadvantage in society. Speech is taken for granted to such a degree by most people that there are often violently strong—although of course unwarranted—prejudices against verbally handicapped people; they may be treated as if they were, at best, a little stupid and, at worst, freaks.

Speech is not only extremely important culturally to us, it is what sets us apart from our fellow creatures on this planet. Biological species are often named for a distinctive characteristic. One prehistoric man is called *Homo erectus*, stressing the erect walking posture that separated him from other primates. Modern man is classified as *Homo sapiens*, 'thinking man,' but it has been suggested that a better name might be *Homo loquens*, 'talking man,' stressing our linguistic faculty.[7]

2-3 Dialect and Register

2-3.1 Dialect

One aspect of language that is immediately apparent to all people, whether they deal professionally with language or not, is the fact that not everyone speaks the same way, even those who supposedly speak the "same" language. The English speak differently from the Americans; the Mexicans speak differently from the Spanish. And yet the concept of "the English language" or "the Spanish language" has some validity, even though these terms refer to a variable entity. The term **dialect** is used to refer to this variability. Dialect is a concept that is often misunderstood and is often approached in an emotional way. We should therefore examine the facts of dialect variability, in order to understand it comprehensively and objectively.

The first important point to consider is that *living languages change over time*. This is a simple fact that cannot be denied: the force of change cannot be resisted (although many purists and traditionalists would like to put a stop to it). You were shown earlier (Section 2-1) a sentence of Old English (the standard form of language spoken in England between 700 and 1100 A.D.). Like virtually any sentence of Old English, it is quite unrecognizable to the uninitiated: not only is it incomprehensible, it does not even look like English.

Middle English looks more familiar but is hard to understand. A few lines from Chaucer's *Canterbury Tales* will make the point (this was written about 1390):

Whan that Aprille with hise shoures soote
The droghte of March hath perced to the roote
And bathed euery veyne in swich licour
Of which vertu engendred is the flour

It is not immediately apparent that this means something like "When the sweet showers of April have banished the dryness of March and bathed every plant with moisture that gives rise to flowers." These examples show that English has changed fundamentally over the past millennium.

To take another example: The Roman troops who invaded and conquered much of Europe about 2000 years ago spoke Vulgar Latin, the everyday language of the Romans. They took this language with them, and it displaced the local language in most of the conquered lands. But of course the modern-day French, Spanish, Portuguese, Italians, and Romanians do not now speak Vulgar Latin; they speak French, Spanish, Portuguese, and so on. The original language has changed or evolved into the modern languages.

Since the example of Latin has been brought up, it should be noted that while living languages all change, dead ones don't. As soon as no one *grows up* speaking a language—that is, as soon as it is no one's native language—that language is "dead." Usually such a language simply ceases to exist, particularly if there are no written records. But if there are written records, or if there is some religious or ritualistic reason for preserving the language, it may remain unchanged virtually indefinitely. Classical Latin (a somewhat artificial creation used for scholarship and oratory) has been preserved in this manner due to the abundance of written records. It has been used in a religious context and until a century ago was the international language of scholarship in the West.[8]

Change in living language is inevitable, but its speed depends on a number of factors. Periods of great social change and the mixing of cultural groups leads to faster language change. Social stability and isolation lead to slower language

[7] Pulgram [1970, p. 310], states: "Clearly man's faculty of speech too is a function of the superior cerebral equipment that evolution has bestowed upon him. *Homo loquens* is therefore no less suitable a name for the species than is *Homo sapiens*." One book on language (Fry, [1977]) goes by the title *Homo Loquens*.

[8] Note that certain archaic Middle English forms have similarly been preserved in a religious context. Nobody uses such forms as *thou* for *you*, *brethren* for *brothers*, or *goeth* for *goes* in everyday speech—these forms are now archaic—but they are frequently used in religious parlance.

change. For example, let us compare the last thousand years of English history to that of Iceland during the same period. England was invaded and settled by both Vikings and the Normans, and it colonized much of the world and engaged in much military conflict. Iceland, by contrast, has been isolated and stable. Thousand-year-old English looks like gibberish to us and takes as much effort to learn as German. On the other hand, a modern-day schoolchild in Iceland can read a 1000-year-old document in Old Icelandic without a great deal of difficulty.

The migration of a group of people to a new location usually leads to slower language change in the group that moved than in the one that stayed home, although *either* group may preserve words or expressions no longer used by the other.

But, quickly or slowly, living languages change over time.

The second point to consider in understanding dialect diversity is that *when groups of people are isolated from one another, language change takes a different direction in each of the two groups.* Let us imagine taking a group of people who speak the same language—a **speech community,** as it is called—and separating it into two groups that are kept separate. The language within each of the new groups would change, but since there are many possible ways in which a language can change, it would be most surprising if the language within each new speech community changed in exactly the same way. So the language becomes different within the two groups, and separate dialects develop.

In the modern world it is perhaps hard for us to imagine the isolation of two groups—we can keep in touch by telephone and through common communication media such as radio, television, and recordings. But we must remember that these are very recent developments, and that the current dialect diversity developed when a short geographic distance was a great impediment to communication.

Regional variation in speech habits is apparent in all countries. Within the United States, for example, there are evident differences between the South, the Northeast, the Midwest, and so on.

But the separation of groups can also be based on other social factors. In some societies religious affiliations may be so powerful as to separate groups of people in close geographical proximity.[9] In some societies there are great differences between the ways the members of each sex talk. (Such differences are small but noticeable in English; for example, male speech often contains more profanity than female speech, although this is by no means a hard and fast rule. Usually female speech contains more questions and tag questions than male speech.) Profession may separate groups, particularly if the work is secretive; underworld slang, for example, is not understandable to most of us. An example of legitimate differences along professional lines is that the words "centimeter" and "respiratory" are generally pronounced differently by medical professionals than by members of the public at large ("SENT-i-meter" and "RESP-ir-a-tory" by the general population; "SONT-i-meter" and "re-SPIRE-a-tory" by health professionals). In multiracial societies where members of the same race tend to interact only with each other, dialect differences will develop along racial lines. Many countries have strong barriers based on socioeconomic group or class, and members of these different classes speak differently.

Let us look at an example of the development of dialect differences created primarily by geographic and political separation. Two hundred fifty to three hundred years ago, general British English and general American English were more similar than they are today. For example, the word *lieutenant* was pronounced "left-tenant" on both sides of the Atlantic; George Washington pronounced it that way. However, the American pronunciation has changed, and the word is not pronounced the same way in the United States as it is in other English-speaking countries. The word *whilst* used to be equally common in the United States and Britain; now it is an ordinary word in British speech but a rare word in American speech.

In a preceding boxed section, it was noted that a language taken to a new location by a migrating group tends to remain more conservative (that is to say, it changes less) than the language that stays

[9]For example, Hindi and Hindustani (or Urdu) are closely related, largely mutually intelligible languages spoken in overlapping geographical areas of India. Hindi is spoken by Hindus and Hindustani by Moslems.

behind in the original location. Again let us compare British and American English, this time looking at some general aspects of pronunciation in light of this tendency.

A distinction between "wh" and "w," as between "which" and "witch" and between "whether" and "weather," was once the norm in English. This distinction is maintained in many areas of the United States, and making the distinction is considered a mark of good speech to many educated Americans. In Britain the speech of the educated no longer makes this distinction. Standard American English has maintained a feature now lost in standard British English.

To take another example, all dialects of English used to have postvocalic r-sounds, that is, the r-sound following vowels in such words as "for," "part," "word," and "cleared." Standard American has retained this feature (as have Scottish, Irish, and Canadian English, among others), whereas standard British has lost it. Once again, American English has preserved a feature now archaic in England, or confined to regional or nonstandard dialects. (Those areas in the United States that have lost postvocalic r-sounds are those areas that had late contact with English traders in colonial times—namely, port cities on the eastern seaboard and the south.)

Vocabularies that have grown up since the separation of the two peoples tend to show the greatest differences. The automobile industry has been strong but separate in the U.S. and England, so many differences exist in vocabulary: *wing* corresponds to *fender*, *gearbox* to *transmission*, *transmission* to *drivetrain*, and so on. An English motorist might say:

> After driving for a couple of hours down the dual carriageway, going under flyovers, being passed by enormous lorries, I decided that at the next lay-by I would pull off the road, get my picnic out of the boot and look under the bonnet to check the fluid level of the windscreen washer.

whereas a North American might say:

> After driving for a couple of hours on the expressway/turnpike/freeway, going under underpasses and being passed by semis, I decided to pull off at the next rest area, get my picnic out of the trunk, and look under the hood to check the windshield washer fluid.

Differences exist *within* countries as well as *between* countries. We have all experienced dialect differences in our everyday living; some people say *pail* where others say *bucket*, some say *sofa* where others say *couch*, and so on.

As we have seen, dialect differences develop because languages change; and when people are separated, the direction of change is divergent. At this point it would be well to clear up a couple of possible misunderstandings. First, our statements about dialect might be construed as supporting an idea that language purists try to promote: namely, that there was once a beautiful, "pure," homogeneous English (or other) language, but then people messed it up by talking badly, and now we have all these awful dialects. The truth is, there *never* was an English that didn't have dialects. *All* languages, unless spoken by only a handful of speakers, *all* have dialects at *all* times in their history. Indeed, it could be argued that there is less dialect variation now than in the past, because mass communication is a great homogenizer.

The second possible misunderstanding is to think that dialect differences involve only vocabulary. The examples given so far have nearly all concerned lexical differences, since such examples are easiest to present. But dialect differences involve any aspect of language: pronunciation, the lexicon, syntax (i.e., how words go together to make sentences), morphology (the building of words from smaller meaningful units), common expressions, and so on. Let us look at a few examples.

1. Pronunciation. "Sumach" is pronounced with "Sue" (/su/) or "shoe" (/šu/) as a first syllable; "creek" may be pronounced to rhyme with "leak" or "lick"; the ⟨r⟩ in such words as "car" and "park" may or may not be pronounced.

2. Syntax. In some dialects, a sentence like "He sick" is the normal equivalent of the more standard "He is sick." In some dialects, it would be normal to say "He's the man bought me a drink," whereas the more standard form would be "He's the man that/who bought me a drink." In another dialect, one might hear, "He's the man what bought me a drink."

3. Morphology. Even though the word *marathon* comes from the name of a Greek city, and the

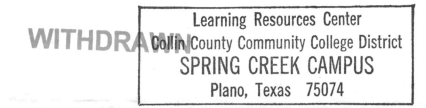

parts *mar* and *athon* have no meaning in themselves, in colloquial English *-athon* means a 'test of endurance,' giving rise to words like *dance-athon, drink-athon,* and *walk-athon.* Most of these words are not part of the standard dialect, although they may become so.

Another example: the word *funnily,* as in the expression "funnily enough," has been formed from the word *funny* by the normal process of forming adverbs from adjectives. This word is common in American speech and is recorded in some American dictionaries but is not listed in British dictionaries.

4. Common expressions. In some places, instead of saying "You're welcome" when someone thanks them, people say "Please." In other places the response to "Thank you" is "uh-huh."

In fact, dialects differ in all of the ways that languages do. The longer the separation between groups, the greater the number of differences that appear. Eventually mutual intelligibility is lost; that is, speakers of the two dialects can no longer communicate. You might think that when mutual intelligibility is lost, it is time to start calling the two dialects *languages.* However, political criteria as often as linguistic ones come into play in choosing whether to call two forms of expression *languages* or *dialects.* For example, Norwegian and Swedish are mutually intelligible and are as similar as some dialects of English. Yet for reasons of national pride the Norwegians call their speech *Norwegian,* and the Swedes call theirs *Swedish.*[10] In a similar way, many Americans call their language *American* rather than *English.* At the other end of the scale, many so-called dialects of Chinese are as different from one another as English and German. But they are called "dialects," not different languages, because the government wishes to stress the political unity of the country.

[10] Of course, *Norwegian* and *Swedish* are the English names for these languages. In the countries in question the situation is complicated by the fact that there are two major dialects of Norwegian: *Nynorsk* and *Bokmål* or *Riksmål.* Additionally, both languages have much dialect variation. But the point remains: no Norwegian would identify his language as *Swedish* or vice versa, even though Norwegian and Swedish are very similar.

2-3.2 Register

Related to the issue of dialect, in that it involves language variation, but a separate issue nonetheless, is the phenomenon of register. The **register** of language involves the manner in which the language is used, as determined by the situation. It is primarily a *social* matter, the correct register being chosen to fit the social situation.

For example, the type of language you would use in addressing a head of state, the President or Queen, is different from that you would use in chatting with the letter carrier at your front door. The type of language you would use as the applicant during a job interview differs from that you would use in addressing a persistent and irritating panhandler on the street. And the language you would be expected to use as a job applicant would vary according to the type of job you are seeking.

Two points to note: First, both *spoken* and *written* language have a range of registers, although the most casual of registers are rarely written and the most formal of registers are rarely spoken (except those used in addressing persons of high rank). Second, while register is determined largely by social criteria, *social* is defined broadly and does not necessarily imply the presence of two or more individuals together. I, the writer of this book, have a certain social interaction with you, the reader, that determines to some degree the type of language I choose and the type of language the publisher accepts.

Joos [1967] identifies five registers, to which he attaches a number of labels:

1. genteel/frozen
2. puristic/formal
3. consultative/standard
4. casual/provincial
5. intimate/popular

While these labels are convenient for noting the range of registers in English, they are not to be interpreted as being precisely defined and mutually exclusive categories. And to these five registers Finocchiaro and Brumfit [1983] have introduced another, which they label **tentative,** a register used to avoid verbal conflict or embarrassment.

The term **frozen** (number 1 in the preceding list) refers to linguistic forms that perhaps were current once but that have fallen into disuse except under certain circumstances. Generally these are the most formal of circumstances. For example, a formal greeting on being introduced is "How do you do." It is frozen in the sense that *How do you do?* is no longer a current way to say "How are you?" any more than *Goes he not there?* is a current form of "Isn't he going there?" (Notice that "How do you do" is often punctuated without a question mark and is usually said without a questioning intonation: It is a frozen form, or fossil, not analyzed for meaning by contemporary speakers.)

Many readers of this book probably never say "How do you do," choosing from a range of less formal greetings:

It's a pleasure.
I'm pleased to meet you.
I've heard a lot about you.
Pleased t' meet ya.
Howdy (a reduced form of "how do you do")
Hi

Similarly, an offer of coffee would be phrased differently depending upon the social relationship between the individuals:

Would you care for a cup of coffee?
Would you like a cup of coffee?
Wouja lika cuppa coffee?
D'ya wan' some coffee?
Coffee?
There's coffee out in the kitchen if you wanna just he'p yourself.

The formal end of the register scale is marked often by frozen lexical items (words) and syntactic structures ("How do you do"; "Would you care for . . .") as well as by careful pronunciation and a lack of shortened, abbreviated, or contracted forms. The less formal end of the register scale is marked by the opposite values of the same set of criteria.

LEXICON. The less formal lexicon may consist of ordinary words as opposed to formal words: "Would you like some coffee?" rather than "Would you care for a cup of coffee?" and "Look, can I get a word in here?" rather than "If it please the court. . . ." It may involve slang words or vulgarisms: "He's on the sauce" rather than "He's been overindulging" (or ". . . drinking too much"), and "Why doesn't somebody give a guy a lousy break?" and so on. (It is hard to present examples containing current slang, because slang tends to change quite rapidly.)

Other words, without going to the extremes of genteel vocabulary or vulgar slang, mark register as well. Speaking to a friend, I would say, "Dad bought a new car"; whereas to someone I knew less well, I would say, "My father bought a new car." (The equivalent to *dad* in other dialect areas might be *pop, paw, the old man,* etc.)

SYNTAX. Syntactic structures, too, mark the degree of formality. The less formal registers avoid certain grammatical forms, such as the subjunctive. So "I think that Wilson should be canned/given the pink slip/shown the door" is less formal than "I recommend that Wilson be dismissed," both for its use of colloquial words and its avoidance of the subjunctive. Actually, it is possible for an archaic or literary syntax to mark an *in*formal register, if it happens to be accepted as slang, or if it is used ironically. For example, the expression "I kid you not" rather than the expected "I'm not kidding you" gained popular currency for a while through the influence of a television personality.

PRONUNCIATION. Pronunciation differences between registers are the most important concern for us in the context of this book. Casual speech (which covers a range of registers) is pronounced differently from formal speech (again, not one register, but a range). In general, it can be said that less formal speech is pronounced less carefully or precisely. This is not to condemn casual speech, but merely to identify its characteristics (very formal speech in a situation demanding casual speech would be as out of place as the opposite).

There are four major manifestations of casual pronunciation:

1. Contractions. The more casual the speaking situation, the more contractions are used. In a for-

mal register one might say, "I am tired of. . . ." This becomes "I'm tired of . . ." in a casual situation. The same goes for "he's," "they're," "she'll," etc.

2. Accommodation and sandhi. Accommodation and sandhi are major topics covered in Chapter 6 and will not be defined in detail here. Both refer to sounds' becoming modified in context. For example, *phone booth* is usually casually pronounced "phome booth," with the "n" of "phone" becoming an m-sound. Such an accommodation is more likely to occur in casual speech.

Sandhi occurs across word boundaries, so contractions like "he's" for "he is" are a kind of sandhi. However, we tend to define as *contractions* only those for which we have a formal spelling. We know that "he's" is a contraction, but we do not immediately recognize that "Ja see 'm?" for "Did you see him?" occurs by the same process. Some sandhi, then, is sanctioned at middle registers, given the name *contraction,* and furnished with "correct" spellings. Other sandhi is more common at even less formal registers and tends to be overlooked because there is no correct way to write it (note the strange spellings I have been forced to use in this section in order to communicate my point).

3. Ellipsis. Ellipsis is the omission of some part of a sentence or word. Ellipsis is more common the more casual the speech. For example, "Coffee?" is a common form of "Do you want some coffee?" and "Leaving already?" is casual speech for "Are you leaving already?"

4. Dialect features. Local dialect features that affect pronunciation tend to be more apparent the more casual or intimate the register. For example, in a dialect area where postvocalic r-sounds (r-sounds following vowels) are dropped, there may be a tendency to insert them in formal speaking situations and to drop them in casual speaking situations. In general, there will be a gradation by which the most casual speech is most local in character and the most formal the least identifiable as to region.

These pronunciation differences between informal and formal speech are pervasive and significant.

The more formal registers (perhaps 1 through 3 on Joos's list of registers) are often the only ones considered in our formal study of language at school, the most casual registers being ignored or dismissed as "wrong" or "ungrammatical." Thus we often act as if these registers did not exist, even though we may use them regularly. Particularly if we are asked a direct question about language, or think about language directly, we tend to think only in terms of the most formal registers. Ironically, this often does not reflect our own pronunciation at all.

While this book does not condone or promote the use of the most casual of registers in formal situations, it does recognize casual registers as a normal part of spoken English, and it does encourage the student to examine the phonetics of everyday, casual speech rather than restricting him/herself to considering only the most formal English. In particular, it emphasizes that a single word pronounced in the most formal register (its citation form) does not reflect the pronunciation of that word in connected casual speech.

2-4 Linguistic Standards, Grammaticality, and Correctness

In this chapter we are looking at dialects in some detail because of the emotional approach many people take to them; this emotionalism may get in the way of an objective study of phonetics. Our discussion brings us logically to the question of what is standard, what is grammatical, what is correct. Let us start with the rise of a standard dialect.

2-4.1 The Rise of a Standard Dialect

The point has been made that at all times in the history of all languages there has been dialect diversity. Let us take the example of English in Great Britain and look at the question historically. At one time there was even greater diversity in the English spoken from one end of England to the other than there is now. The language was different in each region, and in each region people could say whatever they wanted to say without confusion over different forms: any dialect was just as "good" as any other for communication by people who spoke it.

Enter the beginnings of a modern world: books

printed and distributed around the country; poets and playwrights heard around the country; more commerce and travel; more widespread education and literacy; a less purely agrarian economy. Now the dialect differences start to be a problem; there is pressure to conform. One dialect started to take over as the "standard" dialect; that one dialect started to be called "English," although it was only one of many dialects of English.

It is important to realize that no conference was convened to decide which dialect was "best"; nobody sat down to decide which dialect had the most "logical" grammar or the richest vocabulary. All of the dialects were equally good from a communicative viewpoint. The only problem was that no one dialect was spoken by everyone, so whoever's dialect was not chosen would be at a disadvantage. So which dialect became the standard? As in every other country, it was *the one spoken by the people with money and power:* the dialect of the commercial center. For purely geographical reasons, that meant a dialect based on London English. There is always a tendency to speak like those in power. In essence, then, the entire English-speaking world speaks the kind of English it does—and not, say, a type of English based on another British variety—simply because there is a port at London. The port led to London's becoming a commercial center, which gave prestige to the speech of London and made that speech a standard, and that speech was taken around the world with colonization and became the basis for the standard dialects of all English-speaking countries. (Even if you speak, say, midwestern American English and consider standard British English to be strange or foreign or quaint, the fact remains that the influences mentioned in this paragraph shaped the history of your dialect, such that it is primarily based on that one British dialect rather than on any other.)

It is important to realize that the standard dialect of English was chosen for reasons of economic and political power, not because it was the "best" dialect. This is important because we hear so many specious arguments about how standard English is "better."

Let us take an example to make the point. In many nonstandard dialects, double negatives are common: sentences like

I don't have none

or

I ain't got none

are usual. In the standard dialect, one must use only a single negative:

I haven't any

or

I don't have any.

Many grammar teachers point out that this is more *logical,* but if that were the case we would have to say that whole languages, such as French and Spanish (as well as the English of Shakespeare), which regularly use multiple negatives, are "illogical." But it is absurd to claim that a language is illogical: when one Spaniard talks to another, the message is unambiguous. Spanish isn't "illogical," it just has a *different* rule from English. In the same way, standard English isn't *better* or more *logical* than other dialects, it is just that *it is the standard,* and there is much pressure to conform to that standard.

In summary, then, the **standard dialect** (or **prestige dialect**) is the dialect having the greatest prestige, the greatest social acceptance; it is the one people try to imitate if they want to join those with money or power. The other dialects are not "poorer" or "less logical," but rather are other forms of language, which, for historical reasons, did not gain acceptance as the standard. Generally the name of the language—the word *English* or *French* or *Spanish* or whatever—tends to be attached to the standard dialect. Nonstandard dialects are therefore sometimes thought not to "really" be English, although this is a questionable viewpoint.

We should also note that when a language is spoken in several countries, each country has its own national standard. Standard American English is not the same as standard British English, but the two are in most ways more similar than American regional variants are to British regional variants.

It should also be pointed out that, while the historical development of a prestige dialect in England was a primary factor in the establishment of standard dialects throughout the English-speaking world, as stressed in this section, the specific character of speech in different English-speaking countries, and regional dialects within those countries, find their origins to some extent in dialect variations brought from Britain. Britain still has great dialect variation, and the English brought to the United States, Canada, Australia, and other areas, was not homogeneous. For example, differences between general American English and general Canadian English can in part be traced to the higher proportion of Scottish immigrants to Canada than to the United States. As another example, much that is characteristic of Australian speech can be traced to the high proportion of speakers of Cockney who were among the original inhabitants. Much in Appalachian speech can be traced to the regional English dialects of the original settlers.

We can see, then, that the term *dialect* can be used in a specific or a general way. In the context of the English-speaking world, it makes sense to talk of *American English, Canadian English, Australian English, Zimbabwe English, Irish English,* and so forth. However, it is immediately apparent that *American English* is a generalization; it could mean either standard American (the prestige dialect) or the group of all dialects in the United States. Within the United States we would want to distinguish northeastern speech from southern or midwestern. Within the Northeast we would want to make finer dialect distinctions, since the people of New York and Boston talk differently, and so on. Indeed, in some long-settled cities individual neighborhoods have their own speech habits.

2-4.2 Grammaticality

We have noted that the system of a language can be described as a series of *rules*, which are explicit statements about how the structure of the language works. Taken together, these rules form the *grammar* of a language; we stressed that *grammar* does not mean what you should or should not do, but rather is simply the code for converting ideas into utterances and vice versa.

It is obvious that the standard prestige dialect has a grammar. What is perhaps less obvious is that *each and every dialect has its own grammar;* after all, speakers of all dialects convert ideas into utterances, and vice versa, and it is a grammar that permits this. Each dialect has a *different* grammar, and it is this fact that upsets purists.

Let us take an example. In some dialects, it is normal to say

I ain't got none

where standard English says

I don't have any.

The sentence

I ain't got none

does not conform to the grammar of the standard dialect, *but that does not mean that is ungrammatical, because it does conform to the grammar of that dialect.* This is shown by the fact that speakers of that dialect consistently convert the concept of having none into the sentence

I ain't got none

and consistently understand the meaning of that sentence.

Nonstandard dialects are not <u>un</u>grammatical; they simply have a *different* grammar. Truly *ungrammatical* English, like the "sentence"

*None I got ain't

is really exceedingly rare.

One often hears the argument that nonstandard dialects are "simplified." But in fact nonstandard dialects may have a more complex grammar than the standard. For example, in some dialects the following verb forms are used (the difference from the standard is shown in bold type):

STANDARD		CERTAIN DIALECTS	
Declarative	*Negative*	*Declarative*	*Negative*
he can	he can't	he can	he can't
he must	he mustn't	he must	he mustn't
he should	he shouldn't	he should	he shouldn't
he is	he isn't	he is	**he ain't**
he does	he doesn't	he does	**he don't**

Notice that the standard dialect uses a consistent pattern to form the negative. The nonstandard dialect, on the other hand, uses a different form for the negative of certain verbs. Thus the nonstandard dialect has a *more complex* grammar, with special exceptions to the rules. Generally, however, popular colloquial speech is more regular—that is, rules have a broader application—than the form of speech promoted by purists.

In some places a dialect quite radically different from the standard is very widely spoken. Educational authorities promote the standard dialect, but it is considered snobbish, pretentious, or foreign by the everyday speakers. Thus there is great social pressure to conform to the *nonstandard* dialect. In some places almost no one speaks the official standard dialect on a daily basis; people are, however, familiar with the standard, which they hear on television and which they may read and write. Thus these people really deal with two dialects, a situation called **diglossia.**

For example, in the parts of Switzerland where "German" is spoken, what is actually spoken is a language very very different from standard German. Speakers of German cannot understand Swiss German. In fact, Swiss German is not one dialect, but many, and there is no official writing system for them. Speaking standard German (*Hochdeutsch*) is considered pretentious in the "German" areas of Switzerland, but standard German is the written language of books, newspapers, magazines, and official documents, and is the only written language taught in the schools as a first language.

Similarly, although to a lesser degree, some American dialects are very different from the standard. In some areas, and among some social groups, speaking the standard dialect would be interpreted as "putting on airs." But standard American English is the only written language available to speakers of these dialects.

We can now summarize some facts about language and dialect. *Dialect* is not a term with which to put down a form of language we don't like. It is a label to give *any* identifiable variant form of a language, *including the standard form.* It can be used in a broad or a narrow sense. Standard English is one dialect of many, the one having more general acceptance. Nonstandard speech is not *ungrammatical* nor does it display *bad grammar;* it displays strict grammatical structure just as the standard form does. If it is "bad" at all, it is bad only in that its grammar is *different* from the grammar of the standard and may therefore get its speaker ostracized, judged uneducated, or socially penalized in some other way.

2-4.3 Correctness

We have stressed that all dialects have grammatical structure and are legitimate forms of communication for their speakers. Yet there is a danger that an objective discussion of dialect will be interpreted as saying that "anything goes," that linguistic standards should be eliminated, and that there is no such thing as what is correct. This issue is particularly critical if you are correcting the speech of others, as speech therapists or second-language teachers do. Implicit in the notion of correcting the speech of others is some standard of correctness. It is well to ask ourselves how we decide what is correct.

As we have seen, a standard dialect benefits a society through its mutual intelligibility, and there is greater emphasis on standards as the world becomes more and more a "global village." Since different dialects have different lexicons and different grammars, they also have a different correspondence between sentences and meanings, and misunderstanding or a lack of understanding can result. This can lead to serious consequences, irritation, or simply amusement. For example, in some places, the word *gay* still has the primary sense of 'happy' or 'carefree,' whereas elsewhere this meaning has been totally displaced by the meaning 'homosexual.' If an Englishman says that he has "knocked someone up," he means that he has knocked on the door in order to wake up that person. It is easy to see how speakers of different dialects could misunderstand one another badly.

The standard dialect not only has the advantage of wider intelligibility, it has two additional characteristics that are important in a highly educated, literate, and technical world. These characteristics are **codification** and **elaboration.** Let us look at each of these characteristics in turn.

Codification means that the grammar and vocabulary are **codified,** or written down and agreed upon. All dialects have a grammar, but the grammar of the standard dialect is recorded in reference books (called *grammars*, another sense of the word) and is therefore not open to dispute. The sentence

I don't have none

means, in some dialects, 'I don't have any'; but in the standard dialect it means, 'It is not true that I don't have any; I *do* have some.' It is useless, as we have seen, to argue about which sense is more *logical;* what is important is that in the standard dialect the sense is open to verification, because it is codified in grammar books. This means that in an official document (a law, a regulation, a reference book, etc.) the sense is unambiguous and not open to dispute or misunderstanding.

Similarly, spellings are standardized. Standard spelling is not very logical or easy to learn; many nonstandard spellings make a lot more sense. But the advantage of the standard is that it *is* standard; dispute, confusion, and chaos are eliminated.

The second advantage of a standard dialect is that it is **elaborated.** Nonstandard dialects are primarily spoken, not written, and are generally used for everyday conversation. Such a dialect does not permit the wide variety of literary and technical writing needed in a diverse society. Words with specialized senses that would be dropped from a purely spoken dialect are kept in dictionaries and technical vocabularies and are available when needed. Similarly, complex sentences that would never be used in casual conversation are useful for concise written communication, and so their grammatical forms make up part of the standard dialect. Certain sentences with unusual word orders sound fine in songs or poetry but would never be spoken casually. (For example, the famous lines "Stone walls do not a prison make/Nor iron bars a cage" and "Fourscore and seven years ago our fathers . . ." contain syntax or vocabulary that no one would produce in casual speech yet that we all understand it as correct—if quaint, old-fashioned, or literary—English.) The **elaboration** of the standard is the accumulation and codification of a larger vocabulary and more varied syntax than would be supported by a purely spoken language.

These characteristics make the standard dialect essential in the modern world. However, it is important to remember that the standard is primarily a *written* form and is therefore not always the best model of good speech. What is "correct" in a given situation depends upon the national and regional standard and the situation in which the language is to be used. The Queen's English may be a standard of correctness in Great Britain, but it would seem a highly affected form in North America. What is correct in a business letter, a literary work, an official document, a paper delivered at a conference, and a chat over coffee are all different.

Much of what is said about correctness is based on the view that language should not change, that it cannot change without being "debased." Those who express this view often have training in literature, theater, elocution, or traditional (that is, prescriptive) grammar. Traditional grammarians tend to see their role as one of preventing the "debasement" of the language. History shows the debasement argument to be false, as we have seen. After all, each stage of a language can be seen either as having its own merits or as a debasement of an earlier stage. Did Steinbeck, the great American novelist, write in debased Shakespearian English or in good American English? Did Shakespeare write in debased Middle English or in good Early Modern English? Obviously, using an earlier stage of the language as the criterion for what is currently correct leads to absurdities.

Nonetheless, conservative grammarians have in fact succeeded in changing the course of language history through educational influence. But change has been rapid despite their efforts. Distinctions like those between *who* and *whom*, *like* and *as*, *shall* and *will*, and so on are rapidly being lost in North America despite massive efforts to preserve them. The simple fact is that they will be lost.

It is important to recognize that "correctness" in traditional grammar may mean what was done in the past—not the best judge of current usage—but also often means the personal preference of the grammarian. We will see an interesting case involving Noah Webster (Section 2-4.5), but let us take an example to show the often arbitrary nature of statements on what is right. Traditionalists tell us to distinguish between *shall* and *will* as follows:

SIMPLE FUTURE		EMPHATIC FUTURE	
I shall	we shall	I will	we will
you will	you will	you shall	you shall
he/she/it will	they will	he/she/it shall	they shall

This distinction first appeared in an English grammar book written during the Renaissance. It appears to have been the author's personal preference, since it did not reflect the normal usage of the day. Presumably it was accepted as "correct" by other grammarians, as it has been repeated in one (prescriptive) grammar book after another for 500 years. Interestingly, this usage has *never* been normal usage in English and has no historical claim to being right. So much for the objectivity of the authorities.

It is also well to remember that all living languages change (Section 2-3). So what was correct 100 years ago is not necessarily correct today, although, as we have seen, purists often overlook this fact. The speed of the change that has occurred can be emphasized dramatically by considering these facts: Old English, as we saw earlier, is a completely foreign language, as hard for us to learn as German is. An additional sample of Old English is given here in a footnote[11] to further demonstrate this fact. If an average life expectancy has been fifty years over the last millennium, then there have been only twenty nonoverlapping lifetimes since Old English times. On the average, therefore, one-twentieth of the change from Old English to Modern English has occurred during any individual's lifetime. Considering how fundamentally different the two languages are, that's a lot of change witnessed in a lifetime. No wonder the older generation always complains about the speech of the young!

These facts, taken together, demonstrate the value of a standard but make us take the standard with a grain of salt. The standard is not to be rejected out of hand, or replaced by purely personal preferences, but one should consider on whose authority decisions about correctness are made and decide whether that authority should be followed.

Once again, those who are correcting the speech of others must pay particular attention to the notion of correctness. Often people in this position take a very conservative view of correctness and teach only the standard—or worse, the *written* standard—form. It is well to keep in mind that the client of speech therapy or the second-language learner wants *not to be conspicuous by his speech*. If he is taught the most "correct" form in a region where such language is considered snobbish, he has jumped from the frying pan into the fire. If he is taught the literary or written standard and his needs are for a casual form of speech, he will be very conspicuous and may suffer the derision of his fellows. What is correct for that individual is what best serves his communicative and social needs.

2-4.4 Dialects and Phonetics

We have seen that dialect variation involves all aspects of language. In this book, of course, it is *phonetic* differences among dialects and registers that will concern us most. We will not systematically describe the phonetic characteristics of different dialects; that is not the purpose of this book. Rather, we will examine *general* phonetics, and a general North American pronunciation will be assumed. It is hoped that the discussion of dialects will have sensitized you to the fact that when the examples given in this book differ from

[11] The following passage is from a regularized text of an Old English translation of the opening verses of the first chapter of the Book of Genesis. (This text and additional examples can be found on pages 132–133 of Pyles and Algeo, *The Origins and Development of the English Language*, Third Edition, 1982.)

1. On angynne gescēop God heofonan and eorðan. 2. Sēo eorðe sōðlīce wæs īdel and ǣmtig, and þēostra wǣron over ðǣre nywelnysse brādnysse; and Godes gāst wæs geferod ofer wæteru. 3. God cwæð ðā: Gewurðe lēoht, and lēoht wearð geworht. 4. God geseah ða ðæt hit gōd wæs, and hē tōdǣlde ðæt lēoht fram ðām ðēostrum. 5. And hēt ðæt lēoht dæg and þā ðēostru niht: ðā wæs geworden ǣfen and morgen ān dæg.

The following literal, word-for-word translation into modern English is given by Pyles and Algeo:

1. In [the] beginning created God heavens and earth. 2. The earth truly was void and empty, and darknesses were over the abyss's surface; and God's spirit was brought over [the] water. 3. God said then: Be light, and light was made. 4. God saw then that it good was, and he divided the light from the darkness. 5. And called the light day and the darkness night: then was evening and morning one day.

your own speech, neither is the example "wrong" nor are you being told that you "should" pronounce words differently. It is hoped that you will recognize dialect variation as a normal fact and be neither judgmental nor defensive about it. It is hoped that you will sensitize your ear to dialect variations and be able to hear phonetic distinctions that are not made in your own dialect.

2-4.5 Spelling Pronunciations

One aspect of the appeal to correctness that deserves special mention in this, a book on phonetics, is the belief that spelling provides the answers to questions of pronunciation. Simply stated, a **spelling pronunciation** is a pronunciation based on the spelling of a word. It may be a purely idiosyncratic or erroneous pronunciation, or it may be general and end up affecting the standard pronunciation of a word.

If someone pronounced the final ⟨s⟩ of *Arkansas*, it would be a case of spelling pronunciation that was purely erroneous and unlikely to affect the name as pronounced by the residents. The Canadian province of Newfoundland is often mispronounced with the stress on *found*, immediately identifying the speaker as an outsider. The river Thames in England and in Canada is pronounced "temz" (/tɛmz/), but the river of the same name in the United States is pronounced as the word is spelled (/θemz/); the spelling pronunciation has displaced the original pronunciation there. The United States towns of Cairo and Lima are likewise pronounced according to their spelling, rather than like the cities for which they are named.

Current North American pronunciations of *ate* (to rhyme with "fate") and *often* (with a t-sound) are spelling pronunciations that have become accepted and standard. The British pronunciation of *lieutenant* ("left-tenant") already mentioned is likewise a spelling pronunciation (apparently a result of the fact that the letters ⟨u⟩ and ⟨v⟩ used to be written alike). This is an interesting example, because the American pronunciation "loo-tenant" is also a spelling pronunciation, created by the modern forms of the letters, which do not confuse ⟨u⟩ and ⟨v⟩.

Indeed, even *misperceptions* of spellings can lead to pronunciation changes. For example, a piece of outdoor patio furniture in the form of a reclining chair with leg support is called a *chaise longue*, a French expression simply meaning 'long chair.' The French word *longue* is pronounced not very differently from the English word "long" (to be precise, *longue* is pronounced /lɔ̃g/ in French), and the usual way *chaise longue* is pronounced in English is "shaze long." However, the spelling ⟨longue⟩ does not conform to English spelling conventions, and many people mentally (and indeed physically) transpose the ⟨u⟩, giving ⟨lounge⟩, an English word whose sense fits their perception of the function of the item. Thus many people say and write *chaise lounge*. (Such a process is usually called a *folk etymology*, implying that the change occurs because of a folk belief about the origin of the word, but it is clear in this case and others that the *spelling* of the original word plays an important role in the revised pronunciation.)

Spelling pronunciations that are purely erroneous pose no particular problem; standard pronunciations can be verified in a reputable dictionary. Spelling pronunciations that have displaced earlier pronunciations, such as "ate" (no longer rhyming with "bet" in North America), similarly pose no problems, since the new pronunciations are standard and accepted. The matter does become problematical when a person (particularly a speech therapist or language teacher correcting the speech of others) uses the spelling of a word as the authority for pronunciation in the belief that the way a word is spelled indicates how it "should" be pronounced. This belief persists despite the obvious irregularity of English spelling. It has been suggested that this tendency, which is particularly strong in the United States, can be traced in part to the prescriptivist attitude of early grammarians and lexicographers (dictionary compilers) such as Noah Webster. Webster's "spelling" book—which contained advice on pronunciation and points of grammar—sold an incredible 40 million copies[12] at a time when Americans

[12] Laird [1970] has an interesting chapter on Webster, whom he calls "the preeminent cracker-barrel lexicographer." As Laird describes him, "[he] knew all the answers. More a hack of all intellectual trades than a scholar, he was passably schooled but not learned, not even in the subject for which he is now best known. He was intelligent, but he had neither wit nor profundity, and he probably never felt the lack of either quality. He was alert, devout, industrious, patriotic, persistent,

were asserting their political and cultural independence and, as part of the effort to shake off the trappings of colonial status, looked to native-born authorities on correctness in linguistic and other matters. This book undoubtedly had an important influence on the pronunciation of English in the United States.

As we have pointed out, language is constantly changing, and pronunciation changes along with other aspects of language. And since English spelling was mostly standardized at an early time, before certain important sound changes occurred, and was often preserved in the form preferred by certain individual printers, and since we often borrow foreign words in their original spellings, there is little reason to believe that spelling is a valid authority for pronunciation.

However, there are many people who believe that the word *often* "should" be pronounced with a t-sound because the word is spelled that way. They insist that the word *either* "should," on the authority of the spelling, be pronounced with the vowel of "die" and not that of "see." Widespread American pronunciations of such words as *creek, roil,* and *sumach* are judged to be improper for the same reason. Many also promote the careful distinction of pairs of words such as *which* and *witch* and insist that *interest* must be pronounced with three syllables. One may wonder just how we "ought" to pronounce *lamb, hiccough,* and *colonel,* if spelling is taken to be the authority!

More on spelling in Chapter 3.

2-5 Phonemics

In this chapter about language, one aspect of linguistic structure that we should examine is **phonemics.** There is a full chapter on the subject later on (Chapter 8) since you can more easily understand the details once you have studied the articulation of individual speech sounds and have learned their symbols. However, a brief overview of the subject at this point will help you to understand the intervening chapters.

In order for the sound system of a language to serve the function of carrying meaning, there must be a systematic **contrast** among the various sounds. You cannot say that the b-sound (for example) *means* anything; it does not. But in the context of a word—say, "bin"—we understand the meaning because the word *contrasts* with "sin" and "pin" and "win" and "tin" and "din," etc.

This is important, because a particular contrasting sound does not always have a single unchanging phonetic form. Most speech sounds are pronounced in a number of different ways. Let us take a couple of examples. The l-sound in English has two major forms. The "l" in "light" or "lip" is pronounced one way, whereas the "l" of "full" is pronounced another way. You might be able to hear this most easily by pronouncing each word and prolonging the "l": "llllip," "fullllll."

Or, to take another example, the "p" in "pot" is not pronounced the same as the "p" in "spot." You can demonstrate this by putting your hand close in front of your mouth as you say each word. The "p" in "pot" is accompanied by a strong puff of air, whereas the "p" in "spot" is not. This is a very real phonetic difference.[13]

But, as a speaker of English, you recognize the two p-sounds as being "the same" in some sense; in fact it is likely that you need to be convinced that there is indeed some difference between them.

The situation is that the two kinds of "l" and the two kinds of "p" are *different* phonetically, but in English they do not *contrast* with each other. *Either* "p" is recognized as "p," and both contrast equally well with a "t" or a "d" or whatever.

The English "p" is an abstract concept, since what we *pronounce* and *hear* on a given occasion is *one type or the other.* But we *perceive* them as just "p." This abstract "p" is called a **phoneme**

---

public-spirited, conceited, and perverse. Ignorance never dampened his fire, nor did a sense of humor temper his finality" (p. 263). It is obvious that Webster had strong opinions about correctness, and since he wrote a best-selling schoolbook on pronunciation, it is apparent that some American pronunciations can be traced to his whims and preferences.

[13] In these examples of "l" and "p," the facts as stated occur in standard English. But if English is not your first language, the stated phonetic facts may not be true of your speech. Also, while these examples were chosen as being typical of nearly all dialects, it is possible that you speak a dialect that differs from the standard in these respects. This cautionary note pertains equally to all subsequent examples in the book, except that as we go into more detail in later chapters there is even more chance of dialect variation.

and is written with the phonetic symbol between slash marks: /p/. A **phoneme** is a contrasting unit of sound in a given language, and each phoneme often has several different ways of being pronounced. And it is for that reason that the subject must be approached early in a phonetics course. Since each type of "p" is phonetically different, we will talk about those differences in this book. This often confuses the student, since he/she perceives those different "p"'s as the same and wonders what the teacher or textbook is talking about. Remember what we said about language being *arbitrary:* it just happens that English has a couple of types of "p," and it just happens that in English there is no contrast between them. In English, each occurs in combination with particular sounds, or in particular positions in a word (see Chapter 6). But another language could have one or the other or both or neither; and if it had both, it could make a contrast between them. In such a language, the type of "p" in "pot" and the type of "p" in "spot" could be found in the same context and could contrast with each other; to speakers of that language, the two would sound as different as a "p" and a "t" do to you. And just as phonetic facts differ between languages, they also differ between the dialects of English.

A simple analogy might help you to understand the point. Traffic lights—red, amber, green—are a code or signal system. But it is the contrast between them, not the absolute color value of the lights, that has meaning. If you went to another city where the red light was a little pinker or a little more scarlet than what you are used to, you would still understand the message. If the green light were a little more turquoise or a little deeper in hue, it would not confuse you. In fact, when you put on sunglasses, hues change slightly, but the message of a red light does not change.

So our traffic lights do not contrast an absolute shade of red with an absolute shade of green; rather, they contrast some shade of red with some shade of green. In the same way, English contrasts a couple of different "p"'s with several different "t"'s.

Fortunately, the system of traffic lights is international, but it would be possible to imagine a country that used a different set of contrasts. Let us imagine, for example, a traffic light system that is the same as ours, except that a scarlet light means 'stop' and a pinkish light means 'stop if you want to go straight, but you can keep on going if you want to turn right.' Different colors exist and can have any meaning attached to them arbitrarily. In the same way, the types of "p" in "pot" and "spot" are *different phonetically,* and many languages do use them contrastively, although they happen not to be contrastive in the system English has arbitrarily chosen.

If English does not contrast certain sounds, why do we bother to mention them? The simple answer is that when studying phonetics, we must examine the facts as we find them. But there are additional, more concrete reasons. Different dialects often use sounds that are different in small rather than gross ways. Cajun English (spoken in Louisiana) tends toward using the type of "p" in "spot" in *all* contexts. One of our purposes here is to sensitize you to the subtle differences between dialects. Any one dialect has several different pronunciations of many phonemes, as we have seen. Then how can we answer the question, "How is a "p" pronounced?" There is no one answer: it depends on the context of the sound in question. In correcting the speech of others—either misarticulations or foreign accents—one often faces subtle errors: the person is pronouncing a "p" all right, but the wrong *kind* of "p." Studying the different kinds of "p" will sensitize you to this fact. And of course, students of linguistics need to study these details because of the variety of sound systems they will see in their study.

2-6 Intuitions about Speech Sounds

It was stated earlier that our intuitions about speech sounds are often incorrect. Let me state this in a blunter fashion: You know how to pronounce English—you do it all the time—but as soon as anyone asks you how to pronounce something in English, *your answer will very likely be wrong.* Intuitively you know it, but consciously you don't.

There are several reasons for this. One reason is that we generally have little insight into any complex motor activity. It has been noted that a baseball outfielder cannot explain how he judges where a fly ball will land; but he *does* judge it, with uncanny accuracy. Second, our grammar teachers, using their notions of correctness, probably criticized us so much that we have very little confidence in ourselves. Asked how to pronounce something, we respond by saying how we think we *should* say it, instead of how we really *do* say it. This is particularly true if our native dialect differs significantly from the standard, but it is true for all speakers. A third, related, reason is that when asked how a word is pronounced, we tend to choose the pronunciation in the highest register: for example, "would you" rather than "wouja." Fourth, words are modified by their context in flowing speech; when pronounced in isolation, a word is likely to be given an unnaturally precise articulation (the **citation form** of the word is the form as pronounced in isolation).

It is important to pay attention to this fact, since otherwise you may devote too much effort to denying the real facts about your speech, rather than learning about how you actually do speak.

For this reason, there follow a few questions about how English is pronounced. These are designed to help you realize that your intuitions are often wrong and to sharpen your ear.

1. How is the word "to" pronounced? Usually it is pronounced either with *no* vowel, or with a short indistinct vowel (the vowel schwa—/ə/ in the phonetic alphabet). Would you really pronounce it "too" (/tu/) in the sentence "Are you going to the store?" in casual conversation?

2. What is the difference in the pronunciation of these two sentences, when spoken in a normal conversational manner?

I can't do that.
I can do that.

Your first reaction was probably to point to the t-sound of "can't" as the difference between the two sentences. But in normal speech the "t" is usually not pronounced at all; it is assimilated into the following "d." It is the *vowel* of the word "can" that is different in the two sentences. In the first sentence the word "can" is pronounced with the vowel of the word "bat" (/æ/); in the second sentence this word has the short, indistinct vowel found at the beginning of the word "about" (/ə/). Also, the vowel of the word "can" is usually prolonged slightly in the first sentence.

When pronouncing the sentences to check these facts, remember to pronounce them naturally, not in a stilted, hyper-"correct" fashion.

3. How is the word "miss" pronounced? Did you realize that many people pronounce it "mish" (/mɪš/) in the sentence "I miss you"?

4. What sound does the letter ⟨s⟩ represent when it is added to nouns to form the plural? Does it represent an s-sound? Yes, in a word like "cats" it does. But in a word like "dogs" the letter ⟨s⟩ represents a z-sound.

5. What sound does the letter ⟨n⟩ represent? in the word "sin"? in the word "sink"? In the word "sink" it represents not an n-sound but the ng-sound of "sing."

6. What sound does the letter ⟨h⟩ represent at the beginning of a word? Is it pronounced? in the word "honor"? No. in the word "his" or "house"? Before you say yes, consider the casual pronunciation of these sentences:

He's got his books.
The President lives in the White House.

Most speakers do not pronounce the "h" in these contexts.

So, I repeat: Pay attention to the sounds people *really* make when they *really* speak in a normal, casual, everyday way. Forget self-conscious, stilted, hypercorrected pronunciations.

Summary

Language is an arbitrary system of symbolic relationships that permits the encoding of ideas into utterances and the decoding of utterances into their meanings. Language comprises a **lexicon** (vocabulary) and a set of **rules;** both are finite, but they permit an infinite number of sentences. The word **rule** is not a prescription of what to do or not do; it simply reflects one aspect of the systematic structure of a language. The rules together with the lexicon form the **grammar** of a language, or the speaker's knowledge of that language.

Language is manifested in **speech** and in writing. Speech is the primary manifestation of language and the one this book concentrates on.

All languages have different **dialects;** *all* forms of languages are dialects, including the prestige form. Each dialect has a different grammar, and in that sense, all dialects are grammatical; ungrammatical speech rarely occurs. A prestige dialect has developed through the arbitrary functioning of social history. The prestige dialect has become **codified,** that is, agreed upon and written down in reference books. The prestige dialect has the advantage of universality and **elaboration** but was not selected because of its intrinsic qualities.

Dialects differ in pronunciation, vocabulary, syntax, morphology, and other ways. Pronunciation differences between dialects are multiple, so you will find many examples in this book that differ from your own speech. The examples throughout are, unless otherwise noted, in "standard American."

Languages are made up of a variety of **registers** that reflect levels of usage appropriate to different social situations. The rules of English used in a casual chat are different from those used in formal speech or writing. What is **correct** in language means what conforms to the prestige dialect of the region and to the appropriate register. So what is correct in one situation may be "snobbish" or "vulgar" at another place or time. And standards of correctness are constantly changing.

Spelling pronunciations are pronunciations which have been influenced by spelling. Any effort to use spelling as an argument for the "correct" pronunciation is likely to get you into trouble.

The sound system of every language uses **systematic contrasts.** The contrasting sounds are called **phonemes.** Many phonemes have several pronunciations, even though—because of language structure—these different pronunciations seem the "same" to speakers of the language. So in the rest of the book we will from time to time examine phonetic differences among sounds that at first may strike you as "the same."

The actual sounds of your speech are probably very different from what you think they are. If you pay attention to your speech, you will get many surprises. Your first reaction to many examples in the book may therefore be to think that they are wrong.

Vocabulary

accommodation (defined in Chapter 6)
citation form
codification, codified
contrast
descriptive grammar
dialect
diglossia
elaboration, elaborated
ellipsis
frozen
grammar
language
lexicon
linguistic
linguistic competence
phoneme
prescriptive grammar
prestige dialect
register
rule
rule-governed
sandhi (defined in Chapter 6)
speech
speech community
spelling pronunciation
standard dialect

Questions

1. Describe some characteristics of language that you would expect to be universal; that is, characteristics that you would expect all languages to share. Describe some characteristics of English that you would not expect to be shared by other languages.
2. Make a list of the characteristics of *spoken language* as compared to *written language*. Include such terms as *compact, diffuse, analytical, repetitious,* and *spontaneous* in one or the other list. What differences are there between the two in terms of their form and structure, the communication needs they serve, and the constraints on their production? What pitfalls are there in judging spoken language by the criteria applied to written language?
3. In what ways other than speaking and writing do people communicate?

4. What differences are there between your own dialect of English and that which is considered the national standard? If you speak a dialect close to the national standard, then describe a dialect other than your own. Try to find examples of differences that fall under the headings *lexicon, sound system, syntax, morphology*, and other differences.
5. In what ways is the question of dialect likely to be problematic for the speech pathologist? for the teacher of the deaf? for the second language teacher? for the teacher of English to English-speaking students? for the member of a minority group?
6. What dialect features do you think might be diagnosed as errors by a speech therapist unfamiliar with the dialect in question? by an English teacher?
7. How does the theoretical linguist view dialect?
8. It was stated in Chapter 2 that different dialects are equal *linguistically*, but that in *social* terms they differ in their acceptability. In a sense, this is like saying, "Dialects are equally good, except that they are not equally good." Discuss the apparent contradiction.
9. Find some examples of words or constructions that are commonly used but that a prescriptive English teacher is likely to condemn.
10. Find some examples of words or usages that are recommended by the prescriptive English teacher but that you would feel "snobbish" or unnatural in saying.
11. Find examples, in addition to those discussed in Chapter 2, of *rules* of English that the native speaker never thinks about (Section 2-1).
12. It was stated that the *grammar* is what mediates between meanings and utterances. What is meant by this statement?
13. What kinds of attitudes do you expect that verbally handicapped individuals (those with speech dysfunctions, the profoundly hearing impaired, the non-native speaker) have to face in society?
14. If you were a speech therapist or a teacher of a first or second language, how would you decide what is the "correct" form to teach? How would you decide whether someone's pronunciation is "wrong"?
15. In your experience, does diglossia exist in this country? Discuss.
16. Find examples of spelling pronunciations in addition to those given in the text. Remember that there are two types: those that have displaced an earlier pronunciation and are considered correct, at least in one geographical area; and those that are idiosyncratic, if common, errors (such as the one nearly everybody makes upon seeing my family name written).
17. What are some spelling pronunciations common to children? One person is supposed to have remarked that the word *facetious* occurred only in speech but never in writing and that the word "fack-a-tye-us" occurred in writing but never in speech. Has a similar situation occurred with you? With what word(s)? For example, have you ever been confused about the pronunciation of *misled?*
18. Find examples additional to those in Section 2-6 that illustrate the unreliability of our intuitions about the sounds of language.

Readings

In this section and in similar sections in some of the subsequent chapters, suggestions will be made for further reading. For the most part the suggested readings will be relatively general in nature. Full reference information will be found under References at the end of the book.

Speech and Language

Two excellent introductions to the study of language and speech, written in the traditional structuralist framework, go under the same title: *Language*. One is by Sapir [1949], the other by Bloomfield [1961]. The Sapir book emphasizes speech more than does the Bloomfield volume. More recent general introductions include *Our Experience of Language*, by Walter Nash [1971], and *Word Play*, by Peter Farb [1974].

A couple of recent books that, although introductory in scope, are nonetheless written within a modern linguistic theoretical framework, include Fromkin and Rodman's *An Introduction to Language* [1983] and Clark's *Language: Introductory Readings* [1985].

Aitchison's *The Articulate Mammal* [1983] is an introduction to psycholinguistics, and the anthology *Communication, Language and Meaning* (Miller [1973]) looks at language from the psychological viewpoint. Howell and Vetter's *Language in Behavior* [1976] is an examination of language from a social science viewpoint.

Dialect

General discussions of dialect may be found in any of the introductory books just mentioned.

The American dialect of English is described, and its origins examined, in Marckwardt's *American English* [1958] and Mencken's *The American Language* [1936]. *Readings in American Dialectology*, edited by Allen and Underwood [1971], is a collection of articles on dialects of American English. *Americanisms*, edited by Mathews [1966], is a dictionary of words and expressions originating in the United States.

An interesting nontechnical description of the Canadian dialect of English can be found in Orkin's *Speaking Canadian English* [1970].

FOREIGN ACCENTS IN ENGLISH

Wise's *Applied Phonetics* [1957] describes the ways in which speakers of several foreign languages can be expected to pronounce English. It may be a useful reference for those correcting foreign accents. This volume also describes American and British dialects of English.

HISTORY OF THE ENGLISH LANGUAGE

We have briefly mentioned the history of the English language and noted how North American speech has its roots in dialects of Britain. Baugh and Cable's *A History of the English Language* covers its topic exhaustively and interestingly. Pyles and Algeo's *Origins and Development of the English Language* and the accompanying workbook, *Problems in the Origins and Development of the English Language* (Algeo [1972]), are also to be consulted on this topic.

Writing Systems

3

Objectives

To debunk myths many people have about writing and to help separate our knowledge of writing from our knowledge of sound systems.

To show that there are a number of different principles in different writing systems, e.g., *pictographic, ideographic, rebus, syllabic,* and *alphabetic,* and combinations of these.

To show that English spelling is not simply an imperfect alphabetic ("phonetic") system, as commonly assumed, but that it also uses yet another principle: morphophonemic writing.

To show that the study of writing and reading is important to both speech pathologists and linguists.

To introduce the International Phonetic Alphabet.

To explain why different people use the phonetic alphabet in slightly different ways.

3-1 Introduction

In Chapter 2 we looked at a number of aspects of language. One point that was stressed is that our own society places very great emphasis on literacy. We also noted that traditional ideas of what is correct are often based on the written form. As a result, students of phonetics often think too much in terms of how language is *written* and not enough in terms of how it is *pronounced*.

We also have a number of myths about writing and about the writing system we use in English. We often feel that there is a cause-and-effect relationship between the written form and the spoken form; we do not realize that writing systems are primarily *arbitrary*. Writing and speech are different, and often independent, modes of expression.

The phonetic transcription system that is introduced in this book is alphabetic. English writing is loosely based on an alphabetic principle (along with another principle we will examine later). In order to see alphabetic writing from a fresh and objective perspective and to *understand* it rather than take it for granted, we would do well to look at other types of writing systems based on different principles. Then we will look at our own writing system and at phonetic transcription.

3-2 Pictographic Writing

It is said that a picture is worth a thousand words. The principle of **pictographic** writing is to use a picture instead of words.

In such a system, a single picture or, occasionally, several pictures are used to represent a message or short narrative. There is not a one-to-one correspondence between the items in the picture and the words of the message: in fact, the content of the picture could be expressed in many different ways in words. Study the sample pictograph in Figure 3-1.

In pictographic writing, the drawing generally closely resembles the thing it represents; that is, pictographic writing tends to be **iconic.** For obvious reasons, it is easier to think up pictorial representations of concrete objects than of abstract ideas. Although, as Figure 3-1 shows, abstract ideas can be successfully represented in pictographs, this involves some symbolic use of pictorial representations whose meaning may not be immediately obvious: it may be based on cultural convention. (As indicated in Section 3-3, the conventionalized symbols mentioned in this paragraph are perhaps more accurately classified as *ideographs.*) For example, in Figure 3-1 'agreement' is shown by a line connecting the heads (or eyes) of those in agreement, a rather obvious symbolism. Our own culture uses the drawing of a light bulb above a person's head to indicate that the person has just come up with an idea. This is somewhat obscure symbolism and must be learned. The light bulb symbol would have no meaning to a person raised in a technologically primitive culture; indeed, some cultures that use electric light bulbs may not use images of them to mean 'idea.'

Pictographs have been used by many cultures. Among others, many American Indians (that is,

Figure 3-1. A pictograph. Note that certain elements more closely conform to the definition of ideograph. For example, the line linking the eyes, which shows 'agreement,' may be considered to be an ideograph. See text, Section 3-3.1. (Reprinted with permission from *Problems in the Origins and Development of the English Language* [2nd ed.] by John Algeo © 1966, 1972, by Harcourt Brace Jovanovich, Inc.)

indigenous peoples of North and South America) used pictographs. Our own culture uses them in a limited number of contexts. Many political cartoons—those without captions or verbal labels—are pictographs. Advertising may use pictographs, often enhanced by the vivid realism of color photography. One soft drink company has an ad that simply shows a perspiring person on a hot summer day drinking from a distinctively shaped bottle. The message is clear.

Pictographs do not represent *words,* only messages. For example, a pictograph showing a female stick figure and an arrow might be read in any of the following ways (among others):

This way to the women's washroom.
Go down here to get to the ladies' room.
Powder room over there.

The fact that pictographs do not represent words is both their strength and their weakness. The advantages of pictographs are that it is easy to learn the system and make broad interpretations and that the sender and receiver of the message do not need to speak the same language (the latter reason explains their use by the American Indians, who spoke a large number of mutually unintelligible languages). The disadvantages are that the meaning is vague and open to question and misunderstanding, abstract ideas are hard to represent, and some artistic ability is needed to write the symbols. To a phonetician, the greatest disadvantage is that neither words nor sounds are represented at all.

The chief defining characteristics of pictographs are that (1) they are invented spontaneously, and (2) they are easy to interpret without knowledge of a special code.

3-3 Ideographic Writing

In **ideographic** writing (also called **logographic**), each symbol represents a word.[1] The symbol may look like the object it represents, or it may be totally unrelated in form; that is, it may or may not be iconic. Sentences are written with a string of symbols, or **characters.** In contrast to the interpretation of pictographic writing, everyone familiar with a particular ideographic system will read the same message, *word for word,* from a written string.

In English the numerals 1, 2, 3 . . . are ideographic symbols. They each represent one whole word, or one concept, but they are not spelled out as we spell other words. We use many other ideographic symbols, among them %, &, $, *, and #. Sometimes "ideographs" are invented by advertisers for commercial reasons. New York State has been very successful with a bumper sticker reading "I♥NY" ('I love New York'). In fact, signs and bumper stickers using the heart ideograph for 'love' are very common. This particular one stands out because it is very compact: the word *I* contains only one letter, and *New York* is abbreviated, so the whole message is only four characters in length. However, the heart-shaped character meaning 'love' is the only ideograph among the four symbols.

Chinese writing is probably the best example of ideographic writing in use today, although it is by no means a purely ideographic system. Indeed, it would be impossible to find an example of a purely ideographic writing system. In practice, Chinese characters are frequently made to serve a double function through the use of the rebus principle (Section 3-4), but here we will concentrate on those aspects that are, for the most part, in line with the ideographic principle.

The operating principle of the ideographic system is that each character has a meaning, unrelated to the pronunciation of the word it represents. Thus, the characters are combined according to meaning and not to sound. Figure 3-2 gives some examples of Chinese characters. The character for 'tree,' written once, is pronounced "mù"[2] and means 'tree.' Written twice, it is pronounced "lín" and means 'woods.' Written three times in a triangular format, it is pronounced "sēn" and means 'forest.' Notice that while the written element stays constant, the pronunciation changes, just as in English, the words *tree, bush,* and *forest* are unrelated in pronunciation, al-

[1] We are using the term *word* rather loosely. Linguists might use the term **morpheme.** For our purposes, we can think of each character as representing an idea or a word: a single unit of meaning.

[2] These words are romanized according to the standard Pinyin system; they are not written in the International Phonetic Alphabet. The tones marked are discussed in Chapter 7.

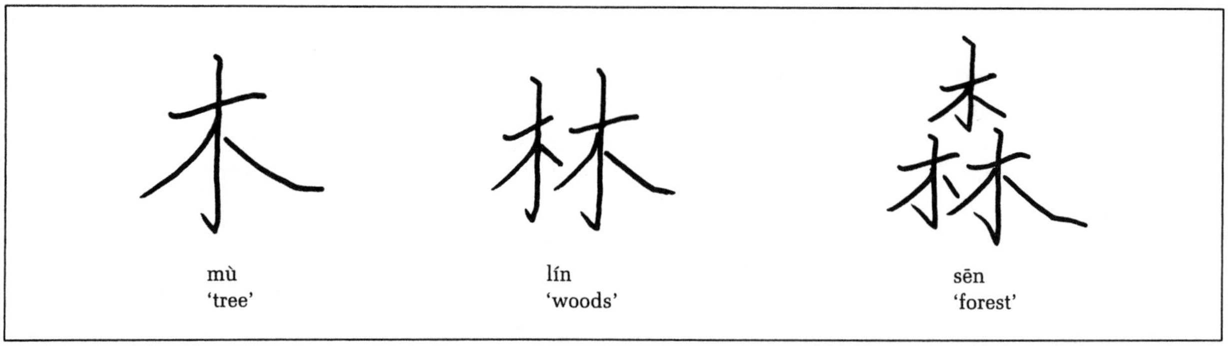

Figure 3-2. Chinese characters may be combined according to meaning and not according to sound. Thus 'forest' is represented in writing with three 'trees,' but the spoken word *forest* (sēn) bears no relation to the spoken word *tree* (mù). Such combinations break from a strict definition of ideographic writing.

though we would have to agree that there is some small connection in meaning among them. These ideographs are based on units of meaning, not units of sound of the spoken word. But there is an exact correspondence between symbols and spoken words. The symbol for "sēn" ('forest') can only be read "sēn" and no other way. A synonym such as "a group of trees" cannot be correctly substituted in reading; as in English, "a group of trees" is written and spoken differently from "forest." It could be argued that if Chinese writing were strictly ideographic, the characters for *tree*, *bush*, and *forest* would be based on unrelated ideographs; they would not all use the character for 'tree.'

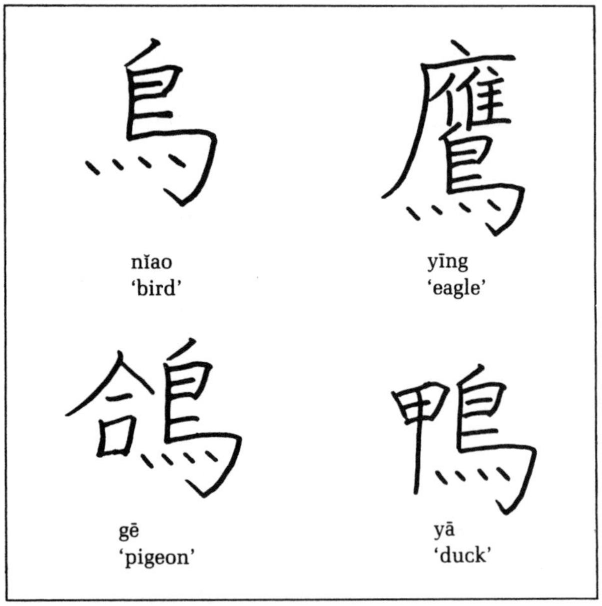

Figure 3-3. The Chinese compound characters for 'eagle,' 'pigeon,' and 'duck' all contain the **determinative** meaning 'bird' and a **phonetic component.** The determinative—in this case "nǐao," 'bird'—is not pronounced in compound characters.

Another feature of Chinese writing (but one that contradicts the strict ideographic principle) is that some written characters are *compound characters,* consisting of two component parts, although the spoken word they represent is *not* a compound word. The compound character consists of a **determinative** and a so-called **phonetic component.** The *phonetic component* is an element that suggests the pronunciation; in most cases the phonetic component has meaning when used alone as a single character, but its meaning plays no role in the compound character. The *determinative* suggests some aspect of the meaning and thus helps the interpretation. In Figure 3-3, for example, we see the Chinese characters for 'bird,' 'eagle,' 'pigeon,' and 'duck.' These are pronounced "nǐao," "yīng," "gē," and "yā," respectively, and it can be seen that, as in English, the pronunciations of the words have nothing in common with one another. However, as illustrated in Figure 3-3, the written name of each of these kinds of bird has the (unpronounced) character for 'bird' as part of it. For example, the compound character for 'duck' contains a phonetic element 甲 that *means* 'first,' a word *pronounced* close to (but not exactly like) "yā." The determinative 鳥 alerts the reader that the *compound character* 鴨 belongs to the category 'birds.' The character therefore represents the word 'duck' and is pronounced "yā."

If this seems terribly complex, it might help to realize that in limited circumstances we do something similar in English. The word pairs *one* and *first* and *two* and *second* have members that are unrelated in sound although related in meaning. But we write *1* and *1st* and *2* and *2nd*. The *2* of *2nd* does not represent the same sound as the *2* written alone, but it *does* represent the same meaning. So the meaning 'two' is conveyed by an ideographic character whose form stays constant even when the pronunciation changes. Similarly the ampersand, &, is an ideograph, representing the word *and*. But it represents the *meaning* of this word, not its sound, as shown by the abbreviation *&cetera*, in which the ampersand replaces the word *et*, which *means* 'and' but doesn't *sound like* "and."

In the preceding section and in Figure 3-3, we saw characters made up of two components but in which one of the components corresponded to nothing in the spoken language. However, Chinese also has spoken compound words that are represented in writing by compound characters. These are directly analogous to the English word *suitcase*, a compound word that is represented in writing by combining the written forms of each of its elements, *suit* and *case*. Some Chinese compound characters are shown in Figure 3-4. For example, the Chinese word meaning 'soft drink' is *qì shŭi*, literally 'steam water.' It is written as 'steam' plus 'water.' The full word for 'bus' is a compound 'public automobile'; both 'public' and 'automobile' are in turn compounds. The compound word 'bus' is written simply by compounding the characters for the various components.[3] Strictly speaking, the Chinese characters shown in Figure 3-3 do not follow the principle of ideographic writing; those shown in Figure 3-4 do.

The main advantage of the ideographic system is that, since it records no sounds, people who speak different languages can use the same system. In fact, people who speak certain dialects of Chinese cannot talk to one another, although they can write to one another, which is one reason the Chinese have resisted changing to the Roman alphabet. The Japanese, whose spoken language is unrelated to Chinese, successfully use Chinese characters in writing (although, as we shall see a little later, they also use a syllabic writing system for some words). In a similar way, our numerals are international.

The main disadvantage of the ideographic system rests in the great number of symbols a person must learn in order to be literate. The numerous symbols also cause problems in typing and typesetting. Inflected languages would not be represented easily by such a system (which, as we shall see, is why the Japanese had to develop a syllabary).

In summary, no strictly ideographic system exists. In principle, each word of the spoken language should be represented by a different symbol (a character), but in Chinese, words are represented by either single or combined characters. Ideographic writing represents the spoken language faithfully; that is, there is only one way to read a written sentence. A perfectly ideographic system—which Chinese is not—in no way represents the sounds of language; it has no phonetic basis.

3-3.1 Distinguishing Pictographic from Ideographic Writing

Pictographic and ideographic writing are often confused, and indeed there is a gray area in which they overlap. The primary difference between them lies in the *conventionality* of the symbol, that is, the extent to which members of the society share a prearranged symbol-meaning link. Pictographs are *spontaneously invented;* ideographs are *conventional*. Pictographs are necessarily iconic; ideographs may or may not be.

As noted, there are gray areas. Pictographs may contain conventionalized elements. The light bulb symbol is an *ideograph* that is usually found

[3] Some readers familiar with Chinese grammar might object to the loose use of the term *compound* to describe such words as the Chinese for 'public' and 'automobile.' This is because the morphemes that make them up are always or usually *bound* morphemes. That is, like the English morpheme *-ty* in such words as *fifty, sixty*, and *seventy*, they may always have to be attached to another morpheme. In the word "gōng gōng," for example, both parts are bound morphemes. *Gōng gōng* may best be described with a term other than *compound;* like the English word *cupboard*, the fact that it is a compound may not be obvious to the native speaker because the sound of the whole word is different from the combination of the sounds of its elements, *cup* and *board*. However, the point of the examples remains: the characters shown in Figures 3-3 and 3-4 are all made up of component parts, but the principle governing how they are read is different in the two cases.

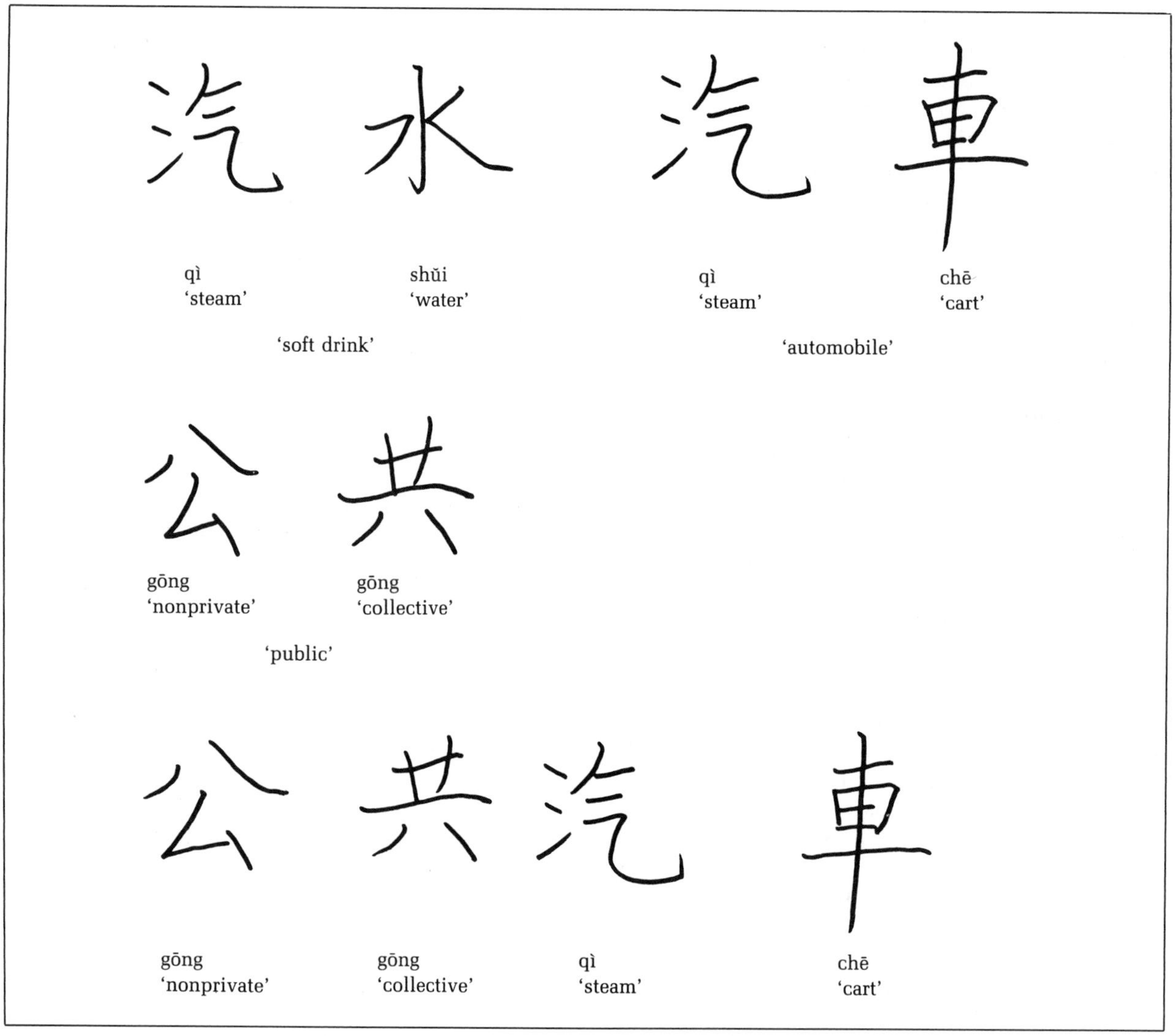

Figure 3-4. In the Chinese characters for compound words, the characters for the individual parts are combined, as one would expect. The spoken word for 'automobile' or 'car,' for example, is the compound word "qì chē," literally meaning 'steam cart' (something like the archaic "horseless carriage"), and is written with the characters for 'steam' and 'cart.' The word for 'public' is a compound made up of parts meaning 'nonprivate' and 'collective,' which happen to be homophonous. The word for 'bus' is 'public automobile' (literally, 'nonprivate collective steam cart'); both the spoken word and the character are four-part compounds. Compare the writing principle illustrated here with that shown in Figure 3-3.

as an element of a *pictograph*. In Figure 3-1, the line linking eyes that shows 'agreement' may well be an ideograph within the culture in which it was used.

A mistake that many people make is to call an iconic ideograph a pictograph. An ideograph is a conventionalized representation; if it looks like what it represents, we call it iconic. That does not make it a pictograph. For example, a common 'No Smoking' sign shows a lighted cigarette with a red circle and red oblique bar indicating interdiction. This is, strictly speaking, an *ideograph*, not a pictograph. Note that the cigarette is always portrayed in the same way: the same angle, always lighted, the same (exaggerated) proportions, etc. It was by no means spontaneously invented by the artist in each case. It is the conventional representation of 'smoking' in our culture. That it is not a pictograph is further indicated by the fact that it refers equally to the smoking of pipes, cigars, and cigarettes.

3-3.2 Blissymbolics: An Example of Ideographic Writing

An interesting use of ideographs, both iconic and arbitrary, is the set of symbols known as *Blissymbolics*. These were developed over the years 1942–1965 by an idealistic individual, C. K. Bliss, as an international written "language." While they have not gained favor in international communication, they are widely used now as a means of communication by the seriously verbally handicapped, such as some individuals suffering from cerebral palsy. With these symbols, often available on a board presenting an array of symbols or on a computer keyboard, the individual can communicate a variety of messages and therefore, one would hope, lead a richer life. A sampling of Bliss ideographs is presented in Figure 3-5. In examining Figure 3-5, note that the use of the terms *pictograph* and *ideograph* in the text supplied by the Blissymbolics Communication Institute is different from the way these terms have been defined in this chapter.

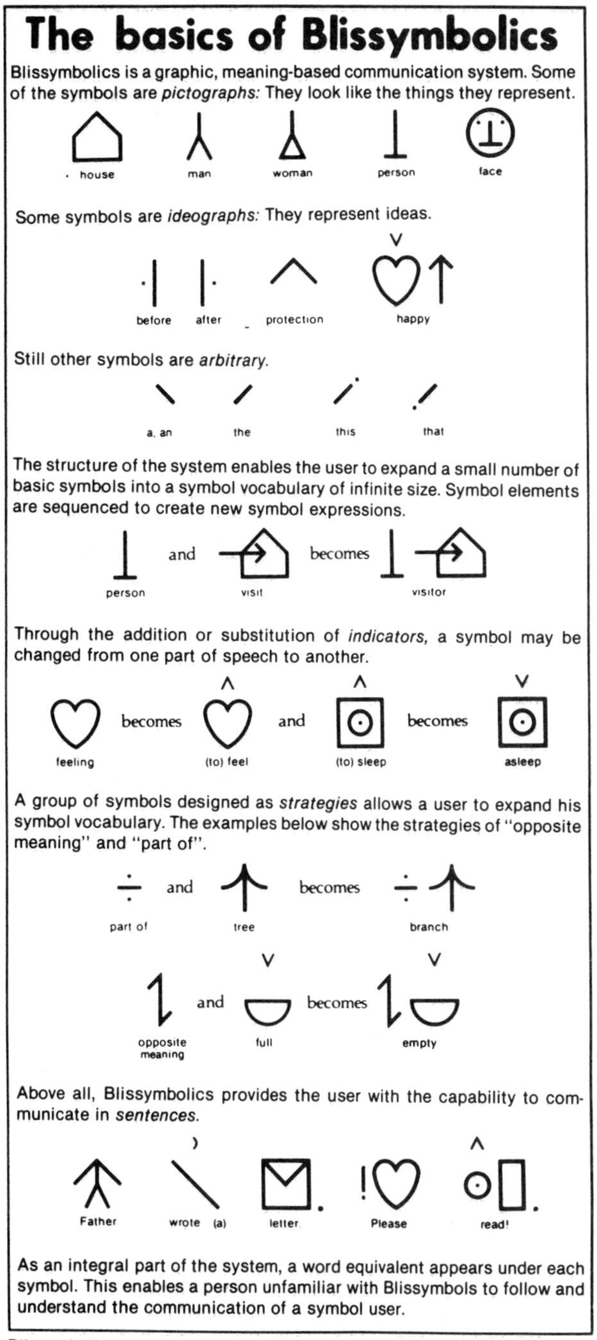

Figure 3-5. Blissymbolics: a guide showing a small selection of the many Bliss symbols. These ideographic characters are used primarily by the verbally handicapped, either on a display board with pointer or on a computer keyboard. Note that the guide's use of the terms *pictograph*, *ideograph*, and *arbitrary* is in conflict with the definitions given in this chapter. What are called *pictographs* above are, by our definition, **iconic ideographs**. What are called *ideographs* and *arbitrary* above are, by our definition, both **(arbitrary) ideographs**. The difference is that what are called *ideographs* are ideographs of content words, and those called *arbitrary* are ideographs of function words. (Blissymbolics used herein derived from the symbols described in the work *Semantography*, original copyright © C. K. Bliss, 1949. Exclusive licensee, 1982: Blissymbolics Communication Institute, 350 Rumsey Road, Toronto, Ontario, Canada M4G 1R8.)

The basics of Blissymbolics

Blissymbolics is a graphic, meaning-based communication system. Some of the symbols are *pictographs*: They look like the things they represent.

Some symbols are *ideographs*: They represent ideas.

Still other symbols are *arbitrary*.

The structure of the system enables the user to expand a small number of basic symbols into a symbol vocabulary of infinite size. Symbol elements are sequenced to create new symbol expressions.

Through the addition or substitution of *indicators*, a symbol may be changed from one part of speech to another.

A group of symbols designed as *strategies* allows a user to expand his symbol vocabulary. The examples below show the strategies of "opposite meaning" and "part of".

Above all, Blissymbolics provides the user with the capability to communicate in *sentences*.

As an integral part of the system, a word equivalent appears under each symbol. This enables a person unfamiliar with Blissymbols to follow and understand the communication of a symbol user.

3-4 Rebus Writing

In ideographic writing, there is the problem of the vast number of symbols needed and the difficulty of finding symbols for such abstract concepts as 'beauty' and 'justice.' The rebus principle makes it possible to extend the use of each character. It is easiest to demonstrate this by example; we will look first at a hypothetical example and then at an example from Chinese.

Imagine that we used the ideographic character —— for *plain*. We could write "Wheat grows best in the ——." Extending the use of the symbol by the rebus principle, we could then write "That is the —— truth" (another sense of *plain*) or even "The carpenter smooths the wood with a ——" (*plane*).

Imagine that we had another character • that meant 'air.' We could write "Fresh • is better than smog." By the rebus principle, we could extend the use of this symbol to another word that sounds the same and write "He is • to a great fortune" (*heir*).

Then we could combine these symbols and write "•——" for *airplane*.

For the rebus principle to work, one must start with ideographic characters. The characters are then used for the *sound value* of the word they originally represented, to represent either homophones[4] or parts of another word. In English, one character would hypothetically do for *sun* and *son*, *brake* and *break*, and so on. Or they could be combined, as we demonstrated with *airplane* above. Similarly, the hypothetical characters for *bee* and *leaf* could be combined to represent *belief*.

Let us move away from these hypothetical examples to actual usage in Chinese. In Chinese the words meaning 'empress' and 'after' are homophones, both pronounced "hòu." As can be seen in Figure 3-6, the same character is used for both, originally that for *empress*. The words meaning 'elephant' and 'compared to' are both pronounced "xiǎng"—the character for *elephant* is used for both.[5] Note that while ideographic characters might be borrowed by one language from another, the rebuses cannot, since they depend on homophony. Only by extraordinarily improbable coincidence would homophones in one language be homophones in an unrelated language. "Empress" and "after" are not homophones in English; and you could not expect the French word meaning 'airplane' to be made up of parts that sound like the French words meaning 'heir' and 'plain.'

后　象

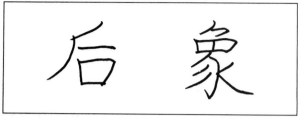

Figure 3-6. The rebus principle. Originally, the Chinese character on the left meant only 'empress,' pronounced "hòu." Now it is also used to represent the homophonous word meaning 'after.' The character at the right originally meant 'elephant'; now it is also used to mean 'compared to.' These words are homophonous, both being pronounced "xiǎng."

As you can see, the ideographic system, when its characters are extended through the rebus principle, becomes rather unwieldy in practice, mostly because of the shifts in operating principle. A character may be used for any of three reasons: (1) it *looks* like what it represents (e.g., the numeral 1 in English), (2) it has an arbitrary relationship to what it represents (e.g., the numeral 5), or (3) it represents another word that *sounds* like the word in question (e.g., "4 sale"). While it is successfully used in Chinese, a language with a

[4]**Homophones:** words that are pronounced alike but are different in meaning and history, such as *son* and *sun; mail* and *male; tied* and *tide; I'll, aisle,* and *isle.* Whether or not two words are homophones is *not* dependent upon spelling. *Well* (satisfactorily) and *well* (a hole dug for the purpose of finding water or oil) are homophones that happen to be spelled alike; their meanings and origins are quite separate. *Passed* and *past* are not true homophones, although they are pronounced identically. They are actually two specialized senses of the same word, as judged on historical and semantic grounds. Indeed, checking an etymological dictionary will show you that *flower* and *flour* are not homophones, but specialized senses of the same word.

[5]These statements are true of the simplified characters in official use in the People's Republic of China and in nonofficial use (as in writing personal letters) outside the People's Republic.

great deal of homophony, it would work less well for a language such as English, in which there is little homophony and many words are long (how would you represent *arbitrary* by the rebus principle?).

For this reason, rebuses in English tend to be limited to puzzles, jokes, children's riddles, and commercial signs designed to attract attention, such as "4 sale." I have seen the business card of a woman named Appleby that pictures a colorful apple and a bumblebee.

3-5 Syllabic Writing

The pictographic and ideographic systems do not represent sound at all. Rebus writing is based on homophony (sounding alike) but does not divide words into consistent units of sound. Syllabic writing is the first system we will examine that consistently links written symbols with units of sound of the spoken language.

A language that uses a syllabic writing system has a group of symbols, roughly corresponding to our alphabet, called a **syllabary.** There is one symbol for each different syllable possible in that language. The number of symbols is usually greater than in our alphabet but far fewer than in the ideographic system.

The phonetic structure of a language needs to be well suited to a syllabic writing system; there should not be too great a number of different syllables. Japanese is a language with a simply syllabic structure and a limited number of different syllables.

English, on the other hand, has a great many different syllables. While we will look at the English syllable in some detail in a later chapter, for the moment you can appreciate its complexity by trying to think of all the different-sounding one-syllable words in English. The number is very large (and there are many syllables found only in polysyllabic words—such as the second syllable of "language"). An English syllable can have zero, one, two, or three consonants before the vowel and from zero to four consonants following the vowel. This creates enormous possibilities for combinations. By contrast, the Japanese syllable consists of either just a vowel (such as "o") or a consonant followed by a vowel (such as "ko").

While Japanese is mostly written in borrowed Chinese ideographic characters, it has a phonetically based way of writing certain words (these include foreign and onomatopoeic[6] words as well as words that have no Chinese equivalent).[7]

Japanese makes use of two syllabaries, often referred to by the Japanese term *kana*. Figures 3-7 and 3-8 illustrate one of these, called the *katakana*. Study the examples given; they will clarify the use of the syllabic principle, in which each different syllable has a distinct symbol. The second *kana* is called the *hiragana*, and has not been illustrated here. Grammatical elements like those mentioned in footnote 7 are written with the hiragana. The katakana is used for foreign words, both borrowings and proper names, and is used for emphasis, much as italics are in English (Morton and Sasanuma [1984]). The native Japanese words in Figure 3-8 would not normally be written in the katakana; it has been done for illustrative purposes only.

Inuktitut (Eskimo) is written in a syllabary that was developed by missionaries. The symbols are based on geometric shapes and give a pleasing appearance on the page. (An alphabetic system is also employed.) In 1821 Sequoya, a Cherokee Indian, developed a syllabary for his native language, a particularly remarkable feat, since he was completely illiterate and therefore had to discover the very principle of writing as well as to develop a system specific to his own language. To this day, whenever Cherokee is written, it is written in that syllabary, not in the Roman alphabet.

The main advantage of a syllabary, if the language is well suited to one, is great economy of writing. The Japanese place name *Yokohama* is written in just four symbols, corresponding to the four syllables of the word. If a language is not well suited to a syllabary, the written form is not economical at all. The Japanese have borrowed many

[6] **Onomatopoeic** words are also sometimes called **imitative.** They are alleged to sound somewhat like the noises they are representing. Words such as "quack," "bark," "squeak," "woof," and "cuckoo" are onomatopoeic.

[7] The grammar of the two languages is totally different, since the languages are unrelated. Japanese has many inflections and function words unlike anything found in Chinese. Thus, Chinese ideographic characters cannot represent every word of spoken Japanese.

	a	i	u	e	o
---	ア	イ	ウ	エ	オ
k	カ	キ	ク	ケ	コ
s	サ	シ 1	ス	セ	ソ
t	タ	チ 2	ツ 3	テ	ト
n	ナ	ニ	ヌ	ネ	ノ
h	ハ	ヒ	フ 4	ヘ	ホ
m	マ	ミ	ム	メ	モ
y	ヤ		ユ		ヨ
r	ラ 5	リ 6	ル 6	レ 6	ロ 6
w	ワ				ヲ 7
n	ン				
g	ガ	ギ	グ	ゲ	ゴ
z	ザ	ジ 8	ズ 9	ゼ	ゾ
d	ダ	ヂ 8	ヅ 9	デ	ド
b	バ	ビ	ブ	ベ	ボ
p	パ	ピ	プ	ペ	ポ

Figure 3-7. The Japanese katakana syllabary. Each symbol represents an entire syllable consisting of a vowel or a consonant followed by a vowel. For example, the symbols in the first column represent the syllables "a," "ka," "sa," "ta," "na," "ha," etc. The second "n" is not the syllable "na" but only the sound "n"; this sound can stand alone as a syllable in Japanese. The last five rows are repeats of symbols above them, modified by diacritics. The consonants are pronounced more or less as you would expect, but note that the vowel symbols have their International Phonetic Alphabet values. Thus, *a* is pronounced as in "f*a*ther"; *i* as in "mach*i*ne"; *u* as in "super"; *e* as in "hey"; and *o* as in "tote". The symbols with numbers beside them are pronounced not as expected but as follows: (1) shi /ši/, (2) chi /či/, (3) tsu /t͡su/, (4) fu /ɸu/, (5) r-like consonant, (6) l-like consonant, (7) o /o/, (8) zhi /ži/, (9) zu /zu/. See examples of words written in the syllabary in Figure 3-8.

English words, and the way many of them must be written in the syllabary is very complex, simply because of the complex syllabic structure of English.

The most important difference between the syllabary and the other systems we have examined is that it is sound-based and therefore provides a way to write new words that come into the language. Also, onomatopoeic words are easier to represent than in an ideographic system.

In English we sometimes use the equivalent of a syllabic system in riddles and advertising. When a company advertises a product as being "E-Z" to use, each symbol represents a syllable. The first syllable has just one sound, like the ee-sound of "meet," while the second syllable is a z-sound

タケシ	Takeshi (a man's name)	
シタケ	shitake (a kind of mushroom)	
ケイト	keito ('wool')	
オサカ	Osaka	
トヨタ	Toyota	
ホンダ	Honda	
ヨコハマ	Yokohama	
カミカゼ	__________	(literally, 'divine wind')
ハラキリ	__________	(literally, 'belly cut')
ラジオ	__________	(a word borrowed from English)
テレビ	__________	(another English borrowing)
__________	kimono	
__________	katakana	
__________	sukiyaki	

Figure 3-8. Examples of the use of the katakana syllabary. Compare the first seven examples with the complete katakana in Figure 3-7. Then write the next four words in the Roman alphabet. Two are Japanese words that are probably familiar to you, and two are English words taken into Japanese. Try writing a few words in the katakana, using as models the symbols in Figure 3-7. Some of these words would not normally be written in the katakana.

followed by the ee-sound. So the letter ⟨z⟩ is not being used as a letter of an alphabet but as if it were part of a syllabary. It represents a whole syllable, in this case made up of two speech sounds.[8] Similarly, if we write "I C U" for "I see you" or "I O U" for "I owe you," we are using these symbols in a syllabic way.

3-6 Alphabetic Writing

In an **alphabetic** writing system, each distinctly different sound[9] of the spoken language is represented by a separate symbol, and each symbol represents only one sound. The written symbols are called **letters,** and they go together to make up an **alphabet** (named for *alpha* and *beta*, the first two letters of the Greek alphabet).

The alphabetic principle is used in most Western languages and many others besides. The principle of one sound to one symbol is followed quite closely in some cases (such as Spanish or Russian) and quite poorly in other cases (such as English or French).

[8] The letter ⟨z⟩ is called "zee" only in the United States. In other English-speaking countries it is called "zed." Syllabic-based terms such as "E-Z" for *easy* or "LA-Z BOY" therefore make no sense outside the United States.

[9] Distinctly different sound: a phoneme. See Section 2-5 and Chapter 8.

3-6.1 A Brief History of the Alphabet

The Sumerians, who had a flourishing culture in Mesopotamia around 3000 B.C., are generally credited with having the first system of writing, a mainly ideographic system. It was developed to serve the needs of a rather advanced commercial trade. A later stage in the development of this system is called **cuneiform** ('wedge-shaped') in reference to the stylized form of the characters written on clay tablets. At the same time, the Egyptians were using a similar system, called **hieroglyphics.** There is some dispute concerning the relationship between cuneiform and hieroglyphic writing; it is likely that the hieroglyphics were an adaptation of the Sumerian script; and certainly the development of the hieroglyphics was influenced by the cuneiform writing.

Both the hieroglyphic and the cuneiform system appear to have undergone a process of **phonetization;** that is, while they started out purely ideographic, they became, at later stages, at least partially phonetic. Apparently the first step in this process was the phonetic use of ideographic symbols through the rebus principle. Some symbols remained purely ideographic, while others came to represent whole syllables; these were combined, as one might combine an ideograph of a *bee* and a *leaf* to represent *belief* (see Section 3-4). As a result of this process, many symbols lost their ideographic value and were interpreted as having purely a sound value. By this means, a syllabary was born. At their most advanced stages, both the cuneiform and the hieroglyphic system remained a mixture of ideographic and syllabic principles. (Some authorities claim that there may even have been a segmental or alphabetic component as well.)

A syllabic form of the hieroglyphic symbols was borrowed by the Phoenicians, a Semitic people who traded on the Mediterranean sea. The *West Semitic Syllabary*, consisting of twenty-two syllabic symbols, had evolved by 1500 B.C.

This syllabary was different from the syllabaries described in Section 3-5 in one important respect: the symbols did not indicate the vowels, only the consonants. It may appear that such a system should not properly be called a syllabary, but rather an incomplete alphabet. Because of the phonetic structure of the West Semitic language (vowels were largely predictable), however, such a system accurately represented the sounds of the words. Also, each symbol represented one consonant followed by one vowel—although the particular vowel was not always specified; thus each symbol was a syllabic character.[10]

Words in the West Semitic language were made up of alternate consonant and vowel sounds and normally began with a consonant. The number of different vowels was fewer than in English, and the particular vowel in a word was at least partially determined by the consonant preceding it. Thus, it is evident that the syllabary would have served well to write the language for which it was developed.

This West Semitic syllabary was borrowed by the Greeks in the tenth century B.C. Like English—and in contrast to the Semitic languages—the Greek language had clusters of consonants together without vowels in between, and thus the Semitic syllabic characters could not represent spoken Greek very well. Unmodified use of the syllabic characters would have resulted in representation of only the consonants, presenting considerable ambiguity to the reader.

The Greeks overcame this difficulty by a simple modification. They used the Semitic symbols to represent only the consonants without the accompanying vowels. Since Greek had fewer consonants than were represented in the syllabary, there were symbols left over to represent the vowels alone, without the Semitic consonant. For example, the West Semitic syllabic character *aleph*, the ancestor of our letter ⟨A⟩, represented the syllable " 'a" in West Semitic. The apostrophe represents the **glottal stop** (written in the International Phonetic Alphabet as [ʔ]: see Chapter 5). This consonant appears in the English expression "uh-uh" (meaning 'no') between the two vowel sounds. The Greeks had no such consonant in their language, so it was a simple matter to let the character *aleph* represent the vowel "a" instead of the syllable " 'a" (or [ʔɑ]). In its most fully developed form, the Greek alphabet had added five letters

[10] The limited evidence available regarding the transition from ideographic to syllabic to alphabetic symbol systems is interpreted differently by various authorities. Some of the sources cited in the Readings differ on this issue.

that did not correspond to any symbols of the Semitic syllabary.

While the Greeks used the first true alphabet, it was not so much their single-handed invention as it was a minor modification of the Semitic syllabary, one small step in the transition from pictographic to alphabetic writing. The modern Greek alphabet is a direct descendant of this first alphabet. Saint Cyril brought Christianity to Slavic peoples, and many Slavic languages, such as Russian and Ukrainian, use the Cyrillic alphabet, also a direct descendant of the Greek alphabet.

The Etruscans, who lived in part of what is now called Italy, borrowed the alphabet from the Greeks and in turn passed it along to the Romans. The Romans adapted the alphabet to the particular phonetic structure of their language, and as they increased their military, political, and cultural influence over Europe, their alphabet went with them.

3-6.2 The Roman Alphabet

The Roman alphabet was well suited to the Roman language, Latin. For the most part there was a one-to-one correspondence between sounds of the spoken language and letters of the alphabet; however, the sound system of Latin was different from that of the modern languages that presently use the Roman alphabet, so this alphabet is less well adapted to those modern languages. Some of the peculiarities of spelling of English and other languages can be attributed to the attempt to make the Roman alphabet serve languages for which it was not developed.

In the alphabet as used by the Romans, there was only one letter corresponding to our ⟨U⟩, ⟨V⟩, and ⟨W⟩ (inscriptions in which a letter ⟨V⟩ is used for both ⟨U⟩ and ⟨V⟩ are not uncommon). Similarly, ⟨I⟩ and ⟨J⟩ were not distinguished, and ⟨Y⟩ was used only to represent the vowel sound of certain words borrowed directly from Greek. These facts partly explain why these letters are used to represent different sounds in various languages. To take one example, the letter ⟨j⟩ is used to represent the sound of our letter ⟨y⟩ (as in "y̲ou") in quite a number of European languages (as well as in the International Phonetic Alphabet).

The letter ⟨C⟩ provides the most confused picture in the original Roman alphabet. It variously represented sounds corresponding to our letters ⟨k⟩ (as in "k̲eep"), ⟨g⟩ (as in "g̲ood"), and ⟨s⟩ (as in "s̲et"). The letter ⟨G⟩ was introduced to reduce the confusion of having one letter represent more than one distinct sound: It was originally a letter ⟨C⟩ with an added crossbar (note the resemblance in form of the upper case ⟨C⟩ and the upper case ⟨G⟩). The fact that the one letter ⟨C⟩ represented both the k-sound and the s-sound, as it still does in the English words "c̲amp" and "c̲ent," is the result of a sound change that occurred in Latin. The k-sounds preceding the vowels ⟨i⟩ and ⟨e⟩ came to be pronounced as s-sounds.

These examples are provided to demonstrate that some of the peculiarities of spelling in English (and other European languages) can be traced either to the peculiarities of Latin itself or to the ways in which the Roman alphabet has been adapted to languages whose sound systems are very different from that of Latin.

The Latin language had fewer speech sounds than many languages that use its alphabet; there are not enough letters in the Roman alphabet to go around. For example, Latin had only five vowels, corresponding to the five letters ⟨a⟩, ⟨e⟩, ⟨i⟩, ⟨o⟩, and ⟨u⟩ (plus ⟨y⟩ in Greek loan words). Most dialects of English have about thirteen vowels (and several diphthongs besides), which must be represented by these five symbols (the use of the letter ⟨y⟩ in English does not help, since ⟨y⟩ is not consistently distinguished from ⟨i⟩). While the lack of consonant symbols is less serious, it is true that Latin had fewer consonant contrasts than English does.

This problem has been solved with varying degrees of success for the various languages using the Roman alphabet. One solution is to add symbols not found in the Roman alphabet. English and several other languages make extensive use of the letter ⟨k⟩; in the Roman alphabet the use of ⟨k⟩ was very restricted. But we would need to add about eleven more symbols, and use each letter that we already have in a distinctive way, in order to have enough for every distinctive sound of English.

In German the letter ⟨ß⟩ has been added to represent the s-sound. Danish has added the vowel letter ⟨æ⟩ to its alphabet. But for the most part, languages using the Roman alphabet have been quite conservative and have not developed new symbols to supplement the old. Indeed, modern English has abandoned several very useful non-Roman letters that were used in Old English (some of these can be seen in the sample of Old English given in Section 2-4.3).

Another way to extend the use of a limited number of symbols to a larger number of sounds is through the addition of **diacritics,** or "accents." French, German, Spanish, Portuguese, Czechoslovakian, and the Scandinavian languages, among others, use various kinds of diacritics to modify Roman letters. Some examples are é, è, ô, ö, ü, ä, ñ, ç, ø, č, and å.[11] English does not make use of diacritics to extend its alphabet.

Another way to extend the alphabet is by the use of **digraphs.** A digraph is a combination of two letters representing one sound. For example, the ⟨ph⟩ of "telephone" represents one sound, as does the ⟨th⟩ of "through," the ⟨ea⟩ of "dean," and the ⟨sh⟩ of "shore," the ⟨oo⟩ of "moon," and so on. Digraphs are used commonly in English and other European languages.

3-6.3 Why English Spelling Is Not Alphabetic

A true alphabetic system uses a one-to-one correspondence between distinctive speech sounds and letters of an alphabet. English spelling violates that principle in several ways.

1. One sound is often represented by more than one spelling. The vowel sound in "tea," "tee," "people," "ski," and "fetus" (also spelled ⟨foetus⟩) is an example, as is the underlined consonant sound in "fellow," "telephone," and "tough."

2. The same letter often represents several different sounds: for example, the ⟨o⟩ in "women," "woman," "bone," "cot," "love," and "port." These variations led George Bernard Shaw, the great playwright and advocate of spelling reform, to suggest that the word *fish* could be written ⟨ghoti⟩ using the ⟨gh⟩ of "enough," the ⟨o⟩ of "women," and the ⟨ti⟩ of "nation" (Shaw [1963, p. xviii]). Clearly, English spelling is not *that* bad, but it does present a number of difficulties.

3. A third problem with English spelling is that it uses digraphs, a practice that violates the basic alphabetic principle of one letter to one sound. Used consistently, digraphs do not cause serious problems, but they can cause confusion in compound words. For example, you might argue that the digraph ⟨ee⟩ is used quite consistently in English to represent one single vowel sound. But note that when two ⟨e⟩'s come together in a compound word such as *re-enter,* the double ⟨e⟩ does not represent the same sound as in "meet." Of course, the hyphen indicates this fact, but the hyphen itself must be inconsistently used because of the use of digraphs in our spelling. We can use a hyphen to separate the two ⟨e⟩'s of *re-enter,* since the digraph ⟨ee⟩ has its own value, but the hyphen is not needed in a word like *recopy* or *reduplicate,* since letters that can form digraphs are not brought together in these compounds. Even this is not a consistent guide, however, since the words *reenter* and *reestablish* may be spelled with or without a hyphen. *Zoology* is never spelled with a hyphen, although the digraph ⟨oo⟩ normally represents as a single vowel; similarly, the words *mishap, pothook,* and *sweetheart* lack hyphens, even though these compounds juxtapose letters that normally form digraphs in English.

4. English spelling is not alphabetic because we sometimes use letters that represent no sound at all. These so-called "silent" letters certainly cause problems for those learning to spell English. We can find examples in such words as *debt, island, right, plate, psychic, pneumatic,* and *castle.*

5. There are sounds that are not represented in the spelling of English words. The word "use," for example, begins with a y-sound, just as the word "you" does. This same y-sound is also left out of the spelling of the word "mute" and other, similar, words.

Above are the *ways* in which English spelling violates the simple alphabetic principle. But that doesn't tell us *why* such an irregular system would have developed. Let us look at some of the causes of irregularities in our spelling.

[11] The use of diacritics is not restricted to European languages or to alphabetic systems. Notice that the last five rows of syllabic characters in the Japanese katakana syllabary (Figure 3-7) are previously used characters with diacritics added.

The spelling system of Old English was quite closely alphabetic, although it did use digraphs. It also used a number of letters not found in our modern alphabet, such as ⟨þ⟩ and ⟨æ⟩. For about 250 years after the Norman conquest of England in 1066, French was the official language of England. Most of the intelligentsia were killed at the time of the conquest, which included most of those who could read and write. So when English regained its status after 250 years of having been written very little, all scribal (that is, writing and spelling) traditions had been lost. English began to be written by those with a Norman French scribal bias and a knowledge of the alphabet as used in Norman French. The letter ⟨þ⟩, used for the th-sound, was dropped and replaced with ⟨th⟩. The vowel "oo" (/u/ in the phonetic alphabet), which was written ⟨u⟩ in Old English, came to be written ⟨ou⟩ according to French usage. In sum, after about 1100 A.D. English began to be written according to foreign, specifically Norman French, spelling conventions.

The second point is that spelling standardization came early and in a helter-skelter fashion in English. In Middle English, spelling was highly personal and very variable. It changed according to personal taste, different regional pronunciations, and even the amount of space on a line. This changeability carried over into the early modern period; Shakespeare is said to have spelled his own name in twenty different ways. While mechanical printing was not invented in England, it did gain widespread distribution there very early. The most influential early printer was William Caxton, who lived in the latter 1400's. Printing was very influential in spelling standardization (as well as in dialect standardization), because more and more printers chose *one* spelling to replace all the variant spellings. For this reason Caxton is single-handedly responsible for many of the modern English spelling conventions. But they also reflect his personal whims and his own dialect preference.

Third, we must consider sound changes. English spelling gained considerable standardization early, and important sound changes have occurred since then. If you have studied other European languages, you may have noticed that many letters—particularly the vowel letters—have a different sound value in English from what they have in most other languages. The letter ⟨i⟩ in most languages usually represents a sound we spell with ⟨e⟩ in English; ⟨e⟩ usually represents a sound we spell with ⟨a⟩; ⟨u⟩ usually represents a sound we spell ⟨oo⟩; and so on. Soon after the initial standardization of English spellings, in the late Middle English and early Modern English periods, all the English long vowels changed pronunciation in what is called the *Great English Vowel Shift*. But the spellings did not reflect the change. Other less dramatic sound changes have occurred that have likewise left spelling and pronunciation out of sync. For example, many words retain the ⟨gh⟩ spelling, although the sound this originally represented no longer occurs in English; words spelled with an initial ⟨kn⟩ or ⟨gn⟩, such as *knife* and *gnaw*, have now lost their initial consonant.

Fourth, one of the results of the appeal to correctness (Chap. 2) is the idea that spelling should reflect the *history* of a word (also called its **etymology**) rather than, or in addition to, its pronunciation. So we spell *telephone* with a ⟨ph⟩ rather than with an ⟨f⟩, because the word is derived from Greek, and ⟨ph⟩ is the "etymologically correct" romanization of the Greek. We spell *psychology* with a ⟨p⟩, even though it is not pronounced in English, because the Greek original had a p-sound. This exercise in etymological "correctness" has gone to some silly lengths. The word *debt* in English is derived from the French *dette;* there has *never* been a b-sound in the English word *debt*. But the word *dette* is derived ultimately from Latin *debitum*, and the person responsible for the standardized English spelling was simply showing off his erudition when he added the ⟨b⟩. A similar attempt with the word *island* shows the height of pseudointellectualism. This word is derived from Old English *ig-lond*, 'island land; land apart.' It has no etymological connection with the word *isle*, which is derived from French and ultimately from Latin (*insula*). Nevertheless, the ⟨s⟩ was inserted into the spelling of *island* in the mistaken belief that it had to be related to *isle*. In sum, many of our spellings are based on etymology, exaggerated notions of etymology, or simply false etymology.

Fifth, English has assimilated a vast non-native

vocabulary; indeed English has one of the highest proportions of non-native vocabulary of any language in the world. A good bit of this vocabulary has come into the language over the last 400 years, during England's colonial times and subsequently. And we have the habit in English of borrowing foreign words in their original spelling or standard romanization, rather than in a way that follows English spelling conventions. So we end up with a hodgepodge of spellings. A few examples will make the point: détente, chutzpah, machismo, machine, khaki, Cointreau, concerto, pizza, blitzkrieg, Czechoslovakia, Pago Pago, colonel, cello, regime, thyme, ghetto, junta, bivouac, chaos, chassis, psalm, prosciutto.

English spelling reform is a subject that crops up frequently in the popular press. There is always someone who feels that we should spell English "phonetically." (As you will soon see, *phonetic* spelling would be an awful everyday system, and of course it is not truly *phonetic* spelling that the reformers are advocating. They really want *alphabetic* or *phonemic* spelling.) The debate is beyond our present purpose, but we can look at a few of the reasons why spelling reform has not caught on. First of all, there is simply conservatism: people do not like change, and those who have learned the present system have a vested interest in maintaining it. Second, the cost would be enormous. Third, present literature, references, etc., would become inaccessible in a short time. But the most critical problem is found in dialect variation: Whose pronunciation will be reflected in the new spelling?

This would not be a problem if all sound correspondences among dialects were regular. If one speaker pronounced the "r" in all words like "car," "beer," and "for" and another speaker did not, both could still use the same regularized spelling. But dialect variations do not always work that way: the word "poor," for example, rhymes in one dialect with "moor" but not with "for," and in another dialect it rhymes with "for" but not with "moor." So (after the initial consonant) should the reformed spelling system spell "poor" like "moor" or like "for"? Not to mention the fact that "poor" rhymes with "truer" in some dialects, but not in others. To cite another example, "sore" and "saw" are homophonous in some dialects but not in others. Satirical entertainer Tom Lehrer, from Massachusetts, rhymed "torture" with "debaucher" in one of his songs; these words do not come close to rhyming in my dialect.

The result is that no system of reformed spelling could be devised for English that would not cause resentment or, at the very least, controversy, because it could not represent all dialects at once.

A fourth impediment to the adoption of a purely alphabetic writing system in English is that there is another principle operating (albeit imperfectly) in English writing. It is a nonalphabetic principle that is widely used in English and represents a regularity that would be lost if truly alphabetic spelling were adopted. The principle is *morphophonemic* writing and is the subject of Section 3-7.1.

3-6.4 Spelling Is Not Pronunciation

Considering the extent to which English spelling is not alphabetic, it is hard to imagine that anyone would think it the authority for pronunciation or would assume that pronunciation is consistently represented by the written word. Yet Chapter 2 has already shown that the phenomenon of spelling pronunciation has changed the pronunciation of many words.

Although it may seem obvious, it should perhaps be emphasized that there is a great difference between spelling and sounds. We hear people talk of pronouncing "letters," but it is of course not *letters*, but *speech sounds*, that are pronounced. These may or may not be well represented by letters in writing. When we say, for example, that someone mispronounces "his s's," of course it is not the *letter* ⟨s⟩, but the s-sound (/s/ in the phonetic alphabet), that we mean. The s-sound is often represented with a ⟨c⟩, and the letter ⟨s⟩ often represents a z-sound. For this reason, talking about pronouncing "letters" can be misleading.

Digraphs deserve special mention. I have heard teachers of English as a second language tell their students that to pronounce the th-sound of a word like "<u>th</u>ought," they should try to pronounce a t-sound and an h-sound together! This is of course completely ridiculous; the th-sound is a *single* sound, no matter how it is represented in writing. There is no reason to assume that the combination of *letters* corresponds to a combination of *sounds*. (In fact, as we have noted, above, the th-sound was represented by a single letter in the Old English alphabet.)

Another problem caused by confusing *letters* with *sounds* is the fact that some sounds are poorly represented by letters in English spelling. For example, there is no such thing as the th-sound. In fact, there are *two* different th-sounds, as in "then" versus "thin" and in "either" versus "ether." The designation "th-sound" does not distinguish between the two.

Many people perceive a cause-and-effect relationship between spelling and pronunciation. However, with the exception of the spelling pronunciations discussed in Chapter 2, *spelling does not cause pronunciation*. Yet many people try to explain pronunciation in terms of spelling. They claim that the word "better," for example, has two "t"'s. It doesn't, of course. It has two *letter* ⟨t⟩'s, but phonetically *only one* t-sound. English pronunciation does not have double consonants such as exist in some languages. Double consonant *letters* are irregularly used in English spelling to represent other phonetic qualities, such as vowel quality or stress placement. The vowel difference between "catty" and "cater" is not *because* one word is spelled with two ⟨t⟩'s and the other with one; rather, the doubling of the consonant letter *indicates* the vowel quality. Only in spelling does *catty* have two ⟨t⟩'s. Similarly, in the words "material" and "matter" the single or double letter indicates the stress pattern. Once again, a spelling convention (such as a double ⟨t⟩) is used to indicate something *unrelated* in the pronunciation of the word (such as vowel quality or stress).

The sound usually spelled ⟨sh⟩ in English is not an s-sound plus an h-sound. Nor does the word "back" contain a c-sound and a k-sound; rather, this combination of letters is used after certain vowel sounds to represent a *single* consonant sound.

This is a book about *phonetics*, and we will be classifying speech *sounds*, not *letters*, into types, primarily vowels and consonants. Phonetically, the number of vowels or consonants in a word *has nothing to do with its spelling*, but only with the sounds it contains. For example, the word "cough" has *two* consonants and *one* vowel. The word "through" has *two* consonants (the th-sound and the r-sound) and *one* vowel. The word "use" has *two* consonants (the y-sound at the beginning and an s- or z-sound) and *one* vowel.

You were probably taught that "the vowels are *a, e, i, o, u,* and sometimes *y*." But this is wrong in the sense in which we are using the word *vowel*. ⟨a⟩, ⟨e⟩, ⟨i⟩, ⟨o⟩, ⟨u⟩, and ⟨y⟩ are *letters* that usually or always *represent* vowels (as just noted, ⟨u⟩ often represents a consonant sound as well as a vowel, as in "use"; ⟨y⟩ may represent a vowel, as in "try," or a consonant, as in "yes"). There are about fifteen or sixteen distinctive vowel phonemes in English; *these* are the vowels of English.

The spelling of words tends to mislead us about pronunciation in another way: we may think that words spelled differently are pronounced differently, even when this is not the case. Most of us pronounce "prints" and "prince" similarly, but the effect of spelling is so strong that we tend to feel that the two words are said differently. Our reaction when told that the two are pronounced alike may be "But *prints* has a ⟨t⟩ in it." The presence or absence of the *letter* ⟨t⟩ in the spelling of the words has nothing to do with whether or not there is a t-sound in the *pronunciation of them*.

In summary:

1. When talking about *sounds*, say "sounds"; when talking about *letters*, say "letters."
2. Don't base conclusions about the right pronunciation on spelling.
3. Don't let your knowledge of spelling distort your perception of speech sounds.
4. Note that, in English, spelling conventions often represent something quite different from what they seem to indicate: a double consonant letter does not represent a double consonant but rather may show where the stress is placed or how a vowel is pronounced.
5. Note that, in phonetics, the vowels or consonants a word contains are tallied with reference to *pronunciation*, not *spelling*.

3-7 Hybrid Writing Systems

A hybrid in the world of plants has mixed parentage: it is a cross between two strains. A hybrid writing system is one that mixes two or more principles. We have already noted that the Japanese have a hybrid system: they use Chinese ideographs plus two syllabaries. The hieroglyphics were a hybrid system: some symbols had a purely ideographic content, and some had a phonetic content through the rebus principle. *All* rebus systems are hybrid, since ideographic symbols must exist before they can be modified to represent a phonetic content.

Some languages, such as Hebrew, have an alphabetic system that transcribes just the consonants, not the vowels. In modern Hebrew, diacritics have been added to show the vowels, especially for children.

When we are writing English quickly, we tend to use special symbols to represent whole words, following an ideographic principle. Other words we write out in full. In fact, all abbreviations short-circuit the alphabetic principle and give a hybrid result.

While the alphabetic principle may be used in reading to "sound out" a new word or to recognize less common words, reading is accomplished, to some extent, by ideographic means. In reading, one does not usually scan each letter of each word; rather, each word is recognized as a whole unit having a certain meaning. An example will show that this is so. If you were to see the word ⟨nea⟩ written, it would probably take you quite a while to realize that what was meant was the joint in the middle of the leg. It is easy to "sound out" this misspelling; but when you simply read it, it makes no sense. The ⟨k⟩ of *knee*, while it plays no role in the pronunciation, helps you to recognize the word in writing. This shows that we read to a certain extent by ideographic, rather than alphabetic, means.

To take another example, look at the emphasized words in these phrases:

A *uniformed* guard stood at the door.
It is a waste of time for *uninformed* people to try to have a debate.

You have no difficulty in reading these sentences, even though the letter ⟨u⟩ at the beginning of each similar italicized word represents a totally different sound (the consonant-vowel combination of "use" in the first case and the vowel of "cut" in the second). The only difference in the spelling of the two words is the fourth letter, ⟨n⟩, of "uninformed"—and certainly there is no regular pattern in English spelling by which the pronunciation of the letter ⟨u⟩ is changed by a letter ⟨n⟩ three letters later in the word. This example shows that we do not read familiar words by "sounding them out" but rather by recognizing them as whole units. Even in an almost perfectly alphabetic language like Spanish, a reader will recognize common words as a unit but will make use of the alphabetic principle for reading less common words.

3-7.1 English Writing: Morphophonemic

On what principle is English writing based? We have indicated that it is *not* purely alphabetic and that, in a sense, it is ideographic (at least to the extent that common words are recognized globally, rather than letter by letter). We have also examined some of the historical reasons for the state of English spelling. But we should turn our attention to the question, Just what principle underlies our writing system?

There are words whose spelling is quite anomalous, such as *yacht* and *junta*, but it is clearly not accurate to dismiss English writing as completely irregular. And there are words such as *cat* and *mop* and *bag* that follow the alphabetic principle closely, but it is clearly not accurate to exaggerate the extent to which our writing is alphabetic: The essential point to notice is that English writing is more *regular* than it is *alphabetic*. That regularity may be described as being **morphophonemic** in nature.

From Chapter 2 you will recall that a morpheme is a meaningful chunk of language that cannot be further subdivided into units having meaning. A morpheme may be a word like *cat* or *dog* or *house*, or it may be a unit that cannot stand on its own: the word *walked*, for example, contains two morphemes, *walk* and *-ed*. The suffix *-ed* (pronounced as a t-sound in this case) has a meaning (namely 'past tense'), although it cannot stand on its own. Similarly, the *s* of *dogs* (pronounced "z") is a meaningful unit ('plural').

Oftentimes the same morpheme can be found in a number of different, related words, even though it may be pronounced differently. Examine the following examples:

nation/*nationalize*
clean/*cleanliness*
create/*creation*/*creature*
state/*station*/*static*
sign/*signal*/*assign*
malign/*malignant*
medical/*medicine*/*medicate*
televise/*television*
indicate/*indication*
discuss/*discussion*
magic/*magician*
produce/*product*
suggest/*suggestion*
presume/*presumptive*
social/*society*
cats/dogs/dish(e)s
walked/bagged/patted

Note that the italicized parts of the words represent the same *morpheme* in each set of example words, and that *in each example the morpheme is pronounced in at least two different ways* (the underlined letters are pronounced differently). Because of historical sound changes and combinatory processes (see Chapter 6), the same morphemes have two or more pronunciations.

The study of the pronunciation of morphemes and its role in phonology (see Chapter 8) is called **morphophonemics,** and it is in this sense that English spelling was described as being morphophonemic.

The tendency in English spelling is to spell a given morpheme the same way, even when its pronunciation changes. For example, the past tense morpheme, although pronounced in three different ways (/t/, /d/, and /əd/), is spelled one way: ⟨ed⟩.[12] The plural morpheme has three pronunciations: /s/, /z/, and /əz/; but only two spellings: ⟨s⟩ and ⟨es⟩. The relationship between the words *sign* and *signal*—that is, the fact that both contain the same morpheme—is clearly indicated by the spelling. A purely sound-based writing system would not show the relatedness of these words, nor would it show the relatedness of *state*, *station*, and *static*, or *discuss* and *discussion*, or *magic* and *magician*, or *analogue* and *analogy*.

This morphophonemic principle is widespread in English spelling and certainly affects the way we read, the way we learn to read, and what goes wrong in reading. Clearly, we do not read the same way as people whose writing systems are purely phonemic (alphabetic), syllabic, or ideographic (see Section 3-8). It is important to realize just how basic this principle is to our way of writing and what the consequences would be of changing this principle through spelling "reform."

Finally, let us note that the morphophonemic principle is not carried through in all cases. For example, the relationship between *pronounce* and *pronunciation* is similar to that between *clean* and *cleanliness* but involves a spelling change reflecting the vowel change. Likewise, there is a relationship between *speak* and *speech* and between *instant* and *instance* that is not reflected in the spelling. The morphophonemic principle is incompletely and imperfectly applied in English.

3-8 Writing as an Area of Specialized Inquiry

As a background to understanding the sound system of English and the use of the phonetic alphabet, this chapter has introduced a number of aspects of writing.

Although it is beyond our scope to discuss this subject in detail, it is well to point out that writing is studied most seriously by people interested in language disorders, linguistics, education, psychology, and development. Let us mention a few of these areas.

The principle upon which a language's writing system is based—be it ideographic, syllabic, alphabetic, quasi-alphabetic, or morphophonemic—affects the way in which speakers of that language read, both out loud and silently, and learn to read (see, for example, Gillooly [1973]). Sometimes children's learning disorders are manifested in an impairment in reading and/or writing (see Taylor and Taylor [1983]). Evidence shows that ability to read and ability to spell do not al-

[12] Actually, a few words in which -*ed* is pronounced /t/ may be spelled—or spelt—with a ⟨t⟩, particularly in British spelling.

ways correlate highly and suggests that these are distinct skills (Frith [1980b]). Neurological language disorders may affect both spoken and written language, but not necessarily both in the same individual. Reading disorders show an interesting—and bewildering—range of characteristics. The affected individual may be able to write but not read, read but not write, or neither read nor write (although he was previously literate); or he may have an impairment restricted to a particular grammatical, orthographic, or semantic class.[13]

3-8.1 The Relationship between Reading and Writing: Disabled Readers

In the preceding section, we noted that there is a relationship between writing and reading. This has become a hot issue academically and educationally, both among those whose interest is theoretical and those who want to know "why Johnny can't read."

Let us briefly mention a few experimental findings in this field.

Japanese is an interesting case in point, since (see Section 3-5) it is written both syllabically and ideographically. The syllabic systems, called **kana,** of which we examined the *katakana,* represent the sound and can be pronounced even when the meaning is unknown. The **kanji** are the ideographic characters, derived from Chinese writing, and contain little if any information as to pronunciation. Many words can be written in only one system or the other, and other words are traditionally written only in one system, but the fact remains that speakers of Japanese read by using two different principles.

Experiments using tachistoscopic presentation of stimuli (which allows extremely brief exposure of stimuli to the visual field corresponding to only one or the other cerebral hemisphere) show differences in the processing of kana and kanji. Single kanji appear to be processed by the right hemisphere of the brain, whereas kana and multiple kanji appear to be processed by the left hemisphere. Additionally, some brain-damaged individuals show a different loss in processing ability with respect to the two types of writing systems. This suggests that the different types of writing systems are processed through different channels (Taylor and Taylor [1983]).

Interestingly, reading disabilities appear to be very rare in Japan as compared to North America. This finding is hard to interpret with certainty, however. It may be because children find it easier to process syllables than phonemes (that they do is well known, but it is hard to say how this is related to the question of reading disabilities among the Japanese). Another possible explanation has nothing to do with writing systems, but with cultural values: there is traditionally a high level of maternal involvement in the teaching of reading to a Japanese child. Another possible explanation for this finding lies in the methodology and criteria used by the researchers—just what constitutes a "skilled" reader, what constitutes a "disability"—such things are hard to compare cross-culturally. However, the fact remains that the type of writing system used certainly influences the process of reading, and may influence it significantly.

The strategies used in word recognition depend upon the writing system in use. One study compared Serbo-Croatian with English. In Serbo-Croatian the writing is alphabetic and adheres closely to phonemic representation, whereas English uses a more morphologically based representation with variable sound values for letters. Under experimental conditions, speakers of Serbo-Croatian tend to rely on phonology (speech sounds) for word recognition, whereas speakers of English rely more on the meaning or the visual appearance of the word (Katz and Feldman [1983]).

Just what significance this has for what goes wrong in reading disorders, and on the efficiency of reading in the normal population, is a matter of some controversy, but the English writing system has been blamed for some children's disabilities

[13] Examples:
Grammatical class: the patient may be unable to read and/or write function words, while having no difficulty with content words.
Orthographic class: the patient may show a marked difference in ability to process words whose spelling is more regular (e.g., *cat*) as opposed to less regular (e.g., *weigh*).
Semantic class: the patient may show differences in ability to write/read words differing on a scale of concreteness/abstractness or of emotional content, or which are restricted to a particular subject area.

in reading and writing. It has been shown that some such children can be taught to use Chinese ideographs, although the value of such a skill for English-speaking disabled readers is questionable. However, it does show that these reading-disabled children can associate linguistic symbols with language (Rozin, Poritsky, and Sotsky [1971]).

The suggestion that a reformed spelling system, with a good symbol-to-phoneme correspondence, would solve the problem of Johnny's not being able to read is not confirmed by the data. Finnish has a highly alphabetic writing system, and a study conducted there showed that a large percentage of grade 6 children were reading at a level that would not permit them to function adequately in the higher grades at school (Vähäpassi [1977]). In other words, while the Finnish writing system permits them to read in the physical sense of 'read,' even unfamiliar material or words, it does not give them any advantage in *understanding* printed material.

It is interesting also that disabled readers appear to have problems that are related only to linguistic symbols (letters, characters, etc.). They do not differ markedly from others with regard to pattern recognition in nonlinguistic symbols.

3-8.2 Is the Alphabet Best?

The study of the history of writing systems suggests a consistent progression of development. Ideographs develop from the standardization of pictographs. Rebuses are based on the homophony of words represented ideographically. From rebuses or similar processes a syllabic or semi-syllabic script may develop. Alphabets, in turn, are born out of syllabaries.

There is thus perhaps a tendency to feel that alphabetic writing is in some sense the pinnacle of cultural development and that writing based on other principles is in some sense more "primitive." Also, the pervasive folklore that English is written alphabetically, albeit imperfectly—when in fact its system is largely morphophonemic—supports the view of the superiority of alphabetic writing and the accompanying notion of the cultural superiority of those who use it.

Such assumptions, if they exist, need to be seriously questioned. The notion that alphabetic writing is better is not supported by the facts. We have seen that, with a perfectly alphabetic writing system, Finnish elementary schoolchildren are not prepared any better for high school than English-speaking schoolchildren. We have seen that the almost unbelievably complex Japanese writing system results, perhaps in fewer reading disabilities, and at least in no more. We have seen that American children with reading disabilities may succeed with an ideographic writing system, at least under experimental conditions. There is evidence that silent reading is faster among ordinary readers of Chinese and Japanese than among ordinary readers of English. There is psycholinguistic evidence that the syllable is a "psychologically real" element, whereas the phoneme is not.[14] While this point is to some extent controversial, the psychological reality of the syllable is generally agreed upon, and therefore the syllable seems a reasonable candidate for the functional unit in a writing system.

Printing considerations must be included in any discussion of this question: the amount of space taken on the page, the time taken to write a message, the amount of ambiguity and redundancy in the written form. The number of different symbols is also an issue, with electromechanical printing devices, and particularly computers,[15] in wide use.

It is by no means a foregone conclusion, therefore, that alphabetic writing is best. But not only are there likely to be universal principles governing reading, which may point the way to the "best" writing system (much research must be done before these are fully understood), there are the phonemic and morphological structure of the language to be considered. The "best" writing system depends upon the language being written.

We noted that some Semitic languages are written without the vowels. Ths wld b trrbl sstm fr Nglsh[16] but is very efficient for those Semitic languages in which the vowels are essentially pre-

[14] A "psychologically real" unit is one that is included in the mental representation of language.

[15] The use of the Roman alphabet and of the kana (syllabaries) has greatly increased in Japan at the expense of the kanji (ideographs), because of the increased use of computers in text production.

[16] "This would be a terrible system for English."

dictable. Chinese writing is very complex, as we have seen, but an alphabetic writing system would result in unmanageable ambiguity because of the enormous homophony in the language.

My own view is that English is best written morphophonemically; that is, written such that morphophonemes maintain an orthographic identity even as their pronunciation changes. This is not to say that English orthography could not be vastly improved; I believe it could with the extension of the morphophonemic principle and the reduction of obviously anomalous spellings. However, in my opinion, English writing and reading would not be improved if English were written according to a strict alphabetic principle. On this point, my view is diametrically opposed to that of spelling reformers who advocate phonemic spelling, such as George Bernard Shaw.

3-9 The International Phonetic Alphabet

By the nineteenth century, Europeans had colonized much of the world: North America, Africa, Asia, the South Pacific. In the process of expansion, many hundreds of groups of peoples were discovered, speaking many hundreds of different languages. The Europeans needed to learn these languages, at least the rudiments of them, for purposes of trade, living side by side in peace, conversion to Christianity, colonial exploitation, and so on. Written records were necessary for the benefit of subsequent travelers in the region. Thus, a hodgepodge of different scripts was developed to transcribe these languages, usually depending upon the native language and even upon the whims of the person who was recording the language. For this reason, as well as for the benefit of the study of philology (word and language history) that was flourishing at the time, some form of standard writing system was needed. The International Phonetic Association was founded in 1886 by the French phonetician Paul Passy, and the Association developed the **International Phonetic Alphabet (IPA).**

The IPA was intended for use in transcribing the sounds of any language that had been discovered or might be discovered in the future. Its aim was to allow anyone familiar with the system, no matter what his native language, to have a very good idea of how to pronounce an unknown language.

The original attempt was very nearly successful, for very few modifications to the system have been made over the years. It should not be expected to be perfect, however, since there are always minor phonetic differences that cannot be recorded. For example, speakers of French, English, and Italian do not produce exactly the same kind of ee-sound (/i/ in the phonetic alphabet), and while the IPA can record some of this difference, it cannot record all of it.

3-9.1 Differences in Phonetic Alphabets

Since the IPA was designed for the purpose of writing down the sounds of all languages, it might be expected to handle English in a simple and consistent way, so it may come as a surprise that different books use slightly different sets of symbols for the same sounds.

The reasons for this are quite straightforward. The IPA is by its very nature a compromise: since it can record with reasonable accuracy the sounds of any language, it is not perfectly suited to any one language. For example, the IPA is not well suited to some of the peculiarities of English, particularly the vowels, so different authors have adapted it to English in slightly different ways. The way the phonetic alphabet is used also depends on just how specific a representation is desired. For example, perhaps it is necessary to record just the gross phonetic form of English words. Perhaps a system is needed that will show subtle differences in dialect. This can require a very fine transcription, with precise use of each symbol. The demands on the phonetic alphabet are again slightly different if it is being used to show a foreigner how to pronounce English. Many readers of this book will use it to record misarticulations and mispronunciations, so that other pathologists can see how a particular client pronounced a word on a particular occasion. This is a purpose for which the IPA was not developed, so some modifications are needed to make it suitable.

There is still another reason for differences in usage of the phonetic alphabet, particularly in North America. Many of the classic letters of the IPA are different in shape from any of the letters available on most typewriters. Common usage has substituted other symbols that can be written more easily without special equipment. For ex-

Table 3-1. The International Phonetic Alphabet Revised to 1951

		Bi-labial	Labio-dental	Dental and Alveolar	Retroflex	Palato-alveolar	Alveolo-palatal	Palatal	Velar	Uvular	Pharyngal	Glottal
CONSONANTS	Plosive	p b		t d	ʈ ɖ			c ɟ	k g	q ɢ		ʔ
	Nasal	m	ɱ	n	ɳ			ɲ	ŋ	ɴ		
	Lateral Fricative			ɬ ɮ								
	Lateral Non-fricative			l	ɭ			ʎ				
	Rolled			r						ʀ		
	Flapped			ɾ	ɽ					ʀ		
	Fricative	ɸ β	f v	θ ð | s z | ɹ	ʂ ʐ	ʃ ʒ	ɕ ʑ	ç j	x ɣ	χ ʁ	ħ ʕ	h ɦ
	Frictionless Continuants and Semi-vowels	w | ɥ	ʋ	ɹ				j (ɥ)	(w)	ʁ		
VOWELS								Front	Central Back			
	Close	(y ʉ u)						i y	ɨ ʉ ɯ u			
	Half-close	(ø o)						e ø	ə ɤ o			
	Half-open	(œ ɔ)						ɛ œ æ	ɐ ʌ ɔ			
	Open	(ɒ)						a	ɑ ɒ			

(Secondary articulations are shown by symbols in brackets.)

Other Sounds.—Palatalized consonants: ƫ, ȡ, etc.; palatalized ʃ, ʒ: ʆ, ʓ. Velarized or pharyngalized consonants: ɫ, ᵭ, ᵶ, etc. Ejective consonants (with simultaneous glottal stop): p', t', etc. Implosive voiced consonants: ɓ, ɗ, etc. ɼ fricative trill. σ, ϱ (labialized θ, ð, or s, z). ʅ, ʓ (labialized ʃ, ʒ). ʇ, ʗ, ʖ (clicks, Zulu *c*, *q*, *x*). ɺ (a sound between r and l). ŋ Japanese syllabic nasal. ɧ (combination of x and ʃ). ʍ (voiceless w). ɪ, ʏ, ɷ (lowered varieties of i, y, u). ɜ (a variety of ə). ɵ (a vowel between ø and o).

Affricates are normally represented by groups of two consonants (ts, tʃ, dʒ, etc.), but, when necessary, ligatures are used (ʦ, ʧ, ʤ, etc.), or the marks ͡ or ‿ (t͡s or t‿s, etc.). ͡ ‿ also denote synchronic articulation (m͡ŋ = simultaneous m and ŋ). c, ɟ may occasionally be used in place of tʃ, dʒ, and ƺ, ƻ for ts, dz. Aspirated plosives: ph, th, etc. r-coloured vowels: eɹ, aɹ, ɔɹ, etc., or eʴ, aʴ, ɔʴ, etc., or ᶒ, ᶏ, ᶗ, etc.; r-coloured ə: əɹ or əʴ or ɹ or ᶕ or ɚ.

Length, Stress, Pitch.— ː (full length). ˑ (half length). ˈ (stress, placed at beginning of the stressed syllable). ˌ (secondary stress). ˉ (high level pitch); ˍ (low level); ˊ (high rising); ˏ (low rising); ˋ (high falling); ˎ (low falling); ˆ (rise-fall); ˇ (fall-rise).

Modifiers.— ˜ nasality. ˳ breath (l̥ = breathed l). ˬ voice (s̬ = z). ʻ slight aspiration following p, t, etc. ‿ labialization (n̫ = labialized n). ̪ dental articulation (t̪ = dental t). ˙ palatalization (ż = ʓ). ̣ specially close vowel (ẹ = a very close e). ̨ specially open vowel (ę = a rather open e). ˔ tongue raised (e˔ or e̝ = ẹ). ˕ tongue lowered (e˕ or e̞ = ę). ˖ tongue advanced (u˖ or u̟ = an advanced u, t̟ = t̪). ˗ or ̠ tongue retracted (i˗ or i̠ = ɨ˖, t̠ = alveolar t). ˒ lips more rounded. ˓ lips more spread. Central vowels: ï (= ɨ), ü (= ʉ), ë (= ə˔), ö (= ɵ), ɛ̈, ɔ̈. ̩ (e.g. n̩) syllabic consonant. ̆ consonantal vowel. ʃˢ variety of ʃ resembling s, etc.

Source: International Phonetic Association. Reprinted by permission.

ample, the first sound of the word "show" is written in the IPA as [ʃ], but North American phoneticians have most frequently substituted the symbol [š] (borrowed from the Czechoslovakian alphabet), since it is easier to write.

Finally, we might mention the temptation to "simplify" in a manner different from that mentioned in the preceding paragraph. In this type of "simplification," symbols of the IPA are used for sounds other than those they officially represent. This may solve an immediate problem, but it creates difficulties when different authors make different "simplifications." Let us look at three common examples:

1. The type of r-sound found in most dialects of North American English is correctly represented as /ɹ/. This is an awkward symbol to write clearly. The letter /r/ exists in the IPA to represent a sound that is not used in North American English (the sound correctly represented by /r/ occurs in Spanish, British English, and other languages). Writers of American books, particularly if their subject is restricted to English, are tempted to use the very handy symbol /r/ and to avoid the nuisance associated with /ɹ/ by not using it.
2. The initial sound of the word "you" is represented in the IPA as /j/. The IPA letter /y/ repre-

sents a vowel not found in standard English. Once again, if one is dealing only with English, one is tempted to use the familiar symbol /y/ in place of /j/, although it contradicts the IPA.

3. In the IPA the symbols /a/ and /ɑ/ are distinguished; they represent different sounds. For purposes of broad transcription of English, it is not necessary to distinguish these sounds; the sound represented by /a/ does not occur distinctively in most dialects. Since the symbol /a/ is generally more available than the symbol /ɑ/, it is often used for the sound value of /ɑ/.

It is the attitude of this book that the type of modification exemplified by the substitution of /š/ for /ʃ/ (as in "show") is reasonable in that no ambiguity results. That is, the symbol /š/ has only one value, even though a student who has learned /ʃ/ will need to learn /š/ if he/she changes teachers or books. However, the type of "simplification" that substitutes /r/ for /ɹ/, /y/ for /j/, and /a/ for /ɑ/ is more problematic because it leaves ambiguity. That is, the reader is no longer sure whether the symbol /a/ represents IPA /a/ or IPA /ɑ/, and so forth. Nonetheless, the convenience argument is quite compelling, particularly for the r-sound. It must be remembered, though, that such substitutions lead to confusion, uncertainty about letter values, and an inability to record small phonetic differences.

In this book the various possibilities will be indicated. Preferences in instruction and laboratory materials may differ, however, so remember that other forms are in use. Since they may be encountered in other books, it is well to have a passing familiarity with the symbols, even though they may not be the preferred usage in this book.

Table 3-1 shows the official International Phonetic Alphabet. In this text we will follow general North American usage as given in the table of symbols at the front of the book. The various phonetic symbols are introduced throughout this book at the appropriate points.

Summary

Although the two are often confused, **writing** is not the same thing as **language;** writing is a means—generally arbitrary—of putting language into a visual medium. Written and spoken language have different purposes and are different in character.

Pictographic writing uses a picture or pictures to convey a message. There is no one-to-one correspondence between aspects of the picture and words of the spoken language. Pictographs are generally **iconic,** but many contain conventional symbols. Our culture uses pictographs in public signs.

Ideally, **ideographic** writing uses a one-to-one correspondence between symbols **(characters)** and words of the spoken language. No pure ideographic system is in use, although major aspects of the Chinese writing system are ideographic. In our culture, such symbols as 1, 2, 3, . . . %, and & are ideographic.

By the **rebus** principle, an ideographic character is used to represent a **homophonous** word. In historical terms, rebuses are important in that they provided the stepping-stone from the non-sound-based ideographic system to the sound-based syllabic and alphabetic systems. In our culture, however, rebuses are generally restricted to riddles and visual puns.

In **syllabic writing,** each symbol represents a syllable of the spoken language. These symbols together compose a **syllabary.** In historical terms, the first syllabic writing system was the first system of writing to consistently link symbols with units of sound. The Japanese make widespread, although not exclusive, use of syllabic writing. In our own culture, we generally restrict syllabic writing to "cute" commercial or jocular uses of letters as syllabic symbols.

Ideally, in **alphabetic** writing, each distinct sound of the spoken language is represented by a different symbol, called a **letter.** Our alphabet, the Roman alphabet, came about through a long historical growth from an ideographic to an alphabetic system.

For historical reasons, English writing does not adhere very closely to the alphabetic principle. English writing is sometimes alphabetic, sometimes anomalous, and often morphophonemic.

The writing system used affects the way people read; it may affect the cerebral processing of written language, and it is likely that it is relevant to reading disorders.

It is important to distinguish between **sounds**

and **letters;** the rest of this book discusses speech sounds primarily. A *consonant*, for example, is a type of *sound*, not a type of *letter*.

The **International Phonetic Alphabet** permits the use of a different symbol for each *different* (not just contrasting) sound. Usage of the IPA varies somewhat, particularly in terms of how it is applied to a given language.

Vocabulary

alphabet
alphabetic writing
character
cuneiform
determinative
diacritics
digraph
etymology
glottal stop
hieroglyphics
homophone, homophonous
iconic
ideographic
imitative
International Phonetic Alphabet (IPA)
kana: katakana, hiragana
kanji
letter
logographic
morpheme
morphophonemic
onomatopoeic
phonetic component
phonetization
pictographic
Pinyin
rebus
romanize
syllabary
syllabic writing
writing

Questions

1. Why did the developers of the International Phonetic Alphabet (IPA) choose an alphabet rather than a syllabic system?
2. Give some examples from your experience of ways in which our culture uses the various types of writing systems. Choose examples other than those given in the chapter.
3. Summarize the relative merits and disadvantages of the various writing systems. For each type, try to think of a situation in which that type would be the best means of written communication.
4. What sound-letter correspondences exist in English spelling? What regular combinatory variants occur? For example, what sounds does the letter ⟨g⟩ represent in such words as "go," "gin," and "right"? What rules govern the sound-symbol correspondence? What exceptions are there to those rules (such as "margarine," "judgment," and "longing")? Examine other letters and digraphs in the same way.
5. In Section 3-6.4 we discussed how certain spelling conventions represent quite unrelated phenomena; for example, consonant letters are doubled not because the consonant sound is doubled but rather to indicate vowel quality or stress placement. Find and discuss other examples of such conventions.
6. Find additional examples to extend the list of morphophonemes in Section 3-7.1.
7. Discuss how the morphophonemic writing principle affects how we read. If spelling were "reformed" so as to be phonemic or alphabetic, what would we gain? What would we lose? How would our reading change?
8. What would an "ideal" writing system for English consist of? Would it be strictly alphabetic? Would it extend the morphophonemic principle? Would it spell foreign words differently from native words? Would it distinguish homophones in spelling? Discuss.

Readings

Exercises in transliteration (changing one script to another) can be found in Algeo's *Problems in the Origins and Development of the English Language* [1972].

There are a good number of short books on the history of writing that give more detail than this chapter. For example, Moorhouse's *The Triumph of the Alphabet* [1953] includes an interesting section on deciphering unknown scripts.

An excellent chapter on the development of scripts and the relationships among them can be found in Pedersen's *The Discovery of Language* [1967].

Technical discussions of issues in reading and writing can be found in the references in Section 3-8 and in Frith's *Cognitive Processes in Spelling* and MacKinnon and Walker's *Reading Research: Advances in Theory and Practice*.

Speech articulation, dynamics, and organization

II

Articulatory phonetics: vowels

4

Objectives

To survey briefly the "organs of speech."

To distinguish vowels from consonants.

To classify vowels on the basis of their articulation.

To present the IPA symbols for vowels.

To introduce vowel length and diphthongization.

To examine vowels not found in English.

To point out that the standard classification contains inaccuracies or, at the very least, overgeneralizations.

4-1 Speech Sounds

Before examining individual speech sounds, we should repeat a point made earlier: that for speech to serve its communicative purpose, it must be made up of **contrasting** sounds, and there must be a considerable number of contrasts.

English, for example, has about forty contrasting speech sounds (the number depends upon the dialect). These sounds can be combined in many ways (although not in just any way, as will be shown in Chapter 8). The result is that an enormous number of different words are possible, without resort to the memory-taxing polysyllabic words[1] that would be needed if there were only a few contrasts. The number of different one- and two-syllable words in English is huge, as an unabridged dictionary demonstrates, and many possible words are not used. If we suddenly needed twice our present vocabulary, we could attain it without inventing new words longer than two syllables. *Strink* and *plick* and so on would be perfectly acceptable new words, having the advantages of being short, pronounceable, easy to remember, and, most importantly, easy to distinguish from other English words; they follow English phonetic **rules,** as the term was used in Chapter 2.

As emphasized in Section 2-5, it is the phonetic *contrasts* of a language that carry meaning. Individual speech sounds cannot be said to have any meaning. For example, the vowel of the word *meet* is meaningless by itself; but in the context of an English word, since it is distinctively different from other English vowels, this vowel indicates that the word spoken is *meet* and not *mate* or *might* or *moat* or *moot* or *mitt,* or whatever. The speaker, of course, is concerned with the meaning of the word *meet* and is not conscious of phonetic considerations. He is able to communicate his meaning through the medium of speech only because there are systematic contrasts among the speech sounds of his language.

4-2 The Supraglottal Organs

We will look at speech physiology in some detail later (Chap. 9), but for our study of articulatory phonetics in Chapters 4–7 we need to familiarize ourselves with the basic form of the supraglottal organs and the anatomical terms used in classifying speech sounds. The supraglottal organs (those above the larynx) and the vocal folds are the speech organs that will be most often mentioned in this book. Figure 4-1 gives a schematized cross section of the head and identifies the important articulatory organs.

We will examine each of these organs in turn, giving each organ its usual name—generally derived from Latin or Greek—and also giving its adjective. These adjectives will be important for referring to speech sounds; for example, a speech sound made with the *lips* is a *labial* sound.

THE LIPS. The lips are used to close the oral cavity in the production of some consonants. They may be rounded and extended in the production of certain vowels. The adjective is **labial** (L. *labia,* 'lips'); when both lips are involved, we speak of a **bilabial** sound.

THE TEETH. Sounds involving the teeth are referred to as **dental** sounds (L. *dentes,* 'teeth'). The upper teeth are involved in speech production more often than the lower ones.

> As the term is most often used, *dental* sounds are those involving the upper front teeth (the upper incisors), as in the f-sound or the th-sound. In fact, other teeth come into play in speech production, but such sounds are *not* called *dental.* For example, the English t-sound is articulated with the sides of the tongue touching the upper molars (back teeth). The English t-sound, however, is not classified as a dental sound.

THE TONGUE. The tongue is the most agile organ of speech; in fact, the word **tongue** means 'language,' not only in English, but in many other languages as well (the word *language* is derived from the Latin word *lingua,* 'tongue'). Many gestures of the tongue are used in speech, and the tongue contacts many of the other speech organs.

The tongue is divided into five regions: the **tip** or **apex,** the **blade,** the **front,** the **back,** and the **root;** these are indicated in Figure 4-1. The **apex** is

[1]**Polysyllabic:** having many syllables.

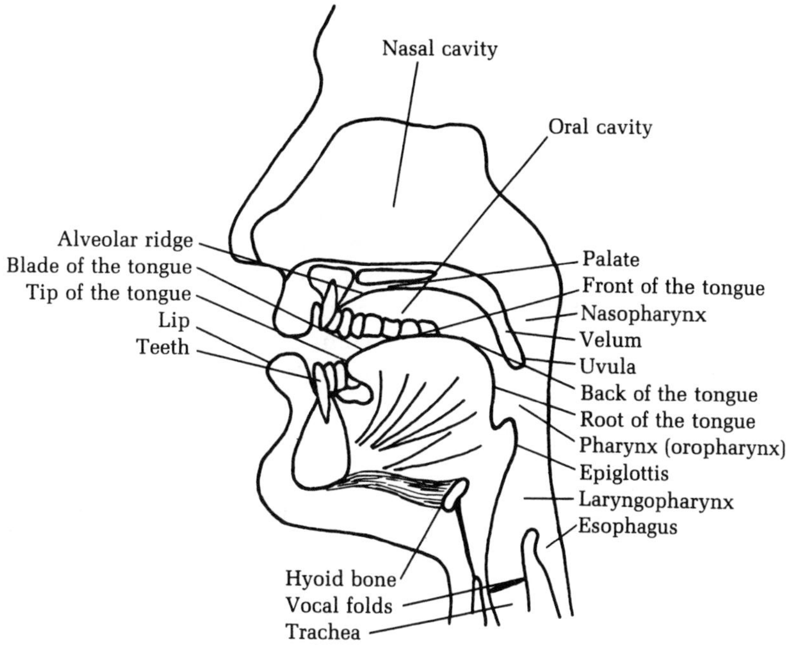

Figure 4-1. A stylized cross section of the head showing the articulators important in the production of speech.

the very tip of the tongue. The **blade** is a very short section of the tongue surface, the part that normally lies below the *alveolar ridge* at rest. The **front** (despite its name) is the middle portion of the oral surface of the tongue, lying below the *palate* at rest. The **back** is the rear portion of the oral tongue surface, lying below the *velum* at rest. The **root** is that part of the surface of the tongue that faces into the *pharynx* or throat cavity. The *front* and *back* are often considered together as the tongue **dorsum.** The adjective for *tongue* is **lingual,** for *tip* is **apical** (L. *apex,* 'tip'), for *blade* is **laminal** (L. *lamina,* 'blade'), and for *dorsum* is **dorsal** (L. *dorsum,* 'back').

THE ALVEOLAR RIDGE (L. *alveus,* 'trough,' 'tray'). Also called the **gum ridge,** this is the ridge directly behind the upper front teeth. The adjectival form is **alveolar.**

THE PALATE (L. *palatum,* 'palate'). The palate is the hard, bony part of the roof of the mouth that extends from the alveolar ridge to the velum. The adjectival form is **palatal.**

THE VELUM (L. *velum* [*palati*], 'veil [of the palate]'). The velum is the soft, muscular rear part of the roof of the mouth that lacks any bony framework. It can be raised and lowered by its own musculature. This movement serves a valving function; when the velum is *raised,* the nasal cavities are closed off from the rest of the vocal tract, as they are during oral breathing or during swallowing. When the velum is *lowered,* the passage (or **velic port**) between the nasal cavities and the oropharyngeal cavity is open, as it is for nasal breathing; this introduces **nasal resonance** and thus imparts a nasal quality to speech sounds produced with a lowered velum.

As with the *alveolar ridge* and *palate,* we use the *velum* as a reference point in describing what position the *tongue* is assuming. If the tongue is arched below the velum, or is touching the velum, we call this a **velar** articulation. Note that in a velar articulation the velum has not done anything. On the other hand, when the velum itself moves, performing the valving function just described, we speak of a **velic** movement or articulation. Be sure to distinguish **velar** (referring to the part of the oral cavity below the velum) from **velic** (referring to the velum itself).

Some authors call the palate the *hard palate* and the velum the *soft palate*. Medical anatomists use the term *palate* in a more general sense, referring to the velum as well as the palate. But in the study of speech, the distinction between the two entities is very important, so phoneticians and speech scientists generally use the clear, unambiguous terms **palate** for the bony part and **velum** for the muscular part.

Note that the **uvula** attaches to the rear edge of the velum. Do not confuse the small uvula with the velum itself; the latter makes up about two-fifths of the roof of the mouth. The uvula plays a role in the articulation of some sounds in some languages, although English has no **uvular** sounds.

THE ORAL CAVITY (L. *os/oralis*, 'mouth,' 'oral'). This cavity is a resonating chamber of primary importance to speech, since its size and shape can be modified so greatly. Its internal volume can be changed by modification of the tongue and jaw positions.

THE NASAL CAVITIES (L. *nasus*, 'nose'). Velic action allows the nasal cavities to be closed or open (or partially open) with respect to the rest of the vocal tract. Opening the velic port allows sound waves to resonate within the nasal cavities, giving a distinctive nasal quality to the speech sounds thus produced.

THE PHARYNX (Gk. *pharynx*, 'throat'). The pharynx is the cavity above the larynx and behind the oral cavity. In everyday language we might refer to it as the "throat cavity" or simply the "throat." For added precision, the pharynx is often divided into three parts:

1. The **laryngopharynx,** which is the lowest part of the **pharyngeal cavity,** or pharynx, just above the *larynx*
2. The **oropharynx,** which is the mid part of the pharyngeal cavity at the very back of the mouth
3. The **nasopharynx,** which includes the nasal vestibule (the entrance to the nasal cavities: entrance, as seen from the pharynx, that is)

THE TRACHEA (Gk. *trachea*, 'neck'; 'place to grab someone to strangle him'). The trachea is the tube that leads from the larynx to where it splits into two **bronchi,** which connect to the **lungs.** It is made up of cartilaginous rings interconnected by connective tissue; it is generally pictured as looking rather like a vacuum-cleaner hose.

THE VOCAL FOLDS. In the *pharynx* at the top of the *trachea* is located a cartilaginous structure called the **larynx.** The larynx with its associated structures serves to protect the lungs from aspiration of food or liquid. Among these structures are the **vocal folds.** The vocal folds vibrate during the articulation of vowels and of many consonants. This vibration is known as **voicing** or **phonation; voiced** sounds are those that are produced with vocal fold vibration, **voiceless** sounds without. The space between the vocal folds is known as the **glottis;** certain articulations of the vocal folds are known as **glottal** articulations. Adjustments of the vocal folds are involved in whispering, intonation, breathiness, and so on (see Chapters 7 and 9).

4-3 Vowels and Consonants

If you were asked to explain the difference between vowels and consonants, you might respond by dividing the letters of the alphabet into those two classifications. As we stressed in Chapter 3, however, phoneticians classify speech *sounds*, not letters, as vowels or consonants. Letters may represent either type of speech sound, although our English spelling system has a poor correspondence between sounds and letters. For example, only six letters in our alphabet represent vowels, but there are about fifteen distinctive vowel sounds in English. In the International Phonetic Alphabet (IPA), there is a better correspondence between letters and sounds, but the terms **vowel** and **consonant** still always refer to *sounds*, never to letters or symbols. The term **phone** or **segment** means a single speech sound.[2] A person does not pronounce *letters*, but speech sounds. Each distinctly different phone is represented by a different IPA symbol.

Phones are classified as vowels or consonants chiefly on the basis of how they are articulated. For the articulation of vowels, the oral cavity is open at least as far as it is for the vowels of "beat" and "boot"—that is, the airflow is unimpeded—and the vocal folds are generally vibrating. For consonants, the airstream is stopped, impeded, or diverted through the nasal passage, and the vocal folds may or may not be vibrating.

In general, your intuition about what is a vowel and what is a consonant will be correct, with the possible exception of some r-sounds and perhaps a few other segments.

This chapter will consider the vowels; the consonants will be considered in Chapter 5.

4-4 Vowels

As we noted in Section 4-3, vowels are articulated with an unobstructed vocal tract and almost always with the vocal folds vibrating. The acoustic nature of vowels is dependent upon the phenomenon of **resonance;** we will examine the acoustic production of vowels in Chapter 10. For the moment suffice it to say that in vowel production the vocal tract is a **resonator,** and that the sound frequencies generated by a resonator depend upon the size and shape of the resonator. We produce different vowels by changing the size and shape of the vocal resonators. Generally phoneticians classify vowels by the position that the speech articulators assume in producing them. So most of this chapter will be devoted to a study of articulatory positions in vowel articulation, as well as to learning the letters of the International Phonetic Alphabet (IPA) used to represent the vowels.

Several major articulatory dimensions are used in classifying vowels. These include:

1. Height. By moving the lower jaw up and down and/or by moving the tongue body up and down within the lower jaw, the oral cavity can be made wider or narrower. This vertical dimension is called the **height** of the vowel.
2. Frontness. Most vowels are produced with a certain arching of the tongue. This arching may be toward the front, the middle, or the back of the oral cavity.
3. Lip-rounding. Vowels may be produced with lips rounded, in a neutral position, or with the corners of the mouth spread.

Those are the three dimensions traditionally used to classify the vowels of English. However, it is apparent that other dimensions are required for articulatory accuracy:

4. Tongue root position. The tongue root may be moved forward or back, widening or narrowing the pharynx. This affects the acoustic quality of the vowel.
5. Velic position. If the velum is lowered, resonance occurs in the nasal cavity as well as in the mouth and pharynx, giving the vowel a nasalized quality. While this adjustment is not distinctive (phonemic) in English, in many languages it is. Also, this dimension is required for a precise description of English vowels in many words.

> 6. Laryngeal position. Some researchers have demonstrated that we adjust the height of the larynx as we talk. Theoretically this should have an effect on vowel quality. However, little research has been done on this question, and any findings have not been integrated into standard vowel taxonomies, so we will not consider it in any detail.

4-4.1 The International Phonetic Alphabet

Before looking at vowel articulation in light of the foregoing dimensions, it might be helpful to discuss briefly the IPA letters that will be introduced in this and the next chapter. As noted in Chapter 3, the IPA was developed in Europe and is based in large part on the Roman alphabet. However, the phonetic values of letters of the Roman alphabet in English are often atypical of the phonetic

[2] The term **phoneme** is sometimes loosely used to mean a speech sound, but this term properly has a more specific meaning, as discussed in Chapters 2 and 8.

values of these letters in most other languages, as well as the IPA. As a result, the phonetic value of these letters, particularly the vowels, may seem unfamiliar or contradictory to the English-speaking person. You may need to pay particular attention to avoid confusion. Furthermore, many symbols in the IPA are not in the Roman alphabet. Pay attention to the exact form of the symbols in writing them, as fine distinctions are often made between them. For example, [ɑ] and [a] are different letters of the IPA, representing different sounds, as are [e] and [ɛ], and [i] and [ɪ]. ([ɪ] may also be represented by [ɩ]). Personalizing letters of the IPA may result in a transcription that is simply wrong.

4-4.2 Frontness and Height

The vowel [i] as in "beet" is produced with the jaw raised. The vowel [æ] as in "bat" is produced with the jaw lowered. Pronounce the two vowels in turn, noting the jaw position and noting also that the tongue stays arched in the forward part of the mouth. Now try the vowels [u] as in "boot" and [ɑ] as in "father." Note that [u] is pronounced with the jaw raised and [ɑ] with the jaw lowered. Also note that the arch of the tongue is toward the back of the oral cavity for both of these vowels. ([u] is pronounced with lip-rounding, but do not let this fact distract you from paying attention to what your *tongue* is doing; we will discuss lip-rounding separately below.) Figure 4-2 shows stylized diagrams of these articulations.

A quadrangle (four-sided figure) has been overlaid on the diagrams in Figure 4-2. This quadrangle is used to specify the tongue position. We will use this **vowel quadrangle** later without the accompanying sketch of the head and tongue.

The four vowels considered so far—[i, æ, u, ɑ]—are produced with the tongue as far as possible from its rest position. If the tongue were raised any more than for [i] or [u], a consonant would be produced. The tongue and jaw positions are as low as practicable for the sounds [æ] and [ɑ]. These vowels, along with others around the periphery of the vowel quadrangle, are called **cardinal** vowels. They are like the cardinal points of the compass, providing reference points for identifying other, **noncardinal,** vowels.

At this point, take time to convince yourself that the preceding descriptions are accurate. Use a mirror and a safely blunt object (such as a tongue depressor) to examine the configuration of your mouth during the production of these vowels. You can also use the technique of prolonging the production of each vowel and concentrate on feeling the position of your tongue or other articulator. The articulatory positions for [æ] and [ɑ] may be particularly difficult to identify. This is because these are the *lowest* (most open) vowels and the tongue is quite flat in the mouth—there may be so little tongue arching that the arch is hard to locate. However, if you alternate pronouncing [æ] and [ɑ] several times rapidly, you will feel the tongue moving forward and back.

We noted that for [i] and [æ] the arching of the tongue is forward in the mouth and the jaw is in the extreme high and the extreme low position, respectively. The jaw can also be between these extremes, as it is for the vowel [e] in "bait."

We noted that for [i] and [u] the jaw is in a raised position and that the arching of the tongue is toward the front of the mouth for [i] and toward the back of the mouth for [u]. The arch of the tongue can be between these extremes, however, as it is for the vowel [ə] in "about."

In classifying vowels, we identify the highest point on the arch of the tongue and consider that point to be the point of articulation of the vowel. That point is described by its position along the **height** and **frontness** dimensions.

In describing vowel height, the vertical dimension, the terms **high, mid,** and **low** are used. The **mid** height may be subdivided into **upper-mid** and **lower-mid.**

In describing vowel frontness, the horizontal dimension, the terms **front, central,** and **back** are used. Do not confuse the terms **central** and **mid.**

In order to identify the point of articulation of a vowel, both dimensions must be given; the height dimension is normally given first. So we identify [i] as a high front vowel, [u] as a high back vowel, [æ] as a low front vowel, and [ɑ] as a low back vowel. As noted, it is sometimes difficult to locate the arch of the tongue in low vowels; the jaw position may be used to identify these as low vowels. Other dimensions must often be specified as well; we will look at them below.

Two notes before we leave height and frontness.

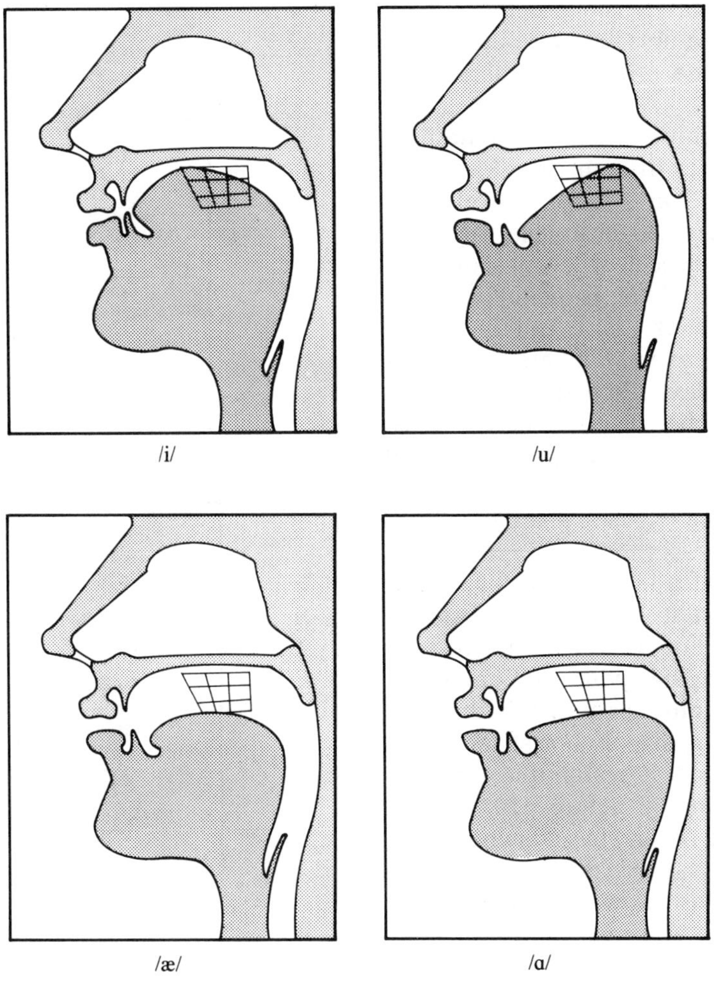

Figure 4-2. The articulation of four cardinal vowels.

First, while the term **height** reflects current usage, this dimension was once called *closeness*. So you may see in other books the term *close* for **high,** *half-close* for **upper-mid,** *half-open* for **lower-mid,** and *open* for **low.** However, those terms are out of fashion and will not be used again in this book.

Second, we noted that vowel height may be achieved either by jaw position or by the tongue position with respect to the jaw. In fact, in rapid, connected speech, the tongue body tends to move up and down *within* the jaw much more than the jaw itself moves up and down.

4-4.3 TENSENESS

Another dimension of vocalic[3] articulation is what has traditionally been called **tenseness.** It had been noted that certain pairs of vowels, although they shared most of the same articulatory features, differed in "tenseness"—one would be classed as **tense,** the other as **lax.** As the name

[3] **Vocalic** is the adjective for *vowel*. The articulation of a vowel is a **vocalic articulation.** A sound following a vowel is in **postvocalic position;** a sound preceding a vowel is in **prevocalic position.** Do not confuse **vocalic,** 'having to do with vowels,' with the word *vocal*, which refers to speech production in general and to vocal fold vibration in particular.

suggests, the tense vowel was thought to be pronounced with a general tension of the speech muscles, whereas these muscles were thought to be more relaxed in the articulation of the lax vowels.

This point of view holds considerable intuitive appeal. If you pronounce [i] as in "beet"—a tense vowel—and [ɪ] as in "bit"—a lax vowel—you will probably feel a greater tension in the facial and other muscles of speech when pronouncing the tense vowel. A second pair is the [u] of "boot" (tense) and the [ʊ] of "book" (lax). And the vowels [e] as in "bait" and [ɛ] as in "bet" are sometimes classed as tense and lax, respectively, although one may also point to height differences in classifying these vowels. In all three pairs, you will probably experience greater muscular tension when pronouncing the "tense" than the "lax" vowel.[4]

However, it is doubtful that the term *tenseness* captures the significant phonetic differences among these vowels. For basic acoustic reasons that will become clear when you read Chapter 10, simply tensing a few muscles will not change a vowel sound unless the size and/or shape of the vocal cavities is changed. Research into the question (Ladefoged [1968], MacKay [1977], and Stewart [1967], among others) has shown that the root of the tongue is advanced (moved forward) in the articulation of tense vowels, widening the pharynx (see Fig. 4-3). You can confirm this fact indirectly by putting your finger on your throat just below the jawbone and pronouncing [i], [ɪ], [u], and [ʊ]. You will note that your finger is forced outward slightly as you pronounce the tense vowels but not as you pronounce the lax vowels.

Even if the tongue root position constitutes the main difference between vowels considered to make up a tense/lax pair, there are other important articulatory differences as well. In the pronunciation of [i], the lips are spread wide (see Section 4-4.4), while they are relaxed for [ɪ]. And [ɪ] is less high and less front than [i]. Similarly, [u] is pronounced with rounded lips, more so than [ʊ], and [ʊ] is less high and less back than [u]. And [e] is a little higher than [ɛ], leading some to suggest that height is the only difference between these vowels; however, the evidence shows that [e] shares some characteristics with other tense vowels, and [ɛ] with other lax vowels; you can demonstrate this by placing your finger on your throat, as described, and pronouncing these vowels.

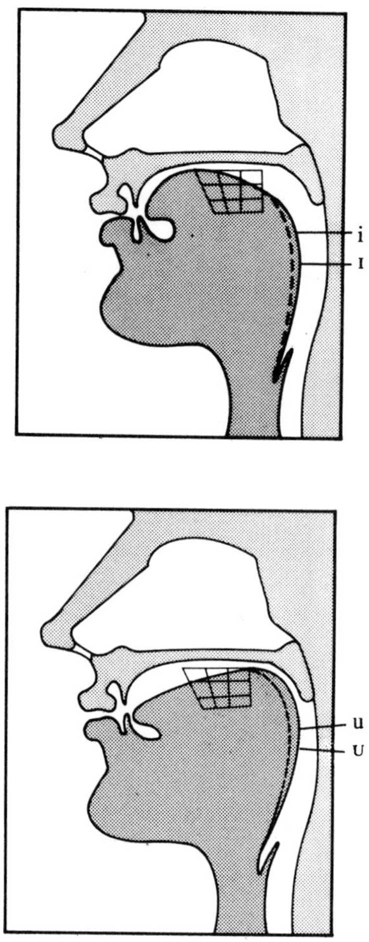

Figure 4-3. The articulation of tense and lax vowels.

Some have suggested that we ought to drop the term **tenseness** and replace it with *advanced tongue root* (ATR). However, the matter is unre-

[4] You may have difficulty pronouncing the lax vowels [ɪ], [ɛ], and [ʊ] in isolation. That is because in English they occur only when followed by a consonant in the same word. When they are pronounced in isolation, there is of course no following consonant. So you may have trouble saying them, just as if they were a foreign sound. This falls under the heading of *phonotactics*, one of the topics of Chapter 8.

solved; and besides, the term *tenseness* is understood to cover *all* the differences between members of a tense/lax pair: tongue root position, lip position, height, frontness, etc.

Also, it is clear that certain muscles *are* tensed in the articulation of tense vowels, in order both to advance the tongue root and to increase the degree of lip involvement. ([u] is more round than [ʊ]; [i] is more spread than [ɪ].)

In summary: (1) Vowel sounds change with a change in the size and/or shape of the vocal cavities, not simply with the tensing of certain muscles; and (2) the terms **tense** and **lax** are understood to refer to a number of phonetic features that appear together, including tongue root position, tongue body position, and lip position.

In guiding others to pronounce this distinction, it is well to heed the words of the influential phonetician Daniel Jones [1932], who pointed out that while he did not accept tenseness to be what others then believed it to be, it is still possible to obtain good results when teaching the sounds in question by instructing students to tense up or relax their tongues.

While phonologists often invoke the tense/lax distinction at all points throughout the vowel quadrangle, it is clear that in strictly phonetic (articulatory) terms the distinction is made among high and mid front vowels and high back vowels.[5] This makes sense if tenseness is primarily a matter of tongue root position; with the tongue body in low and back positions for vowel articulation, the tongue root may be forced back into a position that cannot be changed without moving the tongue body.

[5] **Phonology** is a branch of linguistic study that is concerned, like phonetics, with speech sounds. However, the two fields differ in their objectives and methods. In this, a phonetics text, I am emphasizing the *articulation* of tense versus lax vowels; I am stating that the distinct tongue root positions for tense versus lax vowels occur only with high and mid front vowels and high back vowels. Phonology is more concerned with the systematic *behavior* of segments within the sound system of given languages than with the details of articulation. Many phonologists feel that low and back vowels form pairs that behave the same as the pairs of tense and lax vowels, found in the high and front part of the quadrangle; so they apply these terms to vowels throughout the vowel quadrangle, regardless of whether the articulatory adjustment distinguishing tense and lax is the same between vowels everywhere throughout the quadrangle.

4-4.4 Lip-Rounding

To pronounce the vowel [u], it is necessary to round the lips, but to pronounce the vowel [i], the lips must be spread. In classifying vowel sounds, we sometimes wish to distinguish different degrees of **lip-rounding.** We can do so by using the adjectives **rounded, neutral** (or **unrounded**), and **spread** in describing the vowel.

Many languages distinguish vowels by lip-rounding alone. Such a language may have two vowels that are articulated in the same part of the mouth and whose only difference is that one is rounded while the other is not. In French, for example, there are two high front tense vowels, one rounded, one spread. The French spread vowel, [i], is similar, although not identical, to the equivalent English sound. The high front tense rounded vowel is transcribed [ü][6] and does not occur in standard English. So the French words *pi* [pi] (meaning 'pi,' the Greek letter) and *pu* [pü] ('could') differ only in lip-rounding. There are other pairs of rounded and unrounded vowels in French and other languages, making it necessary in those languages always to specify whether a vowel is rounded or not.

In English, vowels are generally not contrasted by rounding alone. Some vowels are rounded, and others are unrounded, but, with one exception, there are no *pairs* of vowels whose articulation is identical except for rounding. Therefore English vowels are often identified without specifying rounding, since that information would be redundant.

For example, a high back tense vowel in English is always rounded; there is no high back spread vowel in English (although such a vowel exists in some other languages). Whether or not the rounding is specified, however, it remains an important aspect of the articulation of this vowel.

The one exception is the pair of vowels [ʌ] and [ɔ], as in "cut" and "caught."[7] Their place of articulation is similar, but [ʌ] is unrounded while [ɔ] is rounded; so rounding must be specified with these vowels. (In some phonetics texts, [ʌ] is said

[6] The IPA symbol is [y], but the symbol [ü] is replacing [y] among North American linguists.

[7] [ɔ] is the vowel of "caught" in those dialects that distinguish "caught" from "cot."

to be a central vowel, not a back vowel. Such a classification is convenient, since it bypasses the problem of specifying rounding, but it is not an accurate reflection of the articulation in most dialects. Pronounce [ʌ], [ɔ] to see whether your dialect distinguishes them by lip-rounding or by tongue body placement.)

The point rule to remember is that, if in a given language there are pairs of vowels distinguished by rounding alone, then *this feature must be mentioned in describing the vowel.* In French, as we have seen, there are two high front tense vowels, one rounded, one spread. So rounding *must* be mentioned in specifying French vowels. On the other hand, if no vowels in a given language are distinguished by rounding alone, then this feature is often ignored. In English, for example, there is only one high front tense vowel, and it is spread; there is only one high back tense vowel, and it is rounded. So if rounding is not specified, the vowels are still identifiable.

However, *identifying* or *distinguishing* speech sounds is not the same as *describing* articulation. In the descriptions in Section 4-4.8, rounding will be specified.

One other point should be made about lip-rounding, particularly in reference to English. English tends not to use extreme lip postures to distinguish speech sounds, so the spread vowels tend to be less spread than those of many languages, and the rounded vowels tend to be less rounded than in many languages. For example, [u] is classified as a rounded vowel, but if you watch people's lips as they speak English, you will note that the degree of lip-rounding is in fact quite small in most speakers' articulation.

4-4.5 Rhotic Vowels

The word **rhotic** means 'r-like' or 'having an r-quality.' The name comes from *rho,* the letter of the Greek alphabet corresponding to our letter ⟨r⟩. Rhotic vowels are often also called **r-colored.**

A rhotic vowel is a vowel that sounds like an "r." Some examples would be the vowels in the standard North American pronunciation of such words as "bird," "fur," "heard," and "word." Note that while the spelling represents this sound with a vowel letter followed by the consonant letter ⟨r⟩, in phonetic terms *there is just one vocalic sound;* there is no consonant "r" in the example words given.

This English rhotic vowel is a central vowel, transcribed [ɚ]. It is called **schwar.**

> Two points ought to be made concerning transcription. First, the transcription [bɚd] for the word "bird," for example, is a narrowly phonetic transcription correctly indicating that in articulatory terms the vowel and the "r" are inseparable. Phonemic transcription systems, however, often represent this word as /bərd/, which has some intuitive appeal. Do not be misled by such a transcription system into thinking that /ər/ represents a sequence of sounds—any attempt to teach it that way would have peculiar results.
>
> Second, some authors insist on a distinction between [ɝ] and [ɚ]. They use [ɝ] to represent the stressed schwar of "bird," "heard," "her," etc., reserving [ɚ] for the unstressed schwar of "father" and "sister." However, as we shall see in Chapter 7, stress can easily be marked with a special notation, in a way that is the same for *all* vowels. For this reason, this book will use [ɚ] for all schwars and will mark stress separately when necessary.

At least one writer on the subject (Ladefoged [1975]) states that r-coloring of a vowel may come from a number of different articulatory gestures that all produce a similar sound, and that it is therefore better to classify these vowels by sound rather than by articulation. The r-like quality of rhotic vowels may come from some or all of these articulatory gestures: retraction (pulling back) of the front of the tongue; bunching up of the back of the tongue; and retraction of the tongue root into the pharynx. The articulatory drawing at the end of this chapter (see Figure 4-11) may or may not be representative of your speech.

The vowel of such words as "beard," "for," and "board" is made up of a vowel [ɚ] in combination with another vowel. These will be looked at in Section 4-6 on diphthongs.

As you are no doubt aware, many dialects of English lack rhotic vowels. The so-called r-less dialects include many British dialects, and in the United States they include New England, Southern, and Black English. These dialects are not r-less, since they have "r"'s in *prevocalic* position; however, the vowels that are rhotic in other dialects have no r-coloring in these dialects. In them the rhotic vowel is replaced with a non-rhotic central vowel, or else the preceding vowel is lengthened (explained in Section 4-5).

4-4.6 Mid-Central Vowel

The vowel that is articulated at the approximate midpoint of both height and frontness is called **schwa.** Its articulatory point is at or near the rest position of the tongue. This vowel occurs in such words as "terrace," "about," "frustration," "habit," and "prevent" and is transcribed with the symbol [ə]. In standard American this vowel occurs only in unstressed syllables, but in other languages, and indeed in other dialects of English (including many "r-less" dialects), this vowel occurs in stressed syllables. (The interaction between stress and vowel quality is discussed in Chapter 7.)

4-4.7 The IPA Symbols for English Vowels

The articulatory positions of the various vowels discussed are seen in Figure 4-4.

We offer here a list of sample words that will help in identifying the vowels. A word of caution: It is not a good idea to memorize lists of key words as a mnemonic for the IPA symbols. Vowels have slightly different qualities depending on the surrounding sounds, and memorizing key words may hinder more than it helps. It is better to try to associate the symbol with the sound and to avoid thinking of key words once you have identified

Figure 4-4. The vowel quadrangle.

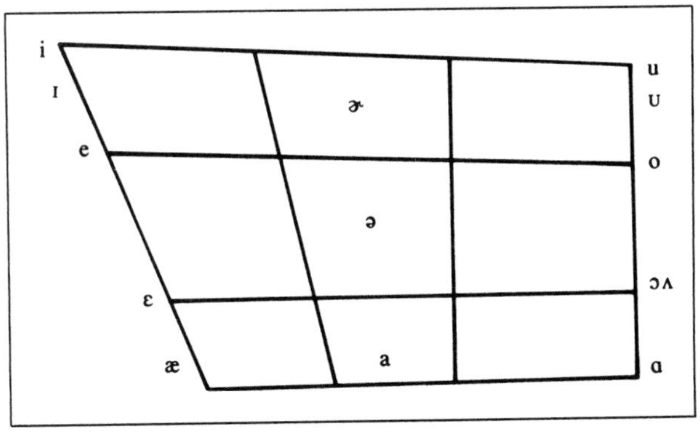

the vowels. Also, there is enormous dialect variation in the qualities of vowels, and the example words given may not be correct for your dialect. The listed words indicate a standard American pronunciation.

VOWEL	EXAMPLES
[i]	bee, heat
[ɪ]	bin, hit, sing
[e]	bay, hate
[ɛ]	bet, hen, test
[æ]	ban, hat, hang
[u]	hoot, boot, food
[ʊ]	hook, took, put
[o]	boat, toast, home
[ɔ]	caught, haughty
[ʌ]	buck, mutt, dusk
[ɑ]	cot, father
[ə]	about, Cuba
[ɚ]	father, butter, bird

The vowel [a] is shown in Figure 4-4. There is no key word for this vowel except in some midwestern pronunciations of "father"; this is the vowel of the French word "la."[8] It is normally used in English only to transcribe diphthongs (see Section 4-6 on diphthongs.

Most of the phonetic symbols are called by their sound or their name as a symbol of the English alphabet. The following symbols have special names:

SYMBOL	NAME
ɛ	epsilon
æ	ash
o	close o
ɔ	open o
ʌ	caret or wedge
ə	schwa
ɚ	(unstressed) schwar
ɝ	(stressed) schwar

[8] The symbol [a] is sometimes used to replace [æ] or [ɑ], since neither of these symbols is available on a typewriter. The problem is that the use of [a] for English vowels is inconsistent (some substitute it for [æ], others for [ɑ]), and therefore it is recommended that [æ] and [a] be correctly and consistently used. The symbol [a] should be reserved for English diphthongs, transcription of fine dialect differences, and foreign languages.

4-4.8 USING THE NOMENCLATURE

So far in Section 4-4 we have introduced various dimensions of vowel articulation. There are several points to keep in mind concerning the nomenclature of these dimensions:

1. The adjectives follow a certain order. [i] is a high front vowel, *not* a front high vowel.
2. As we noted in Section 4-4.4, certain descriptive terms such as **rounded** may be redundant information if we wish to *distinguish* among the restricted set of English vowels. But if we wish to *describe* their articulation, or if we have a list of vowels that includes foreign vowels or those used in nonstandard dialects of English (or those in misarticulated speech), those descriptive terms will be required. In the following list, the terms in parentheses are part of an articulatory description but may be left out if one seeks only to distinguish standard English vowels.
3. It should not be necessary in the long run to memorize this list of descriptions nor to memorize the vowel quadrangle shown in Figure 4-4. Rather, you should use these to confirm your understanding of vowel articulation. You should eventually be able to apply the appropriate description to any vowel, including foreign vowels, those of nonstandard dialects, and those of misarticulated speech.

When we discuss the vowels given in Section 4-4.7, we will use the following articulatory terms:

VOWEL	DESCRIPTION
[i]	high, front, tense, (spread)
[ɪ]	high, front, lax, (unrounded)
[e]	(upper-)mid, front, tense, (unrounded)
[ɛ]	(lower-)mid, front, lax, (unrounded)
[æ]	low, front, (unrounded)
[u]	high, back, tense, (rounded)
[ʊ]	high, back, lax, (unrounded or slightly rounded)
[o]	upper-mid, back, (rounded)
[ʌ]	lower-mid, back (or central), unrounded
[ɔ]	lower-mid, back, rounded
[ɑ]	low, back, (unrounded)
[ə]	mid-central
[ɚ]	central, rhotic, (unstressed)
([ɝ]	central, rhotic, stressed)

Articulatory drawings of the vowels, like those shown in Figures 4-2 and 4-3, are grouped together on pp. 76–80 (Figures 4-6–4-23).

4-5 Length: Vowel Quality versus Quantity

Unfortunately a number of words used in everyday language to describe vowel sounds are in direct conflict with an accurate phonetic description of those sounds. So you will need to pay particular attention to the vocabulary introduced in this section and perhaps to unlearn the meanings you connect with certain words.

The **quality** of a vowel refers to the particular vowel sound that is heard. The quality of each vowel is different because each vowel is different. Quality is also often called **timbre** (pronounced "tamber"). For example, one would say that the quality or timbre of [ɛ] is different from that of [i].

The *quantity* of a vowel, commonly called the **length,** is measured in terms of *time.* A **short** [ɪ] would be spoken quite quickly; a **long** [ɪ] would be prolonged. The terms **long** and **short** do *not* refer to vowel quality. A *long* vowel (or consonant) may also be called **geminate.**

Most of us are in the habit of calling the vowel sound /i/ "long e" and the vowel sound /ɛ/ "short e." The terms "long" and "short," as used in everyday language, refer to vowel quality. The two sounds in question are different vowels (that is, their *quality* is different); they are *not* long and short versions of the same vowel. The reason these (incorrect) terms are used has to do with the historical development of the English language and with our spelling of words. In phonetics, and in the professional description of speech sounds, it is important to remember to reserve the terms **long** and **short** for *temporal length.*

There are two ways to indicate that a vowel is long (in time). The vowel symbol can be written twice (or even many times). This may be a useful method of indicating prolongations in stuttered speech. The other method is to use a **colon** (:) after the vowel symbol to indicate double the length of the sound in question, and to use just one dot to indicate that a vowel is a little longer than normal, but not quite twice as long. For example, if someone prolonged the vowel of the word "bay," it could be transcribed [bee] or [be:]. If the prolongation was slight, it would be transcribed [be·].

While it is not commonly used, the **brevis** mark (L. *brevis*, 'brief') may be employed to indicate a particularly short vowel. A short [e] could be symbolized [ĕ]. This usage should be defined, however, since the brevis is used in classical orthography to indicate vowel quality rather than length, or a combination of both.

Some languages contrast different words by means of vowel length. In Finnish, for example, /tule/ means 'Come' (the imperative), but /tulee/ means 'He comes.' In English, we do not contrast words by vowel length, so we usually do not need to mark the length of vowels at all. Of course, in recording speech that has abnormal prolongations—be it deviant speech, dialect variations, or dramatic use of prolongation—length must be indicated. The speech of stutterers, as well as that of the deaf, frequently contains abnormal prolongations, including prolongations of consonants as well as of vowels.

> While it is true that standard English does not use vowel length distinctively, in the way that Finnish does, for example, this is not to be interpreted to mean that English vowels are all the same length. In fact they vary in length in several ways.
>
> The vowels /i/, /e/, /u/, and /o/ tend to be somewhat longer than other vowels (and they share another characteristic, *diphthongization*, to be outlined next). Vowels such as /ɪ/, /ɛ/, /æ/, and /ʊ/ tend to be rather short.
>
> The length of vowels also depends upon the sound following, if there is one. For example, if you compare the vowel in "bee," "bead," and "beet," you will find that the vowel of "beet" is shorter than the others. This is because it is followed by a *voiceless* consonant (one articulated without vocal fold vibration).
>
> Indeed, vowel length is contrastive in some dialects of English, as it is in many foreign languages. For example, some dialects lacking a rhotic vowel compensate for the missing [ɚ] by lengthening the preceding vowel (Section 4-3.5). Thus, such pairs as "pock" and "park," "Cotter" and "Carter" may be distinguished phonetically by vowel length alone: [pɑk] and [pɑ:k] [kɑtə] and [kɑ:tə]. For the reasons outlined in Chapter 2—because our intuitions are based often on orthographic views of what is "correct"—even speakers of such a dialect are likely to say that the difference between, say, "pock" and "park" is the "r," even when that is missing from the pronunciation and in fact the two words are distinguished by vowel length.

4-6 Diphthongs

A **diphthong** is a vowel whose *quality* or *timbre* changes considerably during its articulation. For example, the vowel of the word "my" is pronounced by starting with the tongue in a low back position and then moving the tongue up to a high front position. You can feel the movement if you pronounce this vowel while paying attention to your articulators.

Because this sound is usually spelled with one letter and forms one phoneme (contrasting sound) in English, some students have trouble hearing that it is actually made up of two parts. The easiest way to hear it is to prolong the pronunciation of the diphthong. As you prolong it, you will hear that you can prolong the first part or the second part, but that at no time are you producing the whole vowel sound.

The standard transcription of diphthongs is intended to show the starting and finishing points of their articulation. So a diphthong whose articulation starts in the neighborhood of [a] and finishes up in the neighborhood of [i] is transcribed [a͜i]. The ligature connecting the two symbols indicates that the two are fused together to form one vocalic element, but in common usage the ligature is often omitted. (More is said about different transcription systems later.)

Figure 4-5 is a stylized drawing of the articulation of a sample diphthong.

More than other vowels in English, the precise quality of the diphthongs varies enormously with surrounding sounds and dialect. The diphthong /a͜i/, for example, may be pronounced [a͜ɪ], [ɑ͜i], [ə͜ɪ], etc. If we wish to transcribe the precise quality of a particular diphthong, we must carefully indicate its starting and finishing points. However, for pur-

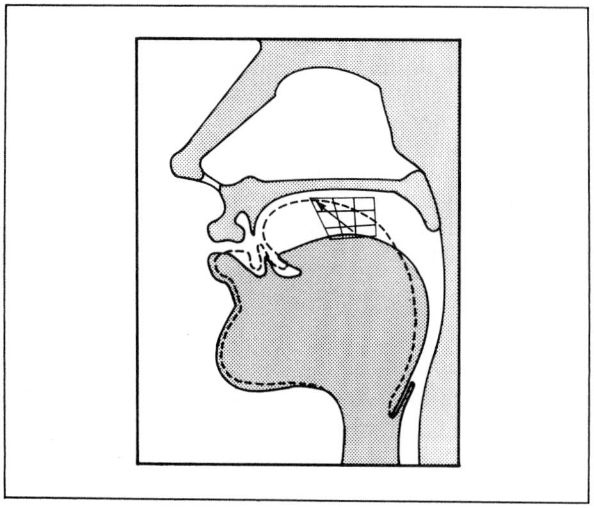

Figure 4-5. The articulation of the diphthong /a͜i/.

poses of broad or phonemic transcription, standardized transcriptions are often used. These are satisfactory as long as the user understands that they are not precise reflections of the pronunciation. The following are the conventional ways of transcribing English diphthongs (after Jones [1972, p. 61] but with the addition of ligatures):

VOWEL	EXAMPLES
/a͜i/	my, buy, eye, I, might, hide
/a͜u/	cow, loud, found, howl, pout
/ɔ͜i/	boy, boil, hoist

It should be reiterated that the quality of diphthongs varies greatly and is not reflected in these standardized phonemic transcriptions. For example, in my own speech, the vowels of "lout" and "loud" are very different, both in length and in quality: something like [lə͜ut] and [la·͜od]. Use of the standard transcription /la͜ut/ and /la͜ud/ would obscure this difference.

When two vowels are juxtaposed in separate syllables, they do not form a diphthong. In the word "doing," for example, the /u/ is in one syllable and the /ɪ/ in another, so no diphthong is formed. This is why the ligature is used: it helps to clarify the transcription. For example, the word "naïve" has two syllables, whereas "knife" has one: /nɑiv/, /na͜if/.

4-6.1 Rhotic Diphthongs

As noted, words such as "beard," "far," and "board" have a diphthong in which the second element is a schwar. Typical dialects have the following diphthongs:

SYMBOL	EXAMPLES
[i͜ɚ]	fear, beer, beard
[e͜ɚ]	bear, mare, chair
[u͜ɚ]	boor, poor, contour
[o͜ɚ]	more, bore, floor
[ɔ͜ɚ]	hoarse, coarse
[ɑ͜ɚ]	bar, far, marble

There exists considerable dialect variation in the rhotic diphthongs, particularly among the lower front ones. Some dialects make a three-way distinction between "marry," "merry," and "Mary"; others make a two-way distinction, and some pronounce all three alike. If need be, one may distinguish [æ͜ɚ], [ɛ͜ɚ], and [e͜ɚ].

Those dialects lacking the rhotic vowel evidence this lack in the rhotic diphthongs as well. In some dialects, such as those typical of New England, a schwa replaces the schwar. In other dialects, such as Southern ones, the vowel preceding the missing schwar is lengthened. And in some dialects, including certain British ones, only the first element of the rhotic diphthong is present, but it takes on a certain rhotic quality. So standard American "for" is [fo͜ɚ], but [fo͜ə] in New England and [foː] in Southern; some dialects will have [foʴ] where the superscript upside-down ⟨r⟩ represents rhotic quality in the vowel; that is, the r-coloring is inherent in the vowel, and no diphthongization occurs.

There is always considerable disagreement concerning the exact quality of the vocalic elements in rhotic diphthongs (as indeed there is with all diphthongs). For example, is "ear" [i͜ɚ] or [ɪ͜ɚ]? Is "boor" [bu͜ɚ] or [bʊ͜ɚ]? What occurs is that the r-coloring may affect tongue root position, making it difficult to tell whether the first element is tense or lax. Additionally there exists much dialectal and personal variation in the pronunciation of these diphthongs. As with other diphthongs, there is some merit in adopting a standard transcription and saving transcribing the fine differences for special purposes such as recording dialect variation.

4-6.2 The Diphthongal Quality of English Vowels

The vowels [i, e, o, u] are identified as long vowels in English, since they are usually prolonged slightly as compared to other English vowels. This prolongation goes hand in hand with another peculiarity about these vowels as they are pronounced in most dialects of English. The long vowels in English tend to be slightly diphthongized. This means that their point of articulation changes slightly as they are pronounced. Pronounce the word "say," for example, and carefully observe your articulatory gestures. Notice that the jaw is not in a constant position throughout the pronunciation of the vowel; the vowel becomes higher as its articulation progresses. Try the words "see," "sue," and "so" and observe the changing quality in them.

It is useful to compare the way a native speaker of French, Italian, or Spanish pronounces these vowels with the way you pronounce them. In English, the articulators move considerably during the production of the vowel; in the other languages mentioned, there is very little or no movement during the production of the vowel. The vowels in these languages are often called **pure** vowels. The term *pure* does not indicate any superiority but simply means that the vowel has a single, unchanging quality. A better term for a pure vowel is **monophthong,** in contrast to diphthong.

While the long vowels in English are generally slightly diphthongized, the short vowels are more monophthongal, or pure. /ɪ/, /æ/, /ɛ/, and the other short vowels do not change in quality during production. However, one frequent peculiarity about the speech of deaf children is their tendency to diphthongize all vowels, short or long. Also, there are dialects, such as those of the American South, in which short vowels are strongly diphthongized: "bit," for example, might be pronounced [bɪ·ət]. Curiously, this same dialect tends to monophthongize certain diphthongs: "my," for example, may be pronounced [ma:].

The transcription symbols that were introduced in this chapter do not indicate the diphthongal nature of these long vowels but represent them as if they were pure vowels. For the most part, this is a satisfactory phonemic transcription system for English; most manuals of transcription use the system indicated in this chapter.

Several systems of transcribing English vowels more precisely are in use, however, and since they may appear in other books, we will mention them briefly. One system was devised by Jones [1972], the other by the team of Trager and Smith (see Ladefoged [1975, p. 64]); the former was developed in England, the latter in the United States. These two systems compare with ours as follows:

THIS BOOK	JONES	TRAGER-SMITH
/i/	/i:/	/iy/
/e/	/ei/	/ey/
/o/	/ou/	/ow/
/u/	/u:/	/uw/

There are other differences among the systems, but for our purposes it is enough to point out the quality of the long vowels and to be prepared for a possible variety of transcriptions of the same sounds. In all cases it is best to pick one system for one's own use and to stay with it consistently.

Of course, it is always possible to use the symbol system introduced here to transcribe accurately the details of the articulation. For example, the English phoneme /e/ of "bay" may, in different dialect areas, be pronounced [ẹi̯], [ɛi̯], [eɪ̯], etc.

In this discussion of transcription of English long vowels let us not lose sight of the practical significance of their diphthongal nature. Once again, if we wish only to *distinguish* /i/ from /ɪ/ from /e/, we can safely ignore their diphthongal quality. But in an accurate *description* their phonetic quality, their diphthongal timbre is important. While the difference between [e:] and [ẹi̯] may be subtle, it is important; pronouncing the word "say" as [se] or [se:] rather than [sɛi̯] sounds strange or foreign. The student learning English as a foreign language or the deaf child learning to speak will tend to pronounce such vowels in an un-English way. Therefore these subtle aspects of pronunciation are extremely important.

In Chapter 6 we will look at some modifications

of vowel quality in the context of words. In Chapter 7 we will look at the effect of stress on vowel quality.

4-7 Summary of English Vowel Articulation

The articulation of all the English vowels we have discussed is summarized in Figures 4-6–4-23. Each shows the tongue and jaw position as well as lip posture. Only one example of a rhotic diphthong is included. In the articulatory drawings of the diphthongs, the starting positions of the tongue, lips, and jaw are shown with a solid line, and the finishing positions are shown with a dotted line.

Several points should be kept in mind in examining these drawings. They are stylized and idealized. They cannot take into account individual variation in vowel articulation (Section 4-9). The jaw movement is exaggerated for graphic clarity; in fact, variation in vowel height in connected speech comes more from tongue movement within the lower jaw than from actual changes in jaw height. The lip postures are also slightly exaggerated for clarity. As we have noted, rounded vowels in English tend to be articulated without the extreme lip rounding and protrusion found in some other languages; the same thing can be said of English spread vowels. Again for clarity, the slight diphthongization of /i/, /e/, /u/, and /o/ has been ignored in the sketches. Furthermore, although there is great variation in the articulation of the diphthongs, one articulation has been shown for these. Finally, in actual articulation in connected speech, it is likely that there is less movement of the articulators than has been shown in the drawings.

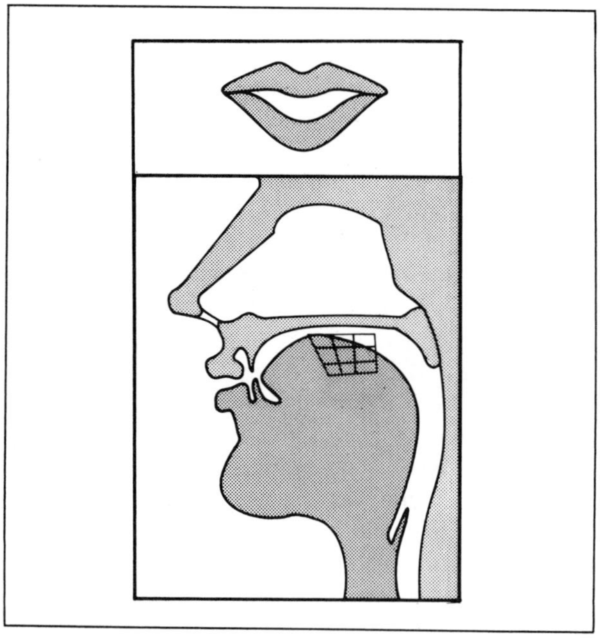

Figure 4-6. /i/

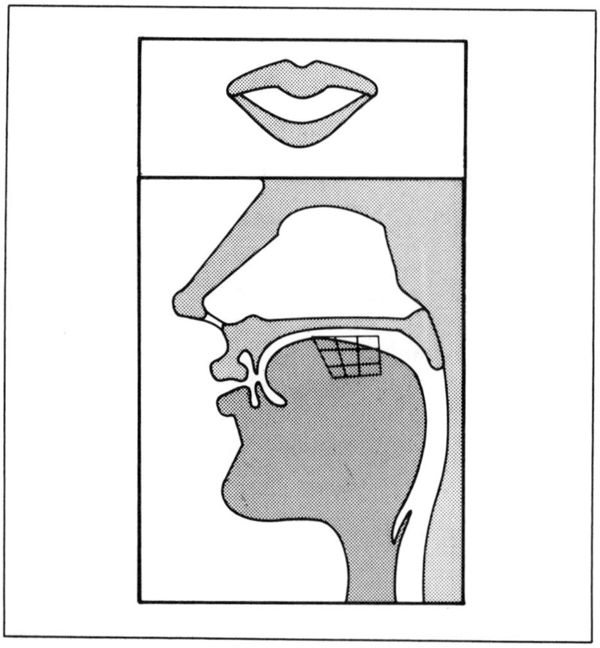

Figure 4-7. /ɪ/

4-8 Other Vowels

Of course, standard English does not have every possible vowel. Many other vowels occur in other languages and in the many dialects of English; indeed, in standard North American English there are many variations of vowel articulation brought about by the influence of surrounding sounds. Let us look at some other vowels.

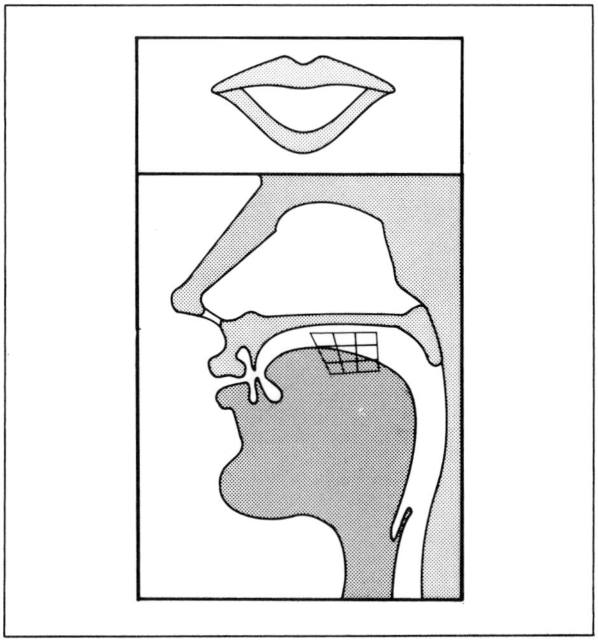

Figure 4-8. /e/

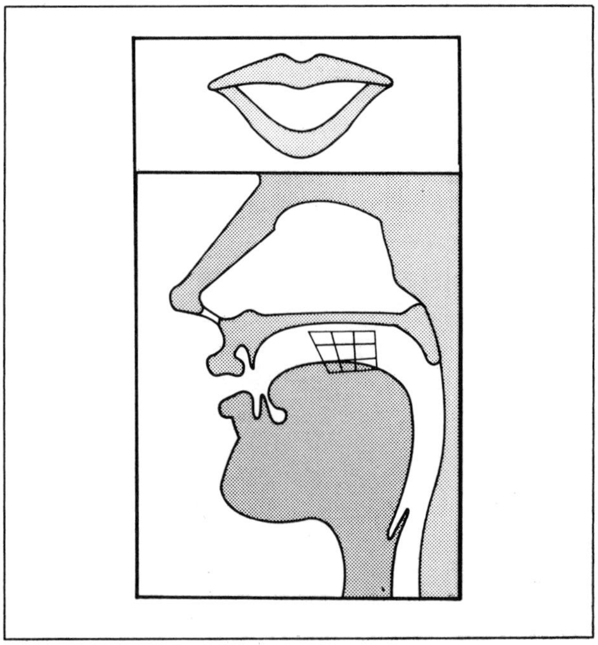

Figure 4-9. /ɛ/

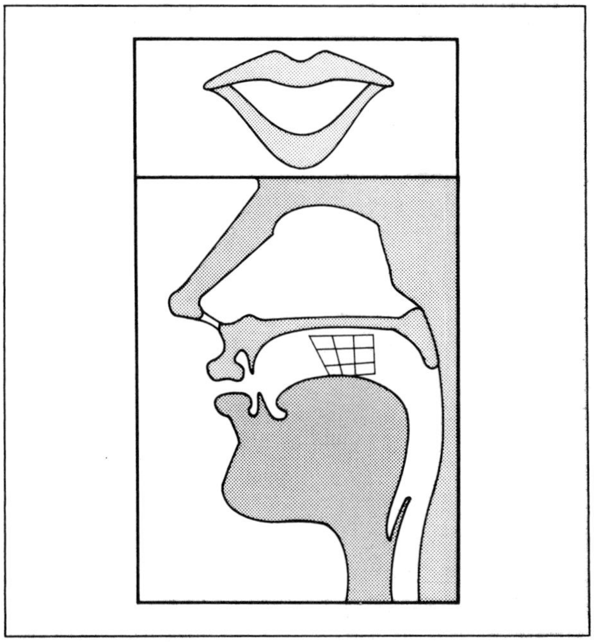

Figure 4-10. /æ/

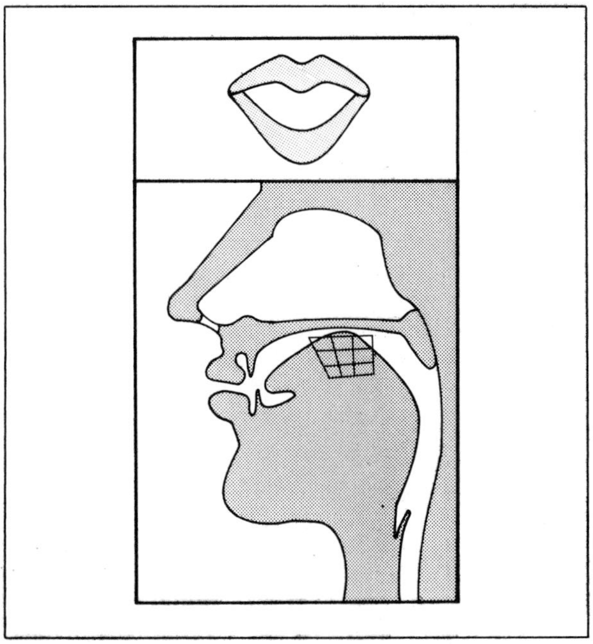

Figure 4-11. /ɚ/

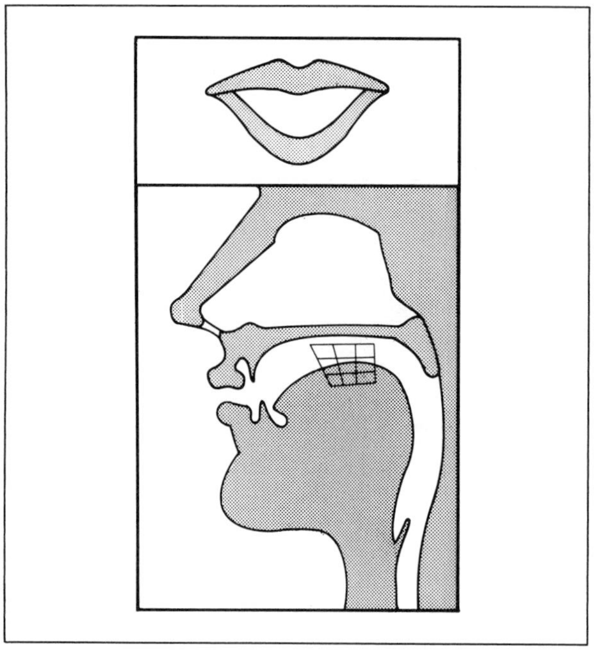

Figure 4-12. /ə/

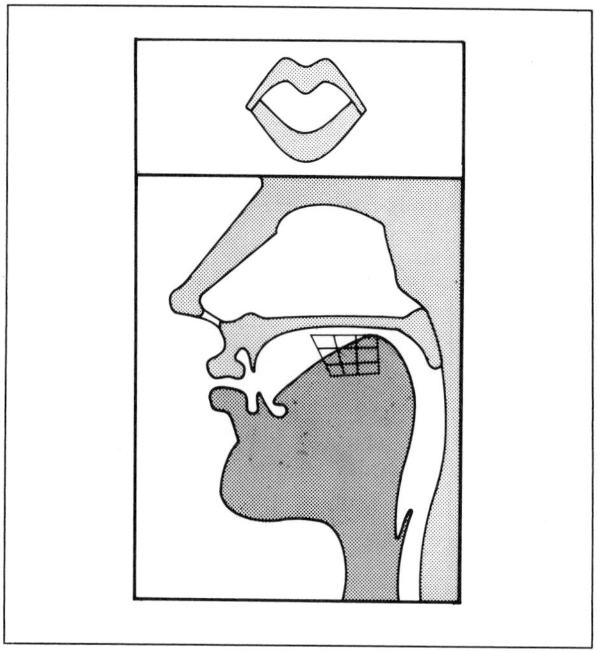

Figure 4-14. /u/

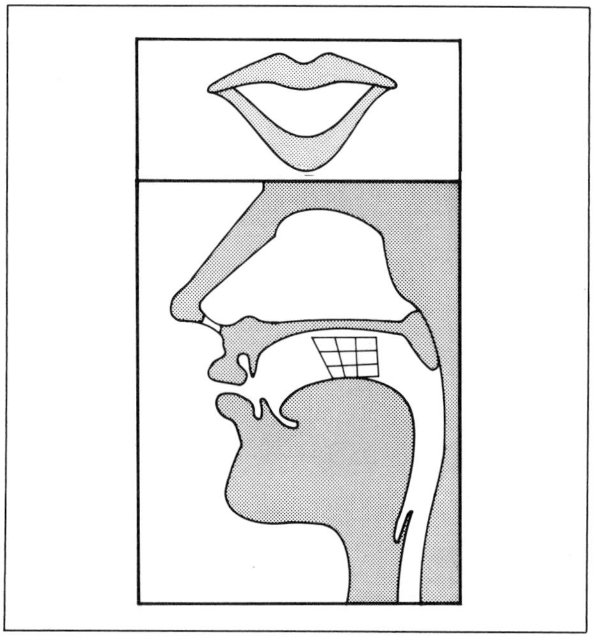

Figure 4-13. /a/

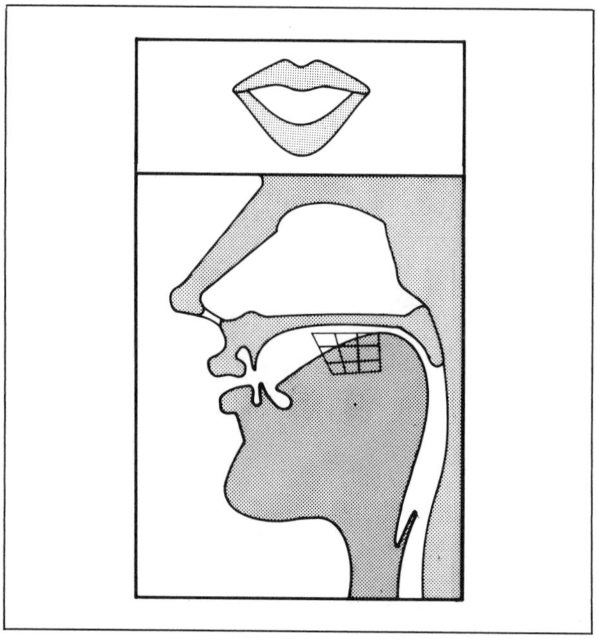

Figure 4-15. /ʊ/

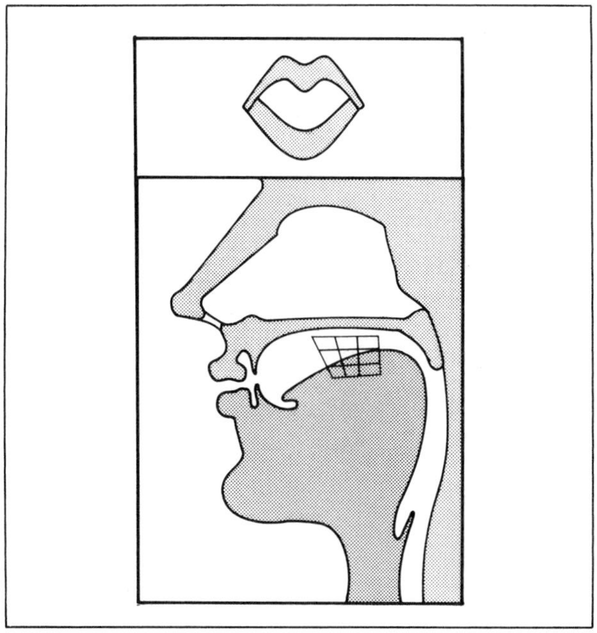

Figure 4-16. /o/

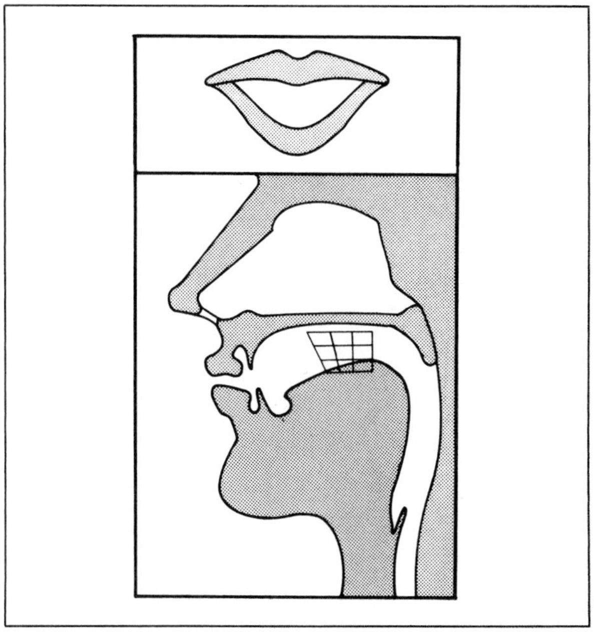

Figure 4-18. /ʌ/

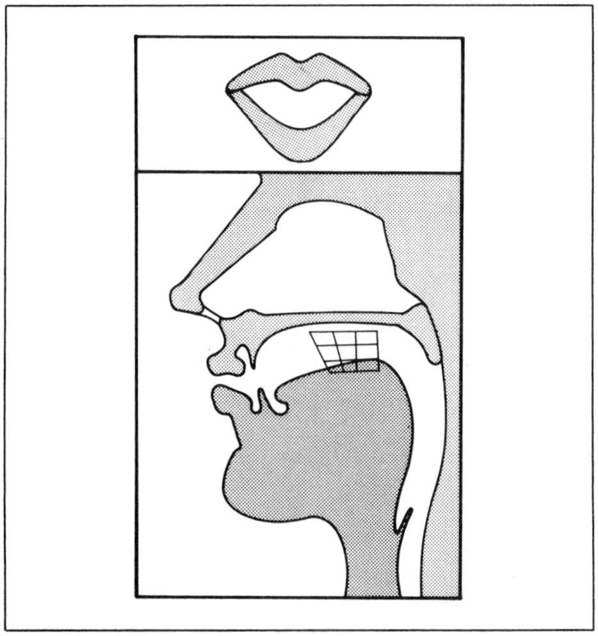

Figure 4-17. /ɔ/

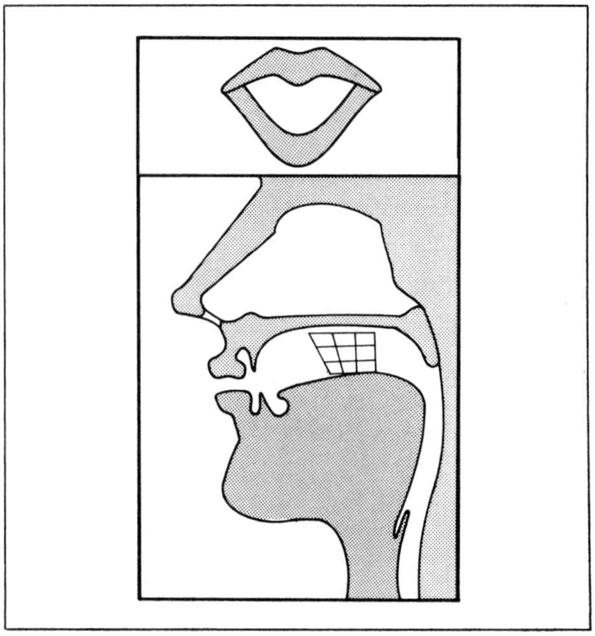

Figure 4-19. /ɑ/

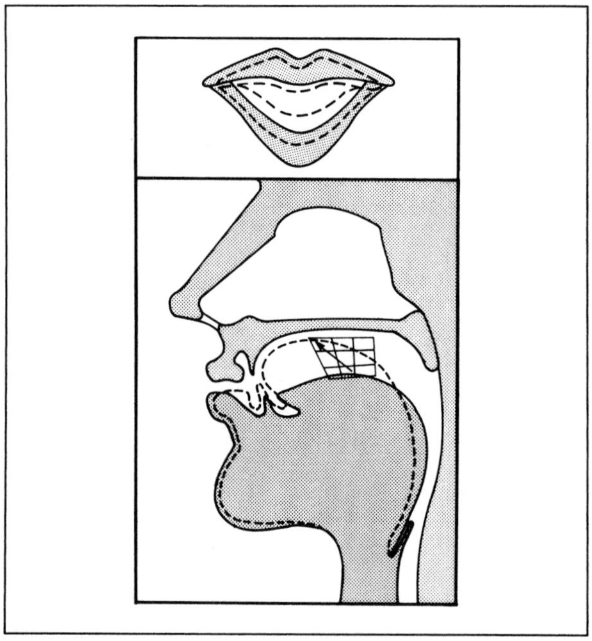

Figure 4-20. /a͜ɪ/

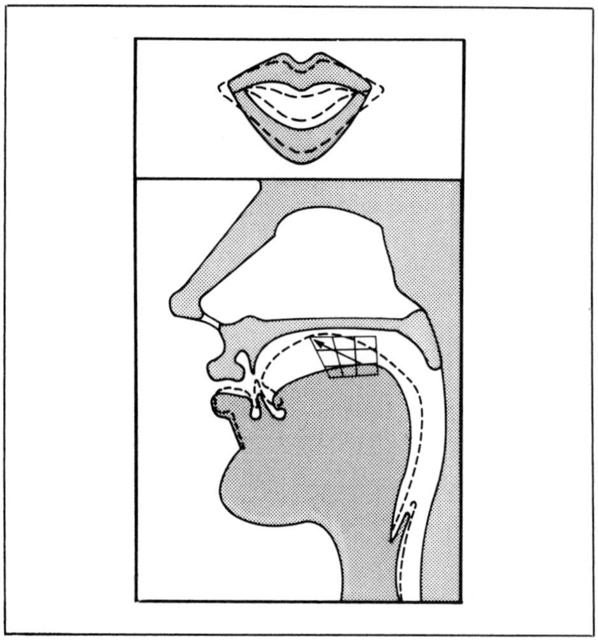

Figure 4-22. /ɔ͜ɪ/

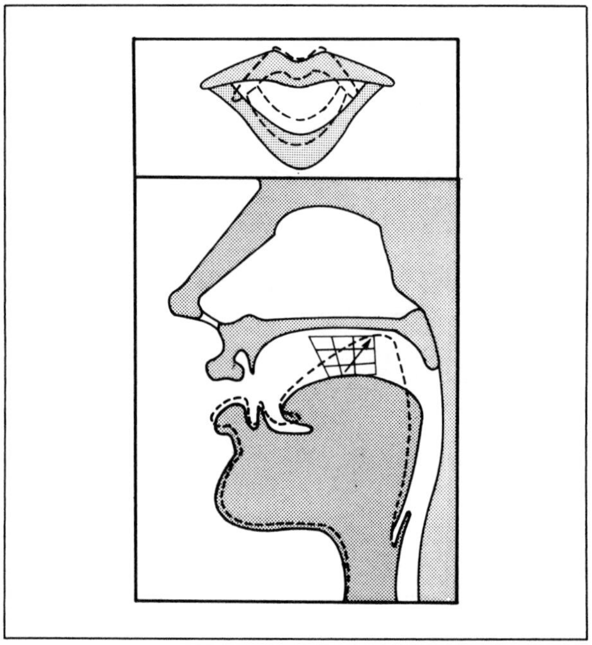

Figure 4-21. /a͜ʊ/

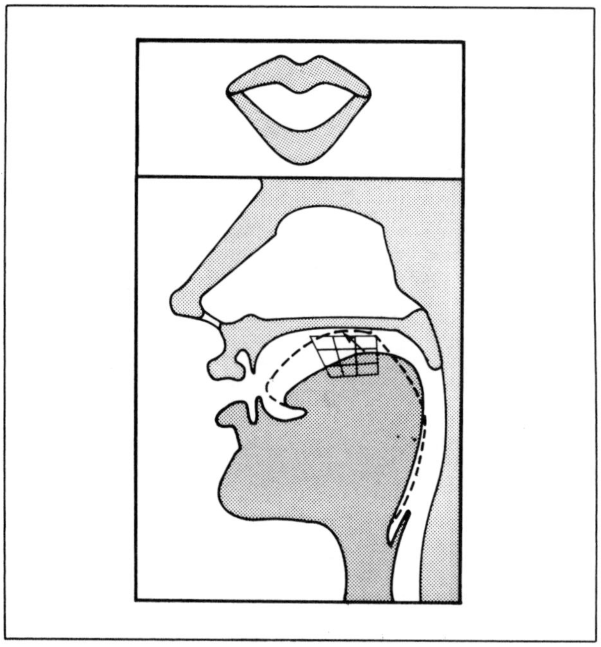

Figure 4-23. /o͜ɚ/

4-8.1 Front Rounded Vowels

All of the English front vowels we have seen are unrounded, that is, they have either spread or neutral lip posture. Front rounded vowels also exist. These have the tongue position of the front vowels /i/, /ɪ/, /e/, and /ɛ/ but are pronounced with the lips tightly rounded and protruded, as for whistling. Practice rounding and unrounding your lips while pronouncing the front vowels. At first you will very likely make an automatic change in tongue position when you round your lips, but with practice you should be able to hold your tongue still while rounding and unrounding your lips. Notice the change in vowel quality that the change in lip posture produces. The symbols for the rounded front vowels corresponding to [i], [ɪ], [e], [ɛ], are [ü], [ʊ̈], [ö], and [ɔ̈], respectively.[9]

These front rounded vowels are used in many languages, including French and German (although the lax [ʊ̈] occurs only in nonstandard dialects of French). In some dialects of English, the vowel [ü] replaces /u/ in some environments. Old English had a full complement of front rounded vowels, which became unrounded in the Middle English period.

4-8.2 Back Unrounded Vowels

Most of the English back vowels are rounded. Many languages have spread vowels corresponding in place of articulation to the back rounded vowels familiar to us. You can pronounce these by pronouncing the back rounded vowel and spreading or unrounding the lips. Again, you may have difficulty at first holding the tongue position while changing lip posture, but practice should pay off.

The unrounded or spread vowels corresponding to [u], [ʊ], [o], and [ɔ] are [ɯ], [ɯˇ], [ɤ], and [ʌ], respectively. [ʌ], as we have seen, is an English vowel (although in some dialects its articulation is more central than back). The English vowel [ɑ] is unrounded; its rounded counterpart is [ɒ].

[9]The traditional IPA symbols, still used in Europe, are [y], [ʏ], [ø], and [œ], respectively. But in North America, linguists are using the umlaut, [¨], as a symbol for front articulation. Notice that [ü] has [u] as its base symbol, a high, tense, rounded vowel. [ü] is also a high, tense, rounded vowel, and the umlaut shows that it is *front*. The other symbols, [ʊ̈], [ö], and [ɔ̈], can be analyzed in the same way.

The high and upper-mid back unrounded vowels occur in a number of languages, some dialects of Chinese among them. But, as we have noted, English "back rounded" vowels are often not very rounded. The vowel of the word "boot," for example, may be closer to [ɯ] or [ɯ͜u] than to [u].

The symbols indicate points on a continuum. [u] represents, theoretically, a very rounded vowel; [ɯ] represents a very spread vowel. But in fact many languages have vowels at neither extreme, and so in practice both symbols represent a vowel tending more toward a neutral lip posture.

4-8.3 Central Vowels

English has several central vowels. Schwa, [ə], a mid-central vowel, occurs in all dialects; and [a], a low central vowel, replaces [ɑ] in some dialects and is the initial element in many English diphthongs. The rhotic schwar, [ɚ], is also classed as central, although we noted that a number of articulatory gestures may be involved in its articulation. There are also high central vowels. Since they are central, their point of articulation is midway between that for [i] and that for [u]. If you pronounce these two vowels alternately, you should be able to locate the arch of your tongue halfway between these two extremes. This high central vowel is [ʉ] if the lips are rounded and [ɨ] if the lips are unrounded or spread. It is claimed that the vowel [ɨ] occurs in many American dialects. In such dialects the words "ros<u>e</u>s" and "Ros<u>a</u>'s" are contrasted, the first having [ɨ] as its second vowel, the latter having [ə] as its second vowel.

The front rounded, back unrounded, and central vowels are shown on the vowel quadrangle in Figure 4-24. Articulatory drawings of the vowels introduced in Sections 4-8.1–4-8.3 are not provided, since they can easily be envisioned on the basis of Figures 4-6–4-23 and Figure 4-24. An articulatory drawing of [ü], for example, would show the tongue position of [i] (Fig. 4-6) plus the lip position of [u] (Fig. 4-14). [ɯ] has the tongue position of [u] (Fig. 4-14) and the lip position of [i] (Fig. 4-6). The lip positions of [ɨ] and [ʉ] are the same as those of [i] and [u], respectively; the tongue position of both is halfway between that of [i] and [u].

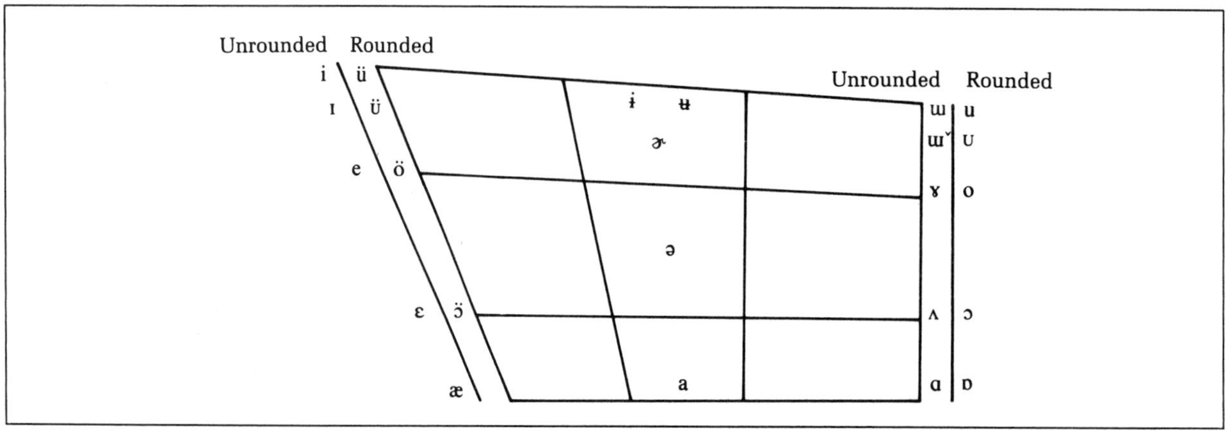

Figure 4-24. The vowel quadrangle, including front rounded, back unrounded, and central vowels.

4-8.4 Diphthongs

Since diphthongs are nothing but a vowel of changing timbre, virtually any combination of starting points and finishing points is theoretically possible. Indeed, nonstandard dialects of English and many dialects of many other languages have a great variety of diphthongs.

Diphthongs are sometimes represented by drawing vectors on the vowel quadrangle. Three standard English diphthongs are shown in this manner in Figure 4-25. Any vector that could be drawn on the quadrangle represents a conceivable diphthong, although not necessarily one attested in any known language.

Front rounded diphthongs such as [ö͜ü] are possible, as are many others.

The Brooklyn dialect replaces the standard North American rhotic vowel [ɚ] with a diphthong whose quality can be represented [ə͜ɪ]. As Figure 4-26 shows, the vector of [ə͜ɪ] closely resembles the vector of standard English /ɔ͜i/. So speakers of standard dialects tend to hear Brooklynese [ə͜ɪ] as /ɔ͜ɪ/ and joke that "bird" is "Boyd" in Brooklynese speech. It is no such thing, of course, but the phonetic similarity causes confusion.

North Americans also may misunderstand Australian (or Cockney) pronunciations of the phoneme /e/. Remember that in standard North American the phoneme /e/ is really somewhat diphthongal in quality: [ɛ͜i]. The Australian equivalent is [ə͜i] or [ʌ͜i], which is quite similar to North American English /a͜i/. Confusion may result when the North American hears /e/ as /a͜i/, as in the story of the American hospitalized in Austra-

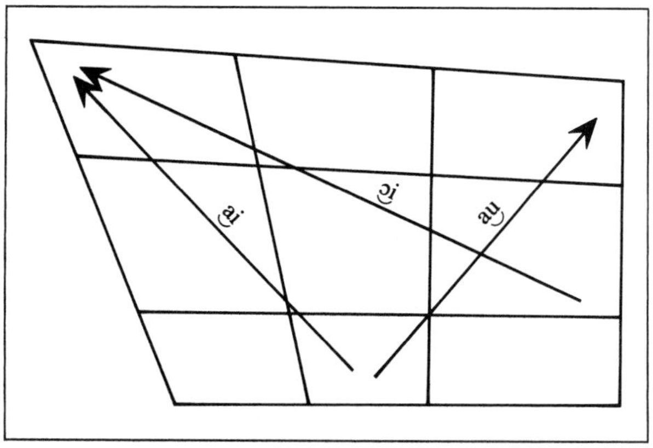

Figure 4-25. Diphthong vectors for the three English diphthong phonemes.

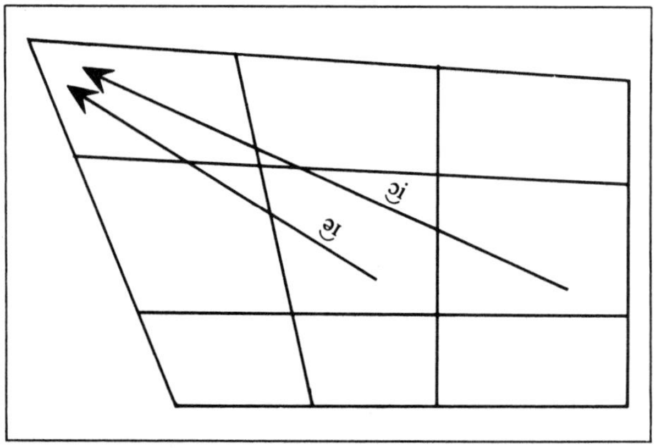

Figure 4-26. Diphthong vectors for Brooklynese [ə͜ɪ] (for standard /ɚ/) as compared to standard English /ɔ͜i/.

lia who is asked by a nurse just coming on duty, "Did you just come in today?" (heard as "Did you just come in to die?").

As noted in Section 4-5, there tends to be somewhat more minor dialect variation in the diphthongs than in other vowels.

4-8.5 Nasalized Vowels

All of the vowels we have examined so far in this chapter have been pronounced with the velum in the raised position, blocking off the nasal cavities. If the velum is lowered during vowel production, then vocal resonance can occur in the nasal cavity as well as in the oral and pharyngeal cavities. This gives a particular timbre to the vowel, which we identify as a nasal quality.

Many languages, including French, Portuguese, Polish, and Gujarati, have distinctive **nasalized** vowel phonemes. You can pronounce these sounds by learning to open (lower) the velum while pronouncing a vowel sound. These steps may be helpful: Pronounce a vowel, such as [ɛ]. Stop pronouncing it, but keep your tongue and lips frozen in position. If you now inhale through your nose, you should feel your velum lowering (it is, of course, always lowered for nasal breathing). Practice trying to hold it in the lowered position while pronouncing the vowel. It may be difficult at first, because you will unconsciously raise the velum as soon as you pronounce the vowel. But patient practice should pay off. (A smoker may find that inhaling smoke first will give a visual clue as to whether or not the velum is lowered. If it is, smoke will pass out through the nose as the vowel is pronounced.) The distinctive nasal timbre of the nasalized vowel should be immediately apparent.

Figure 4-27 shows the articulation of a nasalized vowel, [ɛ̃]. The tilde (˜) is used in phonetic transcription to show nasalization.

All of us regularly pronounce nasalized vowels. The velum must be raised in order to pronounce non-nasal vowels (i.e., all the vowel phonemes of English), but it must be lowered to pronounce nasal consonants. Since the velum cannot move instantaneously, in words having nasal consonants we usually pronounce the adjoining vowel with the velum not completely closed; as a result these vowels are to some extent nasalized.

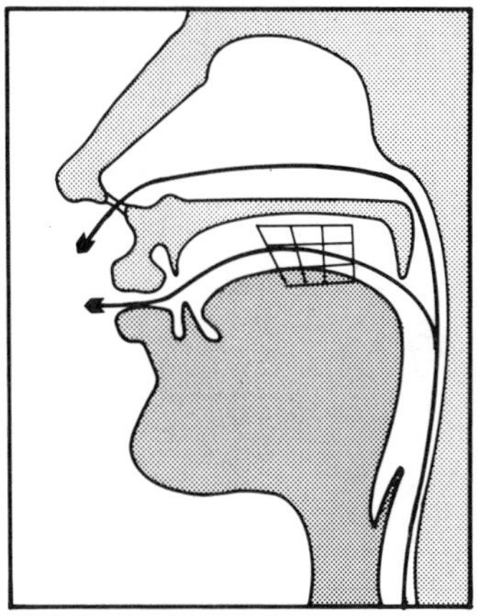

Figure 4-27. Nasalized vowel /ɛ̃/.

Certain dialects of English, typical of the American south central states, have a characteristic pervasive nasality. This is often colloquially called a *nasal twang*.

In certain communication disorders, nasality is poorly controlled. This is often true in the speech of the deaf, since velic movement is not visible and the deaf speaker therefore may not have learned it. Individuals with cleft palate do not learn velic control; since whether the velum is up or down, the nasal passages are connected with the oral passages through the cleft. So after surgical repair or the fitting of a prosthesis, they must acquire velic control. (Some individuals have cleft palate combined with incomplete velic musculature.)

4-9 Accuracy of the Standard Vowel Paradigm

This chapter has presented the standard framework of vowel articulation that has been part of phonetic orthodoxy for many years. There are a number of reasons for doubting its accuracy, however; the following are among them.

1. Ventriloquism. Ventriloquists, of course, neither "throw" their voices nor speak from their stomachs [L. *venter*, 'belly'; L. *loqui*, 'to speak']. What they *do* do is to speak without the usual articulatory movements. They suppress only

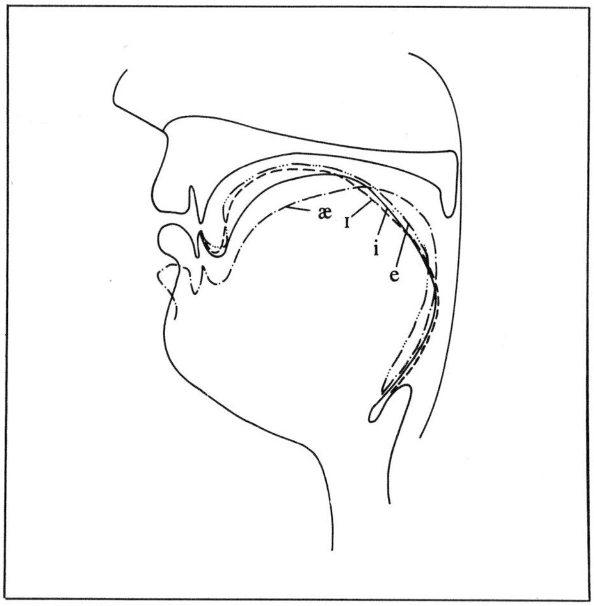

Figure 4-28. Tongue positions for x-ray tracings of vowel articulation. Note the discrepancy between the positions shown and the standard vowel paradigm.

those articulatory gestures that are normally visible, not the gestures within the mouth and throat. The question is, if they still produce intelligible speech, how essential are the gestures normally considered to be part of the articulation of the sounds?

2. Glossectomy and paralysis. Glossectomy is the surgical removal of part or all of the tongue. Many glossectomees (persons having undergone a glossectomy) are able to produce intelligible speech, particularly if the operation was not a radical one. Obviously, such speakers are not using standard articulatory gestures. Similarly, people with partial paralysis of the speech articulators are often able to produce intelligible speech. Once again, it is clear that their articulations are not those shown in standard phonetics textbooks.

3. X-ray evidence. Cineradiography (x-ray moving pictures) would seem a natural tool of phonetic research. However, it is used little because of the health risks it entails. What x-ray evidence of speech articulation does exist variously confirms and contradicts the standard articulatory model. Figure 4-28 shows a tracing from an x-ray study of speech articulation.

It is apparent that more than one vocal tract configuration can produce a given sound. Not all of us make exactly the same movements, as Figure 4-28 shows. The fact that ventriloquists, glossectomees, and those with partial vocal muscle paralysis may produce reasonably normal-sounding speech indicates that they are making compensatory gestures. Just what those gestures are has not been studied.

4. Bite blocks, mashed potatoes, and cigarettes. It is apparent from a simple experiment that standard articulatory positions are not necessary. If you hold a pen or pencil in your teeth, you can still talk in a relatively normal fashion. (Experimentally, a *bite block* may serve the purpose, as in a study by Oller and MacNeilage [1983].) People talk with a cigarette held in their lips, or speak with a mouthful of mashed potatoes. In all of these situations, the standard textbook positions of the articulators are not used.

These facts have implications for both linguists and speech pathologists. Linguists must recognize that phonological models may be based on phonetic "facts" of doubtful validity. Speech therapists should recognize that phonetic output, rather than textbook tongue placement, is the goal in speech correction of the deaf, the dyspraxic, and glossectomees.

Summary

The phonemic **contrasts** of language convey meaning.

The terms **vowel** and **consonant** refer to types of *sounds*. Vowels are produced with a relatively open vocal tract; consonants with the airstream blocked, restricted, or diverted.

A single speech sound is called a **segment** or a **phone.**

The classification of vowels is based on the positions of the articulators in their production. **Height** refers to how close the tongue is to the roof of the mouth. **Frontness** refers to how far forward or back the arching of the tongue occurs. In the case of both dimensions, the point of articulation is taken to be the *highest point on the arch of the tongue*. **Lip rounding, tongue root position,** and

velic position also play a role in vowel articulation.

The **vowel quadrangle** is used to classify vowels according to **height** and **frontness. Cardinal** vowels are vowels around the periphery of the vowel quadrangle that are used as reference points.

In the height dimension we distinguish **high, upper-mid, lower-mid,** and **low** vowels. In some classification systems only three heights are distinguished: **high, mid,** and **low.** In the **frontness** dimension we distinguish **front, central,** and **back** vowels.

Tenseness refers to a traditional classification of vowels into **tense** and **lax** vowels. Tenseness appears to correlate with tongue root position, lip posture, and length.

Three degrees of **lip-rounding** may be distinguished: **rounded, neutral,** and **spread.** Very often only a two-way distinction is made, between **rounded** and **unrounded.**

Rhotic vowels are those having an r-like quality. Standard American English has a rhotic vowel that is spelled with the letter ⟨r⟩; in fact, it is a vowel, not a consonant.

Vowels may be **long** or **short;** this is a measure of their **length.** Do not confuse **length** with **quality** (also called **timbre**), popular usage notwithstanding.

A **diphthong** is a vowel whose quality changes significantly during its articulation. Standard English is said to have three diphthong phonemes, but the phonetic picture is more complicated. There are several (up to ten, depending on dialect) **rhotic diphthongs.** There is enormous dialectal and individual variation in diphthongs. The long vowels are diphthongal in quality, although this fact is often ignored.

Front rounded and **back spread** vowels do not exist in standard English but do occur in many languages. **Nasalized vowels** are not distinctive in English, but many English vowels are nasalized; that is, they are pronounced with the velum at least partially lowered.

There is reason to believe that standard vowel taxonomies are based on idealized articulations, and that in actual speech the articulation is different.

Vocabulary

alveolar
alveolar ridge
apex (of tongue)
apical
back (of tongue)
bilabial
blade (of tongue)
brevis
bronchi
cardinal
central
colon
consonant
contrast
dental
diphthong
dorsal
dorsum
front (of tongue)
front rounded
frontness
glossectomy
glottal
glottis
gum ridge
height
high
labial
laminal
language
laryngeal position
laryngopharynx
larynx
lax
length
lingual
lip-rounding
lips
long
low
lower-mid
lungs
mid
monophthong
nasal cavity
nasalized vowel
nasopharynx
neutral
noncardinal
oral cavity
oropharynx
palatal
palate
pharyngeal cavity
pharynx
phonation
phone
phoneme
phonology
polysyllabic
pure
quality
r-colored
resonance
resonator
rhotic
root (of the tongue)
rounded
segment
short
spread
teeth
temporal length
tense
tenseness
timbre
tip (of tongue)
tongue
tongue root position
trachea
unrounded
upper-mid
uvula
uvular
velar
velic
velum
ventriloquism
vocal folds
vocalic
voiced
voiceless
voicing
vowel
vowel quadrangle

Articulatory phonetics: consonants

5

Objectives

To introduce the nomenclature used in consonant classification.

To examine consonant articulation by manner of articulation: plosive, fricative, affricate, nasal, approximant, etc.

To examine consonant articulation by place of articulation and by voicing.

To discuss airstream mechanisms in natural language and in the laryngectomee.

5-1 Consonants

In the production of consonants the airflow out of the mouth is completely blocked, greatly restricted, or diverted through the nose. This gives consonants a more noisy, less melodic quality than vowels. Note that it is the vowels, not the consonants, that carry the tune when we sing: you can sing an [a], but you cannot sing a [s]!

The way the airstream from the mouth is modified (blocked, restricted, diverted, etc.) provides a means of classifying consonants. This dimension is called **manner of articulation.** We will consider five main types of English consonants according to manner of articulation (plosives, fricatives, affricates, nasals, and approximants) as well as consonants that either occur only combinatorily in English or do not occur in English.

The exact point in the vocal tract at which the airstream is modified—that is, lips, teeth, alveolar ridge, etc.—gives us a second dimension of consonant classification; this dimension is called **place of articulation.**

A third classificatory dimension is **voicing.** A segment is described as **voiced** or **voiceless** depending upon whether or not the vocal folds are vibrating during the production of the consonant. For example, [z] is voiced (the vocal folds are vibrating), while [s] is voiceless (the folds are apart). If you pronounce them out loud, you hear the "buzzing" of the vocal folds accompanying the [z], and you can feel their vibration if you put your hand on the thyroid cartilage ("Adam's apple"). Both the buzzing and the vibration are missing from the voiceless [s]. While it may appear that voicing is either *present* or *absent* (either the vocal folds are vibrating or they are not), and while voicing in consonants is usually taught as if it were an all-or-nothing choice, in fact voicing varies on a continuum. We will discuss this later under the heading Voice Onset Time (Section 5-2.12).

5-1.1 Places of Articulation

The **place of articulation** dimension uses the names of the various parts of the vocal tract introduced in Chapter 4. Let us review those terms, starting at the front of the mouth:

An articulation with the **lips** is a **labial** articulation; with **both lips** it is **bilabial;** the combining form is **labio-,** as in *labiodental.*

An articulation with the upper front **teeth** is a **dental** articulation.

An articulation on or near the **alveolar ridge** is an **alveolar** articulation; the combining form is **alveo-,** as in *alveopalatal.*

An articulation on or near the (hard) **palate** is a **palatal** articulation; the combining form is **palato-,** as in *palatovelar.*

An articulation on or near the **velum** is a **velar** articulation; movements of the velum itself are **velic** movements.

An articulation with the **uvula** is a **uvular** articulation.

An articulation in the **pharynx** (with the tongue root) is a **pharyngeal** articulation (or, more precisely, a *radicopharyngeal* articulation).

An articulation made with the vocal folds themselves is a **glottal** articulation.

An articulation with the **tongue** is a **lingual** or **glossal** articulation, although it is normal practice not to specify the tongue itself unless

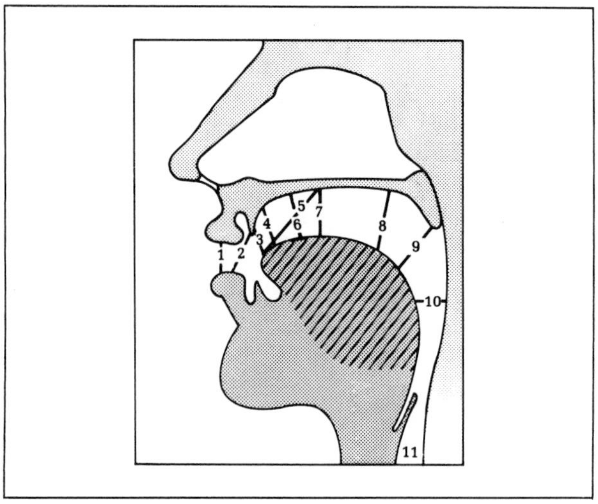

Figure 5-1. A stylized articulatory drawing showing the places of articulation in consonant production. **1, Bilabial; 2, labiodental; 3, dental** (*specifically,* apicodental); **4, alveolar** (*either* apicoalveolar *or* laminoalveolar); **5, retroflex** (apicopalatal); **6, alveopalatal** (laminoalveopalatal); **7, palatal** (dorsopalatal: *actually, the* front *of the tongue on the palate*); **8, velar** (dorsovelar: *actually, the* back *of the tongue on the velum*); **9, uvular** (dorsouvular); **10, pharyngeal** (radicopharyngeal); **11, glottal** (*the* vocal folds, *not shown in drawing*).

one wants to specify the *part* of the tongue involved. An articulation with the **tip** of the tongue is an **apical** articulation; with the **blade** of the tongue, a **laminal** articulation; with the **back** of the tongue, a **dorsal** articulation. The combining forms of these terms are **apico-**, **lamino-**, and **dorso-**, respectively.

See Figure 5-1.

5-1.2 Consonant Nomenclature

The system of nomenclature works as follows. In the articulation of any given sound, it is assumed that one articulator (the **active articulator**) will be the tongue, which will touch or approximate (get close to) a second, **passive articulator.** Usually only the latter is mentioned in naming the segment. For example, if the tongue is raised to touch or approximate the alveolar ridge, the sound is called simply **alveolar;** even though the tongue has done the articulating, it is not mentioned.

However, *both* articulators may be mentioned if

1. Neither articulator is the tongue. In **bilabial** sounds or **labiodental** sounds neither articulator is the tongue, so both are specified (bilabial, 'two lips'; labiodental, 'lip to teeth').
2. A more precise description of the articulation is desired. For example, either the apex of the tongue or the blade of the tongue may touch the alveolar ridge. Usually little attention is paid to this difference, and either type of sound is described as simply **alveolar.** But if you wanted to specify the difference, the two sounds could be called **apicoalveolar** and **laminoalveolar,** terms in which both articulators are named.

Otherwise, though, we usually do not name the second articulator. Replacing the terms **alveolar, palatal, velar,** etc. with *lingua-alveolar, lingua-palatal, lingua-velar,* as some books advocate, simply makes complicated terms that give no additional information. Similarly, calling a sound *dorso-velar* instead of just **velar** normally doesn't add any information, since one would expect the tongue dorsum, rather than any other part of the tongue, to touch the velum. Normally, such a term would only be used contrastively: **dorsopalatal,** as opposed to **apicopalatal.**

5-1.3 Understanding the Nomenclature: A Velar Sound May Not Involve the Velum

One problem with the nomenclature is that it sometimes leads to misunderstandings. Let us consider, for example, a velar consonant. How is a velar consonant articulated? The tongue dorsum is arched up toward the velum (for certain sounds the tongue will touch the velum, for others it will only get close). As long as the sound in question is not a nasal, *the velum itself does nothing in the articulation of a velar sound; it may not even be touched by the tongue.* So in trying to understand what is going on in normal articulation, and what is going wrong in disorders of articulation, do not be tricked by the name of the segment in question into looking for a problem other than where it is. For example, a misarticulated velar does not imply a velic problem. Rather, it is the result of the tongue's not arching as it should under the velum.

5-1.4 Phonemics

The subject of phonemics, discussed in Chapter 2 and mentioned again in Chapter 4, will be dealt with in detail in Chapter 8. Let us see here how it relates to the classification of consonants.

Any system of classifying things is a compromise: Whatever the system used, there are always items that do not fall neatly into the predetermined categories. The categories of speech sounds usually chosen in introductory phonetics books are those corresponding to the **phonemic contrasts** of the language in question. Consider the sound we spell with the letter ⟨t⟩ in the following words: "take," "steak," "train," "cat." In one sense, these are all the "same" sound. But in a strict phonetic sense, they are all different. Each one is articulated in a different manner. If we count the number of consonant sounds by a method that assumes that the various /t/'s are counted "same," we find that there are about twenty-five consonants in English (give or take a few, depending on dialect). If we count by a method in which each different articulation is considered a different sound, there may be more than a hundred consonants in English, since in the same way that there are varieties of "t," there are also varieties of all other segments.

Let us return to the examples above. The /t/ in

the word "train," in many dialects of English, is a retroflex consonant. That is, it is articulated with the tip of the tongue touching the front part of the palate, considerably farther back than the point of contact for the "t" in "take."[1] The "t" of "take" is much more typical of the articulation of "t" in English; in fact, the *only* place in most dialects of English where "t" is retroflex is when it is followed by "r" in word-initial[2] position. Usually when we speak in general terms about the sounds of English, we consider retroflexes to be foreign sounds found only in other languages. But when we look closely, we find that this type of articulation occurs in standard English in this one phonetic environment.[3]

We therefore face a dilemma in presenting the consonants of English: Should we present only the general case and ignore the others? (For example, the "t" of "take," but not the "t" of "steak" or "train"?) Or do we present all the possible types and hope that the detail is not too confusing?

This book takes the approach that the details of articulation *are* important, since the speech therapist is not interested in just the phonemic structure of the language but in the phonetic details as well. It is conceivable that an individual needing phonetic correction will have difficulty with the "t" of "train" but not with the "t" of "take," since they are articulated differently; if your phonetics book tells you they are the same, it is not helping you understand why one is harder to pronounce than the other. The linguistics student needs more than a phonemic inventory as well, be it for sociolinguistic description or theoretical accounting of phonological systems.

In this chapter, as in Chapter 4, the individual sounds are presented thus: Emphasis is given to the basic types of English sounds, and the others are mentioned in boxed sections. In Chapters 6 and 8, considerable space will be devoted to explaining the distribution of these less typical sounds. It is suggested that the student pass over the boxed sections on a first reading, thereby examining only the phonemes of English. On subsequent reading, these sections may be read at their logical point in the text.

[1] Try this to see if it is true in your pronunciation. Say "train" and "take" in a natural way, paying attention to where the tongue blade or apex contacts the roof of your mouth. Most speakers find that they articulate the "t" of "train" farther back in the mouth.

[2] **Word-initial:** at the beginning of a word; refers to the first sound in a word.

[3] The **phonetic environment** of a sound refers to the surrounding sounds and other phonetic features, such as stress, that may influence the pronunciation of the sound in question. This is one of the topics of Chapter 6.

5-1.5 A Note on the Classification of Consonants

The consonants discussed here are organized into major groups by *manner of articulation* and into subgroups by *place of articulation* and *voicing*.

One more note before examining individual consonants. Section 5-9 presents a number of different *airstream mechanisms*, that is, the moving column of air that powers speech may come from different sources. In the following discussion, up to Section 5-9, all consonants are assumed to be *pulmonic egressive*—the air is being pushed out of the lungs.

As in Chapter 4, the articulatory drawings (Figs. 5-6–5-32) are grouped together (see pp. 110–115). You may wish to consult these while reading the text.

5-2 The Plosive

A **plosive** consonant is formed by blocking the oral cavity at some point. During the articulation of most plosives the velum is raised, blocking off the nasal passages.[4] This permits a certain amount of pressure to build up in the oral cavity behind the occlusion; if the velum were not raised, any pressure the speaker attempted to create behind the occlusion would leak out through the nasal passage. The pressure that is built up is released suddenly, as a minor "explosion" or "popping."

[p] as in "pan" is such a plosive sound, as is [t] in "tan." Notice that plosives cannot be pronounced alone. If you try to say a [p] alone, it will invariably be followed by a vowel, usually [ə].

[4] Some non-English plosives are produced with blockage in the pharynx. These do not require velic closure, since the occlusion happens *before* the air gets to the velum. The glottal stop, usually classified with the plosives, is produced by blockage at the glottis, and therefore velic position is not relevant in its articulation.

We usually identify three phases of plosive articulation, although they may not all be present. These three phases are:

1. The **shutting** or **closing** phase, during which the articulators are moving from a previous open state to the closed state.
2. The **closure** phase or **occlusion,** the momentary total blockage of the vocal tract.
3. The **release,** which is the abrupt reopening of the vocal tract. It is sometimes accompanied by a burst of air, if the intraoral pressure has been great.

The term **stop** is also used for plosives.

5-2.1 Bilabial Plosives

The plosive [p] is a **bilabial** sound. For example, the underlined sound in "happy" is a [p]. The blockage of the oral cavity is made with the two lips. [p] is a voiceless sound; the vocal folds are not vibrating. If you attempt to verify this by placing a hand on your throat, it is important not to mistake the voicing of the following vowel for the voicing of the consonant.

If a similar articulatory gesture is produced as for [p], but with glottal vibration, [b] will be pronounced. For example, the underlined sound in "rabbit" is a [b]. [p] and [b] form a pair of sounds produced by similar articulatory gestures, differing primarily in voicing. For the convenience of classification, the consonants will be arranged in pairs.

5-2.2 Alveolar Plosives

Moving toward the back of the mouth, the next point of articulation for English plosives is the alveolar ridge behind the teeth. For the plosives [t] and [d], the oral cavity is blocked by placing the blade of the tongue against the alveolar ridge. The sides of the tongue are placed along the upper teeth, completing the seal. The release occurs when the blade of the tongue is lowered, allowing the pressure to explode over the top. The phonetic symbols [t] and [d] represent the sounds you would expect: [t] as in "material" and [d] as in "Madeira." Note that these sounds are sometimes spelled other ways in English; for example, [t] may be represented with the letters ⟨th⟩ as in "Thomas."

[t] and [d] are **alveolar plosives;** [t] is the voiceless alveolar plosive; [d] is voiced.

5-2.3 Dental Plosives

In some languages, plosives are produced not as in English with the blade of the tongue against the alveolar ridge, but with the tip of the tongue against the upper teeth; they are called **dental plosives.** In Spanish, for example, [t̪] and [d̪] are generally **apicodental** (i.e., the tip—apex—of the tongue is against the teeth), as compared to the most common English articulation, which is **laminoalveolar** (i.e., the blade of the tongue is against the alveolar ridge). The symbol [̪] specifies a dental articulation, as in apicodental [t̪] [d̪] as opposed to laminoalveolar [t] [d]. These dental varieties occur occasionally in English as well.

5-2.4 Palatal Plosives

It is possible to produce a plosive by making an occlusion between the tongue dorsum and the palate. This point of articulation is halfway between that for [t] and [k]; the tongue is arched as for the vowel [i] of "meet." The voiceless palatal plosive is symbolized [c], the voiced one [ɟ]. Usually we do not consider these to be English sounds, but they are often produced by speakers of English instead of [k] and [g], when the latter are followed by certain vowels. For example, the first sound of "coop" (as in "chicken coop") is a [k], but the first sound of "keep" is really palatal, a [c]. Pronounce the two words, and note how your tongue touches the roof of the mouth further forward in "keep" than in "coop."[5] For reasons mentioned at the beginning of this chapter and detailed in Chapter 8, we often consider these sounds to be the "same," despite their differences.

[5]Note that in the examples, the word *spelled* with a ⟨k⟩ ("keep") has the palatal plosive [c]; the word *spelled* with a ⟨c⟩ ("coop") has the velar plosive [k]. This is due to historical developments: the sound [k] in Latin, spelled ⟨c⟩, became [s] before the vowels [i] and [e], and in English ⟨c⟩ before ⟨i⟩ or ⟨e⟩ usually represents [s]. Before the letters ⟨i⟩ and ⟨e⟩, the sound [k] is usually spelled with a ⟨k⟩, whereas the letter ⟨c⟩ is usually used before most other vowel letters.

5-2.5 Retroflex Plosives

Some languages have a plosive produced by placing the tip or apex of the tongue against the forward part of the palatal region. This place of articulation is referred to with the term **retroflex,** since the tongue is *bent* (or *flexed*) *back on itself* (*retro*, meaning 'backward').

In some dialects of English, when a /t/ or /d/ occurs at the beginning of a word before an r-sound, both the plosive and the "r" may be retroflex, as in the words "train" and "drain." But many languages have retroflex plosives that contrast with /t/ and /d/, for example, a number of the languages of India.

Retroflex consonants are symbolized /ṭ/ and /ḍ/, the dot underneath indicating retroflexion. (In the official IPA, these are symbolized with long tails: /ʈ/ and /ɖ/; but the dot diacritic is simpler and is gaining popularity.)

5-2.6 Velar Plosives

The next point at which English produces plosives is with the tongue against the soft palate or **velum.** The two **velar plosives** are [k] and [g]; [k] is voiceless, while [g] is voiced. [k] is as in "cool"; [g] as in "ago."

Note that in the articulation of the velars, the tongue dorsum is raised to meet the velum; the velum is not lowered to meet the tongue. As with other plosives, the nasal passages must remain closed.

5-2.7 Uvular Plosives

Some languages have plosives that are produced on the very back part of the velum, at the point where the uvula is attached. This place of articulation is called **uvular.** The voiceless uvular plosive is symbolized [q], and the voiced one is symbolized [ɢ].

These sounds occur in English when the phonemes /k/ and /g/ occur in the environment of low back vowels, which tend to "pull" their articulation backward. More on this subject in Chapter 6.

5-2.8 Glottal Stop

The **glottal stop** is usually classified with the other plosive sounds, although its manner of articulation is somewhat different. The glottis is the space between the vocal folds. If the vocal folds are brought together and released under pressure, an audible speech sound will be produced. It is not usually counted among the speech sounds of English but is used in several dialects of our language. Speakers of some British dialects, for example, often substitute the glottal stop for [t].[6] Most of us use a glottal stop between the two vowel sounds in the expression "uh-uh," meaning 'no.' The transcription symbol for the glottal stop is [ʔ], like a question mark with a bar instead of a dot. This is a common sound in the languages of the world, occurs in most dialects of English (if only in the interjection "uh-uh"), and substitutes for other plosives quite often in certain speech disorders.

Since the glottal stop involves the vocal folds, there can be no voiced and voiceless varieties; it is classified as voiceless.

5-2.9 Plosive Summary

In summary, English is said to have six plosive phonemes: voiceless and voiced bilabials (/p,b/), alveolars (/t,d/), and velars (/k,g/).

We have also noted that dentals (/t̪,d̪/) and palatals (/c,ɟ/) occur in other languages and occasionally, as positional variants, in English.[7] And we noted that all English speakers produce a glottal stop in certain interjections ("uh-uh"); in some dialects speakers regularly use glottal stops.

Table 5-1 lists plosives by voicing and place of articulation.

5-2.10 Plosives and Communication Disorders

Plosives, as we said, are produced by the build-up and sudden release of oral pressure, requiring closure of the nasal passages with the velum. Individuals with cleft palate have never learned to control the movements of the velum, since, even with the velum raised, air pressure escapes through the cleft into the nasal cavity. After re-

[6] This substitution occurs in certain English (British) and Scottish dialects. The details vary among dialects, but typically [ʔ] replaces intervocalic (between vowels) [t]. For example, the [t] of "matter" and the [t] of "what" in the phrase "What are you doing?" are replaced by the glottal stop.

[7] **Positional variant:** a variant form produced by influence from surrounding sounds. (See Chapter 6.)

Table 5-1. The plosives

	†Bilabial	Dental	†Alveolar	Retroflex	Palatal	†Velar	Glottal
Voiceless	p	t̪	t	ʈ	c	k	ʔ
Voiced	b	d̪	d	ɖ	ɟ	g	

†English plosive phonemes.

constructive surgery or the fitting of a prosthesis, such individuals need guidance in controlling the velum to produce plosive sounds. Very often these individuals substitute a glottal stop for the plosives they cannot pronounce.

Deaf speakers also have articulatory difficulty with plosive sounds and often need guidance to build up sufficient pressure for audible plosives. Deaf speakers often voice *all* plosives, whether or not it is appropriate; this voicing problem is evident with other consonants as well.

5-2.11 Pressure and Aspiration

Plosives may vary in the amount of pressure built up inside the mouth before release **(intraoral air pressure).** In English and in many other languages, the voiceless plosives are produced with considerably greater pressure than the voiced plosives, at least at the beginning of a stressed syllable. This results in their release being accompanied by a sudden puff of air, called **aspiration.**[8] You can test this fact by putting your hand in front of your mouth and saying "pit" and "bit"; you should feel a stronger puff of air accompanying the /p/ than the /b/ sound. A dramatic demonstration of aspiration can be made by holding a lighted match in front of the mouth. "Bit" will usually disturb the flame slightly, while "pit" will usually snuff it. Aspiration is transcribed phonetically by a small raised ⟨h⟩. For example, an aspirated [p] is transcribed [p^h].

The plosives having higher intraoral pressure are often called **fortis,** and those having lower pressure **lenis,** from the Latin words for 'strong' and 'weak.' In some languages, such as Spanish and French, both the voiced and the voiceless plosives are lenis and unaspirated. For this reason, English-speaking people sometimes have difficulty distinguishing /p/ from /b/, /t/ from /d/, etc., in those languages, and this fact contributes to the accent Spanish- and French-speaking people have when speaking English (and vice versa). Voiceless plosives that do not occur at the beginning of a syllable are also lenis in English. Using the test of the hand or match in front of the mouth, compare the /p/ of "pin" (fortis) and "spin" (lenis).

[8] This term will confuse those who know its original meaning. Literally, aspiration is a drawing-in of air, a suction. But in its phonetic sense it refers to a sudden *outgoing* puff of air accompanying release of a plosive.

5-2.12 Voice Onset Time

Related to the questions of pressure, aspiration, and the fortis/lenis distinction, but still independent of them, is the voicing dimension called **voice onset time (VOT).**

Voicing is often considered as if it were, like an electric circuit, either "on" or "off." The difference between "bit" and "pit" is said to lie in the fact that the /b/ is voiced whereas the /p/ is voiceless. A curious fact emerges, however, if one sets about to measure voicing instrumentally: It turns out that, often as not, the /b/ of "bit" is voiceless! /p/ turns out to be even more voiceless. This at first seems puzzling: the vocal folds are either vibrating or else they are not, so how can something be *more* or *less* voiced?

Actually the situation is not so puzzling after all. Vocal fold vibration is initiated by one set of muscles (laryngeal as well as respiratory muscles), whereas the actual occlusion and release of the plosive is effected by another set of muscles (the articulatory muscles of the tongue and/or lips and/or jaw). Just as your legs can move independently of your arms (you can scratch your ear as you walk, for example), so too voicing and articulation are independent. Since they are independent, they don't have to happen simultaneously.

Let us consider the release of a word-initial plosive. This is the point at which the articulators part and any built-up pressure escapes. With this point in time as reference, let us consider the start of voicing. Voicing could start at the same instant as release, before release, or after release. This is what is called **voice onset time** or **VOT:** the *time* with respect to release for the *onset* of *voicing*. If voicing starts *after* release, VOT is considered to have a *positive* value. If release and voice onset

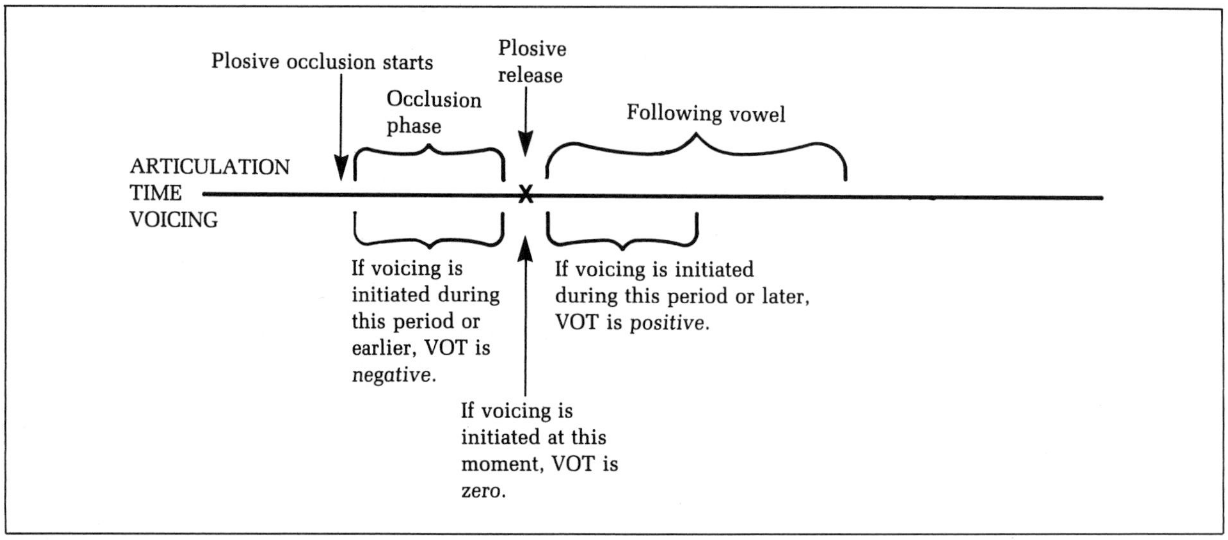

Figure 5-2. Voice onset time (VOT).

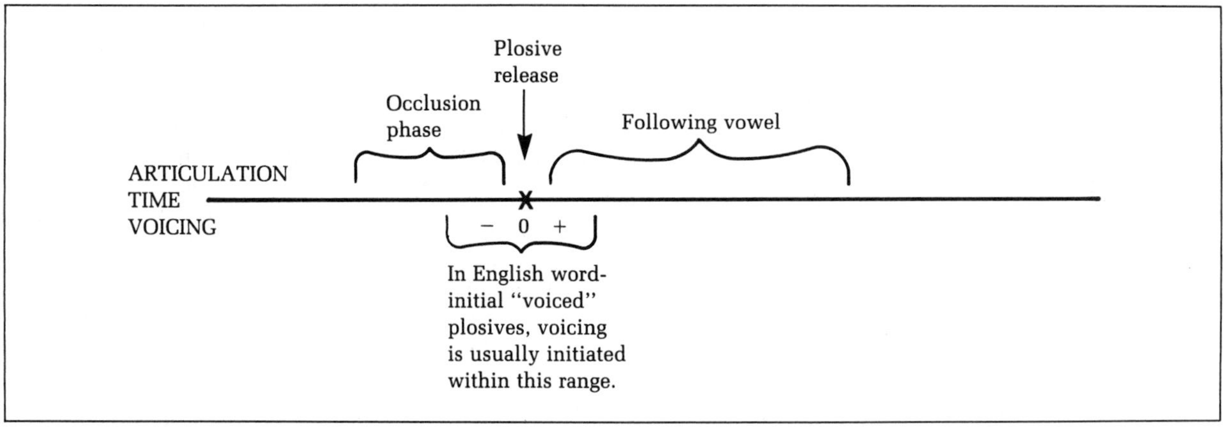

Figure 5-3. VOT of English word-initial voiced plosives.

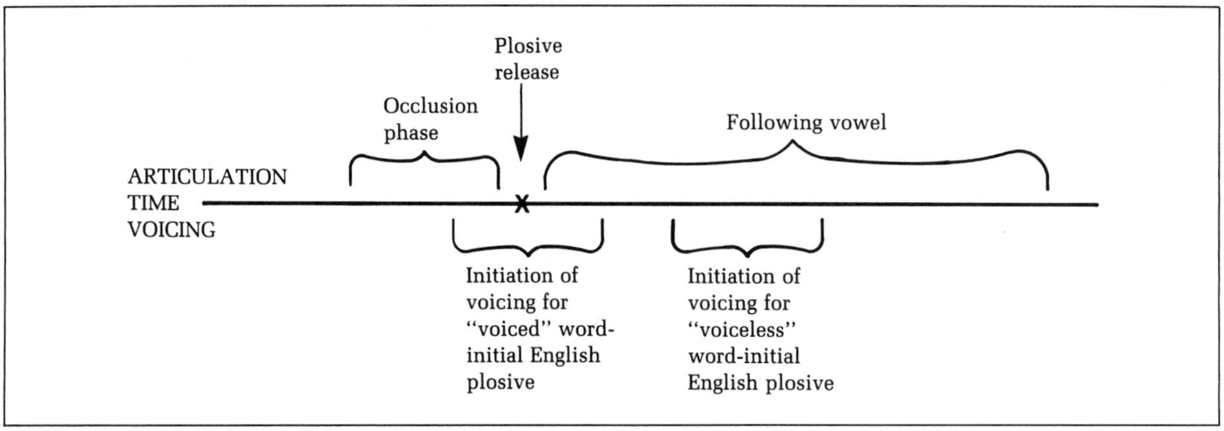

Figure 5-4. VOT of English word-initial voiceless (as well as voiced) plosives.

are simultaneous, VOT is zero (i.e., there is no delay). If voicing *precedes* release, VOT has a *negative* value. Graphically it would look like Figure 5-2 (the line represents time; the point *X* is plosive release).

If one measures VOT in English word-initial voiced plosives, one finds that VOT is usually around zero, either slightly negative or moderately positive (Figure 5-3).

Let us assume that the word spoken was "bowl." The range indicated with a brace in Figure 5-3 shows the range anywhere in which voicing might *start;* once started, it continues throughout the following vowel. Note that the value is often positive, meaning voicing does not start until *after* the release. The occlusion phase is thus *voiceless,* although this is a *voiced* plosive.

What about the voiceless plosive in word-initial position? It will be aspirated, as noted, and have a greater, always positive VOT, as shown in Figure 5-4 (the VOT for voiced plosives is repeated for comparison purposes).

Up to this point we have discussed the VOT of word-initial plosives only. If a voiced plosive is word-medial[9] between two voiced segments, as, for example, in the words "oboe" and "about," voicing continues right through the entire articulation, so the occlusion phase is completely voiced. As the onset of voicing actually occurred with a previous segment, any measure of VOT for the plosive is meaningless.

Let us now consider voiceless plosives in word-medial position. If a voiceless plosive is situated intervocalically[9] at the beginning of a stressed syllable, as in the word "kaput," it is aspirated and has a relatively long positive VOT. On the other hand, if it is situated at the end of a stressed syllable or at the beginning of an unstressed syllable, like the /p/ in the word "capping," it is generally not aspirated and has a rather shorter VOT, more like that of a voiced plosive.[10]

Even more interesting is the case of voiceless plosives following an /s/ in word-initial position, as in "spare," "stick," and "skate." If you were to tape-record a person saying these words and then carefully cut the tape so as to remove the /s/ from each word, what would you hear if you then played the tape? It is natural to assume that you would hear "pare," "tick," and "Kate." But this is not the case: you would hear "bare," "Dick," and "gate." "Voiceless" plosives in this position are not aspirated and have shorter VOTs, falling into the range of voiced plosives in word-initial position so they are heard as voiced plosives if put in word-initial position.

It is paradoxical, but the difference between a voiced and a voiceless plosive depends not only on voicing, but on position as well. The situation is summarized in Table 5-2.

[9] **Word-medial:** at neither the beginning nor the end of a word. **Intervocalic:** between vowels.

[10] /t/'s in intervocalic, unstressed position undergo flapping (discussed later) in North American English. These remarks, therefore, refer only to /p/ and /k/.

5-3 The Fricative

Fricative sounds are articulated by approximating two articulators (i.e., bringing them close together), and then forcing air under considerable pressure through the constriction thus formed. As the air is forced through the narrow constriction, its flow creates a noisy turbulence, like steam escaping through a partially open valve. This hissing or hushing sound characterizes fricatives.

Fricatives can be articulated at the lips, within the oral cavity, with the vocal folds, or, in some languages, in the pharyngeal cavity. For reasons explained in the preceding section, oral and labial fricatives must be articulated with the velum raised. Each place of articulation has a **voiceless** and a **voiced** variety.

As we did with the plosives, we will consider English fricatives in pairs, starting at the front of the mouth and working back.

5-3.1 Labial Fricatives

English has none of the bilabial fricatives that some languages, like Spanish, have. English, however, does have a pair of **labiodental fricatives.** This means that the small passage through which the air must pass is formed with the teeth and the lip. The upper teeth and lower lip are used in English and in other languages that have labiodentals. The voiceless labiodental fricative is /f/; the voiced one is /v/.

5-3.2 Dental Fricatives

English has two fricative sounds produced with the tongue and the teeth. In some dialect regions, the tongue is placed behind the front teeth, producing what we refer to as a **dental fricative.** In other dialect regions, the tongue is placed between the upper and lower teeth to produce an **interdental fricative.** The sound is essentially the same in both cases. This is the sound we spell ⟨th⟩. We do not distinguish in spelling between voiced

Table 5-2. Voice onset time (VOT) of voiced and voiceless English plosives in various environments

Position	Voiceless	Voiced
Word-initial		
Examples	*pan* *tan* *can*	*ball* *doll* *Gaul*
Characteristics	Aspirated VOT: long, positive	Not aspirated VOT: slightly negative through 0 to moderately positive
After word-initial /s/		
Examples	*spare* *stick* *skate*	N.A.
Characteristics	Not aspirated VOT: 0 to moderately positive	
Intervocalic, beginning of stressed syllable		
Examples	*kaput* *retake* (vb) *recoil* (vb)	*rebuff* *redo* (vb) *regard*
Characteristics	Aspirated VOT: long, positive	Not aspirated VOT: not measurable; continuous voicing through preceding and following vowels
Intervocalic, not at beginning of stressed syllable		
Examples	*capping* *matter* *makeup*	*rubber* *madder* *Maggy*
Characteristics	Not aspirated VOT: 0 to somewhat positive. /t/ may be flapped; VOT then unmeasurable	Not aspirated VOT: not measurable; continuous voicing. /d/ may be flapped.

and voiceless varieties, but they are pronounced differently. The voiceless variant occurs in the words "thin," "thought," "ether," and "both." It is transcribed with the Greek letter theta, /θ/. The voiced variant occurs in the words "the," "this," "either," and "lathe." It is transcribed with a symbol called **bar-d** or **eth,** which is a script ⟨d⟩ with a crossbar, /ð/.

The production of both dental and labiodental consonants—as well as some plosives—will be affected by missing teeth. Frequently children are referred to speech pathologists for problems caused by the transition to adult dentition. Usually the problem will correct itself as new teeth grow in. In adults, some speech problems can be corrected through dental work.

5-3.3 Alveolar Fricatives

One pair of fricatives is produced with the blade of the tongue close to the alveolar ridge. These **alveolar fricatives** are /s/ (voiceless) and /z/ (voiced). Another characteristic distinguishing them is that they are produced with the tongue slightly **grooved.** Notice that in pronouncing /θ/, the blade of the tongue is quite flat, but in pronouncing /s/, the sides of the blade are curled up slightly, forming a groove in the center. Fricatives like /θ/, /ð/, /š/, and /ž/ (see Section 5-3.4), which are articulated with a relatively flat tongue, are called **slit** fricatives. The space through which air is forced is a wide thin *slit* as opposed to the rounder groove of /s/ and /z/ (Figure 5-5). Failure to form the groove is responsible for certain types of

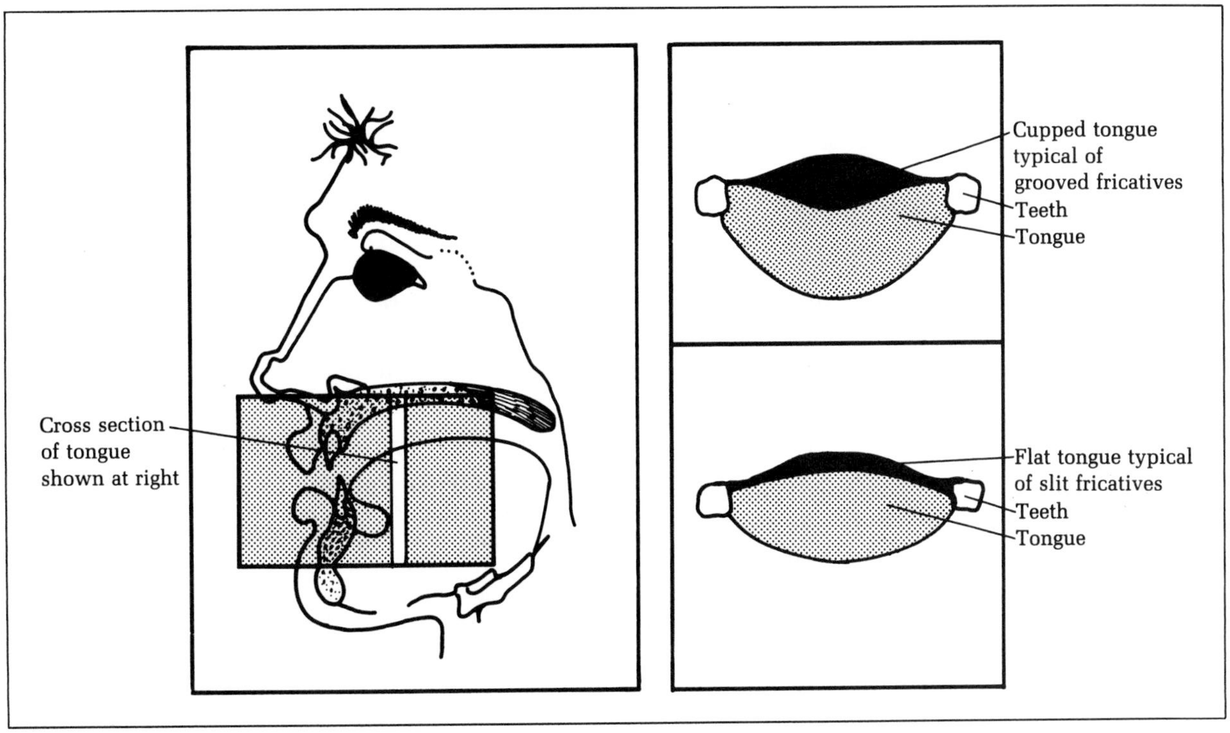

Figure 5-5. Stylized cross section of the tongue, showing its configuration in slit and grooved fricatives.

lisp. If the front teeth are missing, the air will not have to pass by the same route, and a less sibilant fricative sound is produced: an attempt to articulate /s/ produces a /θ/-like sound, which is identified as a lisp.

5-3.4 Alveopalatal Fricatives

The **alveopalatal fricatives** are articulated by bringing the blade of the tongue close to the part of the roof of the mouth where the alveolar ridge and the hard palate join. These are sometimes called *palatoalveolar* or, not very accurately, *palatal* fricatives. Unlike the alveolar fricatives, the alveopalatal fricatives involve no grooving of the tongue; it is more or less flat at the point of constriction. For this reason, they are often called **slit** fricatives, like a number of other fricatives such as /θ/ and /ð/. Both voiceless and voiced alveopalatal fricatives are articulated with lip-rounding (labialization) in English.

The voiceless alveopalatal fricative is usually spelled ⟨sh⟩ in English; it is the sound in the words "shore," "bush," "sugar," and "position." Two symbols are used to transcribe this sound: /š/ and /ʃ/. Either symbol is acceptable, but it is important to be consistent in using one or the other. The wedge over the ⟨s⟩ is called a **hachek;** it is borrowed from the Czech alphabet.

The voiced alveopalatal fricative is less common in English. It is the sound that occurs in the words "measure," "version," and "leisure." It is transcribed either of two ways: /ž/ or /ʒ/.

The symbols [ʃ] and [ʒ] are the traditional symbols for these sounds and are those used officially in the International Phonetic Alphabet (IPA). These older symbols are still commonly used in Europe, but [š] and [ž] have replaced them recently, particularly in North America. I recommend using [š] and [ž] for several reasons: they are easier to write and clearer when handwritten, and the hachek is used in North America for *all* alveopalatal sounds (see Section 5-4).

In some pathological conditions (e.g., cerebral palsy), /s/ and /š/, as well as /z/ and /ž/, are not distinguished. This situation is also labeled with the rather loose term **lisp.**

Table 5-3. English fricatives

	Labiodental	Dental	Alveolar	Alveopalatal	Glottal
Voiceless	f	θ	s	š	h
Voiced	v	ð	z	ž	†ɦ

† [ɦ] is not considered a separate phoneme in English.

5-3.5 Glottal Fricatives

The sound [h] as in "house" is usually classified as a fricative.[11] It is different from the other fricatives in several ways. The supraglottal vocal tract is open; usually its degree of openness is exactly that of the following vowel. The friction comes mostly from the glottis, which is closed to about the degree that it is in *whispering.* (The mechanism of whispering is discussed in Section 9-4.3.) There is also *some* friction from the oral and pharyngeal cavities, particularly in [h] followed by a high vowel. This is called **cavity friction** and combines with the glottal friction to create the characteristic sound of [h].[12] Despite often having more than one source of friction, [h] is generally classified as a **glottal fricative** and is voiceless.

While the vocal folds are producing the friction for [h], it is possible for them to be vibrating and producing a frictional noise at the same time, producing a voiced "h," [ɦ].[13] This **voiced glottal fricative** is heard in some dialects of English when an ⟨h⟩ occurs in intervocalic position; in some dialects it must be not only intervocalic but pretonic[14] as well, as in "be̲hold" and "be̲hind."

Table 5-3 lists English fricatives by voicing and place of articulation.

[11] In the branch of linguistics known as phonology, [h] is often classified as a **glide,** not a fricative. You may have seen it classified that way in another book. The aim of phonology is different from that of descriptive phonetics; phonology studies what is systematic about sound systems, and phonologists are therefore influenced by the fact that [h] *behaves* like [w] or [j] in the sound system of English. On the other hand, our purpose here is to emphasize the *articulation* of speech sounds, so [h] is classified phonetically as a fricative. It is true that [h] is somewhat different from other fricatives. It is more important at this point to understand its articulation than its classification.

[12] Glottal friction is common to all [h]'s. The acoustic characteristics of the cavity friction depend on the position of the articulators—namely, what vowel follows the [h]. This can be easily demonstrated as follows: pronounce the [h] at the beginning of these words by prolonging it; do not pronounce the vowel, just the [h]: "heat," "hot," "hoot," "hat." Each [h] will sound different, and a listener at close range will be able to tell what vowel would have followed the [h] if it had been pronounced.

[13] This glottal mechanism is akin to breathy voicing (see Section 9-4.3).

[14] **Pretonic:** before, or at the beginning of, a stressed syllable.

5-3.6 Other Fricatives

Of course English does not have all possible fricatives, just as we saw that plosives exist that are not used in English. In this section we will look briefly at some fricatives that occur in other languages and some that occur in English only in certain dialects or certain combinations. This is not a complete inventory of all possible fricatives.

Bilabial fricatives exist in some languages. These are produced with a constriction between upper and lower lips. The voiceless variety is symbolized with the Greek letter *phi,* [ɸ]. This sound occurs in Japanese, among other languages; the famous sacred mountain, Mount Fuji, is pronounced not with a [f] but with a [ɸ] in Japanese. To pronounce this sound, spread the lips (smile) with a narrow gap between the lips while acting as if to blow out a candle.

The voiced bilabial fricative is symbolized by the letter *beta,* [β]. Its articulation is similar to that of [ɸ] except that it is voiced. This sound occurs in many dialects of Spanish where the letter ⟨b⟩ or ⟨v⟩ is used in the spelling. (Note, however, that these letters represent the sound [b] or [v] in some dialects of Spanish.)

Grooved dental fricatives, [s̪] and [z̪], exist in some languages. These are like [s] and [z], except that they are slightly farther forward—the constriction is principally between tongue and teeth rather than between tongue and alveolar ridge as for [s] and [z]. Spanish typically has a dental [s̪], and many English speakers produce [s̪] and [z̪], depending on dialect, surrounding sounds, and personal speech habits. Note the use of the diacritic [̪] as for other dental sounds.

Retroflex fricatives also exist. As with other retroflexes, the tongue is bent back, and the constriction is between the apex of the tongue and the alveopalatal or front palatal region. These are

Table 5-4. The fricatives

	Bi-labial	Labio-dental	Inter-dental	Grooved dental	Al-veolar	Alveo-palatal	Retro-flex	Palatal	Velar	Uvular	Pharyngeal	Glottal
Voiceless	ɸ	f	θ	s̪	s	š	ṣ	ç	x	χ	ħ	h
Voiced	β	v	ð	z̪	z	ž	ẓ	j̑	ɣ	ʁ	ʕ	ɦ

Note: [θ] and [ð] may be *dental* or *interdental*. [s̪] and [z̪] are dental but sound very different from [θ] and [ð] by virtue of being grooved and being usually articulated higher on the back surface of the front teeth.

symbolized [ṣ], and [ẓ], using the usual diacritic for retroflexion.[15] These sounds occur in many languages. The s-sound is often retroflexed in the English of parts of Arkansas and Texas. Retroflexed [ṣ]'s are one of the distinctive characteristics of the speech of the comedian W. C. Fields. In many areas of North America, the r-sound following a word-initial [t] or [d] is replaced by a retroflex fricative: the second sound of "train" may be [ṣ], and the second sound of "drain" may be [ẓ].

Palatal fricatives also occur in some languages. The constriction occurs between the arched tongue dorsum and the palate. You can pronounce the voiceless version, symbolized [ç], by holding your tongue in the position for the vowel [i] and blowing air through this constriction. This sound occurs in many languages, German among them. The sound spelled ⟨ch⟩ in German, when next to a front vowel, is pronounced [ç], as in *ich*, *Bächer*, and *Mädchen*. This sound occurs in some dialects of English when [h] is followed by the glide [j] (Section 5-6.1), as in the words "human" and "huge." The voiced palatal fricative is symbolized /j̑/. (The official IPA symbol is /j/, but this provides no distinction from the glide /j/, so common practice dictates using /j̑/. The diacritic /̑/ is explained in Section 5-3.7.)

Velar fricatives exist in many languages. The constriction occurs between the tongue dorsum and the raised velum. You can pronounce the voiceless variety, symbolized [x], by putting your tongue in the position for the vowel [u] (as in "boot") and blowing air through the constriction. You will naturally round your lips to say [u], but this is not essential to saying [x].

Note that while the letter ⟨x⟩ usually represents the sequence /ks/ in English spelling, in the IPA [x] represents a velar fricative.

[x] occurs in some dialects of English, as in the Scottish pronunciation of the word *loch*. It is the sound of German ⟨ch⟩ when next to back vowels, as in *Bach*. Some dialects of Spanish use [x] for the sound spelled ⟨j⟩ or ⟨x⟩, as in *Juana* and *Mexico*, although other dialects use the sound [h].

The voiced variety, symbolized by the letter *gamma* [ɣ], is less common. Some dialects of Spanish use [ɣ] for the sound spelled ⟨g⟩ in certain positions in a word, as in *agua* and *Guatemala*.

Uvular fricatives are produced with a constriction between the raised tongue dorsum and the back part of the velum, where the uvula attaches. The voiceless variety is symbolized [χ], and the voiced variety [ʁ]. The latter has an r-like quality and is the r-sound of many dialects of continental French and of German.

Pharyngeal fricatives are relatively rare. Constriction occurs between the tongue root and the posterior wall of the pharynx. The voiceless variety is symbolized [ħ], the voiced variety [ʕ]. These occur in Arabic, among other languages. The word *guttural* refers to the throat (L. *guttur*, 'throat'), so pharyngeal sounds could be described as guttural, although the latter term is avoided by phoneticians. It is interesting to note how a language such as German is often erroneously described as a "guttural" language. It has no pharyngeals whatever, although it does have velars and uvulars.

Table 5-4 shows the varieties of fricative.

5-3.7 Fricatives and Stridency

Fricatives may vary in the amount of frictional noise (or **stridency**)[16] generated in their articulation. For example, pronounce [s] and [θ] and note how much louder the [s] is than the [θ].

In this example, it appears that [s] is inherently

[15] The traditional IPA symbols are [ʂ] and [ʐ], but their use is waning in favor of the simpler [ṣ] and [ẓ].

[16] The term **strident** is used here in its general sense of 'harsh' or 'noisy' as applied to a sound. While we consider it to have a variable quality, we employ it by and large in accord with its use in generative phonology. However, it should be noted that phonetically *all* fricatives have some degree of stridency, whereas in phonological terms, some are characterized as being nonstrident, since their stridency is below a threshold level.

noisier than [θ]; it is impossible to produce [θ] as noisily as [s]. So the first factor in variable stridency is *place of articulation*. In the same way, it is apparent that [f] is not very strident, whereas [š] is.

A second factor is *voicing*. Compare [s] and [z]. When listening to [z], try to separate in your mind the part of the sound that is glottal vibration or voicing (the "buzzing") from the component that is the s-like noise. You will probably note that, although the [z] can be louder overall (due to the presence of voicing), it actually has *less* frictional noise. What is happening is that less air is passing through the glottis when one is articulating the voiced [z] sound than when one is articulating the voiceless [s] sound. As a result, there is less air passing through the constriction to cause frictional noise. Spectrographic analysis shows the reduced noise component of voiced fricatives.

The third factor controlling the stridency of fricatives is under the speaker's control. When the airflow is increased and/or the constriction made tighter, the fricative becomes more strident. When airflow is decreased and/or the constriction made larger, the fricative is "softer" or less strident.

In order to transcribe a more strident fricative, one may use the diacritic [ˆ] following the regular symbol: for example, [sˆ]. This implies that the articulation is higher (or closer) and thereby more strident. In contrast, one may use the diacritic [ˇ] to indicate that the particular fricative is less strident: for example, [sˇ].

Languages, as well as individual speakers, vary with respect to stridency of fricatives. For example, some dialects of Spanish have the fricative [x]. But among most Spanish speakers it is less strident than the [x] of German. Similarly, many dialects of Spanish having [ɣ] articulate it with so little friction that it may sound like a [w].

The degree of stridency, therefore, is a phonetic variable that contributes to the naturalness of speech. It should be appropriate to the given language; foreign speakers may be expected in some cases to produce fricatives that are too strident or not strident enough. Similarly, in certain speech disorders the degree of stridency may be inappropriate, calling attention to itself.

5-4 The Affricate

An **affricate** is a speech sound made up of a plosive and a homorganic[17] fricative, the two articulated in one movement and acting together as a single unit. In English, the sounds usually spelled ⟨ch⟩ and ⟨j⟩ are affricates. The place of articulation of these affricates ranges from alveolar to alveopalatal; we will classify them as alveolar.

The **voiceless alveolar affricate** occurs in such words as "chin," "batch," and "hatchet." It can be analyzed as [t] followed immediately by [š]. It is usually transcribed [t^{š}], [t͜š], or with the single symbol [č].

The **voiced alveolar affricate** occurs in such words as "jam," "fudge," and "badger." It can be analyzed as [d] followed closely by [ž]. It is usually transcribed [d^{ž}], [d͜ž], or with the single symbol [ǰ]. Speakers of some dialects of American English do not distinguish [ǰ] from [ž]. In most dialects these two sounds are contrasted in such pairs as "ledger" and "leisure" and "pledger" ('a person who pledges') and "pleasure."

The English [t] is usually alveolar, and English [š] is usually alveopalatal. In the affricate [č], both are probably articulated closer to a midpoint, allowing a quick transition. In any case, what characterizes an affricate is that the two elements have similar places of articulation and that the transition from one to the other is rapid such that they act as one unit.

The difference between an affricate and a simple sequence of plosive and fricative can be based on purely phonetic reasons, but it is more often based on phonemic grounds. (Phonemic or phonological considerations have been outlined briefly in footnote 5, Chapter 4, and footnote 11, Chapter 5, and will be dealt with in Chapter 8.)

Phonetic criteria for an affricate would include the following: that the plosive and fricative be homorganic, that they be closely fused by the most direct transitional movement possible, and that the total duration be not much greater than the usual duration of either component part.

The *phonemic* criterion, which is more usual, is that the affricate behave as if it were a single segment in the sound system of a given language.[18] The phonetic and phonemic definitions, therefore, can be in conflict.

For example, in the phrase "chocolate shop"

[17] **Homorganic:** having the same, or a similar, place of articulation.

[18] Just what constitutes the appropriate behavior for an affricate depends upon the phonological (phonemic) theory one accepts. However, the examples given here are quite clear-cut, and the fine details of the argument are beyond our scope.

the affricate [č] appears *twice*, by our phonetic definition: once at the beginning of "chocolate" and again through the combination of the [t] at the end of "chocolate" with the [š] at the beginning of "shop." Whether the [t] and [š] associate intimately enough to be called an affricate phonetically depends upon the individual pronunciation, but it is clear to any speaker of English that the two affricates in this phrase are different in important ways. The [č] of "chocolate shop" clearly *comes from* [t] plus [š], whereas the [č] at the beginning of "chocolate" is *one* sound; it doesn't *come from* the combination of anything. Note that to be able to tell the difference between the two kinds of affricate, you need to know English. If you were a phonetician who spoke no English, you would have no acoustical or articulatory basis for deciding that the two affricates were different.

> Let us take another example to make the point clearer. Many languages have a **dental** or **alveolar affricate** [t͡s]. Such an affricate exists in both German and Italian, and in both of these languages it is written with the letter ⟨z⟩, as in the borrowed words *Nazi* and *pizza*. This affricate also appears *phonetically* in English, as in the expression "bits and pieces" spoken colloquially. Once again, if you know English, you know that the [t] and the [s] that make up the affricate [t͡s] are separable (that is, any speaker of English knows it comes from "bit" plus the plural ending "s"). For this reason, [t͡s] is usually not considered to be an affricate of English. However, a phonetician who was unfamiliar with the languages in question would have no phonetic grounds for considering the [t͡s] of "pizza" as pronounced by an Italian an affricate but the [t͡s] of "bits and pieces" not an affricate.
>
> If someone said the French phrase [odžavɛl] (meaning 'bleach'), as an English speaker you would hear the [dž] as the affricate [ǰ], since it is phonetically so like English [ǰ]. But the French speaker knows that the expression is *eau de javel* and that the [d] and [ž] come from different words, so he would hear them as separate sounds.

In summary, then, even though a plosive and a fricative often combine in fluent speech to form phonetic affricates, giving many different affricates in English speech, we usually define affricates phonemically, based on knowledge of the sound system of the language. So we usually say that English has two affricates: [č] and [ǰ].

> Other languages have other affricates. We have already mentioned the **voiceless dental** or **alveolar affricate** [t͡s], which occurs in German, Italian, and Canadian French, among many other languages. The **voiced dental** or **alveolar affricate** [d͡z] is also common.
>
> The **voiceless labial affricate** [p͡f] occurs in German, among other languages. Other affricates, less common in Western languages, include [t͡θ], [d͡ð], [k͡x], and [g͡ɣ]. Additional affricates are attested in other languages.

5-5 The Nasal

Nasal consonants, as their name suggests, are produced through the nose. The oral cavity is blocked completely during their production, and the velum is lowered to connect the nasal cavities with the mouth and pharynx.

All English nasals are voiced, as they are in most languages. (Voiceless nasals, such as those of Burmese and Icelandic, sound like a snort, which is what they are, at least articulatorily!) For this reason, the nasals of English do not need to be classified according to voicing: the place of articulation and manner of articulation are sufficient. The place of articulation is the point in the oral cavity where there is closure.

The **bilabial nasal** is [m], as in "mouse," "hammer," and "lame."

The **alveolar nasal** is articulated at the same point as [t] and [d]; it is [n], as in "no," "banner," and "fan."

The **velar nasal** corresponds in place of articulation to [k] and [g]. It is usually spelled ⟨ng⟩ and ⟨nk⟩ in English, as in the words "sing" and "sink." It is represented in phonetic transcription by [ŋ]. Note that our English spelling inconsistently represents this sound: The spelling ⟨nk⟩ usually represents the sequence [ŋk], as in "thinker"; but the spelling ⟨ng⟩ may represent either the single sound [ŋ], as in "singer," or the sequence [ŋg], as in "finger."[19] And the spelling ⟨ng⟩, particularly in

[19] In some dialects, particularly in the British Isles, words like "sing" and "singer" are pronounced with [ŋg].

Table 5-5. The nasals

	†Bilabial	Labiodental	Dental	†Alveolar	Retroflex	Palatal	†Velar	Uvular
Voiced	m	ɱ	n̪	n	ṇ	ɲ	ŋ	ɴ

†English phonemes.

the verb suffix "-ing," often represents the sound [n] in colloquial speech. This is often represented with an apostrophe replacing the ⟨g⟩, as in ⟨talkin'⟩, and we say that the speaker "drops his g's," although there were no phonetic [g]'s there to drop in the first place.[20]

A **palatal nasal** occurs in English when an ⟨n⟩ is followed by the y-sound (usually spelled ⟨i⟩, ⟨y⟩, or ⟨u⟩), as in "canyon," "onion," or—in some dialects—"nude." This sound occurs distinctively in French, Italian, and Spanish, among other languages. In French and Italian, it is spelled ⟨gn⟩, as in French *agneau* ('lamb') and Italian *agnello* ('lamb'); it is spelled ⟨ñ⟩ in Spanish, as in *señor*. It is transcribed [ɲ].

A Note on Terminology
Traditionally, the term *stop* was used for both what we have called **plosives** and what we have called **nasals.** These two manners of articulation have in common that air is blocked completely from passing *through the oral cavity*. Thus, *non-nasal stops,* such as [t] and [d], are distinguished from *nasal stops,* such as [m] or [n]. This terminology is no longer widely used, and for that reason, as well as because it is confusing, it is not used here.

A Note on the Articulation of Nasals
I have noticed among my students a very common misunderstanding concerning the articulation of nasals. For this reason, I will stress again the details of the articulation. In the articulation of nasals, the *oral cavity* is blocked at some point, either with the lips, as in [m], or with the tongue and the roof of the mouth, as in [n], [ɲ], and [ŋ]. The velum is simultaneously lowered to open the nasal passages, *but not to close off the oral cavity.* Only in the case of the velar nasal [ŋ] is the oral cavity blocked in the velar region, but even this is not accomplished with the velum alone: the tongue dorsum is arched upward to contact the velum. (See Figures 5-14–5-16.)

5-5.1 OTHER NASALS
As noted, there is a **palatal nasal,** [ɲ] that occurs in English words such as "canyon," but it is not considered to be an English phoneme.

There is also a **labiodental nasal,** articulated with the lower lip and the upper front teeth, much as a [f] or [v] is articulated. While rare in English, it is sometimes articulated when followed by another labiodental, as in "inferior." It is symbolized [ɱ].

Just as there are dental plosives, there is a **dental nasal** [n̪]. The ⟨n⟩ of Spanish and some other European languages tends to be dental, and this sound may appear in English if another dental sound such as [θ] occurs next to the nasal.

Just as there are retroflex plosives in some languages, a **retroflex nasal** [ṇ] also exists in some languages. And finally, there is a **uvular nasal,** articulated just behind [ŋ], symbolized [ɴ]. It occurs in English when ⟨ng⟩ follows a low back vowel, as in the word "bong."

Table 5-5 summarizes the nasals.

5-6 Approximants

In the introductory section of the chapter, we defined consonants as those speech sounds produced with the airstream *blocked* (as in plosives and affricates), *severely constricted* (as in fricatives and affricates), or *diverted* (through the nasal passages, as in all nasals). Not all consonants con-

[20]Those [g]'s probably were pronounced at one time in history; the dialects mentioned in the previous footnote have preserved this archaic feature. Such a dialect, preserving an old trait, is termed **conservative.** Also, many phonologists theorize that, while the [g] in "-ing" is never pronounced in the standard dialect, it *is* present in an abstract sense.

form absolutely to these criteria, however, and we shall examine a number that do not.

The primary sense of the verb *to approximate* is 'to get close to' in a physical sense (the verb *to approach* is related to the verb *to approximate*). To produce one type of consonant, the articulators are brought close together, or *approximated*, although not sufficiently to create the frictional noise of the fricatives. For this reason, they are called **approximants** or, by some writers on the subject, **frictionless continuants.**

These speech sounds have some characteristics of consonants and some characteristics of vowels. Like vowels, they are produced without blockage or severe constriction and therefore have less noise component in their acoustic output than other consonants. They are distributed in language like consonants; that is, they are normally found accompanying vowels in syllables (whereas vowels may stand alone in syllables).

For classificatory convenience, we shall divide these sounds into two groups: the **glides** and the **liquids.**

5-6.1 GLIDES

Glides are the most vowel-like of the approximants. There are several of these sounds in English, the precise number varying according to dialect and system of classification.

PALATAL GLIDE. The place of articulation of the **palatal glide** [j] is dorsopalatal; the lips are slightly spread; indeed, it has virtually the same articulation as the vowel [i]. It is voiced. In English, it is usually spelled with the letter ⟨y⟩, as in the words "yes" and "you."

The sequence [ju] is frequently spelled either with the letter ⟨u⟩ alone[21] or with some combination of letters other than ⟨y⟩: "use," "beauty," "Europe," "mute." Because it is often spelled with one letter, students of phonetics doing transcription exercises often neglect to transcribe both elements of the sequence /ju/. The situation is complicated even further by the fact that, in most dialects of North American English, the [j] of the sequence /ju/ is often dropped following alveolar consonants (namely, [t, d, n, s, l]): e.g., "tube" (compare "too"); "due" (compare "do"); "new" (compare "noon"); "sue" (compare "the Soo" [i.e., Sault Ste. Marie]); and "lute" (the same as "loot" for all speakers).

The pronunciation [ju] after [t], [d], and [n] has prestige as compared to the pronunciation [u], so public speakers, teachers, national TV announcers, and others anxious to maintain "correct" speech tend to say [ju]. However, the rest of us almost always say [u] in this environment. After [s], only the most particular of North Americans will say [ju], a pronunciation which sounds affected or snobbish to most of us. (Outside North America the pronunciation [ju] after [t, d, n] and even [s] is more common.) [j] is nearly universally not pronounced after [l], making "lute" and "loot" identical in virtually all dialects.

A note on symbols: The use of the letter [y] for the glide [j] is very common, and its use is easily explained in terms of English orthography. In the official IPA, [y] represents the high front rounded vowel that we have symbolized [ü]. This book will continue to use [j] for the glide, but your instructor might prefer [y].

LABIOVELAR GLIDE. The place of articulation of the **labiovelar glide** [w] is dorsovelar, and it is rounded (labialized), hence the description *labiovelar*. It is also voiced. Its articulatory configuration is virtually identical to that of the vowel [u]. It is the sound we usually spell with the letter ⟨w⟩ as in "want" and "wink," although it is occasionally spelled in other ways, as in "bivouac."

VOICELESS LABIOVELAR GLIDE. The **voiceless labiovelar glide** is identical in articulatory position to [w], except that it is voiceless and may have a heightened airflow. It is the first sound of the words "which" and "whether" in those dialects that pronounce these words differently from "witch" and "weather." Many dialects do not have this glide, and their speakers pronounce pairs like "whether" and "weather" alike, both with [w]. The symbol for the voiceless glide at the beginning of "whether" is [ʍ]. Unofficially, the symbol [hw] is often used, and it is recommended that you use this symbol in handwritten work,

[21] Some phonologists consider the sequence /ju/ in English to be one single phoneme.

since the symbol [ʍ] is easy to confuse with an ⟨m⟩ unless it is printed very carefully.

5-6.1.1 *The Articulatory Character of Glides*

We noted in the previous section that the articulation of the three glides [j], [w], and [ʍ] is identical to that of the vowels [i] and [u]. An obvious question, then, is, If glides are so similar to certain vowels, how are they different? What distinguishes a glide from a vowel?

The answer is found not in the articulatory *positions* of the sounds, but in the associated *movement*, or, to look at it in a different way, in the *duration* of the segment. *Glides are characterized by a rapid movement toward or away from the articulatory position* said to be characteristic of that glide. Let us compare a vowel and a glide in this respect. Say the word "eat." Now prolong the vowel: [i::::t]. A long [i] still sounds like a [i]. Now say the word "yes." Now repeat it, this time prolonging the glide: [j:::::::ɛs]. Notice that a prolonged [j] does not sound like a [j]; it sounds like an [i]. The rapid movement therefore is critical to the character of a glide, but the essential similarity between glides and vowels remains; indeed, glides were formerly called **semivowels.** The newer term **glide** suggests the movement that is essential to this category of speech sound.

These same facts could be expressed by saying that glides are *nonsyllabic vowels.* Vowels normally form the nucleus of a syllable; such vowels are *syllabic.* A segment that is like a vowel, but that does not form the nucleus of a syllable—that is, another vowel accompanies it that does form the nucleus—is a nonsyllabic vowel, or a glide. The diacritic [̯] is used to indicate nonsyllabicity, so writing [i̯] is the same as writing [j], and [u̯] is the same as [w].[22] I make no suggestion that these more complicated transcriptions should be used routinely; rather, they are mentioned to direct your thinking to the articulatory nature of glides.

Furthermore, some languages have glides whose articulatory positions correspond not to [i] and [u], but to [e] and [o] or elsewhere in the vowel quadrangle. There are no glide symbols that indicate these exact articulatory positions. They can be symbolized thus: [e̯], [o̯], [ɪ̯], and so on. For example, the second sound in many people's pronunciation of "coincidence" may be a velar glide lower than [w], corresponding to [o] in articulatory position: i.e., [o̯].

At this point the reader may well ask: If a glide is a nonsyllabic vowel, or a vowel-like articulation that shifts position rapidly, isn't it a lot like the second element of a diphthong? That is absolutely correct. The diphthong [aɪ͜], for example, is made up of a syllabic vowel (the [a]) and a nonsyllabic vowel or glide (the [i]). This fact could be expressed just as well by the transcription [ai̯] or simply [aj]. The latter transcription is quite common[23] and has simplicity to recommend it. Its use was not suggested in Section 4-6 because it is not flexible enough to record fine differences: for example, [ai͜], [aɪ͜], and [ae͜] would all be transcribed /aj/ using glide symbols. As has been stressed a number of times in this book, the student of phonetics ought to have at his/her disposal the transcription tools to record dialect difference, foreign accent, or misarticulation, even if those tools are not required in every instance.

In a diphthong such as [ai͜], the first vocalic element is syllabic and the second vocalic element is nonsyllabic. Let us examine sequences such as the [jɛ] of "yes" and the [wɑ] of "want" from the articulatory viewpoint. Essentially these are similar to diphthongs, in that there is a close association of a nonsyllabic and a syllabic vocalic element. In the case of "yes" and "want," however, the *first* element is nonsyllabic and the *second* element is syllabic.

Some phoneticians call sequences such as [jɛ] and [wɑ] diphthongs as well. In their terminology, sequences such as [ai͜], in which the first element is syllabic, are called **rising diphthongs.** Sequences such as [jɛ], in which the second element is syllabic, are called **falling diphthongs.** However, common usage dictates that when the term *diphthong* is used unmodified, it refers to sounds of the type [ai͜].

[22] To represent [ʍ] or [hw] in this way, we would have to add the diacritic indicating voicelessness as well, which makes quite a complicated symbol: [u̯̥].

[23] Often as [ay] in those books using [y] instead of [j]. The same principle is used for the other diphthongs: [aw] in place of [au͜] and [ɔj] or [ɔy] in place of [ɔi͜].

> 5-6.1.2 *Non-English Glides*
> As we have seen with other classes of speech sounds, English does not have all sounds in its inventory. Other glides than the ones we have seen exist in other languages.
> Primary among these is a glide corresponding to the vowel [ü], a high front tense rounded vowel. The corresponding glide is like [j], but it is rounded. It is symbolized [ɥ]. Note that this IPA symbol is an upside-down ⟨h⟩, not a ⟨y⟩. This glide occurs in French in such words as l<u>u</u>i and p<u>u</u>is.
> Some languages have glides corresponding to somewhat more open vowels, such as [e] and [o]. Such glides may be symbolized using the diacritic for nonsyllabicity: [e̯], [o̯], etc.

5-6.1.3 */h/ as a Glide*
As noted in Section 5-3, the segment [h] is classified as a glide in many books and articles. Why have we not done the same? The classification of English /h/ as a glide is a phonological, not a phonetic, classification. In phonological classification, the primary criteria are the *distribution* and *behavior* of the sounds in question, rather than their articulation (see footnote 5 in Chapter 4). In English, /h/ behaves like a glide: it occurs prevocalically (before vowels) but not postvocalically (following vowels), for example.

It could be argued that /h/ is a voiceless glide whose articulatory characteristics are those of the following vowel. Since the classification in this book was made on the basis of articulation, /h/ was placed with the fricatives rather than with the glides. For example, /h/ can be prolonged and still remain a /h/, unlike the glides, as we have demonstrated. Both points of view have merit, and the student should not be distracted from the articulatory details by such issues.

5-6.2 The Liquids
A second type of approximant goes by the name **liquid.** The term itself is not very meaningful; but it has been in use since the time of the Roman grammarians and tends to be reused generation after generation, if for no other reason than that it is a convenient cover-term for a group of sounds that share some characteristics. The English r-sound and l-sound are classified as members of this group. Liquids share the characteristics of other approximants: approximation of the articulators, no friction or blockage, and a vowel-like quality.

5-6.2.1 *The Laterals*
The various l-sounds fall into the category of **laterals.** The word *lateral* means 'side,' and in the articulation of laterals, air passes over the sides of the tongue, while the tongue blocks the center of the oral cavity. You can demonstrate this to yourself: Pronounce a [l]. Stop vocalizing, but keep the tongue in position. Now inhale through your mouth, and you will feel the cool air passing over the sides of your tongue.

The English [l] is alveolar, having essentially the same place of articulation as [t], [d], and [n]. Usually the blade of the tongue is used, so the articulation could be described as *laminoalveolar* (as usual, the simple term *alveolar* is sufficient for most purposes). The difference in articulatory terms between a [d] and a [l], for example, is that total oral blockage is required for [d]; so that, while [d] is described as *alveolar,* one has to remember that the sides of the tongue are in firm contact with the upper teeth (molars and premolars). By contrast, the tongue is *narrowed* from side to side in the articulation of all laterals, so that air has space to travel over the sides of the tongue.

Unless otherwise indicated, the laterals we will examine are voiced.

As we have seen, English [l] is an alveolar lateral.

But English has two different l-sounds, although they make up only one phoneme. Pronounce the words "leave" and "dull," prolonging the l-sounds to examine their qualities. You will probably hear a difference between the two. The l-sound of "leave" is described as a *light l.* The l-sound of "dull" is articulated with an additional arching of the tongue in the velar region (the position of [u]), producing a different sound. This latter sound is called a *dark l* or, more properly, a **velarized l** (because of the tongue's arching in the velar region). Generally, prevocalic l's in English are light (except before high back vowels); postvocalic l's are velarized. The symbol for the dark l is [ɫ].

One of the features of approximants in general

is the existence of syllabic versions of the sounds. In a word such as "bottle," the second syllable may have no vowel other than the l-sound. The syllabic nature of the sound can be indicated with a diacritic, thus: [l̩].

One peculiarity of the l-sound in English can be demonstrated by pronouncing such words as "peel" and "cool" and comparing their pronunciation with such words as "peek" and "kook." Notice that the vowel is different when followed by [ɫ]: it has an **off-glide.** "Pool" is not [pʰuɫ] but, rather, [pʰu͜əɫ]. This is a peculiarity of English: the French word *poule* ('hen') is pronounced [pul], with no vocalic off-glide (neither has it velarization of the [l], nor aspiration of the [p]).

The vowel-like nature of l-sounds and the similarity in articulatory position between [l] and [i] and between [ɫ] and [u] has led to some historical sound changes. [l]'s have changed into [i]'s in Italian. For example, Italian *piazza* corresponds to Spanish *plaza* and French *place*. Italian *piano* ('soft,' 'smooth') comes from Latin *planus*, 'smooth,' corresponding to English *plane*. (As the name of the instrument, *piano* is short for *pianoforte*, 'soft-loud,' so named because its loudness could be controlled, unlike the harpsichord that it superseded, which could play at one loudness only.) Similarly, Old French [ɫ]'s changed into [u]'s (although subsequent sound changes have turned most of those [u]'s into [o]'s). For example, English *castle* corresponds to French *château* ([šato]), *veal* to *veau* ([vo]), and *mantle* to *manteau* ([mɑ̃to]). In French, an alternation exists as well: *belle* ([bɛl]) (feminine) means 'beautiful'; *beau* ([bo]) (masculine) means 'beautiful' or 'handsome'; *marteau* ([maʀto]) means 'hammer'; *marteler* ([maʀtəle]) means 'to hammer.'

OTHER LATERALS. If the lateral is produced not in the alveolar region but with the front of the tongue arched against the palate, a sound symbolized [ʎ], a **palatal lateral,** will be produced. This sound occurs in Spanish and is usually spelled with a double ⟨ll⟩ as in *pollo* ([poʎo]). If this sound is difficult for you to pronounce, the following trick may help. Place your tongue in position to pronounce [j]. Now raise it just slightly, so that it makes firm contact with the palate. Pull in the sides of the tongue, so that they are not making contact with the cheeks. Drawing in air through the mouth sharply will tell you if your articulators are in the correct position: you should feel air flowing in over the sides of the tongue, but not over the top.

An l-sound that is **dental** rather than alveolar can be indicated by the usual diacritic for dental articulation: [l̪]. An l-sound made by bringing the tongue tip up to the palate is a **retroflex** articulation. This is symbolized two ways, as with other retroflexes: the traditional symbol is [ɭ], but it is more common now to use the retroflex diacritic: [ḷ].

There are two **lateral fricatives** as well. Strictly speaking, these do not fall into the category of frictionless continuants, since they are fricatives. They are produced with the tongue essentially in the position for English [l], although not narrowed so much. If one blows air out, a fricative noise is created between the sides of the tongue and the upper side teeth and/or the cheeks. If this sound is voiceless, it is symbolized [ɬ]; if voiced, it is symbolized [ɮ].

[ɬ] is the sound spelled ⟨ll⟩ in Welsh. For example, the name *Lloyd* is pronounced with an initial [ɬ] in Welsh. Since [ɬ] does not exist in English, the English ear splits it into two components that exist in English: the *fricative* [f] and the *lateral* [l]. This is the origin of the English name *Floyd*.

5-6.2.2 *Rhotic Approximants*

In Chapter 4 we introduced the term **rhotic,** meaning 'r-like, having an "r" timbre.' This section deals with those approximants (consonants) having an r-coloring. A number of r-sounds in other languages are not approximants, and these will be dealt with in a separate section.

There is great variation in the r-sounds of English, more than in other consonants. As elsewhere in this book, the following discussion assumes a standard North American pronunciation.

The present discussion ignores postvocalic r-sounds in English; these were discussed in Sections 4-4.5 and 4-6.1.

The most typical North American English "r" has an articulatory configuration that is particularly difficult to classify. This difficulty has two causes: the standard classification system has no label for this type of articulation; and there is considerable individual variation in the articulation

Table 5-6. English approximants

	Labial	Alveolar	Palatal	Velar	Pharyngeal
Glide					
Voiceless	(ʍ)			ʍ	
Voiced	(w)		j	w	
Lateral voiced		l			
		ɫ		(ɫ)	
Rhotic voiced			ɹ		(ɹ)

Parentheses indicate secondary articulations.

Table 5-7. The approximants and lateral fricatives

	Labial	Dental	Alveolar	Retroflex	Palatal	Velar	Pharyngeal
Glide							
Voiceless	(ʍ)					ʍ	
Voiced	(w)				j	w	
	(ɥ)				ɥ		
Lateral							
Approximant		l̪	l	ḷ	ʎ		
			ɫ			(ɫ)	
Fricative			ɬ				
Rhotic					ɹ		(ɹ)
				ɹ̣			(ɹ̣)

Parentheses indicate secondary articulations.

(this is not an interdialect variation; within the same dialect, different speakers achieve the same or a similar sound with a different articulation).

The usual term for this type of r-sound is that it is **bunched:** it could be described as a **bunched rhotic approximant.** The term reflects the fact that the tongue is raised and retracted in quite a tight "knot"; there is tongue root retraction into the pharynx. Like the other approximants, it is articulated without closure or friction. It is a resonant sound.

Some speakers articulate it with the tongue blade raised; some with the tongue blade relatively low. The raised tongue blade has led some writers on the subject to classify the sound as a *retroflex;* this is an inaccurate classification for most speakers of English (although a retroflex rhotic sound *can* be produced, as we will see).

Strictly speaking, the correct symbol for this sound is [ɹ]. Common usage, however, is to substitute the much handier symbol [r]. The issue of modification of the IPA was discussed in Section 3-9.1, and for reasons stated there, there is no reason not to use [r].[24]

The rhotic retroflex is produced with an apicopalatal articulation, like other retroflex consonants. Since it is an approximant and not a stop, there is no closure at the apicopalatal point of articulation. The symbol is [ṛ] or [ɹ̣].

In English a retroflex approximant or fricative often occurs when /r/ follows a /t/ or /d/. A word like "train" may therefore be pronounced [tṛen] or [tṣen].

5-6.3 Summary of Approximants

Table 5-6 shows the approximant phonemes of English.

Table 5-7 shows the approximants and lateral fricatives we have examined in this section.

[24] This is particularly true because the IPA symbol [r] in its "correct" usage is ambiguous, and this ambiguity has been eliminated in common usage by the invention of two new symbols to replace IPA [r]: namely [ř] and [r̄], which we will examine subsequently. However, these new symbols leave [r] without any sound value, so its use for the English bunched "r" should cause no confusion.

Table 5-8. The relationship between syllabic and nonsyllabic segments

Nonsyllabic (acts as consonant)	Syllabic (acts as vowel)
j	i
w	u
l	l̩
r	r̩ = ɚ
n	n̩
m	m̩

5-6.4 The Syllabic Nature of Approximants

We have seen that the approximants are very vowel-like in their articulation. We have also seen that the difference between a glide and a vowel is one of the timing and movement. The same may be said of the other approximants. That is, [j] can be said to be a nonsyllabic [i], or, conversely, [i] can be said to be a syllabic [j]. The same can be said of [r] and [ɚ] (which is the same as [r̩]) and of [l] and [l̩].

That is, the difference between "string" and "stirring" is that in "string" the "r" is nonsyllabic, whereas in "stirring" it is syllabic. The word "blue" has a nonsyllabic "l," but in many people's pronunciation "bull" has no separate vowel and has a syllabic "l".

The nasals behave the same way. They may be syllabic in nature: that is, they may form a syllable with no other vowel. Any nasal may do this; however, in English, the only nasal that is commonly syllabic is "n," as in words such as "button" and "hasten."

The relationship between syllabic and nonsyllabic segments is shown in Table 5-8.

In connected speech, the fine dividing line between the syllabic and the nonsyllabic segment may be crossed frequently. For example, the second segment of "beautiful" is [j], but if one is exclaiming "Beautiful!" with great emotion, that second segment easily stretches into an [i:]. Similarly, the word "howdy" comes from "How do you do": the ⟨y⟩ ([j]) of "you" has become the [i] of "howdy."

5-7 Some Other Manners of Articulation

In this section we will examine manners of articulation other than the plosive, fricative, affricate, nasal, and approximant.

5-7.1 The Flap

To produce a plosive sound such as [t], one places the tongue against the alveolar ridge, maintains the closure momentarily, and then pulls the tongue away again by voluntary movement: there is a conscious movement *toward* and a conscious movement *away from* the place of articulation. This is true of all plosives, no matter what their place of articulation. However, another type of occlusion can be made with the light and agile tongue blade. If one makes a very rapid and relaxed movement toward the alveolar ridge, the tongue will tend to "bounce off" and produce a much briefer occlusion than for a plosive. A speech sound made with such a movement is called a **flap,** or, in the terminology of some phoneticians, a **tap.** The movement itself is often referred to as a **ballistic movement.**

There are both **rhotic** and **nonrhotic flaps,** that is, those that have an r-like quality and those that have not.

North American English has a **nonrhotic flap** that occurs as a variety of /t/ and /d/ when intervocalic and posttonic (that is, when between vowels and following the stressed syllable) as in "matter," "ladder," "betting," and so on. This sound is symbolized [ɾ] in the IPA, although many people use upper case ⟨D⟩ in typewritten work. The words listed above are pronounced as follows in casual North American speech: [mæɾɚ] (or [mæDɚ]), [læɾɚ], [bɛɾɪŋ].

A **rhotic flap** is heard in many dialects of British English where the "r" occurs intervocalically; it also is heard in Spanish where there is one orthographic ⟨r⟩. Officially the IPA symbol for this sound is [r], but, as we noted earlier, most phoneticians now use [ř].

Because the rhotic and nonrhotic flaps sound much alike, the British pronunciation of "very" ([vɛři]) sounds like "veddy" ([vɛɾi]) to a North American English speaker.

The articulatory difference between [ř] and [ɾ] probably lies in the tongue root position; the r-like quality of [ř] is very likely associated with some degree of tongue root retraction (narrowing of the pharynx).

5-7.2 The Trill

When an articulator is made to vibrate rapidly (twenty to thirty times per second) by the action of air passing over it, the sound produced is known as a **trill.** This vibration is caused aerodynamically, not directly by muscle contractions, as no muscle can contract and relax twenty times per second. The trill is therefore produced by using muscles to place a relaxed articulator in the correct position so that an airstream over it will set it vibrating.

The tongue blade can be trilled, as can the uvula. (The lips can be trilled as well, and we sometimes produce an inadvertent labial trill when shivering, but this is not a speech sound.) The **alveolar trill** (that is, the **laminal trill**) produces a rhotic sound often called a "rolled r." This occurs in Scottish English (at least, as it is stereotyped by entertainers) as well as in Spanish, where it corresponds to an orthographic double ⟨rr⟩. Spanish, therefore, contrasts a flap and a trill, as in *pero*, 'but' [pɛřo], and *perro*, 'dog' [pɛr̃o].

Officially the IPA symbol for this trill is [r], but as we have seen, [r] is ambiguous, since it is also officially used for the flap. Therefore most North American phoneticians use the symbol [r̃] for the trill. This is not the most satisfactory solution, since the tilde, [˜], is normally used to indicate nasalization, not trilling, but in practice little ambiguity results.

If the uvula is trilled, it produces another sort of rhotic sound used in some languages and symbolized [ʀ]. If this **uvular trill** is voiceless, the diacritic for voicelessness can be added: [ʀ̥]. Both [ʀ] and [ʀ̥] are used in some dialects of French. If a voiced sound is produced at the same place of articulation—at the uvula—but without trilling, the sound is symbolized [ʁ]. This **uvular fricative** r-sound is used in some dialects of German and French.

5-7.3 The Retroflex

Retroflex consonants have been discussed throughout this chapter whenever relevant; however, a recapitulation is made here in order to introduce a comment on the IPA symbols and on the diagnosis of dialect features as articulation problems.

Retro means 'backward' and *flex* means 'bend'; **retroflex** consonants are those produced with the tongue tip bent back so as to articulate with the palate.

The North American English r-sound is sometimes classified as a retroflex, although I have not found a single native speaker for whom this categorization is correct. The bunched articulation involves some retraction of the tongue, but rarely true retroflexion, except in the combination "tr" and "dr" in English, in which there often is some degree of retroflexion of both plosive and "r," although the degree varies with the dialect.

Inappropriate retroflexion may be part of a foreign accent in English and can be expected in individuals whose native language has retroflexes.

In parts of the southwestern and south central United States, s-sounds are produced with retroflexion, as has been noted. In Chapter 2 we discussed dialect variation; one purpose of this discussion was to make the student of speech pathology aware of variation and to caution him/her against diagnosing a dialect feature as a pathological condition. One individual I know was sent, when a schoolboy, by his teacher to a "speech correctionist" because he spoke with retroflex [ṣ]'s, even though this was simply a characteristic of his regional dialect and the school was located in Arkansas near where this dialect feature prevails. Fortunately the speech pathologist knew her job and sent a note back to the teacher saying there was nothing wrong with the youngster.

A second point I wish to make under the heading of the retroflexes (but one that applies quite universally) concerns ethnocentrism and the symbols of the IPA.

The retroflex series is symbolized [ṭ], [ḍ], [ṣ], [ḷ], [ṛ], etc., or [ʈ], [ɖ], [ʂ], etc. In either system, the symbol for a voiceless retroflex plosive is *based* on the symbol ⟨t⟩, that for a voiced retroflex plosive is *based* on the symbol ⟨d⟩, and so on. This gives many students of phonetics the mistaken notion that [ṭ] is a "funny kind of t" and likewise for the other retroflexes. Such a notion is errone-

Table 5-9. The English consonant phonemes, plus consonants that occur in English as variants of phonemes

	Labio-dental	Bi-labial	Dental	Al-veolar	Alveo-palatal	Palatal	Velar	Pharyngeal	Glottal
Plosives		p		t			k		
		b		d			g		
Fricatives	f		θ	s	š				h
	v		ð	z	ž				ɦ
Affricates					č				
					ǰ				
Nasals		m		n			ŋ		
Glides		(ʍ)					ʍ		
		(w)				j	w		
Laterals				l					
				(ɫ)			(ɫ)		
Rhotics						ɹ		(ɹ)	

Normal practice is for voiceless segments to be listed before voiced segments. Parentheses indicate secondary articulations or two places of articulation for the same segment.

ous and ethnocentric. [ṭ] is no more a "kind of" [t] than [p] or [k] is, in the articulatory sense. But we do not make the assumption about [p] and [k] that we do about [ṭ], for a couple of reasons: [ṭ] is substantially a *foreign* sound, so we see it in terms of similarity to the sounds of English. And the phonetic alphabet reinforces this notion by using a symbol that leads us to conclude that there is affinity between the different sounds [ṭ] and [t]. The phonetic alphabet was developed in Europe and has a European bias. Clearly, if it had been developed in India, the retroflexes would not have been assigned symbols suggesting that they were varieties of alveolars.

The phonetic alphabet *does* have a one-to-one sound-symbol correspondence. It does *not*, however, have any claim to neutrality. Do not be misled by the choice of symbols into drawing conclusions about the nature of the sounds represented by them.

5-8 Summary of Consonant Articulation

Table 5-9 lists the consonant phonemes of English, plus additional consonants that occur in English as variants of English phonemes. Table 5-10 lists the consonants we have examined in this chapter.

Figures 5-6 through 5-32 show the articulation of many of the consonants. The phonemes of English are grouped together at the beginning for convenience. To avoid needless repetition, not every one of the consonants listed in Table 5-10 is shown in the drawings. From the place and manner of articulation of a consonant, you should be able to imagine what the articulatory configuration would be (even if you are not a good enough artist to render it on paper). For the same reason, the voiced and voiceless pairs are not drawn separately; there is one drawing for [p] and [b], for example. The differences between them, at the level of intraoral air pressure and vocal fold vibra-

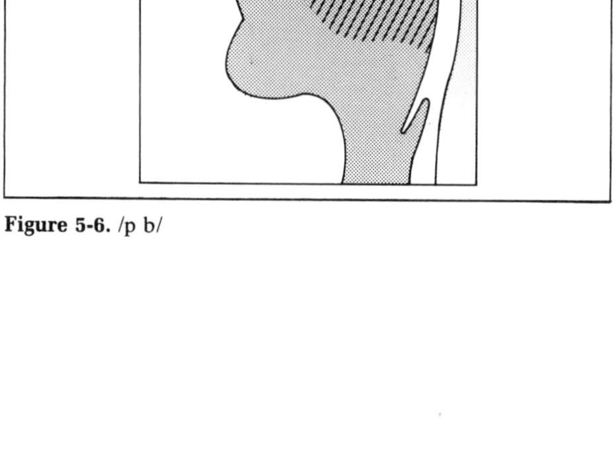

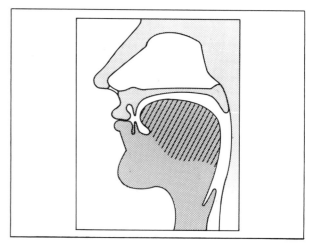

Figure 5-6. /p b/

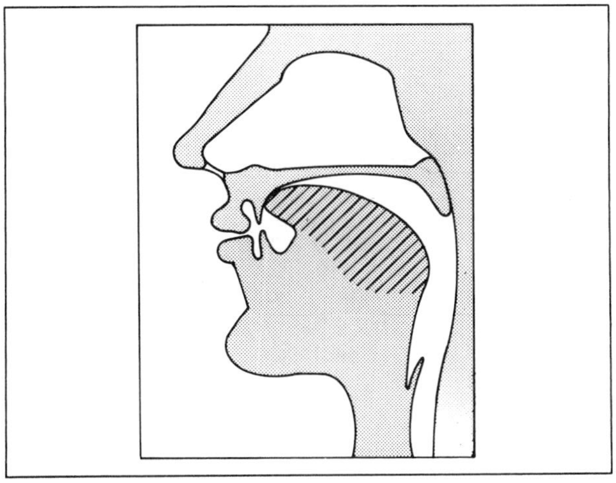

Figure 5-7. /t d/

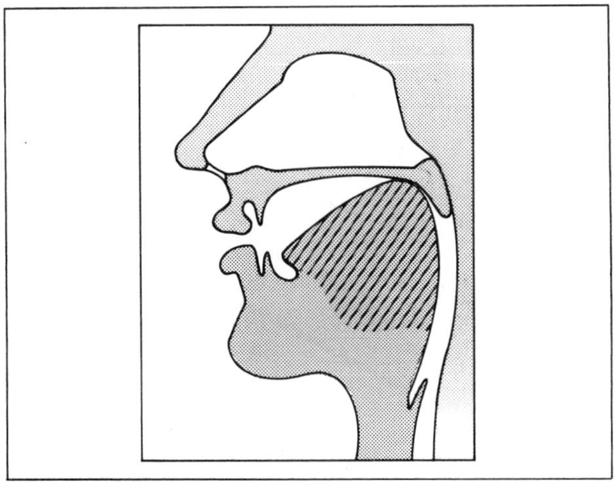

Figure 5-8. /k g/

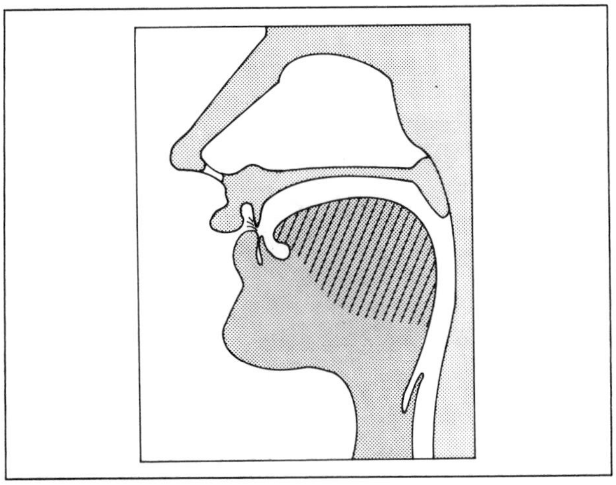

Figure 5-9. /f v/

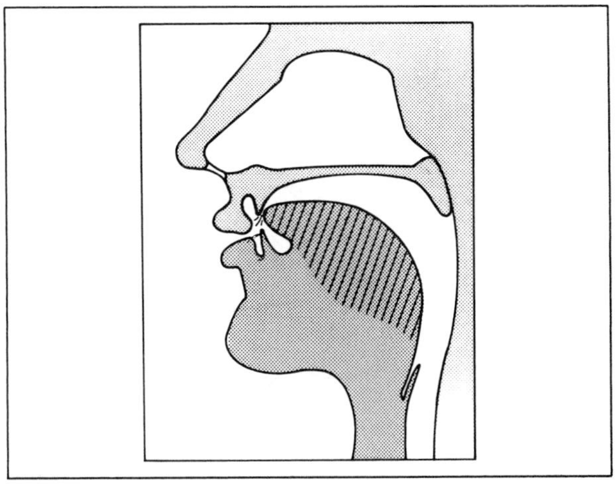

Figure 5-10. /θ ð/

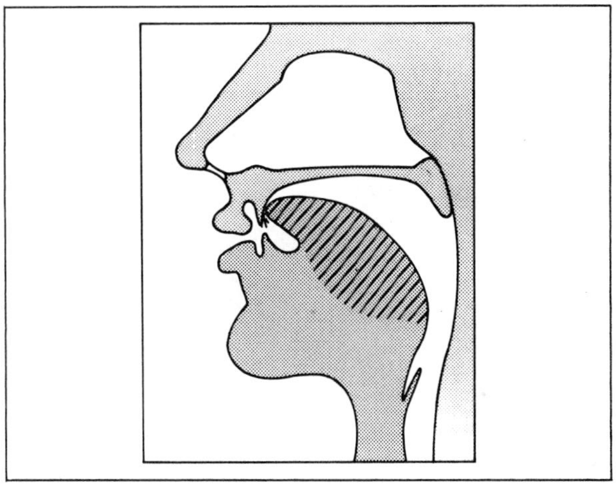

Figure 5-11. /s z/

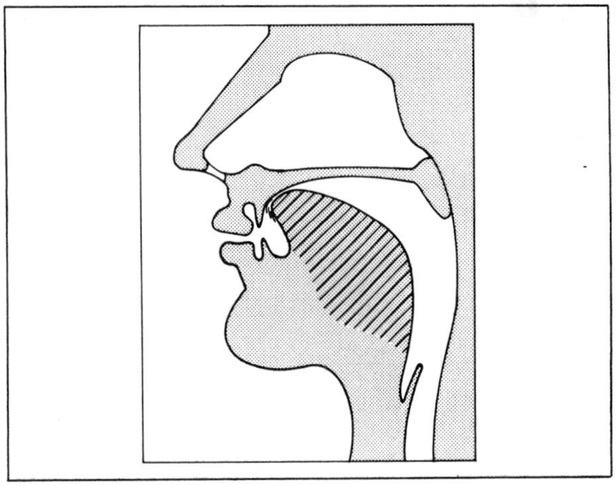

Figure 5-12. /š ž/

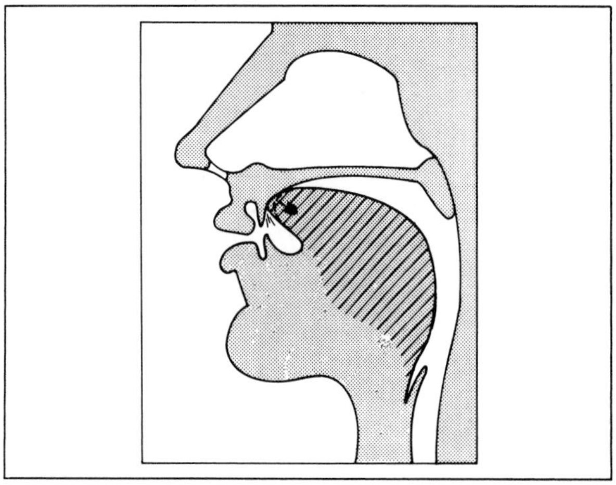

Figure 5-13. /č ǰ/

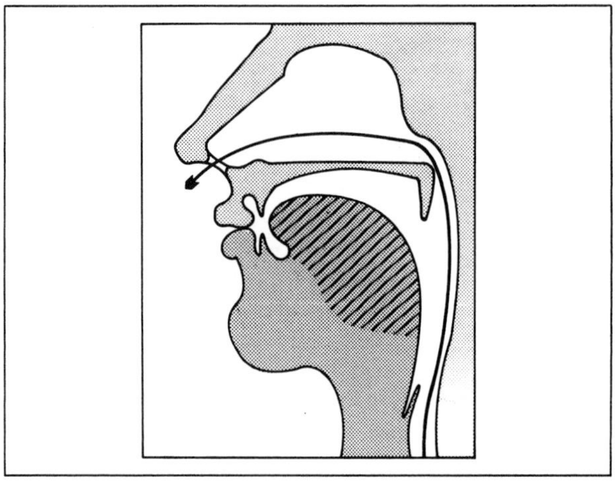

Figure 5-14. /m/

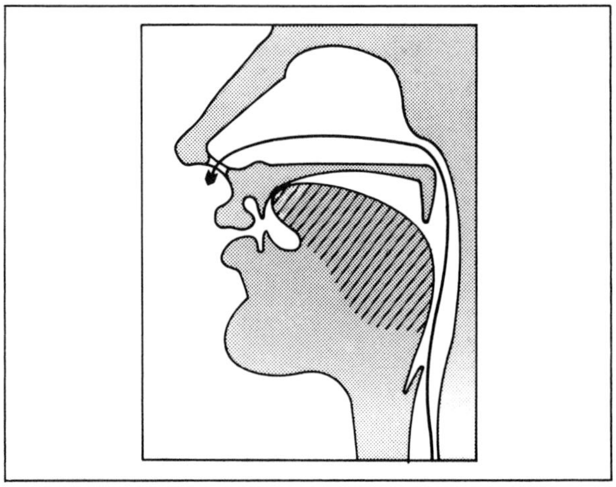

Figure 5-15. /n/

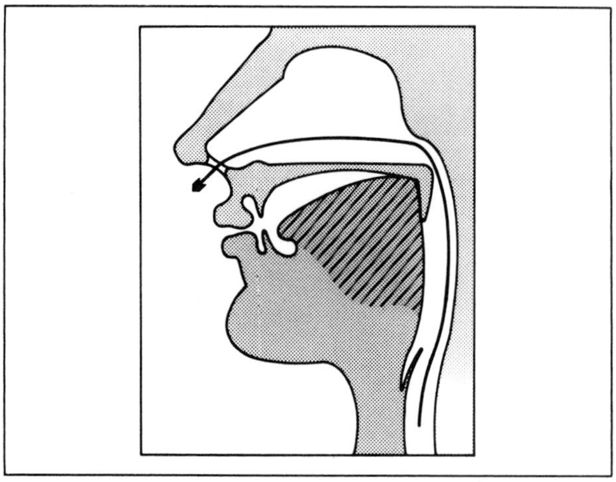

Figure 5-16. /ŋ/

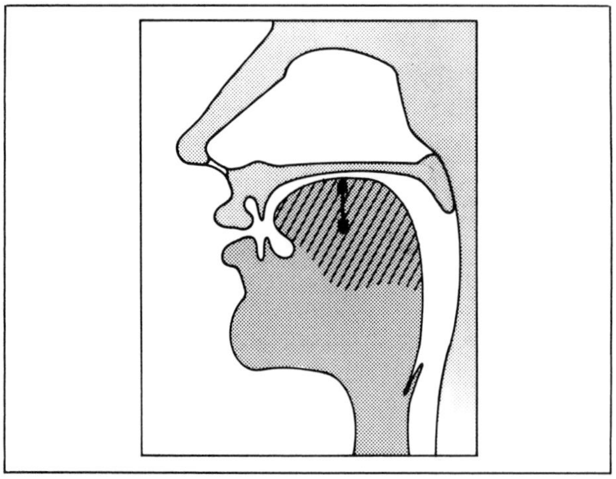

Figure 5-17. /j/

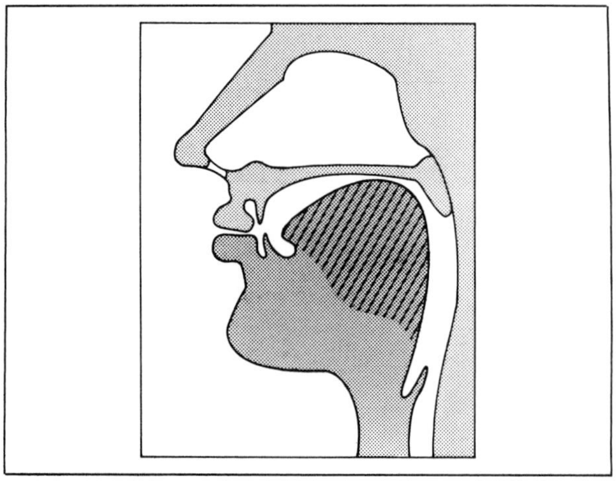

Figure 5-18. /w ʍ/

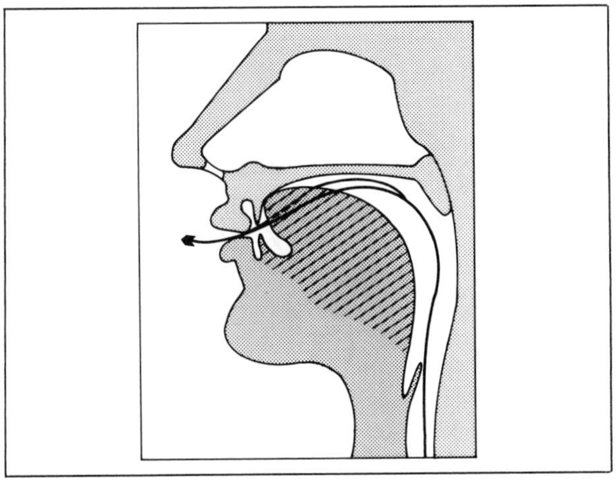

Figure 5-19. /l/

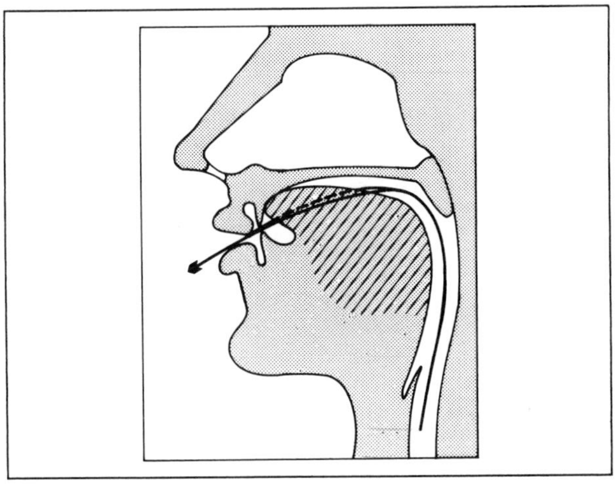

Figure 5-20. /ɫ/

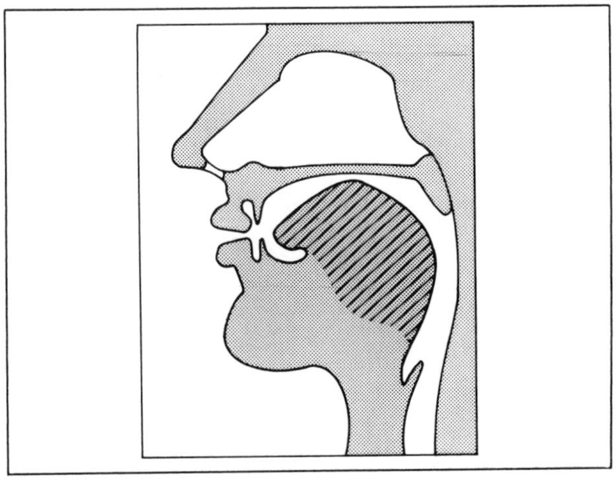

Figure 5-21. /r/ ([ɹ])

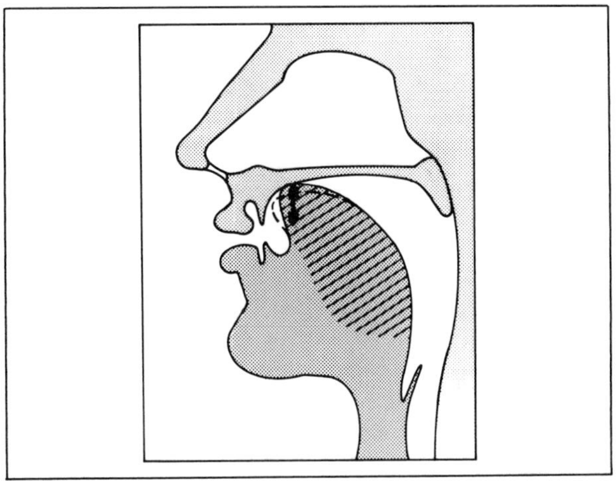

Figure 5-22. /ɾ/

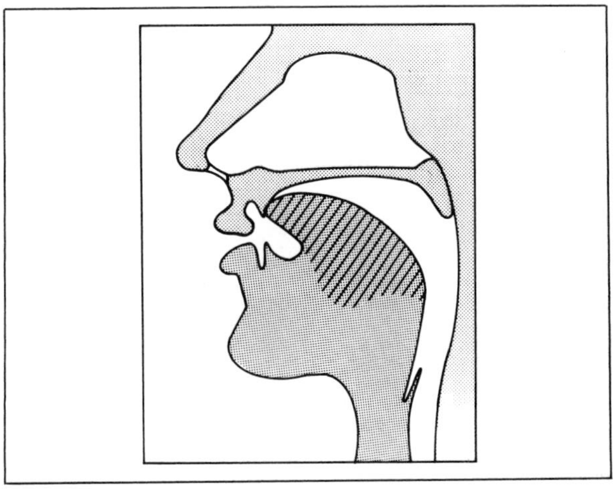

Figure 5-23. /t̪ d̪/ Other dentals have the same place of articulation.

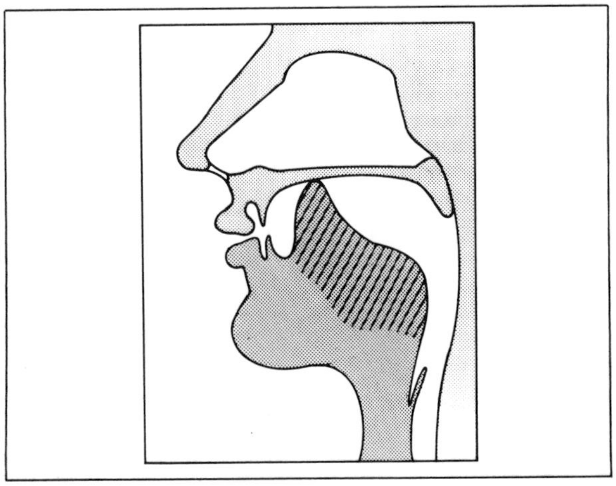

Figure 5-24. /ʈ ɖ/ Other retroflexes have the same place of articulation.

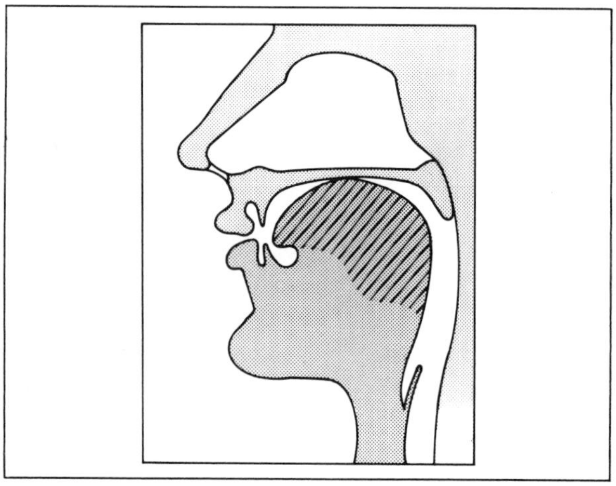

Figure 5-25. /c ɟ/ Other palatals have the same place of articulation.

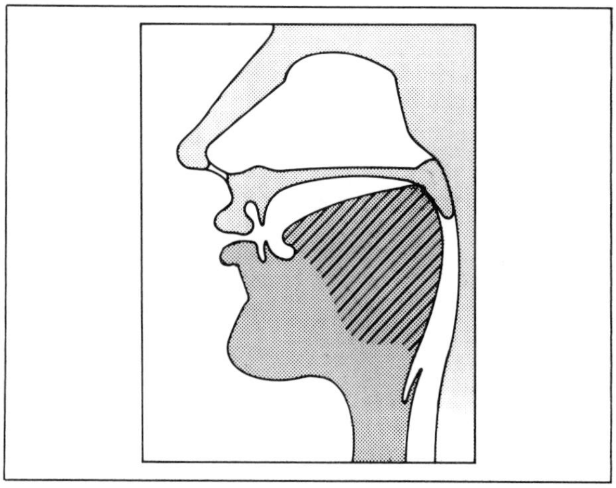

Figure 5-26. /q ɢ/ Other uvulars have the same place of articulation.

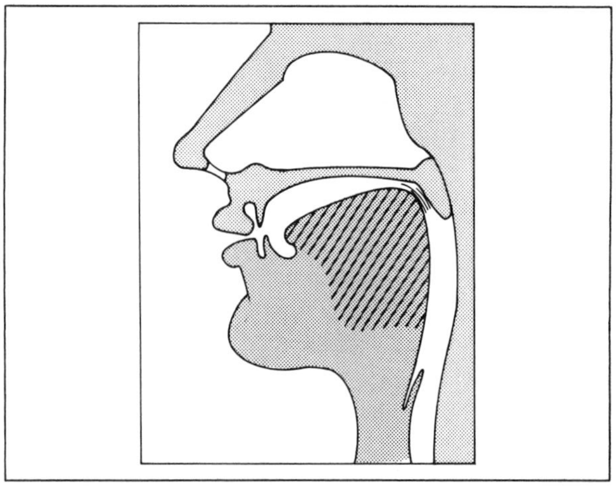

Figure 5-27. /χ ʁ/

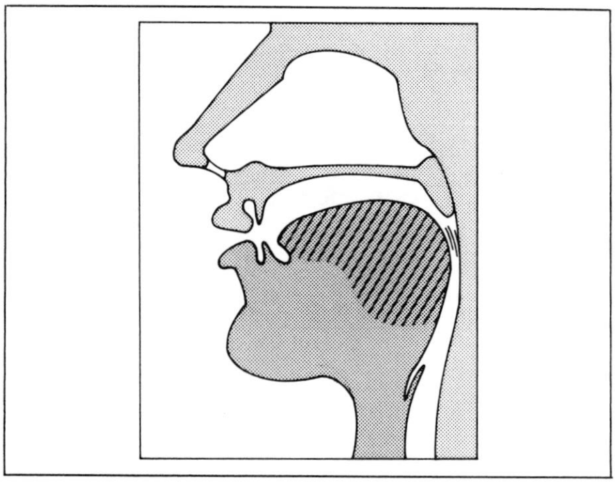

Figure 5-28. /ħ ʕ/

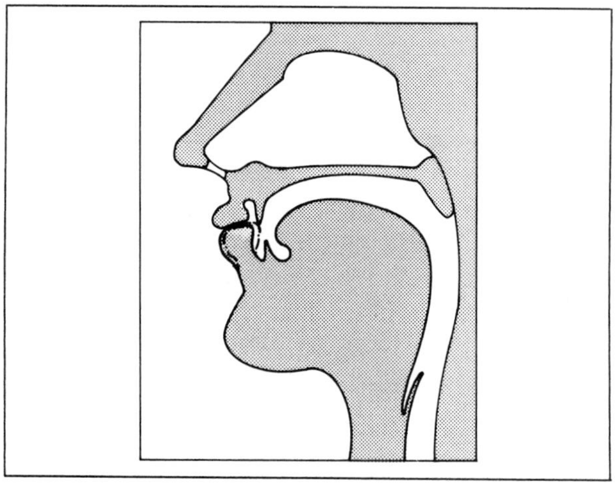

Figure 5-29. /p͡f/

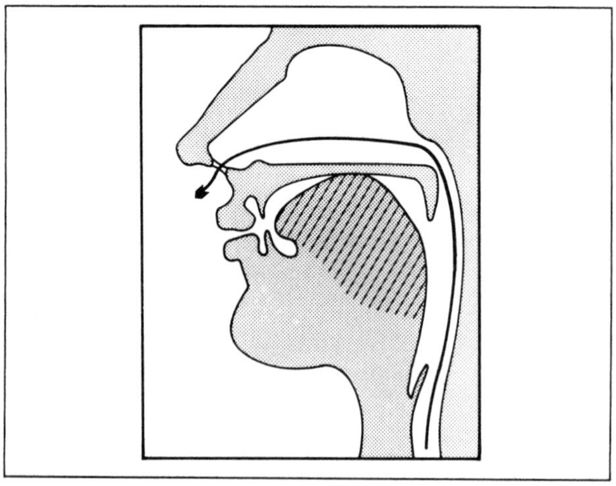

Figure 5-30. /ɲ/

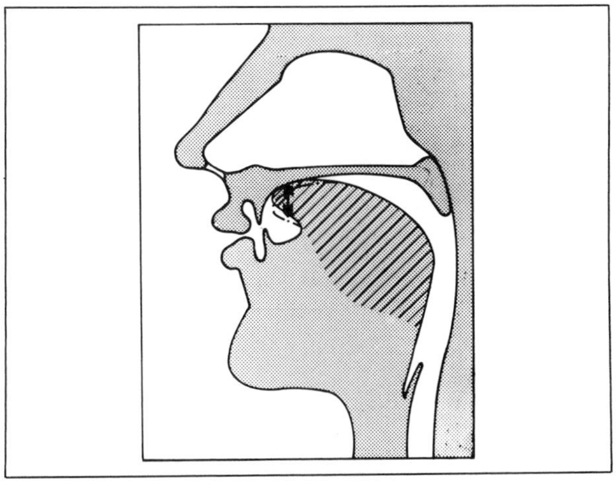

Figure 5-31. /r̃ ř/

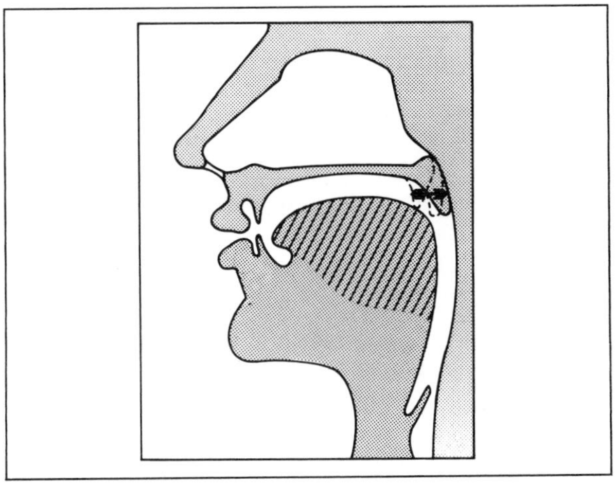

Figure 5-32. /ʀ/

tion, would not show on the articulatory drawing. And finally, the glottal sounds (e.g., [h], [ɦ], and [ʔ] are not drawn, since the critical articulation takes place at the level of the vocal folds, which do not show on such a drawing, and because the position of the other articulators is so dependent upon the sounds that precede and follow the sound in question.

5-9 Airstream Mechanisms and Other Consonant Types

Speech sounds depend upon a column of air, either moving or, if static, under pressure. Several mechanisms exist for creating a moving column of air for speech; these are known as **airstream mechanisms.** All of the speech sounds we have examined in this chapter and in Chapter 4 involved one type of airstream mechanism, namely the **egressive pulmonic** airstream mechanism.

The various airstream mechanisms are named for two parameters: the direction of airflow and the initiating mechanism, or **initiator.** The two directions of airflow are outgoing, called **egressive,** and incoming, called **ingressive.** The terms that refer to the different initiators are **pulmonic** (the lungs), **glottalic** (the larynx or glottis), **velaric** (the tongue at the velum), and **esophageal** (the esophagus).

5-9.1 The Pulmonic Airstream Mechanism

The **pulmonic airstream mechanism** is powered by the lungs (L. *pulmones*, 'lungs'). The details of respiration are described in Chapter 9; for the moment let us note that it is primarily the diaphragm, intercostal muscles, and elastic forces that power airflow into and out of the lungs.

All languages use the **egressive pulmonic airstream,** although many use other airstream mechanisms besides. The **ingressive pulmonic airstream** is normally a variant of the pulmonic egressive airstream used when an individual is in a highly emotional state or is speaking when out of breath. (Typically, someone who has run two blocks to a telephone booth to call an ambulance about an accident will talk using both an egressive and ingressive airstream mechanism.) Sometimes deaf children use an ingressive pulmonic airstream where an egressive one would be appropriate. Occasionally, normally hearing children do the same in the early stages of acquiring linguistic skills.

Some other airstream mechanisms are used in other languages as part of the normal repertoire of segments, and some we will examine are used by individuals with communication disorders.

5-9.2 The Glottalic Airstream Mechanism: Ejectives and Implosives

The **glottalic airstream mechanism** uses the larynx and vocal folds as the initiator (hence the name *glottalic*, from *glottis*, the space between the vocal folds). This mechanism is used for consonants only, primarily plosives.

Table 5-10. The consonants

	Bi-labial	Labio-dental	(Inter) Dental	(Grooved) Dental	Al-veolar	Alveo-palatal	Retro-flex	Palatal	Velar	Uvular	Pharyngeal	Glottal
Plosive	p			t̪	t		ṭ	c	k	q		ʔ
	b			d̪	d		ḍ	ɟ	g	ɢ		
Fricative	ɸ	f	θ	s̪	s	š	ṣ	ç	x	χ	ħ	h
	β	v	ð	z̪	z	ž	ẓ	ĵ	ɣ	ʁ	ʕ	ɦ
Affricate	p͜f		t̪͜θ		t͜s	č	ṭ͜ṣ	c͜ç	k͜x			
	b͜v		d̪͜ð		d͜z	ǰ	ḍ͜ẓ	ɟ͜ĵ	g͜ɣ			
Nasal	m	ɱ		n̪	n		ṇ	ɲ	ŋ	ɴ		
Glide	(ʍ)								ʍ			
	(w)							j	w			
	(ɥ)							ɥ				
Lateral												
Approximant				l̪	l		ḷ	ʎ				
					ɫ				(ɫ)			
Fricative					ɬ							
Rhotic approximant (bunched)							ɹ̣	ɹ			(ɹ)(ɹ̣)	
Flap												
Rhotic				ř̪	ř						(ř̪)(ř)	
Nonrhotic					ɾ							
Trill				r̪̄	r̄					ʀ	(r̪̄)(r̄)(ʀ)	

This is not an exhaustive list of consonants but concentrates on the articulations discussed in the chapter. Parentheses indicate secondary articulations or two places of articulation for the same segment. Only dental *fricatives* are grooved; other segments in the column are simply dental.

The **egressive glottalic airstream** is produced as follows: The vocal folds are closed tightly. Simultaneously the oral articulation is made for the plosive in question (bilabial, alveolar, palatal occlusion, etc.). The velum is raised, so that the space between the glottal and oral occlusions is sealed. Now the speaker raises the larynx in his/her throat. (If you put your hand on your throat and swallow, you will note that the larynx moves up and down; while, as a speaker of English, you may not have learned to make this motion independently of swallowing, you will note that the larynx *can* be moved up or down.) By raising the larynx the speaker compresses the air enclosed between the two occlusions and then releases the oral occlusion, just as for any other plosive. The glottic occlusion (i.e., the closure of the vocal folds) is released *after* the oral occlusion is released.

Plosives produced with this mechanism are known as **ejectives** or, occasionally, as **glottalized plosives.** They are transcribed with the symbol ['], as in [p', t', c', k'].

The **ingressive glottalic airstream mechanism** essentially works in reverse. An oral occlusion is made (bilabial, alveolar, etc.) at the same time as the vocal folds are closed. This time, however, the vocal folds are brought together with the larynx high in the throat (it is at its highest in mid-swallow; you can feel it by putting your hand on your throat as you swallow). In this case, the larynx is *lowered* in the throat during the articulation. Plosives produced with this mechanism are known as **implosives.**

In fact, while the voiceless type of implosive just described is possible, implosives—in languages that use them—are more commonly voiced. This is accomplished by simultaneous use of the *ingressive pulmonic* and *ingressive glottalic* airstream mechanisms, such that voicing occurs as the larynx is lowered.

Implosives are symbolized thus: [ɓ, ɗ, ʄ].

5-9.3 The Velaric Airstream Mechanism: Clicks

The **velaric airstream mechanism** uses the tongue as its chief initiator. This airstream mechanism also goes by the name **oral airstream mechanism,** and speech produced with an egressive velaric airstream is often called **buccal speech** in speech pathology textbooks.

In natural languages,[25] only the *ingressive* **velaric airstream mechanism** is known. The mechanism of articulation is as follows. The oral cavity is blocked off from the pharyngeal cavity in the velar region (this accounts for the term *velaric*). The velum may be raised or lowered, but if lowered, it permits the speaker to breathe normally while making speech sounds with this mechanism. A second occlusion is made at a point forward of the velaric occlusion: because of the velaric occlusion, it is not possible to articulate sounds back of the alveopalatal region.

At this point, there are two occlusions: one velar and one in the labial, alveolar, or alveopalatal region. Now, while maintaining both points of occlusion, the speaker lowers the tongue body *between* these two points, creating a space of low pressure. The front occlusion is then released, and air rushes in, creating the speech sound.

Such segments are known as **clicks.** They are normal speech sounds of some languages, in particular several languages of southern Africa, such as Zulu, Hottentot, and Xhosa. A number of clicks are also produced as interjections by speakers of English. One way that some people smack their lips is by making a bilabial click. The sound of disapproval often written ⟨tsk-tsk⟩ or ⟨tut-tut⟩ is a dental or alveolar click, symbolized [ʇ] in the IPA. The sound given to encourage horses (the "giddy-up" sound) is a click as well; this one is released laterally. That is, the alveolar occlusion is maintained on release, but the sides of the tongue are lowered to release the sound (much like *lateral release* in English; see Section 6-6.4). This sound is symbolized [ʖ] in the IPA. A postalveolar click is sometimes made by humorists; its symbol is [ʗ] in the IPA.

[25]**Natural language:** any human language spoken as a first or mother tongue. Natural languages have the characteristics discussed in Chapter 2.

The clicks [ʇ], [ʖ], and [ʗ] all are used commonly in the southern African languages mentioned. In the usual orthography of these languages, the letters ⟨c⟩, ⟨x⟩, and ⟨q⟩ are used, so the language name *Xhosa* starts with about the same sound as the "giddy-up" click in English.

5-9.4 The Egressive Velaric Airstream Mechanism: Laryngectomees

The **egressive velaric airstream mechanism** is not used in any natural language. However, some laryngectomees make use of it. **Laryngectomees** are individuals who have undergone **laryngectomy;** that is, surgical removal of the larynx. Not having a larynx, they have no vocal folds. And the primary biological function of the larynx is to protect the respiratory system from food, liquid, and secretions—these are directed toward the esophagus and stomach during swallowing by the larynx and associated structures—so the laryngectomee lacks this protective mechanism. If the trachea (windpipe) were connected to the pharynx (throat), there would be nothing to stop food and liquid from being aspirated by ('drawn into') the lungs. Therefore removal of the larynx is accompanied by connection of the trachea to a surgically created hole in the front of the base of the neck; it is through this **stoma** that the laryngectomee breathes. While the stoma solves the vegetative requirements of breathing, eating, and drinking, it is problematic for speech, in that neither the usual mechanism of voicing nor the normal pulmonic airstream is available.

Some laryngectomees speak using an *egressive velaric airstream mechanism*. Its production is just the opposite of the ingressive mechanism used for clicks. There is an occlusion in the region of the velum and one at the point of articulation of the sound the person wants to say, and the tongue between is *raised* to produce an airstream or air pressure. A pseudovoicing may be produced simultaneously, most often laterally by vibration of tongue and/or cheek tissue.

The velaric egressive airstream is not very satisfactory for producing normal-sounding English speech, as you might imagine. No sounds whose place of articulation is palatal, velar, or farther back can be produced successfully—anterior sounds are substituted—and speech produced this way has a "Donald Duck" quality that lowers its intelligibility and its acceptability. However, it may afford certain individuals their only way, or their most comfortable way, of speaking.

Speech pathologists refer to speech produced with the egressive velaric airstream mechanism as **buccal** speech. A related mechanism, known as **pharyngeal** speech, uses the root of the tongue and/or constrictor muscles of the pharyngeal walls to produce an airstream originating in the pharynx. Such a mechanism permits a more successful articulation of palatal and velar sounds than buccal speech.

5-9.5 The Esophageal Airstream Mechanism

The **esophageal airstream mechanism** is used exclusively by laryngectomees; it does not form a normal airstream mechanism in any natural language. As laryngectomees lack both the mechanism for laryngeal voicing and any pulmonary airstream through the mouth, the esophageal airstream is used as a substitute for both. The *esophagus* is the tube leading to the stomach from the pharynx, and essentially the esophageal airstream mechanism is a controlled belch that sets tissue in the lower pharynx and upper esophagus (the *pharyngoesophageal junction*) vibrating in a way that simulates voicing. Air is injected into the esophagus with the tongue; this *charge* of air, as it is called, permits the accomplished esophageal speaker to utter a number of syllables. (The injection of air into the esophagus, permitting willful belching and even the speaking of syllables with the esophageal airstream, are skills possessed by many a mischievous boy, usually to the regret of his mother.)

There are a number of difficulties, including psychological ones, inherent in mastering esophageal speech. One difficulty is that a single charge of air produces far fewer syllables than a lungful of air does, even in the case of an accomplished esophageal speaker who makes very efficient use of the air supply. The result is that speech is slower and more laborious than the speaker is used to. It may also be interrupted or masked by the noise of injecting the charge of air. A second potential problem is that the frequency of vibration of the tissues is around 50 to 80 hertz, a very low frequency even for a male voice. Accomplished male esophageal speakers simply sound hoarse, but female esophageal speakers may worry that their voices sound masculine. However, differences between male and female speech reside in many aspects of the speech signal—acoustic, phonetic, lexical, and syntactic—therefore female esophageal speech is not unfeminine. This has been demonstrated experimentally: blind identification of taped esophageal voices shows a high level of correct sex identification. Finally, many people, having been brought up to believe that belching is rude, worry that others will find esophageal speech unaesthetic. However, accomplished speakers simply sound hoarse, and they find that their speech is both acceptable and intelligible. Roughly two-thirds of those who attempt to learn esophageal speech achieve functional speech and are variably successful in overcoming the problems inherent in it.

The problem of the small air supply that requires frequent renewal is perhaps the most serious difficulty of esophageal speech. A number of surgical techniques and prosthetic devices have been developed in an attempt to use the pulmonary air supply for esophageal speech. All these methods have in common a *tracheoesophageal puncture;* that is, a passageway between the trachea and the esophagus. The trick is to permit exhaled lung air to enter the esophagus when needed for speech, but to prevent any food or liquid from passing through the puncture from esophagus to trachea (and from the trachea to the lungs). One device designed to accomplish this is the Blom-Singer prosthesis, essentially an acrylic tube that is inserted into the stoma, through the tracheoesophageal puncture, and into the esophagus. The design of the tube is intended to prevent food or liquid from entering the trachea, and normal stomal breathing is not interfered with. However, when the individual blocks the stoma on exhalation, the exhaled air is channeled into the esophagus through the prosthesis. This provides a more constant esophageal airstream for speech.

For the student of phonetics, one of the more interesting aspects of esophageal speech involves voicing and its perception. In normal speech, voic-

Table 5-11. Airstream mechanisms

	Pulmonic	Glottalic	Velaric	Esophageal
Initiator	Lungs	Larynx	Tongue	Esophagus
Egressive				
Usage	Universal. All languages have pulmonic sounds. With certain exceptions (interjections, emotional states, dysfunctions), the pulmonic is the only airstream mechanism used in English and other European languages.	Relatively uncommon. Some consonants in some African and Amerindian languages, among others. Plosives (and affricates) only; plosive segments are referred to as **ejectives** or **glottalized plosives.**	Used by some laryngectomees, but not known in any natural language. Called **buccal** speech by speech pathologists.	Used by most laryngectomees but not in any natural language.
Mechanism	Air is forced out of the lungs by the diaphragm and intercostal muscles. Voicing is optional.	Air in pharynx compressed between oral occlusion and vocal folds by raising larynx with vocal folds closed. No voicing possible. Plosive release in oral cavity.	Oral cavity is closed by dorsovelar contact. Air is forced out by action of tongue between velum and place of articulation. Voicing is possible in principle, but this mechanism is not used, except jocularly, by anyone with a normal larynx. Pseudovoicing may occur laterally.	Air (under pressure due to elasticity of esophageal walls) is allowed to escape slowly from esophagus. With tracheoesophageal puncture, air supply is renewed from lungs; without shunt, air supply is injected with the tongue.
Examples, segments	All vowels and consonants of English. /ɑ/, /i/, /p/, /t/, /k/, /b/, /d/, /g/, /m/, /r/, /z/, etc.	Plosives and affricates only. /p'/, /t'/, /k'/	Segments anterior to palate only, since tongue dorsum is used for oral occlusion. No special symbols.	All segments normally produced by the egressive pulmonic airstream. Many phonemically "voiceless" segments pseudovoiced; voiced/voiceless distinction may be carried by cues other than actual voicing.
Ingressive				
Usage	Rare. Usually a variant of the egressive pulmonic airstream, used when speaking excitedly while out of breath. Sometimes used by deaf—and some normally hearing—children.	Uncommon. Plosives made by this mechanism are called **implosives.**	Uncommon. Used in some languages, most notably in southern Africa, for speech sounds called **clicks.** Also used in some languages (e.g., English) as interjections.	N.A.
Mechanism	Air is brought into the lungs by the diaphragm and intercostal muscles. Voicing is possible.	Larynx is lowered, with vocal folds closed or vibrating (aided by ingressive pulmonic airstream). In attested languages, generally the latter mechanism is used. Plosive-like release (with ingressive airflow) in oral cavity.	Two points of closure, one being velar (i.e., velaric). Tongue lowered between points of closure; abrupt noisy inflow of air when anterior occlusion is released.	
Examples, segments	N.A.	Plosives only. /ɓ/, /ɗ/, /ʄ/	Plosive-type segments anterior to the palate only. /ʇ/, /ʖ/, /ʗ/	

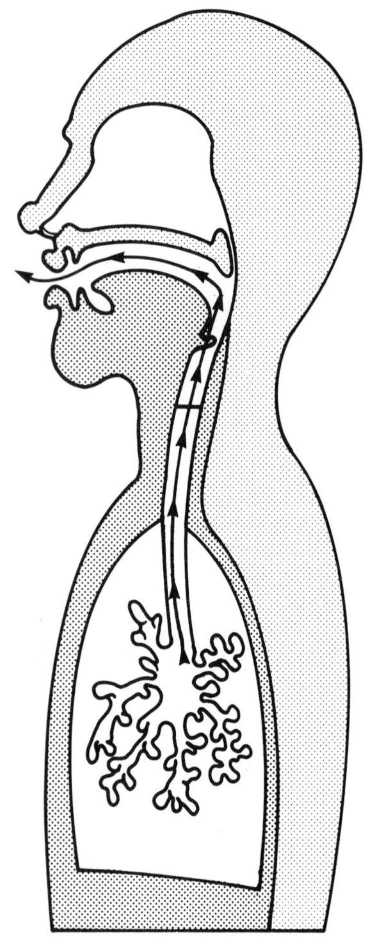

A

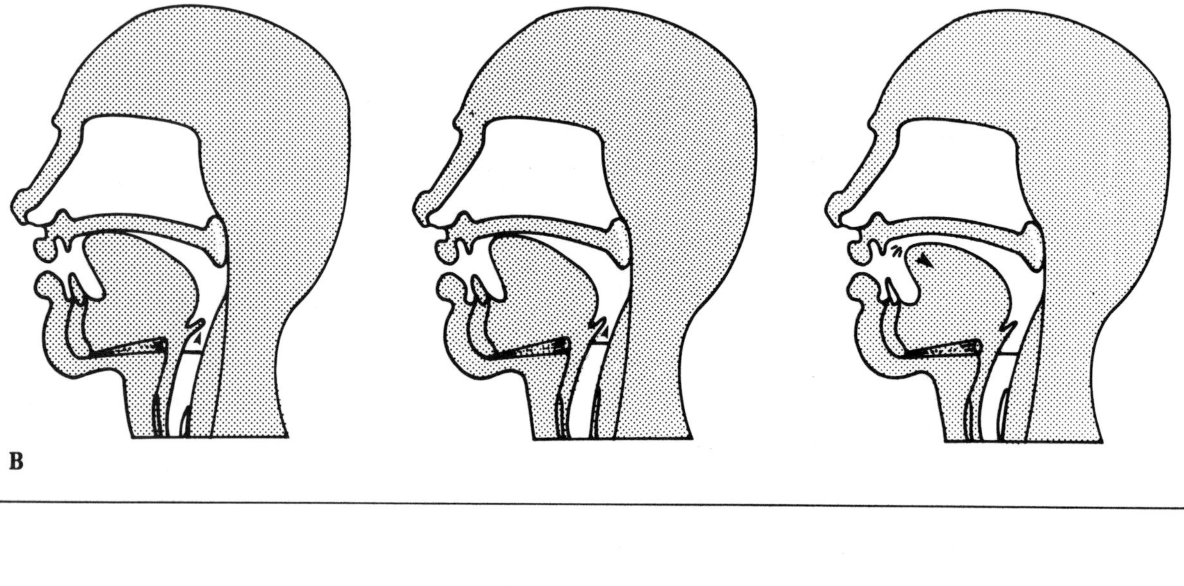

B

Figure 5-33. The airstream mechanisms. *A*. Pulmonic. Air is forced out of or drawn into the lungs by the action of the respiratory muscles. The egressive pulmonic airstream is illustrated. *B*. Glottalic (pharyngeal). Egressive: produces ejectives. Air is compressed between the closed vocal folds and an occlusion as the larynx is raised. *Left*, Vocal folds are shut (adducted); an alveolar occlusion is shown here. The larynx begins to be raised. *Middle*, The adducted vocal folds have been raised. There is increased air pressure between the two occlusions. *Right*, The oral occlusion is released, producing an ejective consonant. Ingressive (not illustrated): produces implosives. Air is rarefied between the vocal folds and an occlusion as the larynx is *lowered*. C. Velaric. Ingressive: produces clicks. *Left*, The tongue contacts the roof of the mouth. *Middle*, The center of the tongue is lowered, rarefying the air between the two points of contact. *Right*, The tongue tip or blade is then lowered suddenly, producing the click. *D*. Esophageal. *Left*, A laryngectomee. The esophagus is connected to the pharynx, as in a normal individual. But the trachea (windpipe) leads only to the stoma; there is no connection between the lungs and the mouth. Pseudovoicing is produced with a controlled belch. *Right*, A laryngectomee with a tracheoesophageal puncture. A plastic tube connects the trachea with the esophagus. A one-way valve at the esophageal end prevents food or liquid from entering the trachea. Air enters and leaves the trachea through the open-air end of the tube and through holes in the tube that are aligned with the trachea. However, if the open-air end of the tube is blocked (as illustrated), exhaled air is forced into the esophagus, providing a continuous source of air for pseudovoicing. For illustrative purposes, the tube is shown larger than it would be in reality.

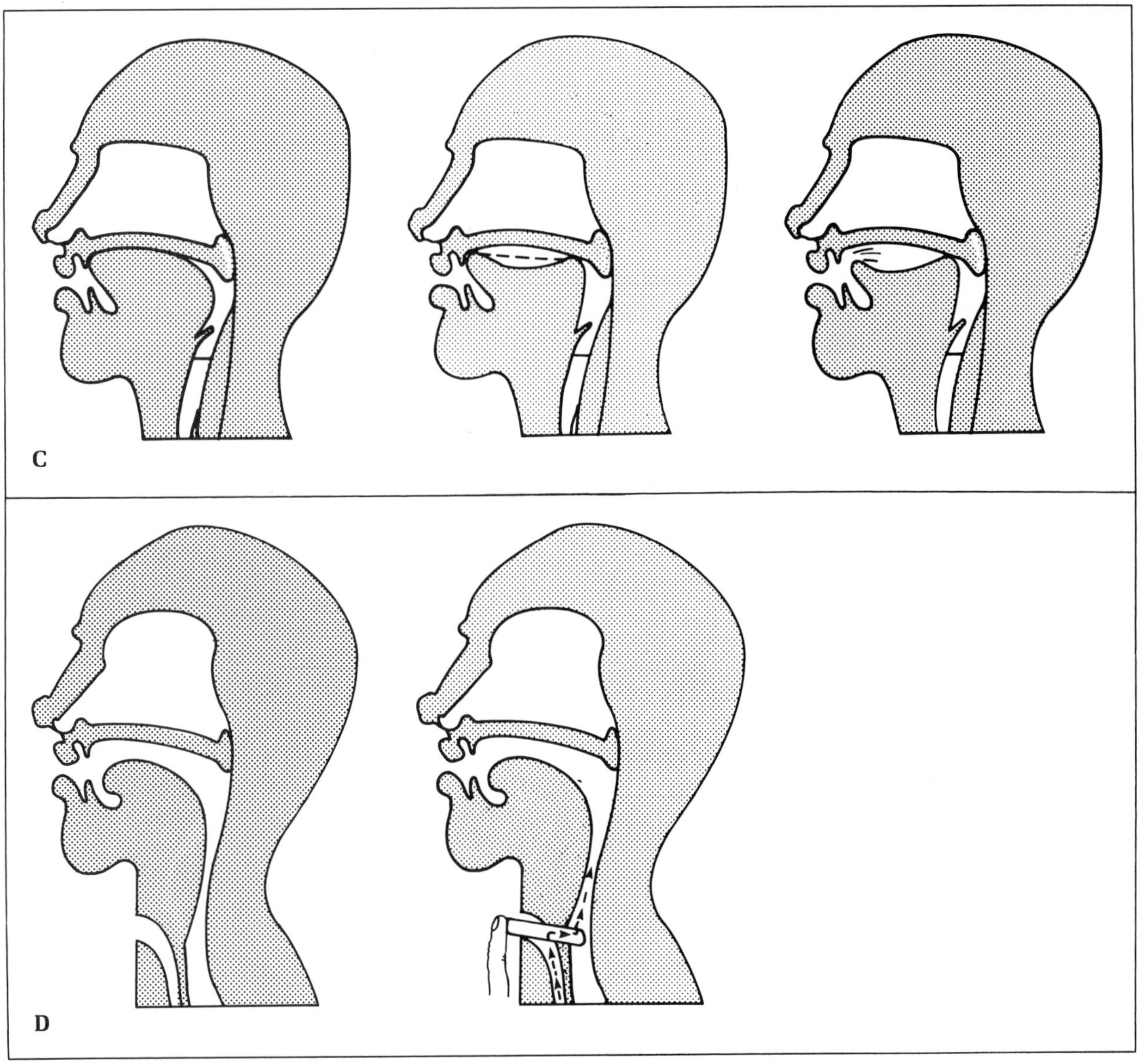

Figure 5-33 (continued)

ing is often initiated and terminated (switched on and off) very rapidly. When one says the word "hippopotamus," for example, voicing is switched on four times and off four times (five times if the preceding word ends with a voiced sound), all in a very short space of time. This rapid switching on and off of voicing is more difficult in esophageal speech, and the result is that many supposedly (i.e., phonemically) "voiceless" segments are in fact pseudovoiced. Yet good esophageal speech remains highly intelligible. Other phonetic cues to voicing are present, such as length of preconsonantal vowels and aspiration of plosives (see Section 8-7.1), and contextual cues help to eliminate ambiguity (see Section 10-11).

Table 5-11 summarizes the various airstream mechanisms, and Figure 5-33 illustrates them. (Figure 10-45 is also relevant to airstream mechanisms.)

Summary

Most **consonants** are articulated with greater constriction, usually creating more acoustic noise, than vowels.

Consonants are classified by **manner of articulation, place of articulation,** and **voicing.**

The usual nomenclature normally involves mentioning the passive articulator only.

Plosives involve total momentary blockage of the vocal tract. Plosives may be aspirated. Voicing in plosives is not "on" or "off" but, rather, varies along a continuum. A measure of the timing of voicing in plosives is known as **voice onset time (VOT).**

Fricatives involve a close constriction through which air is forced.

Affricates involve the close association of a plosive and a homorganic fricative. They are usually defined phonemically rather than phonetically.

Nasals involve oral blockage and velic lowering.

Approximants are that class of sounds involving no blockage or frictional noise but, instead, a narrowing of the vocal tract at some point. Most are voiced.

Glides are vowel-like. They involve movement of the articulators. All glides have vocalic (i.e., vowel) counterparts.

Liquid is the traditional cover-term for approximant laterals and approximant rhotic consonants.

Laterals have a central blockage, with air flowing over the sides of the tongue. There are both approximant laterals and fricative laterals.

The English r-sound is a **bunched approximant.**

Flaps are produced with an exceedingly brief closure, usually laminoalveolar. **Trills** are produced with a rapid aerodynamic vibration of the tongue blade or the uvula.

All vowels and consonants discussed up to this point use the **egressive pulmonic airstream mechanism.** Other airstream mechanisms exist as well. **Ejectives** are produced with the **egressive glottalic** airstream mechanism. **Implosives** are produced with the **ingressive glottalic** airstream mechanism. **Clicks** are produced with the **ingressive velaric** airstream mechanism. Rarely, the **egressive velaric** airstream mechanism is used by **laryngectomees.** The **esophageal** airstream mechanism is regularly used by laryngectomees.

Vocabulary

active articulator
affricate
airstream mechanisms
alveo-
alveolar
alveolar ridge
alveopalatal
apical
apico-
apicoalveolar
apicodental
approximant
aspiration
back
ballistic movement
bar-d
bilabial
blade
buccal speech
bunched
cavity friction
clicks
closing phase
closure phase
consonant
dental
dorsal
dorso-
dorsovelar
egressive
egressive glottalic airstream mechanism
egressive pulmonic airstream mechanism
egressive velaric airstream
ejective
environment
esophageal
esophageal airstream mechanism
eth
falling diphthong
flap
flapping
fortis

fricative
frictionless continuant
glide
glossal
glottal
glottal stop
glottalic
glottalic airstream mechanism
glottalized plosives
grooved
hachek
homorganic
implosives
ingressive
ingressive glottalic airstream mechanism
ingressive pulmonic airstream mechanism
ingressive velaric airstream mechanism
interdental
intraoral air pressure
labial
labio-
labiodental
labiovelar glide
laminal
lamino-
laminoalveolar
laryngectomee
laryngectomy
lateral
lenis
lingual
lips
liquid
lisp
manner of articulation
nasal
nasal stops
non-nasal stops
occlusion
off-glide
oral airstream mechanism
palatal
palate
palato-
passive articulator
pharyngeal
pharyngeal speech
pharynx
phi
phonetic environment
place of articulation
plosive
positional variant
pretonic
pulmonic
pulmonic airstream mechanism
release (of plosive)
retroflexion
rising diphthongs
semivowels
shutting phase (of plosive)
slit fricative
stoma
stop
stridency, strident
tap
tracheoesophageal puncture
trill
uvula, uvular
velar
velaric
velaric airstream mechanism
velarized l
velic
velum
voice onset time (VOT)
voiced
voiceless
voicing
VOT

Readings

Readings on voice onset time (VOT) include "Distinctive Features and Laryngeal Control" (Lisker and Abramson [1971]); "Discriminability along the Voicing Continuum: Cross-Language Tests" (Abramson and Lisker [1970]); "A Cross-language Study of Voicing in Initial Stops: Acoustical Measurements" (Lisker and Abramson [1964]); "Some Effects of Context on Voice Onset Time in English Stops" (Lisker and Abramson [1967]); "The Perception of Voice Onset Time in Polish" (Mikoś et al. [1978]); "Sensitivity of Voice-Onset Time (VOT) Measures to Certain Segmental Features in Speech Production" (Weismer [1979]); and "Voicing Contrast: Perceptual and Productive Voice Onset Time Characteristics of Adults" (Zlatin [1974]).

Readings in esophageal speech and the Blom-Singer technique include "A Comparative Acoustic Study of Normal, Esophageal and Tracheoesophageal Speech" (Robbins et al. [1984]); "Oral Pressures, Vowel Duration and Acceptability Ratings of Esophageal Speakers" (Swisher [1980]); "Vocal Roughness and Jitter Characteristics of Vowels Produced by Esophageal Speakers" (Smith et al. [1978]); "Acoustic Characteristics: Tracheoesophageal Speech" (Baggs and Pine [1983]); "Vowel Duration Characteristics of Esophageal Speech" (Christensen and Weinberg [1976]); "Frequency, Duration and Perceptual Measures in Relation to Judgements of Alaryngeal Speech Acceptability" (Shipp [1967]); "A Study of Talker Sex Recognition of Esophageal Voices" (Weinberg and Bennett [1971]); "An Endoscopic Technique for Restoration of Voice after Laryngectomy" (Singer and Blom [1980]); and "Selective Myotomy for Voice Restoration after Total Laryngectomy" (Singer and Blom [1981]).

Speech dynamics

6

Objectives

To emphasize that speech is a process, not a series of static positions.

To encourage the student to examine the implications of the dynamic nature of speech.

To discuss accommodation (assimilation).

To list some variant forms of English speech sounds in context.

To discuss secondary articulations.

To discuss noncontiguous accommodation.

To discuss various combinatory phenomena, including spontaneous speech errors.

6-1 Introduction

In Chapters 4 and 5 we examined the articulatory characteristics of individual segments. Each one was given its standard articulatory description and was illustrated by a cross-sectional drawing of the head, showing the articulators. While this is a natural way to introduce the subject of speech articulation, it may reinforce the impression most people have of speech: namely, that it is made up of a series of individual static postures, the phonemes of the language, with movements in between. It cannot be stressed enough that this is an entirely false impression.

Speech is a dynamic rather than a static phenomenon, and the articulators are in a state of constant movement during speech. The idealized positions we have seen in Chapters 4 and 5 are nothing more than target positions at which we aim, as it were, while speaking. Sometimes those targets are attained, more often they are not; as a result, speech is often nothing more than a series of approximations. Furthermore, the dynamic nature of speech means that we are planning events before they occur. As a result, we have begun to articulate one segment before completing another; we may be as much as several segments ahead or behind (or both) in our motor activity. The result is that sounds are modified by the surrounding sounds (by their **environment,** as it is called): what a [t] is depends upon what goes before and what follows. This chapter will look at the ways sounds are modified by their environment.

A given segment or phoneme cannot be pronounced in an unchanging way, irrespective of environment. Any attempt to pronounce sounds in a way unaffected by surrounding sounds will result in speech that sounds artificial and stilted (and besides, the attempt will be unsuccessful, since even with conscious effort, the effects of one segment upon another cannot be avoided).

Not only is the *articulation* of segments affected by the surrounding segments, but their *sound* is as well. While speech acoustics and perception are the topics of Chapter 10, we can say at this point that the actual sound you produce when you say a given segment—for example, [s]—is affected by the surrounding segments: the s-sound of "seep" creates different frequencies of sound waves than the s-sound of "sweep." If you were to record natural speech, and then cut the recording up into individual phones and splice these together into words, the results would be at best highly unnatural and distorted and at worst incomprehensible.[1] Even if you recorded whole words, either pronounced in isolation or in sentences, and then spliced them together to form new sentences, they would sound strange.

Individual speech sounds are thus pronounced differently depending upon the neighboring sounds. This phenomenon is variously called **accommodation, coarticulation,** and **assimilation.** (We will use all of these terms and in fact make a distinction among them.) The existence of this phenomenon is extremely important in both practical and theoretical terms. In practical terms it means that the individual being taught to articulate certain sounds (be it a deaf person undergoing aural habilitation, an individual undergoing articulation therapy, or a second-language learner) cannot simply be taught to pronounce a given sound in one simple way. There will surely be modifications to the articulation of that sound; the individual must make those modifications if he/she wishes to have natural-sounding speech. In theoretical terms, the models we devise of phonological systems and of historical sound changes must take into account these variations (either as causes or as consequences, as the case may be).

In this chapter we use the term **accommodation** to refer to any changes in the articulation of a sound that are created by the presence of segments in the phonetic environment. The phenomenon of accommodation will be subdivided in a rough way into **coarticulation** and **assimilation.** Under the heading of speech dynamics we note that other processes than accommodation occur in running speech; these we will look at in the latter part of the chapter.

While the distinction is not an absolutely clear-cut one (and different authors use the terminology differently), we will use the term *assimilation* for

[1] This is why computer-produced synthetic speech often sounds unnatural and may be difficult to understand, unless it is of particularly good quality. In computer speech of ordinary quality, all the instances of a given phoneme are identical, rather than being different in sound according to the environment, as they are in natural speech.

major phonetic changes due to accommodation and the term *coarticulation* for minor changes. Another way of stating this is to say that assimilation generally refers to changes that cross phonemic boundaries (i.e., change one phoneme into another), whereas coarticulation refers to changes that do not cross phonemic boundaries.

Both *assimilation* and *coarticulation* are phenomena of *accommodation,* and there is a gray area in which one might apply either of the former terms equally. In connected speech there are additional combinatory phenomena, some of which also fall under the general heading of accommodation.

The terms **environment, context,** and **phonetic environment** all refer to the sounds surrounding the segment in question. Note that the environment includes not only the surrounding segments but other features of a phonetic nature as well, such as stress and intonation (Chap. 7).

6-2 The Nature of Accommodation

When we speak, conflicting demands are made on the articulators: the tongue blade must touch the alveolar ridge for a [t]; the tongue body must be high and back for an [u]; the velum must be lowered for a [m] or other nasal sound; the velum must be raised for all other segments. All of these demands are made in far less time than is available to fulfill them: normal conversational English is produced at a rate of between 10 and 20 segments per second, implying a maximum of a tenth of a second (100 milliseconds [msec.]) per segment on the average. However, it takes much longer than a tenth of a second to complete any voluntary speech gesture, particularly if one considers the return to the starting point. For example, to lower the velum for a nasal consonant and raise it again afterwards may take as much as half a second: the time it takes to say five to ten segments.

Clearly, "something has to give." What happens is that compromise gestures are made and/or there is carryover of some features of the articulation of one segment onto another. In other words, there is an *accommodation* in the articulatory gestures.

Let us consider a few examples to make the point clear. Consider the nonsense words /iki/, /uku/, and /ɑkɑ/. (Nonsense words are used instead of real words in order to provide the precise phonetic environment needed for the example.) /k/ is a velar consonant, so you would expect a dorsovelar contact, as shown in Figure 5-8. The vowel /u/ is a high back vowel, so its place of articulation is essentially velar, although no linguavelar contact is made, as it is with /k/. By contrast, /i/ is high front, requiring movement of the tongue body forward, and /ɑ/ is low back, requiring movement of the tongue body back. There would be insufficient time in normal speech to make the movements seemingly required to pronounce /iki/, /uku/, and /ɑkɑ/. What happens, therefore, is that the point of contact for the /k/ changes according to the vowel in its environment, as shown in Figure 6-1.

As shown in Figure 6-1A, if you say /iki/, in fact the contact for the /k/ is not on the velum but is brought forward to the palate, the place of articulation of the /i/. This reduces the amount of movement necessary to articulate the word. So in saying the word /iki/, in fact what you say is [ici], with a palatal, not a velar, plosive (see Section 5-2.4).

Similarly with the low back vowel, as shown in Figure 6-1C. Because of the place of articulation of the vowel [ɑ], the point of contact for the /k/ in the word /ɑkɑ/ is farther back on the velum than for a more typical /k/. In fact what you say when you pronounce /ɑkɑ/ is [ɑqɑ], that is, there is a back velar, or uvular, plosive instead of a mid-velar one.

In the case of the word /uku/, the vowel's place of articulation is similar to that of the plosive, so in fact you articulate [uku] when you try to say /uku/ (as in Figure 6-1B).

You can feel the different points of articulation noted in Figure 6-1 and the preceding paragraphs by simply saying the three nonsense words in a conversational manner and paying attention to the point of contact between your tongue and the roof of your mouth.

Now turn your attention to Figure 6-2. Here we are dealing with the words /obo/ and /omo/. Bilabial consonants have been chosen intentionally for this example, in order to avoid lingual coarticulation and concentrate on the velic movements.

In the sequence A–B–C of Figure 6-2 we see three stages in the articulation of the word "oboe"

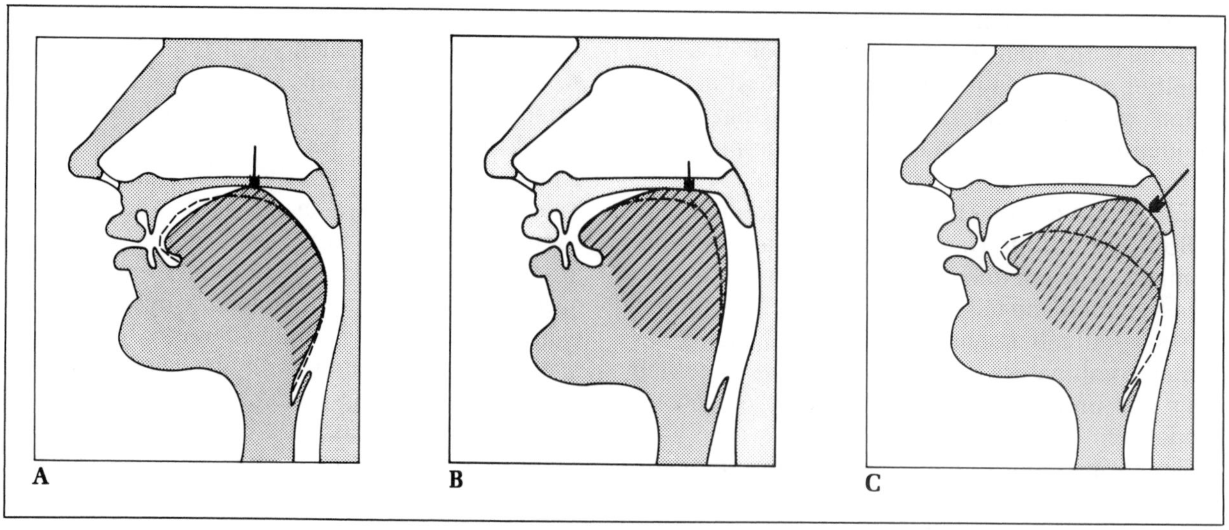

Figure 6-1. Accommodation. **A.** The "word" /iki/, pronounced [ici], with a palatal plosive. **B.** The "word" /uku/, pronounced [uku], with a velar plosive. **C.** The "word" /ɑkɑ/, pronounced [ɑqɑ], with a uvular plosive. Notice the coarticulation affecting the place of articulation. These are normal English articulations. The broken line indicates approximately the vowel articulation; the arrow indicates the actual place of articulation of the /k/.

(/obo/), corresponding to each of the three phonemes. Virtually no coarticulation in lingual or velic gestures is present, and none has been illustrated. Note particularly that since none of the segments are nasal, there is no velic movement.

Now consider the sequence D–E–F of Figure 6-2. Again, each frame corresponds to one phoneme. Again, there is little if any lingual coarticulation, and none is shown. This time, however, the consonant is nasal ([m]). The velum must lower for the [m]. Ideally it should be raised for the vowels, but there is not enough time for that. So the velum lowers during the first [o], or even before it, and rises again during the second [o]. The illustrations are of course static and can show only one point in time; you can interpolate the movement between.

Notice the audible difference between the /o/'s of the two example words; actually, the vowels are [o] in /obo/ ([obo]) and [õ] in /omo/ ([õmõ]). If you pronounce [o] and [õ], you can hear the difference. This trick might help: think of saying /omo/, then start to say it, but interrupt yourself before saying the /m/, and listen to the quality of the vowel. Compare that to an /o/ you say without thinking of a particular word.

Consider now the accommodation shown in Figure 6-3. Here we see the words /ibi/ and "oboe." This time we will consider neither the tongue nor the velum, but the lips. [i] is a spread vowel, and [o] is somewhat rounded (lip positions have been exaggerated for illustrative purposes). Notice the lip posture during the closure phase of the [b]. In both cases the lips are closed—that is essential to the articulation of a /b/—but in /ibi/ they are spread and closed, whereas in /obo/ they are rounded and closed. These are two different articulations of the phoneme /b/—visibly different, although not audibly so.[2]

In these three examples, we have seen accommodation in lingual position, velic position, and labial position. The term **coarticulation** would be appropriate to all three. Literally, *coarticulation* means 'simultaneous articulation,' and in each example we saw that two different phonemes were being articulated simultaneously. In the first example, *one* tongue movement was made for *both* vowel and consonant. In the second example, the correct velic position for the *consonant* was attained during the articulation of the *vowel* (so that

[2] Actually, there is probably a small acoustic difference at the level of the *loci* (see Section 10-10.1).

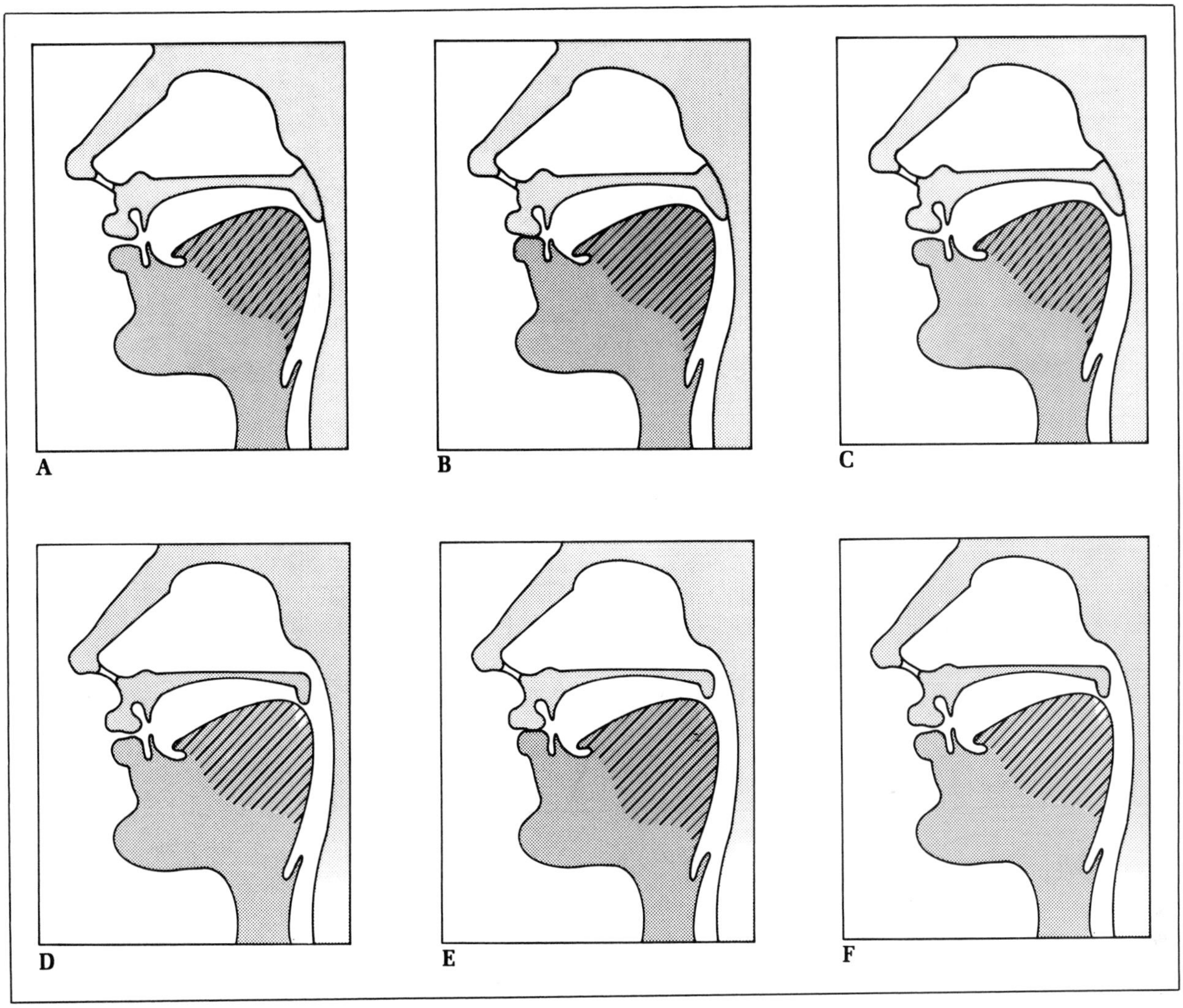

Figure 6-2. Accommodation. **A–C.** The word /obo/. **D–F.** The "word" /omo/, pronounced [õmõ]. Notice the coarticulation affecting vowel nasality.

one feature of the consonant was being articulated at the same time as the vowel). And in the third example, the consonant was being articulated with the lip posture appropriate for the vowel (so that both the consonant and one feature of the vowel were being articulated simultaneously).

Now let us consider an example of **assimilation.** If someone says "I miss you" in normal conversation, the word "miss" is likely to be pronounced "mish" ([mɪš]). This is because the [j] of "you" is palatal and draws the [s] of "miss" back to an alveopalatal or palatal position. (We have not provided a special drawing illustrating this, since the new [š] has essentially its normal place of articulation, as was shown in Figure 5-12.)

Or if you say "phone booth" conversationally, the word "phone" is likely to be pronounced "phome" ([fom]). (The new [m] is essentially the [m] of Figure 5-14.)

As we noted earlier, there is no clear line between coarticulation and assimilation, but it may be useful to make a broad distinction. In assimilation, there is a major change in the place of articulation, manner of articulation, or voicing of a segment, such that it falls into a different phonemic category. In the foregoing examples, [s] is a differ-

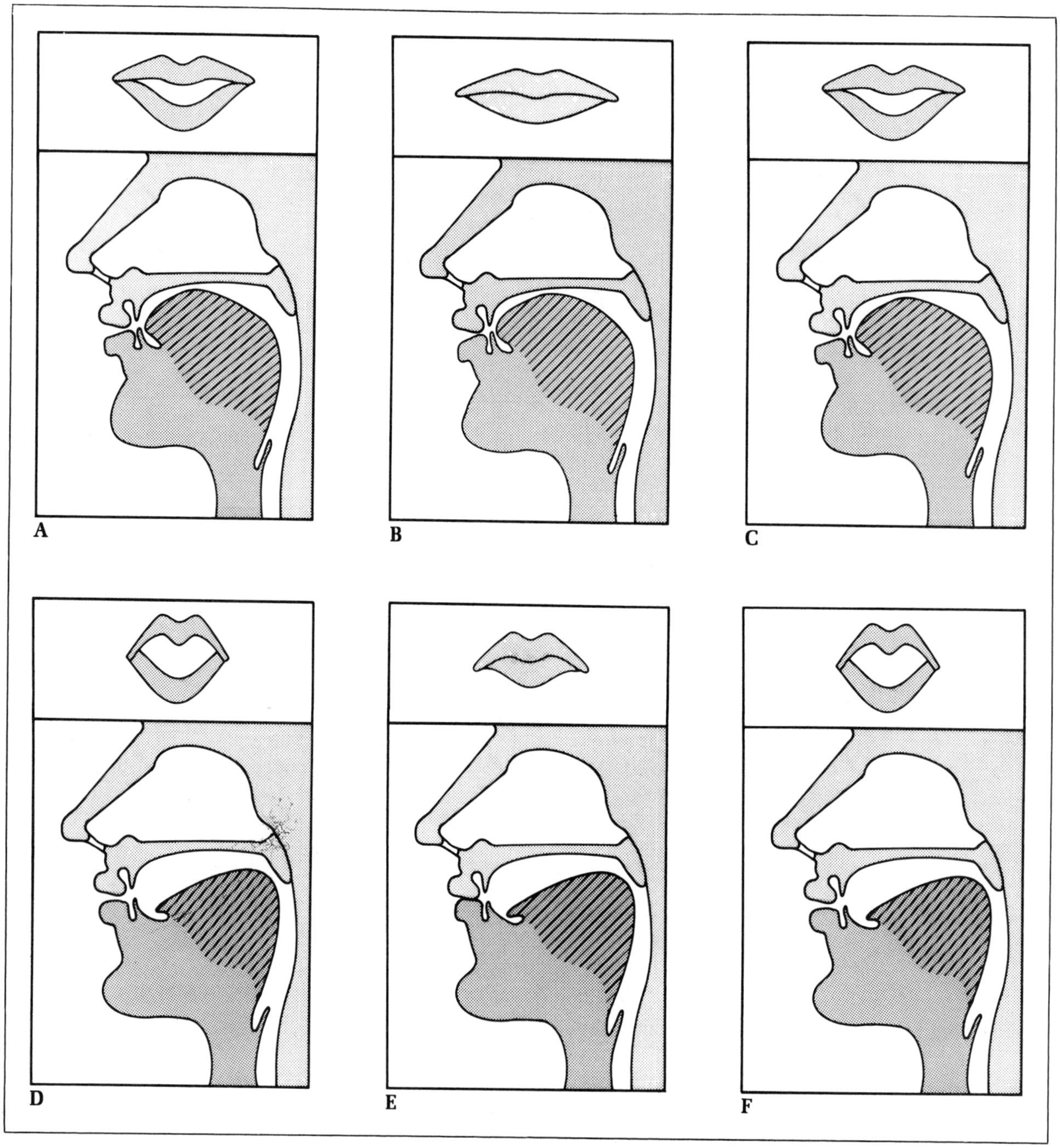

Figure 6-3. Accommodation. **A–C.** The "word" /ibi/. **D–F.** The "word" /obo/. Notice the coarticulation affecting lip-rounding.

ent phoneme from [š]; [m] is a different phoneme from [n]. Coarticulation, on the other hand, occurs when the various segments are different only to the extent of nonphonemic differences. Whether a plosive is palatal, velar, or uvular (i.e., whether it is [c], [k], or [q]) is not a phonemic difference in English, nor is there a phonemic distinction between a /b/ made with rounded lips and a /b/ made with spread lips. (Note that many authors use the term *assimilation* in the general sense we are attributing to *accommodation*.)

6-3 The Causes of Accommodation

Accommodation (that is, coarticulation and assimilation) is a pervasive phenomenon. What causes it?

It is often explained with reference to a "principle of least effort," which invokes the notion that the least effort possible is expended in the production of speech. This explanation accounts for the phenomenon in part but not in whole.

Accommodations are made because there are more segments to produce in a given period of time than there is the possibility of producing them without some adjustments (i.e., "accommodation") in the articulatory gestures. For example, the instance of velic coarticulation illustrated in Figure 6-2 occurs because there simply is no time to lower the velum at the end of the vowel if one does not wish either a pause or an intrusive consonant (see Section 6-4). It is a universal physiological constraint: some amount of nasality will "leak" over to a preceding vowel in *any* language, unless there is an intervening pause or consonant.

But these physiological constraints are not necessarily absolute and cannot be used to explain every instance of accommodation.[3]

For example, the lingual coarticulation shown in Figure 6-1 and accompanying text is correct for most speakers of English. That is, we *do* pronounce /k/ palatally next to a high front vowel. But do we *have* to? The answer is simply No. Some languages make a phonemic distinction between /k/ and /c/ and maintain this distinction in the environment of /i/; that is, speakers of these languages would pronounce [iki] differently from [ici]. So, it is *possible* to say [iki] without making the /k/ palatal; it is just that speakers of English *do not* (not that they *could not*).

One way of looking at the situation is that on a given route there are possible shortcuts; whether or not speakers use a given shortcut depends on the rules of the grammar of that language (a rule in English is that given the sequence /iki/, one takes the shortcut which results in [ici]; a rule in another language might be that one does not take the shortcut). Certain shortcuts may be universally obligatory, such as the nasalization example already mentioned. In other cases, there may be more than one shortcut possible. Looking still at the /iki/ example, another shortcut or accommodation that is physiologically possible is to say [ɯkɯ],[4] that is, to bring the *vowel* articulation *back* to the consonant, rather than to say [ici], where the *consonant* articulation is brought *forward* to the vowel. But speakers of English do not make this accommodation, not because it is not possible, not because it is any less of a shortcut, but simply because it is against the rules of English.

In conclusion, then, accommodations are made either because they must be, for universal physiological reasons (an explanation that is true less of the time than you might think), or because the language in question has a *rule* that a given accommodation be made. In this sense, accommodation is *rule-governed*, as the term was introduced in Chapter 2.

It is important also to realize that accommodation is not the result of "sloppiness" or "laziness." While it is true that accommodation saves muscle movements, and therefore articulatory effort, it does not follow that laziness is its motivating factor. To pronounce each phoneme exactly as illustrated in the drawings of Chapters 4 and 5 would not improve the quality of speech, but it would greatly increase the effort required; a language has a phonetic system with some redundancy, but not too much, because it would simply be inefficient.

An individual speaker says [ici] for /iki/ not out of laziness but because doing so follows the rules of English. It *is* true that dialects and registers of

[3] See also Section 8-3.3.

[4] [ɯ] is a high back tense unrounded vowel having the same tongue position as [u], but with spread or neutral lip posture like [i] or [ɪ] (see Section 4-8.2).

speech (formal versus informal) differ in the amount of accommodation and the particulars of the accommodations made. So speakers of one dialect may feel that the accommodation made in another dialect is in some way sloppy or inferior. And this judgment may be subjectively true from the position of the standard dialect; however, the simple fact of making assimilations or coarticulations is not in itself lazy.

In fact, since accommodations are rule-governed and are part of the grammar of the language, making them *is essential to sounding normal*. The second-language learner often has a hypercorrect pronunciation that sounds strange because it *lacks* the usual shortcuts that speakers take. In this case the second-language teacher has to *promote* accommodations rather than condemn them. A similar situation may occur with the deaf speaker.

Accommodation serves a useful function in speech production in reducing the overall effort required and increasing the number of segments that can be produced in a given amount of time *without loss of clarity*. Speech has a certain amount of built-in redundancy; that is, there is more than one acoustic cue to each segment. The "shortcuts" implied by accommodation reduce the amount of redundancy in the speech signal, but a sufficient level of redundancy remains that speech can be understood even under less than ideal listening conditions. Since a certain level of redundancy remains despite the "shortcuts"—sufficient redundancy for reliable comprehension—there is no virtue whatever in not taking the shortcuts.

However, as discussed in Section 2-4, there is social pressure to conform to the standard dialect, and using a set of rules different from the norm or the standard dialect will sound strange and will be judged "incorrect" by speakers of the standard dialect.

6-4 Can Speech Be Segmented?

One of the most basic assumptions we all share about speech is that it is segmentable: that it is made up of a series of individual speech sounds strung together like so many beads on a string. That these individual sounds, called **segments** or **phones,** are present in speech is a notion that is reinforced by our writing system (even though it is not completely segmental in nature [Chap. 3]) and by the "phonic" method of learning to read, as well as by the way speech sounds are introduced in phonetics textbooks (this one being no exception, as demonstrated by Chapters 4 and 5). While the concept of the segment is very useful in talking about the phonetic—and particularly the phonemic—structure of language, it may well mislead us about the dynamic functioning of speech production.

Let us compare a segmental and a nonsegmental approach to a problem of sound change and see what we can learn from the latter approach.

In many dialects of English, the sequence of /VntV/ is pronounced /VnV/ (where V symbolizes any vowel). Thus, the word "winter" sounds like "winner," and the word "twenty" is pronounced as if spelled "twenny." Let us assume for the sake of this argument that the pronunciations /wɪntɚ/ and /twɛnti/ are "correct" in the historical sense of being older (i.e., they are the "original" pronunciations), and that the pronunciations /wɪnɚ/ and /twɛni/ represent changes. How would you characterize the change in pronunciation of these words? Probably the most common answer would be that the /t/ has been "dropped" in each of these words and in others like them. Such an "explanation" most likely will include a comment on the "saving of effort" displayed by the change (if not the downright "laziness" shown by speakers who do it). This view holds that the word "twenty" is made up of six separate phonemes (or beads on a string) and that the change involves the simple dropping of one phoneme or "bead."

A nonsegmental approach to the description of the difference between, for example, "twenty" and "twenny" gives a surprisingly different result. In what follows, we are concerned with the sequence /VntV/, and so we will ignore the rest of the word and in fact ignore the quality of the vowels. Figure 6-4 illustrates the sequences /əntə/ and /ənə/, representing with the schwa ([ə]) any vowel that might occupy these positions.

One other assumption has been made for the purpose of the illustrations. As you will recall from Figure 6-2 and the explanation of it, coarticulation, due to slow velic movements, results when a vowel is next to a nasal consonant. This

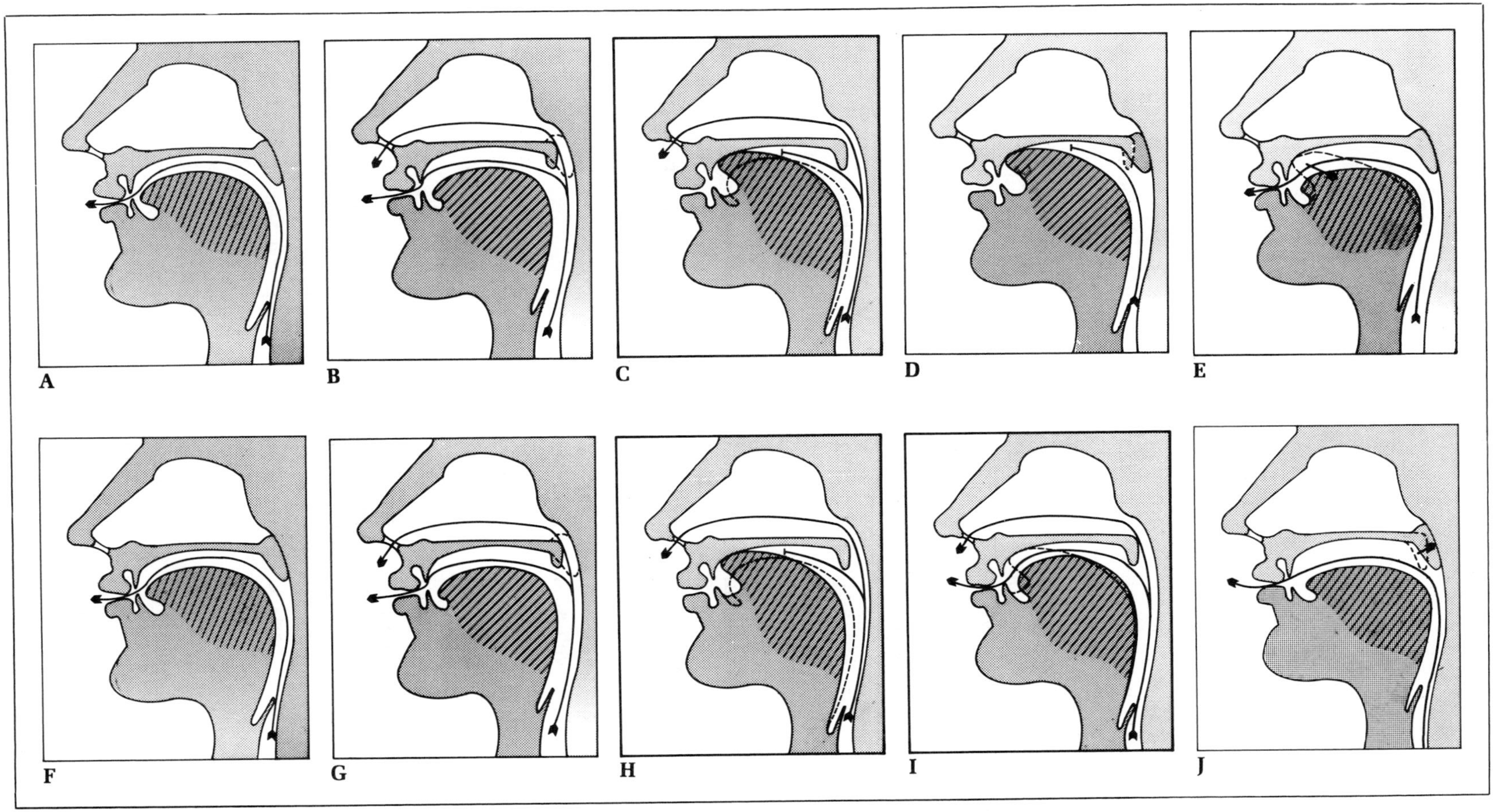

Figure 6-4. The sequences /əntə/ and /ənə/. **A–E.** The sequence /əntə/. **A.** [ə] **B.** [ə̃] **C.** [n] **D.** [t] **E.** [ə] (no nasality). **F–J.** The sequence /ənə/. **F.** [ə] **G.** [ə̃] **H.** [n] **I.** [ə̃] **J.** [ə]. Note that in both sequences the velum is raised, then lowered, then raised. In both sequences the oral cavity is open, then closed with a laminoalveolar articulation, then open again. In /əntə/ the velum is raised *before* the oral cavity is reopened (there is no nasalization of the second vowel). In /ənə/ the velum is raised *after* the oral cavity is reopened (there is nasalization of the second vowel). An additional "segment" involves no additional articulatory gesture.

coarticulation is likely to extend even further than the vowel, so that in a word like "winter" probably not only the /ɪ/ is nasalized, but the /w/ as well; in "winner" the /ɚ/ is likely to be nasalized as well. However, since Figure 6-4 shows only the sequences /əntə/ and /ənə/, the nasalization is shown as happening during the vowels.

Let us examine the articulation of /əntə/, illustrated in Figure 6-4A–E. In part A we see the vowel being articulated; the speaker is anticipating the /n/ following, and velic coarticulation becomes evident in part B. In part C, the velum is still lowered, and laminoalveolar occlusion creates the /n/. /n/ and /t/ have the same place of articulation, so the only articulatory change required (besides voicing) is the raising of the velum; part D illustrates the articulation of the /t/. To pronounce the final vowel, it is necessary to open the oral cavity once more, as shown in part E. Note that the final vowel is not nasalized, as it was preceded by a non-nasal phone.

Now let us examine the articulation of /ənə/, as illustrated in Figure 6-4F–J. The transition from non-nasalized vowel to nasalized vowel to nasal consonant is the same as in the preceding paragraph and is illustrated in parts F, G, and H. At this point, the speaker opens the oral cavity again (shown in part I). Because of the time required for velic movement, the vowel in part I is nasalized, but nasalization is eliminated when the velum is raised (part J).

What articulatory gestures are made for /əntə/ and /ənə/? Are they different? For both /əntə/ and /ənə/, the velum starts from a closed position, is lowered, and is raised again. For both, the oral cavity is open, is closed with a laminoalveolar articulation, and is opened again. Thus both are articulated with the same sequence of gestures. The difference can be found in examining the sequences C–D–E and H–I–J. Both *start* (parts C and H) with oral closure and velic opening. However, in /əntə/, velic closure is accomplished (part D) *before* oral opening (part E); whereas in /VnV/, velic closure is accomplished (part J) *after* oral opening (part I).

In sum, /VntV/ and /VnV/ have the same articulatory gestures in the same order; the difference lies in the *relative* ordering of the same gestures. /VnV/, which has one fewer phoneme than does /VntV/, does *not* have any fewer articulatory gestures. (Of course, there is a difference at the level of the vocal folds; since /t/ is voiceless, there is a cessation of voicing for the /t/ and a reestablishment of voicing afterwards. This is not the case in the sequence lacking the voiceless segment.) Since all of the same articulatory gestures are present in both sequences, it is hardly correct *articulatorily* to say that "winner" has anything less than "winter." And to characterize the difference in terms of the number of segments misses the point articulatorily.

Assume that someone is saying "winner" for "winter" and feels that he should "correct" his pronunciation. He will not correct it by "adding" something that is "missing" but rather by reordering what is already there.

6-4.1 Plosives in Homorganic Nasal Clusters: A Common Sound Change

As has been demonstrated, the difference between /VntV/ and /VnV/ is minimal. The same could be said of the difference between /VndV/ and /VnV/; indeed, the change here is even less, since there is no change in voicing. As you can demonstrate to yourself, exactly parallel arguments may be made to show the minimal difference between /VmpV/ or /VmbV/ and /VmV/, or between /VŋkV/ or /VŋgV/ and /VŋV/.

Since we have seen one example of such a sound change, namely the common colloquial pronunciation in American English of "twenny" for "twenty," and because of minimal articulatory differences in these sequences, we would expect such sound changes to be common in historical terms.

Indeed they are, and they take two forms: the "insertion" of the plosive (known as **epenthesis:** see Section 6-11.3) and the "deletion" of the plosive (known as **elision:** see Section 6-11.1). The words "insertion" and "deletion" are in quotation marks because it has been shown that viewing this phenomenon as a simple presence or absence of a segment misses the point articulatorily.

Examples of epenthesis include the change from Latin *camera* ('room') to French *chambre* ('room, chamber'); from Latin *homo* ('man') to Spanish *hombre* ('man'); from English *loan* to English *lend* (in Old English the verb infinitive had a suffix -*an*, so the /n/ was intervocalic); and from Old English *þunor* (cf. German *Donner*) to Modern English *thunder*.

Examples of elision include the change from Old High German *timbar* (related to English *timber*) to Modern German *Zimmer* ('room') and the change from Middle English *singer* (rhyming with modern English "finger") to the modern pronunciation. The colloquial pronunciations, of "twenty" and "winter" also are examples of elision. Less commonly, this phenomenon extends to /nd/ clusters: in rapid colloquial speech in some dialects, a word such as "indicate" will have no /d/.

In contemporary English, a similar phenomenon of "insertion" can be seen in nasal-fricative clusters. A word such as "prince" is pronounced the same as "prints"; an intrusive /t/ appears between the /n/ and the /s/ of "prince." Similarly, "sense" has just as much of a /t/—or just as little—as "cents." The word "strength" is pronounced /stɹɛŋkθ/ (or, in some dialects, /stɹɛntθ/). The source of the "intrusive" plosive [k] (or [t]) is the same as that of the [t] in the [VntV] sequences we have examined.

6-4.2 The Segment Revisited

It is hoped that this section will have made you question your assumptions about the makeup of speech. The "beads on a string" are not separate—they overlap and interact. We will not abandon the term **segment** in referring to individual speech sounds, but from here on we will use it with a recognition that segments are not autonomous units. We will understand that their articulation represents the overlapping interaction of a number of different articulatory gestures. We recognize that they cannot simply be inserted or deleted like the letters that represent them, without affecting surrounding segments.

6-5 Types of Accommodation

Accommodation refers to the phenomenon of sounds becoming like neighboring sounds. Accommodation may affect the *place of articulation*, the *manner of articulation*, the *voicing*, *other articulatory features* (such as secondary articulations), or any combination of these factors.

6-5.1 Degree of Accommodation

Accommodation may be greater or lesser in its effect. It may affect only the voicing or only the place of articulation or only the manner of articulation, or it may affect more than one of these features. The two sounds in question may become identical as a result of accommodation, or they may become only more similar.

Accommodation is called **partial** if the segment that undergoes change retains some separate character. It is called **total** if the assimilated segment becomes like the assimilating segment in every way.

For example, Italian *Vittorio* corresponds to English *Victor*; *fatto* corresponds to *fact*. In both these words English retains the original [k] (spelled ⟨c⟩). In the Italian words, the original [k] has assimilated *totally* to the following [t]. In a similar way, in a casual pronunciation of "nutcracker," most people say [nʌk˺krækɚ]; the [t] is *totally* assimilated to the following [k]. But when someone says [fombuθ] for "phone booth," a [n] has become a [m] under the influence of the [b]. This is a *partial* assimilation: the place of articulation has changed, but the manner of articulation remains nasal rather than plosive. The [m] is still distinct from the [b].

6-5.2 Direction of Accommodation

Accommodation may be divided up into three types according to the direction of its effect. These are known as **progressive, regressive,** and **double accommodation.**

6-5.2.1 *Progressive Accommodation*

In **progressive,** or **left-to-right,** accommodation, a sound affects one that follows. For example, in the word "dogs" the final ⟨s⟩ is pronounced [z], while in "cats" the final ⟨s⟩ is pronounced [s]. The [g] of "dogs" is voiced, and that affects the following sound; the [t] of "cats" is voiceless, similarly affecting the sound that comes after it.

6-5.2.2 *Regressive Accommodation*

In **regressive, anticipatory,** or **right-to-left** accommodation, a sound affects one that precedes it. For example, when someone says [mɪšjə] for "miss you," the palatal glide [j] has modified the articulation of the *preceding* fricative. When "phone booth" is pronounced [fombuθ], the [b] has affected the place of articulation of the preceding nasal.

6-5.2.3 *Double Accommodation*

Sometimes the segments that precede *and* follow a given segment both exert a similar influence on that segment. In this case the direction of accommodation is said to be **double.** For example, in the word "shear" the vowel is likely to be somewhat rounded. This is because both the [š] preceding the vowel *and* the [r] following the vowel are somewhat rounded. To give another example, the vowels of the words "man," "mat," and "tan" are all likely to be somewhat nasalized. However, the nasalization in "man" is likely to be greater than in the other two words, because the direction of the effect is double; it gets a double dose of accommodation, as it were.

6-5.3 Diachronic versus Synchronic Accommodation

In linguistic science, the term **diachronic** refers to historical events in language. The term **synchronic** refers to contemporary or still ongoing processes. Accommodations may be of either type.

To use an example we have employed several times, the pronunciation [fombuθ] for "phone booth" displays a *synchronic* accommodation, since we pronounce "phone" with a [n] in "phone," and it undergoes the process of accommodation in certain combinations.

To take another example we have seen, Old English *þunnor* has changed to Modern English *thunder*, with a [d] "inserted" as an accommodation. This is a *diachronic* or historical accommodation, since it occurred in the past, and the word is no longer undergoing change (at least in the standard dialect); that is, *thunder* is pronounced with a /d/ in all contexts.

Contemporary (synchronic) processes are particularly significant because they produce variant forms such as the two forms [fom] and [fon] for "phone." Such processes will likely affect other phonetically similar words in a similar way.

6-5.4 Contiguous vs. Noncontiguous Accommodation

Accommodation may affect contiguous segments (those next to one another in a sequence), as has been the case in all the examples we have seen. Or it may affect segments that are at a distance from each other. An example of the latter is the word *orang-utan*, borrowed from Malay, which is often pronounced (and spelled) *orang-utang* in English, the final [n] becoming [ŋ] under the influence of the [ŋ] in the second syllable.

Because there are a number of special examples of noncontiguous assimilation, the subject will be discussed more fully in Section 6-8.

6-5.5 Types of Accommodation

Note that the types of accommodation listed in the preceding subsections are not mutually exclusive categories. For example, **progressive** accommodation could be **partial** or **total:** a **diachronic** accommodation could be **progressive** or **regressive.** Other combinations are equally possible.

6-6 Variants of Some English Segments

In this section we will catalogue a number of examples of variants of phones in English, by way of illustrating the way accommodation works in English.

6-6.1 Release of Plosives

In utterance-final position,[5] plosives in English are often unreleased. That is, when no sounds follow the plosive, the final phase of its articulation, the *release* phase, may not be present. In this case, the accommodation can be seen as being caused by the silence following the segment in question.

For example, if you were to say "Stop!" you might well not release the final [p]. However, if the [p] is followed by another sound (particularly an open sound such as a vowel), as in "Stop, Alice!" the [p] must be released. Note that this, like many other accommodations, is not forced on speakers by physiologic necessity, but is optional,

[5] **Utterance-final position:** the position of the last segment in an utterance, that is, before the speaker stops talking. In this position, a segment is not followed by another segment, and thus no articulatory adjustments (such as release) are forced upon that segment by following segments.

determined by rule in English. In French, by contrast, utterance-final plosives are always released.

There is a lack of standardization in the transcription of nonrelease, but a satisfactory symbol is [˺]; an unreleased [p] would be indicated thus: [p˺]. Hence, "Stop!" may be [stɑp˺]. In English, utterance-final nasals are also often unreleased: "Who was that?" "Jim" ([ǰɪm˺]).

When two similar plosives come together, there may be only one release. For example, in the phrase "canned drink" there normally would be only one release for both [d]'s. In some cases there may be *compensatory lengthening*, that is to say, there may be one plosive whose occlusion phase is prolonged to compensate for the missing release. Single release of two plosives may be transcribed satisfactorily by indicating that the first of the two plosives is unreleased: [kænd˺ drɪŋk].

Even when two juxtaposed plosives have different places of articulation, there may be only one release for the two. For example, in saying "locked," many speakers articulate a velar occlusion for the [k] but do not release it separately from the [t]. That is, they say not [lɔkt] but [lɔk˺t]. This phenomenon may occur even if the two plosives are in different words. In the expression "back to nature," the [k] of "back" may be unreleased.

In diachronic terms, nonrelease may lead to the loss of sounds. Although, as we have noted, all plosives in French are released, this is true of Modern French only. In Middle French, nonreleased plosives were common, and that led to the loss of many word-final consonants. The tendency in English (North American English, at least) toward nonrelease may likewise lead to the loss of final consonants.

6-6.2 Aspiration of Plosives

As we noted in Section 5-2.11, aspiration is the puff of air accompanying the release of plosives. In English, voiceless plosives in certain environments are typically aspirated; voiced plosives never are.

To recapitulate, voiceless plosives at the beginning of stressed syllables are typically aspirated in English: for example, the initial plosives in "pan," "tan," and "can." If you check for this by holding your hand in front of your mouth, you will probably feel the aspiration more for [p] than for [t] or [k]. This is because the point of occlusion, and therefore of release, is further forward, and therefore nearer the hand, in [p] than the other places of articulation. Voiceless plosives in other positions than at the beginning of stressed syllables are typically not aspirated in English: for example, the plosives in "spin," "sting," and "skin."

6-6.3 Nasal Plosion

Plosives are normally released through the oral cavity, either between the lips (for [p] and [b]) or over the tongue (for [t], [d], [k], and [g]). However, if a nasal immediately follows a plosive, the plosive can be released nasally. In the word "shipmate," for instance, the [p] is released nasally; that is, the velum is lowered *before* the lips are parted.

Nasal plosion occurs virtually always when the plosive is followed by a nasal having the same place of articulation. It occurs frequently even when the plosive and nasal have different places of articulation. So it will occur in such words as "shipmate" and "whatnot"; and it is also likely to occur in such words as "batman" and "workman."

There is no standard way to transcribe nasally released plosives, but in the event that it were necessary to indicate it, one could use a small raised N: "shipmate" [šɪp^{N}met].

6-6.4 Lateral Plosion

The plosives [t] and [d] are normally released by separation of the occlusion that has been made between the tongue blade and the alveolar ridge; air escapes over the top of the tongue. (Of course, release is nasal if the plosives are followed by a nasal.) If [t] or [d] is followed by [l], however, the release is lateral; that is, the laminoalveolar occlusion is maintained when the plosive is released. Instead of the blade of the tongue being moved, the sides of the tongue, which have formed a seal along the upper molar teeth in the production of the plosive, are pulled inward; the tongue is narrowed. The plosive release occurs laterally, over the sides of the tongue. This happens in such words or expressions as "little," "battle," and "good luck."

As with nasal plosion, there is no transcription symbol in general use to indicate the phenomenon. Indeed, there is usually little need to indicate it, since lateral plosion can be expected whenever [l] follows [t] or [d] immediately, unless there is a pause between the two sounds. Lateral plosion could, however, be indicated with a small raised L: [gʊdᴸlʌk].

6-6.5 Place of Articulation of [t] and [d]

The plosives classified as alveolars are typically articulated with the blade of the tongue against the alveolar ridge. However, in English the alveolars may be articulated farther forward under the influence of a dental sound or farther back under the influence of a back vowel, a palatal glide, or another consonant. For example, in the expression "both Tom and me," the [t] of "Tom" follows a dental sound, [θ]. The articulation of this [t] may be advanced to the point that it is dental. [t] and [d] may be retracted (articulated farther back) before [š] or [j] or other sound. Thus the /d/ of "dupe" may be a palatal sound in those dialects in which it is pronounced /djup/. Similarly the /d/ of "bad" may be alveopalatal in the expression "Bad shot."

One can expect similar, but less extensive, changes in the place of articulation of [n], [l], [s], and [z].

The diacritic for dental articulation is [̪]; dentals are symbolized [t̪], [d̪], [n̪], etc. The diacritic for fronting is [₊]; this symbol is usually not used with alveolars, since a fronted alveolar is a dental, for which there is a special symbol. However, it may be used with velars, for example. The symbol for retraction or backing is [̠], so a backed [t], as in "meatshop", would be transcribed [t̠].

6-6.6 Place of Articulation of /k/ and /g/

As we noted in Section 6-2, the place of articulation of /k/ and /g/ varies according to the surrounding sounds. These sounds may be fronted, so that they are palatovelar in place of articulation or even palatal, as in the examples given in Section 6-2. They may be backed so that they are postvelar or even uvular in place of articulation. A somewhat fronted /k/ may be represented as [k̟]; if it is fronted such that it is clearly palatal, it would be correctly represented by the symbol [c]. If it were backed somewhat, it could be represented as [k̠]; if backed considerably, the symbol [q] would be correct.

6-6.7 The Articulation of /h/ and Voiceless Segments

The consonant /h/ accommodates in tongue and jaw position to the vowel that follows it in the same syllable. For example, say "heat" and "hoot." Notice that while you are pronouncing the /h/, your mouth is already in the configuration of the following vowel. Except for the voicing and airflow, the accommodation is total. Indeed, [h] could be considered a voiceless vowel with heightened airflow. The symbol for voicelessness is [̥]; so the variant articulations of /h/ could be transcribed as voiceless vowels: "heat" [i̥it]; "hoot" [u̥ut]. This is of course not recommended as a normal transcription of /h/, but rather is done here as a means of showing the extent of the accommodation of articulatory features.

The diacritic for voicelessness introduced in the previous paragraph can be used in combination with any IPA symbol for a voiced sound to indicate **devoicing,** whether the devoicing be due to accommodation, foreign accent, articulation disorder, or other cause. For example, the first vowel in the word "suppose" is often voiceless because of the surrounding voiceless consonants. This pronunciation could be transcribed [sə̥poz]. Or, to take another example, a speaker of French might devoice the final /l/ of "people," as he would do in his native language. This /l/ could be indicated as [l̥]. In the realm of pathological speech, abnormal devoicing, as is common in stuttering, could be indicated with the same diacritic.

Table 3-1 gives a symbol to indicate unusual voicing of otherwise voiceless sounds; for example, the /h/ of "hit" in the phrase "she hit it" may be voiced because of the influence of the vowels that surround it.

6-6.8 Vowels

Vowels, like consonants, are affected by surrounding segments. For example, in English as in many other languages, vowels are lengthened before voiced consonants. The /i/ of "feed" is considerably longer, temporally, than the /i/ of "feet." This is likewise true of the other vowels and diphthongs. The /a͜i/ of "tide" is longer than the /a͜i/ of "tight." Indeed, as far as the diphthongs are concerned, in many dialects there are differences of quality as well as of length as a result of the voicing of the following segment. Compare the quality of the diphthong /a͜u/ in "mouse" as opposed to "browse," and in "about" as opposed to "proud."

A syllable ending in a vowel is known as an **open** syllable; one ending in a consonant is known as a **closed** syllable. Vowels tend to be longer in open syllables than in syllables closed with a voiceless consonant. Those in open syllables are very similar to those in syllables closed with a voiced consonant. The effects on quality as well as length compare with those outlined in the preceding paragraph. Compare "fee," "feed," and "feet"; "tie," "tide," and "tight."

Consonants exert an influence on vowels as well. Vowels preceding /l/ in the same syllable tend to have a schwa off-glide. Compare the /o/ of "hope" and "hole" or the /e/ of "bait" and "bail." R-sounds following vowels tend to combine with them and to modify them, and it was for this reason among others that it was suggested that such sequences be analyzed as diphthongs. For example, the vowel of the word "or" occurs only preceding /r/. While we may transcribe this vowel with the symbol /o/, it is not identical to the vowel in "boat."

6-6.9 Other Accommodations

An exhaustive cataloguing of all assimilations in English would triple in length of this book. Every sentence spoken provides a multitude of examples of accommodation. Once you are sensitive to this, you discover the almost endless variety of ways in which segments are modified by their context. Before looking at a few further examples, remember the point made in Chapter 1, that when words are said self-consciously, they are often said in an unnatural way, and assimilations are blocked. The following examples would occur in natural rapid speech.

In saying the word "pine-cone," most speakers pronounce the /n/ as a [ŋ]. But in saying "pine paneling" they probably pronounce that same /n/ as a [m]. In "that place" the /t/ of "that" becomes an unreleased [p˺]. The /d/ of "broadcast" is usually an unreleased [g˺]. The /n/ of "inferior" is often pronounced as a labiodental nasal ([ɱ]), as it is in "infer," although stress usually prevents this accommodation in a word such as "infamous" (stressed on the first syllable).

The word *sandwich* is often pronounced "sammich" ([sæməč]). The group of 3 consonants -ndw- is simplified initially by "dropping" the /d/ (actually by reordering the gestures such that the /d/ is amalgamated into the /n/); this leaves /n/ followed by /w/. The second step of reducing the number of segments also involves amalgamation: the change of /-nw-/ to /-m-/ involves combining the features of the initial sounds to give those of the resultant sound. /m/ is *nasal* like /n/; it is *voiced* like both /n/ and /w/; it is *bilabial* like /w/.

The pronunciation "punkin" ([pʌŋkən]) for *pumpkin* comes about similarly. In the standard pronunciation, a *bilabial* (the /mp/ complex) is followed by a velar (/k/). In the nonstandard pronunciation, there is accommodation of place of articulation: the entire sequence becomes velar. The old [m] has its *nasal* feature retained in the new [ŋ], and the old [p] is absorbed into the [k], a *voiceless plosive* like [p].

6-6.10 Accommodation and Transcription

When all of the fine details of accommodation are transcribed, the transcriptions become very much more complicated. Inevitably the student will want to know how much detail he/she is expected to transcribe.

While the matter will be clearer after the student has read Chapter 8, there are some things that can be said now. Different instructors will vary in how much detail they demand in students' transcriptions; that is up to them. But there is a more important issue here. We make these accommodations when we speak; and if we did not, our speech would sound very strange indeed. It is natural and normal to make adjustments in our pronunciation of segments in context. It is therefore essential for the student in a phonetics course to become sensitive to this aspect of speech production.

The student of linguistics should note that such modifications have implications for phonological models and for our understanding of historical sound changes.

The student of communication disorders or the second-language teacher must be sensitive to this aspect of speech production in order to be effective. It is not enough to note that someone "talks funny": you need to know *how* in order to do something about it. The foreigner learning English, the deaf speaker, and the individual with an articulation disorder can all be expected to produce speech that either lacks the expected accommodations or contains unexpected accommodations. A sensitivity to these phonetic events provides the teacher or therapist with the resources to analyze and correct these problem areas.

6-7 Primary and Secondary Articulations

In Section 6-2 the example was given of a [b] produced with rounded lips as opposed to spread or neutral lips. Your intuitive reaction to this example was probably to the effect that such a difference would be of minimal importance. Such aspects of articulation are fittingly called **secondary,** as opposed to the more obvious **primary** aspects. The **primary articulation** of a [b] is that it is a voiced bilabial plosive. Additional aspects of articulation, generally resulting from coarticulation, are **secondary articulation;** in this case, the [b] is rounded.

Secondary articulations have a set of labels ending in *-ize* (for the verbs) and *-ization* (for the nouns). We will examine these briefly in this section.

There are a few points to note with respect to secondary articulations. First, while they start out as accommodations, they may gain a life of their own in the sound system of a given language. So one cannot necessarily find a motivating factor in the phonetic environment when one examines the contemporary language. A second point, related to the first, is that while these are called *secondary* articulations, they are not necessarily *unimportant*. The correct secondary articulation in the correct place is necessary for natural-sounding speech, and languages may distinguish between words on the basis of their secondary articulations alone. And third, note that the terms we use for secondary articulations (those ending in *-ize* and *-ization*) are also used in the sense of a change in the primary place of articulation. Examples follow.

6-7.1 Labialization

If a segment is articulated with a rounding of the lips that is not part of its primary articulation, it is said to be **labialized.** For example, compare the [k]'s of the words "kid" and "quid." In the word "kid," the [k] is pronounced with the lips spread; in "quid" the lips are rounded during the articulation of the [k]. The latter [k] can be said to be *labialized*. It is transcribed [k^w]. In English, labialization as a secondary articulation is generally predictable: it occurs when segments are in the immediate environment of a rounded segment.

As a diachronic term, *labialization* means the change from a nonlabial primary place of articulation to a labial segment.

6-7.2 Palatalization

If a secondary articulation occurs in the region of the palate, the segment is said to be **palatalized.** The symbol for palatalization is [^{j}].[6] Russian is a language with much palatalization: it contrasts [p] with [p^j], for example.

As a diachronic term, palatalization refers to a change of the primary place of articulation from a nonpalatal to a palatal one (*palatal* taken broadly to include alveopalatal, postpalatal, etc.). For example, in the history of English, /sjʊgɚ/ became /šʊgɚ/; /sjʊr/ became /šʊr/.

6-7.3 Velarization

Velarization occurs when there is a secondary articulation in the velar region. In Chapter 5 you were introduced to the *velarized* ("dark") /l/, which occurs in the vicinity of high back (i.e., velar) vowels. The official IPA symbol for velarization is [~], but this can result in confusion, al-

[6] The official IPA symbol is a tail on the symbols: [ƫ, ᶁ, ᶊ, ᶎ], etc. However, the symbol [^{j}] is handier, because it can be added as a diacritic, is clearer when handwritten, and can be typed with an ordinary typewriter (by half-spacing up).

though it is commonly used for the velarized [l]: [ɫ]. A completely unambiguous symbol is [ᵚ]; the origin of this symbol is that [ɯ] is a high back unrounded vowel and therefore has the approximate tongue position of velarization.

As a diachronic term, velarization refers to a change of primary articulation to velar.

6-7.4 Nasalization

When a segment that is normally articulated with the velum raised is articulated with a lowered velum, it is said to be **nasalized.** In English, vowels and some consonants are nasalized in the environment of a nasal consonant. In "man," for example, the vowel is nasalized. Note that some languages (French, Polish, and many others) have vowels that are normally pronounced with a velic opening. These are often referred to as *nasal,* rather than *nasalized* vowels, as the nasal quality is contrastive in those languages.

6-7.5 Pharyngealization

Pharyngealization refers to a secondary articulation involving a constriction in the pharynx. The root of the tongue is retracted into the pharyngeal region.

A number of languages have distinctively pharyngealized sounds, and there is evidence that this occurs in English as well. For example, the lax vowels have pharyngeal narrowing as compared to the tense vowels (see Section 4-4.3), and while the term is not usually applied to such vowels, they could correctly be described as pharyngealized. All rhotic sounds are pharyngealized, at least to some extent. This results in nondistinctive pharyngealization as a coarticulatory effect. The [o] of "boat" does not have the same timbre as the [o] of "roar"; evidently the vowel is somewhat pharyngealized in the latter example.

The official IPA symbol for pharyngealization is the same as for velarization, namely [~], and for this reason it is ambiguous. A simpler symbol is [ᶛ], as in [oᶛ] for the pharyngealized [o] of "roar." The origin of this symbol is that [ɒ] is a low back vowel, implying some pharyngeal constriction, and used as a diacritic it represents pharyngealization.

6-7.6 Glottalization

The *glottis* is the space between the vocal folds. The vocal folds may be used in ways other than voicing, including articulation of a *glottal stop* and production of *ejectives* (see Chapter 5). These are all referred to as **glottalization.**

For example, in many dialects of English, a [t] before an unstressed [n], as in "fatten" and "button," is glottalized. What happens is that since the [t] and the [n] have the same place of articulation, and since the velic movement is slow, the speaker opens the velic port at the same time as making the alveolar occlusion. However, with the velum lowered, it is not possible to produce blockage in the mouth to create the stop necessary for the plosive [t], so that blockage is created at the glottis: the [t] is articulated with a simultaneous [ʔ]. This particular type of glottalization could be shown by indicating a **coarticulated stop** (i.e., two stops or plosives articulated simultaneously): "button," [bʌt͜ʔn].

6-7.7 Laryngealization

The use of the vocal folds to produce a different type of voicing, such as *murmur* or *breathy voice* (see Chapter 9), is known as **laryngealization.** Laryngealization in English is restricted to the emotional content of speech, but it is phonemic (contrastive) in some languages.

6-8 Noncontiguous Accommodation

In this chapter, nearly all the examples of accommodation that have been given so far have been of **contiguous** or **contact** accommodation. This simply means that the segment causing the accommodation and the segment affected by it are contiguous: that is, in contact or next to one another.

By contrast, **noncontiguous accommodation** (also called **distant accommodation** or **dilation**) involves accommodation in which the two segments are not in contact—there is at least one segment between them (this is true in an abstract sense only; we argue next that in fact there is no "skipping" of segments).

With consonants, distant assimilation is relatively rare. When it does occur in English, it is often judged to be an error or "slip of the tongue" rather than an acceptable variant form of the word. Such an error might be "No one answered the front door, sho ([šo]) she knocked at the side door," in which the /s/ of "so" becomes like the /š/ of "she." In this case the noncontiguous accommodation is *regressive* or *right-to-left.*

An example of a word that has been changed by noncontiguous accommodation is *orang-utang.* Originally borrowed from Malay as *orang-utan* ('man of the forest'), with /n/ as a final consonant, it has undergone modification such that the final sound is pronounced [ŋ] under the influence of the [ŋ] at the end of the first part of the word. In French, the word *jusque* ('up to', /žüskə/) is often pronounced [žüškə] in running speech. This is an example of progressive noncontiguous accommodation. In neither English nor French is the primary articulation of a consonant often changed by noncontiguous accommodation.

The notion that accommodation "skips" a segment or several is usually valid only in a superficial sense. If one looks at the details of the articulation, particularly in the nonsegmental way that was stressed earlier in this chapter, one usually finds that what is really happening is that the particular articulatory gesture is being carried over through the intervening segments, but that it does not change their character noticeably. For instance, in "sho she," most of the articulatory features of [š], such as the rounded lips, could be maintained through the [o] without adversely affecting its sound in context; so these features can hardly be said to "skip" a segment. In the "jusque," example given, the vowel [ü] is palatal, so one cannot say that the alveopalatal character of [ž] "skipped" the vowel and only reappeared for the following consonant. To cite another example, the word "united" is often pronounced as if spelled ⟨uninted⟩: [junãɪ̯ntəd]. An "intrusive" [n] seems to appear one segment away from the /n/ that is its apparent source. However, the nonsegmental view is that the velic opening is maintained until the /t/. The nasality does not "skip" the vowel, but is maintained throughout. Since nasality is not distinctive in English vowels, however, we do not notice it; all we notice, if anything, is the seemingly intrusive [n]. In subsequent examples, direct your attention toward thinking of how the "noncontiguous" accommodation might be explained in terms of some articulatory feature that is maintained throughout the intervening segments rather than is skipped over.

6-8.1 METAPHONY

Noncontiguous accommodation of consonants is relatively rare, but noncontiguous accommodation of vowels is far more common, although not in Modern English. Any form of noncontiguous vowel accommodation is known as **metaphony;** it may also be called **vocalic dilation** or **vocalic noncontiguous accommodation** or another such compound term. We will examine several specialized forms of metaphony that have their own names. *Metaphony* is the general cover-term.

Since metaphony occurs rarely, if ever, in Modern English, we will examine an example from French. Here are the forms of the present tense of the French verb *laisser,* 'to let, to leave, to permit':

ENGLISH	FRENCH	PRONUNCIATION
I let	(je) laisse	[lɛs]
you (sing) let	(tu) laisses	[lɛs]
he lets	(il) laisse	[lɛs]
we let	(nous) laissons	[lɛsɔ̃]
you (pl) let	**(vous) laissez**	[lese]
they let	(ils) laissent	[lɛs]

Note that the vowel of the verb stem (*laiss-*) is pronounced the same in all forms except the second person plural (*laissez*). All the other forms have either an unpronounced suffix or a suffix containing the vowel [ɔ̃]. However, the second person plural has a suffix containing the vowel [e], very close in pronunciation to the vowel of the stem, [ɛ]. So the [e] modifies the pronunciation of the stem vowel in this case, changing it to [e].

Such an example shows almost random effects of this assimilatory phenomenon; it cannot be said that metaphony is an active, productive process in French, since one has to search quite hard to find a single example. However, in some languages, metaphonic processes are common and widespread. A couple of these that deserve special mention are *umlaut* and *vowel harmony.*

6-8.2 UMLAUT

Umlaut is a form of regressive metaphony specific to the Germanic family of languages, which includes German, English, Swedish, Dutch, and others.[7] Umlaut is a productive process in many Germanic languages, and its effects in several modern languages are widespread. In Modern English, by contrast, it is no longer productive, as it was in Old English. However, its effects are still felt in many umlauted forms retained as linguistic fossils; from the modern viewpoint, these may be considered simply "irregular." The most common such forms in English are certain plurals of nouns, such as *goose/geese*.

Essentially umlaut caused (or causes, in other Germanic languages) the back vowel in the stem or root of a word to become a front vowel when a suffix was added that contained either a front vowel or a palatal glide. Let us look at the example of the word *goose*. In Old English the word was /go:s/. Let us say that the plural suffix was [i].[8] Thus the forms were /go:s/ /go:si/. The process of umlaut fronted the root vowel, giving /go:s/ /gö:si/.

That is all there is to umlaut, but in order to see how it gives us the Modern English forms, we must look at subsequent sound changes. Note that these subsequent sound changes are *not* directly umlaut. The plural /gö:si/ became /gö:sə/ and then simply /gö:s/ as unstressed suffixes decayed and disappeared. The front rounded vowel /ö/ became unrounded to /e/ during the Middle English period; Modern English has no front rounded vowels (in examining this change, note that /o/, /ö/, and /e/ all have the same height; the change from /o/ to /ö/ involves only fronting, and the change from /ö/ to /e/ involves only unrounding). This gives us a singular /go:s/ and a plural /ge:s/. By the massive sound change known as the Great English Vowel Shift, all long vowels were raised (i.e., took on a higher place of articulation: lower-mid to upper-mid; upper-mid to high, etc.); those that could not be raised were diphthongized. By this change, /go:s/ became /gus/ and /ge:s/ became /gis/. These are essentially the modern forms. To recapitulate:

SINGULAR	PLURAL	REASON
go:s	go:si	pre-umlaut forms
go:s	gö:si	UMLAUT
go:s	gö:sə	suffix weakening
go:s	gö:s	suffix disappearance
go:s	ge:s	unrounding of front vowels
gus	gis	Great English Vowel Shift: modern forms

As an example with diphthongs, *mouse/mice* developed essentially as follows:

SINGULAR	PLURAL	REASON
mu:s	mu:si	pre-umlaut forms
mu:s	mü:si	UMLAUT
mu:s	mü:sə	suffix weakening
mu:s	mü:s	suffix disappearance
mu:s	mi:s	unrounding of front vowels
mau̯s	mai̯s	Great English Vowel Shift: modern forms

Umlaut is no longer a productive process in English—that is, we do not pluralize new words this way—but it has left its mark on many words. Note, for example, these pairs: *foot/feet, louse/lice, brother/brethren* (of course, there is also the non-umlauted *brothers*), *old/elder* (again, there is the non-umlauted *older*).

In German, umlaut is still an active process, forming a large part of the plural forms of nouns and affecting the vowels in verbs, adjectives, and adverbs.

6-8.3 Vowel Harmony

Vowel harmony is a process unknown in English, but it is an interesting example of the lengths to which accommodation can go. In a language having vowel harmony, the vowels in a phonological unit must all be of the same type. What constitutes a phonological unit depends upon the particular language: it might be the word, the verb or noun phrase, the clause, or some other unit. What constitutes the "same type" of vowel is also defined by the particular language. In one language the vowels in the unit might have to be either all high or all low. In another language they might have to be all front or all back; all rounded or all unrounded; all tense or all lax; etc.

A particular vowel determines the type of vowel of all others in the same phonological unit. If that vowel is high, all the others will be high. If

[7] The word *umlaut* can also refer to the accent mark, ¨, used in the spelling of German and some other languages. As the term is used here, however, it is not the diacritic, but the *process*, that is referred to. By the way, the word *umlaut* is a German word; *Laut* means 'sound' in German, and the prefix *um* suggests a modification.

[8] The precise form of the original plural ending is not known, and must be reconstructed, which is known as a *proto* form. It is not our purpose to discuss the morphology of proto-Germanic; so we are assuming the plural ending was simply /i/. The argument is not affected by this simplification.

it is low, all the others will be low. Generally, then, the morphemes of the language have two forms, one with each of the two types of vowel.

Turkish is a language having vowel harmony. In Turkish, the plural ending on nouns is either *-ler* or *-lar*. Examine the following words to see if you can determine the rule that governs which plural ending is used (the words are given in their usual script, not in the IPA, but you can assume approximately IPA values for the vowels):

TURKISH SINGULAR	ENGLISH SINGULAR	TURKISH PLURAL	ENGLISH PLURAL
diş	'tooth'	dişler	'teeth'
çocuk	'child'	çocuklar	'children'
asker	'soldier'	askerler	'soldiers'
kedi	'cat'	kediler	'cats'
masa	'table'	masalar	'tables'
gece	'night'	geceler	'nights'
baba	'father'	babalar	'fathers'
kuş	'bird'	kuşlar	'birds'

As you can see from these examples, Turkish adds *-ler* in the plural if the noun stem contains front vowels, and adds *-lar* in the plural if the noun stem contains back vowels.

In Akan, a West African language, the verb, the future tense marker (equivalent to English *will*), the object (English *it, him, her, them, us, you*), and the subject (English *I, we, you, he, she, they*) are considered together as one unit. Depending upon the vowel of the verb, all these words must contain a tense vowel or all must contain a lax vowel. Each word, except the verb, has two forms: one that goes with verbs having a tense vowel and one that goes with verbs having a lax vowel. In this language the equivalent of *you* is /wʊ/ (lax) or /wu/ (tense), and the equivalent of *I* is /mɪ/ (lax) or /mi/ (tense), and so on.

6-9 Stress and Accommodation

Accommodation happens most in speech that is rapid and casual. The slower the speech, and the more formal or careful it is, the less the various types of accommodation occur. Indeed, this is why it is difficult to teach the phenomenon of accommodation to students of phonetics: When the professor or the textbook gives an example, such as the "phone booth" example given a number of times in this chapter, the students very often "pronounce" it silently to themselves. But this "pronouncing" is a careful, precise pronunciation: a *citation* form. Being a careful, slow citation form, it does not contain the accommodation the professor or textbook claims is present. At first the students may conclude that their instructor is wrong; finally, I hope, they will recognize that the absence of an assimilatory process in careful speech does not imply its absence in casual speech.[9]

Just as the speed of speech and its formality plays a role in the accommodations made, so too does the related phenomenon of *stress*. Stress will be discussed in Chapter 7, along with *emphasis* and *rate*. The effects of stress and other suprasegmentals upon accommodation will be discussed at that time. At this point, it will suffice to point out that the greater the stress on a syllable, the greater the emphasis on a word, the slower the rate of speech, or the greater the formality of the speech, the less the accommodation which occurs.

6-10 Sandhi

Sandhi is a term that originally meant *accommodation* or *assimilation* but that has now taken on a special meaning. *Sandhi* is the Sanskrit word for 'juncture,'[10] and its use in this context dates from the time of the ancient grammar of Sanskrit written by Pānini. As the term is used by some, a distinction is made between *internal sandhi* and *external sandhi*. *Internal* and *external* refer to position with respect to words, so **internal sandhi** simply means accommodation within words, what we have been calling *accommodation* throughout this discussion. **External sandhi** means accommodations that occur across word boundaries; that is, those that might affect the final segment(s) of one word and/or the initial seg-

[9] Of course, the remarks made in Chapters 1 and 2 concerning dialect apply here: a student may be completely correct in believing that the example cited does not occur in his/her dialect.

[10] Sanskrit /sɑn/ 'together'; /dʰə/ 'to put, to hold'; /i/ *noun ending*. Hence, 'juncture.'

ment(s) of the following word because of the combination of sounds that occurs when these words are in sequence. In modern terminology, the term *sandhi* unmodified refers to external sandhi, that which occurs across word boundaries.

Sandhi certainly exists in English, but not in so widespread a way as in some languages. In French, a sandhi phenomenon called **liaison** occurs. Many words in French have lost their final consonant through historical change, but this "lost" consonant is pronounced when the word is followed within the same phrase by a word starting with a vowel. The specifics are relatively complex and vary with the individual word, the dialect, and the speaker, but two simple examples will illustrate the process. The French plural article meaning 'the' is *les*. It is pronounced [lɛ], except when followed by a word beginning with a vowel, when it is pronounced [lez] (actually the [z] is attached to the beginning of the following word). Thus the French equivalent of 'the courses' is *les cours* ([lɛ kuʀ]), but that of 'the animals' is *les animaux* ([lezanimo]). The word meaning 'tall' in the masculine is *grand*, pronounced [gʀɑ̃]; but the final consonant is pronounced (as a [t], not as a [d]) if preceding a word starting with a vowel. Thus, 'tall professor' is *grand professeur* [gʀɑ̃ pʀɔfɛsɔ̈ʀ], but 'tall man' is *grand homme* [gʀɑ̃tɔm]. (The ⟨h⟩ in *homme* is not pronounced, so this word begins with a vowel.) What is important to note from these examples is not the details of French, but rather the fact that the result of sandhi is that a given word is pronounced differently in different contexts; there may be several pronunciations of the "same" word.

Let us look at a few English examples. The word "you" is often pronounced [jə] in unstressed positions, and in these positions it often combines with a preceding verb, as in "did you" [dɪǰə]. The [d] and the [j] combine to give [ǰ] by processes that should be familiar to you at this point in the chapter. Other similar examples are "could you," "would you," "had you," and, with a different consonant, "miss you," as mentioned earlier. Similarly, "wanna" for "want to," "gonna" for "going to," "shoulda" for "should have," etc.

The forms often called *contractions* result from sandhi as well. In English some of these are optional and depend upon the formality of the speaking situation (the register): "I'll" for *I will*, "won't" for *will not*, "he's" for *he has* and *he is*, "ain't" for *am not*.[11]

The preceding examples of liaison in French are not really exotic; English has essentially the same phenomenon, some dialects to a greater degree than others. For example, in all dialects the indefinite article has a form determined by whether the following word begins with a vowel: "*a* car"/"*an* apple." Since, historically, *a*/*an* is just an unstressed form of the word *one*, you can see that the argument for liaison where a "lost" final consonant "reappears" before a vowel is a valid one, diachronically at least. That is, the [n] of "an" is not *inserted;* rather, in "a" it is *dropped*. In some dialects the pronunciation of "the" changes depending upon the first sound of the following word: "th<u>e</u> car" ([ðə]), "th<u>e</u> apple" ([ði]). In the latter case, a [j] is likely to appear between the vowels to make the transition.

In certain nonrhotic ("r-less") dialects there is another kind of liaison. Word-final [r] or [ɚ] is not present unless the next word begins with a vowel. For example, "the ca<u>r</u> came" /ðə kɑ kem/ but "the ca<u>r</u> is" /ðə kɑrɪz/.

In other nonrhotic dialects a similar, related phenomenon occurs. The details are the same as those just described, except that in addition to inserting a [r] where it is justified etymologically (i.e., where there is an ⟨r⟩ in the spelling), this dialect also inserts a [r] between any word that ends in a [ə] and any word that begins with a vowel. Thus, "father" is pronounced [fɑðə], but "fathe<u>r</u> is" has a [r]. But so does "Canader is" ("Canada is") and "ideer is" ("idea is"). This is a sandhi phenomenon as well.

Sandhi can go quite far in some dialects. The following story has been told of a number of different places. Two residents meet on the street at about noon. The first asks the second [ǰit?]. The

[11] Originally *ain't* was a perfectly respectable contraction for *am not*. Indeed, *I ain't* has far more justification than *I aren't*, which one hears. However, it spread to other verb forms such as *you ain't* and *he ain't*. This gave *ain't* a bad name, and grammarians declared it "incorrect" even in the form where it is justified. Pity.

second replies [n̩čεt]. They have had a conversation about lunch.[12]

6-10.1 Sandhi and the Language Learner

Sandhi has implications for the individual learning a new language. Simply put, if the words of the language have different phonetic forms, particularly when the writing system represents them as the same, it can confuse the language learner, since he may not recognize what he hears as the same word as that given in a citation form.

An obvious example in English is "Did you go?" This is a very simple sentence, and a beginner in English as a second language would very likely understand it. However, his teacher has probably been careful to pronounce it very precisely, and the student is completely mystified when he hears ordinary people say [dɪǰəgo] or just [ǰəgo]. Some speakers may consider this pronunciation "bad," but people say it, and it is doing no favor to the foreign language learner to hide from him the sandhi phenomena that occur in the speech of ordinary people. Similarly, we are taught (and we teach foreign learners) that "and" is pronounced [ænd], but I suggest that you try pronouncing it that precisely when you order "ham and eggs" in a restaurant, and see what kind of a look you get. Recall the example given in Chapter 1 of the pronunciation of the word "to": in context, it is often pronounced [tə] or simply [t]. Once again, it cannot be stressed enough that if speech is to sound natural, the speaker must take the "shortcuts" other speakers take, neither more nor less, and the foreign learner must not be the battleground on which we fight issues of what is the "right" way to pronounce the language.

Note that the native speaker of a language is generally unaware of sandhi, unaware that he/she has more than one pronunciation for a given word. A teacher of English as a second language said her students complained that in a sentence such as

You said you'd do it if you could.

they found it impossible to hear the " 'd" of "you'd"; how were they supposed to know whether the speaker said "would" or not? If you compare these two sentences:

You said you'd do it if you could.
You said you do it when you can.

you will see that there is *no* difference between "you'd do it" and "you do it" because of the sandhi phenomenon of single release of two plosives. The native speaker of English *thinks* he hears the " 'd" in the first sentence, but that is because he knows the rules of grammar (in the unconscious sense used in Chapter 2). Since the verb at the end of the sentence (*could*) is in the conditional, there must be a *would.* Another way to put this is that the " 'd" must be there, because *"You said you do it if you could" is an ungrammatical sentence. The foreign learner doesn't necessarily know that, so he doesn't "hear" the " 'd" that the native speaker "hears." In fact, of course, neither hears it, since it is not pronounced separately from the following [d]. See also Section 10-11.4.

6-11 Other Combinatory Phenomena

This chapter has dealt primarily with accommodation, the most pervasive and therefore the most important aspect of speech dynamics, and how it occurs as segments combine to form words, phrases, and sentences. In this section we will briefly consider a number of other phenomena that occur in running speech or that occur diachronically and thus change the language permanently.

6-11.1 Elision

When a segment or several segments are left out of a word when it is pronounced, we say that the sounds have been **elided. Elision** may occur diachronically and alter the word forever; it may have occurred in some dialects; or it may occur synchronically as a function of the speed and formality of speech.

An example of permanent historical change is the words *vehicle* and *article,* which originally had a vowel before the final [l]. This vowel shows up in the related words *vehicular* and *articulate* but has been *elided* in the forms *vehicle* and *article.*

[12] I will put the translation down here in the hope that you will try to work out what they said before looking for the answer. The first asks, "Did you eat?" and the second replies, "Not yet."

As an example of dialectal differences in elision, take the words *inte̸resting* and *secreta̸ry*. In England both words contain three syllables; the marked vowel is not pronounced. In the United States both words contain four syllables.[13] The marked vowels have been elided in British English. In American English it is not so much that these vowels were not elided, but rather that the elided vowels were put back again as spelling pronunciations under the influence of Noah Webster, as noted in Chapter 2.

An example of synchronic processes is the word *po̸lice*, which may be pronounced [plis] in rapid speech, eliding the first vowel, and the word *pho̸netics*, often quickly pronounced as [fnɛɾəks], eliding the first vowel.

6-11.2 Haplology

Haplology is like elision in that it involves leaving something out, usually as a diachronic change. In the case of haplology, one of two identical or similar syllables, situated in sequence, is elided. For example, the adverb *probably* is not pronounced "probable-ly"; this is haplology at work. The term for the scientific study of mammals is *mammalogy* and not *mammalology*. The term *morphophonemic*, used in Chapter 3, has undergone haplology and exists also in the form *morphonemic*. In this latter case, both haplologized and non-haplologized forms exist, the latter being the preferred form.

6-11.3 Epenthesis

Epenthesis is the insertion of a sound, without etymological justification (i.e., the sound was not there before), generally to break up consonant clusters[14] or to provide a transition between sounds. Epenthesis may be totally idiosyncratic or dialectal, or it may result in a permanent change in a word (i.e., it may become acceptable). Epenthesis is also common among foreign language learners who find certain combinations of sounds in another language difficult to pronounce; similarly it may happen in children as they learn their native tongue or in individuals with a certain speech dysfunction.

An example of idiosyncratic epenthesis is that some individuals insert an epenthetic vowel into such words as "film" ([fɪləm]) and "athlete" ([æθəlit]).

An example of dialectal epenthesis is that dialect of English that inserts a [r] between any word ending in a vowel and any word beginning with a vowel. In this case, one may say that an epenthetic [r] is separating the vowels.

The foreign speaker may make many epentheses, depending upon the phonetic structure of his native language and that of his target language. For example, while Old English had such clusters as [kn-] and [gn-] at the beginnings of words (this spelling is still retained in such words as *knight*, *knife*, *gnaw*, and *gnat*), Modern English does not. So the English speaker learning German, a language having these clusters, is likely to separate the consonants of the cluster with an epenthetic vowel. German *Knecht* 'servant' should be pronounced [knɛçt], but is likely to be pronounced [kən . . .] by the English speaker. Speakers of foreign languages learning English can be expected to insert epenthetic vowels to break up unfamiliar consonant clusters, or epenthetic consonants to break up unfamiliar vowel sequences. (However, vowels and glides are more often epenthetic segments than are consonants.) What is originally an epenthetic segment may become permanent, particularly in the case of words borrowed from foreign languages. For example, French borrowed the English word *knife* in Middle English times, when the initial [kn] cluster was pronounced and the vowel was [i], not the modern [ai̯]. The modern French word meaning 'pocket knife' or 'penknife' is *canif*, pronounced [kanif], the [a] originally being epenthetic.

The term *epenthesis* is also used to describe the transitional sounds that occur as native speakers correctly pronounce their own language. In English, vowels juxtaposed in adjacent syllables are usually separated by (or, perhaps more correctly, the transition from one to the other is made by) a glide: [j] following a front vowel and [w] following a back vowel. For example, the two vowels of "being" have a [j] between them; the two vowels of "doing" have a [w] between them. Such

[13] In Canada, ever schizophrenic in linguistic matters, *interesting* is pronounced as in England, *secretary* as in the United States.

[14] A **cluster** is a group of consonants together in the same syllable (word-initial clusters are often called *blends* by reading teachers).

sounds, too, may be called epenthetic or **transitional.** These transitional sounds might well be described as "making the word easier to say." But in fact they are as much a result of arbitrary rule as of physiological necessity. Many other languages have such sequences with no (or far less of an) intervening glide.

6-11.4 Metathesis

Metathesis or **inversion** is said to occur when two adjacent segments are reversed, either as an error, a historical change, or a dialect feature. For example, in some English dialects the word *ask* is pronounced [æks].[15] Examples of historical metatheses abound; often *both* forms of a word exist either in different languages or in different dialects. For example, compare the names *Roland(o)* and *Orlando;* compare Italian *formaggio* ('cheese') with French *fromage;* compare English *burn* with German *brenn(en);* compare English *through* and *thorough* with German *durch.*

While metathesis is traditionally explained as merely the exchange of two segments, it is hoped that your understanding of speech dynamics is such that you question this simple view, understanding that segments overlap articulatorily. When a rhotic sound (any type of r) is next to a vowel, for example, there is a great deal of overlap in their articulation. One cannot say, in articulatory terms, that the [r] precedes or follows the vowel in any absolute way. They are blended together. Thus metathesis is not a historical game of leapfrog with speech segments, but rather a slight or a gradual reordering of overlapping motor commands, such that the perception of which "segment" is first changes.

6-11.5 Dissimilation

Languages sometimes change in such a way that the best explanation of the change is that similar sounds **dissimilate,** or become less alike. The change may affect identical sounds or similar sounds. No very persuasive theoretical explanation of dissimilation has been advanced, but the historical phenomena remain; in the absence of an explanation, a label is always useful and gives the appearance of knowledge. A few examples will suffice to illustrate the process.

French *marbre* gave English *marble.* French *pourpre* gave English *purple.* In both cases one of two r-sounds (two identical sounds in the same word) *dissimilated* to [l], a similar sound. Another example is the French word *colonel,* in which both ⟨l⟩'s are pronounced as [l]. In the borrowed English word, one [l] has dissimilated to [ɚ] (and the second vowel has been elided). To take another example, the old Germanic form of the word 'heaven' was *himmen;* this was its form in Old English. Pay attention to the second and third consonant sounds which are underscored above. Note that these are two similar sounds, both nasals. The modern English is *heaven,* in which the second consonant has dissimilated to [v] (still a voiced labial sound). Modern German is *Himmel,* in which the third consonant has dissimilated to [l] (still a voiced alveolar).

Notice that in these examples, dissimilation affects noncontiguous segments. It is conceivable that examples of contact dissimilation could be found.

Convincing theoretical accounts of dissimilation are lacking; there is difficulty in determining what force would motivate it. By contrast, the motivation for accommodation is obvious. One plausible explanation is that dissimilation does not, in fact, exist; only accommodation does, and apparent examples of dissimilation result from accommodation. To cite the *heaven* example, it is conceivable that a form such as *hivel* existed; one or other of the two consonants in question changed to a nasal by a perfectly ordinary historical sound change, and then the other assimilated to it. However, the changes did not affect all dialects, and therefore parallel forms existed. Because of the paucity of written records, we may be able to attest (that is, have a definitive written record of) only one of several forms. For example, perhaps Old English *himmen* is not the ancestor of Modern English *heaven.* Perhaps in some other dialect of Old English from which we have no

[15] In this case it is interesting to note that the standard form "ask" is the one that has been metathesized; the Old English word was *axian* (where *-ian* was a verb suffix). When one criticizes the "mistakes" speakers of certain dialects make, it is well to check the facts about who is "right." In this case, naturally, "ask" is the correct modern form, but "aks" has a historical claim to being "correct."

written records, the form *hivven* existed and is the ancestor of Modern English *heaven*. It just happens that in the dialect of which we have records, the form *himmen* came about by accommodation.

6-12 Speech Errors

In the previous section we examined a number of combinatory phenomena not directly related to accommodation. One of the other things that happens when sounds go together to make up words, sentences, and, most importantly, discourse, is that people make speech errors. Such errors have been of academic interest for at least a century; Freudians believe that errors may reveal subconscious wishes, fears, etc. Modern speech researchers are likewise interested in spontaneous errors in running speech, not for their psychopathological content but for what they tell us about the process of speech planning.

Speech errors, examined for their phonetic content, fall into a number of types. These include **exchanges, elisions, insertions, perseverations,** and **iterations,** not all of equal frequency. **Exchanges** involve the switching of segments, as in the classic **Spoonerisms** (discussed next). **Elisions** involve the dropping of segments, **insertions** the insertion of segments (usually related to exchanges). **Perseveration** involves the prolongation of the articulation of a given segment, and **iteration** its repetition. Perseveration and iteration are found in the speech of stutterers, but they are also found quite normally in speech errors of all individuals.

Other types of errors exist, too. These include the substitution of whole words or the blending of two words, such as when a person is undecided between saying "pretty" and "beautiful" and says instead "prettiful." While interesting for what they show about morphological processing, these errors are not strictly phonetic in nature and will not therefore enter into the present discussion.

6-12.1 Spoonerisms

Spoonerisms are exchange errors that result in a sentence having a new meaning that is amusing or cute. Actually, these are extremely unlikely to arise naturally as errors, for a couple of reasons. First of all, the chances that an exchange error will happen to result in a pithy new sentence, which makes sense and is witty into the bargain, are vanishingly slim. Second, when one makes an exchange error, one generally stops short; one does not go on to complete the sentence.

However it may be, the Reverend William A. Spooner, preacher and lecturer at Oxford University, became renowned for making this type of error. It is likely that he did not make many of the lapses that are attributed to him; however, they are amusing, and for that reason a few will be repeated here. The Reverend Spooner (who lectured in History) is reported to have said to a lazy student with whom he was disgusted, "You have hissed my Mystery classes; you have tasted the whole worm." In a sermon he is supposed to have called God "a shoving leopard." He had a predilection for riding around the campus on "a well-boiled icicle." Apparently his affliction was catching (such is the nature of reputations); an usher at one of his church services is reported to have said to a parishioner seating herself at a reserved place, "Mardon me, padam, but this pie is occupewed; may I sew you to your sheet?"

6-12.2 Real Speech Errors

As you might imagine, the reality of speech errors is far less witty. However, they are very interesting in their own right. They are studied for what they reveal about the nature of motor planning in speech and the nature of linguistic units in speech planning.

When a process is not observable, but a scientist wishes to understand it, what it is observed to do when it breaks down can tell the scientist a lot about how it operates normally. Let us take a simple analogy from everyday experience. Imagine that you wished to know how paper is put on toilet rolls; specifically, you want to know whether the paper is produced in 4-inch wide form and rolled onto 4-inch cardboard tubes, or whether it is produced in wide sheets, rolled onto long tubes, and *then* cut into the width in which you buy it. Of course, the obvious thing to do is to visit a paper factory and observe, but let us imagine that, like the speech and language centers of the brain, toilet paper production cannot be observed directly. One way of getting information, then, is to see what goes wrong in its production. You can look at a million perfectly formed rolls of tissue without learning anything more than by looking at one. However, by examining one deformed roll, you can learn a lot. If you find one roll whose end is at an angle rather than square, you know that the paper is rolled first in wide sheets, and then cut. You know this because it would be virtually impossible to form the paper in a long, narrow sheet of varying width such that, when rolled up, it would have a perfectly angled end. The angled end on a tissue roll is a mistake from the manufacturer's viewpoint, but to the observer it reveals something about the process of the manufacture. Speech errors do the same for an understanding of the process of speech production.

Essentially, there are two aims to research into speech errors. One is to determine the nature of the linguistic units in the sound systems of language, and the other is to examine the nature of the motor planning process in speech: we wish to obtain insight into both speech and language. While it is beyond our scope to examine these issues in detail, a brief outline may prove useful.

With respect to the linguistic units, recall that Chapter 2 introduced the notion of the *phoneme*, which will be examined in greater detail in Chapter 8. The phoneme is only one unit that has been proposed as the basic unit of sound systems. There is much controversy among phonologists and psycholinguists as to the nature of the units in phonological systems. Speech errors may serve as evidence. For example, if speech errors of the exchange type always involved only the phonemes proposed in a given theory, that would constitute evidence in favor of the theory (although not absolute proof, of course). For instance, are the affricates [č] and [ǰ] single phonemes in English, or are they simply the juxtaposition of their component parts [t] and [š], [d] and [ž]? If spontaneous speech errors involve exchanges of one component and not the other, it is apparent that the two parts are not as intimately related as they would be if speech errors always showed the whole affricate being exchanged.

On the other hand, some speech researchers are interested in *performance* models of speech; in other words, what events take place as a person speaks (performs the act of speaking). The issues here conclude the steps in planning for speech (planning at a cerebral and motor level), and the phonological units involved.

6-13 Accommodation and the Teaching of Speech Sounds

We have already stressed the importance of accommodation and other combinatory phenomena to normal-sounding speech. But they can also play a role in the teaching or correcting of speech sounds, as by the foreign language teacher or speech therapist.

From a study of accommodation you have come to understand that the transitions between different sounds make some combinations easier to articulate than others. This means that a given sound will be easier to pronounce in some environments than others, due to some articulatory similarity between that sound and the sounds in the environment. This similarity may be one of voicing, manner of articulation, place of articulation, or some other feature of the articulation. Note that while a different terminology is used in classifying vowels and consonants, articulatory similarities may remain. For example, front vowels are articulated with the tongue arched under the palate and thus share tongue position with palatal consonants. Back vowels are articulated with the tongue arched under the velum and thus share tongue position with velar consonants.

A particular target sound will be easier to produce in certain environments than others; by designing the environment, one can render a given sound easier to pronounce. Designing the appropriate environment is a matter of putting general knowledge of speech articulation to work, as in the following examples.

On one occasion I was teaching English to speakers of French and was helping a student who was having difficulty pronouncing /θ/ and /ð/, a common problem for learners of English. The student was quite frustrated, trying to pronounce "there" and always substituting a /d/ for the /ð/. I suggested that he try first with words like "brother" and "father" rather than with words like "there" and "then." The student succeeded in pronouncing these words after a few tries, and while no miracle was performed, he did approach the subsequent pronunciation exercises with heightened optimism as a result of his success. Why did this work? Fricatives like /θ/ and /ð/ are continuant sounds; that is, there is no interruption to airflow in their production. They "flow" more easily in intervocalic position. Another clue to this is the fact that in the history of many languages, intervocalic plosives have turned into fricatives, suggesting that fricatives are easier to pronounce in this environment.

To take another example, if an individual were having difficulty pronouncing /s/ or /z/ sounds, what contexts would provide the greatest ease of pronunciation? Would there be any difference in difficulty, for example, in pronouncing the /z/ in "easy" and "ozone"? In the word "easy," the /z/ is surrounded by high front vowels having a similar tongue placement to the /z/. The vowels surrounding the /z/ in "ozone" have a very different tongue position from the /z/ itself, and this disparity complicates the articulation of the difficult consonant.

Would there likely be any difference in the difficulty of pronouncing the /s/ in the words "beets" and "beaks"? Again, notice the similarity of tongue position between /t/ and /s/ (indeed, /t͜s/ is a common affricate in many languages), and the dissimilarity of tongue position between /k/ and /s/. For an individual having difficulty pronouncing /s/, "beats" would probably be easier to say.

In general, when compiling lists of practice words for those with specific articulation problems (or difficulties resulting from a difference between their native language and the one they are learning), you may generate earlier success and reduce frustrating and self-defeating failure by carefully selecting words that place the difficult sound in helpful environments. Exercises may then be graded in difficulty up to the most troublesome environments for the target sound. In certain cases, of course, there is no getting around a complex group of consonants.

Summary

Speech is a dynamic, not a static phenomenon. The target articulatory positions are usually not fully attained in connected speech. Sounds are modified therefore by their phonetic **environment.**

To the extent that sounds are modified so as to become like those sounds in the immediate environment, the phenomenon is known as **accommodation,** which may be roughly subdivided into **assimilation,** the term for accommodations involving large changes that cross phonemic boundaries, and **coarticulation,** the term for smaller changes of a subphonemic nature.

Accommodation results in changes in the articulatory features of segments, changes that range from voicing to place of articulation to manner of articulation to the addition of **secondary articulations.**

Accommodation may be due to physiological constraints or may be due to nonconstrained rule-governed adjustments.

A view of speech simply as a string of phonemes, like a string of beads, misses the point of the interactive nature of sequenced speech sounds; oftentimes a nonsegmental view of speech is more useful in determining what processes are at work. However, the term **segment** is still a useful one.

Accommodation may be **partial** or **total** in its effect. It may be **progressive, regressive,** or **double** in direction. It may be a **synchronic** phenomenon, that is, contemporary and productive, or it may be **diachronic,** having left certain changes in the contemporary language through historical change. It may affect **contiguous** or **noncontiguous** segments (although many examples of "noncontiguous" accommodation are in fact contiguous ones).

Some examples in English of variant forms of segments include nonrelease of plosives, aspiration of plosives, nasal and lateral release of plosives, place of articulation of alveolar and velar consonants, length and quality of vowels.

Secondary articulations include **labialization, palatalization, velarization, nasalization, pharyngealization,** and **laryngealization.** Secondary articulations may become primary over time.

Noncontiguous accommodation is also known as **dilation.** Consonantal dilation is relatively uncommon. Vocalic dilation is more common; it is called **metaphony.** Two forms of metaphony are **umlaut** and **vowel harmony.** Umlaut is the name given to a fronting of stem vowels under the influence of the suffix in Germanic languages.

Accommodation is reduced by increased **stress** and by more formal register.

Sandhi is the term used to mean accommodation and other combinatory phenomena crossing word boundaries. **Contractions** and **liaison** are two examples of sandhi.

Other combinatory phenomena include **elision, haplology, epenthesis, metathesis, dissimilation,** and **speech errors.** The latter are studied for their contribution to our understanding of speech production.

Knowledge of accommodation and combinatory processes can be useful in teaching speech sounds.

Vocabulary

accommodation
anticipatory
assimilation
closed
cluster
coarticulated stop
coarticulation
context
contiguous
diachronic
dilation
dissimilate, dissimilation
distant accommodation
double accommodation
elision, elide
emphasis
environment
epenthesis
exchange
haplology
insertion
inversion
iteration
labialization, labialize
laryngealization
left-to-right
liaison
metaphony
metathesis
nasalization, nasalize
noncontiguous accommodation
open
palatalization, palatalize
partial
perseveration
pharyngealization
phonetic environment
primary articulation
progressive
rate
regressive
right-to-left
sandhi
secondary articulations
speech errors
Spoonerism
stress
synchronic
total
transitional
umlaut
velarization, velarize
vocalic dilation
vocalic noncontiguous accommodation
vowel harmony

Questions

1. Give some examples of assimilations from casual speech.
2. Have you noticed any dialect differences in assimilations? If so, give some examples.
3. Many of us find it difficult to hear the modifications to speech sounds brought about by assimilation, and often we are even disbelieving of the assimilatory changes in our own speech. Why do you think that this is so?
4. What is the difference between a labial and a labialized phone, a nasal and a nasalized phone, a laryngeal and a laryngealized phone, etc.?

Readings

Stemberger [1983] gives a complete overview of speech errors and their theoretical significance. See also Fromkin [1971], [1973], and [1980].

Suprasegmentals

7

Objectives

To define and discuss suprasegmentals: stress, emphasis, intonation, rate, rhythm, and tone.

To describe both the phonetic form and the linguistic function of each.

To indicate the practical implications of suprasegmentals.

7-1 Introduction

In this chapter we will examine a number of phonetic phenomena that affect several segments at once: stress, intonation, rhythm, and others. The term **suprasegmental** indicates that these phenomena occur *above* (supra) the level of the *segment* (language being viewed as a hierarchy of levels).

We have noted several times in this book that the technical terminology used in phonetics may lead to confusion if attention is not paid to its exact meaning. In the area of suprasegmentals this is particularly true, since such terms as *accent* and *intonation* are used very loosely in everyday speech. Once again, therefore, I suggest that you pay close attention to the definition of terms.

One other factor to which you should pay attention is the grammatical level at which a particular suprasegmental operates. You will note that some phenomena operate within words, whereas others operate within sentences or larger units. Often, two different phenomena (such as stress and emphasis, or tone and intonation) are similar phonetically but differ in their grammatical role.

The primary types of suprasegmentals we will be examining in this chapter are stress, emphasis, timing, intonation, and tone.

7-2 Stress

As with other phonetic phenomena, the role of stress is different in different languages; it happens to be very important in English. Its importance is shown by the fact that misplaced stress can render otherwise correct English completely unintelligible.

The term *accent* is sometimes used in place of **stress,** but *accent* has a number of meanings and is therefore not sufficiently precise for our needs. (A foreign "accent" may involve anomalies in vowels, consonants, accommodation, or other aspects of speech besides stress. An "accent" or diacritical mark may indicate stress but more often indicates other aspects of pronunciation.)

Like other suprasegmentals, stress is often given short shrift in introductory books and courses in phonetics. It is therefore important to emphasize that while stress may be a less tangible phenomenon than consonants or vowels, it is nonetheless of great importance. Its correct placement is essential for comprehension. The student of speech pathology should note that stress is highly susceptible to distortion by the deaf speaker, foreign speaker, or individual with certain voice disorders. The student of linguistics should note the great importance of stress in historical (diachronic) sound change and in contemporary (synchronic) phonological processes.

7-2.1 Locating the Stressed Syllable

If you are a native speaker of English, you may never have paid much attention to stress, particularly since English spelling uses no consistent device for recording it. For this reason, many speakers (who use stress in a completely natural way when they talk) have difficulty locating or identifying stress.

Simply stated, **stress** is an accentuation of, or a giving of prominence to, one syllable (or more) of a polysyllabic word. For example, if you compare the words "payment" and "invent," you will see that they are stressed differently: "payment" on the first syllable and "invent" on the second syllable.

If this is difficult for you to perceive, a trick may be helpful to you in locating the stressed syllable. Intentionally stress each syllable in the word. When you stress the wrong syllable, it will sound strange to you.[1] By a process of elimination, therefore, you can locate the stressed syllable. For example, say "PAYment" and "payMENT," stressing the first, then the second, syllable. When you stress the second syllable, "payMENT," the word will rhyme with "invent." This is obviously the wrong pattern for the word "payment," so the stress must fall on the first syllable.

Let us look at a three-syllable word to find out which syllable is stressed: "discover." If you have a good ear for stress, you need only say the word (out loud or, better yet, to yourself) to find the stressed syllable. If you are not used to locating the stress, you will need to use the test of stressing the wrong syllable. Say the word "discover" three times, each time stressing a different syllable: DIScover, disCOVer, discovER. The second one

[1] Of course, this trick will help only if you have native fluency in English. If you do not, you may not recognize the wrong stress pattern as being wrong.

should sound most natural to you. After you have used this technique for a while, you should be able to abandon it and find stress in a word just by saying the word to yourself.

7-2.2 Levels of Stress

The degree of stress carried by a particular syllable varies on a continuum from weakest to strongest. In fact, not just one but several factors contribute to stress, and each factor is variable (these factors will be enumerated in Section 7-2.3).

However, while stress can vary continuously, it is convenient and linguistically relevant to identify a number of levels of stress.[2] For most practical purposes, the continuum from strongest to weakest stress is divided into three identifiable **levels of stress.** (A fourth level, which comes into play in phrases and sentences, is distinguishable; we will disregard it in this section.) The three levels are **primary** (the strongest), **secondary** (medium), and **weak** or **tertiary.**[3]

A word like "pimento," for example, has three levels of stress in English. The most strongly stressed syllable is the second one, /mɛn/. The last syllable, /to/, has less stress than the second syllable but more than the first. The first syllable has weak stress. These different levels of stress are generally marked ´, `, and ˆ, respectively, for primary, secondary, and weak. These symbols are convenient, because they are available on a typewriter with an international keyboard. The word "pimento" could be transcribed /pə̂mɛ́ntò/.

Other systems are sometimes used to mark stress. For example, the syllable with primary stress may be written in capitals, as was done earlier. The disadvantage is that only two levels of stress can be marked. The official IPA system uses a raised vertical line to mark primary stress, a vertical line at the level of the base of the letters to mark secondary stress, and nothing to mark weak stress: /pəˈmɛnˌto/. This system forces the transcriber to divide every word into syllables, which is not always convenient.

Note that it is a characteristic of *English* that three levels of word stress need to be distinguished. Other languages have different systems of stress.

7-2.3 The Phonetic Effects of Stress

A stressed syllable sounds louder to us; we consciously perceive stress as loudness. In fact, loudness is not the only characteristic of stress, and it may not be the most important factor in our unconscious perception of stress. Let us compare the "same" syllable in a stressed and an unstressed environment. Take the syllable *ment* in the words "payment" and "mental"; it is unstressed in the first word, stressed in the second.

Certainly there is a difference in loudness between the two. But there is also a difference in length. (Remember that length is a matter of duration or time, not of quality.) The vowel and the whole syllable are longer in the stressed syllable. The vowel quality also changes: it is a distinct /ɛ/ in the stressed syllable; it is not so distinct in the unstressed syllable, probably being reduced to schwa.

As stressing of a syllable may be accompanied by a heightened subglottal air pressure (i.e., a momentarily heightened pressure of air coming from the lungs), both amplitude and frequency may be affected. Often the F_0[4] is slightly increased in stressed syllables, although, interestingly, some researchers have noted that stress is sometimes accompanied by a decrease in F_0.

Another factor that changes in stress is degree of accommodation. A strongly stressed syllable resists many of the assimilatory forces from surrounding syllables; a less strongly stressed syllable may undergo more assimilatory changes.

[2] Chopping a continuum into discrete units is something that is done by necessity in phonetics. In a similar way, there is an infinite variety of vowels—there is no limit to the number of points between /ɛ/ and /æ/, for example—but we divide the continuum into discrete units. Oftentimes the cutoff points depend upon the particular language.

[3] Unfortunately, in this area also there has been little standardization of terminology. Ladefoged [1975] uses the terms *stressed, unstressed,* and *reduced,* respectively, for what are here called **primary, secondary,** and **weak** stress. Furthermore, if four levels of stress are distinguished, the terms **tertiary** and **weak,** which are synonymous here, must be differentiated in order to have four different names to identify the four levels. The terms used in this chapter are in widespread use, and they will be used consistently to prevent possible confusion, but sometimes inconsistencies in terminology will be encountered in reading.

[4] **F_0:** the abbreviation for **fundamental frequency** of the voice, the frequency of vibration of the vocal folds. This concept will be discussed in Chapters 9 and 10.

In summary, the more strongly stressed a syllable is, the more it may show the following characteristics:

1. It may be longer
2. Its vowel may be more distinct
3. It may be louder
4. Its segments may be less modified by those in surrounding syllables
5. Its F_0 may be raised (or, less usually, lowered) as compared to surrounding syllables

The word *may* has been used intentionally in this list. The phonetic manifestations of stress are highly variable; any combination of factors may mark stress in a given pronunciation of a given word.

7-2.3.1 The Effect of Stress upon Vowels
One of the effects of weak stress is that the vowel tends to be **reduced** to schwa. What is a reduced vowel? It tends to be shorter in duration and to have a less distinctive quality. This results from the fact that in unstressed syllables the tongue movements tend to be more relaxed and not to arrive at articulatory positions distant from the mid-central position. However, it is not accurate to think of vowels as either reduced to schwa or not reduced. There is a continuum, and any point between the extremes may be represented in an actual articulation. Syllables having secondary stress are reduced as compared to those having primary stress, and syllables having weak stress may be completely reduced.

Are there any differences between vowels in syllables having primary stress and those in syllables having secondary stress? The differences are small but are important in contributing to a natural-sounding pronunciation of English. For that reason, it is important to pay attention to them. What are these differences? A good way to start, as usual, is to listen analytically to some speech sounds. The syllable /to/ in the word "pimento," as has been shown, is an example of secondary stress; in the expression "tow truck," it has primary stress. When these two are pronounced out loud in a normal voice, some small difference will be noticed between the syllable /to/ in "pimento" and in "tow truck." There is less

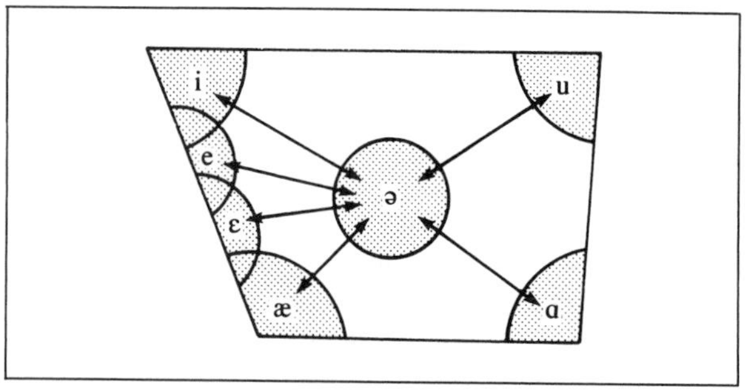

Figure 7-1. Vowel reduction. For the sake of clarity, not all vowels are indicated. When stressed, the vowels are articulated nearer to their cardinal positions, close to the outer edges of the vowel quadrangle. When weakly stressed or unstressed, they tend to be reduced toward schwa ([ə]) or pronounced nearer the mid-central position of the vowel quadrangle.

of a diphthongal character to the vowel in the syllable having secondary stress, and it is shorter in duration. Furthermore, its position of articulation may be a little more central.

What is occurring is that for each vowel there is a point anywhere between schwa and the full value of that vowel that can be pronounced. We must therefore make a judgment about which end of the continuum a pronunciation is closer to. In the vowel quadrangle shown in Figure 7-1, the arrows represent the continua along which each vowel might be pronounced. The enclosed areas in Figure 7-1 represent the range of pronunciations that would be clearly and consistently identified as particular vowels. Note that while not all vowels are included in this diagram, the same principle applies to /o/, /ɔ/, and the other vowels.

Suppose we consider one vowel, say /e/, in greater detail. Figure 7-2 shows that, depending upon stress, there are numerous realizations of an English vowel (as before, the principle applies equally to vowels not shown in the diagram). Although it is not diagrammed, a very important phonetic change brought about by stress is the fact that /e/ under primary stress is diphthongized (see Section 4-6.2), but under secondary stress it is not or is less so. All four of the English long vowels (/i, e, o, u/) behave similarly. For example, compare the pronunciation of /i/ in the words "foresee" and "hippy." Further examples will be found below.

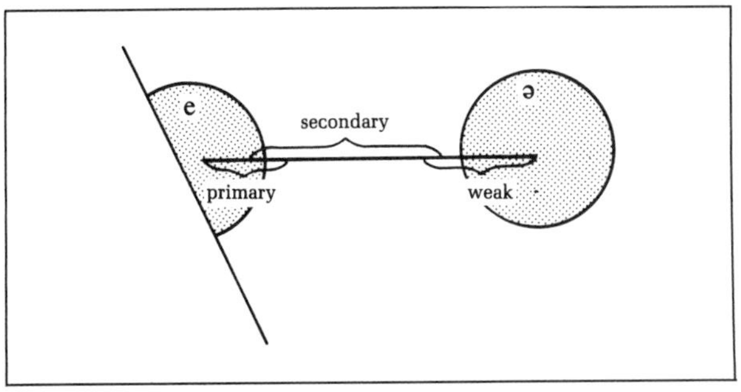

Figure 7-2. Levels of stress for /e/. An enlargement of a portion of the vowel quadrangle in Figure 7-1, showing the approximate position of articulation of the vowel /e/ under primary, secondary, and weak stress.

The high front vowels present a special problem, though, in many dialects of North American English. They tend to remain high when they are reduced, resulting in a high central vowel. On the vowel quadrangle, this vowel is located midway between /i/ and /u/, above /ə/; its IPA symbol is /ɨ/. This vowel is present in many speakers' pronunciation of the word "roses" (as opposed to "Rosa's," which has /ə/). Usually the symbol /ɨ/ is not used in the broad transcription of English, although of course it is used for detailed transcription as in the case of fine dialect differences or communication disorders. The result of the slightly peculiar behavior of /i/ and /ɪ/ under reduced stress is that a number of different—and therefore confusing—conventions are used in the transcription of these vowels when they do not have primary stress. These conventions will be examined later.

It seems apparent in general that the idealized full articulatory movements for vowels are made only under primary stress and that reduced stress leads to articulatory gestures that do not fully reach their target. As noted in our discussion of vowel articulation in Chapter 4, tongue position is not the only factor in vowel articulation. Lip posture and tongue root position play a role as well. It is apparent that each of these features, too, will vary along a continuum and that stress will influence whether or not the idealized articulatory position is reached. For example, an /i/ under secondary stress will have a more neutral (i.e., less spread) lip posture than an /i/ under primary stress. This leads some phoneticians to identify /i/ under secondary stress as an /ɪ/ and contributes to the differences in transcription systems that we will examine in Section 7-2.3.3. In addition, the tongue root position, which varies according to the "tenseness" of a vowel, may be subject to some variation according to level of stress and thus may contribute to some of the acoustic differences between a vowel under primary stress and the same vowel under secondary stress.

7-2.3.2 The Reduced Forms of Vowels

Let us now look at some examples of English vowels under the influence of different degrees of stress. At this time it would be well to recall a point that is relevant throughout this or any other phonetics book: namely, that the examples may not be appropriate in all dialects. In Table 7-1, the vowels may not in all cases be appropriate to *your* pronunciation.

It may at first seem arbitrary that a certain reduced vowel is stated to be a reduced form of a particular cardinal vowel. For example, why is the ⟨e⟩ of "homogenize" a reduced /i/ and not, say, a reduced /e/? By looking at a related word in which the particular vowel is stressed, one can find the "true"[5] value of the vowel. In this case, the word "homogeneous" provides the clue to the value of this vowel. If there is no related word in which the particular vowel is stressed (as, for example, "orchard"), knowledge of the history of the word (often reflected in spelling) is used in making this judgment.

Table 7-1 indicates various English vowels and diphthongs under the three levels of stress. Several aspects of the influence of stress on vowels should be noted in the examples.

1. Note that the long vowels (/i, e, u, o/) are fully diphthongized under primary stress but are shorter and "purer" under secondary stress. And, like the short vowels, they are reduced to schwa under weak stress. Let us take the vowel /e/ from Table 7-1 and look at it in greater detail. Under

[5]This "true" value is what phonologists call the **underlying** vowel. As the word "homogenize" is pronounced (its **surface** form), one can only tell that there is a schwa. An examination of related words (e.g., "homogeneous") shows that this sound is an /i/ that has been reduced to schwa through the operation of phonological rules. Thus the underlying vowel is /i/; the surface vowel is [ə]. (See Chapter 8.)

Table 7-1. Reduced forms of vowels

Vowel	Primary stress	Secondary stress	Weak stress
i	scheme homogeneous	schematic hippy	 homogenize
ɪ	simple morbidity	simplistic morbid	simplistic insipid
ɛ	tempestuous	tempestuous	tempest
e	maintain Canadian grade	 gradation	maintenance Canada
æ	Canada nationality extrapolate	 extrasensory acknowledge	Canadian nationalism extra
u	moving	removability	
ʊ	hoodwink	motherhood	
o	photo Oklahoma	photosynthesis Oklahoma	photograph
ɔ	auction	auctioneer	
ʌ	confront	confrontation	
ɑ	monotone	monocular	(carbon) monoxide
a͜i	license digest (noun)	licentious digestion	 digest (verb)
a͜u	sauerkraut	sauerkraut	
ɔ͜i	employ	employability	
ju	refute	refutation	jugular
Rhotic vowels:			
ɚ	circle imperfect	semicircle imperfection	circumnavigate perfection
iɚ	commandeer ethereal		commander ether
e͜ɚ	primarily	primary*	primary*
u͜ɚ	injurious		injury
o͜ɚ	laborious professorial record (verb)	laboring	labor professor record (noun)
ɑ͜ɚ	partner		orchard

*Depends upon dialect.
Note: There are considerable dialect differences in the degree of stress placed on each syllable. Also, the stress may be modified when the word is used in a sentence as compared to being pronounced in isolation.

primary stress, as in "grade" and "Canadian," the vowel /e/ is highly diphthongized. It might be symbolized [ei], [ɛi], etc., depending upon dialect. Under secondary stress, as in "gradation," the vowel quality is retained, but the vowel loses some of its length and most (or all) of its diphthongal nature. It is an [e], pure and simple. Under weak stress, as in "Canada," it is completely reduced to schwa, [ə].

2. Note that there are few examples of the diphthongs /ai/, /au/, and /ɔi/ under weak stress. Because of the historical development of these sounds, most are in syllables taking primary or secondary stress. There are a few examples of fully reduced diphthongs, however. The noun "digest" (*Reader's Digest*) has primary stress on the first syllable, /dáíǰɛ̀st/; but this syllable is reduced in the verb form ('to digest food'): /dəǰɛ́st/ (although in many dialects the verb is pronounced /daìǰɛ́st/. Again because of historical development, diphthongs often alternate with different vowels: for example, "pronounce" and "pronunciation," "denounce" and "denunciation," "imply" and "implicit."

3. Notice that the reduced form of /ju/ is usually /jə/; that is, the /j/ glide is retained under weak stress. Exceptions to this are common, depending upon dialect and the individual word. For example, the word "manufacture" is commonly pronounced [mænəfækčɚ] rather than the expected [mænjəfækčɚ].

4. A vowel followed by an r-sound is generally reduced to one single vowel, /ɚ/ or /ə/, depending on the dialect. For example, note the relationship between "laborious" and "labor."[6]

7-2.3.3 The Transcription of Stress

It is normal practice in transcription to differentiate two levels of stress in our representation of *vowels;* that is, when a vowel has weak stress, it is transcribed with a schwa, but when it has either primary or secondary stress, it is transcribed with its full quality (/e/, /i/, etc.). Thus, while the three levels of stress can be indicated with stress marks, there is no generally accepted way of transcribing the effect of secondary stress on vowel quality.

This lack is usually not a problem. For one thing, the stress marks are available when needed; and for another, it is often satisfactory to ignore the differences in vowel quality under primary and secondary stress *for the purposes of transcription,* although one *cannot* ignore the phonetic differences for the purposes of speech correction. The real phonetic differences between vowels under primary and secondary stress contribute to natural-sounding speech. Individuals wishing to improve their pronunciation will need to become aware of the subtle differences in vowel quality resulting from stress in order to achieve that improvement.

Some confusion is created by the use—recommended by a number of authors—of the symbol /ɪ/ for an /i/ under secondary stress. Certain authors suggest transcribing the word "happy" as /hæpɪ/. However, in most dialects, /ɪ/ under primary stress is different from /i/ under secondary stress, so this usage is confusing. In a broad transcription, I would recommend transcribing /i/ under primary or secondary stress with the symbol [i] and marking the stress where required.

LONG VOWELS. Chapter 4, on vowels, showed that all long vowels in English are to some extent diphthongs. We discussed the fact that some authors prefer to show that these are diphthongs in the transcription, while other authors feel that if one is dealing only with English, the simpler system is better. The vowel in the word "boat," for example, can be written /o/, /ou/, or /ow/.

Long vowels tend to be more diphthongized in syllables of primary stress. In syllables of secondary stress, they tend to retain their distinct character—the long vowel does not become a schwa—but they are less diphthongized. So, in those transcription systems that indicate the diphthongal character of long vowels, sometimes the diphthongal quality is not marked in secondary stress syllables. For example, "tow truck" [tou] *but* "pimento" [pəmɛnto]. The syllable with the /o/ has primary stress in "tow truck" but secondary stress in "pimento."

The important point here is that, phonetically,

[6] Alternations such as labor/laborious provide one argument for calling a sequence such as the ⟨-or-⟩ of "laborious" a diphthong rather than a vowel plus consonant.

there is less of a diphthongal character to long English vowels in syllables having secondary stress than primary stress; this is true no matter what system is used to transcribe the vowels.

DIPHTHONGS. The diphthong phonemes, like /a͜i/ and /a͜u/, retain their diphthongal character in positions of secondary stress. They are a little shorter in duration, and the starting and finishing points of the diphthong may both be a little closer to the neutral rest position of the tongue, than if the diphthong were under primary stress, but the best transcription is to use the same symbol as for the fully stressed versions. For example, in the expression "White House" (meaning the president's residence), "House" has secondary stress. If you have a good ear, you may be able to detect the fact that the diphthong in "House" is a little reduced from its realization in a stressed articulation of "house." But the best transcription is to use the same vowel for both and, where necessary, to mark stress separately.

The foregoing examples should make it clear that the first two levels of stress are not well distinguished by transcribing different vowels according to degree of stress. A much better system, when it is important to mark stress, is to use the accent marks given earlier in this chapter, in conjunction with the full vowel quality for both primary and secondary stress; and to use schwa for the vowels under weak stress.

7-2.4 How Languages Use Stress

Different languages use word stress differently. We can arbitrarily divide the world's languages into four types according to their use of stress, but we will take a detailed look only at those like Modern English. The student who is familiar with the languages given as examples may find cases that do not behave exactly as stated. In general the principles operate as stated; an effort has been made to select familiar languages rather than exotic ones that might serve as more perfect examples.

In a language such as French, every syllable has equal stress. There is a schwa in French, but it is not a reduced form of some other vowel, it is a separate and distinct phoneme.[7] In such a language, stress cannot be used to contrast two words that are otherwise similar.

In some languages, such as Old English, the syllable that takes primary stress is determined by simple rules. In this type of language, stress is completely predictable; it does not have to be learned for each word the way it does for Modern English. However, two words could not differ by stress placement alone. For the most part, Modern German has predictable stress, and stress placement is not used to carry meaning distinctions.[8]

In a language such as Spanish, the syllable taking primary stress is *usually* determined by rule. There are a fair number of exceptions, however, and contrasts are made on the basis of stress alone. In Spanish spelling, stress is unmarked when it is predictable by the rule, and it is marked with an accent if it falls on a syllable other than the one predicted by the rule.[9] For example, these words contrast in Spanish: *termino* ('I terminate'; stress on the second syllable, unmarked because it is where the rule predicts), *término* ('term'; unpredictable stress as marked), and *terminó* ('he terminated'; unpredictable stress as marked). The characteristic of this type of language is that while stress is predictable in most cases, stress alone can be used to carry meaning differences in the exceptional cases.

In a language such as English, stress might be placed anywhere in a word, so the stress pattern must be learned separately for each word. (This is

[7] Students familiar with spoken French will realize that this is not quite true; polysyllabic French words take a slight stress on the final syllable. The two essential factors remain: there is no reduction of vowels in other syllables, and stress cannot be used to contrast words. Additionally, the speaker may strongly stress a syllable other than the final one for emotional or theatrical effect, but this is not contrastive.

[8] There are exceptions to this general rule as a result of prefixes being perceived as part of the word in some cases and as separate prefixes in other cases. For example, *übersetzen* means 'to transfer' or 'to ferry,' whereas *übersétzen* means 'to translate.' However, the stress is not marked in German spelling, as it has been in the latter word.

[9] The rule in Spanish is that stress falls on the penultimate (second to last) syllable if the word ends in a vowel, an ⟨s⟩ or ⟨n⟩; otherwise the stress falls on the final syllable.

In monosyllabic words, the accent mark may be used for a different reason: namely, to distinguish homographs (words spelled alike) such as *tu* and *tú*. This usage of the accent mark has nothing to do with stress.

not to say it is totally random: there is some regularity. But the rules are complex and full of exceptions; they are also sensitive to the history of the word.) This system offers the advantage of allowing meaning contrasts: the same string of phonemes may have different pronunciations and therefore different meanings according to the stress placement.

In summary, some languages stress syllables equally, others give different stress to different syllables. Of those stressing syllables unequally, stress may be predictable or not. Only if it is unpredictable can it be used to carry meaning difference.

7-2.5 English Word Stress

As noted, Old English had a stress system in which the placement of primary stress in a word was predictable. This is not true of Modern English; the reason is chiefly that the vocabulary that is borrowed from other languages is usually borrowed with the foreign stress pattern.

The Old English system worked this way: the first syllable of a polysyllabic word took primary stress, unless that syllable was a prefix; in that case the first root syllable took primary stress. Indeed, for those English words that have changed little since the days of King Arthur, this rule remains true. The word "fáthêr," for example, has primary stress on the first syllable. The word "fòrbíd" has primary stress on the first root syllable. (*For* is in this case a prefix, as it is in the word "fòrgét." But in the word "fórtỳ," the syllable *for* is the root, and it takes primary stress.) A similar pattern can be found for most other English words of Germanic origin. Over 50 percent of the words in our vocabulary have been borrowed from foreign sources, most from the Romance languages (Latin, French, etc.), but from dozens of other languages as well. In most of these words, either the stress pattern of the original language has been retained or an attempt has been made to imitate the original stress pattern when the word has been adapted to English pronunciation. As a result, we have words like "vocábulary," "pajáma," and "automátic," which have unpredictable stress patterns different from those of original English words like "fáthêr" and "bérrỳ."

While stress placement may be mostly unpredictable in English, stress remains a fundamental part of the phonetic shape of any English word. As stated earlier in the chapter, incorrect stress placement often renders a word completely incomprehensible. This can be demonstrated by taking a few polysyllabic words and pronouncing them with incorrect stress placement. Try, for example, [ə̂nkɔ́rə̂kt], [ǽnə̂ðɚ̀], and [mə̂ntʰɛ́zə̂mɑ̀].[10] Our understanding of spoken words depends on correct stress; it is unlikely that anyone would understand the words if they were pronounced as just suggested. This should convince us of the necessity of paying attention to stress in correcting speech.

Words in English can be contrasted on the basis of stress alone, without any other phonetic difference to signal the contrast (except, of course, the change in vowel quality that is a direct result of the stress change). Let us look at some examples of this. Noun-verb pairs are often contrasted in English by stress:

NOUN	VERB
cónflìct	cônflíct
cóntràst	côntrást
défèct	dêféct
dígèst	dîgést or dìgést
éxpòrt	êxpórt
ímpòrt	împórt
récôrd	rècórd
súbjêct	sûbjéct

There is considerable dialect difference concerning whether all such pairs are contrasted. You may find that in your own speech you have the two pronunciations of "subject" but only one for "digest" or "import." However, all of us will agree that there are some pairs whose form is distinguished by stress. Thus we can conclude that stress serves a contrastive function. In fact, the effect of stress may be so strong psychologically that we do not even think of the two forms of "defect" as even being the same word. (This can be seen in the expressions "a défèct in materials" and "the spy will dêféct to the other side.") The noun-verb pairs listed demonstrate that words can

[10] "Incorrect," "another," and "Montezuma."

differ on the basis of stress alone in English (vowel quality, of course, is changed as a result of stress). Other words are similarly distinguished. "Personal" and "personnel" are distinguished by stress, as are "plastic" and "plastique" (a kind of explosive), "moral" and "morale," "local" and "locale," and "human" and "humane."[11]

But if stress plays a truly distinctive role in English, stress differences should not be limited to pairs of related words, such as the noun-verb pairs and doublets just given; that is, there should be pairs of words that just happen to be stressed differently. And indeed, such pairs exist; for example, *insight/incite, debtor/deter, decade/decayed* (in most dialects), *bellow/below, demon/demean, desert/dessert, Concorde/conquered, weakened/weekend,* and *coral/corral.*

From the example words listed in this section—whether or not the words are related—it can be seen that the same sequence of phones can form different words depending upon stress placement and the other phonetic changes (in vowel quality) that result directly from stress placement.

7-2.6 Contrastive Stress

Contrastive stress involves giving an unusually strong stress to a syllable in order to prevent possible ambiguity or confusion. For example, the words "illusion" and "allusion" would normally be pronounced similarly, since the first syllable of each word carries weak stress and its vowel is reduced to schwa, but if it was thought that a listener misunderstood, the speaker might say, "I said állusion, not íllusion," stressing the distinctive syllables. Similarly, "gorilla" and "guerrilla" may be pronounced alike unless contrastive stress is used to differentiate them; the pair "lumbar" and "lumber" would also be subject to such stress for contrastive purposes. Of course, context usually supplies the cue; only in unusual circumstances is contrastive stress used. One of the most common instances in everyday speech is numbers: "thirteen" is often confused with "thirty," "fourteen" with "forty," and so on. Here, context is often an inadequate guide to the speaker's intentions, since either number may be possible in the context, so contrastive stress is used.

Even when there is considerable phonetic difference between two words, a speaker might still want to give a word contrastive stress to be sure the listener understood. In discussing styles of art, primary stress might be given the first syllable of "impressionism" to be sure to distinguish it from "expressionism."

7-2.7 Stress and Spelling

English spelling, for the most part, does not record stress. This lack does not create much of a problem for the native speaker, who has learned the stress pattern and spelling of each word separately, but it does create a problem for two groups in particular, the deaf individual and the foreigner learning English, since the written word offers few clues to the pronunciation.

Stress is reflected in one way in our spelling, however, although for most of us it is simply an additional spelling problem rather than a clear representation of spoken English. When a suffix whose first letter is a vowel is added to a word ending in a consonant, the question arises as to whether to double the final letter of the word. Usually when the final syllable of the root word is stressed, the consonant is doubled. So we have ⟨timber⟩/⟨timbered⟩ but ⟨infer⟩/⟨inferred⟩ (however, note ⟨inference⟩, a word that is stressed on the first syllable). Double consonant *letters*—remember not to confuse a doubled letter with an actual long consonant[12]—are often, although irregularly, used in English to indicate stress patterns. A doubled letter often indicates that the *preceding* syllable is stressed. Compare "material" and "maternal" on the one hand with "matter" and "mattock" on the other. The latter two

[11] These pairs of words are examples of what etymologists call **doublets:** the same word being borrowed twice. In each pair, the first word was borrowed from French early in the history of English and became stressed on the first syllable to conform to usual English pronunciation. The second word in each pair was borrowed later in history (for example, the word *personal* was used in English in the fourteenth century; *personnel* was not used in English until the nineteenth century). The second of each pair is stressed on the final syllable, in imitation of the French pronunciation and in contrast with its doublet.

[12] Some languages have contrastively **long, geminate,** or **doubled** segments, either vowels or consonants (see Sections 4-5 and 8-6.4). Standard English does not, and as noted in Section 3-6.4, a double *letter* in English is often used to indicate another aspect of pronunciation than the length of the sound so represented.

are stressed on the first syllable; the former two on the second syllable. But the marking of stress is highly irregular. In the words "catty" and "cater," both stressed on the first syllable, the number of ⟨t⟩'s relates to the vowel quality and not to stress placement.

7-2.8 Stress and Non-normal Speech

All the facts presented in this section should lead to a serious consideration of the importance of stress in speech correction. An individual may pronounce the individual phones of a word correctly, but if they are stressed incorrectly, the word will be quite unintelligible to the native speaker. This can result in considerable frustration—and even an attitude of defeat and noncommunicativeness on the part of the speaker—if the speaker does not realize the nature of his/her difficulty. (Some of the disorders mentioned in this section are briefly described in Section 9-7.)

7-2.8.1 *The Foreign Speaker*

The foreign speaker of English must be taught the importance of stress, both as it affects his intelligibility and contributes to his foreign accent, although the extent of his problem will depend on the use of stress in his native language. Speakers of languages like French, which lack contrastive word stress of the sort found in English, can be expected to have particular difficulty. Another type of difficulty is created by international words—those that appear in many languages but may have different stress patterns in each language. Or the individual's native language may make use of borrowed English words whose stress pattern has been modified; a foreign speaker may think he is using an English word, yet it is not recognizable to the native speaker.

The problem of spelling has already been mentioned. A foreign speaker who has learned English by reading (or from teachers who were not fluent) may make stress errors in pronunciation, although he reads or writes without difficulty. The beginning foreign speaker may benefit if the teacher exaggerates stress to emphasize its importance. Furthermore, just as it is necessary to learn the grammatical gender of each new word when one studies Spanish, German, or French, the student of English must learn the correct stress patterns of polysyllabic words along with their spelling and meaning.

7-2.8.2 *The Deaf Speaker*

The problem facing the deaf speaker is in some ways similar to that of the foreign speaker, although for vastly different reasons. Not having heard words spoken, and not being helped by English spelling, the deaf speaker is likely to make inappropriate use of stress. Indeed, the most typical problem is one of placing too much stress on syllables that ought to contain reduced vowels. One approach to this problem is for the teacher to make use of an instrument that displays amplitude (loudness) on a television-like screen. By this means the deaf speaker receives visual feedback as he attempts to imitate the patterns for words and sentences.

7-2.8.3 *The Stutterer and Others*

The stutterer, too, may make inappropriate use of word stress. After blocking on a word, the speaker may finally release the initial consonant very abruptly, with great pressure. This gives the impression of heavy stress on the initial syllable. In the case of the stutterer, inappropriate use of stress is tied directly to the main problem of stuttering—it cannot be separated and dealt with alone, as it can in the case of the foreign or deaf speaker (it is true that some approaches to therapy work toward a reduction of subglottal air pressure; this is only one aspect of stress).

Those suffering from other communication disorders—be they voice (laryngeal) disorders, dysphasia, or whatever—may show disruptions of stress patterns in their speech. In dyspraxia, disruptions of stress patterns may be caused directly by a lack of muscle coordination; in a voice disorder, these disruptions may be caused by difficulty in regulating subglottal air pressure. In any case, the therapist may want to evaluate the situation and decide whether the individual's overall intelligibility can be improved through direct efforts to improve the use of stress, or whether stress and anomalies will be corrected automatically through a broader approach to the individual's problem.

7-3 Prominence

In the preceding section we examined *stress*, which plays a role at the level of the word in English grammar. In physiological and acoustic terms, stress is a giving of **prominence** to a specific syllable or syllables, and this distinguishes words from one another. The term *stress* says something about the grammatical role of this phenomenon in English. The term *prominence*, on the other hand, is a grammatically neutral term that simply indicates that a segment or group of segments is made to stand out from the others. This is accomplished by a number of features that have been mentioned in the preceding section. They include such things as an increase in loudness, an increase in duration, a reduction of accommodation, and/or a change in fundamental frequency.

Phonetic prominence can play other roles than stress, other roles than distinguishing words from one another. It can also play a role at the level of the phrase or sentence. In this case prominence affects whole words, or even groups of words, and also affects the interpretation of the sentence (or phrase) as a whole. Prominence therefore can play a role in the *syntax* of the sentence, whereas stress plays a role in the *lexicon* (vocabulary). Prominence at this level goes by a number of names, depending upon the precise role it plays. While there is quite some variation in the terminology used by different authors, we shall distinguish between **phrasal stress, emphasis,** and **contrastive emphasis.**

To reiterate: *prominence* refers to a group of phonetic variables that make segments or sequences of segments stand out. If it operates at the level of the lexicon (word), it is called *stress*. If its grammatical role is different, operating within sentences or phrases, it is called *phrasal stress, emphasis*, or *contrastive emphasis*, depending upon its function. These last will be discussed below.

7-3.1 Weak Forms

We have mentioned the *citation form* a number of times in this book. The citation form of a word is that pronunciation a person would give if that word were pronounced in isolation. However, as a result of the patterns of prominence in sentences, words (particularly common, short words having little semantic content: prepositions, articles, and the like) are often rendered in a much reduced form known as the **weak form.**

A few examples of common weak forms follow:

WORD	WEAK FORM
the	[ðə], [ð]
a	[ə]
to	[t], [tə], [ə] (as in "gonna")
and	[ənd], [nd], [n̩]
you	[jə], [j]
he	[i]
-ing	[ən]

Whatever one may say about its "correctness," "He is going to go" is often pronounced [izgənəgo]. The second-language learner is often confused by such colloquial (albeit normal) pronunciations, because second-language teachers and second-language textbooks often give only citation forms, and, usually as a result of exaggerated standards of correctness, do not even mention the way that people really talk. Despite this attitude, the use of weak forms is a pervasive and normal aspect of speech, and the second-language student should be exposed to it.

Note that the use of weak forms is constrained by the syntax (grammatical structure) of the sentence. For example, the words *going to* are often realized as "gonna" ([gənə] or [gɔnə]). But note the constraint: When *to* is part of a verb infinitive, the weak form is permissible, but when *to* is a preposition, it is not. Consider these sentences:

He's *going to* take a trip.
He's *going to* England.

Notice that *going to* may be rendered in its weak form in the first sentence but may be rendered only in its strong form in the second (the vowel may be reduced or elided, but the /t/ will remain).

7-3.2 Phrasal Stress

Prominence is used within the phrase in English to show the grammatical and semantic relations among the words in the phrase. (A **phrase** is not a random collection of words or a common expression, but a grammatical unit, e.g., noun phrase, verb phrase.)

For example, in an adjective-noun combination, the adjective usually takes secondary stress, while the noun takes primary stress:

Ìt's â whìte hóuse.
Ìt's â blàck bóard.

This pattern contrasts with compound nouns made up of an adjective plus noun or two nouns:

Ìt's thê Whíte Hoùse (or Whíte Hôuse).
Ìt's â bláckboàrd.

The second element in a two-part compound may take secondary or tertiary stress. Of course, the situation is complicated if either or both elements have more than one syllable. Note that many compound words in English are orthographically *two* words, not one. They are two words on paper, but in speech they are one compound word. "White House" is a compound noun, as are the italicized words below:

He's reached *middle age*.
He's just a *lame duck* (a helpless, ineffectual person).

Contrast the stress pattern of these phrases with the following ones.

It happened in the *Middle Ages*.
It's a *lame duck* (a duck with a broken leg).

Just as word stress provides a means for signaling meaning differences, so too phrasal stress allows a distinction in speech between *blackbird* and *black bird*, between *hot dog* (frankfurter) and *hot dog* (overheated canine), between *English teacher* (teacher of English literature or language) and *English teacher* (a teacher whose nationality is English), and between *German shepherd* (a kind of dog) and *German shepherd* (German sheepherder).

7-3.3 Emphasis

Prominence at the level of the sentence is called **emphasis.** In emphasis, certain words are given more prominence than others. Emphasis is governed by syntactic and semantic considerations and thus relates to the overall meaning of the sentence.

In English generally, content words are given more prominence than function words. Content words are those containing the greatest meaningful information, usually nouns, verbs, adjectives, and adverbs. The function words are those required for grammatical completeness but generally having a low semantic content. They include prepositions, articles, and so on: this category overlaps with that of words having weak forms, already considered.

Let us examine a sentence to see that this is so:

The man came to the party.

Notice that "man," "came," and "party" have considerable prominence, whereas the two instances of "the" and the word "to" are greatly reduced, i.e., are in their weak forms. Notice that, as we saw in Section 7-3.1, the grammatical role of the words governs their degree of prominence. In the foregoing sentence, the word "to" is greatly reduced in a colloquial pronunciation, but the word "to" may have different grammatical roles that change its prominence. For example, in the sentence

The (unconscious) man came to.

the word "to" is not reduced. In this sentence the word *to* is a particle of the verb: that is, the verb is not *come* but *come to* ('regain consciousness'). The effect is that *to* carries more meaning and is therefore not reduced.[13]

This phenomenon causes there to be a great deal of difference in the pronunciation of words depending on their situation. The citation form of "to" is [t^hu], but in "The man came to the party,"

[13] Notice the effect of leaving to out of each sentence:

The man came the party.

sounds like it has a foreign accent, but it is understandable. On the other hand

The (unconscious) man came.

does not mean the same as

The (unconscious) man came to.

to may be reduced to [t] and form an affricate with the [ð] of "the." In the sentence "The man went to the party," *to* may disappear (perhaps except as a slightly prolonged occlusion of the [t] of "went.") Or, in either sentence, the pronunciation [tə] might be heard. In the sentence "The man came to," *to* would have greater prominence and a full vowel. In the sentence "The children came, too," *too* may have considerable prominence and a full, diphthongized vowel.

To take another example, examine the word "out" in the following sentences:

He was kicked *out* of the bar.
He was knocked *out* in the fifth round.

In the former sentence, "out of" is likely to be pronounced [a͜uɾə], whereas in the latter sentence, "out" is probably pronounced nearly in its citation form.

It is apparent that stress and emphasis interact in some way. Polysyllabic words as well as monosyllabic ones will occur in situations of greater or lesser emphasis. In this case, the degree of prominence of a given syllable will be a combination of the *stress* of that syllable within the word and the *emphasis* of the word as a whole. Generally the *relative* degree of prominence will be retained. That is, in a polysyllabic word, the weakest syllable stays weakest, and the strongest stays strongest, but the *absolute* level of prominence of the syllables may change as the whole word is given more or less emphasis. For example, the word "pimento" will have three levels of stress internally, whatever its level of emphasis.

For this reason, in analyzing levels of prominence in sentences, we generally distinguish *four* levels, called **primary, secondary, tertiary,** and **weak.** (That is, the terms *tertiary* and *weak* are distinguished in this context, although they are often used interchangeably in regard to word stress.) These four levels are symbolized ´, `, ^, and no symbol, respectively.

7-3.4 Contrastive Emphasis

Just as word stress can be used contrastively (íllusion, not állusion), so, too, can emphasis. Very often it serves the purpose of what is called **focus** or that goes under the name of **new information** versus **old information.** In connected speech (discourse), there is normally a theme or narrative. In any given sentence, some words will serve simply to set the scene by making reference to what the listener already knows, and other words will give *new information;* that is, they will serve as the *focus* of the sentence.

For example, let us imagine a discourse about a customer's complaint against a merchant. If the listener asked (emphasized word in italics):

You *went* to the store?

the context would be that the listener *knew* that the speaker had communicated with the store but was confirming (i.e., focusing on, finding out new information) that it was by going there in person rather than, say, by telephoning. But if the listener asked:

You went to the *store?*

the context would be that the listener understood that the speaker had traveled somewhere to make his complaint, but wanted to verify that it was the store rather than, say, the warehouse, the head office, or the Better Business Bureau.

Generally, then, new information is given more emphasis than old information. This is accomplished by increased prominence in the phonetic sense as well as by syntactic devices that place the words in more prominent locations. This is a pervasive device in English. Let us look at another example. Examine the differences in meaning of the following sentences:

I didn't break it.	(Yes, I agree that it is broken, but I deny responsibility for breaking it.)
I *didn't* break it.	(I strongly deny the accusation in general.)
I didn't *break* it.	(Okay, I'll admit I did something to it, but I didn't break it; I only disassembled it: I can put it back together again.)
I didn't break *that.*	(Okay, you caught me breaking some other stuff, but you can't pin this one on me. [Notice that *it* is replaced by *that* in a position of emphasis.])

Whichever word is emphasized is new information; the others are old. In the third sentence, for example,

I didn't *break* it.

break is new information. The rest is old information: it is accepted that *I* did something to *it*. What is under focus (being disputed in this case, as the sentence is negative) is the question of whether *break* properly describes what happened.

Let us look at another example:

I'm a member of the party.	(Statement of fact; no special focus.)
I'm a member of the party.	(Not anyone else; me.)
I'm a *member* of the party.	(I admit to membership but not to . . . [commitment, demonstrating, lobbying, agitating, etc.])
I'm a member of the *party*.	(. . . but I'm not a member of . . . .)

In a similar way, this technique is used to clarify distinctions. One might say

Bill Báker is bringing the soft drinks.

if there were another person named "Bill" with whom he might be confused.

7-4 Intonation

Intonation is the "melody" of speech, the changes in the frequency of vibration of the vocal folds during speech. (See Chapter 9 for a discussion of the mechanism of vocal fold vibration.) The frequency of vocal fold vibration is often called the "pitch" of the voice, although the term *pitch* properly has another meaning. *Intonation* is one of those terms that is commonly used in a very vague way in everyday speech, and you should therefore pay attention to the specific way it is used here.

While the details will be given in Chapter 9, we can say now that the speed or frequency of the vibration of the vocal folds is under voluntary control, within limits, and that changes in their frequency of vibration are used in all languages as a phonetic cue. The frequency of their vibration is known as the **fundamental frequency (F_0)** of the voice.

Not all languages make the same use of changes in F_0. In this section we will look at those that use such changes at the level of the sentence. In a subsequent section (7-6) we will examine changes at the level of the word.

The first thing to note in examining intonation patterns is that many sentences, particularly the longer ones, are divided into phrases having their own internal intonation patterns. These phrases are called **breath groups,** although it is not obligatory that the speaker take a breath at every breath group division. These breath groups correspond to syntactic divisions within the sentence. Note the natural divisions in the following sentences:

Bob and Jim and some of the guys down in Marketing | bought a few tickets for last week's lottery draw | but they didn't win a darned thing.
I asked her | what all the fuss was about.
Can you tell me | who they elected president of the association?

Some sentences are short enough and simple enough syntactically to contain only one breath group. In others, there may be more than one way the same string could be divided into breath groups.

Intonation plays a role in revealing the grammatical structure, and therefore the meaning, of a sentence. For example,

You're going.

and

You're going?

have different meanings. While this difference may be shown (inadequately in many cases) on paper with punctuation marks, it is shown in speech by intonation, changes in the frequency of the voice.

Let us examine a few common intonation contours.

In a statement, usually the intonation is relatively level, with a slight rise near the end and a fall at the end:

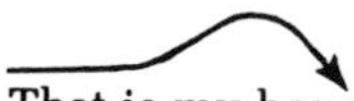

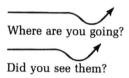

That is my house.

In a question, the pitch level is generally higher throughout, often with a brief drop near the end and a rise at the end:

Where are you going?

Did you see them?

The exclamation has a pattern similar to that of the statement but with a sharper fall in pitch at the end. This is probably combined with other markers such as louder voice and greater prolongation:

You can't go!

In a very short sentence, often the intonation pattern of a long sentence of similar syntactic type is compressed into the few syllables of a short sentence:

"May I go?" "No." "No?" "No!"

Each breath group may have its own intonation pattern:

If he doesn't arrive by tonight, I'll have to leave

without him.

In lists, the individual items are marked intonationally, and so is the end of the list:

I have to buy butter, eggs, cheese, and milk.

It should be noted that it is the *relative* pitch of the voice rather than its absolute pitch, that is used in intonation. Since a male's voice is generally lower than a female's, it will start lower and end lower than the female's voice but will have rises and falls of pitch relative to its normal frequency. The female's voice will rise and fall around *her* normal frequency. Her *lows* may be higher than the average male's *highs*, but this poses no problem, as the listener attends to the relative, not the absolute, pitch.

Section 10-10.6 and Figure 10-43 relate to the acoustic aspects of intonation.

7-5 Timing

The timing of speech involves several factors: the rate of speech, the use of pauses, and the rhythm of the syllables.

7-5.1 Rate

In English, the **rate** of speech of a casual, unexcited nature is about 12 segments per second. It slows down in very formal speech, in speech where there is interference or background noise, and in the speech of a person talking to someone whose hearing or command of the language he/she supposes to be not good. On the other hand, it speeds up considerably (to as much as 20 segments per second) when the speaker is excited, speaking informally but hurriedly, or arguing.

In a rough way, the faster speech is, the greater will be the dynamic influences discussed in Chapter 6. Accommodation, particularly coarticulation, will be greater. Similarly, sandhi will increase. The number of segments elided will increase, and in general the articulatory target of the speaker will be less frequently and less completely attained.

All of this stands to reason: the causes of coarticulation, explained in Chapter 6, become all the more compelling as the number of segments per second increases. If nasality spreads onto three or four other segments at normal speed, it will spread further at greater speed. One cannot, however, assume that coarticulatory effects will spread twice as far at twice the speed. This is because the articulatory gesture subject to spreading may itself be made more cursorily: lip-rounding, for example, may not extend over twice the number of segments, because the rounding itself is likely to be less; nasality may not extend twice as far, because the velum may not open as far when speech is being produced at higher speed.

7-5.2 Pauses

The title of this section is misleading. **Pauses,** in fact, do not occur very often in speech. We tend to think they are frequent because of orthographic conventions: the space between words on paper, the use of commas, periods, and other punctuation marks that suggest pauses. One place pauses do occur is when the speaker is inhaling; inhalation pauses are generally related to breath groups, discussed earlier.

What is far more common in speech than actual pauses are **prolongations** and **hesitation noises.** Very often what we perceive as a "pause" in speech turns out, upon acoustic examination, to be a prolongation of the preceding sound. That is, the final segment or segments of the word preceding the "pause" are stretched out, such that there is in fact no pause in the sense of a silent period. There is constant vocalization throughout the "pause."

Another way such "pauses" are filled is with hesitation noises, those sounds often written as "um" or "ah" or "er." These are very characteristic of a given language. Very often a person who has learned a second language well has mastered most aspects of the sound system but uses the hesitation noises characteristic of his native language. They give his speech a very "foreign" character, even if he otherwise speaks well. This is true particularly if, as is often the case, the foreign speaker has to search for words more often than the native and so uses hesitation noises more often: if those noises are foreign, he will draw attention to his searches for vocabulary and increase the impression of "foreignness" of his speech. Experience shows that second-language speakers can make enormous increases in the acceptability of their speech by learning the appropriate hesitation noises.

7-5.3 Rhythm

The **rhythm** of speech in fact means the rhythm of the syllables. In some languages that rhythm is quite regular. In others it is quite staccato, although not random and disorganized: rhythm is governed by the grammar and is therefore ordered.

As shown earlier, not every syllable is stressed in an English sentence. Prominent syllables occur at intervals depending on syntactic, semantic, and emphatic considerations. It is these strongly stressed syllables, and not the total number of syllables, that determine the rhythm of an English sentence. For example, consider these sentences:

The *dog barked.*
The *doberman panted.*

In each sentence there are two prominent syllables: "dog" and "barked" in the first; "dob-" and "pant-" in the second. The first sentence has three syllables, the second has six: twice as many syllables. *But the length of time to say these sentences is very nearly the same;* the length of time between prominent syllables is very nearly constant.

The word "doberman" takes more time to say than "dog" *in isolation.* But in the context of a sentence, the timing is determined not by the number of segments or the number of syllables, but by the *number of prominent syllables.* In this context, then, "dog" and "doberman" are approximately equal in length: "dog" is lengthened; the unstressed syllables of "doberman" are much compressed.

To take another example, examine the following sentences:

The *cow ate grass.*
The *cow ate* the *grass.*
The *cow* has *eaten* the *grass.*
The *cow* has been *eating* the *grass.*

In each sentence, there are three prominent syllables: the first is "cow," the second "ate" or "eat-," the third "grass." Once again, a normal rhythm in English will give all these sentences approximately the same length. It will stretch and compress syllables to compensate.

At first you may find this difficult to believe. One reason may be that you read the sentences carefully, pronouncing each syllable. This distorts the natural rhythm of English. A number of times in this book allusions have been made to the citation form of words and to the distortions created by hypercorrect self-conscious pronunciations.

In the present case there is great likelihood of such distortion. Try saying the sentences with the prominent syllables in time with the beats of a metronome, or beat your knuckles on the desk in time with the prominent syllables. Note that when the time between the prominent syllables is constant, the sentences sound quite natural.

Of course there are limits to the compression that will occur. In the sentence

The cow has been leisurely eating grass.

there are just too many syllables between "cow" and "eat" for the time to be the same as that of the earlier sentences. Indeed, even the fourth sentence of the "cow" sequence is getting to the limit.

This type of rhythm, in which timing is essentially constant between prominent syllables, is called **stress-timed rhythm.** It is the rhythm of English and many other languages. It has a particularly staccato pattern, since there is an uneven and changing number of syllables between successive prominences.

Many other languages, of which French is a good example, have a type of rhythm based on the total number of syllables. Each syllable is given approximately equal time, so the overall length of a spoken sentence depends on the number of syllables in it. Such a system is called **syllable-timed rhythm.**

It is an oversimplification to say that there are just two types of rhythm patterns. Rather, there is a continuum along which languages fall. English is not a "pure" case of stress timing; as we noted, a greater number of syllables between prominences will result in a slight increase in time. However, English leans heavily in the direction of stress timing.

If English is spoken with a syllable-timed rhythm, it will sound unnatural, stilted, perhaps pedantic. The foreign learner of English whose native language is syllable-timed can be expected to carry over his native timing when learning English. For teaching purposes, a dramatic demonstration of the appropriate rhythm can be made by speaking in time to a metronome, or to knuckles pounded on the table. An unnatural rhythm is also to be expected in the speech of the deaf and in a number of other speech disorders.

7-6 Suprasegmentals Are Used Together

Note that the various suprasegmentals are used together in a complex interaction. Stress, emphasis, intonation, timing features, and even voice quality (Section 9-4.3) combine to communicate subtle shades of meaning.

For example, in the sentence

I didn't break it.

which we examined in Section 7-3.4, the various meanings are communicated by prominence as well as by a number of other vocal devices.

7-7 Tone

A language such as English, which uses the intonation patterns in the sentence to carry certain aspects of meaning, is often classed as an **intonation language.** By contrast, some languages, such as Chinese, many other Asian languages, many Amerindian languages, and many African languages, use the fundamental frequency (pitch) as a distinctive and inherent part of the *word*, not the sentence. Such languages may be referred to as **tone languages.** In fact, a two-way distinction such as this is a simplification; for example, Lehiste [1970] makes a four-way distinction. There are intermediate types, such as Swedish, whose tonal properties will be described later. For the purposes of this text, we will make the broad distinction between languages in which pitch functions at sentence level and languages in which pitch functions at word level.

Tone languages are little known in Western culture, because Indo-European languages are not tone languages. However, this does not mean that tone languages are exotic or rare; indeed, it has been estimated that *more than half* of the languages of the world are tone languages.

The first point to recognize in understanding the principle of tone languages is that the physiological mechanism of adjusting the vocal fold tension and configuration to achieve pitch changes is exactly the same in a tone and in an intonation

Table 7-2. Tones of the Common Tongue (Mandarin) dialect of Chinese

Tone number	Tone name	Pitch at start and end*	Quick or slow change	Example word	English meaning
1	High level	4 → 4	Not applicable	m→a	'Mama' (mother)
2	High rising	3 → 5	Quick	m↗a	'Hemp'
3	Low rising	2 → 1 → 4 or 5	Slow	m√a	'Horse'
4	Falling	5 → 1	Quick	m↘a	'To scold'
—	Neutral	Depends on preceding tone	Not applicable	ma	Question marker

* A pitch of 3 corresponds to the speaker's normal fundamental frequency; 5 is the highest pitch, 1 the lowest. Do not confuse the tone number, used as a name, with the pitch.

language. Both types of language use pitch changes to carry meaning. The difference lies in the level of the grammar at which the pitch changes operate. Tone occurs at the level of the word; intonation occurs at the level of the sentence. A comparison could be made with prominence: prominence at the word level is stress, and at the sentence level is emphasis. Stress and emphasis play different roles grammatically but are similar physiologically and articulatorily.

In an intonation language like English, as we saw, pitch plays a role at the level of the sentence and of discourse. Pitch plays a role in the syntax of the language: we distinguish "We're going" from "We're going?" by intonation (patterns of pitch changes).

In a tone language such as Chinese, pitch is not a part of the sentence; it is part of the word. In English, we do not expect "ban" and "pan" to be related in meaning just because there is some phonetic similarity between them. In Chinese, do not expect "m↘a" and "m↗a" to be related in meaning just because there is some phonetic similarity between them (the arrows indicate rising and falling pitch). To a speaker of Chinese, the words "m↗a" and "m↘a" sound as different as "pan" and "ban" do to you; they are unrelated words.

To illustrate tone, we will use the example of the Mandarin or Common Tongue dialect of Chinese. Imagine a scale of pitch running from 1 to 5. 1 is the lowest pitch, and 5 is the highest pitch, with 3 being the middle point, close to a person's natural fundamental frequency. The points 1 and 5 are the lowest and highest pitches normally used in speaking without emotion; they do not represent the extremes of a person's musical range. (Speakers of tone languages no more use their full range in normal speech than do speakers of intonation languages.) No absolute musical values can be assigned to these pitch levels, since the levels are relative. There are considerable individual differences in the absolute frequency and range of the voice.

A set of contrasting words is given in Table 7-2. You will note that not only are the pitches indicated, but the speed of change is as well. For example, the two rising tones (tone 2 and tone 3) are different in speed of change, and it is likely that this feature is as important or more important in perception than the pitch level differences between tone 1 and tone 2.

Examine Table 7-2, which gives the tone patterns of Mandarin applied to the phoneme string /mɑ/. In a Chinese sentence, the situation is complicated by the fact there is a kind of sandhi between successive tones. The tone for the word *horse* would be different from that given in Table 7-2 in the context of a sentence such as "[The] horse runs." This is similar in principle to the accommodation and sandhi of segments in English that we examined in Chapter 6.

In English, a one-word sentence has the intonation pattern of a longer sentence compressed into one word. So the sentence "No?" has a rising intonation, and the sentence "No." has a falling intonation. What is the difference between this example and the Chinese word "ma" said with a rising and with a falling tone? There may in fact be no *phonetic* difference. However, there is an enormous difference grammatically. If you asked an English speaker whether "No." and "No?" were the same word, he would answer that of course they are. The two have the same denotative or dictionary meaning, although the different intonational patterns give a slightly different interpretation to the utterance as a whole. On the other hand, if you asked a Chinese speaker whether "má" and "mà" were the same word, he would answer that of course they are not. That would be like asking a speaker of English if there were any difference between "other" and "udder," between "boss" and "bus," or between "tin" and "thin." A pair such as "má" and "mà" has nothing common in meaning, unless by coincidence.

Mandarin Chinese has been given only as an example of the principle. Many tone languages exist; each has its own tone system. As few as two different tones may be distinguished; over a dozen may be distinguished. There may be a combining of tone with other phonetic features, such as the speed of change noted in the Chinese example. Fall-rise or rise-fall patterns like tone 3 in Chinese are also common. There is no universal transcription system for tone; there are too many varieties.

Swedish, a language closely related to English, has a grammatical feature akin to tone (some scholars class it as tone, others use a different term, noting essential differences from the phenomenon in Chinese; as we have noted, the classification system varies). Swedish is an intonation language like other European languages, but it uses a kind of tone as well. Most polysyllabic words are pronounced with a rise-fall tone pattern. This tone pattern, the *unmarked* or normal tone, called tone 1, is used for the vast majority of polysyllabic Swedish words. But certain words, which would otherwise be homophonous, have a fall-rise-fall tone pattern, as well as a lengthening. This is tone 2, the *marked* or distinctive tone. Certain otherwise homophonous pairs are distinguished in pronunciation by the two tones. For example, *tanken* pronounced with tone 1 means 'the tank'; with tone 2 it means 'the thought.' Said with tone 1 *komma* means 'comma'; with tone 2 it means 'to come.' The tone and intonation of Swedish combine in ways similar to the interactions of stress and emphasis in English.

7-8 Practical Implications of Suprasegmentals

Suprasegmentals make a major contribution to speech; they are governed by complex rules. Inappropriate use of stress, timing, emphasis, intonation, etc. will lead to speech that is at worst unintelligible and at best stilted and unnatural. Thus in working in speech correction, deaf education, or second-language teaching, one must pay attention to these aspects of speech.

The rhythm of the sentence is one of the areas most susceptible to anomalies. The hearing-impaired individual may tend to give equal stress to all syllables and thus to speak with syllable-timed rhythm rather than stress-timed rhythm. Similarly, an individual learning English as a second language may use syllable-timed rhythm if that is appropriate in his native language. A metronome or the rapping of knuckles on a desk, as already described, may make this point clear. Contrastive emphasis does not usually present problems, particularly to second-language learners, since its use is probably universal, but the stressing of content words and reduction of function words may not be handled appropriately by the second-language learner or the hearing-impaired.

Intonation patterns present problems to the hearing-impaired for the obvious reason that the patterns are not heard. However, individuals whose hearing loss is not profound may, with the help of amplification, be able to pick out the intonation contours of speech. Since the fundamental frequency is generally below 300 Hz, many hearing-impaired individuals with high-frequency hearing loss can pick out the fundamental frequency although missing many of the individual segments.

Intonation patterns may be inappropriately used by the learner of English when the patterns are different from those of his/her native language. The intonation patterns of most European languages are similar in the main to those of English but usually differ greatly in detail. Many second-language teachers do not pay much attention to their students' use of intonation. There are several reasons for this. First, second-language courses often stress the written word at the expense of any significant training in speech. Second, many second-language teachers lack training in phonetics and cannot put their finger on just what is wrong with their students' pronunciation. And finally, the second-language teacher may prefer to put up with the students' errors rather than to correct them.

But since intonation is so important a part of natural-sounding speech, some effort should be put into teaching it, along with the other suprasegmentals. One method that has been used successfully is to have students say model sentences. Sentences are chosen as exemplifying various intonation patterns. Some teachers make use of numbers (much as we did in the example of Chinese tones) in teaching intonation. If both teacher and students are musically inclined, musical notes may be used to demonstrate intonation contours.

The second-language learner whose native language is a tone language can be expected to have particular difficulties with intonational contours. This is because to him pitch is an inherent part of the word, not of the sentence.

Evidence shows that a good mastery of suprasegmentals makes the speech of the language learner far more acceptable to native speakers. For this reason it should be stressed far more than it usually is by the second-language teacher.

The laryngectomee who uses esophageal speech (see Section 5-9) can be expected to have some difficulties with stress and intonation. This is because esophageal speech has less pitch and dynamic (loudness) range than laryngeal speech, and because it has a discontinuous nature caused by the necessity of renewing the air supply. As a result, the laryngectomee may not be able to make full use of stress and intonation to signal meaning. Phrasing may circumvent the problem. If the intonation needed to distinguish "You're going" from "You're going?" is inadequate, it will still be possible to distinguish "You're going" from "Are you going?" or "You're going, eh?" Similarly, if the stress necessary to say "*John* did it" may be lacking, the emphasis may be indicated by saying "It's John who did it."

Summary

Suprasegmentals are those phonetic features that occur above the level of the segment.

Prominence results from a combination of phonetic cues and makes certain segment(s) stand out from the others. In English, prominence is used at the level of the word and at the level of the sentence.

At the level of the word, prominence is called **stress.** English is said to have three levels of stress. English uses stress to distinguish among words, which means that it is not always predictable in English. It is predictable in some languages.

At the level of the sentence, prominence is called **emphasis.** For syntactic and semantic reasons, some words carry more emphasis in an English sentence than others. Emphasis may also be used contrastively.

The **fundamental frequency** of the voice, also called its **pitch,** can have a role at the level of the word or at the level of the sentence. In English, it plays a role only at the level of the sentence. It is called **intonation.** Intonation contours depend upon the syntactic structure of the sentence and serve to reveal that structure to the listener.

Timing features of speech comprise **rate,** the use of **pauses,** and the **rhythm** of speech. The rhythm of English is normally **stress-timed.**

Some languages (in fact most languages, English not among them) use the pitch of the voice at the level of the word. This is called **tone.** In tone, pitch is an inherent part of the word.

Suprasegmentals have a number of practical implications in second-language teaching and speech therapy.

Vocabulary

breath group
contrastive emphasis
doublet
emphasis
F_0
focus
fundamental frequency (F_0)
hesitation noise
intonation
intonation language
levels of stress
new information
old information
pause

phrasal stress
primary
prolongations
prominence
rate
reduce, reduced, reduction
rhythm
secondary
stress
stress-timed rhythm
stressed
suprasegmental
syllable-timed rhythm
tertiary
tone languages
underlying form
unstressed
weak
weak form

Exercises

1. Find additional examples of pairs of words distinguished by stress (including accompanying vowel changes).
2. Give some examples of dialect differences in the stress pattern of individual English words. What about "controversy," "laboratory," "decal," "respiratory," and "corollary"? Find additional examples.
3. Give some examples from your own experience with foreign speakers, deaf speakers, or individuals with some communication disorder who have pronounced the right word with the wrong stress, causing problems of comprehension.
4. "What?" is often heard as the response to a statement. How does the speaker signal that "what" means 'I don't believe it'; 'I am shocked'; or 'Please repeat; I didn't hear you'? Say the word such that it has each meaning, and describe the phonetic devices used to signal the various meanings.

*5. [14]Speech has certain resources for conveying meaning that writing can represent imperfectly at best. Say this sentence aloud in a way that will convey each of the meanings indicated below: "He's a very enthusiastic person."

I am simply giving you the fact.
I like him; his enthusiasm is to his credit.
I dislike him; his enthusiasm is depressing.
I am hesitant or reluctant to describe him.
I mean him, not her.
I am asking you, not telling you.
Is that what you said? I can hardly believe it.
The degree of his enthusiasm is quite remarkable.
Enthusiasm is the only good thing about him, and it isn't much; I could say more, but I won't.

Describe as precisely as you can how the various meanings are signaled. Can any of these meanings be shown in writing by punctuation or typographical devices?

6. Make up a sentence, and give it a variety of meanings through the use of stress, pause, and intonation. Paraphrase the meanings, and describe the devices used to achieve the meanings.
7. Do different dialects use suprasegmental features differently (besides stress, already covered in question 2)? Find examples of differences in emphasis, intonation, rate, etc.
8. What special problems are involved in suprasegmental remediation of the student of English as a second language, of the hearing-impaired, and of the laryngectomee? What methods might the teacher/therapist apply?

*9. Can these pairs be distinguished in speech? If so, how?

blue blood (aristocrat)	blue blood (cyanotic condition)
red eye (cheap whiskey)	red eye (bloodshot eye)
hot line (direct telephone line to Moscow)	hot line (heated cord)
New Year (January 1)	new year (fresh year)
long shot (kind of bet)	long shot (shot-putting at a far distance)
short order (quickly cooked food)	short order (brief command)
big head (conceit)	big head (large skull)
a man's store (store selling men's clothing)	a man's store (store owned by a man)
a fishing pole (rod for fishing)	a fishing Pole (Polish fisherman)
a bull's-eye (center of a target)	a bull's eye (eye of a bull)

[14] Starred exercises in this chapter are from *Problems in the Origins and Development of the English Language* (second edition) by John Algeo © 1966, 1972, by Harcourt Brace Jovanovich, Inc., and are reprinted with their permission.

*10. Can these pairs be distinguished in speech? If so, how does the distinction differ from that of the pairs in the preceding list [question 9]?

New Jersey (the state)	new jersey (blouse purchased recently)
old maid (spinster)	old maid (serving-woman of advanced years)
little woman (wife)	little woman (small female)
Long Island (the place)	long island (any elongated island)
good and hot (very hot)	good and hot (hot and good)

*11. Each of these sentences is ambiguous in writing. Say each sentence in two different ways to make the potential meanings clear. Describe the means you use to make the spoken sentences unambiguous.

Old men and women should be the first to abandon ship.
The doorman asked her quietly to telephone the police.
She gave him an order to leave.
They went by the old highway.
He painted the picture in the hall.

*12. Are these sentences usually distinguished in speech? Can they be distinguished?

He came to.
He came too.

He found a pear.
He found a pair.

The staight way is best.
The strait way is best.

The mathematics department is teaching plane geometry.
The mathematics department is teaching plain geometry.

The directions read, "Leave address with Miss Jones."
The directions read, "Leave a dress with Miss Jones."

13. What problems are there in writing a tone language alphabetically? Do you think these problems had anything to do with the fact that Chinese is written in a primarily ideographic fashion? Are there any tone languages written alphabetically? How do they cope with the problem?

Readings

Chomsky and Halle [1968] discuss several aspects of stress, including rules for predicting word stress in English words. Their volume was extremely influential in modern phonology. Stress is discussed at some length in Ladefoged [1967] and Lehiste [1970].

Lehiste [1970] discusses suprasegmental phenomena in general and attempts to integrate them into linguistic theory. Lieberman [1967] discusses the perception and production of intonation, its linguistic significance, and the extent to which it is a central part of speech. Pike [1945] discusses intonation both from the viewpoint of analysis and from the viewpoint of utilization of intonation in the teaching of speech. Liberman [1978] is a study of the intonational system of English.

Many available books contain exercises in emphasis and intonation. Many are designed for the learner of English as a second language; others are designed for the more general goal of speech improvement. A selection includes *Drills* [1967], Gordon [1974], Lado and Fries [1954], and Prator [1957].

Phonemics and phonotactics: sound contrast in language

8

Objectives

To distinguish in some detail the phonemic from the phonetic level in language.

To define and provide tests for the phonemic status of speech units.

To indicate some complications of phonemic analysis.

To provide some non-English examples of phonemic analysis.

To show that units other than segments have phonemic or equivalent status.

To indicate practical outcomes of phonemic theory.

To indicate how phonemic judgments relate to transcription.

To define and explain the importance of the syllable as a unit.

To define and explain the importance of phonotactic constraints.

To demonstrate how phonotactics can play a role in practical problems.

8-1 Contrast in Language

The point has been made several times that for spoken language to function effectively, there must be a systematic **contrast** among the sounds of the language and quite a number of such contrasts for efficiency. The study of **phonemics** is the study of the system of contrasts.

In spoken English, the sound /t/ contrasts with other speech sounds. It is because of the contrastive role of /t/ that we perceive the word *tin* when someone says it, and we know that the person meant 'tin' and not 'sin' or 'bin' or 'pin' or 'din' or 'gin' or 'fin.' It is easy to conclude that /t/ is a separate sound in English and that it is **distinct** (that is, a *different sound*) from /d/ or /s/ or other sounds. This seems obvious, hardly worthy of mention.

However, the matter is complicated because, as shown in Chapter 6, there is not just one kind of /t/ in English, but many. For example, /t/ may be aspirated or nonaspirated, released or unreleased. It may have an alveolar, alveopalatal, or dental place of articulation. When released, it may be centrally, nasally, or laterally released (depending upon the sound that follows). It may even be pronounced like a "d," as [ɾ]. Indeed, a careful acoustic study would show that virtually every instance of /t/ is slightly different.

Why is it that we group all these quite different sounds together and call them simply /t/? Is it perhaps because they all sound so much alike that it would be impossible to differentiate them? This is undoubtedly true of some varieties of /t/, but not of all. For example, it is easy to hear the difference between an aspirated and an unaspirated /t/, and the speakers of some languages make that distinction all the time.

Or perhaps we group them together because of accommodation; that is, since the various kinds of English /t/ are determined mostly by the phonetic environment, is it simply impossible to produce certain kinds of /t/ in certain environments? This again is only partly true. It would be pretty hard to produce a centrally released /t/ just before an /l/ without putting in any intervening sound. But there is no physical reason that we could not pronounce an unaspirated /t/ where we pronounce an aspirated one, and vice versa.

No, the reason why we, as speakers of English, group these different sounds together as "one" speech sound is not because we could not hear the distinction and not because we could not pronounce the distinction everywhere. Rather, it is because we are speakers of English, and the English language happens to work that way. You cannot assume, just because two phones seem to you to be slightly different forms of the "same" sound, that they will seem that way to speakers of every language.

The speakers of some languages distinguish between aspirated and unaspirated /t/: to them, these are different sounds. Speakers of another language may distinguish, at the ends of words, between a released and an unreleased /t/: they do not feel, as English speakers do, that either one can be used.

A group of phones, or sounds, that go together in a certain language to form what the speakers of that language feel to be one sound, and that are never used in a contrastive way, form what is called a **phoneme** of that language. The various forms of that one sound, such as the aspirated, unaspirated, dental, alveolar, and laterally released /t/'s of English are called **allophones** of that phoneme. We can say, therefore, that /t/ is a phoneme of English and that its allophones include all the various kinds of /t/ mentioned here and in Chapter 6.

Note to Students of Linguistics

The approach this chapter takes to the question of sound contrast in language represents a theoretical viewpoint that is no longer current among most linguists. The field is now called **phonology,** rather than **phonemics,** as it once was. And the approach presented here uses what is now referred to as the **autonomous phoneme,** whereas most phonologists now take the approach of the **systematic phoneme.** They view the phoneme, not as a single entity, but as a bundle of features representing different aspects of its articulation.

However, this chapter takes a traditional approach to sound contrast in language for a number of reasons. First, traditional phonemics is relatively intuitive: it makes sense, and thus provides a good introduction to the problems linguists face in analyzing phonological systems. Second, approaches to phonology are many and varied, with many substantive issues still to be decided. The purpose of this book is to introduce phonetics and phonetic issues, rather than to take a particular approach to phonology. So, through traditional phonemics, this chapter will alert you to the dual nature of linguistic sound systems—that is, that there is a concrete phonetic level, involving articulatory gestures and sound waves, and there is also a level of phonological contrasts. Third, as a student of linguistics you will study modern phonology as a distinct subdiscipline, so you would reap no benefit if the material were covered in your phonetics textbook. Finally, many users of this book will apply their knowledge to clinical practice or second-language teaching, and I felt that a traditional approach was most useful in those applications (but I must reiterate that traditional phonemics is the usual starting point for linguistics students learning modern phonology).

As a linguistics student, therefore, you should view this chapter as an introduction to the problem of systematic sound contrasts in language, and not as the current solution to that problem.

8-2 The Phoneme

The idea of the phoneme is somewhat abstract; that is, you cannot put your finger on *the* phoneme /t/. It is not a single, unchanging entity. Rather, it is an abstraction from the many, many different instances of /t/ that are heard in speech, some of which are almost unrecognizable (particularly in rapid speech).

The idea that the phoneme is abstract should not be disconcerting, nor should it make the concept seem terribly complex. Virtually every word we use in everyday conversation is abstract, and in the same way that the word *phoneme* is.

Take, for example, the familiar word *tree*. While there are different kinds, a mental picture of a typical tree can be conjured up without much difficulty. It is of no consequence (or it should not be) that every single tree in the whole world is different; they are still trees, even when some of the "typical" characteristics are lacking. For instance, the typical tree may have leaves, but many trees do not. The typical tree may be quite large, but it does not matter that there are dwarf trees that may stand only a foot high, although they may be a hundred years old. So, while the mental picture of a typical tree is idealized, it is a recognized fact that there are many varieties of trees, some of them quite unlike the accepted image, and these must be acknowledged as trees.

Just as our mental picture of a tree is somewhat idealized, so is the definition of a particular phoneme in a certain language. All instances of the phoneme /t/ in English are different, ranging from those that are almost identical with our idea of a typical /t/ to those that are acoustically deviant (a stuttered /t/, for instance, may be highly anomalous).

So, when we speak of the particular phoneme /t/, we mean a typical /t/, but we also take into consideration all the various forms that that phoneme may have in the English language. Even the various allophones cover a broad range of possible articulations; if we speak of the laterally released allophone of /t/, each instance will be a little different, but the term is still useful for grouping together speech sounds that share many common features.

Of course it is possible to be specific or general with the terminology. Heavily aspirated, moderately aspirated, and lightly aspirated /t/'s can be distinguished. Or they can all be grouped together as /t/'s and referred to, for example, as the aspirated allophone of /t/.

8-2.1 Some Allophones of English Phonemes

Let us reinforce the notions of phoneme and allophone by reviewing some of the material from Chapter 6, using the new terminology. In the examples, note that we place the symbols for phonemes between slash marks (/t/) and the symbols for the allophones between square brackets ($[t^h]$).

1. The phoneme /t/ in English has many allophones:

ALLOPHONE	TYPE	EXAMPLE	ENVIRONMENT
[t]	Unaspirated /t/	*stop*	Following word-initial /s/
$[t^h]$	Aspirated /t/	*top*	In word-initial position
[t˺]	Unreleased /t/	*bought two*	Before another similar plosive or optionally in utterance-final position
[ɾ]	Flapped /t/	*butter*	Intervocalic, posttonic (i.e., preceded by the stress)
$[t^N]$	Nasally released /t/	*whatnot*	Before a nasal
$[t^L]$	Laterally released /t/	*little*	Before a lateral

ALLOPHONE	TYPE	EXAMPLE	ENVIRONMENT
[t̪]	Dental /t/	*both Tom and I*	Before or after a dental
[t̠]	Back (alveopalatal) /t/	*meatshop*	Before or after an alveopalatal
[ʔ]	Glottal stop	*button*	Before unstressed syllabic [n̩]

2. The phoneme /p/ in English has many allophones:

[p]	Unaspirated /p/	*spot*	Following word-initial /s/
$[p^h]$	Aspirated /p/	*pot*	In word-initial position
[p˺]	Unreleased /p/	*stop*	Optionally in word-final position

3. The phoneme /l/ in English has three main allophones:

[l]	"Light" (non-velarized) /l/	*limb*	Word-initial, particularly before front or low back vowels
[ɫ]	"Dark" (velarized) /l/	*mole*	Post-vocalic, particularly after high or mid back vowels
[l̩]	Syllabic /l/ (generally velarized in English, but, for clarity, not indicated)	*little*	Generally word-final following a consonant; no other vowel in the syllable

4. The phoneme /e/ in English has a number of allophones:

[e̯i]	Diphthongized /e/	*fate*	In a syllable carrying full stress
[e]	Shorter, non-diphthongized /e/	*gradation*	In a syllable carrying secondary stress
[ə]	Schwa (unstressed)	*Canada*	In an unstressed syllable

Note also that /e/ may have long or short allophones, depending upon the voicing of the following consonant:

[e:]	Long	*made*	Before a voiced consonant or in an open syllable
[e]	Short	*mate*	Before a voiceless consonant

Both of these are diphthongized, but for clarity this is not indicated.

This listing is by no means exhaustive. An important point is demonstrated by these few examples, however: all information is not necessarily given if it is not relevant. For example, /e/ may be long or short, diphthongized or not. In the foregoing table, long and short /e/ were listed [e:] and [e]; diphthongization was not marked, since we were at that point concentrating on length. It can be seen, therefore, that it is allowable to record only what is necessary for clarity. A second point to note is that the allophones, while phonetically more specific, are still abstractions. For example, each instance of a laterally released /t/ will be a little different from every other one.

8-3 The Predictability and Contrastiveness of the Phoneme

A phoneme is made up of a group of allophones; the allophone, in turn, represents a number of articulations that vary in small ways among speakers, among phonetic environments, and according to the particular occasion on which it was said. In a list of allophones of some English phonemes, it is evident that the various different types of /t/, for example, properly belong together. However, the *feeling* that they belong together does not constitute a definition, and that feeling is likely to cause difficulties in the phonemic analysis of a foreign language. What are the criteria for deciding that a certain group of phones should be grouped together as allophones of a certain phoneme?

The first criterion is **phonetic similarity.** The allophones of a phoneme are generally quite similar: that is, their place of articulation is the same or nearly the same, and their manner of articulation is usually the same or similar (the phoneme /t/ may have [ɾ] as an allophone; flaps and plosives are similar). One would not expect a bilabial nasal to have a velar fricative as an allophone.

The second criterion has to do with the **functioning** of sounds in a particular language. Functioning is reflected in the **predictability** of a sound or its **contrastiveness.** While these two notions may seem quite distinct, they are actually two sides of the same coin. Let us look at each aspect in turn.

8-3.1 Contrastiveness of the Phoneme

Why do we group [p] and $[p^h]$ together as one phoneme, and count [b] as a separate phoneme? (Of course, it is perfectly obvious to the English speaker that we do this; here, we are trying to answer the question of why we are doing it.) The most obvious reason that [p] and [b] are considered to be separate is that the difference between them alone can be used to signal the difference between words: "pit" has a different meaning from "bit." These two words form what we call a **minimal pair;** that is, a pair of words whose sounds (not necessarily spelling) differ by *one* segment only. In this case, the sound difference between the words /pɪt/ and /bɪt/ lies in the difference between /p/ and /b/.

The existence of this minimal pair tells us that the difference between these two sounds can *signal a meaning difference* in English: it is **contrastive.** We can confirm this by finding other minimal pairs: *putter/butter; lap/lab; pan/ban; rapid/rabid; post/boast.* Of course, not every word will have such a mate; there is a word "prairie" but no word *"brairie" (the asterisk indicates a nonexistent word). It may be quite difficult to find minimal pairs for some sounds; sometimes, because of an accidental gap in the language or because of phonotactic restrictions (the subject of a later section of this chapter), there are no minimal pairs. If any can be found, however, an important discovery has been made about the functioning of the phones under question: they are contrastive. "Pan" has a different pronunciation and meaning from "ban," and therefore /p/ contrasts with /b/. We may therefore say that they are separate phonemes.

Let us now try the test of contrastiveness on [p] and [p^h]. The first thing to notice is that no minimal pairs can be found; that is, there may be a word [p^hɪt], but there is no word *[pɪt]. There may be a word [spɪt] but no word *[sp^hɪt]. It will not be possible to find a pair of words whose only sound difference is the difference between [p] and [p^h]. Let us try substituting one sound for the other: say [pɪt] instead of [p^hɪt]. There is no difference in meaning. It may sound a little strange, but it is still the same word. Try saying [sp^hɪt] instead of [spɪt]. Again, it may sound a little odd, but the word has not changed.

Since substituting one for the other does not change the meaning, *the two sounds are not contrastive.* We conclude that they are **allophones** of the same phoneme.

In summary, the test of contrastiveness reveals whether two sounds are separate phonemes or are allophones of the same phoneme. When the substitution of one sound for the other can totally change the meaning of the word, two separate phonemes are involved; when it cannot, allophones of the same phoneme are involved.

At this point, it must be stressed that the *absence* of a mate to form a minimal pair does not *prove* that the sounds in question are allophones. Positive evidence is conclusive; negative evidence is not. For example, in trying to determine the status of /t/ and /d/ in English, we might check to see if there were a word *"dask" to go with "task." The absence of this word is an accidental gap in English and proves nothing. Even if we found twenty other words with no mates, we would not have proved that the sounds in question were allophones. Only one contrastive pair is needed to prove that the two sounds are separate phonemes: "tot" and "dot." For some sounds, particularly among the vowels, the clear-cut evidence of minimal pairs may be difficult or impossible to find. In such cases, other tests may be applied.

8-3.2 Predictability and the Phoneme

The second way the function of a sound is revealed is through its **predictability.** An example will demonstrate how to test for predictability.

Imagine being presented with this transcription, in which one symbol is replaced by a hyphen: [-æt]. If the choice were given of replacing the hyphen with either [p] or [p^h], could it be predicted which would go into the space? Yes, the correct answer must be [p^h], as long as we know it is an English word. This must be the case, since the word-initial /p/ is aspirated in English. Notice that this prediction could be made even without knowing the word. Try the same exercise with the nonsense word *[s-æš]. Is the hyphen replaced by [p] or [p^h]? This time the answer must be [p]. You can make this prediction whether or not you know what the word means and whether it has any meaning at all. All you need to know is that it is English.

Now try the same test with [p] and [b]. Given the transcription [læ-] with one symbol left out, can you predict which of the two sounds belongs? No. The answer will be that it depends upon the meaning of the word. If you are given a nonsense syllable and asked to perform the same task, as with *[stɪ-], you will see that there is no way at all to predict which sound is the correct one.

In summary, the choice between two allophones is normally predictable, while the choice between two phonemes is not (except, as will be shown, as a result of phonotactic restrictions).

The various allophones of a phoneme are normally found each in its own environment and not in the environments of the other allophones. The environments, therefore, are for the most part mutually exclusive; this idea is expressed by saying that the allophones are in **complementary distribution.** Things that are **complementary** go together to make a coherent whole,[1] and indeed the environments of each of the allophones go together to make up the environment for the entire phoneme. As an example, we could say dark and light /l/ are in complementary distribution in English. That is, all of the environments of [l] plus all of the environments of [ɫ] are mutually exclusive; they, along with the environments of syllabic [l̩], make up the environment of all English /l/'s. Another way to express this idea is to say that the allophones are **conditioned variants, variants** because they are variant forms of the same phoneme, and **conditioned** because they are conditioned (determined) by their particular phonetic environment.

Certain allophones, it should be noted, are in so-called **free variation.** For example, if asked to predict whether a word will end with a released or a nonreleased /p/, you will have to admit that you cannot, that either one is acceptable. But this does not mean that the two are separate phonemes. Here the test of contrastiveness would provide the answer: [stɑp] and [stɑp˺] both have the same meaning and are both perfectly acceptable pronunciations of the same word.

8-3.3 Intrinsic and Extrinsic Allophones

Different allophones occur in different environments, as we have just seen. It would be well at this point to examine just why this is so.

It appears that some allophonic variation must be due to the inevitable effects of coarticulation, and some must be due to arbitrary rules of a given language. The terms **intrinsic** and **extrinsic allophones** have been used for these types (Ladefoged [1968b], after Wang and Fillmore [1961]).

An **intrinsic allophone** is one that is generated by the coarticulatory effects of neighboring sounds. The lateral release of /t/ when followed by /l/ is an example of such an intrinsic allophone, since it is impossible to release /t/ centrally in such an environment without generating an intrusive intervening sound. If the adjustment is an intrinsic one, the same allophonic distribution can be expected to occur universally in all languages.

An **extrinsic allophone** is one produced systematically by speakers of a given language, although no physiological reason compels them to do so. In English, the aspiration of /t/ word-initially and the nonaspiration of /t/ following word-initial /s/ are such examples, since it is perfectly possible to produce each variant in the other variant's environment. The distribution of extrinsic allophones can be expected to be different in different languages.

This distinction is an important one for the student of phonetics to consider. As in other matters of a phonetic nature, we have a strong tendency either to consider that the way things are in our native language are that way for a good logical reason, even when the reason is arbitrary, or else to fail to notice those phonetic facts because we are so used to the way things are in our native tongue. To reiterate: the distribution of allophones in English is due partly to speech physiology and partly to arbitrary rules of English grammar.

However, the **intrinsic-extrinsic** distinction should not be taken in too absolute a sense; there is a gray area between. Peter Ladefoged, a phonetician with much experience with West African languages, states, "In studying the phonetic structure of a wide variety of languages I am sometimes surprised by finding that speakers take care not to make an articulatory adjustment which I had considered to be an inevitable coarticulation and a language universal" [1986b, p. 292]. That is, what seems to be an *intrinsic* allophonic adjustment may not be so.

By the same token, what seems to be an *extrinsic* allophonic adjustment may fall into the

[1] Not to be confused with *complimentary*, meaning 'flattering.'

gray area. For example, in English, word-initial voiceless plosives are aspirated and voiced ones are not. We may be tempted to say that this is an extrinsic allophonic adjustment, since voiceless plosives *can* be nonaspirated in this position. And voiced ones *can* be aspirated. But the aspiration pattern of English is quite common among languages in general; aspiration of voiced plosives is quite rare. There may be, and probably is, a physiological reason that this adjustment is *more likely* or *easier to articulate,* but that does not *preclude* a different articulation in which the adjustment is not made.

To take another example, the English phoneme /k/ is articulated palatally (as [c]) before palatal vowels (as in the word "key"); it is articulated as a back velar (as [q]) in some dialects before [ɑ] (as in the word "cot"). It is articulated as a front or mid velar [k] when followed by low front, central, or high back vowels. Such an adjustment is a natural consequence of coarticulation, but it is *possible* to pronounce [q] before a front vowel or [c] before a back vowel. One could therefore argue as to whether the English allophonic distribution is intrinsic or extrinsic.

In summary, we may distinguish three types of allophonic distribution: **intrinsic,** in which physiologically constrained coarticulatory effects force the adjustment; **extrinsic,** in which the language systematically makes an adjustment without physiological motivation; and an unnamed type (properly a subtype of extrinsic) in which the adjustment has very strong, but not compelling, physiological motivation.

8-4 Functional Units in Language

Languages, as we said before, depend upon sound contrasts in order to carry or convey meaning. But what languages contrast is not segments, but phonemes. In English, /t/ is contrasted with /p/. The choice between /t/ and /p/ depends upon whether a particular word happens to have one or the other; a substitution of one for the other is not usually tolerated (except in accommodation).

If a particular word contains a /t/, however, the particular type of /t/ is selected on the basis of the sounds around the phonetic environment. We may say that the major selection between phonemes is based on a criterion dependent upon meaning; the small choice between allophones depends upon the surrounding sounds.

Unfortunately, this simple picture is made a little more complex by some situations that do not fit neatly into it. Let us consider a few of these.[2]

8-4.1 Morphophonemics

The first problem we come across in a phonemic analysis is that sounds that appear to be contrastive sometimes are not. For example, we can use the test of minimal pairs to demonstrate that /s/ and /z/ are contrastive in English: *sip/zip; bus/buzz.* But then we note that the English plural ending, usually spelled ⟨-s⟩ or ⟨-es⟩, is pronounced according to the surrounding sounds: [s] in the word "cats" and [z] in the word "dogs" (and [əz̆] in the word "buses," but we will ignore this for the moment). Now, "cats" cannot contrast with *[kætz], nor can "dogs" contrast with *[dɑgs] (or *[dɔgs]; the vowel varies with the dialect).

In this case, phonetic considerations are mixed with other aspects of the grammar. A **morpheme,** you will recall, is the smallest *meaningful* unit of language. The word *cats,* for example, contains two morphemes: *cat,* which means what you think it does, and *-s,* which means 'more than one' (plural). Some morphemes, like *cat,* can stand alone; these are called **free** morphemes. Other morphemes, like *-s,* must be attached to another morpheme to form a word; these are called **bound** morphemes. Both types of morpheme may have more than one form. The morphophonemic situation being discussed in this section occurs most commonly with bound morphemes, such as the plural *-s.*

The morpheme *-s* must be attached to a word, and its pronunciation depends on the phonetic shape of the word to which it is attached. The change in pronunciation is not a small one—that is, the choice of one or another allophone—but is between two phonemes. Normally, a change from one phoneme to another changes the meaning of the word, but not here.

[2] Students of linguistics should note that the weight of evidence provided by the various problems brought up in Section 8-4, as well as other theoretical issues, eventually led to the abandonment of the autonomous phoneme as presented in this chapter and to its replacement by other phonological theories, most notably **distinctive feature analysis** and **generative phonology.**

The solution to this problem is to propose the existence of the **morphophoneme,** a morpheme having more than one different phonemic realization. This concept was introduced in Chapter 3. Elsewhere the difference between /s/ and /z/ is a **phonemic** or **contrastive** difference, but in this specific morphophoneme (the plural), the difference between [s] and [z] depends upon the phonetic environment (as is usually the case for allophones of one phoneme).

Another example would be the negative prefix spelled *in-* or *im-* and pronounced [ɪn], [ɪm], or [ɪŋ]. Since two of the variants are reflected in the spelling, these tend to be thought of as different prefixes, but they are actually different pronunciations of the same morphophoneme. Three of the main variants can be seen in these words:

SAMPLE WORD	PHONETIC SHAPE OF MORPHOPHONEME
indistinguishable *inordinate*	[ɪn]
impossible	[ɪm]
incredible	[ɪŋ]

The test of contrastiveness will confirm that /n/, /m/, and /ŋ/ are separate phonemes. But in this prefix, the choice among these phonemes depends upon the following sound. Usually, only the choice between allophones depends upon the following sound.

8-4.2 NEUTRALIZATION

The second problem we find in phonemic analysis is that certain pairs of phonemes lose their phonetic contrastiveness in some environments. As an example, the difference between /t/ and /d/ in English is phonemic or contrastive. Minimal pairs such as *tin/din* and *mitt/mid* show this to be true.

When the sounds /t/ and /d/ are in intervocalic position, however, and the preceding vowel is stressed, the distinction between /t/ and /d/ is often not made in speech. For example, the words "betting" and "bedding" are often both pronounced [bɛɾɪŋ], with the voiced flap [ɾ] replacing both /t/ and /d/. In this case, two sounds that are normally contrastive are *no longer* contrastive and are not used to signal a meaning distinction. Of course, context supplies the clue to meaning, and no confusion for the listener generally results.

How do we analyze this situation *phonemically?* We say that /t/ and /d/ are separate phonemes and are contrastive but that this contrastiveness may be **neutralized** in one phonetic environment. There are two points to notice in this example. First, neutralizations may be optional or obligatory. In this example, the neutralization is optional in North American English; "bedding" may be pronounced [bɛɾɪŋ] or [bɛdɪŋ]; "betting" may be pronounced [bɛɾɪŋ] or [bɛtɪŋ]. Other neutralizations may be obligatory.

The second point is an important, although somewhat abstract, one. While the word "betting" may be *phonetically* pronounced [bɛɾɪŋ], it is still *phonemically* /bɛtɪŋ/; that is, even when the word is pronounced with the flap [ɾ], the speaker of English knows that the basic sound is /t/; in fact he probably thinks he *hears* /t/. One reason for this is that the neutralization is restricted to one phonetic environment; in the related words *bet/bed* and *bets/beds,* for example, the contrastiveness between /t/ and /d/ remains.

8-4.3 VARIANT PRONUNCIATIONS

Another problem for phonemic analysis is optional pronunciations. The word "either" may be pronounced /a͜iðɚ/ or /iðɚ/, and the first sound in "economics" may be /i/ or /ɛ/. The problem here is that since /i/, /a͜i/, and /ɛ/ are different phonemes, a change from one to another should change the meaning. "Might" and "meet" (/ma͜it/ and /mit/) are different words with different meanings, but /a͜iðɚ/ and /iðɚ/ are not.

Variant pronunciations are really not a great problem, since the number of words in this category is small. Certain words have more than one acceptable pronunciation, and /a͜i/ and /i/ are still separate contrastive phonemes despite the two pronunciations of "either."

8-4.4 DIALECTS

The fourth problem found in phonemic analysis is that different dialects of the same language make different phonemic contrasts. For example, we have noted that some dialects distinguish /ɔ/ and /ɑ/, whereas others do not. Thus, some speakers distinguish "caught" and "cot," while these words are homophonous to speakers of other dialects. Not only is the exact phonetic shape of the segments different, in different dialects, but the *contrasts* made are different as well. Some dialects have two separate phonemes corresponding to /ɑ/ and /ɔ/; others have but one phoneme (which may have the two phones as allophones). Small phonemic differences such as this generally do not cause communication problems.

To take another example, the Cockney dialect of English has leveled the distinction between /f/ and /θ/ and between /v/ and /ð/. Just the sounds [f] and [v] are pronounced. The words "thought" and "fought" are pronounced with an initial [f] sound; the words "that" and "vat" are pronounced with a [v] sound. Thus, Cockney lacks two *segments* of standard English and correspondingly lacks two standard English *phonemes*.

Two dialects may differ in their inventory of speech sounds *without* differing in phonemic structure. Let us take the example of Cajun English, a dialect spoken in Louisiana, in which aspiration of initial voiceless plosives is reduced or not present at all. Thus, /p/ does not have the aspirated allophone of standard English. Cajun therefore has one less *segment* but the same number of *phonemes* (with respect to this point).

Two dialects may differ in having phonetically different realizations of the same phoneme. For example, the consonant /r/ in intervocalic position is quite different in North American English than in upperclass British English. The North American /r/ tends to be more of a liquid sound (properly symbolized [ɹ]); the British /r/ is generally closer to a flap than a liquid in articulation (properly symbolized [r] or [ř]). The two dialects have different *segments* but the same *phonemic* structure (with respect to this point).

8-5 Languages and the Phoneme

We will next take a few examples from languages other than English and examine their phonemic structure. The purpose of these examples is to see how the phonemic systems of languages can vary; the specific details of these particular languages are not the point of the examples. Rather, non-English examples are used to emphasize the principle of phonemics, which may be obscured by our intuitive knowledge of our native tongue.

8-5.1 Some Examples

In Spanish, [d] and [ð] are allophones. They are in complementary distribution; [ð] occurs intervocalically (or between a vowel and certain resonant consonants such as [ř]), and [d] occurs everywhere else. Both are spelled with the letter ⟨d⟩ in the Spanish spelling system. The word *nada*, for example, is pronounced [nɑðɑ]. The Spanish-speaking person has both sounds in his phonetic repertoire but does not contrast them. There could not be a pair of words whose only difference was that one had the sound [d] where the other had the sound [ð]. The speaker of Spanish who is learning English has difficulty learning to distinguish "other" from "udder," or "den" from "then," even though he can pronounce both sounds. He distributes the two sounds as they are distributed in Spanish: he says "other" for both "other" and "udder," and "den" for both "then" and "den," and has difficulty recognizing his error.

The French or German speaker learning English also usually has difficulty with [ð], but for a different reason. This segment is lacking in those languages.

Thai provides us with an example of a language that contrasts aspirated and unaspirated voiceless plosives. Both English and Thai have the phones [p], [p^h], and [b], but the two languages differ in their phonemic structure. Fromkin and Rodman [1983] give the example of these three contrasting Thai words:

/pɑɑ/	forest
/p^hɑɑ/	to split
/bɑɑ/	shoulder

The example demonstrates that [p] and [p^h] are contrastive in Thai, since we have found a minimal pair. We know that [p] and [p^h] are in complementary distribution in English and are not contrastive, so the same three phones must function as two phonemes in English but as three in Thai:

THAI PHONEMES	SEGMENTS	ENGLISH PHONEMES
/p/	[p]	/p/
/p^h/	[p^h]	
/b/	[b]	/b/

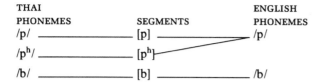

To take another example, Japanese has a sound very similar to English /l/ and a sound very similar to English /r/. These are not separate phonemes, however; they are allophones of the same phoneme. The l-like sound occurs with certain vowels; the r-like sound with other vowels. The Japanese speaker can produce both sounds but only in certain environments. English speakers often say that the Japanese reverse the /r/ and /l/ when they speak English, but this is not true. The correct or incorrect variant may be used, in accordance with the distribution in Japanese.

Other examples could be given. In Russian, the difference between dark and light /l/ is phonemic. In Old English, [f] and [v] were allophones, as were [s] and [z].

8-5.2 Phones and Phonemes

When speakers of English hear [t], [t˺], [t̬], [t^h], or another variant of the /t/ phoneme, they "hear" the sound /t/. The difference between the variants, when appropriately used, is not significant for communication. Even in the case of neutralization, the phone uttered will correspond specifically to one or another phoneme. So [bɛɾɪŋ] is interpreted as /bɛtɪŋ/ or as /bɛdɪŋ/, depending on context; we will "hear" /bɛtɪŋ/, even when the speaker *said* [bɛɾɪŋ], if that is what makes sense in the context. The question of whether [bɛɾɪŋ] or /bɛtɪŋ/ is *transcribed* is a matter of how much need for detail there is; this question will be dealt with in Section 8-8. Here we must realize that there is a basic phoneme /t/ that is perceived by the listener, even if it is not pronounced differently from a /d/ by the speaker.[3] The word "betting" contains the phoneme /t/, even if its pronunciation is indistinguishable from that of "bedding."

One segment that exists in three different languages will illustrate how one phone may correspond to different phonemes. The affricate [t^s] exists as a segment in German, one dialect of French, and English, but its status as a phoneme is different in each case. In German, the affricate /t^s/ has a separate status as a phoneme. This can be demonstrated by minimal pairs (pay attention to the phonetic transcription, not the standard spelling):

Ziegel	[t^sigl̩]	tile
Tiegel	[tigl̩]	saucepan
Zank	[t^sɑŋk]	quarrel
Tank	[tɑŋk]	tank

These examples prove that /t^s/ is not a variant of /t/. Could it be a variant of /s/? No, since /s/ does not occur in word-initial position in German. Could it be a variant of /z/ (as its spelling might suggest)? No, there is a minimal pair:

Zank	[t^saŋk]	quarrel
sank	[zaŋk]	sank

In a similar way, the possibility that /t^s/ is a variant of any other phoneme in German can be eliminated, so it must have its own status. The word *Zank*, for example, must have /t^s/ as its basic first sound.

In the French spoken in Quebec, the phoneme /t/ is pronounced [t^s] when it precedes a high front vowel, /i/ or /ü/. So a word such as *type*, pronounced /tip/ in standard French, is pronounced [t^sip] in Quebec French, but a word such as *tout* is pronounced [tu] in all dialects. In Quebec French, /t/ has two allophones, [t] and [t^s], which are conditioned by their environment. We cannot find a minimal pair, as we could in German. So when a speaker of Quebec French says [t^sip], the basic sound is /tip/. The two phones do not have separate phonemic status.

In English, the sequence of /t/ followed by /s/ is often pronounced as an affricate when spoken quickly. So "bits and pieces" may be pronounced [bɪt^sən . . .]. However, while *phonetically* an affricate is pronounced, from the point of view of *pho-*

[3] This is true, however, only where neutralization normally occurs. If /d/ were said for /t/ elsewhere, the listener would either recognize the error or would misunderstand the message.

nemics or basic sounds it is simply a /t/ followed by an /s/. The English speaker hearing [t^s] interprets it as /ts/.

Consequently, while the same phone exists in all three languages, its function in each is very different, and it will be heard differently by the native speakers of each language, because each has a different set of phonemic contrasts.

LANGUAGE	SEGMENT	SAMPLE WORD (USUAL SPELLING)	BASIC SOUND OR PHONEME
German	[t^s]	*Zank*	/t^s/
Quebec French	[t^s]	*type*	/t/
English	[t^s]	*bits and pieces*	/ts/

8-5.3 PHONEMICS AND PHONETICS

Phonetics has as one of its objectives a *universal* system of classifying speech sounds on an articulatory basis. Phonemics, on the other hand, devises a simpler classification system that captures only the distinctions necessary for a particular language. One result of this is that the meaning of a transcription of a statement is occasionally misunderstood. Sometimes students are confused by statements that appear to be contradictory; often the apparent contradiction results from a confusion over whether the statement is true *phonetically* or *phonemically*.

The vowel [ʌ], for example, is described as a *central* vowel in many phonetics textbooks. Chapter 4 (Section 4-4.4) stressed that it is a *back* vowel in most (but not all) dialects. However, the contradiction is not as serious as it first appears. In Chapter 4, the details of the articulation were stressed, as that was the objective of that chapter.

When we are interested only in the *distinctiveness* of English phonemes, there is economy in classifying [ʌ] as a central vowel. As noted, rounding (labialization) is a redundant feature of all English vowels with the exception of the pair [ʌ]-[ɔ]. That is, for all other *English* vowels, rounding is predictable from other articulatory information: no high front vowel is rounded; no high back vowel is spread; no low vowel is rounded (in most dialects); and so on. This is an aspect of the overall phonemic system of English; and this generalization can be captured by calling [ʌ] a central vowel (which is not far from the articulatory truth). We can then generalize that front vowels are unrounded and back vowels are rounded ([ʊ] is an exception because it is lax, and the only remaining exception, [ɑ], can be explained by the fact that its rounded counterpart, [ɒ], is rare in all languages). Such a classification does not cause any problems among central vowels, since most English dialects have [ə] only in unstressed (weak) syllables and have [ʌ] only in syllables with primary or secondary stress.

Thus, in an analysis of the *phonemic* system of English, [ʌ] may be classed as central for the sake of economy in classification. The only problem arises when a person mistakenly assumes that the *phonemic analysis* is supposed to be a precise *articulatory description*, which it is not.

Another case in which the two types of analysis are in apparent conflict is the sound [ɚ]. Many transcription systems will transcribe the word "bird," for example, as /bərd/, while this book has suggested [bɚd]. Again, the contradiction is not one of substance. From a purely phonetic point of view, the standard North American dialect of English has one rhotic, nondiphthongized vowel in the word "bird": the vowel cannot be separated from the /r/ in the articulation (of course, these remarks do not apply to the so-called r-less dialects or to certain British dialects with flapped intervocalic [ř]'s).

From the point of view of a phonemic analysis, the transcription /bərd/ may best indicate the contrastive system of English. Historically, schwar developed from the sequence of a vowel plus the consonant /r/. Schwar makes no phonemic contrast with the consonant /r/, and our intuition as speakers of English is that "bird" contains a sequence of vowel plus consonant /r/.

Your instructor therefore may choose the transcription system in which "bird" is transcribed as /bərd/. We have stressed the existence of schwar in English because it is of practical importance to realize that a word like "bird" will sound odd if an attempt is made to pronounce a sequence of vowel plus consonant /r/.

8-6 Phonemic Status of Phonetic Units Other Than Segments

When we examine the sound systems of languages with a view to discovering what the contrasts are, we find that phonetic units and phonetic phenomena other than segments serve a contrasting role like that of the phoneme. Let us look at some of these.

8-6.1 The Phonemic Role of Stress

In Chapter 7 we noted that English words are often contrasted on the basis of stress (and the resultant changes in vowel quality). So a pair of words such as "défect" (noun) and "defect" (verb) are contrasted by stress alone.

We can therefore say that stress is **phonemic** in English; that is, stress plays a *contrastive role* in the sound system of English.

> In the terminology of linguistics, the suffix *-eme* means 'a significant or contrastive unit of.' We have already seen the terms **phoneme,** a contrastive unit of sound, and **morpheme,** the smallest meaningful (therefore contrastive) unit into which words can be broken.
>
> In the same way, the term **prosodeme** is sometimes used to refer to the contrastive unit of stress (stress being a *prosodic* feature of speech). However, the fact can be expressed simply by stating that stress is phonemic.

In Chapter 7, examples were given of some languages that do and some that do not use stress phonemically. We noted that, in Spanish, stress is used contrastively: 'término' and 'terminó' are different words. Thus, *stress is phonemic in Spanish,* as it is in English, although the details of its frequency, its orthographic (spelling) representation, and the effects of stress on vowel quality are very different in the two languages.

We noted that, in German, stress is almost always predictable, although its placement is not according to the usual rule in certain borrowed words, and there are a few words in which stress is contrastive (the two different words spelled *übersetzen* are one example). One could therefore say that stress is not phonemic in German, although there are minor exceptions to this rule.

We noted that, in French, stress is not contrastive. But note that *not contrastive* is not the same thing as *not present.* We noted that polysyllabic words in French are stressed lightly on the last syllable (unless the vowel is schwa, in which case the penultimate syllable is lightly stressed). Thus, there *is* stress in French, and misplaced stress will sound strange to the speaker of French, but stress is not *contrastive* or phonemic in French. As a consequence, misplaced stress does not have as serious an effect on comprehension in French as it does in English.

8-6.2 The Phonemic Role of Juncture

The division between words, usually represented with an orthographic space when language is written, has a phonemic status. For example, there is a difference between

a nice man

and

an ice man

even if the iceman has been gone from our neighborhoods for many decades. In a similar way

Rick's truck

and

Rick struck

are different. The difference lies not in which set of phonemes makes up the utterances nor in the order in which those phonemes are found. A phonemic transcription of both would show the same phonemes in the same order. Yet the two expressions are clearly different. The position of the juncture is the difference.

In phonemic transcription, juncture is usually marked with an orthographic space, although this is inaccurate phonetically (there is no corresponding silent pause). When one wishes to be unambiguous in marking juncture, the crosshatch (#) is used. Thus:

/rɪk strʌk/

versus

/rɪks trʌk/

or

/rɪk#strʌk/

versus

/rɪks#trʌk/.

Note that the foregoing are broad phonemic transcriptions; a detailed phonetic transcription would show such characteristics as aspiration, retroflexion, and other effects of the different place of juncture (see Section 8-9).

Juncture can be said to be phonemic as it distinguishes phrases.

8-6.3 The Phonemic Role of Tone

In Chapter 7 we noted that some languages, such as Chinese, use the fundamental frequency of the voice to distinguish between words. Such a phenomenon is called **tone.** We can say that tone is phonemic in Chinese, since words are contrasted by tone alone.

> The term **toneme** is sometimes used to refer to the contrastive role of tone.

8-6.4 The Phonemic Role of Length

We also noted that some languages use **length** contrastively. Recall that **length** refers to the temporal duration of a vowel or consonant and is not to be confused with vowel timbre, everyday usage of the term notwithstanding.

Note, for example, the following vowel contrasts in Finnish (in Finnish orthography, a double letter indicates a long segment):

tuli	'fire'
tuuli	'wind'
puhu	'speak' (imperative)
puhuu	'she/he speaks'

Similarly, note the following consonant contrasts in Finnish:

palo	'fire'
pallo	'ball'
kuka	'who'
kukka	'flower'

On the basis of these examples, we can say that length is phonemic in Finnish (as it is in many languages).

8-6.5 The Phonemic Role of Voice Quality

In Section 9-4.3, we will discuss modes of vocal fold vibration. These include *normal voice, falsetto, whisper, breathy voice,* and *creaky voice.* While in English breathy voice and creaky voice may be personal affectations or displays of emotion, these two voice qualities are phonemic in some languages. That is to say, in a given language two different words could have the same sequence of segments and differ only in that one is said in normal voice and the other in breathy voice; such a language phonemically distinguishes normal voice from creaky voice. In some languages, the special voice quality is used for certain segments or sequences of segments rather than for the whole word.

There is some evidence that special voice quality, used phonemically, may develop into, or develop from, phonemic tone in the history of a given language.

8-6.6 The Phonemic Status of Phonetic Variables

In Section 8-6 we have seen that a number of phonetic variables are used differently in different languages. Voice quality, for example, is a phonetic variable available to every human speaker. Some languages use very little variation in voice quality, even at the phonetic level. Other languages may use it to show emotion (such is the case in English). In yet other languages it may be *phonemic,* which is to say that variation in that quality changes the meaning of words as interpreted by a speaker of that language.

This section should alert you to the fact that a

phonetic variable having no linguistic significance in English may be fundamental in the phonemic system of another language. But a variable (such as the tenseness of vowels) that is critical in English may have no particular significance in another language.

Similarly, in the phonemic system of a child learning English, a foreigner learning English, or the individual with some sort of speech disorder, distinctions may be made that differ from those made in standard English.

8-7 Realization of Some Phonemes in English

In Chapter 6 and in Section 8-2.1, we examined a number of different variants of English phonemes. These are correctly called **realizations** of phonemes, in that the phoneme is an abstract representation and the actual noise you make when talking is how you *realize* ('make real', 'put into action') that abstraction.

It is well to note that the actual physical (acoustic and articulatory) realization of a phoneme may in many cases be very different from that which is expected. A good example is juncture: "a nice man" is different from "an iceman." However, there is no pause in speech corresponding to the space on the page between words. Instead, a number of juncture phenomena (see Section 8-9) come into play in signaling the word boundary. Among these are *aspiration:* a /t/ at the end of a word will not be aspirated, whereas one at the beginning will. The speaker thus signals whether the /t/ is word-final or word-initial by aspirating it or not. Another such signal is *length.* While length is not phonemic in English, it is used to signal other features that are themselves phonemic. For example, one of the differences between "an ice man" and "a nice man" is the length of the /n/: it is longer in "a nice man" (Hoard [1966]).

Length also signals the "presence" of postvocalic /r/ in r-less dialects, as we have noted (see Section 4-5). The difference between the pronunciation of "Kotter" and of "Carter" may reside solely in the length of the vowel: it will be longer in "Carter." One may say that this dialect has a phoneme /r/ that is never realized as such postvocalically but that is realized as a lengthening of the preceding vowel.

Another example of unexpected realizations of phonemes lies in *voicing.* It is clear that English has, in plosives, fricatives, and affricates, a voiced-voiceless distinction that is phonemic: /p/ is a different phoneme from /b/, /f/ from /v/, /č/ from /ǰ/, and so on. But is the difference truly one of vocal fold vibration? As we noted in regard to voice onset time (Section 5-2.12), word-initial plosives in English *all* may be voiceless, in the sense that the vocal folds are not vibrating while the occlusion is made; voicing starts generally *after* release. Voicing is initiated sooner for "voiced" plosives than for "voiceless" ones. Also, in certain environments, aspiration is a sign of voicing: only "voiceless" plosives are aspirated. So how do we know whether the speaker said "bought" or "pot"? Not by whether the initial plosive was actually voiced or voiceless—neither was—but because the voicing of the vowel gets started sooner in one than in the other, and because one is accompanied by the noise burst of aspiration. Other cues are used as well.

In a word such as "spot," the voice onset time of the /p/ is about the same as the voice onset time of the /b/ in "bought" (see Section 5-2.12 and Table 5-2). And there is no noise of aspiration to help. However, *phonotactic constraints* (the topic of a later section in this chapter) come to the rescue: no word in English starts */sbV/, so the sound must be /spV/ (remember that the symbol V in a phonetic transcription represents *any* vowel).

What about voicing in postvocalic plosives: how is the phonemic difference between /mæt/ and /mæd/ realized? *Phonemically,* of course, the difference is that one word ends in a voiceless segment, the other in a voiced segment, but is this true *phonetically*? No, it is not. The difference lies in the length of the vowel; the /æ/ is longer preceding /d/ than preceding /t/. Indeed, you can make a recording of "mad" sound like "mat" by chopping out a bit of the vowel.

Note also that there may be *no* realization of a phonemic difference. For example, the difference between "betting" and "bedding" may simply be nonexistent phonetically. There may be no difference at all between "prints" and "prince" in a strict phonetic sense, but there is all the difference in the world phonemically.

8-7.1 Phonemics versus Phonetics

Let us take, as an example of phonemic "reality" and phonetic "reality," the difference between /t/ and /d/. These two are undoubtedly different phonemes in English, as the difference between them distinguishes many pairs of words. Asked "What is the difference between /t/ and /d/?" you might answer simply, "/t/ is voiceless, whereas /d/ is voiced."

However, I wish to bring it to your attention that the truth is not that simple. The difference between the *abstract phoneme* /t/ and the *abstract phoneme* /d/ may well be characterized as one of voicing, but that does not mean that the *concrete, physically real segments* differ *phonetically* in that way. If we look at instances of these phonemes in different environments, we find that they differ in a variety of ways, not simply in voicing.

Example 1

"tock" versus "dock"

What is the difference between /t/ and /d/ in the context of this pair of words? The /t/ has a longer voice onset time (VOT)—that is, it is less voiced than /d/—and is aspirated, which /d/ is not. In this situation, in which /t/ and /d/ are word-initial, the phonetic difference might be loosely said to be one of voicing—or at least VOT—keeping in mind that there may be no actual voicing during the occlusion phase of the /d/.

Example 2

"stock" versus *"sdock"

How do we know that "stock" is phonemically /stɑk/ and not */sdɑk/? After all, if we record an English speaker saying "stock" and then cut the [s] off, we hear "dock" and not "tock." So the so-called /t/ in "stock" is phonetically like a word-initial /#d/. Why, then, do we think it is a /t/? Let one thing be clear: the reason is not that it sounds like a /t/ or that it is phonetically like a word-initial /#t/. Rather, English has a rule that a plosive following /#s/ at the beginning of a word must be "voiceless": "spot," "stock," and "skirt" are possible, but never anything like *"sbot," *"sdock," and *"sgirt." We have simply defined these as voiceless, despite the fact that they are phonetically like word-initial voiced plosives. Orthographic conventions, too, support this notion: we spell these sounds with ⟨p⟩, ⟨t⟩, and ⟨k⟩ (or ⟨c⟩ or ⟨q⟩) and never with ⟨b⟩, ⟨d⟩, or ⟨g⟩. Later in this chapter we will examine the domain of phonotactics in some detail, but for the moment let us note that it is convention, or rule, rather than any supposed phonetic "facts" that leads to the conclusion that the second segment of "stock" is /t/.

Example 3

"mate" versus "made"

How do we know that "mate" has a /t/ and "made" has a /d/? Is it because the final plosive of "made" is more voiced than the final plosive of "mate"? No. The difference lies in the vowel length, and a recording of "made" will sound like "mate" if a portion of the vowel is chopped out. What, then, is the phonetic difference between "mate" and "made"? The voicing of the final segment? No, the length of the vowel.

Example 4

"latter" versus "ladder"

In colloquial speech, /t/ and /d/ between vowels and following the primary stress are flapped to [ɾ] (concisely, /t/ and /d/ are flapped when intervocalic and post-tonic; i.e., between vowels and after the stress). While not obligatory, this modification is very typical of North American English, and avoiding it (i.e., saying [t] and [d] in this context) tends to sound pedantic. In this discussion, it will be assumed that flapping occurs as a matter of course.

The question to be asked here is the same as in

the previous examples: When you hear someone say "latter" or "ladder," how do you known which was said? Does voicing give the clue? Again, the answer is no, since voicing continues right through both. Is there *any* phonetic difference between the words at all? This time, the answer is also no. So the answer to the main question, How do we distinguish the words? must be found in the context. You "hear" a /t/ where the context demands the word 'latter,' and you "hear" a /d/ where the context demands the word 'ladder.' (When a person is talking about scaling the side of a building, he is unlikely to do it with a "latter," and the opposite of "the former" is not likely to be "the ladder.") Section 10-11 discusses the listener's interpretation of what he hears; for the moment, let us note that what you "hear" depends at least partly on what makes sense.

Let us return to phonemic and phonetic "reality." It is certainly true that English has, for example, a /t/ and a /d/ and that these are different phonemes. They have some kind of existence, in an abstract sense. But it is a mistake to conclude that because English has a contrasting /t/ and /d/, the /t/ is invariably "a voiceless alveolar plosive" and the /d/ is invariably "a voiced alveolar plosive." When you think you hear a /t/ rather than a /d/, there are reasons other than voicelessness that signal it. Furthermore, "hearing" a /d/ rather than a /t/ does not necessarily mean that the voicing was actually there to hear.

In practice, how does one describe the pronunciation of an English /t/? The answer is that it depends; no general description can fit all normal instances of /t/ in connected English speech. What is the difference between a /t/ and a /d/? Again, it depends. The /t/ of "stock" is much like what a /d/ would be if it were at the beginning of a word; the /t/ of "latter" and the /d/ of "ladder" may be identical. Note that these details are true for North American English only. In British English, the *latter/ladder* example is not true. In foreign languages having a /t/-/d/ distinction, /t/ in a context like "stock" might not be the same as one in a context like "dock." But these dialects and languages have their own variability. Ultimately each language and dialect defines its own phonemes and defines what variability is permissible.

The most important thing to learn from this section is that phonemes do not correspond to invariable phonetic entities.

8-8 Practical Implications of Phonemics

A study of phonemic (phonological) systems in language is obviously a question of theoretical interest to linguists. However, it must be stressed that phonemics also has practical implications in the areas of second-language learning, child language acquisition, and some communication disorders. This is so because the phonemic structure of language corresponds to something that has a certain degree of reality in the mind of the speaker.[4]

In the following examples, keep in mind what was said in Chapter 2 concerning language and dialect, namely that each form of language—including those that are not considered "correct"—is governed by a grammar. In this section examples will be given of child language, foreign accent, and speech anomalies. An infant does not have the adult grammar in his head, but he does not speak haphazardly, either: his speech is governed by a grammar. The phonemic system of that grammar (and of other forms of anomalous speech) is the topic of this section; as we will see, an analysis of nonstandard grammar can be useful. The point is that as long as we consider an anomalous speech pattern to be a hodgepodge of "errors," we learn nothing; but once we realize that many of these "errors" in fact reveal systematic differences between the anomalous grammar and the standard grammar, we have made an important discovery, and often the systematic nature of the anomalous speech suggests approaches for correcting the problem.

In approaching this subject, it is important to keep in mind the concept of an **inventory** of sounds of a given language or of the speech of a given individual. But a study of phonemics has

[4]The issue of the "psychological reality of the phoneme" is one that has been debated at length by phonologists and psycholinguists. The debate often revolves around theoretical issues in phonology, and, as has been noted several times, those theoretical issues are beyond the scope of this chapter. What *is* being stressed in this section is that there is an intuitive "reality" to phonemic distinctions—after all, the student of phonetics often has difficulty even in hearing subphonemic differences—and that a simple phonemic analysis of anomalous speech can reveal important aspects of its structure, which often have practical significance.

shown us that there are *two separate inventories* of any given speech system: there is the inventory of *phonemes*, and the inventory of *segments* or *phones*. The inventory of segments is invariably longer. For example, the inventory of standard English *phonemes* includes /p/, /t/, and /k/. But the inventory of English *segments* includes quite a number of varieties of each phoneme type: aspirated, nonaspirated, released, unreleased, nasally released, etc. It is also important to keep the notion of *neutralization* in mind when examining the practical implications of phonemics. In the example given earlier in this chapter, it was stressed that while "betting" and "bedding" are pronounced alike by most North American speakers of English, the one *phonetic* realization is always interpreted by the listener as corresponding to one or another phoneme: that is, /t/ and /d/ are neutralized *phonetically*, but not *phonemically*.

Let us turn our attention to some anomalous language systems.

Most children go through a stage in which they pronounce /r/ and /w/ alike, as [w]. Initially, no phonemic distinction is made: the child has *one* phoneme /w/, corresponding to the adults' /r/ and /w/. Most children then go on to perceive the difference and to establish two phonemes in their grammar, as in adult grammar, but *they neutralize them phonetically*. They still say "wabbit," but it is clear that they have two phonemes, because if an adult says "wabbit," the child will object. (This is often amusing, as the child may disdainfully correct the adult, saying, "No, it's not wabbit, it's *wabbit!*") Normally the child goes on to master [r] (a difficult sound to articulate), and the "baby talk" disappears. If at the middle stage, someone perceives a problem in the child's speech and tries to "teach" the child the difference between "rut" and "what," "run" and "won," etc., the effort is wasted, as the child already perceives the difference. But it is quite a different matter if the child develops in a much less common way: he can say [r] and [w], but produces them in complementary distribution: for example [r] preceding front vowels, and [w] preceding back vowels. This is a different problem: here the child produces both *segments* but doesn't distinguish the *phonemes*.

Let us emphasize the latter situation by taking an example of foreign accent. In Spanish, [ð] and [d] are allophones, in complementary distribution: [ð] occurs intervocalically, and [d] elsewhere. The Spanish-speaker learning English will tend, therefore, to pronounce "udder" and "other" the same (with [ð] in both), and "den" and "then" the same (with [d] in both). The problem often is that he does not perceive that the difference between [ð] and [d] is *contrastive* in English. This is quite a different problem from teaching the French speaker to pronounce English: for him [ð] is a very difficult sound to articulate, so the teacher must help him to pronounce it. The Spanish speaker, by contrast, can pronounce it perfectly well but needs to learn to *distinguish* it from [d]. The phonemic status of a sound therefore suggests a strategy for correcting it.

It is often useful to go beyond asking what *sounds* are being articulated. It is useful to ask what *contrasts* are being made and what allophonic distributions are present. This is true of child language, foreign accent, and articulation disorders as well.

A common articulation disorder is failure to distinguish /t/ from /k/. But there may be a number of quite different manifestations of this. An individual may produce *both* sounds, but not distinguish them phonemically; that is, they may be in complementary distribution (for example, [t] preceding front vowels and /k/ preceding back vowels is a possible distribution). Or the individual may produce only one of the two sounds but still retain the phonemic distinction (like the child who *says* "wabbit" but recognizes this pronunciation as an error in adult speech). That is, the person recognizes the distinction between "tap" and "cap," but pronounces these two words alike. Or the individual may lack both the phonetic and the phonemic distinction, neither recognizing nor articulating the difference between "tap" and "cap."

Each situation is different in that articulation therapy is less important when the individual can pronounce both sounds; instruction in the contrastive role of the two sounds is redundant if the individual makes the *distinction* (even when not supported by a phonetic difference).

One of the reasons why the phonemic level is so important is that we tend to perceive sounds in ways that correspond to the phonemic distinctions in our own language. English does not make a phonemic distinction between aspirated and unaspirated plosives—as some languages do—so speakers of English are likely to have trouble hearing that distinction. French does not make a distinction between /i/ and /ɪ/,[5] and speakers of that language therefore have trouble even hearing [i] and [ɪ] as different sounds.

We often hear it said that a Japanese accent in English "reverses r's and l's." In fact, the situation is more complex: Japanese has a sound similar to English /r/ and a sound similar to English /l/. The two form *one* phoneme and are in complementary distribution (the conditioning factor being the neighboring vowels). When the Japanese speaker speaks English, the sounds are distributed according to the neighboring vowels rather than according to whether the English phoneme /r/ or /l/ belongs. There are two points to note in this example: first, speakers of English tend to *hear* either /r/ or /l/, even though what the Japanese speaker tends to produce is neither; and second, speakers of English tend to hear only the "wrong" variant, not the times the speaker has it right (which occurs about half the time, depending on the neighboring vowel). It is clear that the Japanese speaker does not reverse r-sounds and l-sounds. It is also clear that phonetic correction with such an individual, if based on the false assumption of "reversal," would not get very far.

Note that an ability to *pronounce* certain segments is not a substitute for distinguishing them phonemically. An individual's speech will still be anomalous—even if he can pronounce the segments in question—if he does not make the phonemic distinction. We have already seen the example of the Spanish speaker who is capable of pronouncing [ð] but still substitutes [d]. Let us take another example: many American dialects substitute /u/ for /ju/ following /t/, /d/, /s/ /l/, and /n/. So these dialects distinguish "booty" from "beauty" and "moot" from "mute," but do not distinguish "do" from "due" or "too" from the first syllable of "tuna." Likewise "new" is pronounced as [nu], and so on. Many speakers perceive the [ju] pronunciation as "better" or "more educated" and so adopt it. Generally they have no difficulty *pronouncing* "due" as [dju], or "new" as [nju], but since they do not *distinguish* words such as "do" and "due" *phonemically* in their mental lexicon, they tend to overgeneralize the "correction" and say things like [njun] for "noon" and [dju] for "do."

Similarly, when North Americans try to imitate a "British accent" by replacing the vowel [æ] with [ɑ] in such words as "fast" and "can't," they often produce laughable results. Not because they cannot pronounce the vowel [ɑ], which of course they can, but because they do not know which words to put it in. Standard British English has a different vowel phoneme in the words "fast" and "hat," but for most North Americans these words have the same vowel phoneme. So North Americans who say [hɑt] for "hat" or [ɑnt] for "ant" ("ant" and "aunt" not being distinguished in the speech of most North Americans) are mistaken in thinking they are imitating British English. The most ridiculous example I have heard is that of a North American church minister who adopted a slightly British accent (or what he thought was an elegant and very correct speech style for a preacher) while delivering sermons. In North American English, the word *ass* meaning 'donkey' and *ass* meaning 'stupid person' are pronounced alike, with the vowel [æ]. In British English, the former is pronounced with the vowel [æ], the latter with the vowel [ɑ] (and is usually spelled ⟨arse⟩, although there is no [r] in the pronunciation). The minister in question had Christ riding an [ɑs] rather than an [æs]. An English-educated person in the congregation was quite startled by the news.

Such an example points up why correction of a pronunciation problem is not just a question of helping the person to *pronounce* individual segments. Knowledge of the phonemic structure of the target language is also necessary for correct pronunciation. (Of course, this is not to say that an explicit study of phonemic theory by the language learner or client of speech therapy is desirable or useful; rather, it is to stress the importance of the contrastive role of sounds.)

Let us complete this section on the practical side of phonemics with a quotation from Charles Van Riper, the most influential of American

[5] [ɪ] occurs as an allophone of /i/ in some dialects, notably that of Quebec; but most dialects lack [ɪ] altogether.

speech pathologists. In his classic textbook *Speech Correction* [1972], Van Riper argues for what he calls a "phonetic analysis" (actually a sort of phonemic analysis) of the speech of those with articulation errors, and he cites the following case:

> One of our student speech therapists gave an articulation test to a boy of seven and came out with the astounding summary that although he had thirty-two defective sounds, his speech was perfectly intelligible. When we checked her findings we found that the child actually was doing only one thing incorrectly: He was *forming* the final sounds of every word, but was not pronouncing them audibly. The student therapist had been right in finding that thirty-two sounds were defective, but this actually had no significance or importance. Our therapeutic task was clearly to teach the child to strengthen his terminal sounds [p. 189].

In this child's speech, every phoneme had a nonaudible allophone in word-final position. He went through the same process to form the non-normal allophone of each phoneme. In this case, it is quite obvious that the therapist should attack the problem not as a case of thirty-two misarticulations but as *one* articulation defect.

8-9 Transcription and the Phoneme

The notion of the phoneme plays a role, whether we are aware of it or not, in how we transcribe "phonetically." This section will describe how the phoneme affects transcription and how some specific aspects of transcription are used to record non-normal speech. Linguistics students will probably want to skim the references to non-normal speech, but the principles of transcription outlined in this section are relevant to them as well as to students of communication disorders.

8-9.1 Phonemic and Phonetic Transcription

As noted previously, sometimes we want a transcription to contain more detail, sometimes less. The more detailed type is called a **phonetic,** or **narrow,** transcription, whereas the less detailed type is called a **phonemic,** or **broad,** transcription.

We put a **phonemic** or **broad** transcription between slash marks[6] (/ /). Each symbol represents a phoneme. So the symbol /p/ represents the unaspirated allophone, the aspirated allophone, and the unreleased allophone. We do not use a separate symbol for each type of /p/, since all types are just instances of the same phoneme, /p/. Similarly, the effects of coarticulation are not marked, and the effects of assimilation are marked only when a segment crosses a phoneme boundary. Therefore, we would not indicate that the /d/ in the word "handle" is laterally released, since laterally released /d/ is not a separate phoneme; but we would mark the fact that someone pronounced the /s/ of "miss" as /š/ in the expression "miss you," since /s/ and /š/ are separate phonemes.

This is the most common form of transcription. But what happens when someone reads it? Does he or she make errors in reading, since so much phonetic information is left out? Generally not, since most of the information left out is predictable. For example, it is not necessary to tell a person to release the /t/ of "little" laterally; the person does that automatically. If that information were left out of a transcription, the reader would supply it unconsciously. He or she would also aspirate the plosives when appropriate, if the speech that was recorded was normal English speech. This is very important: the predictable detail is predictable only in a *normal* pronunciation of a *known* dialect of a *known* language. Aspiration is predictable in English, so it is left out of a phonemic transcription, but aspiration is *not* predictable in Thai or Punjabi, so it would have to be included in a phonemic transcription of those languages. And the details of aspiration are different in Cajun English from what they are in general American, so one cannot expect that the same type of broad transcription would work for both dialects.

And what if a speech pathologist wants to record some non-normal speech and indicate that the plosives are not appropriately aspirated? If the therapist uses a broad, phonemic transcription, it will not accurately record what is unusual about the speech, since the error being recorded is not phonemic but subphonemic: the wrong allophone is being used. In this case, we would need the other type of transcription, in which these details are marked.

We put a **narrow** or **phonetic** transcription be-

[6] Properly, but not often, called **virgules.**

tween brackets[7] ([ ]). Here each different allophone has a different symbol, and we carefully mark the effects of coarticulation and assimilation. We mark every relevant phonetic detail.

Suppose we were recording speech in which aspiration is not used as it usually is in English. If *all* voiceless plosives were aspirated, we could simply use a broad transcription and write a note to this effect. If *none* of the plosives were aspirated, a note would suffice as well. But if some plosives were aspirated, and some were not, in a pattern differing from standard English, our transcription would have to show this. In a narrow transcription, aspirated and unaspirated /p/ would be marked: [pʰ] and [p]. Similarly, we would use different symbols for dark and light /l/, and so on.

The narrow transcription is not useful to the speech pathologist alone. It may also be used in recording a dialect other than our own or to record the way a foreigner speaks English. In sociolinguistic studies, fine details of articulation are often relevant as markers of dialect.

You will note that as a result of combinatory processes (accommodation, among others) certain epenthetic or **intrusive** sounds appear, and you may wonder whether you ought to transcribe these. For example, the word "buy" would be transcribed /bai̯/ in the system introduced in earlier chapters. But what about the word "buying"? The student with a good ear for sounds will note an intrusive /j/ approximant inserted between the /ai̯/ of *buy* and the /ɪ/ of *-ing* in most people's speech. If it is recorded, the transcription would be [bai̯jɪŋ]. Do you record this intrusive sound? In a very narrow phonetic transcription, it should be included, since it is, after all, a sound that is articulated. But for the purposes of a broad phonemic transcription, there is no need, because the insertion of /j/ is *predictable* and does not represent a separate and distinct phoneme. Whenever the *-ing* suffix is added to a word whose final sound is /i/, /e/, /ai̯/ or /ɔi̯/ (that is, a high or upper mid front vowel), the /j/ is automatically and unconsciously inserted, as in the words "being," "baying," "buying," and "annoying." Otherwise, it is not; notice the words "testing," "teasing," and "jawing," as well as others like them. (You may also have noted that if the word ends with a high or upper-mid *back* vowel, the approximant /w/ is inserted.) Since the insertion of this sound is predictable, there is no more need to indicate it in a broad transcription than there is to indicate the aspiration or nonaspiration of /t/. However, the same caution applies here as elsewhere: if you are recording speech that is not typical, be it a foreign accent, an unusual dialect, or the speech of someone with an articulation problem, the use of such intrusive sounds may not be predictable and should be recorded carefully.

In summary, slash marks enclose a broad, phonemic transcription, while brackets enclose a narrow, phonetic transcription. It is important to use these symbols correctly, since the meaning of the letters of the phonetic alphabet changes depending on the enclosing marks. For example, the symbol /p/ means *both* aspirated and unaspirated variants, but [p] means *only* the unaspirated variant.

It should be noted that there is not a simple two-way choice between narrow and broad transcriptions. There is a continuum running all the way from very broad transcription to transcription containing extremely detailed information about the articulation of each and every phone. Most transcriptions are somewhere in the middle, with broad transcriptions tending toward less detail and narrow transcriptions tending toward more detail. Also, it is common practice to include a narrow transcription of certain sounds, while letting other sounds be represented in broad transcription. Almost never do we achieve a completely phonemic transcription; almost always some subphonemic distinctions are recorded.

One particularly important point to remember about broad transcription is that it lumps together under one symbol sounds that are different (the allophones). It may be easy to think that sounds that are represented with the same symbol are in all important respects the "same." However, as we have seen, the various allophones of one phoneme may be, from a phonetic and articulatory viewpoint, quite different.

[7] [ ] are properly called *brackets*, but most people say *square brackets*.

8-9.2 Specialized Transcription for Speech Therapists

A number of conventions used in the recording of non-normal speech are not in general use by phoneticians and so are not usually included in books on phonetics. A few important ones will be mentioned here.

If an individual substitutes one phoneme for another, this can be recorded with a broad transcription, thus: /wæbət/ for "rabbit." If an individual makes subphonemic substitutions—that is, substitutes one allophone for another—a narrow transcription is needed, at least with respect to the affected sound, thus: [spʰɪt] for "spit," if the /p/ is aspirated. This sort of transcription can be employed to show subphonemic substitution and indeed must be used when the individual makes inconsistent substitutions.

When the individual consistently makes the same substitution or distortion in the same phonetic environment, however, a kind of shorthand employing abbreviations is used. The letters (I), (M), and (F) in parentheses refer, respectively, to initial, medial, and final position in a word. They mark the position at which the distortion usually occurs. If the distortion occurs in all positions, all positions are marked. The minus sign (−) is used to indicate that a sound has been omitted; the plus sign (+) is used to indicate that a sound has been inserted; and the diagonal or slash (/) is used to indicate a substitution or distortion. Let us look at several examples:

t/s (I, M, F) means [t] substituted for /s/ in all positions.
θ/s (I) means [θ] substituted for /s/ in initial position.
−l (F) means that the final /l/ is omitted.
+ə (M) means that the vowel [ə] is inserted medially where it is not appropriate.

While the concept of "medial" position is widely used among speech therapists, note that it is often an inadequate specification of the environment. In Chapter 6 we looked at some coarticulatory and assimilatory effects in normal speech. We noted that the environment in which these effects occurred was often highly specified. For example, /t/ is replaced with [ɾ] only between vowels and only when the first of the two vowels is stressed. Simply stating that /t/ is flapped "medially" is quite incorrect. It is therefore sometimes important to specify environments.

Some speech therapists make use of symbols borrowed from generative phonology and modified for the purpose of specifying anomalous articulations. Their use is recommended, as it permits great precision.

A substitution is indicated with an arrow, which can be read "is realized as" or "is pronounced as." The symbol ø means 'nothing' and is used for insertions and omissions. For example,

/s/ → [t] '/s/ is pronounced as [t]'
ø → [ə] 'schwa is inserted' (i.e., nothing becomes [ə])
/l/ → [ø] '/l/ is deleted' (i.e., [l] becomes nothing)

In this system, a single oblique line separates the statement of substitution (the foregoing three examples) from the statement specifying the environment. It is read "in the environment." For example:

/t/ → [ɾ] / . . .

is read as '/t/ is pronounced as [ɾ] in the environment . . .'

This statement is still not complete, since we have not specified the environment. Several special symbols are used in the environment statement. A dash (_) replaces the sound in question, the sound undergoing change. The symbol # means 'word boundary' and may be used to specify the beginning or end of a word. V specifies any vowel, C any consonant, N any nasal, and P any plosive. Let us look at a few examples to clarify the system. The statement

/t/ → [ɾ] / V́_V

means '/t/ is pronounced as [ɾ] when it occurs between vowels, the first of which is stressed';

/l/ → ø / _#

means '/l/ is omitted in word-final position' (the dash, which represents the /l/, occurs before the word boundary; therefore it is in word-final position);

p → pʰ / #s_

means 'plosives are aspirated following word-initial /s/' (this rule is incorrect for standard English, of course);

/s/ → [θ] / #_

means '/s/ is pronounced [θ] in word-initial position.'

As can be seen, this symbolism can be used to specify very precisely the environment of omissions, substitutions, and deletions.

A familiarity with some of the less frequently used IPA symbols can also be useful to the speech pathologist and to the second-language teacher recording unusual substitutions. If, for example, an individual substitutes a dark or velarized /l/ for the light /l/, the appropriate symbol, [ɫ], may be used. Or, if an individual has a certain type of bilateral lisp that is similar to the voiceless lateral fricative [ɬ], this substitution can be indicated without complicated explanation.

Some therapists employ the usual English spelling to indicate substitutions, but there are disadvantages to this practice. For example, if one writes ⟨th⟩ for /θ/, there is considerable ambiguity; ⟨th⟩ may indicate either the voiced or the voiceless dental fricative, whereas /θ/ is specific. And using ⟨th⟩ for /θ/ makes it difficult to distinguish an aspirated from an unaspirated /t/, which may be important in some cases. It is a good idea to avoid transcribing speech with English spelling. As more and more speech pathologists have training in the IPA, there should be more consistency in the use of symbols.

8-10 The Syllable

Let us turn our attention to the syllable. The syllable is important for a number of reasons. It is clearly a fundamental unit of phonetic structure. It may play a role in phonetic memory, production, and perception. We are looking at it now because it plays a role in phonotactic restrictions, the subject of the last part of this chapter.

The syllable has recently gained importance in phonology and in performance models of speech. While many models of the syllable exist, to a large extent the theoretical arguments behind these differences are beyond our present purpose. Let us examine the syllable in light of a composite of typical current analyses.

First and foremost, the syllable has *structure*. In examining that structure, we need to use several new terms. The first of these is **cluster.** A cluster is a group of consonants together in the same syllable. For example, there is a cluster [kr] at the beginning of the word "crust"; the cluster [st] is found at the end of the same word. In the word "tactic," however, there is no cluster. The consonants [kt] are juxtaposed, but they are in different syllables (at least in the usual analysis), so they do not form a cluster. And remember that spelling has nothing to do with clusters; the word "though" has no clusters; the ⟨th⟩ at the beginning represents *one* consonant; the ⟨gh⟩ at the end is merely an orthographic anachronism.

The usual analysis divides the syllable first into an **onset** and a **rhyme.** The onset is the initial consonant or cluster that precedes the **nucleus** (for the moment, the vowel). Of course, it is possible that there be no onset, as in these one-syllable words: "eye," "eight," "own." The **rhyme** is the rest of the syllable, consisting of the nucleus and any consonant or consonants that follow.

The **rhyme** is further subdivided into the **nucleus** and the **coda.** The **nucleus,** also called the **peak,** is usually a vowel or a diphthong that is central to the syllable. However, as we shall see, the nucleus may be a segment other than a diphthong or vowel. The *coda* is the consonant or consonants following the nucleus. There need not be a coda, as in such unisyllabic words as "boy," "go," "straw," and "through." The onset may be missing; the coda may be missing; but there is always a nucleus. There is also always a rhyme, whether or not that rhyme contains a coda.

The usual way of showing the structure is with an **immediate constituent** diagram, as follows. The structure of the one-syllable word "crowds" is shown.

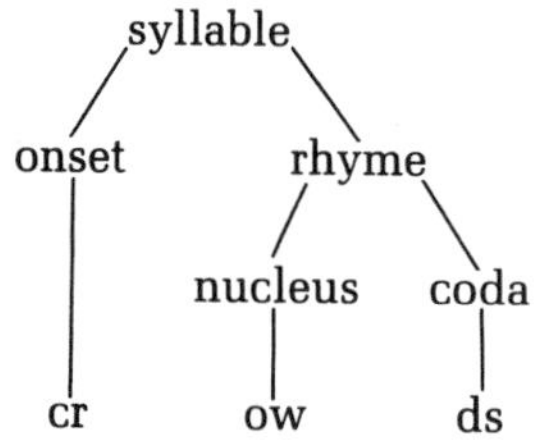

The immediate constituent "slots" are left blank if those constituents are absent. For example, the word "eye" has a nucleus, but neither onset nor coda. The word "though" has onset and nucleus but no coda. The word "at" has nucleus and coda but no onset.

Any of the three constituents may have greater or lesser complexity. The word "sixths" has four elements in its coda. The word "splash" has three elements in its onset. The word "sit" has a simple vocalic nucleus, whereas "crowds" has a diphthongal nucleus.

Another model of the syllable concerns itself with the relative "strengths" of the various elements, noting that the rhyme is "stronger" than the onset, and that within the rhyme the nucleus is "stronger" than the coda.

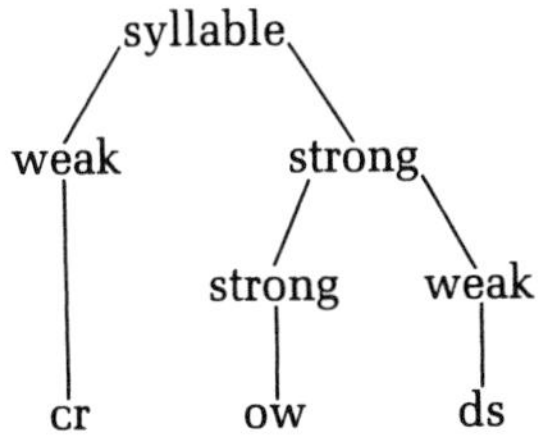

In this model, there are additional complications: both the coda and the onset are further analyzed in terms of the relative strengths of their components. For our present purpose, however, the model as shown above is sufficient and makes intuitive sense. Rhyming is a more powerful literary device than alliteration. And note that slight off-rhymes are permitted if the segment that is "off" falls into the coda rather than in the nucleus.[8]

Another feature of syllabic structure is revealed in what is known as the **sonority hierarchy.** Sonority is the degree to which a speech segment is vowel-like. A vowel is the most sonorous (low vowels more than high vowels); plosives are the least sonorous. Voiced segments are more sonorous than voiceless. The other segment classes fall in between, roughly in this order: vowels, glides, liquids, nasals, fricatives, plosives. A syllable nucleus may always be a vowel, but it may be a less sonorous segment if that segment is surrounded by segments that are less sonorous still. For example, the English interjection "Pssst!" may be seen as a syllable whose nucleus is [s:::]. The surrounding segments, [p] and [t], the onset and coda, have even less sonority than the nucleus. In a less extreme case, the [n] of "happen" and the [l] of "bottle" are often syllabic, as are similar consonants in similar environments in English, and are transcribed with the syllabic diacritic [n̩], [l̩].

The sonority hierarchy explains why a word like "rhythm" has two syllables. Let us write the segments phonemically: /rɪðm̩/. The /m/ and the /ɪ/ both are *more* sonorous than the segment /ð/ between them; therefore there must be a syllable boundary at the point of low sonority. The transcription might be written /rɪ$ðm̩/, where the dollar sign ($) signifies a syllable boundary.

For speakers who pronounce "film" and "elm" as two syllables, [l] must have less sonority than [m]. In the standard dialect, in which these words have one syllable, [l] has greater sonority than [m].

Another important concept of syllabicity may fly in the face of what you have been taught about dividing words into syllables. There is usually *one* proper way to divide words for purposes of orthography (writing correctly). For this purpose, the dictionary is the authority, and nothing said in this section contradicts what are in essence spelling conventions in English. However, the fact that a certain place is where a certain word ought to be divided for *spelling* purposes says nothing as to how that word is divided *phonetically* when spoken. It has been observed that certain consonants in polysyllabic words do not seem to belong definitively to one or the other syllable. Such consonants may be said to belong to both syllables simultaneously. The consonants of "ladder," "coming," "happy," etc., fall into this category. They may be classed as being **ambisyllabic,** part of two syllables at once.

Ambisyllabicity, or at least reinterpretation of syllabic structure, has been responsible for historical changes. For example, the word "apron" once had a [n] at the beginning (it is related to the word *napkin*), but "a napron" became reinterpreted as

[8] In poetic *rhyming*, one has a series of words whose **rhymes** (i.e., **nuclei** plus **codas**) are the same, but whose **onsets** differ; for example, "bright," "night," "cite," "bite," and "write" rhyme. In *alliteration*, one has a series of words with the same first-syllable **onset** (or the same first sound of the onset, if the onset comprises a cluster), for example, "beautiful bright bouncing baby." Notice that the **rhyme** is a *strong* element whereas the **onset** is a *weak* element in the model of the syllable presented in this paragraph. And notice that rhyming, as a literary device, imposes itself more strongly on literary form than does alliteration.

An off-rhyme is an "almost" rhyme, such as frequently occurs in popular songs of doubtful literary merit. Such "rhymes" as "time"/"fine," or "drape"/"fate" are examples of off-rhymes. (The segments that are off share many of the same articulatory features.) Off-rhymes are satisfactory if the element that is off falls in the coda (a *weak* element in this model) rather than in the nucleus (a *strong* element in this model). No one would attempt an off-rhyme such as "hate"/"fight," in which the segment that is off is in the nucleus.

"an apron," and the change stuck. The previously absent [n]'s at the beginning of "newt" and "nickname" became attached by a similar process, opposite in effect.

Syllabic boundaries may shift in other ways as well. In my dialect, for example, it is common for the expression "Not at all," spoken colloquially, to be said in the following way: "notatall." In fact, rather than being attached to the beginning of the following words, the [t]'s in question probably become ambisyllabic; they are flapped like other ambisyllabic [t]'s in similar environments: [nɑɾəɾɑl].

A few technical terms may help to describe phonetic environments in a few words. A syllable that has a consonantal coda is known as a **closed** syllable. A syllable that has no coda, that is, that ends with a vowel, is known as an **open** syllable. The first consonant in the onset is known as the **releasing** consonant in the syllable. If the onset contains a cluster, the whole cluster may be called the *releasing cluster*. The last consonant in the coda is known as the **arresting** consonant of the syllable. If the coda contains a cluster, the whole cluster may be called the *arresting cluster*.

8-10.1 The Phonetics of the Syllable

There have been a number of attempts to find a specific phonetic (physiological or acoustic) correlate of the syllable; the best known is that of Stetson [1951], who believed he had located a "chest pulse" corresponding to the syllable. However, that finding did not stand up under scrutiny. Indeed, there is no specific articulatory event that corresponds to the syllable, other than the obvious one of the presence of the nucleus.

What constitutes a nucleus is something which is governed by the rules of the language in question. English, for example, permits a syllable like "Pssst!" in an interjection, but not in any words.

It is clear therefore that the syllable is a *phonologically* rather than strictly phonetically defined notion. The syllable is rather like the phoneme, in that it is an abstraction; it is found at a higher level of analysis but does not necessarily have a specific and constant physical reality. The result is that speakers of the same dialect will generally agree on the number of syllables present (although not necessarily on their boundaries). But in cases other than the simple, obvious one in which the syllable nucleus is a vowel, the phonetician is hard-pressed to specify its nature.

8-10.2 The Importance of the Syllable

The foregoing may seem to negate the importance of the syllable: if the syllable cannot be precisely defined, why deal with it, you may ask. Indeed, its existence is not questioned, only its precise realization. The syllable is more and more being considered an important unit in terms of speech production and perception. Consider the following:

1. Phonotactic restrictions (the subject of Section 8-11) are mostly based on the syllable.
2. There is evidence that speech errors (Chap. 6) tend to fall into patterns that can be most efficiently described with reference to the position of the error within the syllable.
3. Some languages are written syllabically; the alphabet developed out of syllabic writing; there is evidence that reading is faster with syllabic writing than with phonemic writing (Chap. 3).
4. The syllable is an important unit for the rhythm of speech in many languages, and while this is less true of English (being stress-timed: Chap. 7), it is still apparent in poetry and song.
5. Psycholinguistic evidence is mounting for the syllable as a unit in the representation of speech. For example, Lieberman [1975, p. 9] states

> The coding and decoding of speech in terms of syllables is an essential aspect of human linguistic ability. Children who have severe reading "disabilities" can, for example, be taught to read with 3 to 6 hours of tutoring by making use of a syllabic notation [Rozin et al., 1971]. Traditional methods of teaching reading essentially assume that the phonemic level of language is basic (roughly the alphabetic level). Much of the difficulty in teaching children to read can be overcome if intermediate units, representing syllables, are used to introduce reading.

In an experiment by Shumsky [1977], children with reading deficiencies were taught "pig latin," an encoded form of English used as a "secret language" by children. The rule of pig latin involves moving the releasing consonant to the end of the word and adding the vowel [e]. The children with reading deficiencies achieved little success in mastering pig latin. However, when the same children were taught "syl-latin," in which the entire first syllable was moved to the end of the word, the level of success was higher.

One interpretation of such results is that a phonemically based manipulation of language is somehow on a higher, or less fundamental, level than a syllabically based manipulation. Children with reading deficiencies may lack certain linguistic skills and therefore may perform better at more "basic" tasks. Therefore the syllable is more basic than the phoneme, goes this line of reasoning (by no means the only interpretation of such results).

6. There is an acoustic-perceptual argument for the primacy of the syllable. We will examine acoustics and perception in Chapter 10, but for the moment let us note that a syllable such as [pɑ] is nonsegmentable acoustically. Anomalies in the acoustic patterns of syllables that are perceived similarly suggest that perception occurs in a global fashion, rather than strictly segment by segment, particularly in the case of plosives. Of course, one might want to segment the articulatory gestures involved in producing a syllable, but strictly speaking the syllable is not segmentable acoustically.

Such facts as these underline the degree to which the syllable, rather than the segment or phoneme, is a basic phonetic unit in speech.

8-11 Phonotactics

8-11.1 Introduction

One of the factors that characterizes the sound system of a particular language (or, indeed, of a particular dialect) is its phonemic inventory. English, for example, counts /θ/ and /ð/ among its phonemes, whereas French and German do not. Another characteristic of a language is its inventory of allophonic variation. For example, Spanish counts [ð] as an allophone of its phoneme /d/, whereas English does not; it has both as separate phonemes. The specific segments in a language also characterize it. For example, English has both [i] and [ɪ]; it counts them as separate phonemes: /i/ and /ɪ/. Standard French has /i/ as a phoneme but does not have [ɪ] at all. Quebec French, like English, has both [i] and [ɪ], but their status is different from their status in English: in Quebec French the phoneme /i/ (unlike standard French) has an allophone [ɪ].

The taking of such inventories, however, is only part of the story of the characterization of the sound system of a given language. The combining and ordering of those sounds is also important. This is the domain of **phonotactics.**

Let us look at an example to make the point. Both English and Spanish have phonemes that could be characterized /s/, /t/, /r/, and /e/.[9] In both languages these could be ordered /tres/ to form a word (English *trace*, Spanish *tres*). In English these phonemes can be combined thus: /stret/, but in Spanish such a sequence is not permitted. No Spanish word begins */#str-/, so, while /stret/ can be said to be made up of Spanish phonemes, it cannot be said to conform to Spanish phonotactic rules.

8-11.2 The Phonotactics of the English Syllable

The English syllable (with rare exceptions, such as the interjection "Pssst" already alluded to) contains a vocalic nucleus. It contains from zero to three consonants in the onset. It contains from zero to four consonants in the coda, although the final cluster is often simplified. Table 8-1 shows the various possibilities in one-syllable words and gives a number of examples. There are a couple of points to remember in examining the table. First of all, many dialects simplify the coda when it contains more than one consonant. The table therefore shows what is possible; it does not purport to indicate the "correct" pronunciation for any given word. Second, note that the table lists one-syllable words only. Polysyllabic words do not contain more complex syllables than one-syllable words, but they may contain different syllables. For example, the vowel [ə] is never found in a one-syllable word when that word is stressed in a sentence, but schwas are common in polysyllabic words.

[9] In fact, of course, the exact phonetic quality of these phonemes is different in the two languages. /s/: English [s], Spanish [s̪]; /t/: English [tʰ] or [t], Spanish [t̪]; /r/: English [ɹ] (although we usually write [r]), Spanish [ř]; /e/: English [e͜i], Spanish [e]. However, both languages have phonemes of similar phonetic quality, and that is what is relevant to the example.

Table 8-1. Phonotactics of the English syllable

Number of consonants before vowel	Number of consonants after vowel	Some sample words
0	0	oh, ah, I, eye
0	1	at, up, ought, in
0	2	ask, oust, eighth, elf, apt
0	3	asks, ousts
1	0	to, how, pea, though
1	1	tot, hut, thought
1	2	task, takes, rats
1	3	tasks, pests
1	4	sixths
2	0	tree, spy, through, schwa
2	1	stick, stop, steak, trap
2	2	stops, steaks, trust
2	3	trusts, tramps
2	4	twelfths
3	0	spry, squaw, straw
3	1	streak, squeak, straight
3	2	strains, squeaks, scrapes
3	3	sprints, splints
3	4	strengths [strɛŋkθs]

Note: These one-syllable words are arranged in order by the number of consonants preceding and following the nucleus (vowel or diphthong). As always, it is pronunciation and not spelling that matters. The final word ("strengths") might not be counted, because the [k] is epenthetic rather than phonemic. Note that polysyllabic words may contain some syllables not found in any one-syllable word; for example, schwa does not occur in one-syllable words when stressed but may be contained in one or more syllables of a polysyllabic word.

Some of the information in Table 8-1 could be summarized in this formula: (CCC)V(CCCC). The parentheses indicate optional segments. The formula can be read as follows: the English syllable contains from zero to three consonants followed by an obligatory vowel (or diphthong), followed by from zero to four consonants.

A number of issues come into play in this formula.

1. How are affricates counted? As one consonant or two? Because of the way that affricates behave as single phonemes in English, they are counted here as one consonant.
2. How are epenthetic segments counted, such as the plosive that appears between a nasal and a fricative? Is "fence" /fɛns/ (two consonants in the coda) or /fɛnts/ (three consonants)? There is a *phonetic* [t] present, but not a *phonemic* /t/. So it is not counted as a phoneme in the formula.
3. Is a sequence such as that found in the English word "or" counted as a diphthong or as a sequence of vowel plus consonant? As pointed out in Section 8-5.3, both are correct at different levels of analysis. In standard North American English, the word "or" is pronounced with a *phonetic* diphthong, but *phonemically* it may contain the sequence /or/, vowel plus consonant.

The *number* of consonant or vowel segments in a syllable is one aspect of phonotactics. A syllable of the form CCVCCCCC simply could not be an English syllable, although it may be possible in certain other languages. However, there is more to phonotactics: there are restrictions concerning *where* certain consonants can go in the formula. For example, CCV is an acceptable form for an English syllable, but */pti/ is not, even though it is made up of English phonemes. If a releasing cluster contains a plosive, then it must take one of two forms: (1) /s/ followed by a voiceless plosive, as in "speed," "stop," and "skate"; or (2) a plosive followed by an approximant, as in "please," "blue," "pray," "brat," "beauty" (/bjuti/), and "gray." /w/ combines with voiced nonalveolar plosives only in borrowed words "bwana," "Gwen," and "guano"),[10] whereas it combines freely with voiceless (nonlabial) plosives in native English words: "quack" and "twin." /j/ follows /t/ and /d/ in some dialects only: "tube" and "duty."

In all cases in which three consonants precede the vowel, the first must be /s/, the second a voiceless plosive, and the third an approximant: "streak," "squeeze," "spleen," "spew," "scrape," etc.

A releasing cluster may be formed of a fricative and certain approximants: "thwart," "slip," "flip," and "fright." Notice that the fricative is voiceless: we have "slip," but never a word like *"zlip."

Alveopalatal fricatives cannot enter into releasing clusters like other fricatives: we have "flip" and "slip" but nothing like *"shlip." German and

[10] *Bwana* is from Swahili; *Gwen* and similar names are Welsh in origin; *guano* is Spanish, originally from Quechua; with the voiced alveolar plosive [d], native words combine with [w]: *dwell, dwindle,* etc.

Yiddish permit /š/ in releasing clusters, and some words have been borrowed into American English in this form, but these are generally restricted to dialects in geographical regions where one of these languages is commonly spoken. More commonly, borrowed foreign words are changed so as to conform to English phonotactic patterns. The word "strafe," which comes from the German *strafen* (/štʀɑfən/, 'to punish'), has been so modified.

Notice that there are phonotactic restrictions even for single consonants in the onset. For example, the sound /ŋ/ is restricted to postvocalic position in English: it never precedes the vowel; we have "rum," "run," and "rung," as well as "mutt" and "nut," but no "ngut." There is no physiological reason why [ŋ] cannot be pronounced as an onset; it occupies the onset position in many languages (as in the common Vietnamese name Nguyen), but English has a phonotactic rule against it. Notice how powerful the rule is: English speakers generally regard a [ŋ] in word-initial position as unpronounceable. We make other nasals syllabic—[m̩] when humming, [n̩] as in "button"—but we look in great wonderment at the Chinese name Ng, a syllabic /ŋ/: [ŋ̍]. Most of us will pronounce this name [ɪŋ] to avoid the /ŋ/ in word-initial location.

The consonant /ž/ similarly has special restrictions. In many dialects, it is found only intervocalically. So "measure" is pronounced with a /ž/, but "garage" is not. Similarly, a borrowed word such as "genre" with /ž/ in the onset, or "rouge" with /ž/ in the coda, causes puzzlement among speakers of some dialects: those dialects have phonotactic restrictions prohibiting /ž/ in those positions.

There are restrictions on the nucleus as well. For example, in English lax vowels occur only in closed syllables. Tense vowels, on the other hand, occur in both open and closed syllables. So we have words like "beet," "bead," "bean," and "bee," but with the lax vowel only "bit," "bid," and "bin," never a word like *[bɪ].

8-11.3 Phonotactics at the Phonemic and Phonetic Levels

It would be useful for us to distinguish between phonotactic patterns at the phonemic and phonetic levels. Let us take an example to see how this applies. In a word such as "sixths," we note that the coda contains the four-phoneme sequence /ksθs/. However, the typical speaker is likely to say [sɪks]. That is, the actual phonetic output differs from the phonemic structure of the word. Usually, as in this example, the difference results in a simplification. But in practice, such dynamic adjustments may result in more complex phonetic than phonemic clusters. For example, the word "phonetics" has a simple one-segment onset in its first syllable: /f/. However, in speech the first unstressed vowel is likely to be elided. Thus, the /f/ of the first syllable and the /n/ of the second (original) syllable combine in the new first syllable: [fnɛɾəks]. In this casual pronunciation, we find the releasing cluster [#fn], which is not a permissible releasing cluster at the phonemic level in English. There are many examples of differences between the set of phonemes (and their groupings) on the one hand and the actual (phonetic) segments produced (and their groupings) on the other.

8-11.4 Dialect Differences in Phonotactic Restrictions

Dialects differ with respect to the clusters permitted and other phonotactic considerations. For example, it is quite common in North American speech for the arresting cluster /st#/ to be pronounced [st#] but for the arresting cluster /sts#/ to be pronounced [s#]. Thus, "test" is [tɛst], but "tests" is [tɛs]. Similarly with the verbs and nouns "beast," "breast," "best," "baste," "cast," etc. Also, there is often simplification of other final clusters from three to two segments. A dialect may permit /ft/ as a final cluster, but not */fts/. So "craft" has a final [ft], but "crafts" has a final [fs].

Another common dialect feature is the simplification of codas with two plosives: "fact" is pronounced [fæk], and "wrapped" (/ræpt/) is pronounced [ræp]. Homorganic clusters are similarly simplified: "tend" and "ten" are pronounced alike, as are "wind" and "win," and so on.

Other, particularly rare, clusters may be simplified in certain speech areas. For example, in regard to epenthesis (Chap. 6) we mentioned the word "film" and the fact that it is often pronounced [fɪləm], with an epenthetic schwa. The arresting cluster /Vlm/ is rare and may simply be nonpermissible in some dialects.

These are but a few examples of such differences; listening to the speech around you, you will find many others.

8-11.5 Language Differences in Phonotactic Restrictions

Languages differ greatly in their phonotactic restrictions, and it would be well to give a few additional illustrations of this fact. Naturally, there being thousands of languages in the world, we can give only a few examples. We will avoid giving the most exotic examples and stay for the most part with languages familiar to North Americans.

An important point to notice in starting is to distinguish between spelling conventions and phonotactic restrictions. Other languages have spelling conventions that are naturally unfamiliar to us unless we know the language in question. A group of letters together does not necessarily signal a group of consonant *sounds*. The English spelling ⟨th⟩ does not represent a [t] and a [h], nor does the Italian spelling ⟨gh⟩ (as in *ghetto*) represent a [g] and a [h]. It is misleading, therefore, to look at an unfamiliar language and to assume that certain combinations of sounds are permissible on the basis of its spelling.

We have mentioned elsewhere the case of German, which permits /#kn/ as a releasing cluster as well as /#gn/. Old English did the same, and this cluster persisted into Middle English times and is generally retained in Modern English spelling (not pronunciation), as in "gnat" and "knife."

In French, virtually any consonant may be followed by /w/ in a releasing cluster, as in *bois* /bwɑ/ 'woods,' *voit* /vwɑ/ 'sees,' *pois* /pwɑ/ 'peas,' *roi* /ʀwɑ/, 'king,' *trois* /tʀwɑ/ 'three,' *moi* /mwɑ/ 'me,' *soi* /swɑ/ 'self,' *loi* /lwɑ/ 'law,' etc. Most of these combinations are quite unfamiliar to the speaker of English and may therefore be difficult to say at first.

Some languages have far simpler phonotactic restrictions than English. Many languages, for example, have no coda, ever. All syllables are open in such languages. Japanese broadly fits this category. You may examine its syllabic structure by examining the syllabary developed to write it (see Fig. 3-7). Essentially, the syllable structure is (C)V; that is, either a vowel, or one consonant followed by a vowel. Complications are that /n̩/ may serve as a syllable, and C may be an affricate (not a cluster).

There are no languages that permit only closed syllables, but since some languages permit only open syllables, it is posited that open syllables represent a simpler state of affairs than closed syllables. All languages permit consonants in onset position, although which consonants and how many together differs from language to language.

8-11.6 Phonotactic Restrictions: Part of the Grammar

Phonotactic restrictions form part of the *grammar*, as this term was used in Chapter 2, that is, part of the knowledge of a speaker. The complex limitations on phonotactic patterns in English, which were only outlined in bare bones fashion in this section, are part of the knowledge of a speaker by the time he/she is five or six years old.

This fact is manifested in a number of ways. One way is that all "nonsense" words or invented trade names conform to phonotactic restrictions. Any time a child invents a word; any time an adult produces a nonsense word (for example, Lewis Carroll's *Jabberwocky*); any time an adman invents the name of a new washday miracle, the result is never nonsense, at least not *phonetic* nonsense, in the sense that phonotactic rules are always followed. Occasionally, spelling conventions are broken—particularly in brand names, to increase identifiability (as, for example, *Exxon*, with its double ⟨x⟩)—but never phonotactic restrictions.

Another manifestation is our difficulty in overcoming these restrictions in learning a foreign language, or even a different dialect of our own language, when its phonotactic restrictions are significantly different from those of our native dialect. We tend to pronounce the other language (usually badly) in accordance with the phonotactic restrictions we are used to.

8-11.7 Phonotactics and Language Teaching and Speech Disorders

Imagine that you were trying to learn German and said [kənɑbə] instead of [knɑbə], and your teacher concluded that you just could not pronounce a [k] or a [n]. He/she would be way off base, of course. You can pronounce both [k] and [n]; you just have difficulty putting them together into a releasing cluster with no epenthetic vowel between. Yet very often second-language teachers, in correcting foreign accents, and speech pathologists, in dealing with articulatory disorders, conclude quite erroneously that their student or client cannot say a particular sound. They may then concentrate on having the student/client pronounce that sound individually. This often misses the point: the individual can say the sound, but because of a conflicting phonotactic constraint, does not do so in certain combinations.

The teacher or therapist in this situation would do well to examine the individual's output: Are particular combinations difficult, or is it, indeed, the individual sound? If it is the combination, or the position in which the sound is found, then it is a good idea to find situations in which the sound is correctly said and to use those as stepping-stones to the correct pronunciation.

For example, the German teacher might do well to find words in English that have /kn/ juxtaposed. The English speaker has no trouble with "breakneck," for example. By saying it several times, he will gain a sense of what it feels like to pronounce that combination. He will also realize he *can* pronounce it. Or take the French teacher whose English-speaking students balk at saying [ž] in word-initial position. The teacher would do well to have his students say the sound in English words like "vision" and "leisure." (Being a fricative, this sound can be prolonged, to emphasize its isolated pronunciation.) The person will realize he can say the sound, and transfer this to word-initial position.

It is often useful to appeal to the individual's casual pronunciations. For example, it would not be surprising if an English-speaking student had considerable difficulty pronouncing an initial [#fn] cluster. But that same person probably casually pronounces "phonetics" with an initial [#fn] cluster (although if you *ask* him how to say "phonetics," you will get the citation form, not the casual pronunciation). The creative teacher in this case would point out that if the student can say [fnɛɾəks] for "phonetics," he can pronounce an initial /#fn/ cluster.

While the preceding examples have come from second-language teaching, the same principles apply in articulation therapy. If the client has the ability to pronounce a certain sound in some contexts but not in others, work from his ability, trying to add to the contexts in which the sound is correctly said. As with phonemic errors (see Section 8-8), the problem the client is having here may be a matter of a faulty rule in his grammar rather than an actual inability to articulate a given sound.

Summary

Sound systems in language operate by means of sound contrasts. Each contrasting sound has one or more phonetic realizations. The contrasting sounds are called **phonemes;** the variants of these are called **allophones.**

The allophones of a given phoneme are in **complementary distribution** for the most part; that is, they are found in mutually exclusive environments. Some allophones may be optional. In any given language, the phonemes *contrast* with one another; allophones do not. For the most part, allophones are *predictable.*

Intrinsic allophones are generated by coarticulatory effects, whereas **extrinsic** allophones are produced by speakers without compelling physiological motivation; their production is rule-governed.

In examining phonemic systems, we see that traditional phonemic theory is self-contradictory unless we recognize the existence of the **morphophonemic** level. We also see that phonemic distinctions may in certain environments not be supported by phonetic differences; this is known as **neutralization.**

Dialects may differ from one another phonemically as well as phonetically. What are essentially the same segments may correspond to different phonemic contrasts in different languages.

Stress, tone, length, and voice quality may be phonemic or contrastive, just as segments are. Of these phonetic features, stress is the only one considered to be contrastive in standard English.

When looking at anomalous language systems, be they the speech of children, second-language learners, or those with certain communication disorders, we find that a phonemic analysis allows us to distinguish between anomalies that are purely phonetic and those that occur in the phonemic structure of the speech. This distinction has implications for the approach to be taken in correcting the problem.

A transcription that uses a different symbol for each phoneme but the same symbol for all allophones is known as a **broad** or **phonemic transcription**. Such a transcription is placed between slash marks. A transcription that uses a different symbol for each different segment is known as a **narrow** or **phonetic transcription.** Such a transcription is placed between brackets.

Speech pathologists may make use of special transcription symbols not found in the IPA to transcribe anomalous articulations.

The **syllable** is a unit having internal structure. It is usually considered to consist of an **onset** and a **rhyme.** The latter is further subdivided into the **nucleus** and the **coda.** A **cluster** is a group of consonants together in the same syllable. There is psycholinguistic evidence of the importance of the syllable as a unit of speech and language.

Phonotactics examines the positions and combinations that specific segments may occupy within the syllable or word. The English syllable contains a vowel or diphthong preceded by zero to three consonants and followed by zero to four consonants.

Dialects differ in their phonotactic constraints, as do different languages.

Phonotactic constraints have practical outcomes in terms of the invention of "nonsense" words, in terms of the learning of a second language, and occasionally in the patterns of errors in disordered speech.

Vocabulary

Terms in parentheses have been mentioned in this chapter but will be defined more fully in a later chapter.

allophone
ambisyllabic
arresting [consonant, cluster, etc.]
autonomous phoneme
bound [morpheme]
brackets
(breathy voice)
broad [transcription]
closed [syllable]
cluster
coda
complementary distribution
conditioned, conditioned variants
contrast, contrastive, contrastiveness
(creaky voice)
distinct
distinctive feature analysis
extrinsic allophone
(falsetto)
free [morpheme]
free variation
generative phonology
immediate constituent
intrinsic allophone
intrusive
inventory
length
minimal pair
morpheme
morphophoneme, morphophonemic
narrow [transcription]
neutralization, neutralize
nucleus
onset
open
peak
phoneme, phonemic, phonemics
phonemic transcription
phonetic similarity
phonetic transcription
phonology
phonotactics
predictability
prosodeme
realization
releasing [consonant, cluster, etc.]
rhyme
sonority hierarchy
syllable
systematic phoneme
tone
toneme
variant
virgule
(whisper)

Questions

1. Make a phonemic analysis of English; that is, make a list of all the phonemes of English. Compare your

list with that of your classmates. Discuss the reasons for any differences. Use minimal pairs to demonstrate the phonemic status of pairs of segments.

2. Take the list you have made for question 1, and beside each phoneme indicate the conditioned variants it has and the environments in which they appear.
3. What **phonemic** differences have you noted among various dialects of English? Leave out any phonetic differences that do not reflect phonemic differences; also ignore differences in stress, rhythm, or intonation.
4. Make a phonemic analysis of a sample of misarticulated speech or of a sample of English as spoken by someone learning it as a second language.
5. Discuss the phonemic system of a foreign language with which a substantial number of the students in the class are familiar. Note similarities and differences with English, both in phonemic and in phonetic inventories. What allophonic variants does each phoneme have? If you cannot find a language with which enough students are familiar, use data from the exercises in Gleason [1955] and Pike [1947] for this question.
6. We sometimes say, when a spelling error such as ⟨nite⟩ for ⟨night⟩ is made, that the word was spelled "phonetically." Is this true? Should an ideal spelling system for a language be phonetic? or phonemic? (or, as noted in Chapter 3, morphophonemic?) Discuss.
7. Comment on the phonotactic patterning of consonants in these words: "sphere," "Sphinx," "thwart."
8. Analyze phonotactic regularities in arresting clusters. What combinations are possible? What restrictions on other positions are created by a given segment (for example, in releasing clusters, if the third position is occupied, it must be an approximant, and the first position must be occupied by /s/)?
9. Examine the following words: *bdellium, mnemonic, knight, limb, sing, pneumonia, pterodactyl, ptomaine, psychology, wrong, xenon, agnostic,* and *fox* versus *vixen.* Consult an etymological dictionary (one that shows word histories) and find out which words reflect a change in English phonotactic patterns, which reflect foreign phonotactic patterns that were modified when the words were borrowed into English, and which reflect peculiar spelling conventions. Where relevant, make statements about different phonotactic restrictions in other languages. Find additional examples.
10. An interesting historical phonotactic change has taken place in English, illustrated by the following set of words. Examine the words:

limb	limp
jamb	camp
comb	tramp
sing	sink
sang	sank
fling	frank
pinned	pint
wind	hint
hind	went

a. What overall pattern do you see? What exceptions are there?

b. There is a dialect in which the following words (and words like them) are pronounced as indicated. How does this fit the pattern established above?

wind	[wɪn]
went	[wɛnt]
bend	[bɛn]
faint	[fent]

c. Let us call the first set of data dialect A, and the second set of data dialect B. Is dialect A or dialect B considered more standard? Is dialect A or dialect B more regular in the application of the phonotactic rule illustrated by the data? Discuss.

Readings

A set of exercises in determining the phonemic status of phones in a number of languages can be found in Gleason's *Workbook* [1955]. Pike's volume [1947] contains theory and useful exercises on phonemics as well. Both are highly recommended for practice.

Jones]1967], Twaddell [1966], and Bloomfield [1961] give classic accounts of phoneme theory. Discussions can also be found in Abercrombie [1967], Brosnahan and Malmberg [1970], Fromkin and Rodman [1983], Lyons [1968], and O'Connor [1973].

The modern view of the syllable in phonology is surveyed in Selkirk [1982]. Other works in this area include Kahn [1976] and Lowenstamm [1979].

Whorf [1956] has a very complete outline of the phonotactic restrictions of one-syllable words in English (pp. 223 ff.). Scholes [1966] examines phonotactics very thoroughly. There is a discussion in O'Connor [1973] and in Chapter 6 of Hill [1958].

Foundations of phonetics

Physiological phonetics: the anatomy of speech

9

Objectives

To discuss the concept of "speech organs."

To enumerate, describe, and define the roles of the supraglottal organs and the larynx.

To discuss phonation, its mechanism and its linguistic function.

To discuss respiration, its mechanism and its role in speech.

To enumerate the major muscles of speech in terms of the articulations they facilitate.

To summarize briefly some physical anomalies that affect speech production.

9-1 The "Organs of Speech"

This chapter will deal with the anatomical structures and physiological processes involved in the production of speech. We will begin with a naming of major anatomical landmarks; that will give us a vocabulary with which to classify speech sounds by their articulatory positions. We will then examine vocal fold vibration, respiration, vocal musculature, and anatomical and physiological[1] anomalies affecting speech production. It should be stressed that the overview of speech physiology given here is rather superficial. Students of speech pathology will surely have an entire course devoted to this subject. Several excellent textbooks and atlases of speech anatomy and physiology are listed at the end of the chapter, and the interested student is encouraged to read further in this area. It should also be noted that since this is an introductory *phonetics* book, much technical vocabulary in the area of anatomy has been intentionally avoided.

The study of physiological phonetics is basic to an understanding of both normal and pathological speech. The human repertoire of speech sounds depends fundamentally upon the geometry of the vocal tract. The kinds of sounds we make, the kinds of transitions we make between sounds, the combinations of sounds that are possible, and the kinds of sound changes that occur throughout the history of a language all are intimately tied to our vocal equipment.

It has been demonstrated that chimpanzees are capable of acquiring some limited form of human language,[2] but they cannot learn to *pronounce* any words in a recognizable way. They are restricted to some form of manual language output—the sign language of the hearing-impaired or the manipulation of symbolic tokens. This is because their vocal tracts are different from ours in small—but essential—ways. Human vocal tracts are capable of a wider range of sounds. So, to know what our phonetic capabilities are, and why, we must begin with our anatomy.

It is traditional to say that speech is an *overlaid function*. That is, we have no unique "speech organs" not found in other mammals. Lungs, larynx, tongue, teeth, lips, and brain are all found in lower animals; these structures all have more primary biological functions than speech. In one sense, then, speech has been "overlaid" on these organs. Such a view is simplistic, however, in that it overlooks both the high degree of cerebral specialization unique to human beings and the degree to which our speech organs have been shaped through evolution for the specific task of speech. The specialization of the higher brain centers for speech is incredible in its complexity, not only permitting retention of the rules of grammar and the vocabulary of language, but also making possible the fine control and minute synchronization of the various muscles brought into play in speaking.

Philip Lieberman, in his fascinating *On the Origins of Language* [1975], claims that the form of all our "speech organs" was influenced by adaptive selection through evolution, which favored speech over more basic functions. Using computer-assisted acoustic modeling of various vocal tracts and soft-tissue reconstructions from prehistoric skulls, he traces the development of the human phonetic potential. He points out, for example, that the right-angle bend in our vocal tract (between mouth and throat) and the low placement of our larynx (low as compared to neonate humans and our closest living relative, the chimpanzee) are essential for our phonetic virtuosity but are nonadaptive in other ways. This right-angle bend and low larynx interfere with swallowing, increasing the chance of asphyxiation due to choking. Similarly the form of our vocal folds is such as to permit fine variation in pitch and very efficient phonation, but they get in the way of rapid, deep breathing in a way that a horse's, for example, do not; thus our athletic potential is reduced by an adaptation for speech. Such adaptive capacities as risk-free swallowing and rapid gas exchange through breathing seem so basic that they would be "traded" through evolution only for something of exceptional adaptive potential. In Lieberman's view, this "something" is speech. In that sense, then, speech is not "overlaid";

[1] It is perhaps useful at this point to distinguish **anatomy** from **physiology.** Simply stated, *anatomy* is a study of *structures* (bones, muscles, tendons, etc.): where they are, how they are shaped, and so forth, whereas *physiology* is the study of the *functioning* of those structures. What is generally called *physiological phonetics* includes both anatomical and physiological concepts.

[2] Very limited, restricted to naming, according to most linguists who have examined the problem.

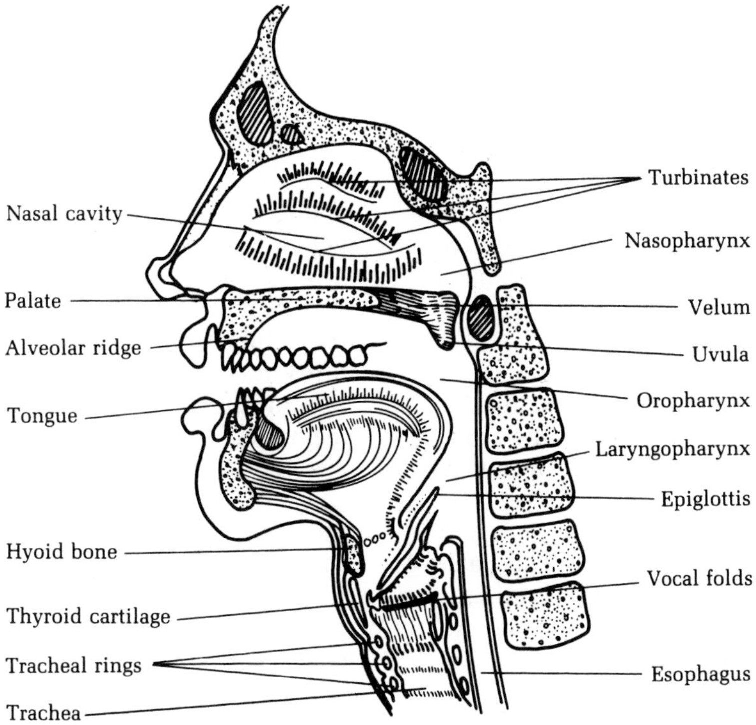

Figure 9-1. A cross section of the head, showing speech articulators and associated structures.

rather, our speech organs are the shape they are because of speech.[3]

9-2 The Supraglottal Organs

The supraglottal organs (those above the larynx) and the vocal folds are the speech organs mentioned most often throughout this book. Figure 9-1 gives a schematized cross section of the head, with the important articulatory organs identified. We have already examined these briefly in Chapter 4 and will review them here.[4]

THE LIPS. The lips are used to close the oral cavity in the production of some consonants. They may be rounded and extended in the production of certain vowels. The adjective is **labial** (L. *labia*, 'lips'); when both lips are involved, we speak of a **bilabial** sound.

THE TEETH. Sounds involving the teeth are referred to as **dental** sounds (L. *dentes*, 'teeth'). The upper teeth are involved in speech production more often than the lower ones. As noted in Chapter 4, the upper side teeth (molars and premolars) are used in speech production, as for [t]; the tongue creates a seal along them. Since that is not considered the place of articulation, only sounds with apicodental or laminodental contact are called *dental*.

THE TONGUE. The tongue is the most agile organ of speech. Many gestures of the tongue are used in speech, and the tongue contacts many of the other speech organs. The tongue is divided into five regions: the **tip** or **apex,** the **blade,** the **front,** the **back,** and the **root;** these are indicated in Figure 9-1. The **apex** is the very tip of the tongue. The **blade** is a very short section of the tongue surface,

[3] To take an analogy, whales are descended from four-legged land-walking mammals. It would be simplistic to say that swimming is "overlaid" on the legs and arms of a whale; those "legs" and "arms" have been fundamentally modified by adaptation to an aquatic environment.

[4] Some of this section repeats parts of Chapter 4, because some instructors may assign this chapter first. In certain cases greater anatomical detail is given here.

the part that normally lies below the *alveolar ridge* at rest. The **front** (despite its name) is the middle portion of the oral surface of the tongue, lying below the *palate* at rest. The **back** is the rear portion of the oral tongue surface, lying below the *velum* at rest. The **root** is that part of the surface of the tongue that faces into the *pharynx* or throat cavity. The *front* and *back* are often considered together as the tongue **dorsum.** The adjective for *tongue* is **lingual,** for *tip* is **apical** (L. *apex*, 'tip'), for *blade* is **laminal** (L. *lamina*, 'blade'), and for *dorsum* is **dorsal** (L. *dorsum*, 'back').

THE ALVEOLAR RIDGE (L. *alveus*, 'trough,' 'tray'). Also called the **gum ridge,** this is the ridge directly behind the upper front teeth. The adjectival form is **alveolar.**

THE PALATE (L. *palatum*, 'palate'). The palate is the hard, bony part of the roof of the mouth that extends from the alveolar ridge to the velum. The adjectival form is **palatal.**

THE VELUM (L. *velum* [*palati*], 'veil [of the palate]'). The velum is the soft, muscular rear part of the roof of the mouth that lacks any bony framework. It can be raised and lowered by its own musculature. This movement serves a valving function; when the velum is *raised*, the nasal cavities are closed off from the rest of the vocal tract, as they are during oral breathing or during swallowing. When the velum is *lowered*, the passage (or **velic port**) between the nasal cavities and the oropharyngeal cavity is open, as it is for nasal breathing; this introduces *nasal resonance* and thus imparts a nasal quality to speech sounds produced with a lowered velum.

As with the *alveolar ridge* and *palate*, we use the *velum* as a reference point in describing what position the *tongue* is assuming. If the tongue is arched below the velum, or is touching the velum, we call this a **velar** articulation. On the other hand, when the velum itself moves, performing the valving function just described, we speak of a **velic** movement or articulation. Be sure to distinguish **velar** (referring to the part of the oral cavity below the velum) from **velic** (referring to the velum itself).

Some authors call the palate the *hard palate* and the velum the *soft palate*. Medical anatomists use the term "palate" in a more general sense, referring to the velum as well as the palate. But in the study of speech, the distinction between the two entities is very important, so phoneticians and speech scientists generally use the clear, unambiguous terms **palate** for the bony part and **velum** for the muscular part.

Note that the **uvula** attaches to the rear edge of the velum. Do not confuse the small uvula with the velum itself; the latter makes up about two-fifths of the roof of the mouth. The uvula plays a role in the articulation of some sounds in some languages, although English has no **uvular** sounds.

THE ORAL CAVITY (L. *os/oralis*, 'mouth,' 'oral'). This cavity is a resonating chamber of primary importance to speech, since its size and shape can be modified so greatly. Its internal volume can be changed by modification of the tongue and jaw positions.

THE NASAL CAVITIES (L. *nasus*, 'nose'). Velic action allows the nasal cavities to be closed or open (or partially open) with respect to the rest of the vocal tract. Opening the velic port allows sound waves to resonate within the nasal cavities, giving a distinctive nasal quality to the speech sounds thus produced.

In phonetics textbooks, the nasal cavity is generally shown in lateral cross section (side view). In such a view, it appears to be a large, open chamber that should have a rich resonance. However, a frontal cross section would show that each side of the cavity contains three curled scroll-like membranes called **turbinates,** which swirl the air in the cavities, presumably to increase olfactory (smell) sensitivity and to warm cold air before it gets to the lungs. These structures partially fill the nasal cavity and cut up the remaining space into small passageways. The importance of this phonetically is that the nasal cavities, far from being a large, open resonator, in fact form a poor resonator. Notice how muffled nasal consonants sound, and note that they cannot be shouted very effectively.

THE PHARYNX (Gk. *pharynx*, 'throat'). The pharynx is the cavity above the larynx and behind the oral cavity. In everyday language we might refer to it as the "throat cavity" or simply the "throat." For added precision, the pharynx is often divided into three parts:

1. the **laryngopharynx,** which is the lowest part of the **pharyngeal cavity,** or pharynx, just above the *larynx;*
2. the **oropharynx,** which is the mid part of the pharyngeal cavity at the very back of the mouth; and
3. the **nasopharynx,** which includes the nasal vestibule (the entrance to the nasal cavities).

The pharynx is the critical area in which the food passageway and the air passageway cross and are common for a distance. Air is normally inhaled through the nose, enters the *back* of the pharynx through the velic port, and passes through the larynx on its way to the lungs at the *front* of the laryngopharynx. Food enters the *front* of the oropharynx during swallowing and passes through the *back* of the laryngopharynx, where it enters the **esophagus** (Gk. *aesophagos*, 'eating food'), the passage leading to the stomach.

THE TRACHEA (Gk. *trachea*, 'neck'; 'place to grab someone to strangle him'). The trachea is the tube that leads from the larynx to where it splits into two **bronchi,** which connect to the **lungs.** It is made up of cartilaginous rings, interconnected with connective tissue; it is generally pictured as looking rather like a vacuum-cleaner hose. We will examine it further in Section 9-5.

9-3 The Larynx

The **larynx** (Gk. *larynx*, 'upper part of the windpipe')[5] is a complex cartilaginous structure situated at the upper end of the trachea, below the pharynx. Popularly called the "voice box," it is extremely important both for speech and for more basic biological functions. It is fundamentally important to speech because it contains the **vocal folds,** which vibrate, producing a tone necessary for the production of most—and the distinction between some—speech sounds. In terms of biological functioning, the larynx serves several purposes. The vocal folds and the **epiglottis** (Gk. *epiglottis*, 'on top of the glottis'), internal parts of the larynx, serve to prevent intrusion of food or liquid into the lungs during swallowing. If a foreign substance does enter the windpipe, a coughing reflex is triggered that involves the vocal folds. And during muscular exertion of the arms and torso, the vocal folds shut tightly, trapping air in the lungs. This keeps the lungs inflated, so that the **thoracic cage** (the rib cage) remains a stable base and fulcrum for the levers that are our arms. (To demonstrate that this is so, try to talk while lifting or pushing something heavy, and note how difficult it is.)

The larynx is made up of five cartilages (Figure 9-2). These are the **epiglottis** (which serves no function in speech), the **thyroid cartilage,** the **cricoid cartilage** (which is in effect the topmost tracheal cartilage), and the two **arytenoid cartilages.**

Locate the larynx in your own neck. The thyroid cartilage faces frontward. Most commonly in men, part of this cartilage (the "Adam's apple") protrudes conspicuously at the front of the neck. Of course, the same cartilage exists in the same place in women and children, but it is generally smaller and the angle formed by its two faces is flatter, so the larynx does not show as much. Once you have located the thyroid cartilage, locate the V-shaped notch in the front of it. This is a handy reference point for locating other structures. (Because of the relative size of this cartilage in men and women, and because of the distribution of subcutaneous fat, women often have more difficulty than men in locating this notch.) Above the notch, you should be able to palpate (locate by feel) the **hyoid bone,** also pictured in Figure 9-2. The hyoid bone, the only bone in the body not contiguous with any other bone, is attached to the thyroid cartilage by the latter's **superior horns** and by a membrane (descriptively called the **thyrohyoid membrane**) that fills the space between the bone and the cartilage. Below the thyroid cartilage, you should be able to palpate the **tracheal**

[5] Aristotle defined *larynx* as 'the part of the vocal apparatus used in sounding vowels.' In biblical Greek, *larynx* meant 'speech.'

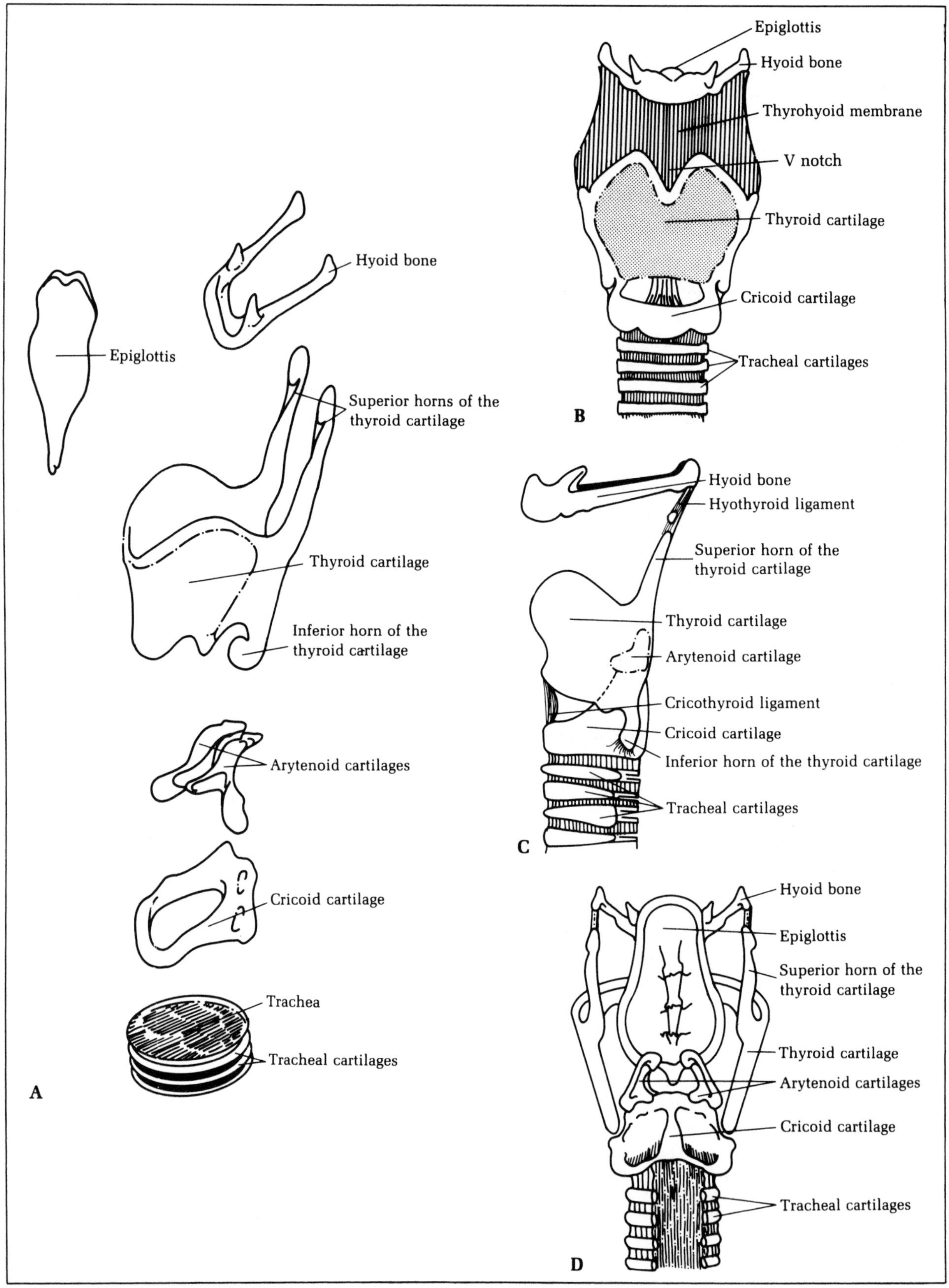
Hyoid bone
Epiglottis
Superior horns of the thyroid cartilage
Thyroid cartilage
Inferior horn of the thyroid cartilage
Arytenoid cartilages
Cricoid cartilage
Trachea
Tracheal cartilages
A
Epiglottis
Hyoid bone
Thyrohyoid membrane
V notch
Thyroid cartilage
Cricoid cartilage
Tracheal cartilages
B
Hyoid bone
Hyothyroid ligament
Superior horn of the thyroid cartilage
Thyroid cartilage
Arytenoid cartilage
Cricothyroid ligament
Cricoid cartilage
Inferior horn of the thyroid cartilage
Tracheal cartilages
C
Hyoid bone
Epiglottis
Superior horn of the thyroid cartilage
Thyroid cartilage
Arytenoid cartilages
Cricoid cartilage
Tracheal cartilages
D

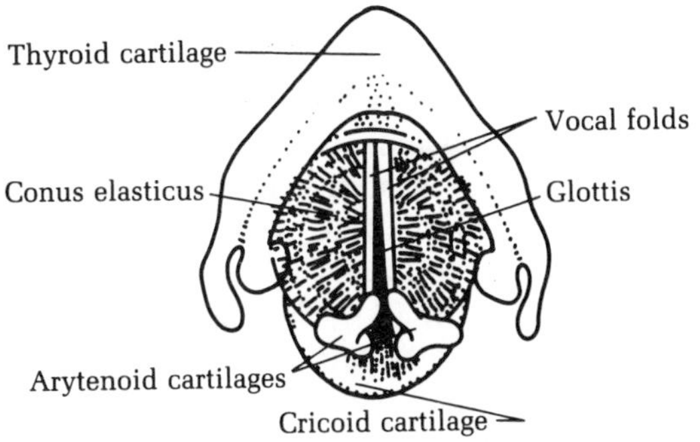

Figure 9-3. The conus elasticus and the vocal folds as seen from above.

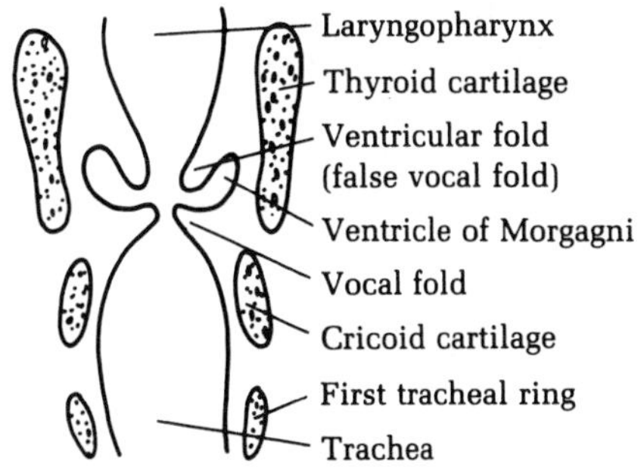

Figure 9-4. The vocal folds in schematic cross section.

cartilages and the **cricoid cartilage,** although it may be hard to tell for certain that you have located the latter. Look at Figure 9-2 when feeling for these structures, and try locating them on a friend if you have no success on yourself.

From the phonetician's viewpoint, the laryngeal cartilages are interesting to the extent that they serve to support the **vocal folds**[6] and associated speech muscles (Figure 9-3). The vocal folds are two bands of tissue, made up of muscle and ligament, which serve as a variable valve for air passing into and out of the lungs. The roughly triangular space between the vocal folds is called the **glottis** (Gk. *glottis,* 'mouthpiece of pipe in which reed is inserted'; 'mouthpiece of trumpet'; metaphorically, 'mouth of windpipe'). When the vocal folds are **adducted**[7] the glottis disappears; like the hole in a doughnut, it is nothing in itself but is defined by what surrounds it.

The vocal folds attach at the front to the inside of the thyroid cartilage below the V notch. This point of attachment is the apex of the triangular glottis. The rear ends of the vocal folds attach one to each arytenoid cartilage. The arytenoid cartilages sit on the upper edge of the cricoid cartilage; they both slide and pivot, and in doing so they bring the rear ends of the vocal folds together or apart. The vocal folds form the edge of a membrane that stretches from the vocal folds to the cricoid cartilage at the sides and back and to the thyroid cartilage at the front. This so-called **conus elasticus** ('elastic cone') ensures that air can pass only *between* the vocal folds (through the glottis).

The vocal folds are seen in cross section in Figure 9-4. Note that above them is another pair of folds of soft tissue, called the **false vocal folds** or **ventricular folds.** These are separated by a pair of *ventricles* (anatomical terminology for a 'chamber' or 'cavity') called the **ventricles of Morgagni.**

9-4 Phonation

The production of many speech sounds requires that the vocal folds vibrate. This vibration is known as **phonation, voice,** or **voicing** (the word *voice* also has a more general sense, of course). The vocal folds make other linguistically significant articulations, and these are often lumped together under the term *phonation* as well.

9-4.1 Voice Production

Let us turn our attention first to *voicing,* the normal vibration of the vocal folds that occurs in about three-quarters of speech sounds. Voicing is

[6] The **vocal folds** are sometimes called the *vocal bands, vocal cords* or *vocal chords.* The latter terms suggest, falsely, that they are situated like the strings of a musical instrument. The term **vocal folds** is currently the most usual term.
[7] To **adduct** the vocal folds is to bring them together, or close them. To **abduct** the vocal folds is to separate them, or open them.

◀ **Figure 9-2.** The larynx and the laryngeal cartilages. A. An oblique view of the laryngeal cartilages exploded. B. A front view of the larynx (thyrohyoid membrane shown). C. A side view of the larynx (thyrohyoid membrane not shown). D. A rear view of the larynx.

the quasi-periodic[8] vibration of the vocal folds, occurring on the order of 100 to 160 times per second (or **hertz,** abbreviated **Hz**) in adult men and on the order of 170 to 300 Hz in adult women. In children, this frequency can fall within the female range or can be considerably higher, particularly in infants. I have measured frequencies up to about 500 Hz in the cries of young infants.

This speed of vibration is called the **fundamental frequency** of a voice (abbreviated FF or F_0).[9] It depends to an extent upon the age and sex of a speaker and is partly under voluntary control. Singing involves changes in F_0 that follow the tune of the song. The transition from childhood to adulthood involves some deepening of the voice (that is, a lower F_0) in both men and women, due to the enlargement of the larynx along with the rest of the body and as a **secondary sexual characteristic.**[10] In men the degree of enlargement is greater than in women. The thyroid cartilage grows disproportionately, forming the protruding "Adam's apple"; as a result, the angle between the two faces of the cartilage is sharper, and the vocal folds, which attach inside this angle, are longer. This results in a lower F_0 due to the increased mass of the folds. At puberty, boys often experience a "breaking" or "cracking" of the voice; in the same way that adolescent growth spurts in the leg bones result in awkwardness and lack of coordination as the muscles and brain adjust to the unfamiliar limbs, so too the rapid growth in the length of the vocal folds upsets the fine muscular coordination required for phonation. (Since girls undergo some laryngeal enlargement at puberty, some girls experience a "breaking" of the voice as well.)

Muscles can make repetitive movements only about twelve times per second at the very most, so it is obvious at once that the high rates of vocal fold vibration are not created by any muscles contracting and relaxing several hundred times per second. Some other process must be at work. Several explanations of vocal fold vibration have been advanced;[11] they take into account various factors, including muscular forces, aerodynamic principles, tissue elasticity, and mass (inertia).

Essentially, phonation works like this: The vocal folds are adducted (closed) gently by the speaker (Figure 9-5A). The speaker creates a heightened subglottal air pressure (air pressure below the glottis), which exerts a static force against the adducted vocal folds (Figure 9-5B). Since the vocal fold tension and subglottal pressure have been precisely regulated by the speaker to this end, the static force of the air is greater than that which the vocal folds can withstand. The vocal folds are therefore pushed apart (Figure 9-5C–E); in the most usual mode of vibration the separation first appears toward the back (arytenoid) end, and then works toward the front (thyroid) end. Since the vocal folds are now abducted (open), the tension of the vocal folds is no longer working against a static air pressure, but rather against a moving or *dynamic* air column. Aerodynamic forces thus come into play, namely the **Bernoulli** or **Venturi effect.**

To understand the Bernoulli effect, imagine a pipe through which air is being pumped at a constant flow rate (Figure 9-6). As long as the pipe is a closed system, and as long as the diameter is constant, the pressure within it will be constant. However, if the diameter of the pipe is reduced, the pressure at the constriction will be **lower** than at other points. At first this fact may be counterintuitive: it seems backward. It may help to think of it in this way: Since the system shown in Figure 9-6 is a closed one—that is, the air has nowhere to go but through the pipe—the *quantity* of air per unit time passing through the constriction is the same as through the rest of the pipe. But since the passageway is narrower, the air must be traveling *faster* at the constriction than elsewhere in the pipe. Since the air is traveling *faster*, there is greater turbulence and therefore greater distance between the molecules. And what is pressure but a measure of how compactly the molecules are

[8] **Quasi-periodic:** almost, nearly periodic; that is to say, almost cyclical or regular. The vibration of healthy vocal folds is very nearly regular and rhythmical. The term *periodic* will be defined more fully in Chapter 10.

[9] The abbreviation F_0 is read "F-zero" or simply "fundamental (frequency)." The reason for the abbreviated form will become clear in Chapter 10.

[10] **Secondary sexual characteristics** are sexual characteristics that appear at puberty, as opposed to **primary sexual characteristics,** which are apparent at birth or shortly thereafter.

[11] See, for example, Van den Berg [1958].

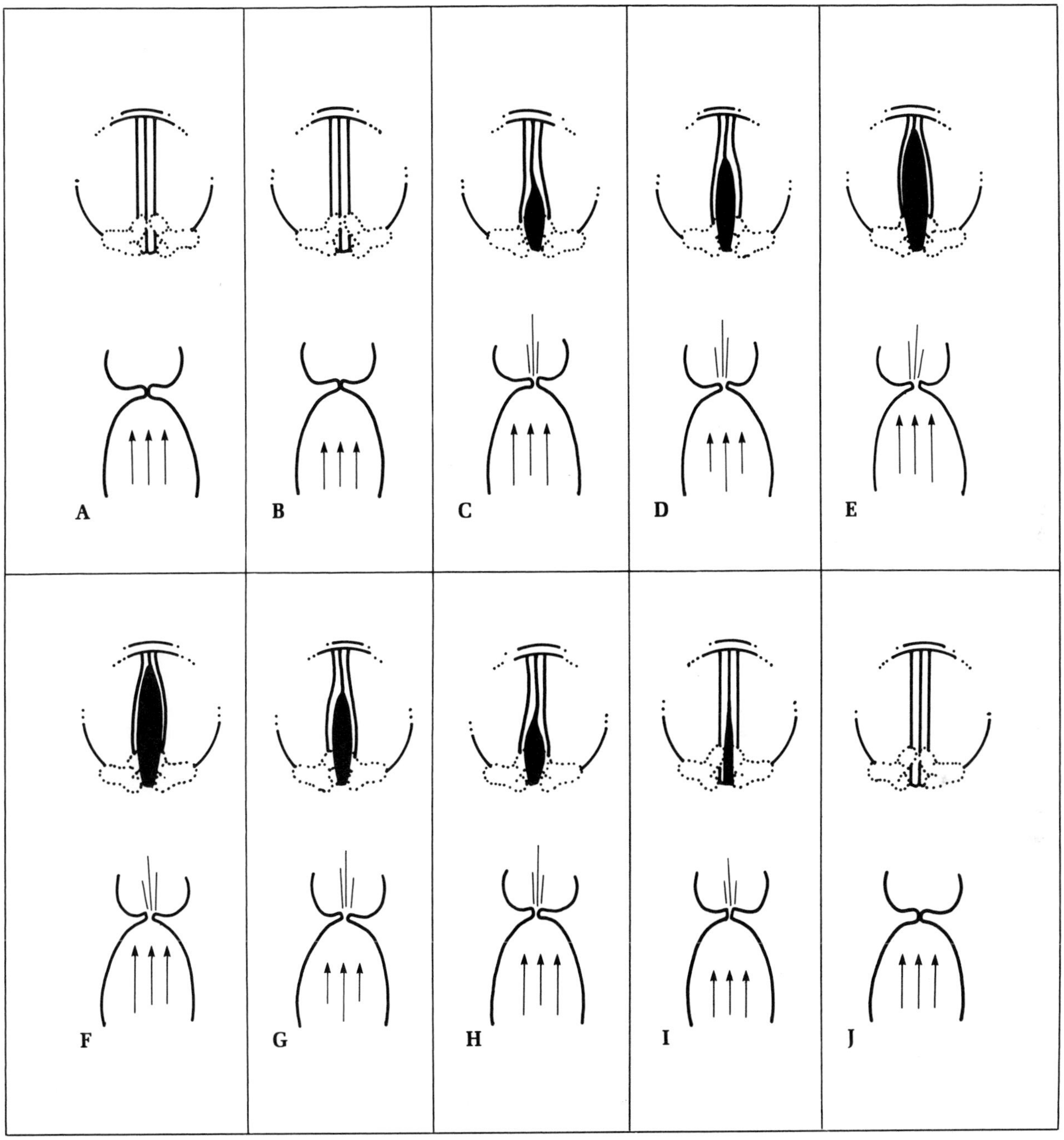

Figure 9-5. The vocal folds in simplified cross section as seen from above during a glottal cycle divided into 10 equal time periods. A, B. Static subglottal air pressure presses against the adducted vocal folds. C. The air pressure begins to force the vocal folds apart. D, E. The vocal folds are forced farther apart by air pressure. In the mode of vibration illustrated, the glottal chink first appears at the posterior (arytenoid) end and moves anteriorly toward the thyroid end, but this is not the only mode of vocal fold vibration possible. F. Aerodynamic principles mean reduced air pressure through the glottis, insufficient to maintain vocal fold separation. G–I. The vocal folds return to their adducted position, since muscular forces and tissue elasticity are exerting greater force now than is the air pressure. J. The vocal folds are completely adducted, and airflow stops. Once again, static air pressure is acting against the vocal folds, and the cycle is ready to begin again.

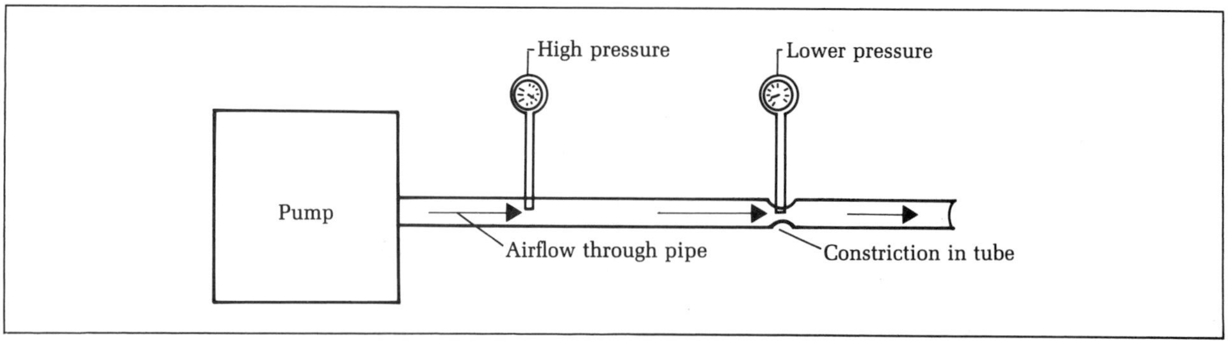

Figure 9-6. The Bernoulli effect. The pressure of air being pumped through a pipe is lower at a constriction.

packed? Hence, *the pressure is lower at the constriction.*[12]

Back to the vocal folds: As we said, in Figure 9-5E the vocal folds have been pushed open by a static pressure and are now contending with an air*flow*. The air is passing through a constriction, the glottis, and due to the Bernoulli effect, the pressure at the glottis is reduced. This reduced pressure is insufficient to hold the vocal folds apart against the muscular and elastic forces that are working to adduct them. Thus the vocal folds begin to close again (Figure 9-5F–I). Finally, they close completely (Figure 9-5J). The subglottal pressure remains, however (Figure 9-5J). Since the vocal folds are now closed (Figure 9-5A,B,J), they are once again contending with a static pressure that is greater than they can withstand under their present degree of tension. So they begin to open again (Figure 9-5C), and the cycle repeats.

This explanation of the mechanism of vocal fold vibration, presented here in its barest essentials, takes into account *muscular forces, aerodynamic effects,* and *tissue elasticity.* It is therefore called (after Van den Berg [1958]) the **myoelastic-aerodynamic theory of voice production** (*myo-* is a combining form from Greek meaning 'muscle'). More recent theories are more sophisticated, taking *inertia* and *tissue viscosity* into account, as well as treating the contact face of the vocal folds as two (coupled) masses rather than as one mass. See, for example, Ishizaka and Matsudaira [1972].

[12] This, by the way, is how airplanes fly: the distance across the top of the wing is greater than across the bottom of the wing, so as the plane moves forward, the air must pass faster over the top than over the bottom. Thus the air pressure is lower above the wing than below it: the greater pressure beneath the wing supports the weight of the airplane.

9-4.2 Fundamental Frequency

The glottal cycle is repeated anywhere from fifty or so times a second to several hundred times. This frequency is known as the **fundamental frequency** of the voice and is abbreviated F_0, as we have noted.

Each individual has a fundamental frequency (F_0) that is most *natural* to him or her. This is the frequency that can be maintained with the least strain to that individual's laryngeal musculature and the least damage to the contact surfaces of the vocal folds. This frequency is called the individual's **natural frequency** or **natural pitch.**

Each individual also has his or her own characteristic **range;** that is, the full extent, from the lowest to the highest, of the frequencies he or she can produce.

Be sure not to confuse the range of possible **natural frequencies** of the human voice with the **range** of a particular individual. We have noted that most adult males have a natural frequency falling somewhere between 100 and 160 Hz. That means that most adult men have a natural frequency that falls within these frequencies. But each individual man will have his own **range.** One man might have a natural frequency of 150 Hz, with a range from 100 to 300 Hz. Another man might have a natural frequency of 100 Hz, with a range from 50 to 250 Hz. Similarly, most women have a natural frequency of between 170 and 300 Hz, but each has her own characteristic range.

The **natural frequency** depends primarily on innate characteristics; a person's **range** can be increased with vocal training.

The speed of vocal fold vibration—the frequency of the voice—depends on a number of factors: vocal fold length, size, mass, and tension, among other things. We noted that for phonation, there has to be a critical balance between subglottal pressure and vocal fold tension: too little pressure or too much tension, and the vocal folds will not be forced apart; too much pressure or too little tension, and the airstream will hold them open. But there is more than one balance point: you can phonate with a lower pressure and tension or a greater pressure and tension. Both frequency and volume will be affected by this adjustment.

The mass of the vocal folds also affects their frequency. To demonstrate this principle, hold your clenched fist in front of you, elbow bent. Now move your fist back and forth as rapidly as possible. Now hold a compact but heavy object in your hand, and once again move your hand back and forth as fast as possible. You will note that the increased mass slows down the speed at which you move your hand back and forth. In the same way, greater vocal fold mass will result in a lower frequency. When people have colds, their voices often have a lower pitch. The main reason is that inflammation of the vocal fold tissue adds to its mass and hence slows down the rate of vibration. Such inflammation may also have the effect of stiffening the vocal folds. Also, phlegm may stick to the vocal folds, increasing their mass. Not only *rate* of vibration but *voice quality* as well may be affected, giving a *hoarseness* to the voice. The inflammation and stiffness of the vocal folds may affect their mode of vibration as much as it does their rate of vibration, and phlegm on the contact surfaces may affect vibration and airflow.

The length of the vocal folds also affects their speed of vibration. Their length can be adjusted somewhat, as shown in Figure 9-7. The thyroid cartilage pivots with respect to the cricoid cartilage; the axis of this movement is at the **cricothyroid joint,** where the **inferior horns** of the thyroid meet the cricoid. As you will recall, the front ends of the folds are attached to the thyroid cartilage, and the rear ends to the arytenoids. The arytenoids are, in turn, situated on the cricoid. So when the thyroid pivots as shown in Figure 9-7, the length of the vocal folds changes.

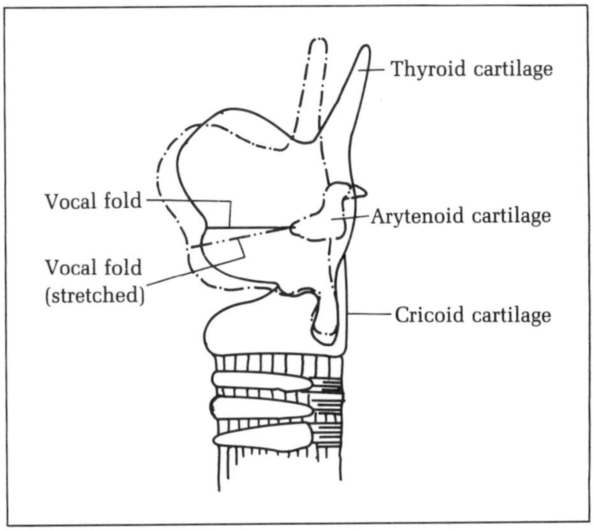

Figure 9-7. The rocking motion of the thyroid cartilage with respect to the cricoid cartilage. The thyroid cartilage can change its angle relative to the cricoid cartilage by pivoting about the cricothyroid joint. The anterior end of the vocal folds are attached to the thyroid cartilage, and the posterior end to the arytenoid cartilages (and ultimately, therefore, to the cricoid cartilage). Thus, the pivoting action changes the length of the vocal folds, which affects their mass, and thus changes their frequency of vibration.

This is an easy effect to palpate. Put your index finger in the V notch of your thyroid cartilage. Hum or say "ah," and go through your whole vocal range—from lowest note to highest and back again. You should feel the thyroid cartilage rocking, as illustrated in Figure 9-7.

Note that a *lower* frequency is produced with *longer* vocal folds, and vice versa. While this may be counterintuitive, it is in fact true. Apparently the change in *mass* affects the frequency of the vocal folds more than the change in *length.*

9-4.3 Modes of Vocal Fold Vibration

The discussion up to this point has concerned the most common form of vocal fold vibration (phonation). Other forms exist as well, some of which have linguistic significance at one level or another.

We noted that usually the glottal chink appears at the arytenoid end of the vocal folds and works forward. The end of the cycle sees the reverse situation: the vocal folds come together first at the thyroid end, and the closure moves rearward. (See Figure 9-5.) In another mode of vibration, the chink starts in the middle and works outward in both directions. This different mode of vibration affects **voice quality,** that aspect of voice that is individual to each person.

Falsetto, also called "head register" as opposed to the more usual "chest register," is another mode of vocal fold vibration. Not only is falsetto of a much higher frequency than the normal register, but the vibration is different in nature. We noted that normal vibration is quasi-periodic, that is, close to being regularly cyclical. In falsetto, the vibration is much more periodic, sinusoidal in wave form, and poorer in harmonics.[13]

One characteristic of the normal register of phonation is that it is remarkably efficient, efficient in two ways. First, a maximum amount of sound energy is generated from a given mechanical input (generated by lung muscles creating an airstream). Second, since air is not wasted, phonation can continue for a long time without interruption. A speaker can say twenty or thirty syllables without renewing his air supply, although the number is usually smaller in normal speech.

The mode of **breathy voice** makes rather less efficient use of the air supply. In breathy voice, the vocal folds are never completely adducted; they always remain slightly apart, perhaps as for whispering. As the name suggests, it has a breathy, sometimes husky, quality. It is affected by certain actresses, since breathy voice in females is considered sexy by some in our culture. On the other hand, breathy voice in males is considered by many to be effeminate. But the interpretation of breathy voice is language- or culture-specific; in some languages breathy phonation is *phonemic* (rather than having emotional/sexual content), that is to say, some pairs of words differ only in that one is said with breathy voice and the other with normal voice. Speakers of such a language recognize these as different words, as different as "bit" and "pit" sound to us.

Another mode of vocal fold vibration is **creaky voice,** so-called because it sounds to some like the creaking of a rusty hinge. Creaky voice is produced by an extremely tense phonation; the vocal folds are very tense, and so the subglottal pressure must be very high to produce voice. The result is a tense, irregular phonation with a popping quality. (For this reason, it is sometimes called **vocal fry,** after the sound of frying bacon.) This is the kind of voice you will produce if you try to talk while lifting a very heavy object. (You may be able to produce creaky voice just by imagining you are lifting a heavy object.) "Vocal fry" is a common voice disorder: one response to anxiety is a tensing of all muscles, including the laryngeal ones, giving a very tense voice quality.

Just as breathy voice is phonemic in some languages, so too is creaky voice. In such languages, two different words may be exactly the same except that one is produced with creaky voice, the other with normal voice.

Whisper is another mode of phonation, although it does not involve vocal fold vibration. In whispered speech, the glottis is left slightly open—usually there is a triangular chink at the arytenoid end—so that the air passing through creates a noisy turbulence. This noise replaces the usual vocal fold vibration to excite resonance in the vocal cavities.

Two other linguistically significant laryngeal articulations should be mentioned before we leave the subject. [**h**] is produced by a glottal configuration like that for whispering. And the **glottal stop** [ʔ] is produced by closing the glottis and opening it abruptly.

The various glottal configurations are shown in stylized fashion in Figure 9-8. In the laboratory or clinic the glottis is viewed and photographed by means of **indirect laryngoscopy** ('indirect larynx-viewing'). The traditional method has been to hold a mirror at the bend of the throat (after using a local anesthetic to numb the gag reflex), and to view or photograph through the open mouth. Nowadays, a fiberoptic device called a *fiberscope* is most often used for this purpose. Indirect laryngoscopy is shown in Figure 9-8.

9-5 Respiration

Phonation and ultimately speech depend upon a moving column of air produced by the respiratory system; it is to this system that we will now turn

[13] *Sinusoidal* describes the shape of the sound wave produced. *Harmonics* are overtones or multiples of the F_0. Both these concepts are defined in detail in Chapter 10.

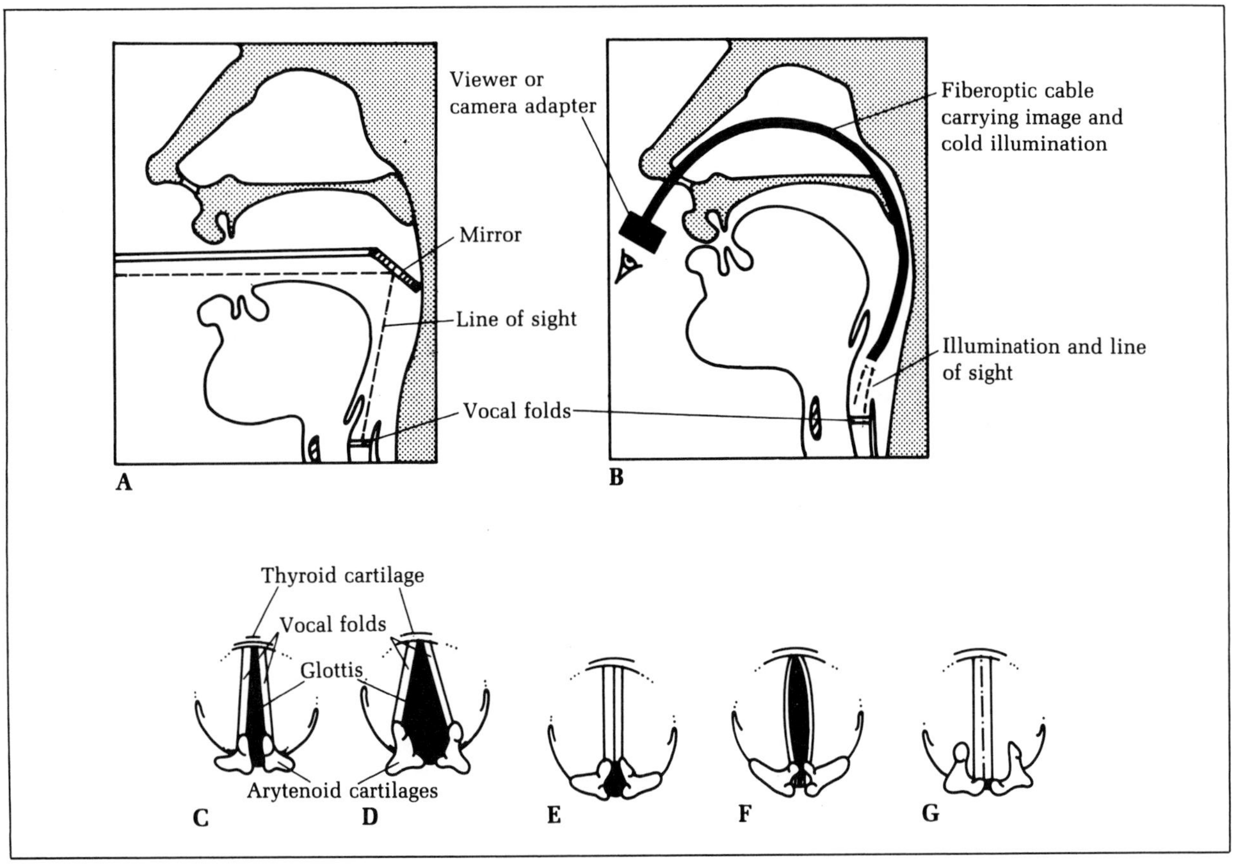

Figure 9-8. Indirect laryngoscopy (A,B) and glottal configurations (C–G). The interior of the larynx cannot be seen directly, so it is viewed indirectly by mirror or fiberscope. A. The traditional method of indirect laryngoscopy with a mirror. B. Laryngoscopy with modern fiberscope. The fiberoptic cable carries both the image and a cold illumination source. Viewing is achieved directly by eye through an eyepiece, or, more usually, by videocamera and monitor. C. Normal respiration. The vocal folds are somewhat abducted. D. Forced respiration, as during aerobic exercise. The vocal folds are fully abducted for maximum airflow. E. Whispering. There is a small triangular chink at the arytenoid end, creating a restricted, noisy airflow. F. Phonation. The vocal folds at the most open phase of their cycle. G. Phonation. The vocal folds at the point in their cycle at which they are completely adducted. Note also: During short-term heavy physical exertion, particularly with the upper body and arms (such as in lifting), the vocal folds are completely and forcibly adducted.

our attention. What follows is necessarily a simplified view, but one that will outline the essentials.

The **trachea** (windpipe) descends into the chest cavity from the larynx. It is held open by cartilaginous rings, as already noted. The trachea branches into two **primary bronchi,** one leading to each lung. The bronchi further subdivide into smaller and smaller tubes[14] until they reach the **alveolar sacs.** The latter are the small chambers in the lungs in which gas transfer takes place. For purposes of describing speech physiology, we often consider the lungs to be empty bags or balloons; this is a useful analogy, but it is well to remember that the vital function of the lungs is carried out in thousands of tiny sacs having a combined surface area of about 70 square meters.

[14] Called, in descending order, secondary bronchi, bronchioles, terminal bronchioles, respiratory bronchioles, and alveolar ducts.

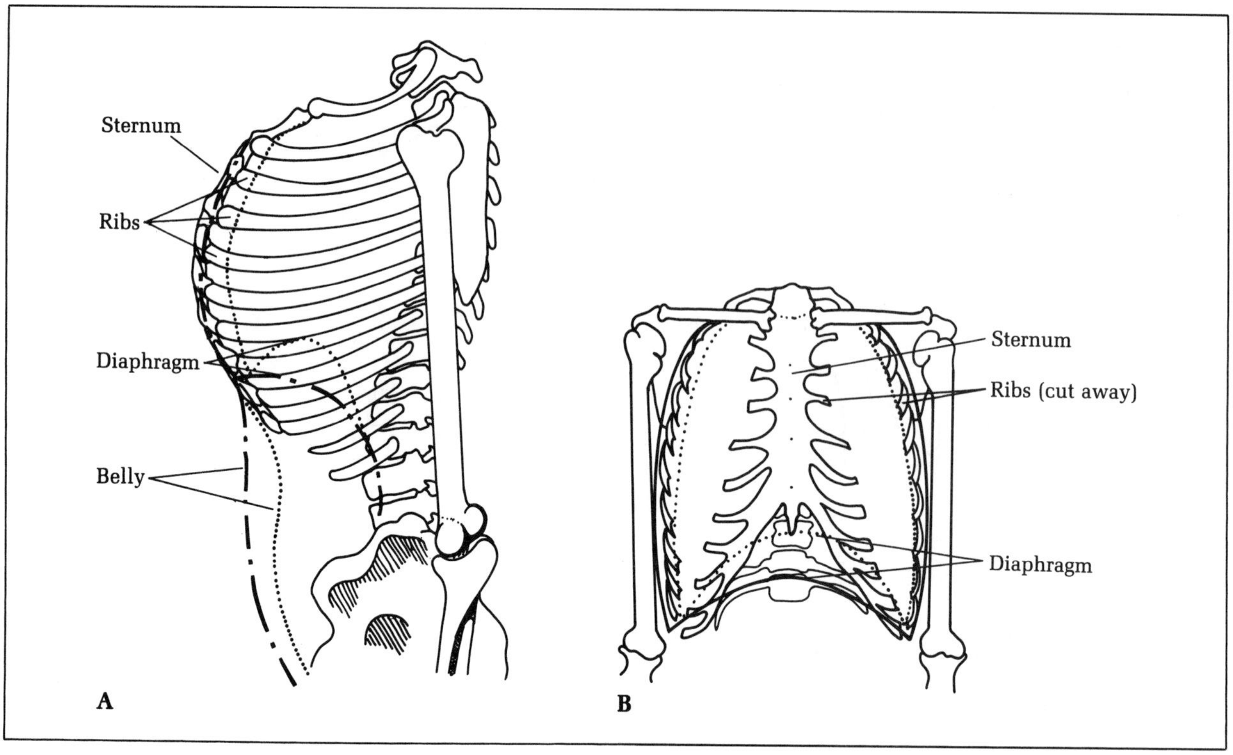

Figure 9-9. The thorax in inspiration and expiration. In inspiration, the internal volume of the thorax is increased, and in expiration, its internal volume is decreased. The internal volume can be increased either by raising of the sternum or by lowering of the diaphragm (which divides the thoracic and abdominal cavities). The internal volume may be decreased by the chest being flattened somewhat, and/or by the abdominal contents pushing up against the lower thoracic area. A. In this lateral view, the dashed line shows maximum thoracic volume. The sternum is high, and the diaphragm is contracted, pushing down against the abdomen. The dotted line shows minimum thoracic volume. The sternum is lower (the ribs would therefore angle slightly lower toward the sternum, but the drawing shows the ribs in one position only). Abdominal muscles have pulled in the belly, forcing the diaphragm up. B. Frontal view. The outline represents maximum volume, the dotted line, minimum.

Each lung is encased in a membrane called the **visceral pleura.** Another membrane, called the **parietal pleura,** lines the two halves of the thorax (chest cavity). These two pleural membranes are in contact, with a fluid filling any space between them (the **pleural cavity**). As the space inside the thorax increases through movements of the rib cage or diaphragm, the parietal pleura moves with the thorax. The visceral pleura follows, although it is not directly attached, because of surface tension[15] and the inflow of air into the lungs to balance atmospheric air pressure with that inside the lungs. Puncturing the pleural lining will allow the lungs to "collapse," since it destroys the linkage between the two pleura.

The thorax is bounded by the **rib cage** and the **diaphragm.** The rib cage comprises the **vertebral column** (popularly, but not very accurately, called the "spine" or "spinal column"), the **ribs,** and the **sternum** (the "breast bone"). The ribs are all attached at the vertebral column, and all but the lower two are attached to the sternum. The ribs are joined to the vertebral column and to the sternum in such a manner as to permit limited movement. Thus the sternum can rise and fall (relative to a standing posture) with respect to the vertebral column. This rise and fall has the effect of increasing and decreasing, respectively, the volume or space within the thorax (Figure 9-9).

[15] Other mechanisms are probably at work, too. See, for example, Dickson and Maue-Dickson [1982, p. 82].

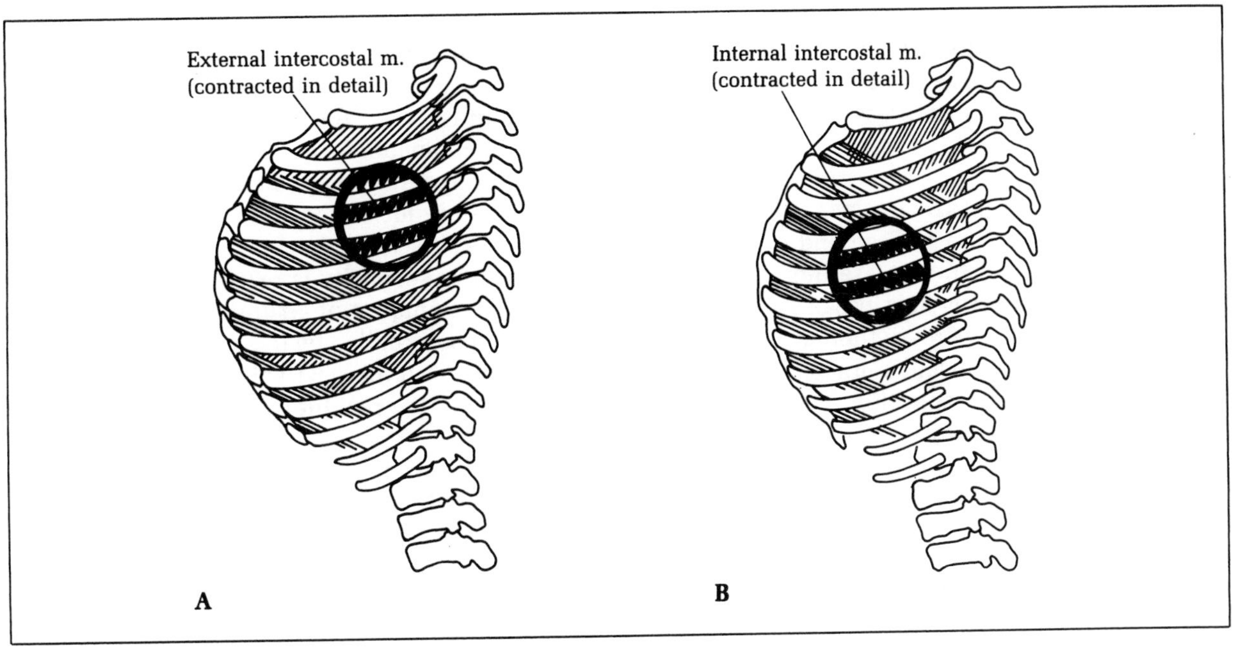

Figure 9-10. The intercostal muscles in inspiration and expiration. The intercostal muscles run between the ribs, essentially in two layers: the **internal** and **external intercostal muscles.** The external intercostals have fibers running in the direction of those in the detail of part A, i.e., from higher at the spinal (back) end to lower at the sternal (chest) end. The internal intercostals lie beneath at approximately right angles to the externals and have fibers running in the direction of those detailed in part B, i.e., high at the sternal end and low at the spinal end. A. Inspiration. The external intercostals contract to raise the sternum (detail). B. Expiration. The internal intercostals contract to pull the sternum down (detail). In fact, as noted in the text, contraction of the internal intercostals occurs only in maximum expiration. In normal, shallower respiration, it is the external intercostals that act in expiration to slow down the elastic recoil of the lungs.

9-5.1 The Muscles of Respiration

The diaphragm is a muscular wall separating the thoracic cavity from the **abdominal cavity.** It, too, plays a role in respiration, as shown in Figure 9-9, since a downward movement of the diaphragm has the effect of enlarging the thoracic cavity.

The **muscles of respiration** therefore include the diaphragm and the muscles that control the rib cage, which are many in number. While popular belief has the diaphragm as *the* muscle of respiration, and while voice students are told to do this or that with their diaphragms, in fact many muscles besides the diaphragm are involved in breathing.

The most important of these are the **intercostal muscles** (*intercostal* means 'between the ribs')[16] (Figure 9-10). There are essentially two layers of intercostals, with fibers that run at approximate right angles to one another. Descriptively, the outer layer is called the **external intercostals** and the inner layer the **internal intercostals.** It is only a slight oversimplification to say that the external intercostals serve to elevate the sternum for inhalation and that the internal intercostals serve to lower the sternum in exhalation. The mechanism of this is shown in Figure 9-10.

Other muscles can change the thoracic capacity as well. Muscles of the back, neck, and abdomen may play a role in breathing, though there is some controversy as to whether certain muscles whose position may suggest their having a role in respiration do in fact actually play that role. Textbooks of speech anatomy, some of which are mentioned in this chapter's Readings, list many potential respiratory muscles; a summary of evidence for the role of these muscles can be found in Dickson and Maue-Dickson [1982]. While we will not enumerate them all here, two such groups of **accessory respiratory muscles** should be mentioned. Cer-

[16] These are the muscles that make up the meat of "spareribs."

tain muscles of the neck, notably the **scalene muscles,** serve to elevate the ribs in inhalation. Certain abdominal muscles serve to pull in the abdomen; abdominal contents thus press against the diaphragm in exhalation.

9-5.2 The Mechanism of Respiration

In review, elevating the ribcage and/or lowering the diaphragm serves to increase thoracic capacity. Conversely, lowering the ribcage or raising the diaphragm serves to decrease thoracic capacity.

However, strictly muscular forces are not the only forces at work in respiration. The elasticity of the tissues involved is also a major factor. The lungs inflated by inhalation can be likened to a toy balloon or an air mattress. Their walls are stretched when inflated. A release of the neck of a balloon results in a rapid deflation without the application of additional forces; you do not need to squeeze the air out of a balloon. The deflation of the lungs when full to capacity, if all muscles were relaxed, would not be as dramatic as that of a toy balloon, but the effect would be essentially the same. The air supply would be exhausted rapidly. For both speech and quiet breathing, such a mechanism would not be efficient. A force must be applied that will slow down that deflation of the lungs that is brought about by elastic recoil. It is easy to see that the same muscles used to *inflate* the lungs would, if kept contracted, *keep the lungs inflated.* If these muscles were *relaxed slowly,* the lungs would *deflate slowly.* This is in fact what happens. So, in the initial stage of *exhalation,* it is the muscles of *inhalation* that do the work. Indeed, in quiet respiration the muscles of inhalation (primarily the external intercostals) do all of the work; the expiratory muscles are at rest. On the other hand, in rapid deep breathing, both inspiratory and expiratory muscles are at work.

Another dimension comes into play in speech. The analogy we used of a toy balloon is not useful here, since a balloon more or less *completely* deflates by itself. We will therefore look at an air mattress for comparison. When the plug is first pulled from an inflated air mattress, the air comes out rapidly. The air flow becomes slower and slower, however, and eventually a point of equilibrium is reached at which the air mattress is far from empty of air, but no more air flows out spontaneously. It is then necessary to force the rest of the air out, by rolling up the mattress or lying on it.

In a similar way, the fully inflated lungs will deflate spontaneously to a certain volume, the **functional residual capacity;** air pressure and speed of flow out of the lungs will become less and less as this point is neared. When the functional residual capacity is reached, there is still a considerable amount of air in the lungs. Much of this air can be expelled by the action of the expiratory muscles, but there will always remain a small amount of air, the **residual volume,** which cannot be expelled.

In speech, air is drawn into the lungs rather more quickly than in quiet breathing, so as not to interrupt the flow of conversation any more than necessary. Initially speech is produced with the airflow controlled by the *inspiratory* muscles. As the functional residual capacity is reached, *expiratory* muscles may start to play a role in maintaining the necessary air pressure. If one continues to speak after the functional residual capacity is reached, more and more expiratory muscles come into play. In normal conversation, people do not continue talking much beyond the functional residual capacity; rather, they take a fresh lungful of air, usually at a point corresponding to a grammatical break. However, people may continue nonstop when reciting poetry or the lines of a play, singing, arguing emotionally and trying to avoid a pause that would let the opponent break in, or saying a long sentence that has no convenient grammatical break. In regard to this last point, there is evidence that, when talking, we plan our breaks ahead, so that we are rarely caught in the position of having reached the functional residual capacity without an appropriate grammatical break at which to draw air.

The needs of speech modify the respiratory cycle in more than one way. Talking does not require a simple constant subglottal pressure. Rather, the pressure required to maintain phonation at the speech volume we desire varies with syllable structure, stress, emphasis, and other phonetic factors. Therefore the muscles controlling the air pressure within the lungs are making constant minute adjustments during speech.

9-6 The Muscles of Speech

Let us turn our attention now to the muscles of articulation and phonation. The complex actions of speech production are made up of individual muscle movements. In order to understand how speech articulation functions normally and how it is affected by various disorders and abnormalities, we should look at the individual speech muscles. Once again, remember that this discussion is simplified and that the technical vocabulary used by anatomists has been kept to a minimum; only major muscles are shown.

A number of preliminary remarks should be made. First, a muscle is capable of exerting a force only by *contracting*, thus by *pulling in one direction only*. Muscles do not push. If a muscle connects points x and y, it is capable of drawing x and y closer together or of resisting some other force that would draw x and y apart, nothing more. Once the muscle in question has drawn x and y closer together, some other force must draw them apart. Normally this other force is another muscle or group of muscles that serve to pull in the opposite direction, although tissue elasticity, aerodynamic forces, or even gravity may provide the opposing force. In typical anatomical drawings, the alignment of muscle fibers is shown by lines or striations. The direction of pull is parallel to these lines.

Second, whether x or y or both move when the muscle that connects them contracts depends on what other forces are acting on x and y. Consider Figure 9-11. Here we see structures x and y connected by a muscle that we will call *muscle x-y*. If muscle x-y contracts, x and y will be drawn closer, as we know. But which will move? That depends on whether muscle x-*w* or muscle y-z is contracted at the time. The contraction of x-y might *raise* y or might *lower* x, or do both, depending on the contraction of other muscles. So, from the anatomical drawings in this chapter and in other books, it is generally easy to see what the functional potential of a given muscle is. But note that it has two possible effects.

A third point concerns the terminology. The names of the muscles are much more straightforward than first appears. Most are named for either their *function* (e.g., *levator palati*, the muscle that *elevates* [raises] the [soft] *palate*) or their points of attachment and insertion (e.g., the *cricothyroid* runs between the cricoid cartilage and the thyroid cartilage). Understanding these two principles makes the names easier to remember. It should be noted, though, that the names of some structures might be unfamiliar. For example, the tongue is referred to by the term *gloss* in these muscle names: *hyoglossus, genioglossus, palatoglossus,* etc.

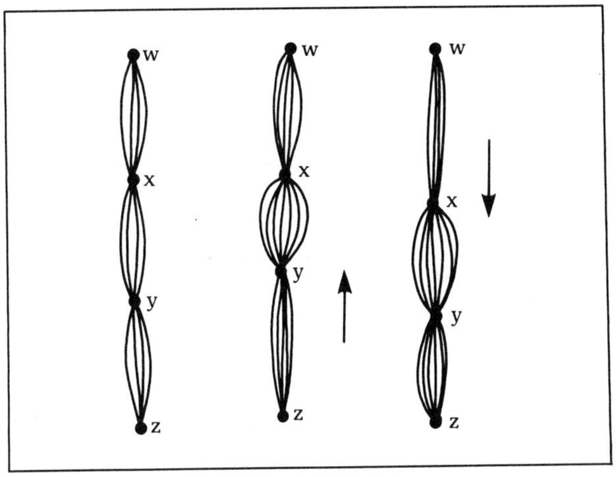

Figure 9-11. The effect of muscle contraction. If muscle x-y contracts, it will bring x and y closer together. But whether y is raised or x is lowered depends upon the contraction of other muscles.

9-6.1 Articulatory Muscles

In this section, we will examine the major muscles involved in speech articulation and will consider them in terms of what they do in the production of speech segments. Because the scope of this book is articulatory phonetics rather than anatomy, we will look at them globally rather than in detail. Figures 9-12 through 9-21 show major types of articulatory gestures as a function of the muscles responsible for their production.

9-7 Physical Anomalies Affecting Speech Production

In this section we will introduce some common anatomical anomalies, caused by birth defects, disease, vocal abuse, aging, or surgery, that can affect speech production. With what you have

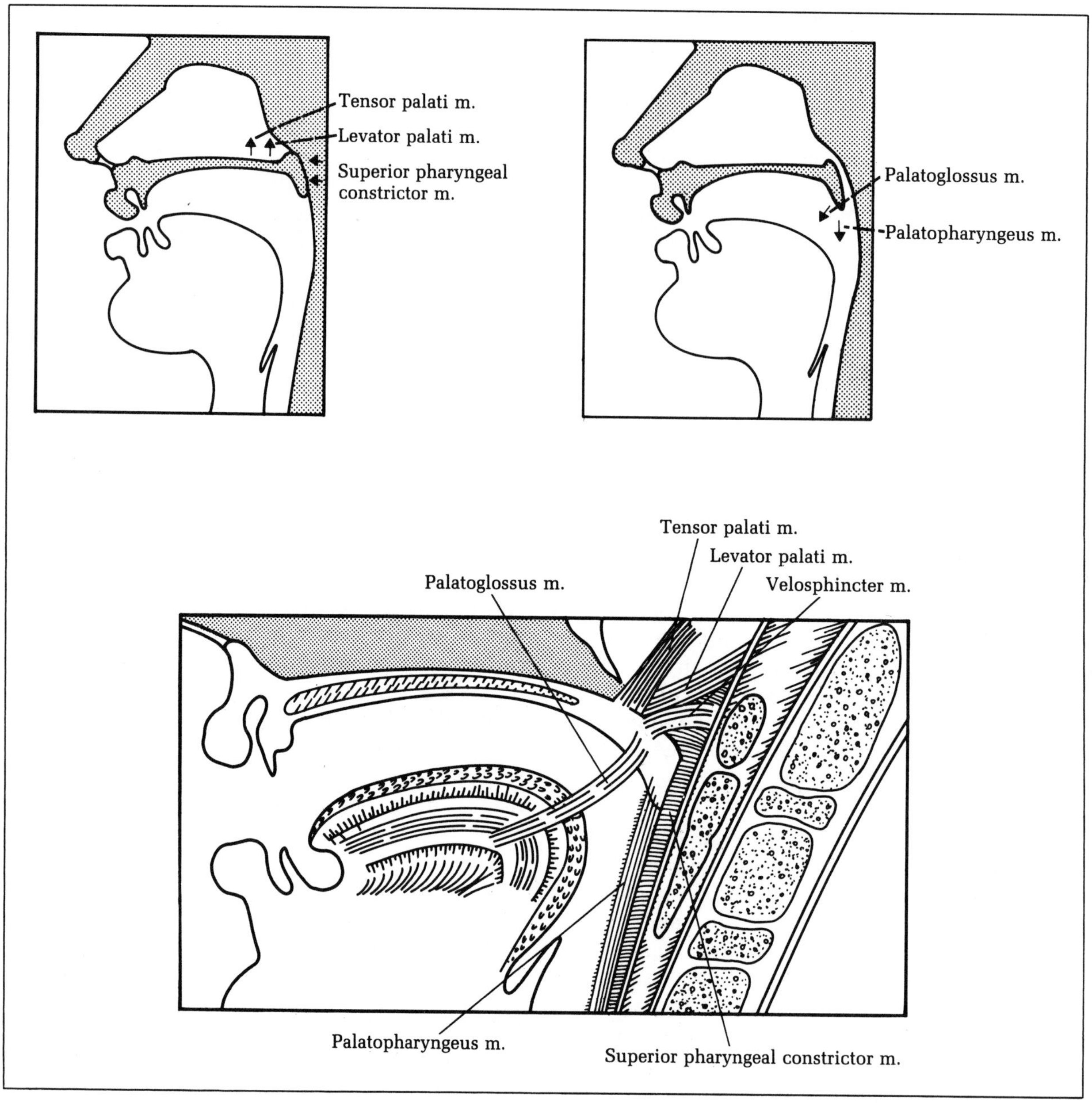

Figure 9-12. Nasal versus non-nasal articulation. Nasality is controlled by the velum. When the velum is raised, an oral sound may be produced. When it is lowered, a nasal sound may be produced. The muscles that raise it are the **tensor palati** and the **levator palati.** The muscles that lower it are the **palatoglossus** and the **palatopharyngeus.** The palatoglossus will raise the back of the tongue if the levator palati and the tensor palati are tensed. These muscles are situated in bilateral pairs; that is, there are two of each muscle, one on either side. The **superior pharyngeal constrictor** may play a role in velic closure as well, by drawing forward the posterior pharyngeal wall.

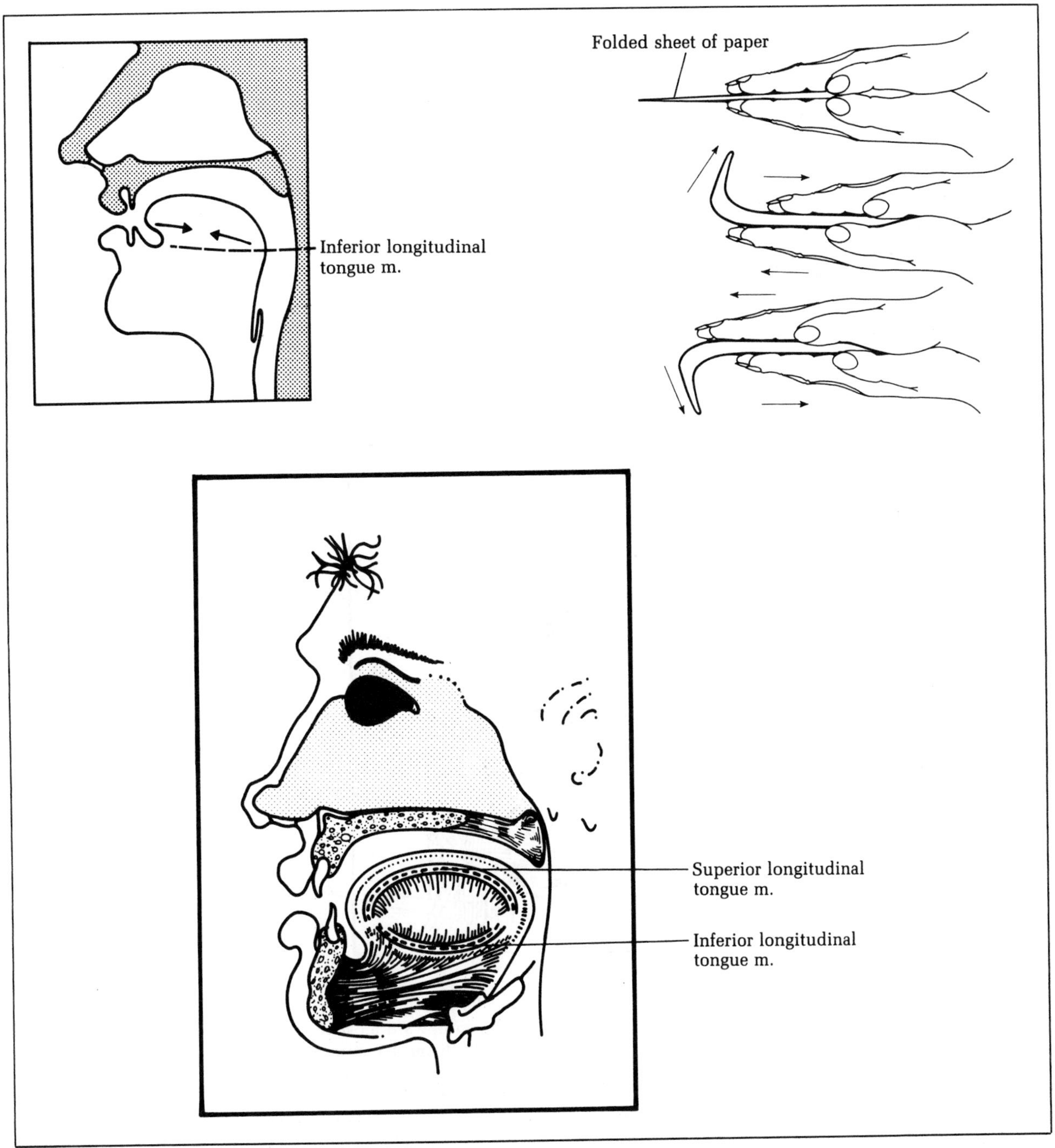

Figure 9-13. Tongue arching, as for palatal sounds, velar sounds, and high or mid vowels. If the **inferior longitudinal tongue muscle** is contracted, the tongue will arch up in the middle. The two longitudinal tongue muscles lie one above the other, and whichever is contracted will cause a curling in that direction. This is analogous to pulling on one or the other side of a piece of folded paper: it will curl to the side pulled. Compare Figure 9-15.

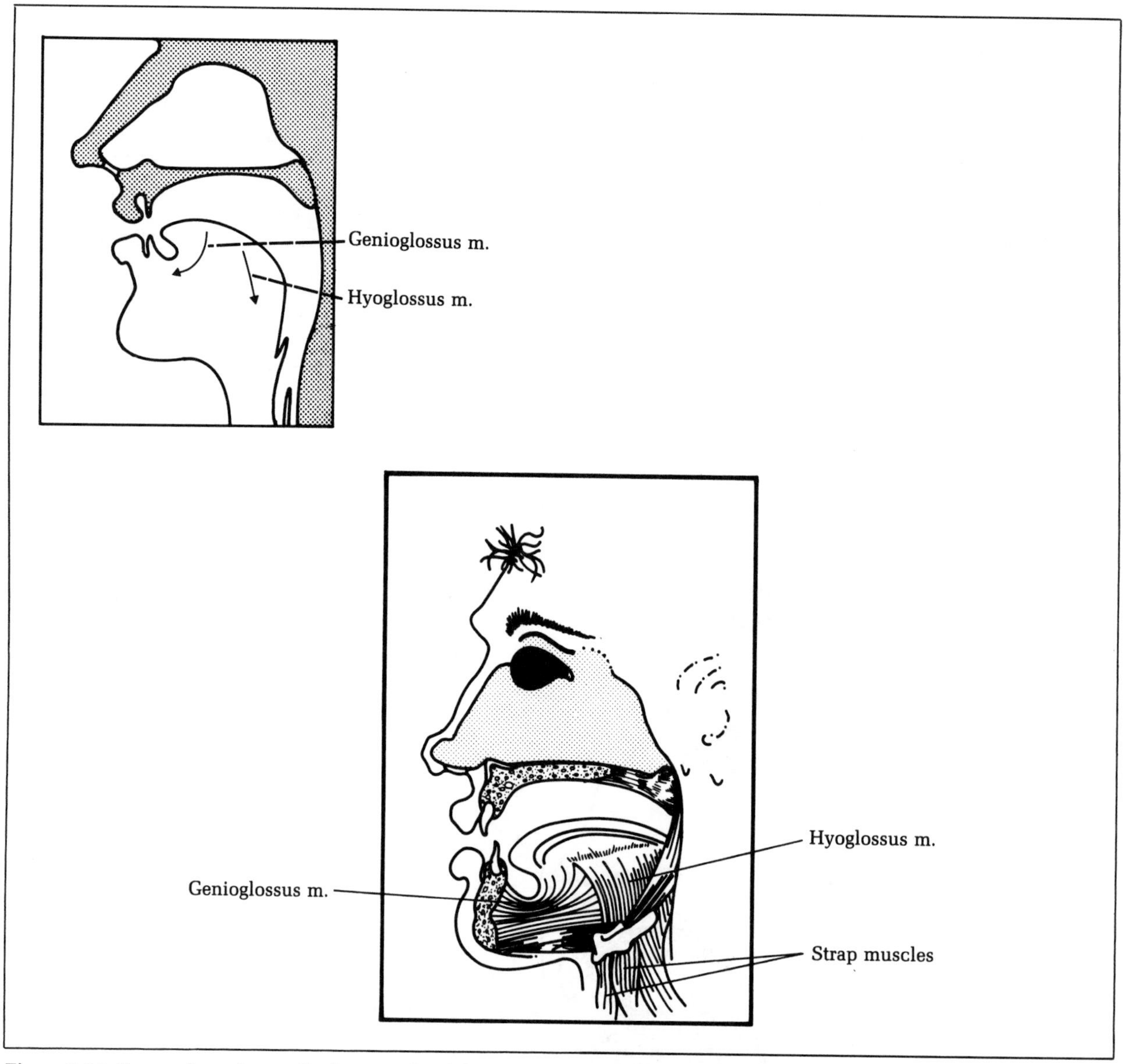

Figure 9-14. Tongue lowering, as for low vowels. If the **genioglossus** and **hyoglossus muscles** are contracted, the tongue will lower within the jaw. The genioglossus has something of a forward pull, the hyoglossus a backward pull. These two forces are balanced differently for a low front as compared to a low back articulation. The **vertical tongue muscle,** seen in Figure 9-16, contributes to lowering as well. In order that a contraction of the **hyoglossus muscle** results in a downward movement of the tongue body rather than an upward movement of the hyoid bone, several muscles in the neck contract at the same time (see Figure 9-11). These so-called strap muscles run between the **hyoid bone** or the **thyroid cartilage** at the top and the **sternum** (breastbone), **clavicle** (collarbone), or **scapula** (shoulder blade) at the lower end (see Figure 9-21).

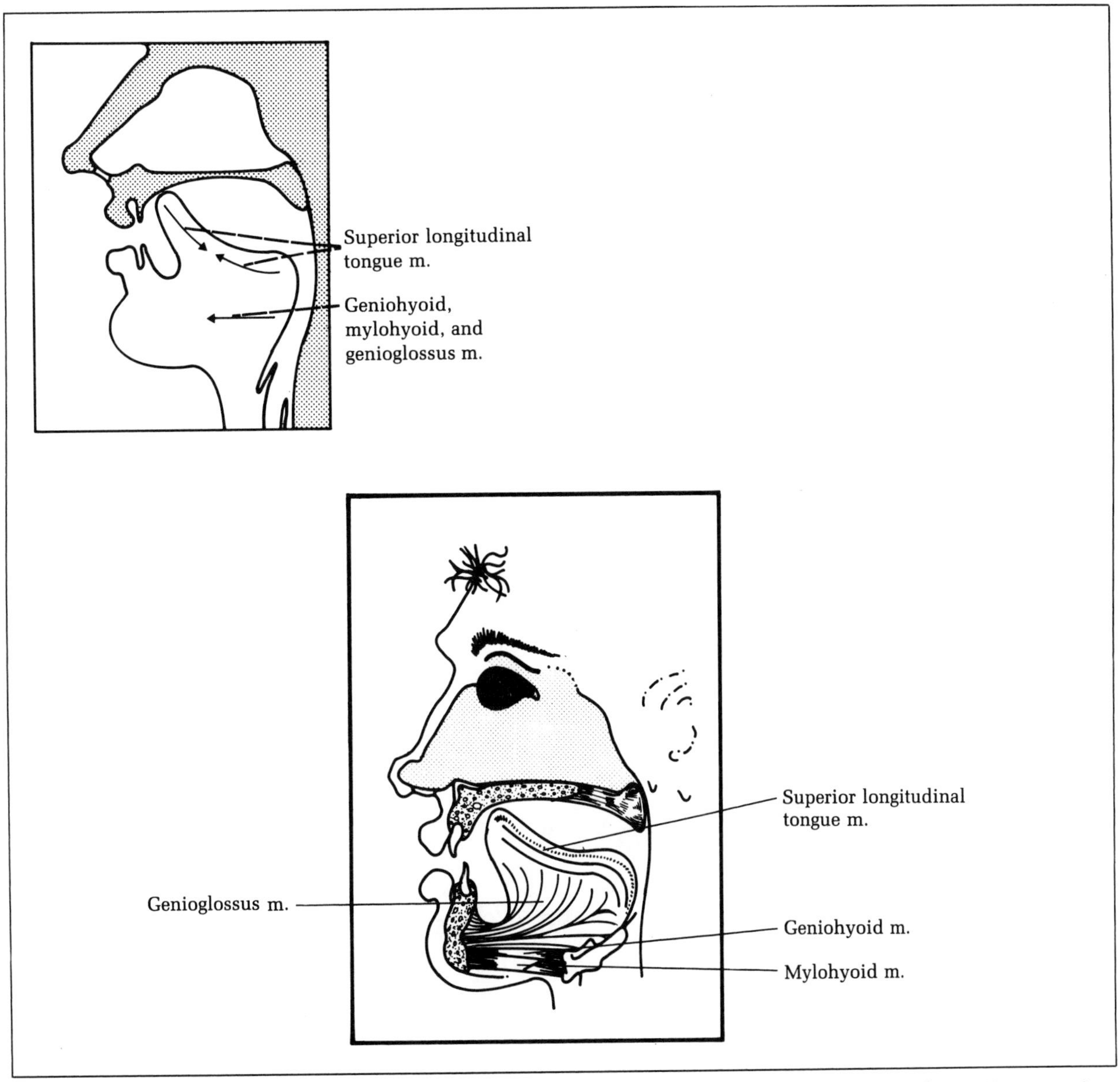

Figure 9-15. Tongue-tip raising, as for alveolars and dentals. If the **superior longitudinal tongue muscle** is contracted while the **inferior longitudinal tongue muscle** is relaxed, the tongue will arch in the opposite direction to that seen in Figure 9-13. The tip will be raised up off the floor of the mouth. Simultaneously the tongue body may be drawn forward by action of the **geniohyoid, mylohyoid,** and **genioglossus muscles.** The **vertical tongue muscle** (see Figure 9-16) serves to flatten and thereby broaden the tongue. This is important in the production of [t], [d], [n], [s], and [z], where there must be a positive seal between the sides of the tongue and the upper side teeth (molars and premolars). Failure to make this seal leads to lisped fricatives and lisped, affricated, inaudible, or otherwise deviant stops.

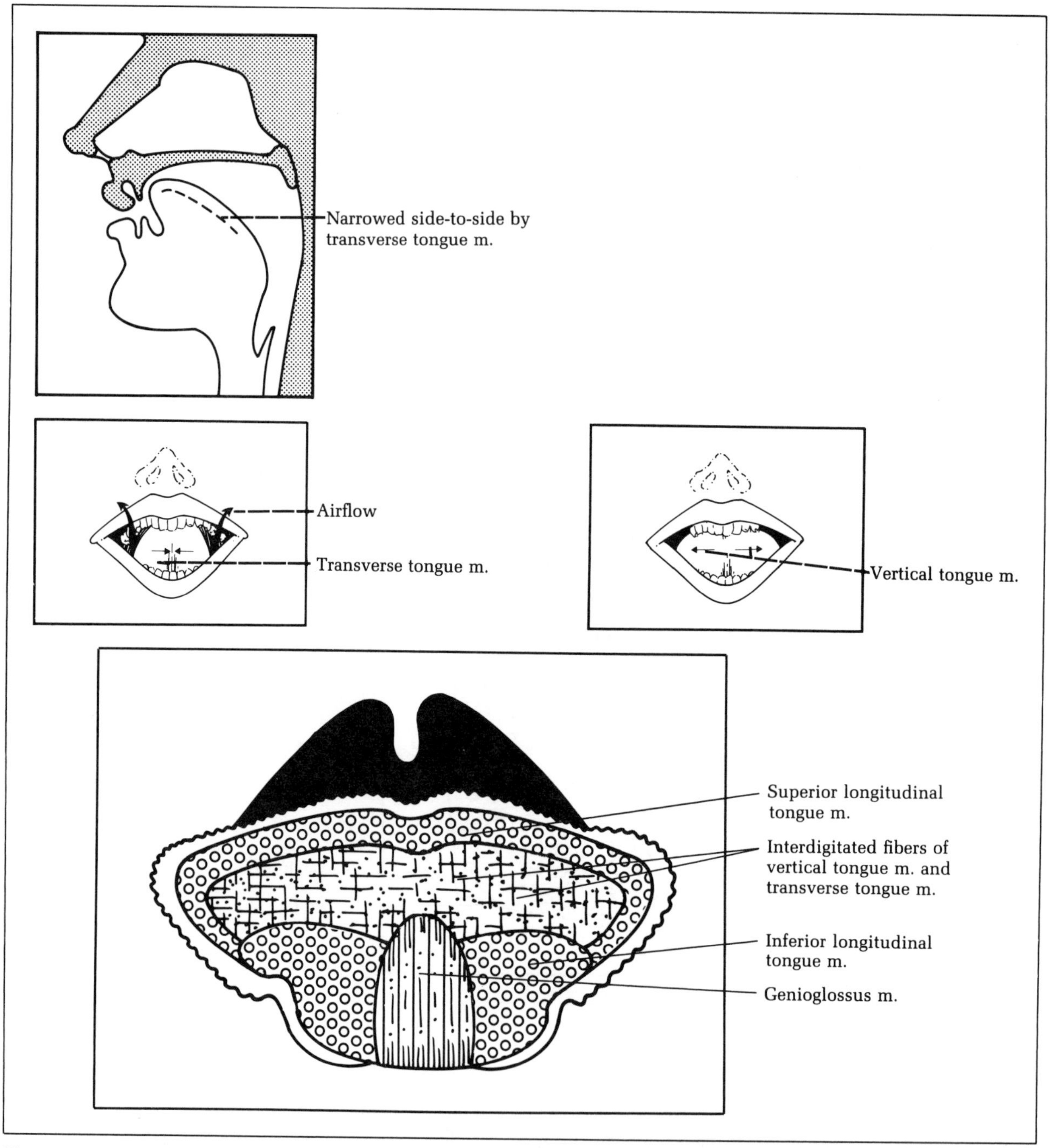

Figure 9-16. Tongue width adjustment, as for laterals versus nonlaterals. The **transverse tongue muscle,** when contracted, narrows the tongue from side to side (along the dotted line, *top left*), the opposite effect to that described for the **vertical tongue muscle** (see Figure 9-15). This allows space for air to flow between the sides of the tongue and the molars, as in the articulation of [l] and other laterals (*middle left*). In the articulation of nonlateral alveolars such as [d], the vertical tongue muscle contracts, flattening and thus widening the tongue, which makes a seal along the molars (*middle right*). The fibers of the vertical tongue muscle and the transverse tongue muscle are finely interdigitated (*bottom*). Those of the vertical tongue muscle are oriented vertically. Those of the transverse tongue muscle are oriented horizontally, running from side to side.

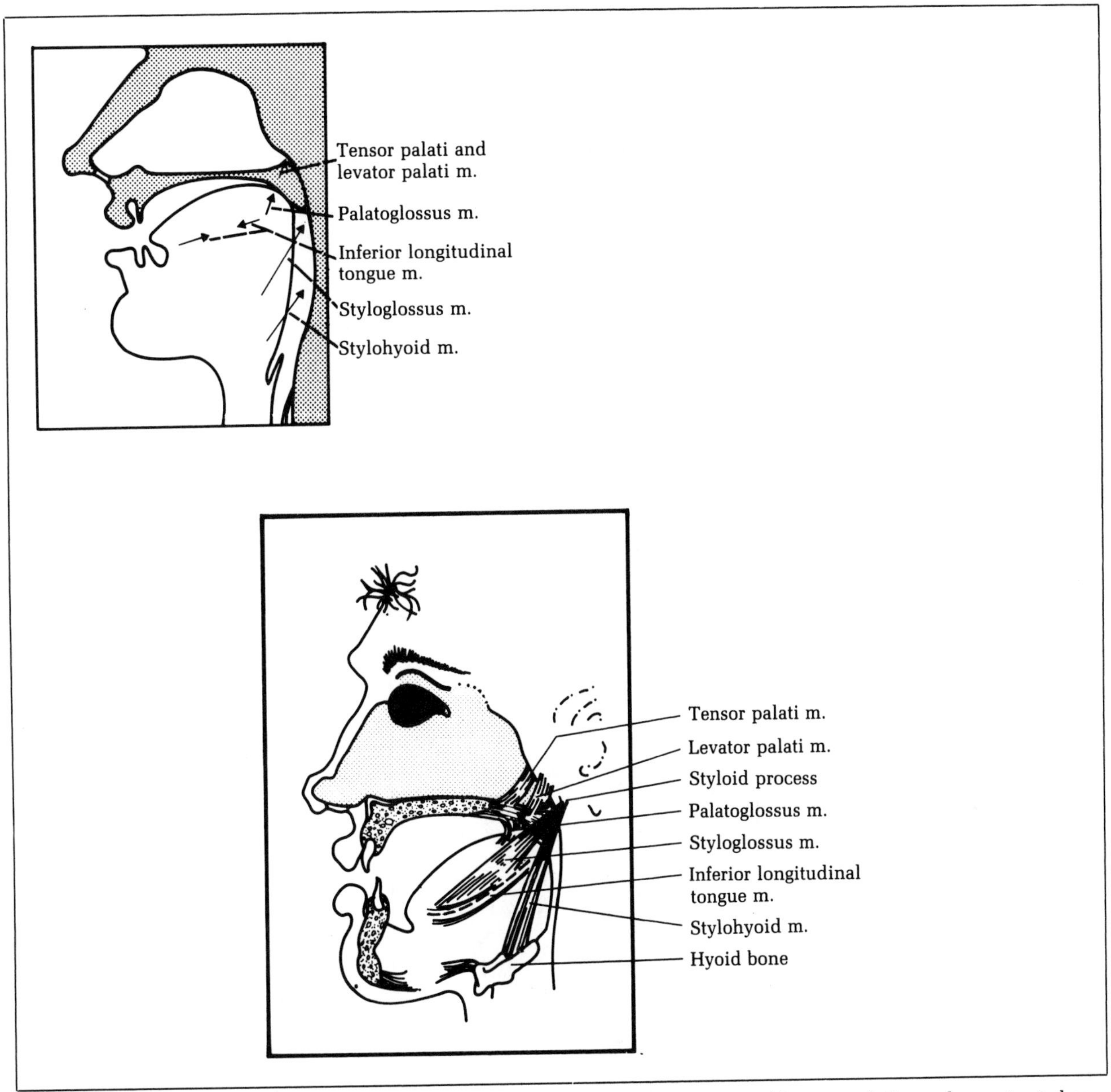

Figure 9-17. High back articulation, as for high back vowels and velar consonants. To raise the back of the tongue, the tongue is arched (see Figure 9-13) with the **inferior longitudinal tongue muscle.** The back is raised with the **palatoglossus** (**tensor palati** and **levator palati** muscles contracted so that the tongue dorsum is raised rather than the velum lowered; see Figure 9-12) and with the **styloglossus muscle.**

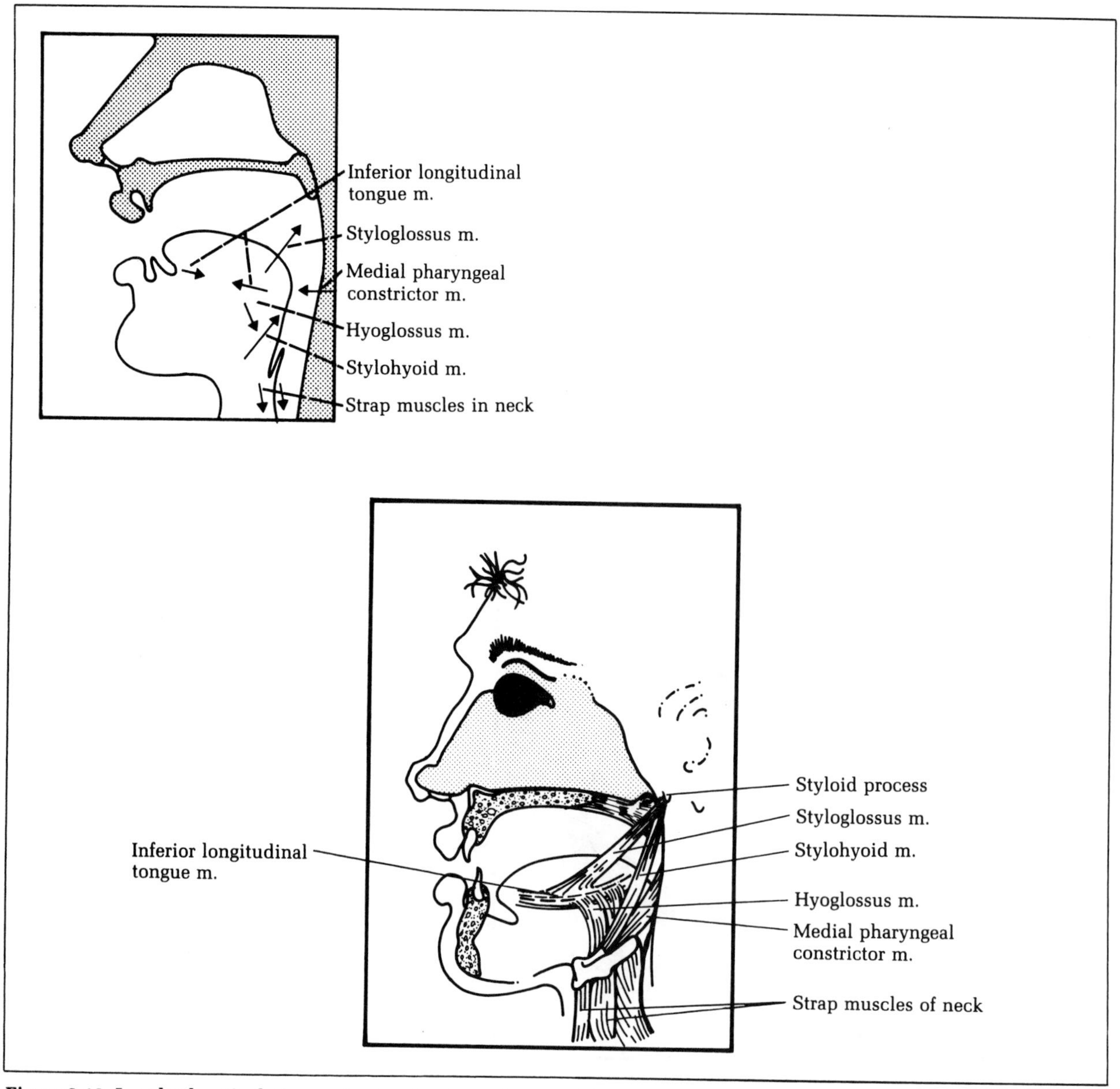

Figure 9-18. Low back articulation, as for low back vowels and various rhotic sounds. To constrict the pharynx for low back sounds (e.g., [ɔ]), rhotic sounds (r-sounds), lax vowels, and pharyngealized sounds (such as Arabic emphatics), the tongue body is drawn back with the **styloglossus** and **stylohyoid muscles** and probably with the **medial pharyngeal constrictor** as well. The **hyoglossus** lowers the back of the tongue body (as described in Figure 9-14, neck muscles come into play). There may be some bunching of the tongue with the **inferior longitudinal tongue muscle.**

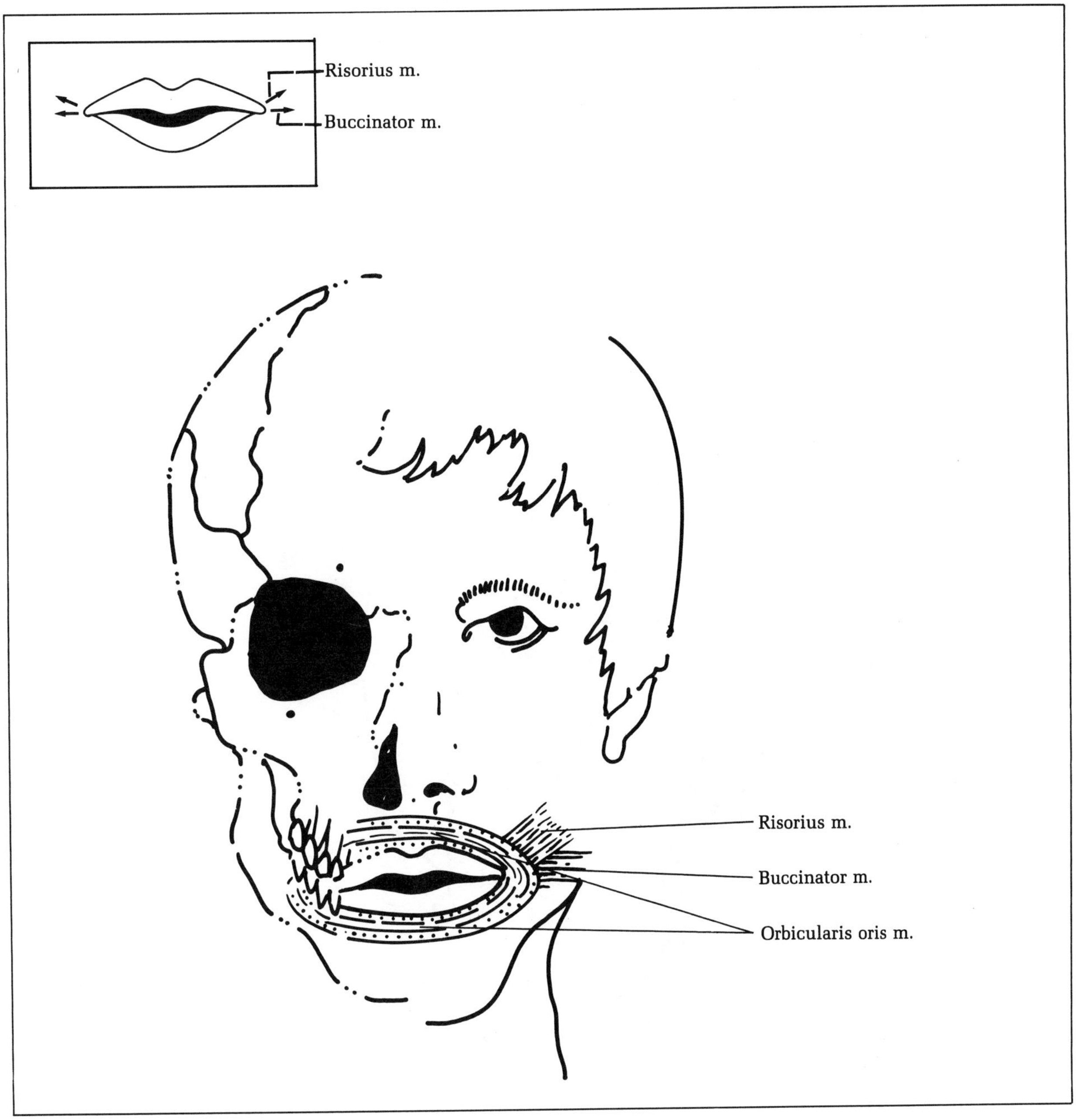

Figure 9-19. Lip-spreading, as for [i], [e], **and** [j]. The **buccinator muscle,** assisted by the **risorius muscle,** pulls back on the corners of the mouth for spread sounds.

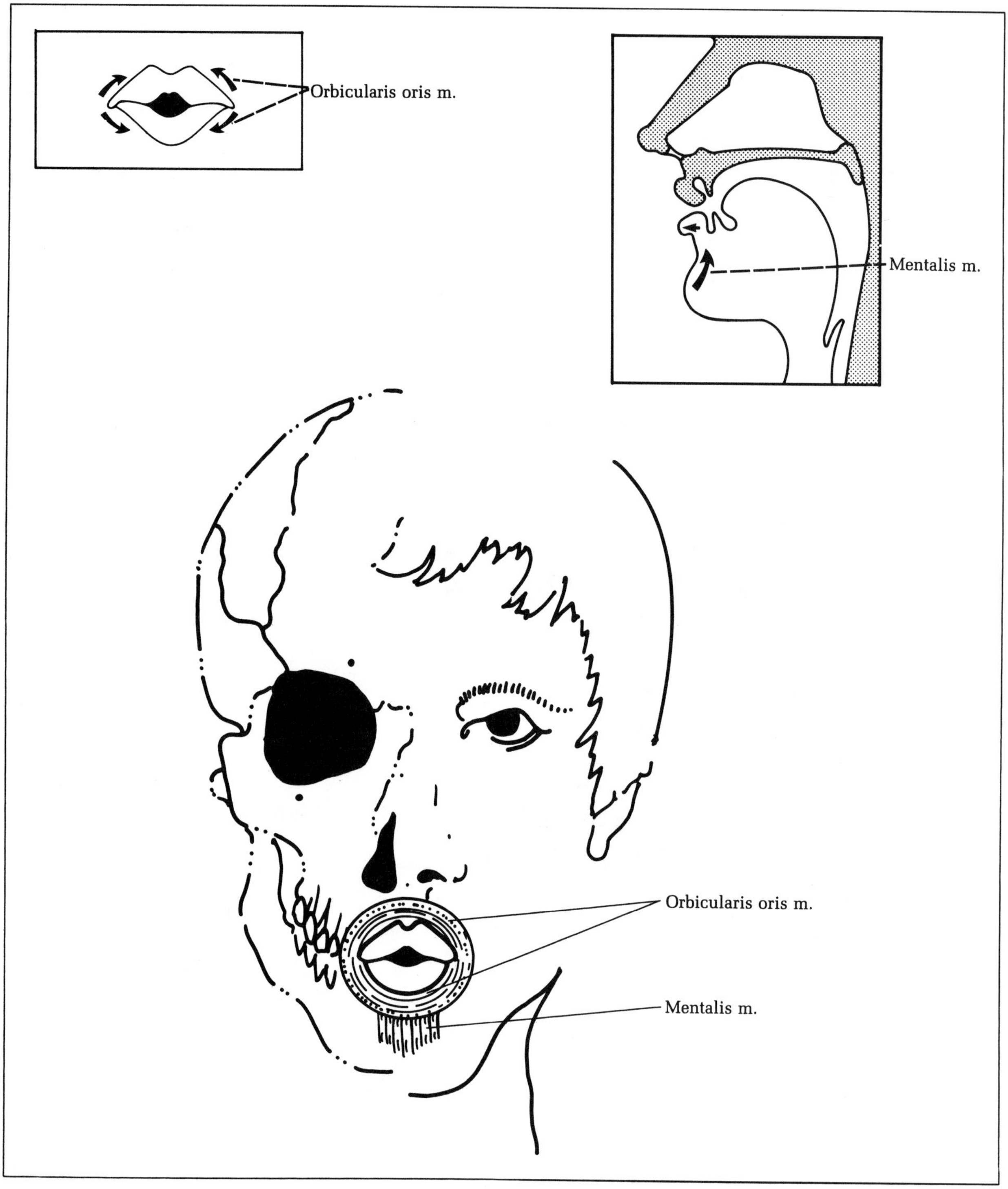

Figure 9-20. Lip-rounding, as for [u], [o], [š], [r]. The **orbicularis oris muscle** rounds the lips. **Eversion** (curling outward) of the lower lip, which may accompany lip rounding, may be assisted by the **mentalis muscle.**

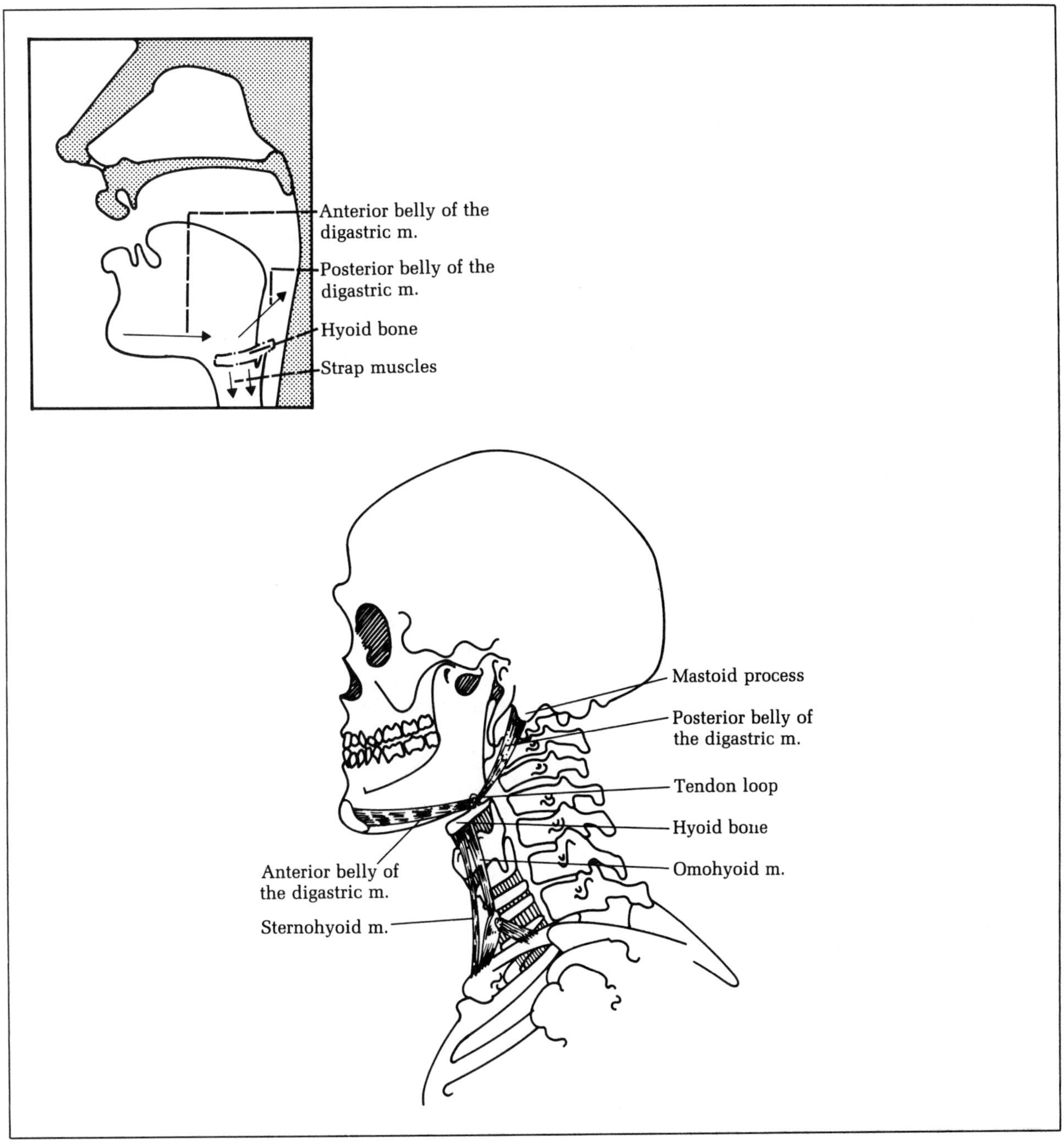

Figure 9-21. Jaw opening, as for all speech sounds, especially low (open) ones. The **digastric muscle** lowers the jaw. Strap muscles in the neck (see legend, Figure 9-14) maintain the position of the hyoid bone, so that the pull of the **anterior belly of the digastric muscle** has the desired effect. The **posterior belly of the digastric muscle** likewise has more of an anchoring effect on the hyoid bone than an opening effect on the jaw. Two strap muscles have been illustrated; there are a number of others.

learned about speech articulation in Chapters 4–7, you should be able to see how these anomalies can affect the production of speech.

LARYNX AND VOCAL FOLDS We already noted in Chapter 5 the drastic effect of **laryngectomy.**[17] The laryngectomee must use other than the normal airstream mechanism and normal source of voicing. Possible alternative airstream mechanisms were outlined in Chapter 5.

Other anomalies of the **larynx,** caused by injury, disease, or abuse of the voice, can prevent the normal vibration of the vocal folds. These may result in **voice disorders** which can be either **organic** (physical in cause) or **functional** (the cause may be psychological or a result of use). An example of an organic voice disorder is **unilateral** or **bilateral vocal fold paralysis,** generally due to nerve dysfunction. An example of a functional voice disorder is **hysterical dysphonia,** essentially psychological in origin. **Spastic dysphonia** is a condition whose cause is not yet entirely understood; it results in an extremely strained phonation.

Disorders that affect **voice quality** and that result from growths or a change in the form of the vocal folds include **contact ulcers, polyps,** and **vocal nodules. Contact ulcers** are sores generally associated with vocal abuse and phonation below a person's natural frequency, often in association with smoking and alcohol consumption. **Polyps** are abnormal growths, usually unilateral, that affect voice quality through changes in vocal fold mass and/or airflow through the glottis. **Vocal nodules** are, in essence, calluses on the contact surfaces of the vocal folds. They are generally due to vocal abuse that results in the slamming together of the vocal folds. This may be caused by yelling, loud singing, inappropriate pitch (as in the case of AM disk jockeys), and strenuous activity such as weightlifting.

[17] **-ectomy** is a suffix referring to the surgical removal of an organ. The suffix **-ectomee** refers to an individual who has undergone such an operation. Thus, a **laryngectomy** is the surgical removal of the larynx; a **laryngectomee** is a person whose larynx has been removed. The same convention is used for **glossectomy** (surgical removal of the tongue) and **glossectomee.**

PALATE AND LIP. **Cleft palate** is a surprisingly common congenital defect in which the nasal and oral cavities are connected through a cleft or split in the palate. If unrepaired, its effects upon speech are serious. Not only does it give a nasal quality to speech and prevent normal production of many consonants (see Chapter 5), it also prevents the child from learning normal velic movements. Since the oral and nasal cavities are connected in this condition no matter how the velum is placed, the child does not learn proper velic control. The result is hypernasality or hyponasality, even after the cleft is repaired.

Cleft lip is a congenital split in the upper lip, which may extend to the upper jaw and teeth. It may or may not be associated with cleft palate. It may be surgically corrected at an early age. It is commonly called *harelip,* although professionals avoid this term.

VELUM. Abnormalities of the **velum** and its musculature may prevent the proper closure of the nasal cavity from the oral cavity. Such **velic deficiencies** may accompany cleft palate; an unrepaired cleft palate will aggravate any velic deficiency for reasons outlined previously.

TEETH. Normal **dentition (teeth)** plays a role in speech production. Certain speech problems can be traced to dental problems.

TONGUE. Removal of the **tongue** and supporting structures severely disrupts speech production. Such surgical removal is called **glossectomy.** Through the use of compensatory movements of the remaining structures—notably the lips and the floor of the mouth—many glossectomees produce intelligible speech; the degree of retained intelligibility is primarily a factor of the remaining tongue mass.

Laryngectomy and glossectomy are both usually performed as treatment for cancer, and both correlate very highly with smoking.

THE COMMON COLD AND INFECTIONS. *Temporary physical states* that interfere with speech production are as prevalent as the common cold. The nasal passages may be blocked, interfering particularly with nasal resonance ("I've got a bad cold id by dose"). Inflammation of throat tissue (pharyngitis) may interfere with velic closure or other articulatory gestures. Vocal fold vibration may be disturbed by a buildup of mucus and/or inflammation of the vocal folds, which may change voice quality or prevent phonation altogether.

HEARING. Normal *hearing* is essential not only for the development of speech in the child but for the maintenance of speech in adults. Our reliance upon self-monitoring is demonstrated by the deterioration in the speech of individuals who become deaf as adults. Therapy may be used to reduce this deterioration.

BRAIN. Injury to the *brain*, often the result of a stroke, may result in an impairment known as **aphasia** (**dysphasia** in less serious forms). The aphasic individual generally has difficulty both in producing and in comprehending spoken and written language. It is a *language* disorder more than a *speech* disorder, since the articulators are undamaged. (See also Chapter 3 on reading disorders.) However, aphasia may be accompanied by **dyspraxia (apraxia).** Dyspraxia is the inability to program a motor movement or sequence in the absence of a paralysis that might explain such an inability. Dyspraxia results in inconsistent sound errors. **Dysarthria** is an impairment of speech motor movements resulting from damage to the cranial nerves. The patterns of misarticulation are consistent.

Summary

The **"organs of speech"** have other primary biological functions, but in man they have been modified fundamentally so as to permit speech.

Speech physiology can be divided into three systems: the supraglottal, the laryngeal, and the subglottal. These systems provide articulation, phonation, and respiration, respectively.

Speech sounds are generally named for the supraglottal organs involved in their articulation.

Phonation refers to the vibration of the vocal folds. There is more than one mode of vibration of the vocal folds. All modes involve a combination of contributing forces that can be classified as *muscular, aerodynamic,* or *elastic* in nature.

Respiration is accomplished through a combination of muscular and elastic forces.

Articulation of speech is accomplished by a complex set of muscles in the face, lips, tongue, neck, and surrounding area.

Speech production can be adversely affected by a number of physical states and disorders. These can affect phonation (voice), articulation, or the central processing of language.

Vocabulary

The terms in parentheses are those mentioned as an aside and are considered less important than the other terms, taking into account the scope and objectives of the chapter.

abdominal cavity
abduct, abduction
accessory respiratory muscles
adduct, adduction
alveolar ducts [lungs]
alveolar ridge [mouth]
alveolar sacs [lungs]
anatomy
apex, apical
aphasia
apraxia
articulation
arytenoid cartilages
back [of tongue]
Bernoulli principle
bilabial
blade [of tongue]
breathy voice
bronchi
(bronchioles)
buccinator muscle
cleft lip
cleft palate
contact ulcer
conus elasticus
creaky voice
cricothyroid joint
cricoid cartilage
dental
dentition

diaphragm
digastric muscle: anterior belly, posterior belly
dorsum, dorsal
dysarthria
dysphasia
dysphonia
dyspraxia
epiglottis
esophagus
eversion
external intercostals
false vocal folds
falsetto
F_0
front [of tongue]
functional residual capacity
fundamental frequency
genioglossus muscle
geniohyoid muscle
glossectomee
glossectomy
glottal stop
glottis
gum ridge
hertz
hyoid bone
hyoglossal muscle [*also:* hyoglossus muscle]
hypernasality
hyponasality
indirect laryngoscopy
inferior horns
intercostal muscles
internal intercostals
labial
laminal
laryngectomee
laryngectomy
laryngopharynx
larynx
levator palati muscle [*also:* levator veli palatini]
lingual
lips
longitudinal tongue muscle: superior, inferior
lungs
muscles of respiration
mylohyoid muscle
nasal cavity
nasopharynx
natural frequency
natural pitch
oral cavity
orbicularis oris muscle [*also:* orbicular muscle of mouth]
organs of speech
oropharynx
palate, palatal
palatoglossus muscle
palatopharyngeus muscle [*also:* palatopharyngeal muscle]
parietal pleura
pharyngeal cavity
pharyngeal constrictor muscle: superior, medial
pharynx
phonation
physiology
pleural cavity
polyp
(primary bronchi)
quasi-periodic
range
residual volume
respiration
(respiratory bronchioles)
rib cage, ribs
risorius muscle
root [of tongue]
scalene muscles
(secondary bronchi)
secondary sexual characteristic
sternum
styloglossus muscle
stylohyoid muscle
superior horns
teeth
tensor palati muscle [*also:* tensor veli palatini]
(terminal bronchioles)
thoracic cage
thyrohyoid membrane
thyroid cartilage
tip
tongue
trachea
tracheal cartilages
transverse tongue muscle
turbinates
uvula
velar
velic

velic deficiency
velum
ventricles of Morgagni
ventricular folds
Venturi effect
vertebral column
vertical tongue muscle
visceral pleura
(vocal bands)
(vocal chords)
(vocal cords)
vocal folds
vocal fold paralysis
vocal fry
vocal nodule
voice
voice disorder
voice quality
voicing
whisper

Readings

Textbooks in speech anatomy include Dickson and Maue-Dickson [1982], Palmer [1972], Singh [1980], Kaplan [1971], Zemlin [1968], and Shearer [1979]. Vennard [1967], while chiefly concerned with singing rather than speech, is also useful.

Speech acoustics and perception

10

Objectives

To explain the nature of basic acoustic processes, including sound waves, periodicity, frequency, amplitude, phase, wavelength, and harmonics.

To explain the nature of resonance through the concepts of Fourier's theorem and the standing wave.

To apply these principles to the vocal tract in speech production and thus to explain the acoustic nature of speech.

To discuss the nature of the processes by which speech is perceived.

We have considered speech production and speech physiology. It is now time to turn our attention to the physical aspects of the speech signal. In this area, there are three basic questions that the student of phonetics should address. First, by what processes are the articulatory positions and movements we have studied converted into the sounds of speech? Second, what are the parameters or characteristics of speech sounds (that is, acoustically what is a /ɑ/, a /p/, etc.)? And third, how is speech perceived?

These questions are relevant to an understanding of speech, since the very noises we make are defined by our physical form and by acoustic principles. Fantasy films often show giants, dwarfs, animals, or grotesque aliens speaking everyday English. However, the premise is absurd, because if a speaker had a mouth shaped like that of—for example—a dog or a horse, the sounds produced *could not* be the same as those produced in the mouth of an average-sized normal human being. Even if a dog were smart enough to talk, it could not make the same kinds of noises you and I do when we talk, because of the size and shape of its mouth; acoustic laws would not permit it.

We need to examine basic acoustics in order to proceed to the questions posed in the first paragraph. Let us start by considering *sound*.

10-1 Sound

Sound is the passage of a disturbance through the air or another medium. Sound is energy, specifically **acoustic energy,** and it has the potential to do work. It vibrates eardrums and windows, for example. Sound must have a medium in which to travel; it does not pass through a vacuum. It advances by causing vibratory motion of the molecules of the medium through which it is traveling. It travels through the air at a rate of about 1100 feet per second (approximately 330 meters per second) and considerably faster through denser media such as water or steel.

Sound travels by a wave motion, in a pulsating fashion. The analogy is often made that sounds travel in air as ripples do in a pond. This analogy is a useful one for introducing the behavior of waves, since we have all experienced water waves. There are some important differences between surface waves on the water and sound waves in the air, but these differences will be considered after we have examined the points of commonality.

10-2 Wave Motion

If we throw a pebble into a still pond, we see that a series of ripples fans out in all directions from the source of the disturbance. These ripples or waves move onward, while individual water molecules return to their original location after the wave has passed. Let us look at how this works.

In Figure 10-1, a stone has just been thrown into a body of water, and ripples are beginning to move away from the source of the disturbance. Individual molecules of water move up and down as a result of the disturbance. The high points are called **crests;** the low points, **troughs.** Let us look at one particular drop of water on the surface, say the point x in Figure 10-1. It may help to visualize a cork riding on the surface of the water. What happens to this cork (or drop) as the wave approaches? As the crest approaches, it rides *up* to its highest point. As the crest passes, it rides *down* to its original position, and it continues riding down to a low point in the trough of the wave. As the next crest approaches, it rides up past its starting position and back to the peak of the next crest. This continues as long as there are waves passing the spot. Note that this individual drop of water has ridden up and down, up and down, but has *not moved forward or backward.* The same drop of water is part of each successive wave that passes.

It is essential to recognize the fact that while the wave moves continuously forward, the individual particles of the material through which it travels

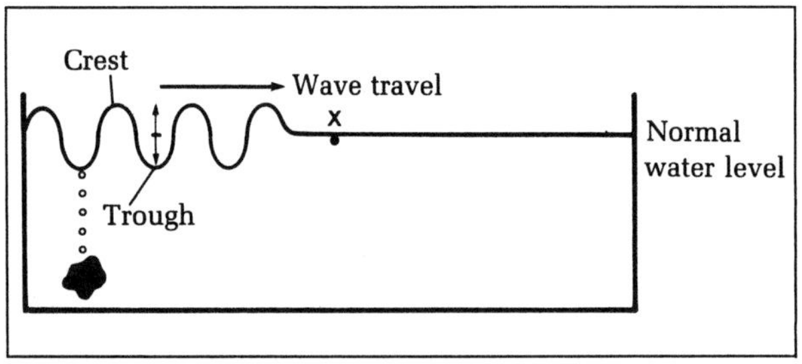

Figure 10-1. A surface wave on water. As the wavefront advances, individual spots on the water surface rise and fall.

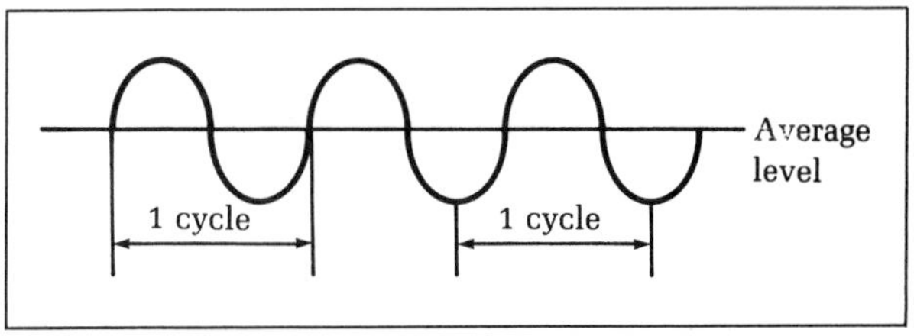

Figure 10-2. The cycle of a wave.

(in this case, water) do *not* move a great distance; they just oscillate around one average, or rest, position.

10-2.1 Dimensions of Waves

Since waves can vary in a number of ways, it is useful to have a vocabulary to describe their dimensions. First, a term is needed to indicate one single unit of a wave. One **cycle** refers to one complete wave, that is, one complete crest and trough. One cycle can be measured from crest to crest, but it is more usual to indicate one cycle as starting at the baseline, rising above it, falling below it, and rising back up to it again (Figure 10-2). The word **cycle** does not indicate any dimension; it simply means one complete wave. Cycle implies something repetitive, and indeed we expect one cycle to be followed by another that is just like it.

Waves can vary both in their physical dimensions (their size) and in their temporal dimensions (their timing).

10-2.2 Physical Dimensions of Waves

Waves have physical size. They can be bigger or smaller, longer or shorter. Special terms are used for these dimensions.

One physical dimension of waves is how high the crests are and how deep the troughs are. (This is related to the amount of energy that is behind the wave.) It is called the **amplitude.** The greater the amplitude, the higher the crests of the waves.

The second physical dimension is the length of one cycle: how far is it from one crest to the next? This dimension is called the **wavelength,** descriptively enough. It can be measured in any unit of length: inches, feet, centimeters, meters, etc. (metric units are most commonly used, as in other scientific measures). Figure 10-3 illustrates amplitude and wavelength.

10-2.3 Temporal Dimensions of Waves

If we were to decide on a particular constant period of time, say 1 minute, and count the number of cycles (that is, the number of complete waves) that occurred during that period of time, we would have a measure of how often or how frequently the wave cycle repeats itself. This measure is descriptively called the **frequency** of a wave. The 1-minute time period would probably be useful for counting waves on the ocean, but in dealing with sound, the time period of 1 second is found to be most useful. Thus, the standard unit of frequency is **cycles per second (cps),** or the number of complete wave cycles that occur each second. The term cycles per second has been replaced by the less descriptive term **hertz (Hz),** and we shall use the term **hertz** from here on.

The **speed of propagation** of a wave refers to the speed at which it **propagates** (travels) through a medium. In the case of ripples on a pond, this speed is easily measurable. A stopwatch will measure the time it takes for the wavefront to cross the pond. Knowing the distance across the pond allows us to calculate the speed. In the case of sound in air, the speed of propagation is a little less than 1100 feet per second (330 meters per second).

The speed of propagation—or speed of travel—is *not* related to frequency. This fact is important in any discussion of sound, since high-frequency (high-pitched) sounds travel at the same speed as low-frequency (low-pitched) sounds.

The **period** is the other temporal dimension of waves. Frequency answers the question, How many cycles occur in one standard time period? **Period** answers the complementary question, How long does it take to complete one cycle? There is a direct relationship between the frequency and the period: the more cycles there are per second, the shorter time each cycle must take. Mathematically, one can state the relationship between the two measures as a reciprocal. For example, what is the period in a measured frequency of 10 cycles per second? If there are 10 cycles in 1 second, then each cycle must take $\frac{1}{10}$ of a second. If the frequency is 150 Hz, the period will be $\frac{1}{150}$ of a second, and so on.

In summary, we have introduced two physical dimensions of waves, the **amplitude** and the

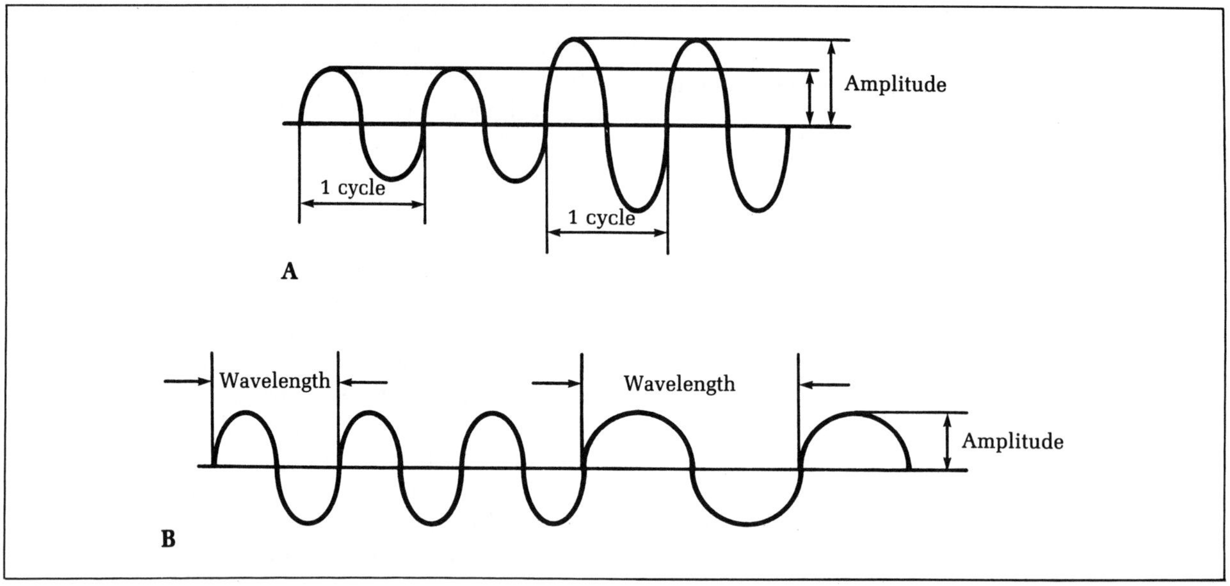

Figure 10-3. Amplitude and wavelength. A. Same wavelength, different amplitudes. Amplitude is a measure of energy and is shown graphically by the displacement from the baseline. B. Same amplitude, different wavelengths. The wavelength is the physical length of one cycle (in inches, centimeters, feet, meters, or other unit of length).

wavelength; and three temporal ones, the **frequency,** the **speed of propagation,** and the **period.** The rest of this chapter will build on these basic concepts.

10-2.4 PERIODICITY

Every statement made so far has implied a wave with a rhythmical type of motion, in which each cycle is exactly like the preceding and following cycle. Such a wave motion is called **periodic,** like the wave shown in Figure 10-4A.

Some types of naturally occurring wave motion are not rhythmical; each cycle is unlike the others. Such a wave is termed **aperiodic,** since it has no regular period (see Figure 10-4B). Because the cycles are not occurring at regular intervals, one cannot speak of the *frequency* of such a wave motion, and while it might be possible to measure the *wavelength* or *period* of a single cycle, these terms are usually reserved for periodic waves.

While it is true that the terms *frequency* and *period* are not appropriate to describe aperiodic waves, since each cycle is different, it may be that *most* of the cycles in a given aperiodic wave have periods that fall into a particular range. As periods correspond to frequencies, and since it is usual to specify sound waves in terms of frequencies, such an aperiodic wave might be said to cover a certain frequency range, say 4000 to 8000

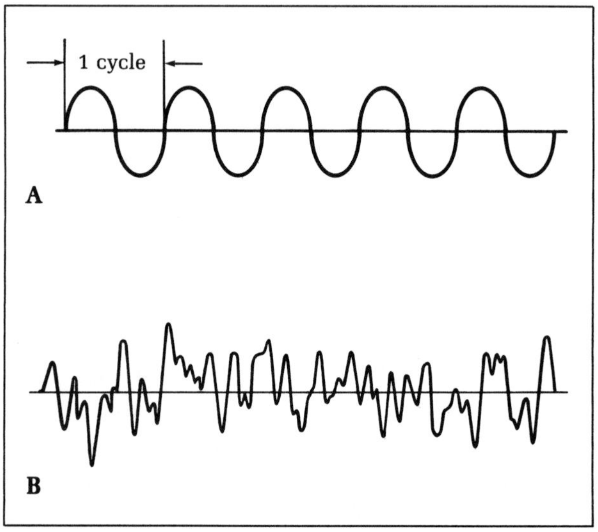

Figure 10-4. A. A periodic wave. Each cycle has the same shape and period. B. An aperiodic wave. Each cycle has a different shape and period.

Hz (or 4 to 8 kilohertz [kHz]). That means that this particular sound wave contains irregular cycles, but that most or all of those cycles have periods corresponding to frequencies between 4 and 8 kHz. We shall see that this is important in describing the acoustic character of fricatives.

10-3 The Wave Motion of Sound

We have looked at the behavior of waves in general and at water waves in particular. This has allowed us to become familiar with the basic dimensions of waves. If we wish to understand the wave motion of sound in air, however, we must realize that the water wave analogy has its limitations; there are some important differences between the two kinds of waves.

The first difference between the two kinds of waves results from the differences in the media through which they travel. Air is a gas, and like all gases, it completely fills the space that contains it, distributing itself equally throughout. Air can be compressed and rarefied. Water, on the other hand, is a liquid. It will take up the same space whether it is placed in a large container or a small one.

The second way in which sound is different from ripples on a pond is that waves on the water are **surface** waves; they result from a rise and fall in the surface of the water. Sound waves in the air, by contrast, are actually *in* the medium. Sound does not travel along the surface of the air (there is no surface of the atmosphere like the surface of a lake); it travels *through* the air.

There is a toy that is called a Slinky. It is a long, springy coil several inches in diameter, like a big soft spring. Imagine a long Slinky lying on the top of a table, stretched and held at both ends. If one end is quickly pushed and pulled back to its original position, the shock so generated will travel the length of the Slinky. In fact, if the far end is securely held, the shock may bounce off and travel back to the starting point.[1] The way that the shock travels the length of the Slinky is very much like the way sound travels through the air. Notice that no part of the Slinky moves up and down like the surface of the water.

This brings us to the third difference: in the surface waves on the water, the surface of the water is moving up and down, while the wave front is moving forward, at right angles. In the Slinky, each individual spot oscillates back and forth about its resting place. This back-and-forth movement follows the same path as the wave. In this respect, the motion of the Slinky is like that of air molecules disturbed by the passage of sound. Each molecule of air is displaced back and forth on the path the sound travels (Figure 10-5).

What is happening at a particular point in space that is being bombarded by sound? There is a rhythmical rise and fall in air pressure as a result of the passage of the disturbance. Suppose some disturbance originates a sound wave. This disturbance compresses nearby air molecules, or forces them more tightly together, creating a place of higher-than-average air pressure. Being elastic, the group of molecules springs back to its normal spacing. This springing brings the air pressure back to normal, but the molecules, in springing apart, continue past their starting point and end up farther apart than they began. This results in a lower-than-normal air pressure. They return to normal spacing, and therefore normal pressure, after the passage of the disturbance. Also, in springing apart so far, the group of molecules disturbs the next group of molecules, compressing them in turn. By this means the disturbance is passed from molecule to molecule (Figure 10-6). The nature of sound at any one place is an alternate rise and fall in air pressure. In other words, there is an alternate **compression** and **rarefaction** of the air molecules.

Figure 10-7 shows two periodic sound waves, graphed above a representation of the compression and rarefaction of air molecules. Each undulating wave tracing looks like the earlier diagram of a water wave, but there is an important difference. In the water wave, the rise and fall of the tracing in the graph represented a rise and fall in the surface of the water. In Figure 10-7, the rise and fall of the tracing does *not* represent an up-and-down motion of air particles. Rather, it represents a rise and fall in air *pressure*.

[1] This demonstration, however, would work best on a surface of ice or with the Slinky suspended horizontally along its length by strings from the ceiling to reduce the friction of rubbing the tabletop. However, a plastic laminate tabletop provides a surface with little enough friction for the demonstration to work.

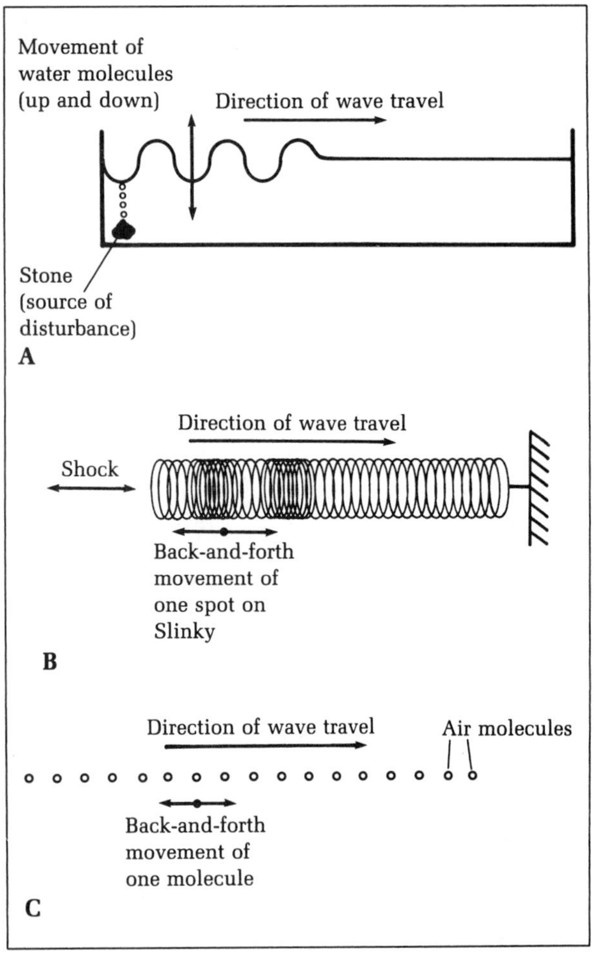

Figure 10-5. Wave motion on water, in a Slinky, and through the air. In each case the wave propagates (travels) in a single direction (although it may reflect back later), whereas a particular molecule or a particular spot moves back and forth around a single place. A. Waves on water, showing that the wave travel is perpendicular to the direction of travel of water molecules. B. A shock wave traveling through a Slinky, showing that wave travel is parallel to the direction of travel of a spot on the Slinky. C. As a sound wave passes through the air, each molecule of air moves back and forth along the same path that the wave travels.

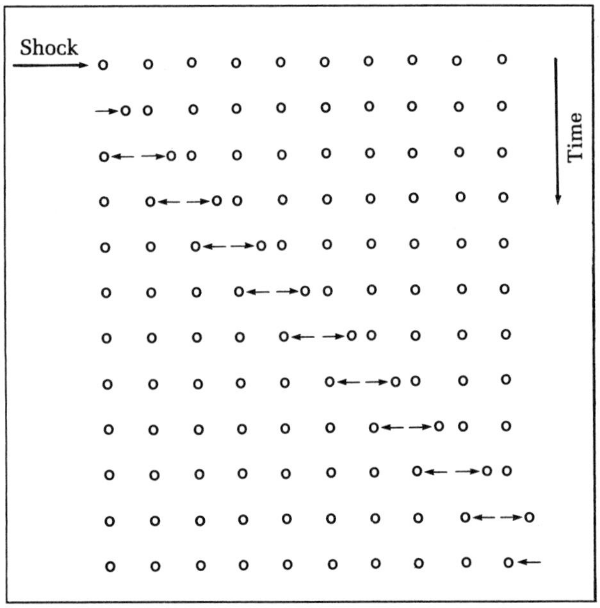

Figure 10-6. Passage of a shock wave (a single cycle of a wave) through the air. The circles represent individual air molecules. Each successive row down is a moment later in time. The oscillation of individual air molecules is passed from molecule to molecule. By this means, the shock moves along the row, but each individual molecule returns to its original place. If there were a continuous sound rather than a single shock, the cycle would repeat itself many times per second.

Below the undulating tracing of the wave in each part of Figure 10-7 is a drawing that represents the disturbance created by a continuous wave emitted from a loudspeaker. The vertical lines represent molecular proximity: where the lines are close together, the molecules they represent are close together (i.e., the air is compressed). Notice that the undulating wave is *above* the baseline at the point corresponding to the compression, such as at point *p*. Where the vertical lines are farther apart, the molecules they represent are far apart (i.e., the air is rarefied; pressure is low). This corresponds to the part of the undulating graph *below* the baseline, such as at point *q*.

The undulating graph line in parts A and B of Figure 10-7 is the standard way that a sound wave is represented graphically. But notice that the x-axis or baseline in part A is labeled "time" whereas in part B the x-axis is labeled "distance." The two look identical but the labeling of the x-axis indicates that something very different is represented by the graph line in each part. Much confusion results from a failure to recognize that, while similar graphically, the two are different conceptually.

Part A shows air pressure *varying over time at one place*. Imagine that a microphone (a device sensitive to minute changes in air pressure) were

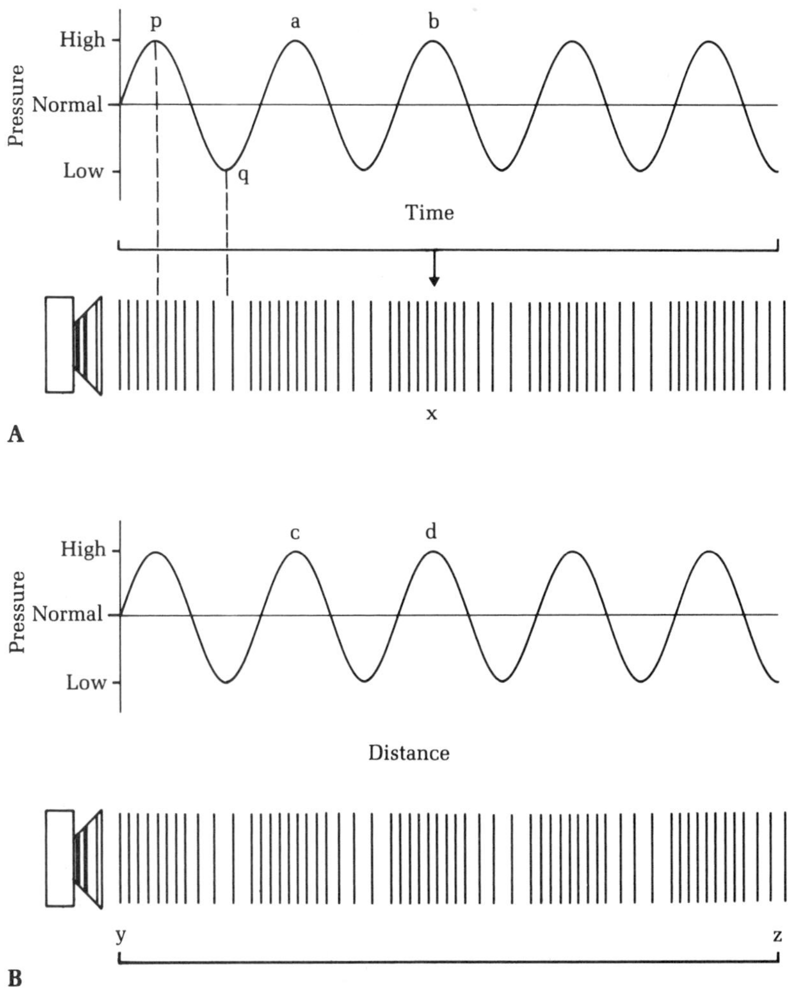

Figure 10-7. Variations in air pressure (A and B, upper part) and molecular displacement (A and B, lower part) in a sound wave. In both A and B the graph lines are pressure tracings and the vertical lines beneath represent molecular proximity (see text for a detailed description). A. Air pressure is monitored from the vantage point x, a fixed distance away from the sound source. As time passes, the amount of pressure at point x is plotted, forming a tracing that shows the variation of pressure over time. Points *a* to *b* indicate the *period* of the wave. B. Air pressure is measured at different distances away from the sound source. The pressure at all points from *y* to z is measured at the same time. The graph shows the changes in air pressure corresponding to the molecular compression and rarefaction depicted beneath. Points *c* to *d* indicate the *wavelength* of the wave.

placed near a sound source (the loudspeaker shown below the graph), at the point x, let us say. As the sound wave propagates (travels) through the air past point x, the pressure *at that point* will rise, then fall, then rise, then fall, etc. That is what is graphed: the rise and fall of pressure over time, at one point in space. This would be akin to watching a highway through a tiny observation slit that permitted you to see only a few feet of the road. All you could do is to report whether or not you could see a car at that moment: "Now I see a car, now there is no car, now I see a car, etc." You could even make a graph of your sightings of cars as a function of time, a graph in the style of part A.

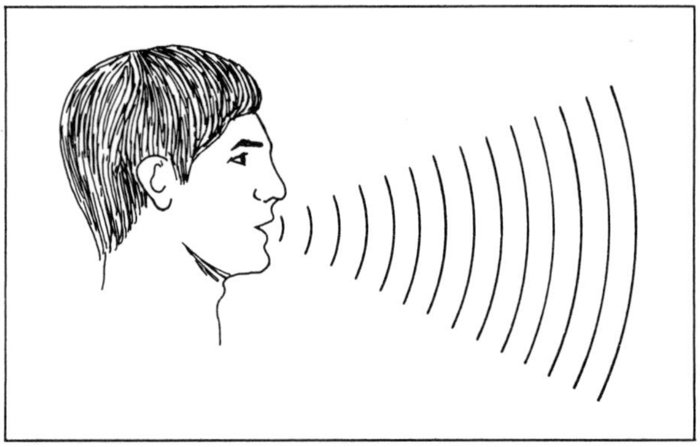

Figure 10-8. Sound waves moving away from a point source. The solid lines represent high pressure, or crests; the midpoints of the spaces between the lines represent points of low pressure, or troughs. Of course the sound is radiating three-dimensionally, not in one general direction only.

What part B shows is very different. Here the point of time is fixed, and the change of pressure is measured at different distances from the sound source. Imagine again that the loudspeaker is producing a continuous sound and, further, that we had some sort of special camera that could take a picture of the density of air (that is, how close together the molecules are). If we took a picture with this camera, we would obtain a photograph like lower part of Figure 10-7B, showing the molecules closer together and farther apart as a function of their distance from the loudspeaker. This imaginary photograph shows *different points* at the *same moment*. This would be like an ordinary snapshot of a section of highway; it would show cars at different places at the same moment (the moment the photograph was taken).

Another way to consider the difference between the concepts shown in parts A and B is to ask yourself what one cycle represents on each graph. In part A, since the x-axis is marked in *time*, one cycle (e.g., from point *a* to point *b*) represents the *time* of a cycle, namely the **period.** In part B, since the baseline is marked in *distance*, one cycle (e.g., from point *c* to point *d*) represents the *distance* of a cycle, namely the **wavelength.**

Be sure, whenever you look at a graph of a sound wave, to check what units the x-axis is marked in, and thus to understand what the graph is showing.

While surface waves on water are different from sound waves in important ways that have been explained in this section, *sound* propagates through water by essentially the same process as it propagates in air, although at a faster speed.

The movement of sound waves in air is three-dimensional; that is, sound radiates in all directions from a source. This is indicated in Figure 10-8, in which the solid lines represent points of high pressure and the spaces between the lines represent points of low pressure.

10-4 The Dimensions of Sound Waves

We will see in this section how the various dimensions of waves apply in the specific case of sound waves.

10-4.1 Periodic and Aperiodic Waves

A periodic wave will be perceived as having a musical or tonal quality, as does a single note from a musical instrument. An aperiodic sound will be perceived as being "noisy," like a hiss. A prolonged vowel sound, such as [ɑ:::], is predominantly periodic; a consonant sound such as [s] or [š] is aperiodic.

10-4.2 Frequency

The frequency of sounds that we hear is much greater than that of waves on the water. A very good, young human ear can hear sounds between a low of 20 Hz and a high of 16,000 to 18,000 Hz[2] (abbreviated 16 to 18 kHz, where *k* stands for *kilo*, meaning 'thousand'). Sounds whose frequency is below 20 Hz may be felt as vibration or heard as a series of individual clicks, and sounds whose frequency is above 18 kHz are not perceived at all, although many animals (e.g., dogs and bats) can hear sounds of higher frequencies than humans can. It is a universal fact that age reduces our range of hearing, as well as our acuity throughout the range that we do have.

Sounds of a high frequency are perceived as being high-pitched; low-frequency sounds are low-pitched. To get an idea of what particular frequencies sound like, consider the following examples: If you turn up the volume control on a record-

[2] The range of human hearing is often listed as 20 Hz to 20 kHz. This upper figure makes a convenient, easily remembered round number, but is in fact higher than what most children and virtually all adults can hear.

player amplifier without playing a record, you hear a humming sound. The frequency of this sound is 60 Hz, because the amplifier operates from 60-cycle alternating current in North America. Middle C on the musical scale is 256 Hz. The octave scale in music is based on a doubling of frequency: C above middle C is 512 Hz, C above that C is 1024 Hz, and so on.

10-4.3 Amplitude

The amplitude of sound waves corresponds to the amount of compression and rarefaction that occurs. A bigger original disturbance will cause air molecules to be displaced further; this causes a greater rise and fall in air pressure. In turn, this causes the eardrums to move a greater distance back and forth. Greater amplitude is perceived as increased loudness.

Our ears respond to a remarkable variation in amplitude. The minimum amplitude that can be perceived corresponds to the slight pressure needed to displace the eardrums by about the diameter of a hydrogen molecule. The maximum sound amplitude that can be endured without pain corresponds to a pressure about *one million times* as great as the minimum amplitude that can be perceived. The range of amplitudes available in a signal is known as its *dynamic range*. The dynamic range of the ear is enormous, much greater than the best stereo system.

Amplitude and frequency are independent of one another; one dimension can be varied without affecting the production of the other. While a change in one of these dimensions can affect our *perception* of the other (see the following section), it is still true that a high-pitched or low-pitched sound can be loud or soft.

10-4.4 Psychological Dimensions of Sound

We have noted that a change in frequency corresponds to a change in pitch and that a change in amplitude corresponds to a change in loudness.

Frequency and **amplitude** are concrete, physical dimensions of sound that can be measured accurately and reliably with instruments. On the other hand, **pitch** and **loudness** refer to perceptual or psychological dimensions that can be measured only through subjective reports. That is, pitch can be measured only by asking people what pitch they hear, often in relation to a reference tone. These perceptual dimensions are not as reliably measured as the corresponding physical dimensions, because of the variability of the human machine, extraneous factors such as fatigue, and the interaction between the two dimensions. For example, a certain amplitude may sound loud if its frequency is 1500 Hz, but that same amplitude will seem soft if its frequency is 150 Hz. The ear is simply less sensitive at this lower frequency.

In everyday speech we use the term **volume** to mean the same as **loudness.** Technically, however, psychoacousticians use the term **volume** to refer to the extent to which a sound is perceived to *fill* a given space; this is different from how *loud* the sound is.

10-4.5 Phase

Imagine two sound waves that are identical in all ways except that their peaks and troughs do not line up, as shown in Figure 10-9B. The difference between these two cannot be described using any of the terms we have met so far. The two waves in Figure 10-9B–D are said to be **out of phase,** whereas the two waves in Figure 10-9A are said to be **in phase.**

The extent to which two waves are out of phase is measured in **degrees.** There are 360 degrees in a circle, so one-quarter of that is 90 degrees, one-half is 180 degrees, and so on. Notice how this applies to sound waves in Figure 10-9A–E. In Figure 10-9E we see two waves whose starting points are 360 degrees out of phase; however, if we consider a point somewhere in the middle of the figure, rather than at the right or left end, we could not tell whether the waves were *in phase* or *360 degrees out of phase.*

10-4.6 Wavelength

Wavelengths for sounds can easily be calculated if we know the speed at which sound travels and the particular frequency involved. The speed of sound through air is about 1086 feet per second at sea level and normal barometric pressure (barometric pressure will affect the speed of sound slightly).

A simple multiplication of the velocity of sound by the period of a particular wave will give

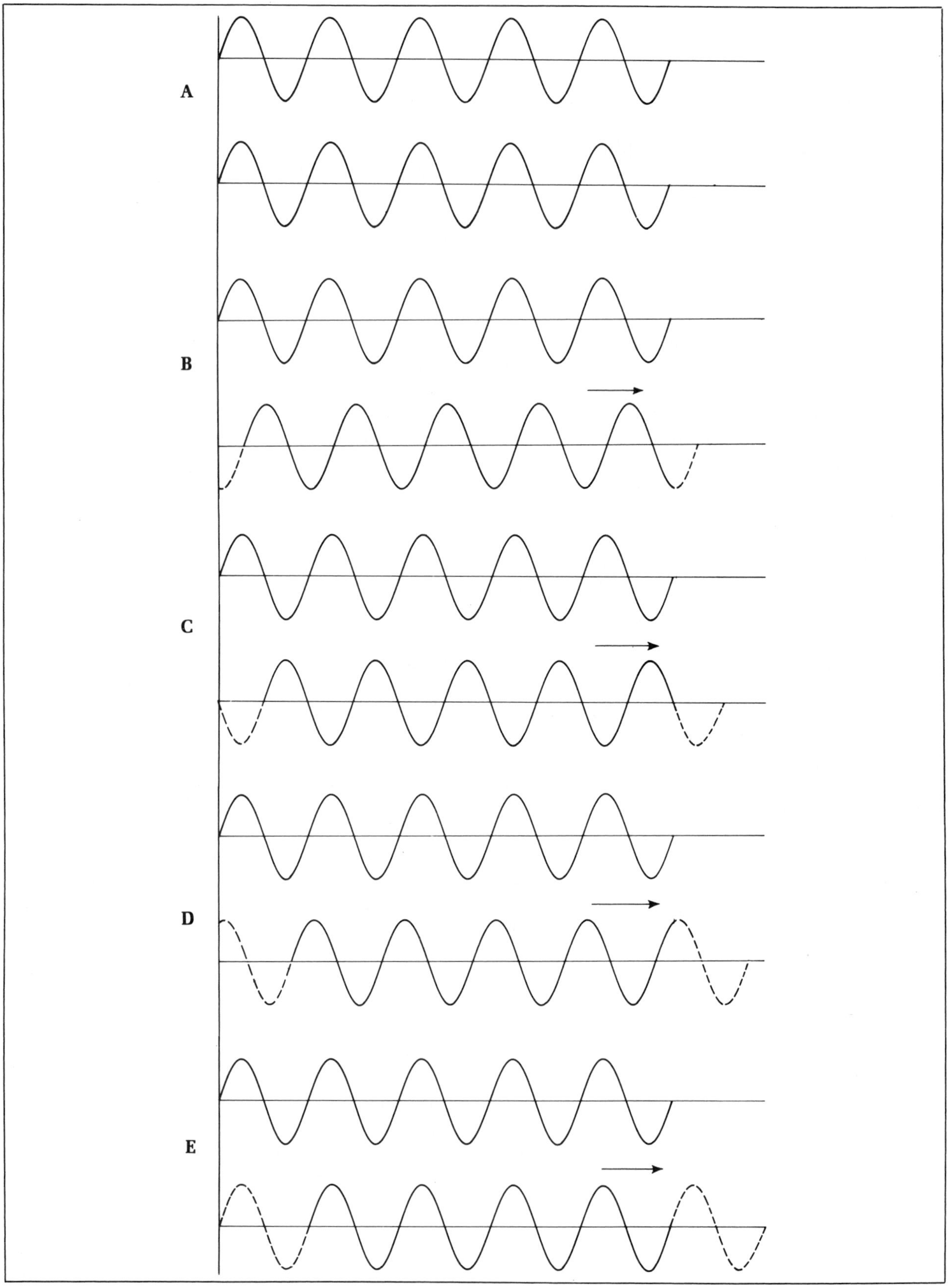

A
B
C
D
E

its wavelength, as shown in the following examples. (In using this formula, it is important to keep the unit of time constant in both velocity and period; here the unit is 1 second. Writing the units out clearly, as has been done in the examples, will help prevent confusion about the meaning of the answer, since the time unit can be seen to cancel out.)

$$20\ \text{Hz:}\ \frac{1086\ \text{feet}}{\cancel{1\ \text{second}}} \times \frac{\cancel{1\ \text{second}}}{20\ \text{cycles}} = 54.3\ \text{feet (per cycle)}$$

$$18\ \text{kHz:}\ \frac{1086\ \text{feet}}{\cancel{1\ \text{second}}} \times \frac{\cancel{1\ \text{second}}}{18{,}000\ \text{cycles}} = 0.060\ \text{foot}$$

$$256\ \text{Hz:}\ \frac{1086\ \text{feet}}{\cancel{1\ \text{second}}} \times \frac{\cancel{1\ \text{second}}}{256\ \text{cycles}} = 4.24\ \text{feet}$$

The lowest pitch human beings can hear—20 Hz—corresponds to the longest wavelength in the examples, over 54 feet (about 16.5 meters). The shortest wavelength corresponding to a sound a young human ear can hear—18,000 Hz—is 0.060 foot, or about three-quarters of an inch (just under 2 cm). The wavelength of middle C is about 4¼ feet (about 1.3 meters).

It is apparent that, for certain frequency ranges, human beings make use of wavelength in localizing sound (that is, in determining from which direction a sound originates); since our ears are several inches apart, we can perceive whether or not the waves reaching our two ears are in the same phase of their cycle. Indeed, one of the greatest problems for individuals suffering from a unilateral (one-sided) hearing loss is difficulty in localizing. Fortunately, phase is not the only cue for localizing, so such individuals retain some localizing ability.

Wavelength is dependent upon the speed of propagation of the sound. For example, sound travels through a steel bar at about sixteen times the speed it travels through air. So the wavelengths in steel would be about sixteen times as long as they would in air for the same frequency.

Figure 10-9. Phase. The cycle is considered as if it were a circle of 360 degrees. A. Two waves are *in phase*. B. The lower wave has moved to the right a quarter cycle; the two are *90 degrees out of phase*. C. The lower wave has moved to the right another quarter cycle, so that it is now a half cycle or *180 degrees out of phase*. D. Another quarter cycle means that the two waves are *270 degrees out of phase* (or 90 degrees out of phase, if considered from the opposite end). E. Another quarter cycle means one full cycle or *360 degrees out of phase*. Since in a periodic wave each cycle is identical, this is really the same as being *in phase* or *0 degrees out of phase*.

10-5 Harmonics

If a sound source is producing a periodic tone of a given frequency, there normally are additional frequencies present that are whole-number multiples of the basic or **fundamental frequency.** These additional frequencies are called **harmonics** by physicists and speech scientists, but if you have musical training they may be familiar to you under the name **overtones.**

For example, a fundamental frequency of 100 Hz will have harmonics of 200, 300, 400, 500, 600, and 700 Hz, and so on. A fundamental frequency of 175 Hz will have harmonics of 350, 525, 700, 875, and 1050 Hz, and so on. These are called the *second, third, fourth, fifth* harmonic, and so on. There is no first harmonic; the second harmonic is twice the fundamental, the third harmonic three times the fundamental, and so on.[3]

Because of harmonics, one rarely hears a pure tone; mostly we hear combinations of tones: the fundamental plus a number of harmonics of different amplitudes. For example, when you hear a note—say, middle C—played on different musical instruments, this "same" note sounds different. In fact, the 256-Hz fundamental will be the same, but the number of harmonics, and the relative amplitude of each, will be different, accounting for the different sound quality of the same note on each different instrument.

The source of harmonics can be found in the nature of the vibrating object that generates the sound. If that object is rigid, and vibrates as a whole, few or no harmonics will be generated. But if the object is supple, undulating as it vibrates, it will generate many harmonics. The analogy is often made of a rope. Imagine a rope attached to the wall at one end and held in your hand at the other. Now vibrate the rope up and down—once per sec-

[3] Some physicists use a different numbering system in which what we are calling the *second* harmonic is called the *first* harmonic. Technically this is more logical, but it is also more confusing, since the *second* harmonic is then *three* times the fundamental, and so on.

ond, let us say, in order to have a round number. The *whole* rope will be oscillating at 1 Hz, its fundamental frequency. But each *half* of the rope, if considered on its own or viewed with high-speed photography, is vibrating at 2 Hz, the second harmonic. If you consider the thirds of the rope, each is vibrating at triple the fundamental; the quarters are vibrating at four times the fundamental, and so on. These different frequencies—or **modes of vibration** as they are called—are possible because the rope is flexible.

The sound generated by a tuning fork will, by contrast, have almost no harmonics. Each tine of the fork vibrates as a rigid whole, with none of the undulatory movement of the rope. The sound of a tuning fork is as nearly free of harmonics as anything most of us ever hear; although used for tuning musical instruments, tuning forks generate a sound that is very unmusical, owing to its pure (nonharmonic) nature.

10-5.1 Harmonics in the Voice

We noted in Chapter 9 that vocal fold vibration is undulatory (see Section 9-4). Normally the glottal chink appears first at the arytenoid end and progresses forward in a rippling motion to the thyroid end. In this way, the vocal fold vibration is much like the motion of the rope in our earlier analogy; vocal fold vibration is rich in harmonics.

Most adults, as we noted in Chapter 9, have fundamental frequencies ranging from a low of 100 Hz to a high of 300 Hz. But most of us produce harmonics up to 4000 or 5000 Hz, or even beyond. Voices that we perceive as being "rich" or "resonant" have strong harmonics; those we perceive as "weak" or "thin" or "brittle" are poorer in harmonics. Falsetto tends to be poor in harmonics. Figure 10-10 shows spectra of the sound produced by the vocal folds of a couple of typical adults, one male, one female.

There are several points to note in Figure 10-10. First, the graph shows what is called the **glottal source,** that is, the vocal fold vibration *alone*. The pattern of glottal frequencies is modified by the pharyngeal, oral, and nasal cavities, as we shall see later in the chapter; it serves as a *source* for vocal resonance, but it is *not* vocal output. Second, this is a different type of graph from what we have seen up to now. It shows a *spectrum*, that is, all of the component frequencies in the signal. It shows the amplitude of each component, and its frequency. The graph consists of a series of lines, because the components are *discrete*, that is, there is no sound energy of any frequency between the harmonics. Third, notice that there is a gradual falling off of the amplitude of the harmonics as frequency increases; each harmonic has less amplitude than the next-lowest harmonic. The fall-off is about 6 to 12 dB (decibels) per octave for the average voice. The graph shows these harmonics abruptly ending below 4000 Hz, while in fact they continue to higher frequencies; however, beyond 4000 or 5000 Hz, they become too low in amplitude to be of much concern in the study of speech.

10-6 Addition of Waves

In the previous section we discussed a situation in which one sound source produces periodic sound waves of several frequencies at once. But the sound waves discussed and illustrated in the early part of this chapter (except for the aperiodic wave) consisted of *one* frequency alone. What happens in a sound wave when several waves are produced simultaneously? How do they combine?

Several simple sound waves can be added together to form a new **complex** sound wave, which is the sum of the component parts, as shown in Figure 10-11. This figure illustrates the sum of a 100-Hz sound wave plus a 200-Hz and a 300-Hz wave. Remember that the rise and fall of the graph line represents the rise and fall of air pressure at a point in space. If two waves, both in the rising phase of their cycle, arrive at the same point at the same time, the resulting rise in pressure will be doubly fast and doubly great. But if the two waves arrive out of phase—that is, one in the rising phase of its cycle and the other in the falling phase of its cycle—they will cancel each other out, since, if the pressure is being influenced to rise and fall simultaneously, it will stay balanced in the middle. It can be seen in Figure 10-11 that when several waves are added together, the amplitude of the resultant wave at any one point is sometimes *increased* by an additive effect of the component waves and sometimes *decreased* by a subtractive effect of the component waves.

Waves A, B, and C in Figure 10-11, like the waves in Figures 10-2, 10-3, and 10-4A, are

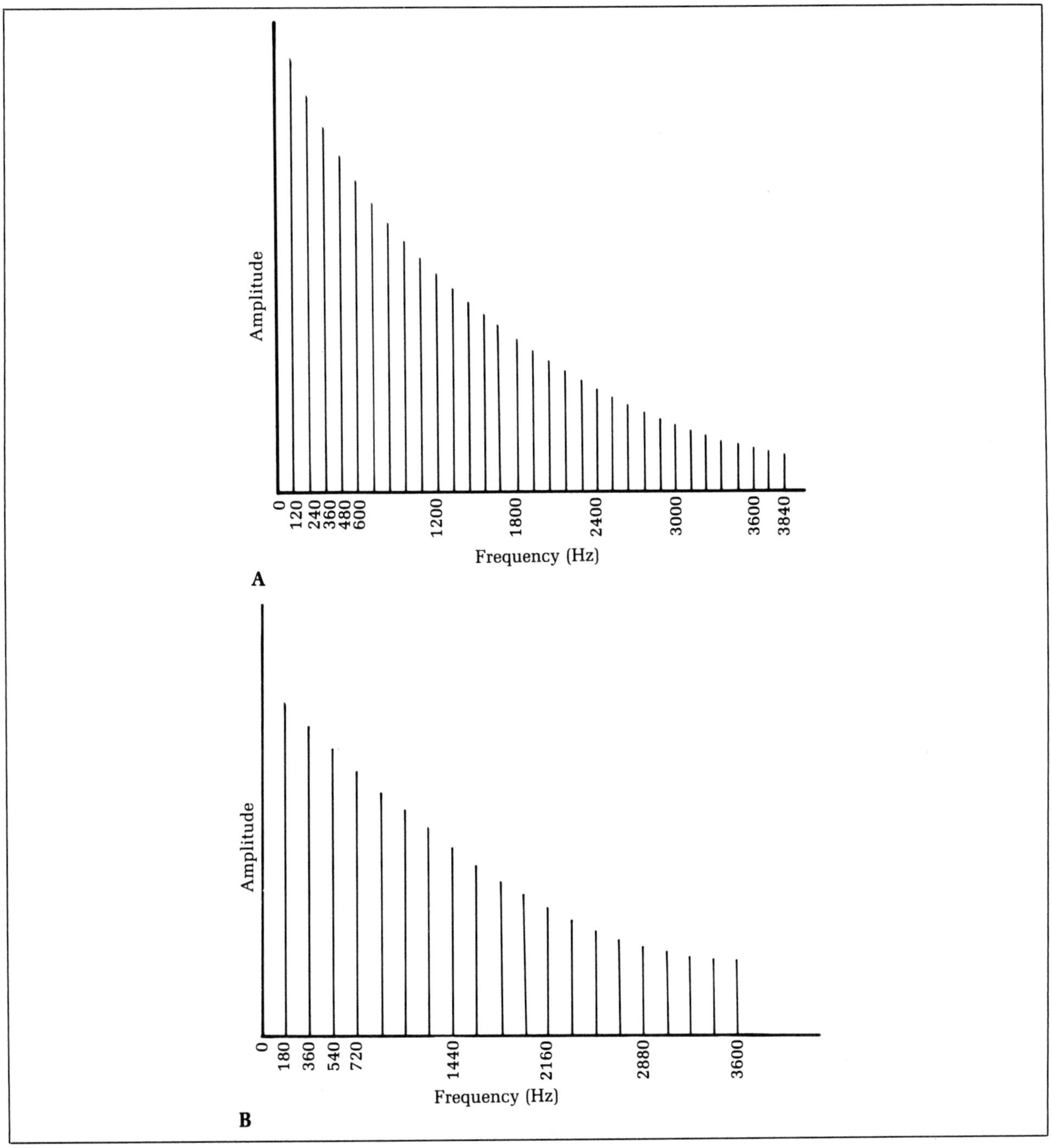

Figure 10-10. Spectra of the glottal source of the voice. Frequency is shown on the x-axis, amplitude on the y-axis. A. The graph shows no energy between 0 and 119 Hz, then a lot of energy at 120 Hz, then nothing from 121 to 239 Hz, then a lot of energy at 240 Hz, etc. The F_0 is 120 Hz, a typical adult male F_0. B. The F_0 is 180 Hz, and represents an adult female F_0. Note that there are a larger number of spectral peaks in a voice having a lower F_0.

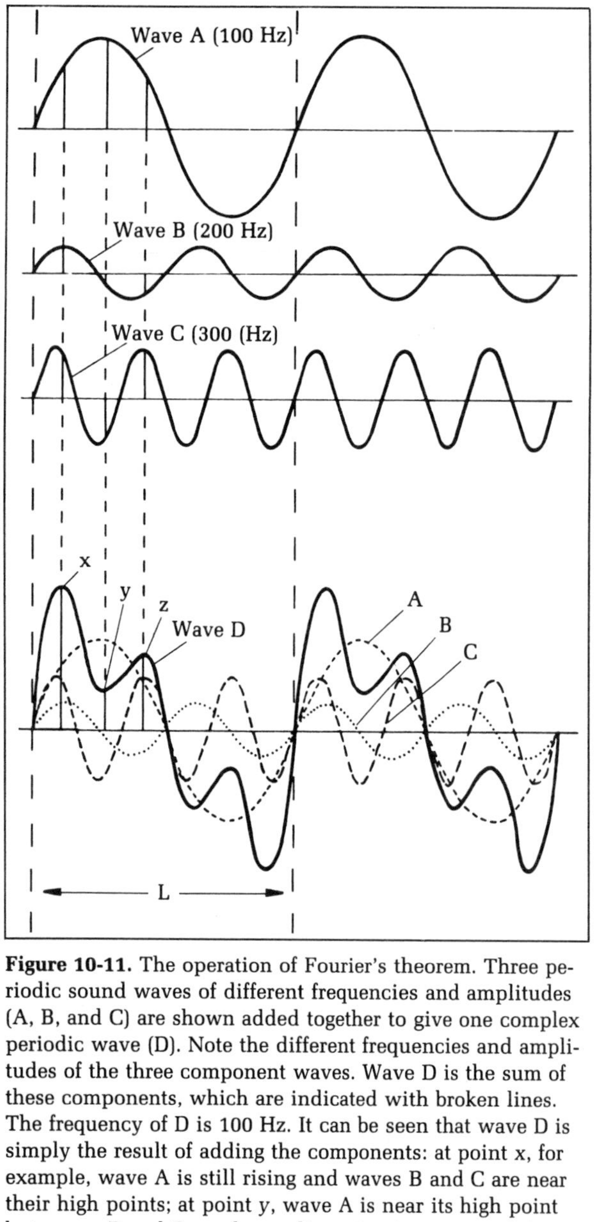

Figure 10-11. The operation of Fourier's theorem. Three periodic sound waves of different frequencies and amplitudes (A, B, and C) are shown added together to give one complex periodic wave (D). Note the different frequencies and amplitudes of the three component waves. Wave D is the sum of these components, which are indicated with broken lines. The frequency of D is 100 Hz. It can be seen that wave D is simply the result of adding the components: at point x, for example, wave A is still rising and waves B and C are near their high points; at point y, wave A is near its high point but waves B and C are descending; at point z, wave A is starting its descent, wave B is near its low point, and wave C is at its high point. Any other point along wave D can similarly be found to be the sum of the components. The rise and fall of the graph line represents rise and fall in pressure, so it is apparent that when one component wave is influencing the pressure to rise, and another is influencing it to fall, the result will be the sum of those influences: an intermediate point. When all component waves are influencing the pressure to rise, the overall rise will be the sum of all the component waves. Distance L corresponds to one cycle of waves A and D, two cycles of wave E, and three cycles of wave C.

termed **simple** or **sinusoidal** periodic waves, or simply **sinusoids.**[4] When these are added together, the resultant wave (like wave D in Figure 10-11 and any of the waves in Figure 10-12) is termed **complex.** *The complex wave will be periodic if all of its component waves are.*

Complex periodic waves may have relatively simple or extremely complex shapes (a few are illustrated in Figure 10-12).[5] But no matter how intricate the shape of a complex wave, it is easy to tell if it is periodic or not. If it has a pattern that is repeated, it is periodic; if it has no repetitive pattern, the wave is aperiodic.

Any complex periodic wave can be divided up into component sinusoidal waves, according to **Fourier's theorem,** named for the French mathematician who first proposed it. This means that any complex periodic wave, such as any of those shown in Figure 10-12 (and any of an infinite number of others), can be seen as the sum of simple sinusoidal waves of varying frequencies and amplitudes. (Their precise physical properties can be discovered through the application of Fourier's theorem, which involves mathematics that remain difficult and time-consuming even in this day of computers.) The fact that wave D in Figure 10-11 is the combination of sinusoids is easy to accept; it is perhaps harder to see how such wave forms as the square wave in Figure 10-12A can possibly be the sum of sinusoids. It is far beyond the scope of this book to demonstrate the mathematical derivation; suffice it to say that *any* periodic wave is the sum of a number of sinusoids.

If the sinusoidal components of a periodic wave are different in frequency by more than a few hertz, then our ears hear the complex wave as having a different quality from a simple wave of the same frequency. (People with a good ear for music can often identify the components.)

As Figure 10-12 shows, a complex periodic wave has a cycle that can be identified. As with the simple periodic waves we saw earlier, each cycle is exactly like those that precede and follow.

[4]The term **sinusoid** is derived from the trigonometric function of the same name, whose shape, when graphed, is like the shape of a graphic representation of a simple wave. The name is often shortened to **sine,** both in mathematics and in discussion of the shape of sound waves.

[5]Figure 10-12 contains graphs of some vowel sounds; vowels are discussed in Section 10-9.

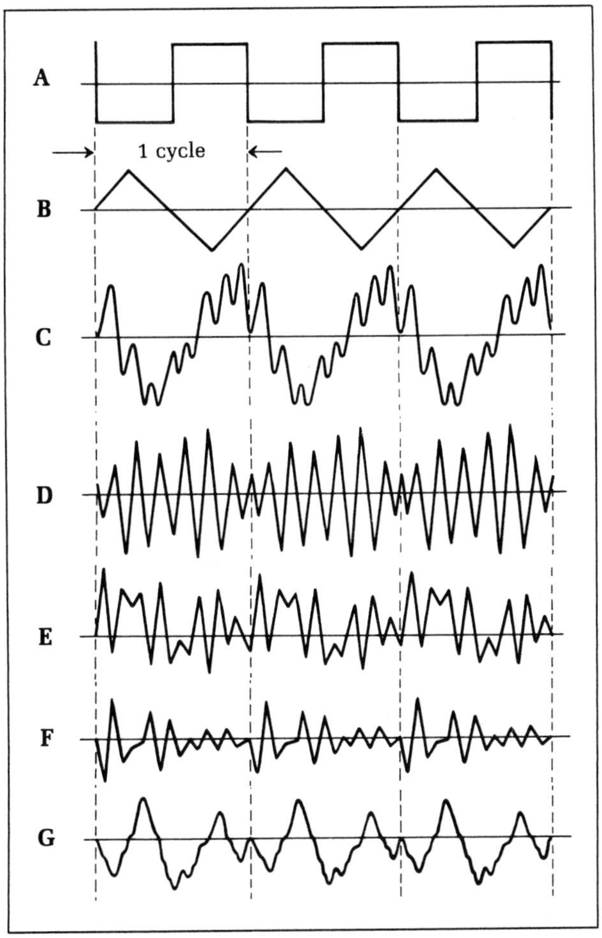

Figure 10-12. Some complex periodic waves. Illustrated are seven of the infinite variety of complex periodic waves. A. A "square" wave. B. A "triangular" wave. C. The sum of a 300-Hz, a 2055-Hz, and a 2350-Hz wave. D. The sum of a 400-Hz, a 500-Hz, and a 600-Hz wave. E. The sum of a 100-Hz, a 500-Hz, and a 600-Hz wave. F. The author pronouncing the vowel /ɑ/ (F_0 about 120 Hz). G. The author pronouncing the vowel /u/ (F_0 about 120 Hz). For ease of comparison, the seven waves have been drawn to different scales to make the length of one cycle the same for all. The fundamental frequency of the wave from which C was drawn is 300 Hz; of E, 100 Hz; and of F and G, about 120 Hz. These different frequencies of course correspond to different wavelengths and periods, so in scale drawings the lengths of the cycles would differ (for example, E would be four times as long as D). They have been made to appear the same length in this drawing so that you can compare the different wave shapes.

The frequency of a complex wave is measured the same way as the frequency of simple waves: the number of times the cycle repeats itself each second. Of course, the components of the complex wave each have their own frequencies, higher than the frequency of the overall complex wave.

A complex periodic wave, like simple periodic waves, will have a somewhat melodic quality, as contrasted with an aperiodic wave, which has a harsh or "noisy" quality. *Melodic,* however, does not imply that the sound is necessarily pleasing musically, only that it is not harsh and noisy. For example, if you pronounce a sustained vowel such as "ah," you are producing a complex sound wave that is predominantly periodic.

With a minimum of equipment you can produce sounds that have the auditory quality of complex periodic waves as opposed to that of simple periodic waves. A tuning fork, tuned to a particular frequency—say, the note A on the musical scale—will produce a simple periodic wave. The same note played on any musical instrument will have the *same frequency* but will be complex rather than simple. It strikes the human ear as being "richer" than the note produced by the tuning fork. As mentioned earlier, musical instruments tend to emphasize certain harmonics and deemphasize others. The same note played on different instruments will have the same frequency but will be a complex wave of a different shape, again depending on which harmonics are emphasized. (It is a curious fact that we find certain combinations of harmonics "rich" and others discordant.) Many phonetics and acoustics laboratories are equipped with oscillators that can produce sine waves, square waves, and sawtooth waves of the same frequency.

The additive nature of sound waves, and the fact that a complex wave can be seen as the sum of a number of simple waves, is basic to speech. The resonant speech sounds, such as vowels, result from the combination of several frequencies or tones into a complex wave form.

10-7 Standing Waves

Let us turn our attention to an acoustic phenomenon that plays a fundamental role in resonance and hence in speech production, namely the standing wave.

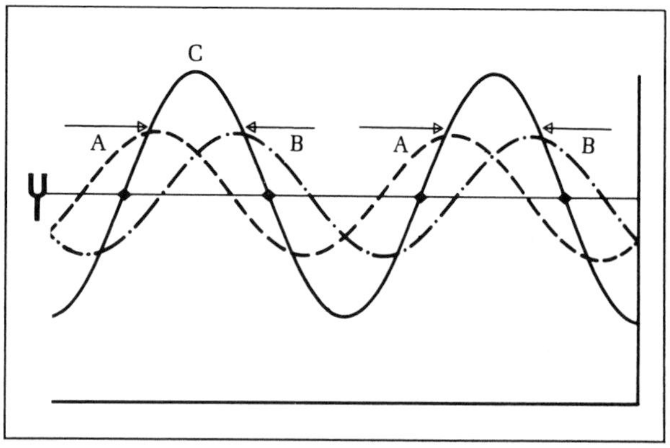

Figure 10-13. A reflected wave. Wave A (*broken line*) represents sound radiating from the tuning fork. Wave B (*dash-dot-dash*) represents sound being reflected from the wall. Notice that the wavelength fits exactly twice between the tuning fork and the reflecting wall. Wave C (*solid line*) is the sum (by Fourier's theorem) of waves A and B. Its *points of zero influence* (baseline crossings) are always in the same place, if the distance from wall to tuning fork is a whole number of wavelengths.

Recall that for any given speed of propagation, the wavelength depends on the frequency. The higher the frequency, the shorter the wavelength. Each frequency has a *unique* wavelength in a given medium.

Imagine a sound source, say a tuning fork, that produces a frequency of 108.5 Hz. By the formula in Section 10-4.6, you could calculate the wavelength in air of that frequency. If you did, you would find that it is 10 feet. Now imagine that the tuning fork is exactly 20 feet from a wall. Sound waves will travel from the tuning fork to the wall and will rebound off the wall back to the tuning fork. (In fact, sound waves would go in all directions, but for the moment we are considering only those that follow this direct path.) It is easy to see that two complete wavelengths would fit between the tuning fork and the wall. The fact that there is an exact fit leads to a special situation when the outgoing wave and the returning wave interact. (Naturally these two waves have the same wavelength, and since little energy is lost in reflection, we can assume for the purpose of illustration that they have the same amplitude.) In Figure 10-13 we see a portion of the waves from the tuning fork as they hit the wall and rebound. By the principle we examined in Section 10-6, these two waves add up to give a wave of double amplitude. But because of the exact fit of the wavelength, the resultant wave has a special property: the points where it crosses the baseline (that is, the points of normal air pressure or *points of zero influence*, as they are called technically) *are always in the same place*. If you consider Figure 10-13, you can see why this is so. Waves A and B will each advance the *same* distance in any given time period, and so the points at which they cancel each other out always land at the same place.

In Figure 10-14, one cycle of the wave has been cut into twelve equal parts, so you can follow, step by step, the combination of the two waves.

This type of wave is called a **standing wave,** because it seems to be standing in one place. This is because the points of zero influence (normal air pressure), called the **nodes,** stay in the same place. The distance between the nodes is *one-half the wavelength* of the wave.

If the waves could be made visible, they would appear as in Figure 10-15. (Remember that the crests and troughs represent air pressure, not the rise and fall of air molecules.)

In the examples given, we considered *one* original wavetrain[6] and *one* reflected wavetrain. The same situation would apply if the sound source were in the middle of a room of the correct dimensions. In that case, however, we would have to consider the continuous reflection back and forth. That reflection would mean that the resultant wave would have an even greater amplitude.

The standing wave pattern occurs if the distance between source and reflector, or between two reflectors, is any multiple of the distance between nodes. For this reason, it is apparent that the critical factor is not the wavelength, but one-half the wavelength.

10-8 Resonance

Resonance is the property of an object to vibrate at a certain frequency. For example, a tuning fork or a guitar string will vibrate at a particular fre-

[6] A **wavetrain** is several or many continuous connected cycles, as in a normal continuous acoustic output (rarely would a sound be produced that was only 1 cycle long, the duration of its period). Figure 10-12 shows 7 different wavetrains, each 3 cycles long.

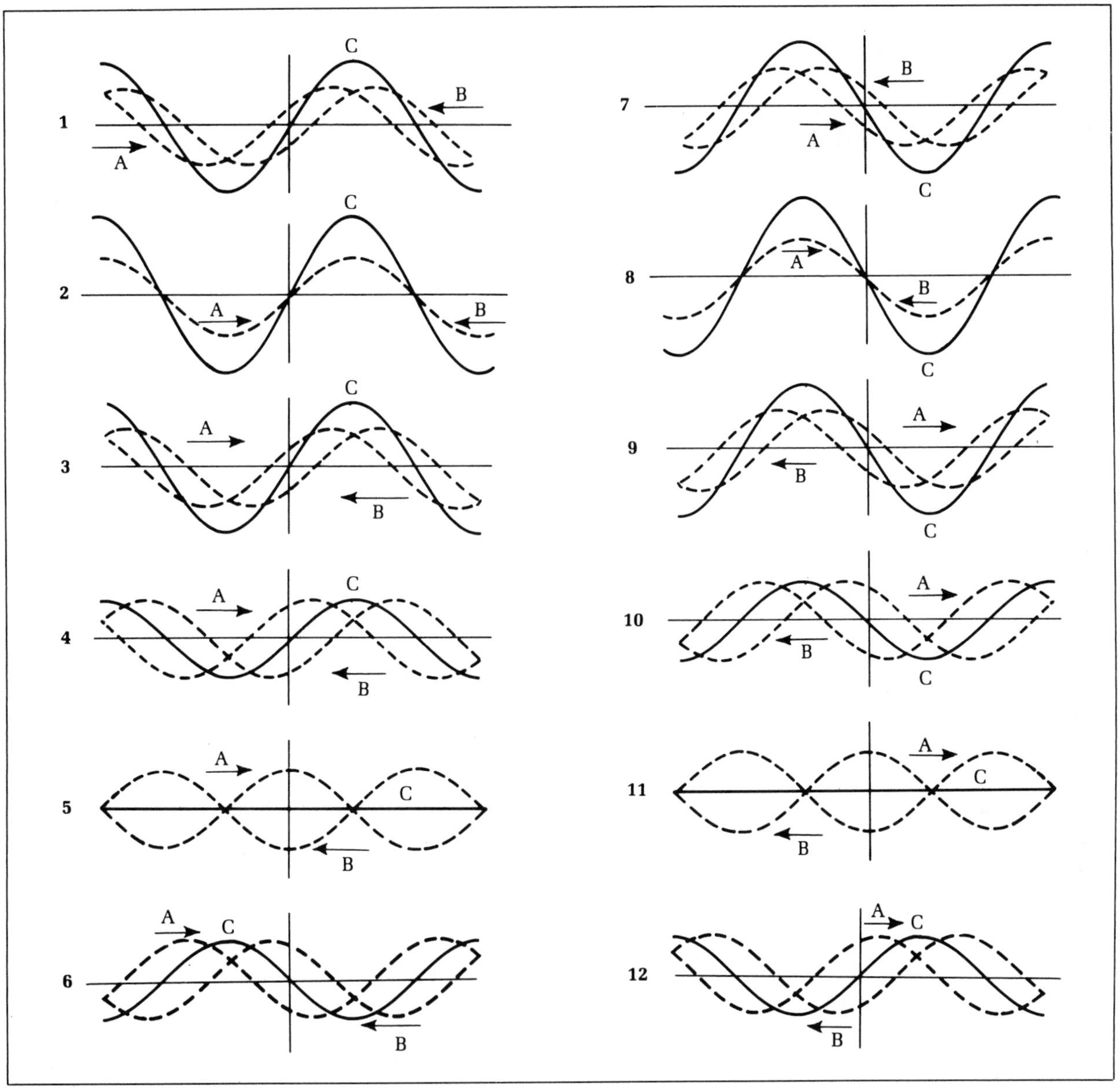

Figure 10-14. A standing wave. The two waves shown in Figure 10-13 are reproduced here, divided into twelve parts. In each successive drawing, waves A and B have been advanced by one-twelfth of a cycle or 30 degrees (remember that *both* A and B are advancing at the same rate). Wave C shows the resultant wave. Note the special properties of wave C: its points of zero influence (the points at which it crosses the baseline) *are always the same*. This is different from other sound waves (such as A and B in this drawing or, perhaps more clearly, the waves in Figure 10-9), whose points of zero influence move forward or back.

quency if an external force (a strike or a pluck) supplies the appropriate "push." Notice that a given tuning fork has only one natural frequency: strike it hard or softly, quickly or gently, and it will always vibrate at the same frequency. (The only way that it could be made to vibrate at any other frequency would be to fasten it to another vibrating object: put it in a paint shaker, for example. Or you could change its physical proper-

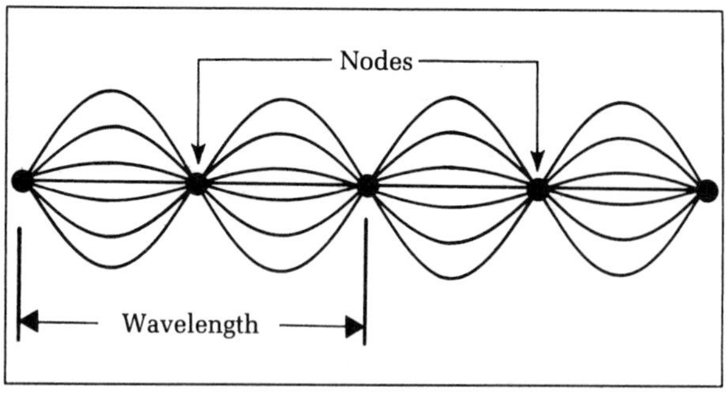

Figure 10-15. A standing wave. Viewed over time, the crests would rise, fall, become troughs, and rise again to crests, as shown in this view at different moments in time, but there would be no apparent movement forward or back. The points of zero influence (baseline crossings), called **nodes** in the case of a standing wave, stay at the same point. There is a node every *half* wavelength (you can see why by examining Figure 10-14).

ties, say by filing away some of its metal, but that would simply give it a *new* natural frequency.)

This resonant vibration can be imparted by an outside oscillation. If you took two tuning forks having the same frequency, set one in vibration, and brought the two close together, the second one would begin to vibrate. But this phenomenon of *sympathetic vibration* is selective: if you took two tuning forks having *different* frequencies (being careful not to choose frequencies that were multiples of one another), the second would *not* pick up the vibrations. This phenomenon also occurs outside the laboratory; we see examples often in everyday life. Most of us have been in a car that rattles only when the engine is idling at a certain speed. The part that rattles has its own natural frequency and is set in vibration only at a certain engine speed, because at that speed the engine emits a series of pulses whose frequency matches the resonant frequency of the loose part. At other engine speeds, the frequencies do not match, and no sympathetic vibration occurs. Or, to take another everyday example of sympathetic resonance: most of us have had the experience, when playing a radio or stereo, of finding that a certain note makes some object in the room vibrate. In the case of cheap radios or TVs, that object might be the grill on the loudspeaker. Whatever the object is, every time a certain frequency is emitted by the loudspeaker, that object rattles.

It is important to understand that the object is free to vibrate all the time, but that it does not vibrate in sympathy to just *any* sound, *only* to a sound whose frequency matches its own natural resonant frequency. In this way, resonance is *selective;* it acts as a *filter.*

10-8.1 Air Chamber Resonance

So far in this section we have examined solid objects that vibrate. However, when dealing with speech, we need to look at resonance in air-filled chambers, such as the mouth, pharynx, and nasal cavities.

Recall from Section 10-7 that when there is a sound wave whose half-wavelength fits exactly any number of times into an enclosed space, a standing wave pattern will be established. Because of the addition of the original and reflected waves, that specific frequency will be emphasized by the enclosed space. The air chamber will *resonate* at that specific frequency.

Other frequencies whose half-wavelength does not divide evenly into the length of the chamber will not be reinforced by the chamber, since the wave and its reflections will not be synchronized to create a standing-wave pattern. The air chamber resonator is selective, just like the solid object resonators we saw earlier in this section. If we took an air chamber resonator tuned to, say, 256 Hz, and introduced a 256-Hz tuning fork into it, that frequency would sound louder. But the sound of, say, a 200-Hz tuning fork would not be reinforced.

Although the air chamber resonator is selective, it is not selective for one frequency only. If you double a given frequency, you cut the wavelength in half. Therefore, if the original wavelength fits evenly into a given distance, so will half that wavelength (and other multiples of the frequency as well). (See Figure 10-16.)

Now imagine an air chamber resonator like that we considered earlier, but different in that its walls are slightly curved (Figure 10-17B). You can see that the distance between the walls is slightly variable. As a result, it is not tuned to a specific frequency; rather, *any* frequency within a small range will set up a standing wave, since a slightly longer wavelength (i.e., a lower frequency) will set up a standing wave where the walls are farther

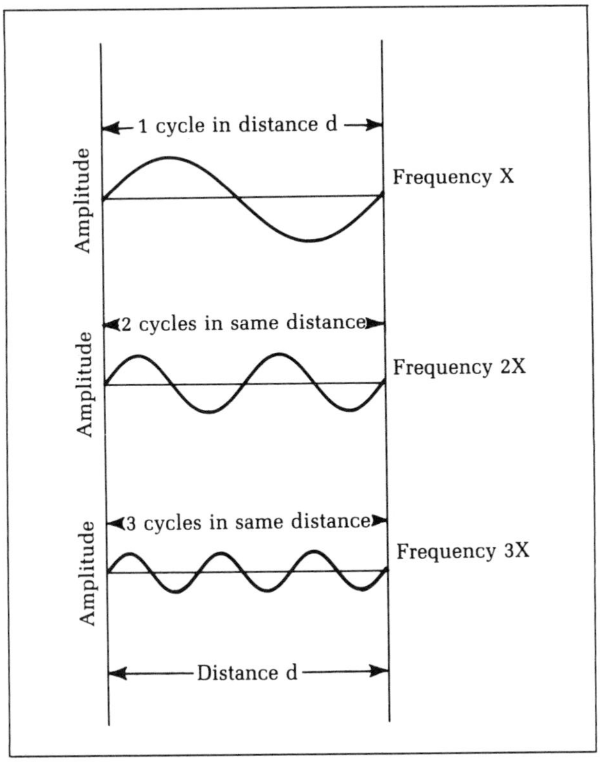

Figure 10-16. Resonance. If a wave of frequency X Hz has a wavelength that fits exactly into a resonator, then other frequencies, such as 2 X, 3 X, etc., will also fit exactly into the resonator. Thus a resonator tuned to a particular frequency will also be tuned to whole-number multiples of that frequency.

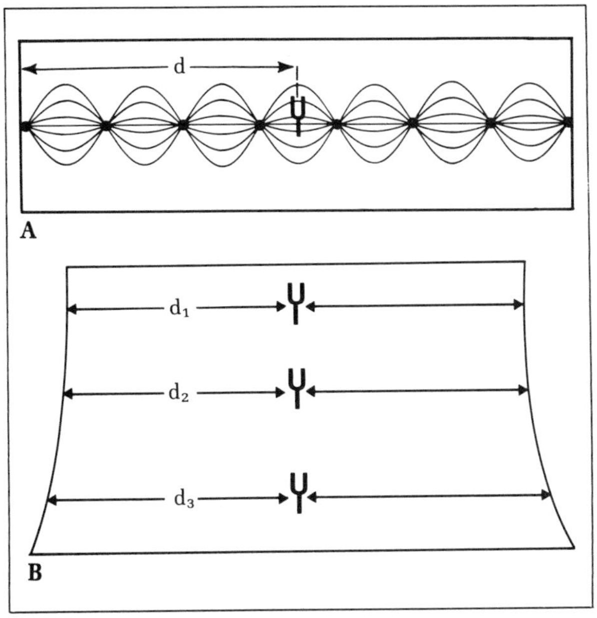

Figure 10-17. Tuning. A. A resonator with straight end walls. Because the distance (*d*) from source to reflection does not vary, this resonator resonates at a precise frequency, X Hz, and its multiples. B. In a resonator with curved walls the distance (d_1, d_2, d_3) from source to reflection varies, meaning that slightly different wavelengths will set up standing waves, or resonance. Therefore any of a *range* of frequencies, say 0.9 X to 1.1 X, will set up a standing wave. Resonator A is said to be sharply tuned, resonator B not sharply tuned.

apart, and a slightly shorter wavelength (a higher frequency) will set up a standing wave where the walls are closer together. So this resonator will reinforce a *range* of frequencies, whereas the straight-walled resonator (Figure 10-17A) is tuned to a very specific frequency. The resonator in Figure 10-17A is said to be **sharply tuned,** whereas that in Figure 10-17B is not sharply tuned.

Figure 10-18 shows the output spectrum of a sharply tuned resonator (as in Figure 10-17A) versus one that is less sharply tuned (as in Figure 10-17B). *The speech resonators, having complex shapes, tend not to be very sharply tuned.* Note that a resonator acts in a sense as a filter, in that it transfers some frequencies (those that establish standing waves) well, and that it transfers those frequencies that do not match its properties (i.e., no standing wave) poorly.

One more theoretical issue must be examined before we can look at how all of this applies to the vocal tract. The air space resonators we have looked at so far have had solid walls between which there is reflection. But the vocal tract (as well as piccolos, flutes, trumpets, etc.) is in effect *an open-ended tube* (the mouth is open throughout most of speech). How can there be reflection off the open end of a tube? There is, however. The reason is that, within the tube, the standing wave sets up rapid oscillations of pressure. Where these oscillations meet the relatively stable pressures outside the tube, there is such a mismatch of pressure and particle speed that there might as well be a solid wall. (An analogy might help at this point. Water is soft and will not support your weight if you try to stand on it. But if you belly-flop onto the water from a 10-meter diving board, you might as well have landed on a brick walkway. Similarly, a fast-moving stone will skip on the surface

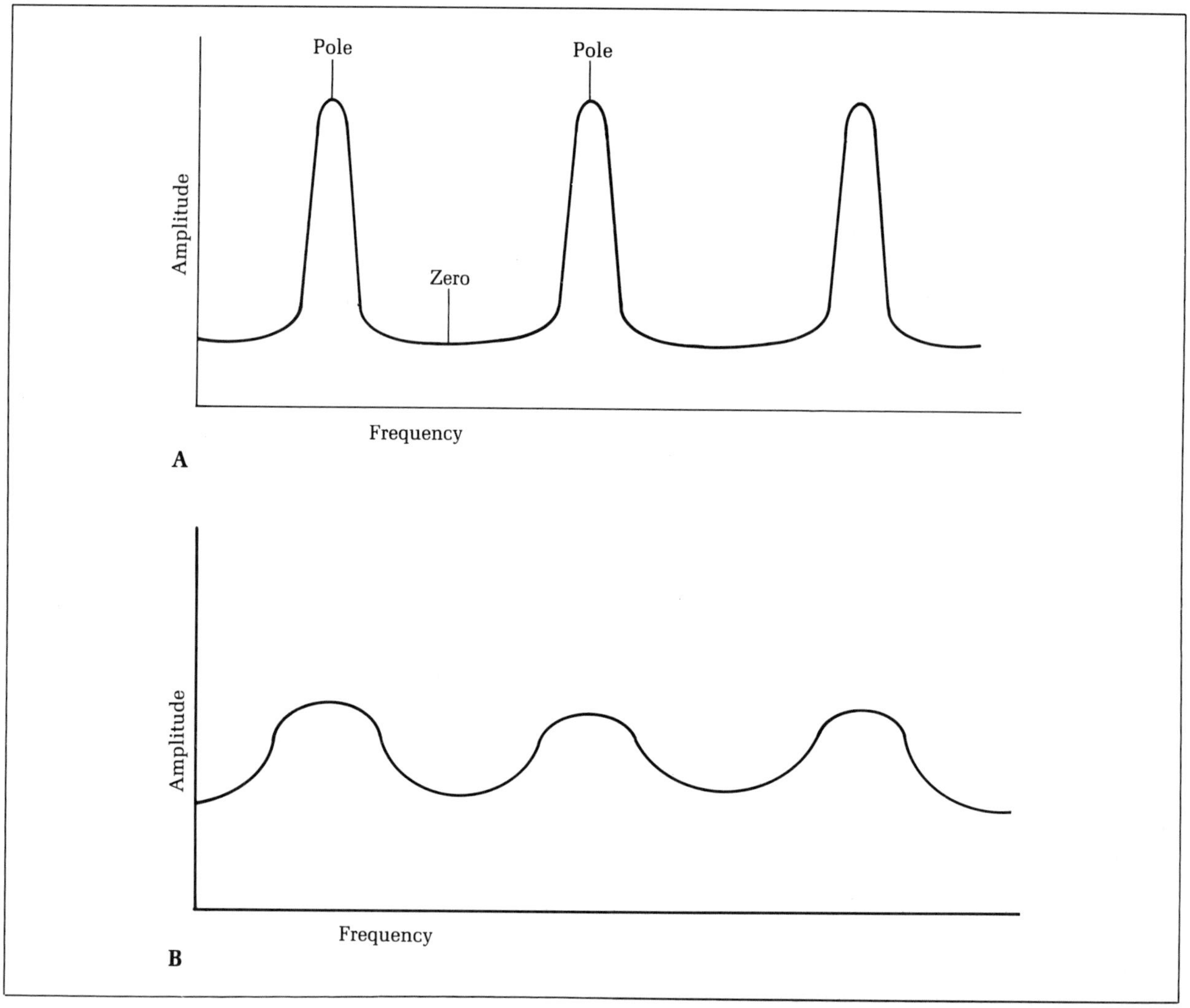

Figure 10-18. Tuning. A. A spectrum of a sharply tuned resonator, as in Figure 10-17A. B. A spectrum of a less sharply tuned resonator, as in Figure 10-17B. Both these spectra show the *transfer* through a given resonator. The peaks (technically, *poles*) are at frequencies that set up standing waves; the valleys (technically, *zeros*) are at frequencies where wave patterns cancel each other out. These spectra can be viewed as *filter* functions, in that they map the acoustic filtering of a given resonator.

of the water, but a stone that is not moving will sink. In the same way, the fast-moving pressure oscillations within an open-ended tube meet the still air outside the tube and are partially reflected.)

The point of reflection occurs in that part of the cycle where the air pressure is maximally different from normal air pressure (i.e., at a peak or trough in a graphic representation like Figures 10-2 and 10-3), so *in an open-ended resonator it is the one-quarter wavelength or three-quarter wavelength that is critical*, not the half wavelength as in the completely enclosed resonator. This is shown in Figure 10-19.

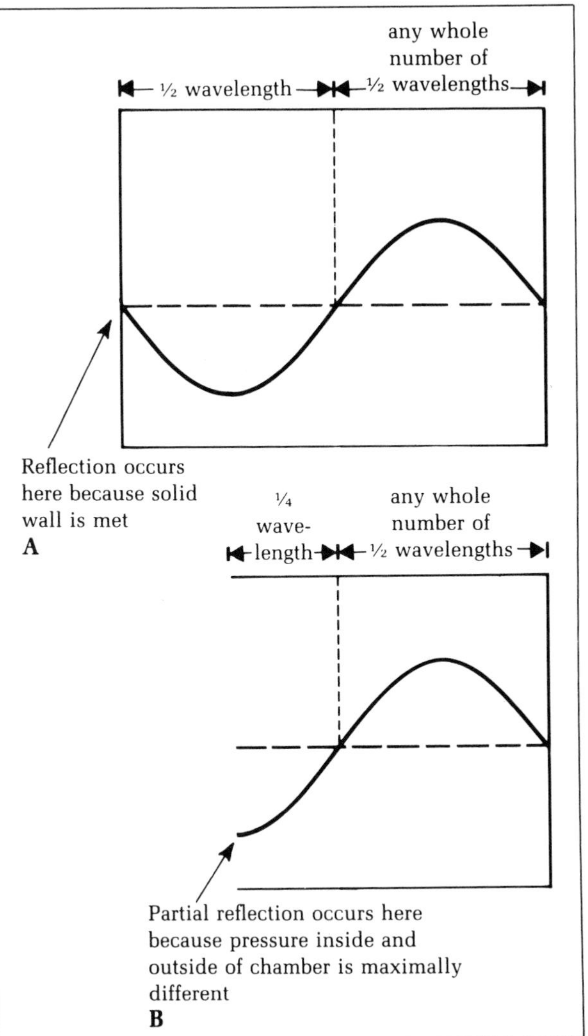

Figure 10-19. Resonance in open and closed resonators. A. Resonance within a closed resonator, the type we have examined up to this point. For resonance, there must be a whole number of nodes fitting within the length of the resonator, so the length of the resonator must be a multiple of the half-wavelength. B. Resonance within an open-ended resonator, such as the vocal tract. Reflection occurs at the open end at the point of maximum difference from normal air pressure (i.e., at a crest or trough, halfway between nodes). Halfway between nodes is one-half of a half wavelength, or one-quarter of a wavelength. Thus the critical length for resonance of an open-ended resonator must be either one-quarter or three-quarters of a wavelength (but not two-quarters or four-quarters, because there are nodes there). In both cases the neat fit is required—that is to say, some exact multiple of a fraction of the wavelength—because otherwise each successive reflection would put the crests and troughs at a different point. Hence there would be no standing wave and no reinforcement of that frequency.

An open-ended air space resonates when some external sound source introduces sound waves of the correct frequency or frequencies. This external source is said to **excite** resonance. The resonator resonates at its own natural frequency (frequencies), which is (are) dependent upon its physical dimensions. In this way it selects from any number of external frequencies the one or ones that match its own properties.

Try holding a drinking cup next to your ear in a room where music is playing loudly. You may hear it resonate every time a certain note is played.

Another everyday example: Blow across the neck of a bottle. The bottle emits a loud tone. What is creating this tone? Imagine that the bottle were separated from its neck and that you were blowing across the neck alone. The noise at the neck would be a hushing noise, an *aperiodic* sound (see Figure 10-4B), and that is all you would hear. But with the bottle intact, the neck is attached to a resonator that has its own natural frequencies. It selects from among all the different cycles of the aperiodic sound those that happen to coincide with the bottle's own frequency. Just those few cycles are enough to set up a standing wave, and the bottle emits a loud tone whose frequency corresponds to the wavelength of the standing wave.

Figure 10-20 shows a spectrum of a soft-drink bottle. This spectrum was obtained with a speech spectrograph (sonagraph), a sound analysis device used by phoneticians and speech scientists. The spectrum made with this device—called a **spectrogram** or **sonagram**—is oriented differently from the spectra shown in Figure 10-10 and 10-18. In Figure 10-20, frequency is shown on the y-axis (the vertical axis), time is shown on the x-axis (the horizontal axis), and amplitude is shown by the darkness of the shading. If you imagined the dark bands to be mountains rising out of the page, and you viewed those mountains from the right edge of the page, the graph would resemble Figure 10-18. However, Figure 10-20 shows changes over time, which Figure 10-18 does not, and that is why the graph has this form: speech is not a constant sound, but one that is changing over time, so the spectral graph must show change over time. Later in this chapter we will see spectrograms of speech.

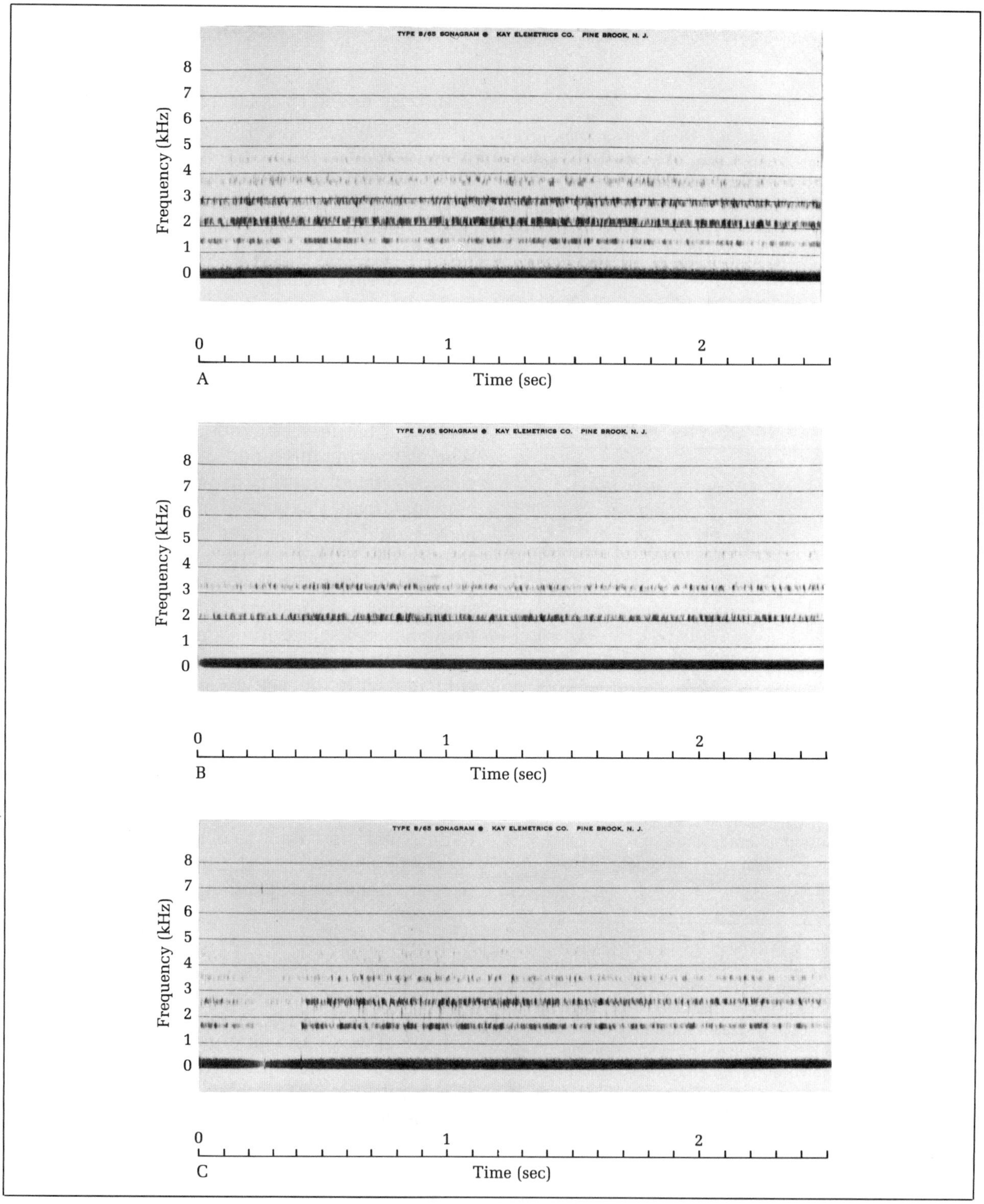

Figure 10-20. Spectrograms of soft-drink bottle resonators. The same bottle has been used each time, but its characteristics have been changed by filling it partially with different amounts of water. A. The empty bottle shows strong resonances at below 400 Hz, at about 1400 Hz, at about 2100 Hz, and at about 2900 Hz, with a weaker resonance at about 3800 Hz. B. The bottle partially filled with water shows strong resonances at below 400 Hz, at about 2100 Hz, and at about 3300 Hz, with a weaker resonance at about 4600 Hz. C. The same bottle with a different amount of water. What are the resonant frequencies this time?

In any case, Figure 10-20 shows that the soft-drink bottle chosen for the test has a strong resonant frequency below 400 Hz, one at about 1400 Hz, one at about 2100 Hz and one at about 2900 Hz. It is likely that both the height and the width of the bottle set up resonances.

If we chose a soft-drink bottle of a different size and shape, or if we put water in the original bottle to change the effective size and shape (as in Figure 10-20B,C), the resonant frequencies of the bottle would be different, since the standing wave would be set up in a different-sized dimension. You can demonstrate this to yourself by changing bottles or adding water: you can hear that the tone produced is different.

10-9 Acoustic Principles Applied to the Vocal Tract: The Vowels

We are now in a position to examine the speech production mechanism in light of the acoustic principles we have been examining. In this first part we will be looking at resonant, voiced speech sounds; that is, the vowels and a few consonants. Later we will look at nonresonant speech sounds such as the fricatives.

As explained in Section 10-5.1, the vibrating vocal folds emit an acoustic signal. This *glottal* signal has its own *fundamental frequency*, and it is accompanied by *harmonics* that are significant up to about 5000 Hz. Figure 10-10 shows the spectrum of this glottal or laryngeal signal. The glottal signal is relatively weak and would sound rather like a party noisemaker if it did not pass through the vocal cavities.

This glottal signal is produced in the throat, and any sound emitted must pass through the pharynx (throat cavity) and the oral cavity and/or the nasal cavities. These cavities together form an open-ended bent tube (if both oral and nasal cavities are open, it has two open ends). This tube has its own acoustic characteristics, which modify (filter) the signal passing through it.

What distinguishes this tube from, say, the soft-drink bottle we examined is that it has a highly complex, irregular shape and that its size and shape may be changed with tongue, velic, mandibular (jaw), and pharyngeal movements.

Each different configuration of the vocal tract has its own resonant frequencies, and the act of speaking involves moving the articulators into the appropriate positions in order to emit the appropriate frequencies.

The vocal tract, having a complex shape, resonates at several frequencies at once. For example, the arching of the tongue in the articulation of most vowels effectively separates the vocal tube into two parts: from the larynx to the arch, and from the arch to the lips. In complex resonators there tends to be interaction between the standing wave patterns in different parts of the vocal tract, giving rise to multiple resonances.

Resonant speech sounds tend to be characterized by three resonant frequencies; these are called **formants.** (Most vowels are recognizable if only the first two formants are audible but sound more natural if the first three are heard.) Higher-order formants (a fourth, fifth, sixth) are generally present in the acoustic signal, but they tend to be characteristic of the particular individual's voice quality rather than of the particular vowel.

The vowel /i/, for example, has formants at about 300, 2700, and 3300 Hz. Resonance at each of these frequencies is excited by the harmonics of the fundamental frequency. If there is a slight mismatch between the formant frequency and the harmonics, this is not a problem, since the vocal resonators are not sharply tuned. For example, if there is a formant at 2700 Hz and harmonics at 2600 and 2800 Hz (the fundamental being 200 Hz), both the harmonics are emphasized, and the listener hears the prominence in the 2700-Hz range.

The formants are numbered from lowest to highest: 300, 2700, and 3300 Hz are the *first formant, second formant,* and *third formant,* respectively, of the vowel /i/. This is abbreviated F_1, F_2, and F_3. The fundamental frequency of the voice is often considered the "zero-th" formant, and this explains the abbreviation F_0 for fundamental frequency introduced in Section 9-4.1.

Each vowel has its own characteristic set of formant frequencies. The vowel /ʊ/ has these frequencies: F_1, 470 Hz; F_2, 1160 Hz; and F_3, 2680 Hz; which are different from those of /i/ and of all other vowels.

When two different speakers pronounce the "same" vowel, they will not produce identically the same formant frequencies. Resonance depends upon the physical dimensions of the resonator, and after all we do not all have the same size of mouth. However, the *pattern* of frequencies, or ratio between them, tends to be constant. Adult males average lower formant frequencies than adult females, since on the average men's vocal resonators are larger. Children average still higher formant frequencies, but the *pattern* of all three groups is similar. Men, women, and children produce the "same" vowel with slightly different formants and very different fundamentals, but the similar *pattern* of formants leads us to perceive the vowel as the same.

You can change the F_0 without affecting the formants. Say /ɑ/ on a low note, a middle note, and a high note. If you keep the articulators fixed, the formants will be the same. The F_0 will change, and so, of course, will its harmonics, but in normal speech there is always a harmonic near enough to each formant to excite resonance at that formant.[7]

Figure 10-10 showed the spectral output of the glottal source. Figure 10-18 showed the resonant characteristics of a bottle resonator. If we made a graph of the resonant characteristics of a particular vocal tract configuration (in the style of Figure 10-18) and superimposed on it the glottal output of Figure 10-10, we would see the spectral characteristics of the given sound (Figure 10-21). The resonant characteristics of a resonator can be conceptualized as a filter, since the resonator lets pass much energy at frequencies corresponding to spectral **poles** (peaks) and does not let much through at the spectral **zeros** (valleys). The result, illustrated in Figure 10-21, is often called the **source-filter theory of speech production.**

Before looking at the spectra of the various vowels, we should reiterate the effect of the articulatory gestures on acoustic output. The shape and size of the vocal resonators are changed by the various articulatory gestures. In vowels, the arched tongue divides the oral cavity into two tubes (this is evident in all but low front vowels). The back vowels show this most clearly: the *high back* vowel makes a break in the front velar region, the *upper mid back* in the back velar region, the *lower mid back* in the upper pharyngeal region, and the *low back* in the mid pharyngeal region. In this series, the front tube (lips to arch) has gotten progressively longer, while the back tube (arch to larynx) has gotten progressively shorter, affecting the frequencies of F_1 and F_2 (Figure 10-22A–C).

Lax vowels are produced with a narrower pharynx than tense vowels: the width of the pharynx affects the acoustic characteristics of the vocal tract.

The shape and size of the opening at the lips is modified, although to a lesser extent in English than in some languages. While we did not examine the acoustic theory behind this adjustment, it is true that the shape and size of the opening of an open-ended resonator affects acoustic output. Compare, for example, /i/, having a narrow slit opening, with /ɪ/, having a slightly more open mouth configuration. This, along with tongue root position, accounts for some of the acoustic difference.

In some languages rounded vowels are articulated with greater rounding and protrusion of the lips than in English, and this has two acoustic effects: the rounding changes the shape of the opening, as noted in the previous paragraph, and the lip protrusion actually lengthens the resonating tube. The vowel /ü/, for example, is articulated exactly like a /i/, except that the lips are tightly rounded and everted (protruded) as for whistling. The two vowels sound very different (see Section 4-8.1). The difference in vocal tract length brought about by lip-rounding and spreading is illustrated in Figure 10-22D and E.

The very low vowels may be produced with a resonator so high (from palate to tongue) that the height of the oral cavity has its own resonant contribution to make.

Nasalized vowels are produced with a lowered velum, permitting resonance within the nasal

[7] Opera sopranos sometimes hit such high notes—500 or 600 Hz—that there is a great gap between harmonics. As a result, there is sometimes no harmonic anywhere near a formant, so resonance is not excited at the formant frequency. Since the formants are the essential information needed by the listener, the vowel is unintelligible if they are missing. For this reason, operatic singing is often unintelligible at the higher ranges.

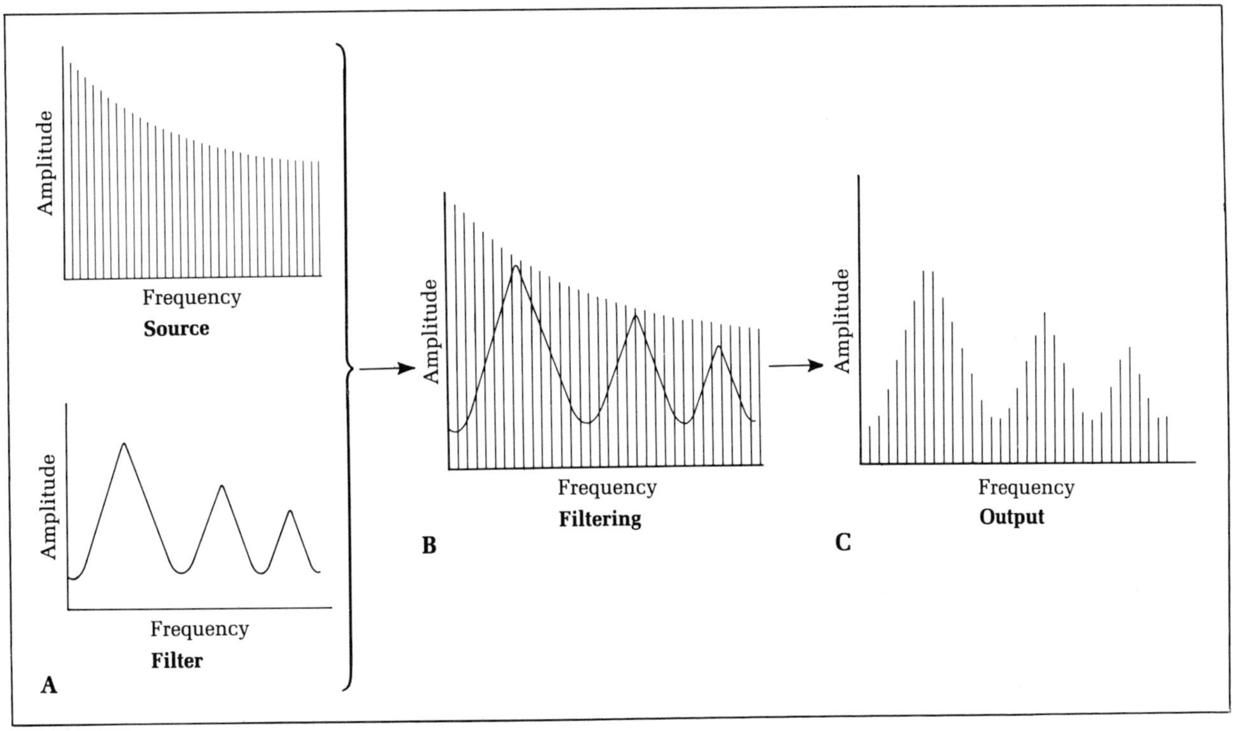

Figure 10-21. The source-filter theory of vowel production. A. *Top*, a spectrum of the *glottal source* as shown in Figure 10-10. This is the *input* or **source.** *Bottom*, the resonant characteristics of the vocal tract, as in the style of Figure 10-18. The vocal tract resonator can be conceptualized as a **filter,** since it transfers some frequencies better than others. B. The **filter** superimposed on the **source.** C. The resultant vocalic output, as explained by the **source-filter theory.** Those harmonics that fall at or near the peaks (poles) of resonance are transferred with high amplitude and are heard by the listener. Those harmonics that fall in the valleys (zeros) of resonance are transferred with low amplitude and are heard less well.

cavities. But as noted in Section 9-2, the turbinates in the nasal cavities break up these cavities into small passageways that are poor resonators. The effect is that the nasal passages are considered to be **antiresonators.**

Let us look now at Figures 10-23 through 10-31, which are spectrograms of the vowels of American English. They show the acoustic components of the vowel sounds of the speech of an adult male and were made with a commercially available Kay Elemetrics Sona-Graph digital sound spectrograph.[8] Other details of technical interest are that a wide-band filter was used in the analysis and that the sounds were recorded with a high-frequency preemphasis normally used for speech.

The salient features to look for in the spectrograms are as follows: (1) The **frequency scale** is shown along the vertical axis. (2) the **time scale** is shown along the horizontal axis. (3) The **amplitude** is shown by the darkness of the shading: the darker the shading, the greater the amplitude. (4) The **formants** show up as darker bands (a few have been labeled to aid identification). (5) The **vertical striations** visible in the spectrograms reflect individual cycles of the glottal frequency, each vertical line representing the opening of the vocal folds (the higher the pitch of the voice, the closer together these would be). (6) The formant frequencies change for the diphthongs. (7) The long vowels /i,e,o,u/ are slightly diphthongized, as shown by the change in formant frequencies.

[8]Kay Elemetrics Corporation, 12 Maple Avenue, Pine Brook, New Jersey 01058.

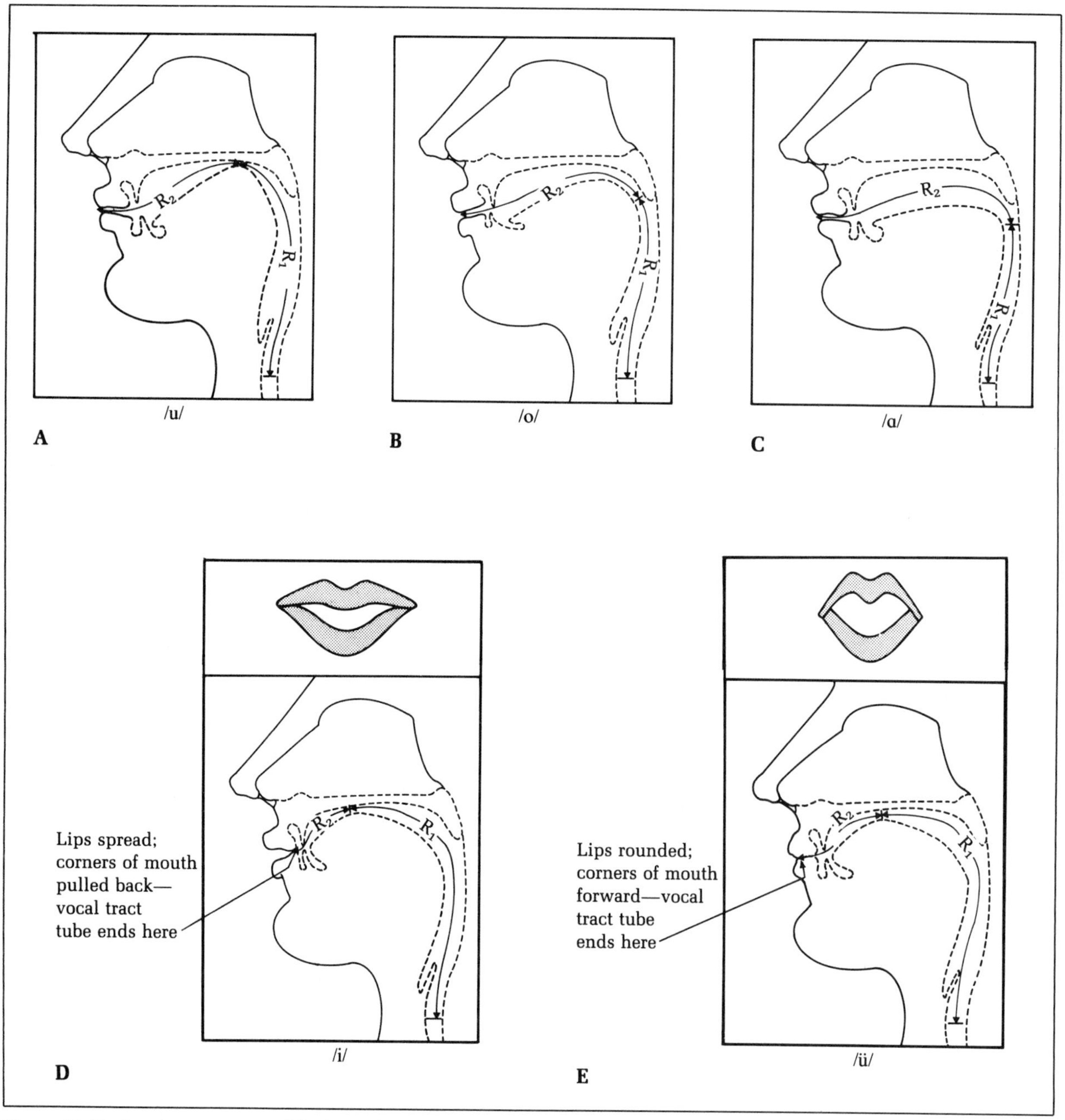

Figure 10-22. A two-resonator model of speech. A simplified view of vowel production is that there are two resonators responsible for F_1 and F_2 (this ignores interactions but is a useful starting point). Note that different articulations change the size of the resonators and therefore of the formant frequencies. A. /u/. B. /o/. C. /ɑ/. Notice that, in progressing through this sequence of vowels, the pharyngeal resonator (marked R_1) gets shorter (therefore resonating at a higher frequency), and the oral resonator (R_2) gets longer. D. /i/. E. /ü/. Notice that the tongue position is the same for these vowels, although /i/ is lip-spread and /ü/ is lip-rounded. Notice how lip-rounding extends forward the point at which the vocal tract "tube" ends (that is, meets the external normal air pressure). Thus the forward resonator (R_2) is much longer in rounded than in spread vowels. (In addition, the size of the opening of a resonating tube plays a role in the acoustic effect; the much smaller oral opening in rounded than in spread vowels is likely to affect acoustic output. However, the acoustic theory behind this has not been introduced in this chapter.)

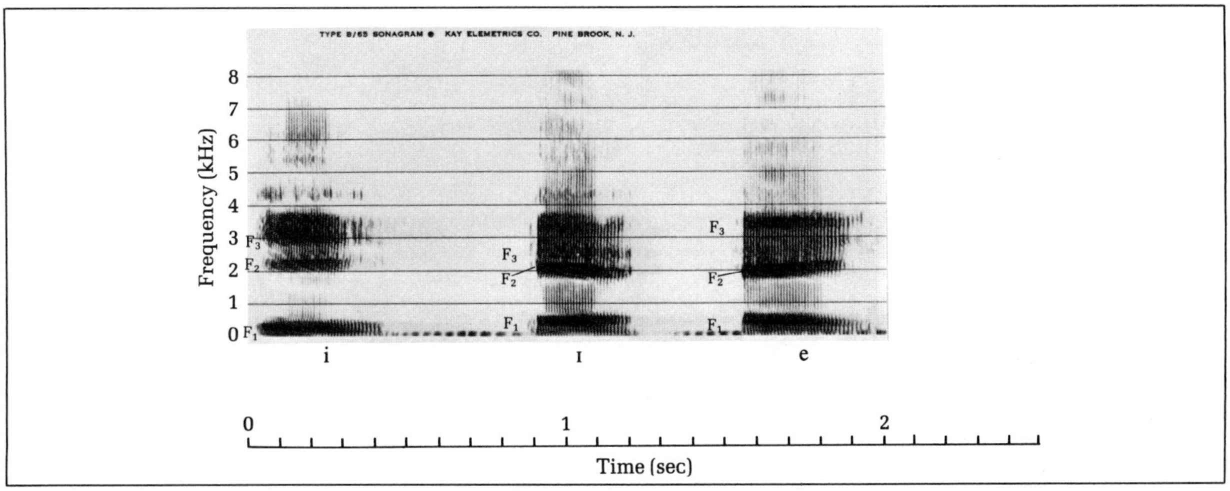

Figure 10-23. Spectrogram of [i ɪ e]. The formants have been marked for you on this spectrogram only.

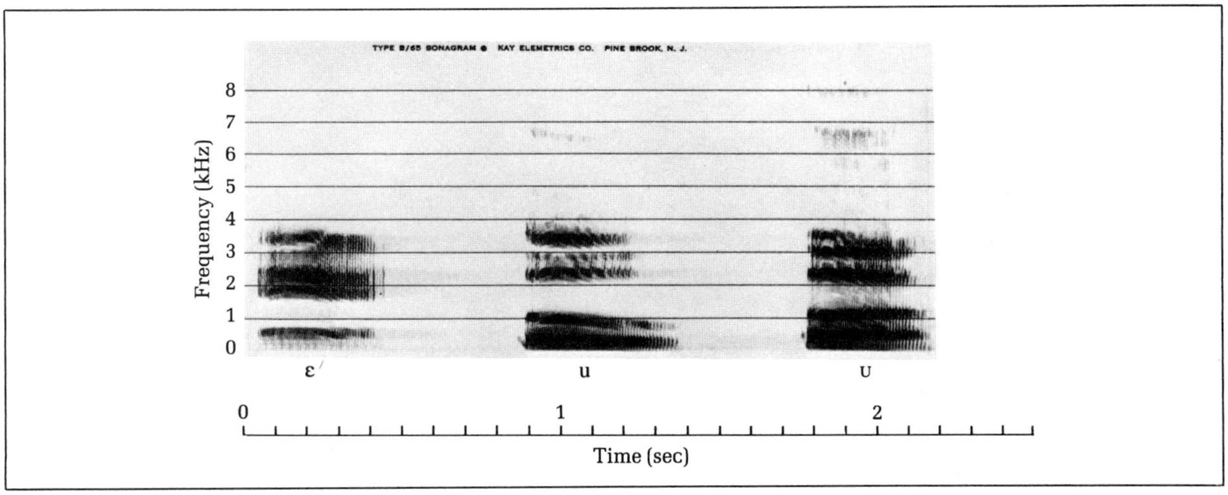

Figure 10-24. Spectrogram of [ɛ u ʊ].

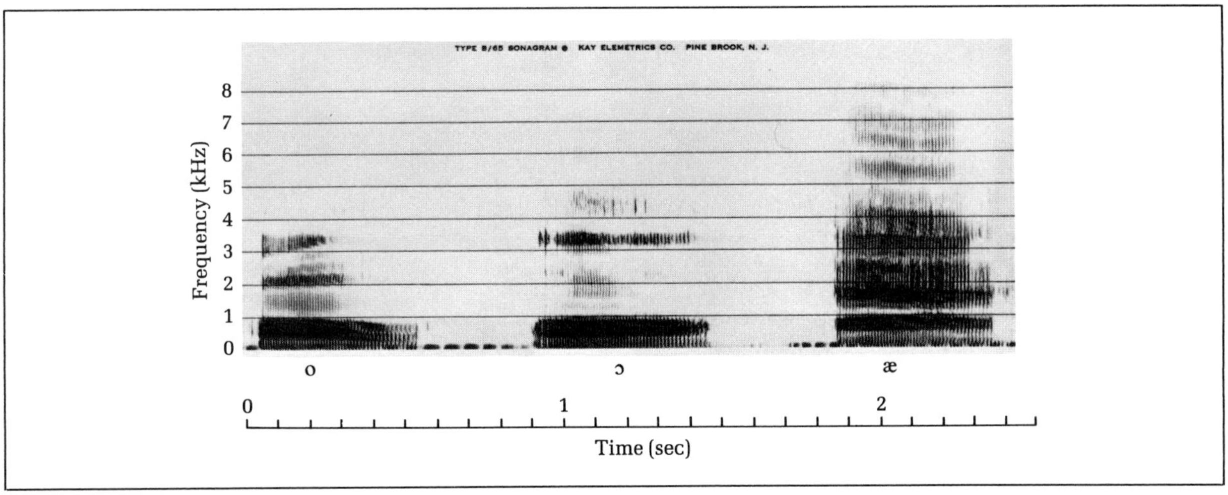

Figure 10-25. Spectrogram of [o ɔ æ].

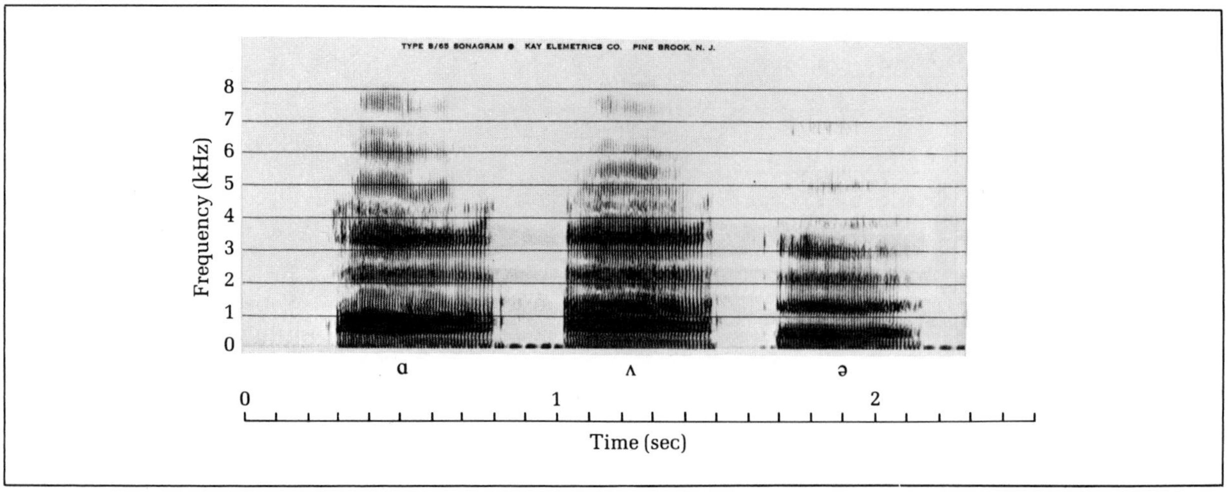

Figure 10-26. Spectrogram of [ɑ ʌ ə].

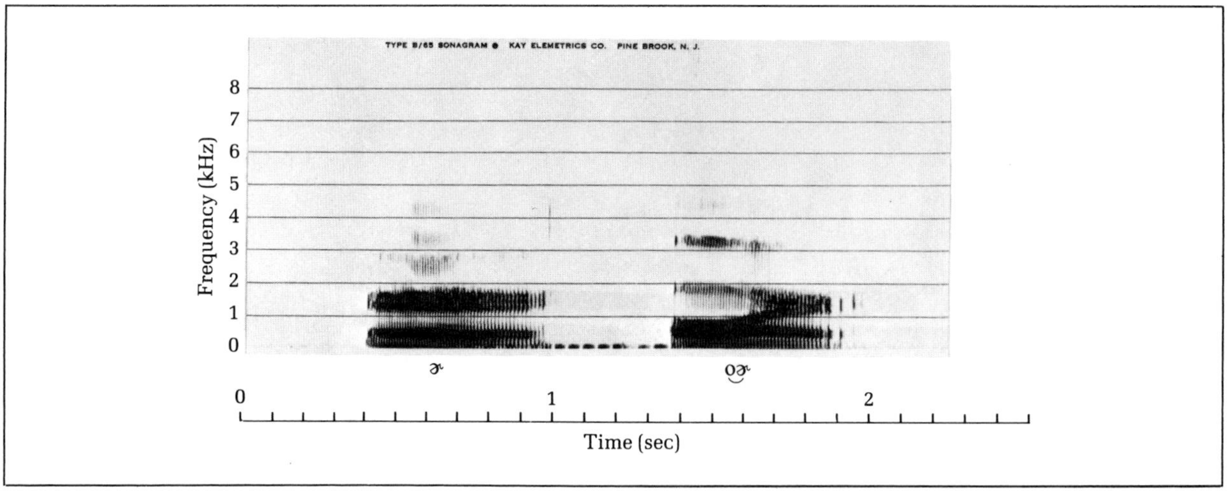

Figure 10-27. Spectrogram of [ɚ o͜ɚ].

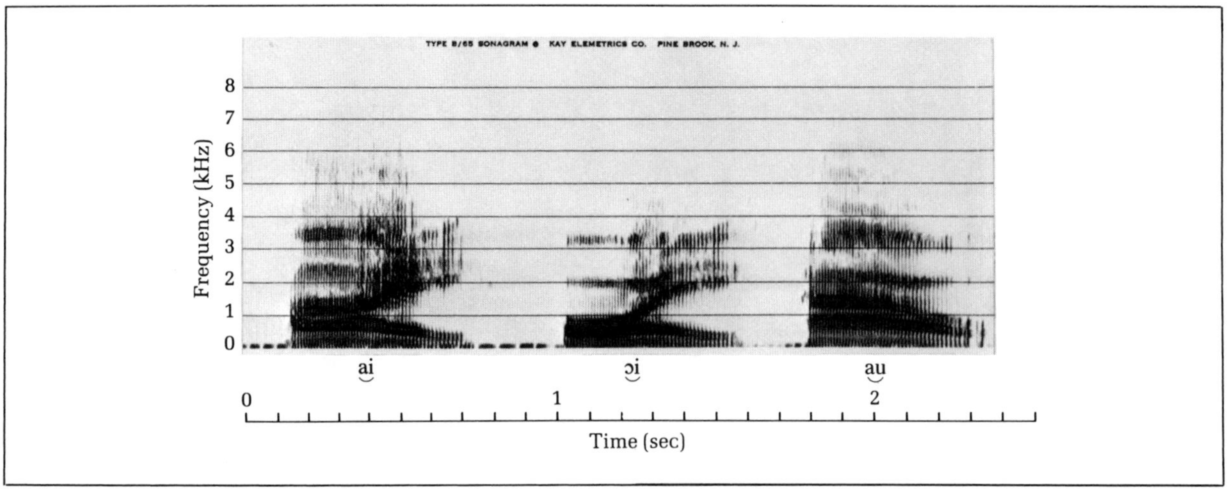

Figure 10-28. Spectrogram of [a͜i ɔ͜i a͜u].

10-10 Acoustic Principles Applied to the Vocal Tract: The Consonants

10-10.1 The Plosives

Of all the speech sounds, the plosives have the most peculiar acoustic pattern, for after all, during most of the time that the plosive is being articulated, the mouth is closed and little or no sound is coming out. During this phase of the articulation, the spectrogram is primarily blank, showing relative silence.

You recall that English voiceless plosives in certain positions are articulated with greater intraoral air pressure and are released with a stronger puff of air than the voiced stops. This puff of air is called **aspiration** and is visible on the spectrograms of the voiceless plosives. It shows up in Figure 10-32 (p. 277) as a shading covering a wide frequency range at the end of the blank occlusion phase, very brief in duration, and immediately preceding the second vowel. (The vowel begins with the visible vertical striations representing voicing.) Often the aspiration shows up as an abrupt vertical pattern on the spectrogram (seen most clearly in Figure 10-32 in the spectrum of /ətɑ́/) and may therefore be called an *aspiration spike*.

The presence of the aspiration noise serves two functions in the perception of speech. First, its presence is one cue to voicelessness. Second, it appears that the characteristics of this burst of noise vary with the place of articulation. So aspiration provides one cue to place of articulation.

Figure 10-33 shows a spectrographic analysis of intervocalic voiced plosives in English. As you will recall from Section 5-2.12, such plosives are fully and continuously voiced because the preceding and following segments are also voiced. During their occlusion phase, the mouth is closed, and not much sound is allowed to escape. The voicing shows up on the spectrogram as a low-frequency **voice murmur** during the occlusion phase (the phase that shows up blank on spectrograms of voiceless plosives). This can be seen in Figure 10-33.

> In Section 5-2.12 we discussed voice onset time (VOT) in a number of situations. The voiced plosives in Figure 10-33 are continuously voiced, so VOT does not apply (there can be no *onset* of voicing in one segment if the sequence of sounds is continuously voiced). *Voiceless* plosives, on the other hand, have a *positive* VOT, as you will recall, which means that voicing starts *after* release. In Figure 10-32, release is visible as the *aspiration spike* mentioned previously, and you can see that the vowel starts a little later than the spike; this delay is the positive voice onset time.
>
> VOT in *word-initial voiced* plosives, as you will recall from Section 5-2.12, may be slightly negative, zero, or slightly positive. Since there is no (or very little) aspiration in voiced plosives, their release usually makes no noise, and is therefore seldom visible on a sound spectrogram. In order to make VOT measurements of voiced plosives and of nonaspirated voiceless plosives, special equipment is needed that senses the articulatory movement of release and translates it such that it is visible on the spectrogram. Thus it becomes possible to see relative timing of release and the voicing of the following segment, and VOT can be measured.
>
> VOT is an important perceptual cue to voicing in plosives; it helps distinguish /p/ from /b/, /t/ from /d/, and /k/ from /g/.

Figures 10-32 and 10-33 show that F_1 and F_2 of the vowel following the plosive change in frequency in the first 40 to 50 milliseconds (thousandths of a second) after the release of the plosive and that the pattern of this change is different for each plosive. Thus, the main acoustic difference distinguishing plosives having different places of articulation is a small change—lasting a few milliseconds—in the frequency of the formants of the following vowel. These changes are called **formant transitions,** and they represent the primary feature that the ear receives and the brain decodes to perceive individual plosives.

Let us look at these formant transitions in isolation, in stylized drawings. In Figure 10-29, the basic transitional patterns are shown for plosives followed by the vowel /ɑ/. What happens when a different vowel follows the plosive? As can be seen in Figure 10-30, the transitions are different for each combination of plosive and vowel. However, this does not mean that the syllables /di/, /dɛ/, and /dɑ/, for example, have nothing in common. Let us superimpose the stylized formants for these syllables (Figure 10-31). Notice that the F_2 transi-

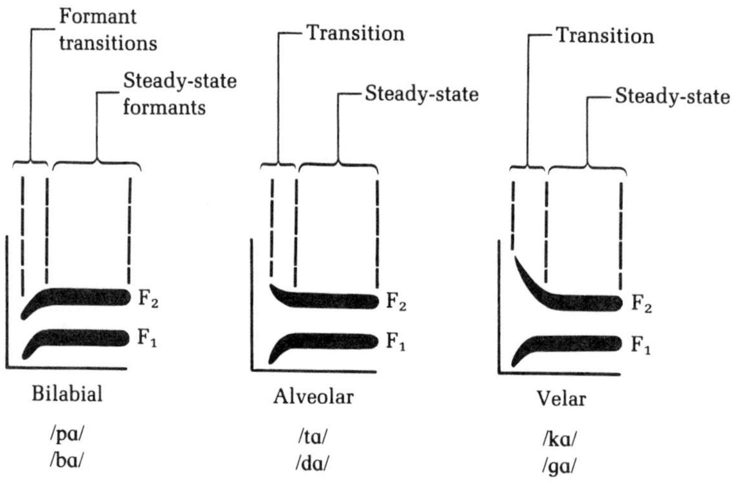

Figure 10-29. Stylized spectrograms showing formant transitions for plosives of each place of articulation and the vowel [ɑ]. The formants are determined by the vowel (note that these remain constant for all syllables containing the vowel [ɑ]), but the shape and direction of the transition is determined by the place of articulation of the plosive. Thus the transitions for [pɑ] and [bɑ] are similar, as are those for [tɑ] and [dɑ], as well as those for [kɑ] and [gɑ]. The members of the pairs are distinguished by other factors, as discussed in the text. The formant transitions (in concert with other acoustic factors) are perceived by the ear as the plosive consonant; the stable period is perceived as the vowel.

tions for all the syllables beginning with /d/ point to the same spot; the F_1 transitions all point to another, different spot. The other syllables beginning with /d/ would have transitions pointing to the same spot as well. Each of these spots (x in Figure 10-31) is called a **locus** (plural, **loci**); notice that their actual location on the spectrogram is in the silent portion of the plosive articulation. As can be seen by extrapolating the formants in Figure 10-30, the labials and velars each have distinctive loci, and the locus for F_2 is different for each place of articulation. (That is, extend the formant transitions backward in the direction they point to, such that they meet, as was done in Figure 10-31. The meeting point for all the extrapolated F_2 transitions of syllables beginning with the same plosive indicates the frequency of the locus for that place of articulation. Note that there are two different F_2 loci for velars; the division comes between /gɑ/ and /go/ in Figure 10-30.)

The formant transitions appear at the *end* of the vowel when the plosive *follows* the vowel, and if the plosive is situated between two vowels, there are two sets of transitions: those leading into and those leading out of the plosive. For this reason, plosives are likely to be more intelligible when situated intervocalically than at the beginning of a word, preceding a vowel. Plosives situated at the end of a word are least intelligible.

Finally, note in Figure 10-39 that the final /t/ of the sentence is not released; therefore no aspiration indicative of release is visible in the spectrogram.

The acoustic shape of plosive consonants suggests that our perceptual mechanism is quite remarkable. Consider, for example, the fact that if formant frequencies change slowly, we perceive a diphthong, while rapid formant transitions are perceived as a sequence of consonant plus vowel. As another example, a plosive consonant such as /d/ does not have a single unchanging acoustic quality; rather, the syllables /di/ and /dɑ/ appear to be less similar acoustically than are /bi/ and /di/. Apparently our perceptual mechanism abstracts the loci and identifies them, even though they are just hypothetical dots on a graph in a period of relative silence.

In summary, several acoustic cues lead to our perception of different plosives: (1) voiced and voiceless plosives having the *same* place of articu-

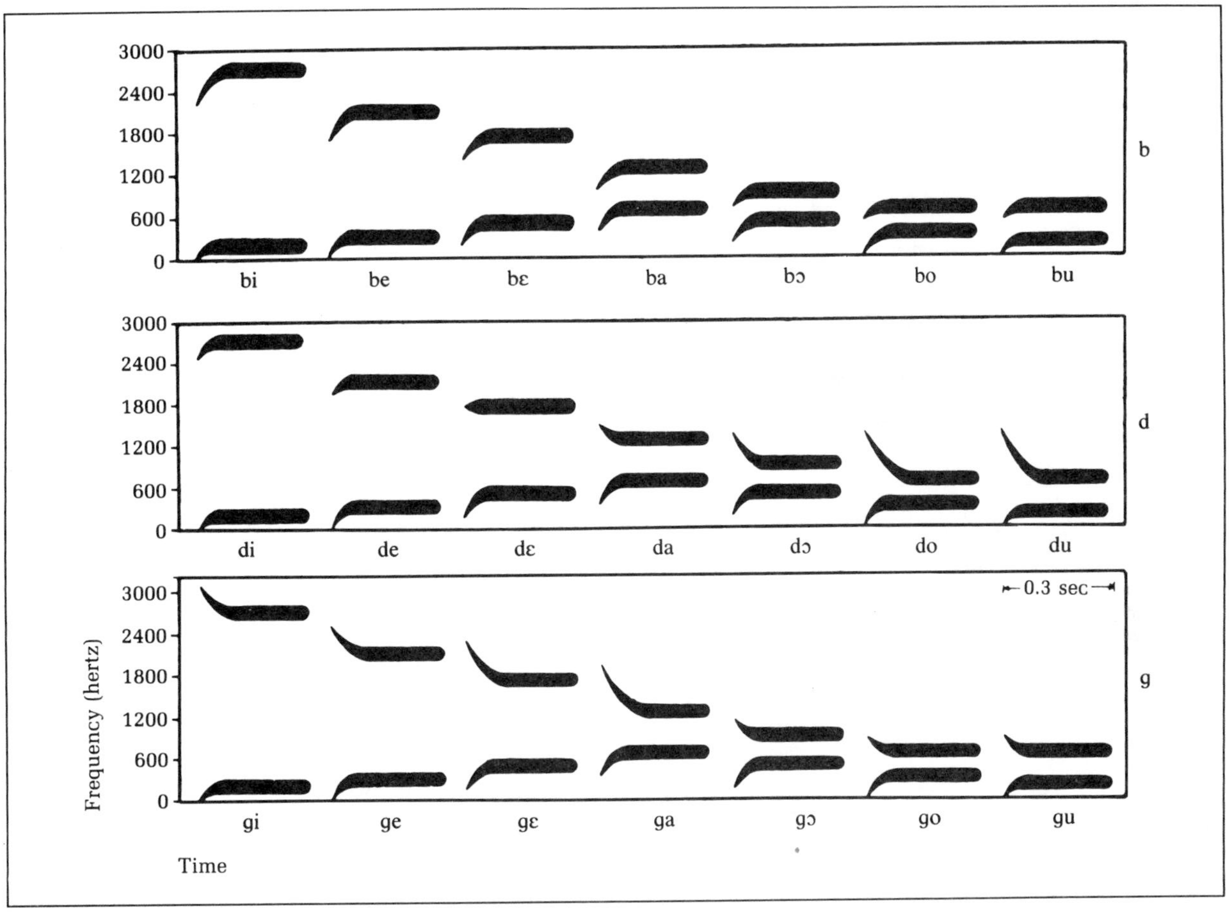

Figure 10-30. Spectrograms of synthetically produced syllables, showing second-formant transitions that produce the voiced plosives before various vowels. (From Pierre C. Delattre, Alvin M. Liberman, and Franklin S. Cooper, Acoustic Loci and Transitional Cues for Consonants. *Journal of the Acoustical Society of America*, Vol 27, July 1955. Used by permission of the authors and the American Institute of Physics.)

lation are distinguished by aspiration and voice onset time; and (2) different places of articulation are distinguished by patterns of formant transitions, as well as by the noise burst of aspiration, when this is present.

10-10.2 The Fricatives

Fricatives are produced with audible air turbulence. This turbulence creates "noise," that is, sound that is aperiodic in nature. Aperiodic sound shows up on the spectrogram as an uneven shading across a wide frequency range. (Aperiodic sounds have no regular period, but contain individual cycles having many different periods. So when they are analyzed acoustically, they show their various components, which appear on the spectrogram as a shaded area extending over a range of frequencies corresponding to the component cycles of the aperiodic wave.) Aspiration, mentioned in Section 10-10.1, is aperiodic; acoustically it is like a fricative.

In order to produce the frictional sound of a fricative, a certain minimum airflow must pass through a minimum constriction. The shape of the constriction is also relevant and plays a role in the sound produced; hence the importance of the slit fricative–grooved fricative distinction mentioned in Section 5-3.3. Also, the acoustic output is subject to modification as a result of resonance within the oral cavity; this accounts for the importance of lip-rounding in producing [š].

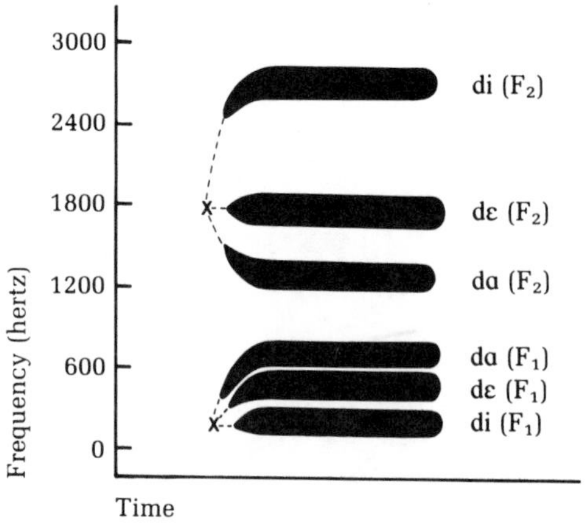

Figure 10-31. The loci of the formant transitions of the alveolar plosives /d/ and /t/. While the shape of the formant transition changes according to the formant frequency of the following vowel, the locus remains constant. That is, the formant transitions of the alveolar plosives always "point" to the same frequency (x in the illustration), no matter what vowel follows. It is thus the frequency of the locus that our ear perceives in identifying the place of articulation of the plosive consonant.

Figure 10-34 shows that each of the voiceless fricatives has a distinct pattern of aperiodic noise: /f/ has a frequency of 1500 to 8000 Hz (actually higher, but the upper limit for the standard spectrogram is 8000 Hz); /θ/ has a similar frequency range, although its lower limit is closer to 1000 Hz and it is much weaker overall; /s/ has a frequency of 3500 to 8000 Hz; and /š/ has a range from about 1500 to 7500 Hz. Each fricative is identified by a distinctive frequency range, and this agrees with our intuitions. For example, /s/ sounds higher to us than /š/.

You will note another difference among the fricatives. Some show up darker than others on the spectrograms. Darkness is an indicator of amplitude (loudness), so you can see that there are differences in loudness among the various fricatives. /s/ and /š/ appear as the loudest; /f/ is considerably less loud; and /θ/ shows up as being quite weak. This agrees with our intuition, for it is easy to demonstrate that /s/ can be said much louder than /θ/. (This was discussed in regard to *stridency* in Section 5-3.7.)

Thus, the fricatives are perceived through their two salient acoustic features: (1) the frequency range of their aperiodic sound and (2) their relative loudness.

A third feature, voicing, comes into play to distinguish voiceless fricatives from their voiced cognates. This can be seen in Figure 10-35, the spectrogram of the voiced fricatives. Note that vertical striations, representing voicing, are visible as the fricative is articulated. They tend to obscure the aperiodic sound to some degree on the spectrogram, but for the most part it should be possible to see the simultaneous voicing and aperiodic sound.

In all cases, the aperiodic noise of the voiced fricatives has less loudness than that of the voiceless fricative. This is clearly visible when the spectrograms of /əsɑ́/ and /əzɑ́/ are compared. The reason relates to the articulation of these sounds. In voiced sounds, the amount of air that may pass out of the lungs is restricted by the vocal folds, which open and close rhythmically. The decreased amount of air and decreased pressure reduce the amount of turbulence and hence the loudness of the voiced fricative sounds.

10-10.3 The Approximants

Figure 10-36 gives spectrograms of four approximants surrounded by the vowels /ə/ and /ɑ́/. These syllables resemble diphthongs as much as they do consonant-vowel sequences. The approximants show distinct formant patterns, just like the vowels. This is most obvious in the case of /j/. It is less apparent on the spectrograms of /r/, /w/, and /l/ because of the degree of oral closure, which renders the upper formants (F_3, F_4, etc.) very weak.

10-10.4 The Nasals

As can be seen in Figure 10-37, the nasals have formant patterns, similar to those of the vowels, that serve to identify particular speech sounds. The nasals show a slightly reduced loudness as compared to the accompanying vowels. This is the result of oral closure.

10-10.5 The Glottal Stop and Fricative

In Figure 10-38 the glottal stop appears to be similar to the plosives in having a period of silence and a slight delay in the onset of voicing; however, it lacks the formant transitions characteristic of other plosives. The formant transitions in the other plosives are a result of the changing resonant qualities of the oral cavity as the articulators move from the position for the plosive to the position for the following vowel. With the glottal stop, there is no such movement and therefore no formant transitions.

The glottal fricative /h/ (Figure 10-38) shows an acoustic pattern as do the other fricatives. One essential difference is that the aperiodic noise tends to center around the frequencies of the formants of the following vowel. This is because /h/ is pronounced with the oral configuration of the following vowel, which means that the oral cavity has the same resonant characteristics as it does for the vowel that follows; and while there is no glottal pulsing (voicing), noise at or near the formant frequencies is emphasized. Like the tone produced from a soft-drink bottle, the source is an aperiodic sound, in this case created primarily at the narrowed glottis. Those cycles of the aperiodic sound that match the resonant characteristics of the vocal tract excite resonance. /h/ therefore is in effect a *noise-excited vowel*. Figure 10-38 also shows [ɦ], a voiced glottal fricative, in fact produced with breathy voicing (see Section 9-4.3).

10-10.6 The Sentence

Let us look at the spectrogram of a sentence (Figure 10-39) in order to see what can be learned about the acoustic shape of units longer than one syllable. Some of the features mentioned here are the subject of more detailed discussions elsewhere in the book.

Perhaps the most immediately apparent feature of the sentence is the way that the words are run together. Because of the emphasis placed on writing, we tend to think of words as distinct items separated from other words by a space, not only on paper but in time as well. In speech, however, there is usually no space of time left between words. The sentence "Joe took father's shoe-bench out" is pronounced as if it were a single seven-syllable word. Remember that plosives are characterized by silence during their closure phase, and so the apparent space between "Joe" and "took" is only the articulation of /t/, not a pause.

Second, notice the way similar sounds are modified in context. In the sequence "father's shoe-," there is a /z/ followed by a /š/, but notice that only the /š/ shows up; the /z/ is not pronounced. Such phenomena were considered in Chapter 6.

Third, examine the vertical striations representing individual pulses of the vocal folds. Notice how the distance between them varies. A change in this distance represents a change in the fundamental frequency; the further they are apart, the lower is the fundamental frequency. Notice how the frequency drops through the phrase "Joe took father's," rises sharply on "shoe," and drops to its lowest point on "out." Such patterns of frequency are known as **intonation,** which was discussed in Chapter 7.

10-10.7 Flaps and Trills

Figure 10-40 shows a flap and a trill. Note the very brief occlusion for the flap and the rapid series of occlusions for the trill. A third rhotic sound is also shown.

10-10.8 Stress

As shown in Chapter 7, stress is a combination of factors. No single factor is a sine qua non for the perception of stress. A reduction in assimilation, an increase in length, a change in F_0 (a rise or a fall), or an increase in amplitude may signal stress.

Even amplitude changes do not function in a simple fashion. That is to say, one cannot simply assume that greater stress corresponds to some given level of amplitude. The low vowels are produced with a more open vocal tract than the high vowels. More acoustic energy is therefore emitted during their production. An [ɑ], for example, normally has greater amplitude than an [i], so an [ɑ] under **secondary** stress may actually have greater amplitude than an [i] under primary stress. However, the degree of stress perceived by the listener is relative to the normal range of amplitude of the vowel in question, not to an absolute measure of amplitude. So, while a primary-stressed [i] may actually be less loud than a secondary-stressed [ɑ], the listener still perceives it as having greater stress.

While stress information is carried primarily by the vowels, individual consonants have their own characteristic amplitudes. The release of plosives in particular often has a strong burst of energy, especially the aspirated voiceless ones. The overall amplitude of the syllable may thus be affected by the consonant that begins it. Again, our perceptual mechanism factors this out, since we know the "normal" amplitude of each consonant.

These facts mean that we cannot simply build a machine to measure amplitude and use it as an instrumental measure of what we perceive as stress in words. This should be borne in mind in looking at spectrograms that show an amplitude analysis (Figures 10-41 and 10-42). Remember, too, that F_0, length, and assimilation may override amplitude in the perception of stress. Figures 10-41 and 10-42 use two nonsense words in which there are no differing vowels and consonants, so that it is possible to concentrate on the amplitude alone. The nonsense words "zozozo" and "beebeebee" were pronounced with the stress pattern of the word "pimento" and were said in a natural fashion as if they were ordinary English words. This yielded the pronunciations [zə̂zózò] and [bə̂bíbì] with normal vowel reductions.

An amplitude analysis has been added to the upper part of each spectrogram. It is synchronized with the usual spectral analysis; that is, the amplitude analysis "lines up" with the usual spectrographic display. Amplitude is shown by a line that rises with higher amplitude and falls with lower amplitude.

In Figure 10-41, the relative amplitudes of the three vowels can be seen. They follow the expected pattern: the highest peak is in the primary-stressed (second) syllable; the second-highest peak is in the secondary-stressed (final) syllable; and the lowest peak is in the weakly stressed (first) syllable. Notice other cues to stress visible in this spectrogram: the second syllable is the longest syllable, and its vowel is more diphthongized than those of the other syllables.

In Figure 10-42 ([zə̂zózò] and [bə̂bíbì]), the situation is complicated by the high-amplitude plosive release, whose result is that all syllables seem to have high energy. The first syllable, actually the most weakly stressed, appears to have quite high amplitude because of the strong release of the word-initial plosive. The amplitude level of all three syllables appears to be quite similar, so clearly other cues to stress are present. The primary-stressed (second) syllable holds its high amplitude for a longer period than the final syllable, whose amplitude level drops quickly. The second syllable shows more diphthongization than the final syllable (shown by the formant frequencies). The weakly stressed (first) syllable is short, and the formant pattern of its vowel indicates that it is reduced to schwa.

In summary, we have seen in Figures 10-41 and 10-42 several acoustic parameters that play a role in the perception of stress: (1) amplitude (relative to the normal amplitude for that vowel or consonant), (2) length (relative to the intrinsic length of the sounds in question), and (3) vowel quality (including reduction and diphthongization). The role of F_0 and accommodation has not been shown in these spectrograms.

Figures 10-43 through 10-46 show acoustic analyses of intonation, whispered speech, esophageal speech and speech with an electrolarynx (synthetic larynx), and computer-synthesized speech, respectively.

10-11 Speech Perception

In this section we will look briefly at the process by which speech is perceived. Research into speech perception is ongoing, and a single definitive theory has not been established. A detailed discussion of the merits of the various current theories of speech perception is beyond the scope of this text; rather, our purpose will be to start you thinking about the process of perceiving speech. Most of the readers of this book will be students of communication disorders or linguistics or language teaching rather than students of speech science per se. Therefore it would be useful at this stage of study to learn about the nature of the process rather than the details of the arguments of the various theories, although we will summarize those theories in Section 10-11.6.

10-11.1 Acoustic Features

What all theories of speech perception have in common, naturally enough, is that they pay some attention to the acoustic parameters of speech. That is, the various acoustic characteristics of speech that we examined briefly in Sections 10-9 and 10-10 must be important cues to what was said. What the various theories differ about is the way in which those cues are used. More on this later. In the meantime, we would do well to examine further some fallacious assumptions that are

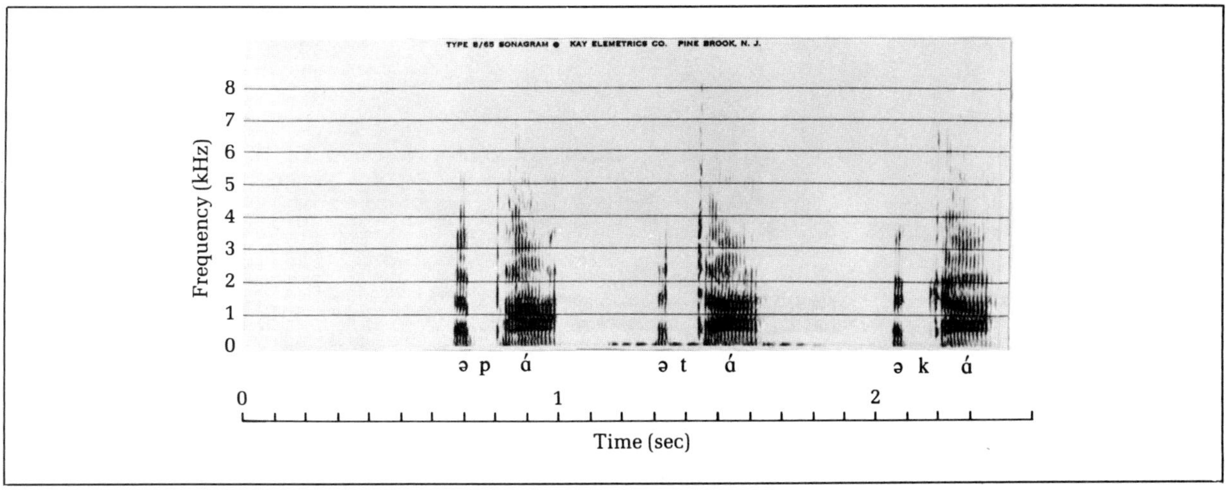

Figure 10-32. Spectrogram of [əpá] [ətá] [əká].

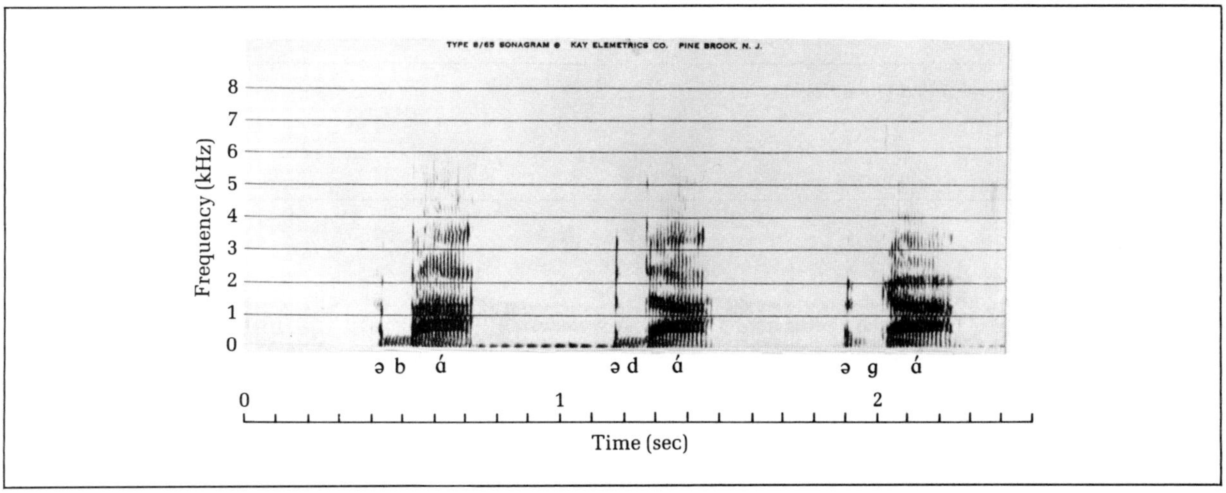

Figure 10-33. Spectrogram of [əbá] [ədá] [əgá].

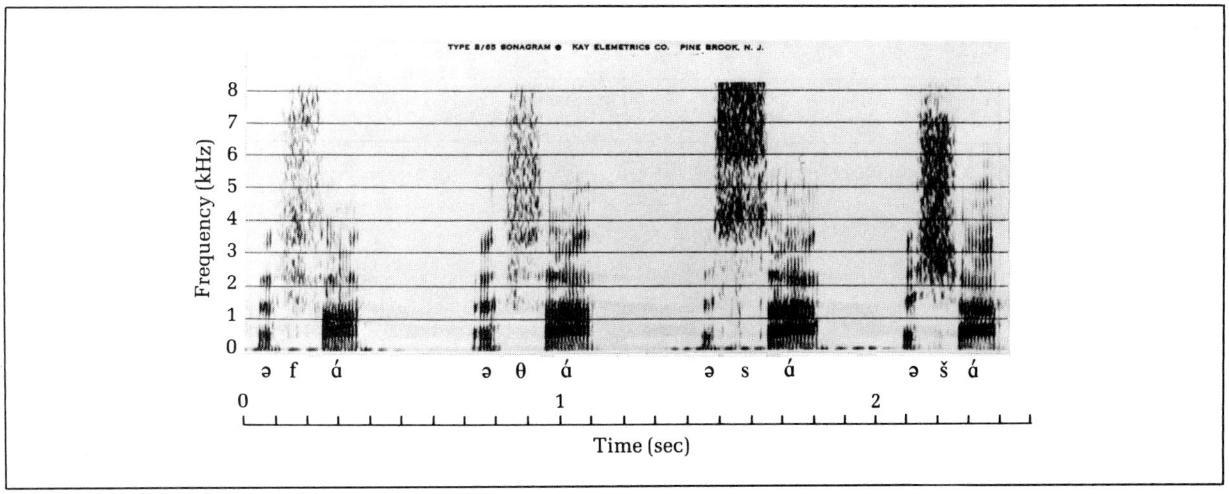

Figure 10-34. Spectrogram of [əfá] [əθá] [əsá] [əšá].

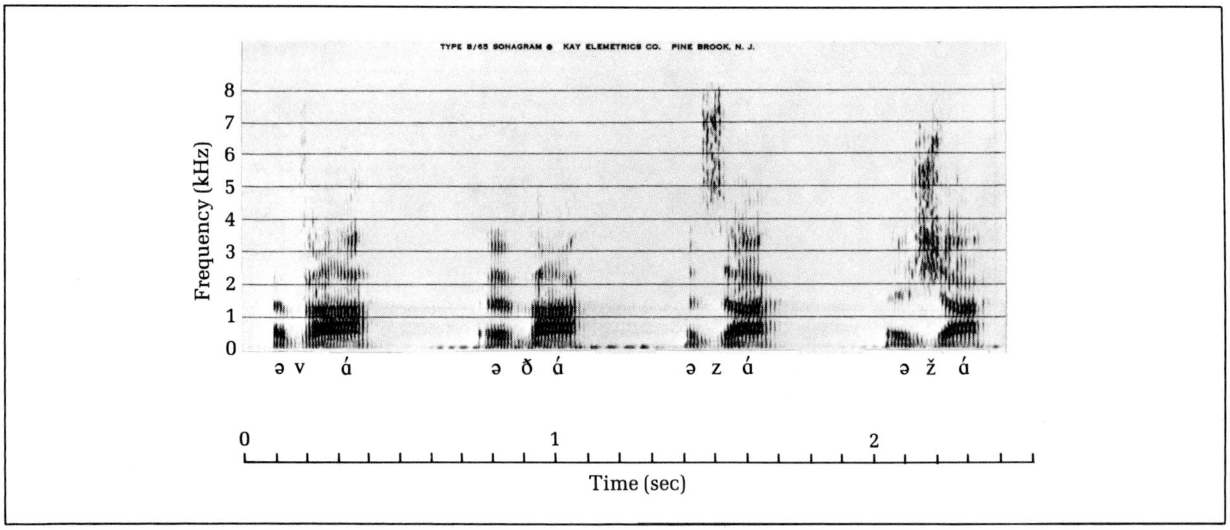

Figure 10-35. Spectrogram of [əvá] [əðá] [əzá] [əžá].

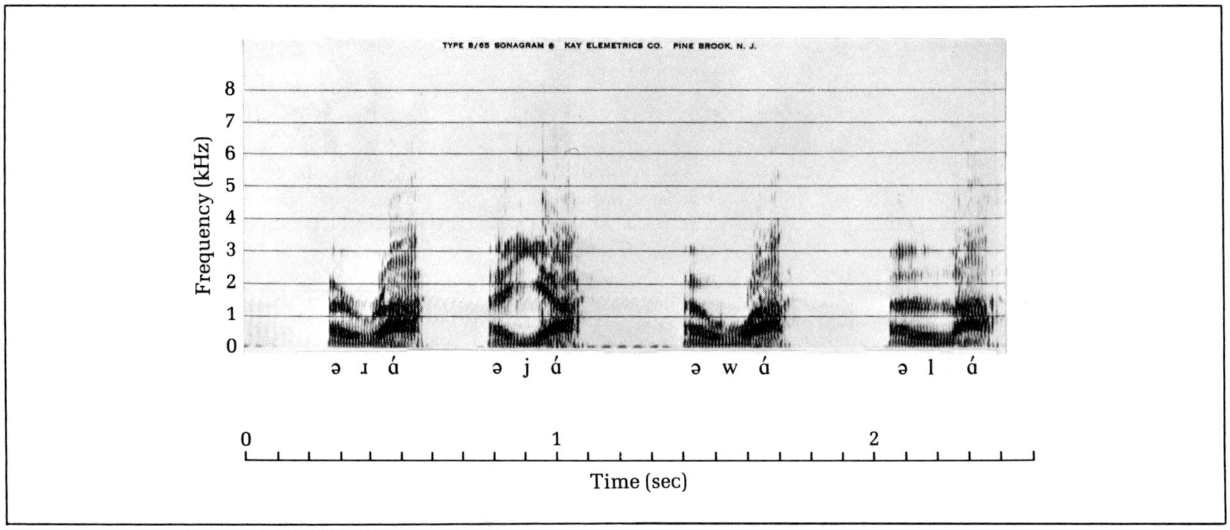

Figure 10-36. Spectrogram of [əɹá] (or [ərá]) [əjá] (or [əyá]) [əwá] [əlá].

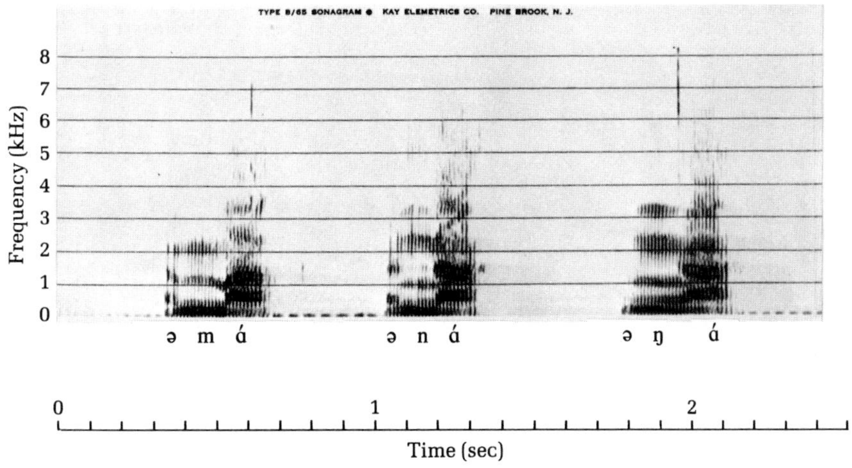

Figure 10-37. Spectrogram of [əmá] [əná] [əŋá].

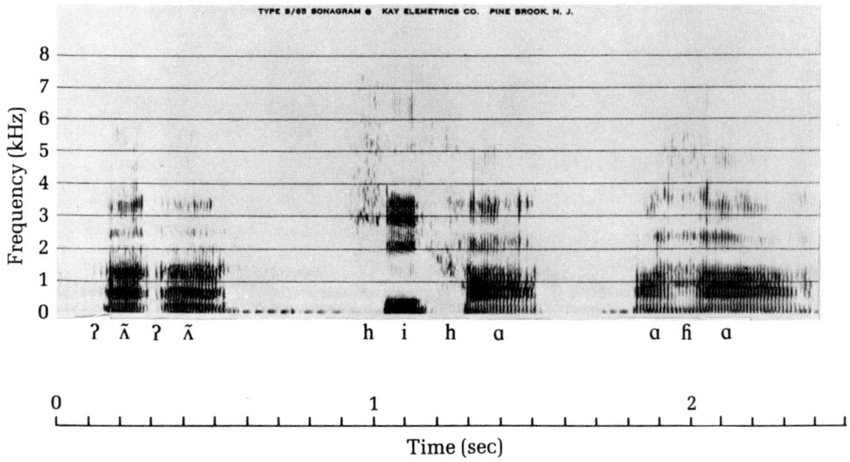

Figure 10-38. Spectrogram of [ʔʌ̃ʔʌ̃] [hihɑ] [ɑɦɑ]. Notice that [h] is voiceless (no vertical striations), while [ɦ] is voiced (vertical voicing striations).

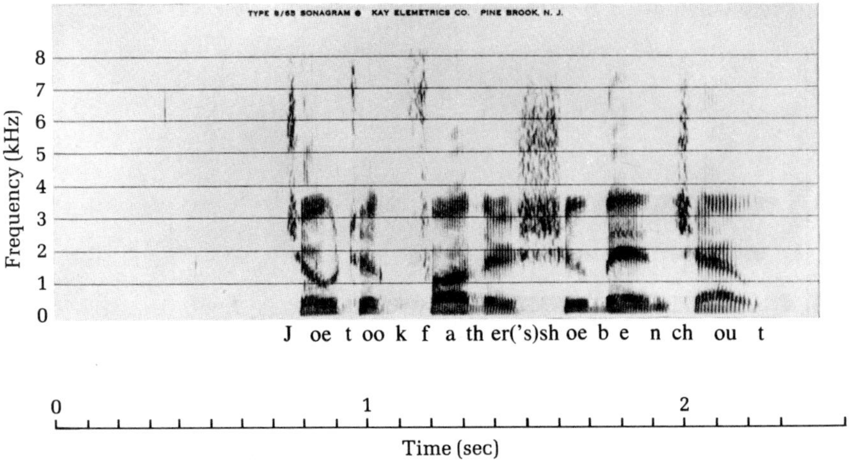

Figure 10-39. Spectrogram of the sentence "Joe took father's shoe-bench out."

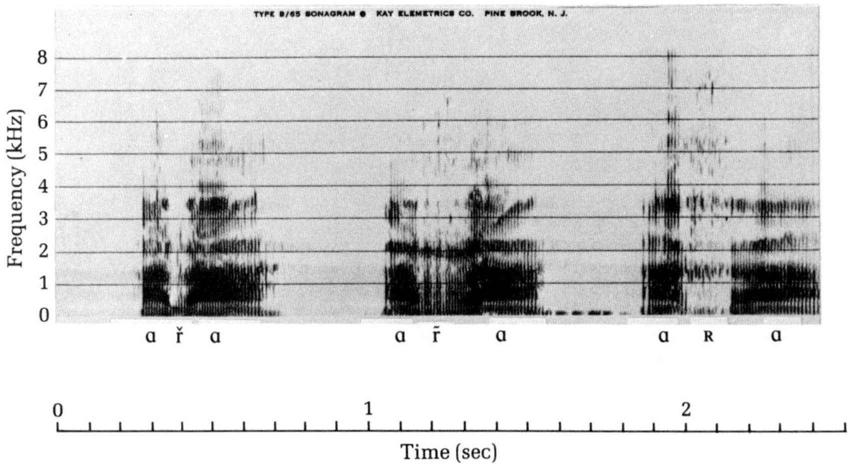

Figure 10-40. Spectrogram of [ɑřɑ] [ɑr̄ɑ] [ɑʀɑ]. Notice that the flap [ř] looks somewhat like a voiced plosive (compare Figure 10-33), except that the occlusion is shorter and not so complete—the formant patterns can be seen during the occlusion. [r̄] shows a series—in this case, three—of occlusions of very brief duration. And [ʀ], the French or German r-sound, has a fricative pattern.

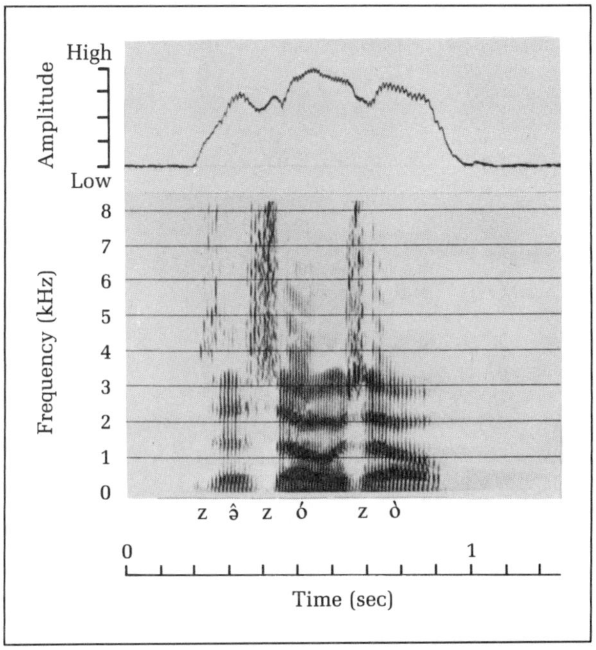

Figure 10-41. Stress and amplitude. An instrumental measure of amplitude has replaced the higher frequencies of this spectrogram. The nonsense word *zozozo* was pronounced with the stress pattern of the word *pimento* [zə̂zózò].

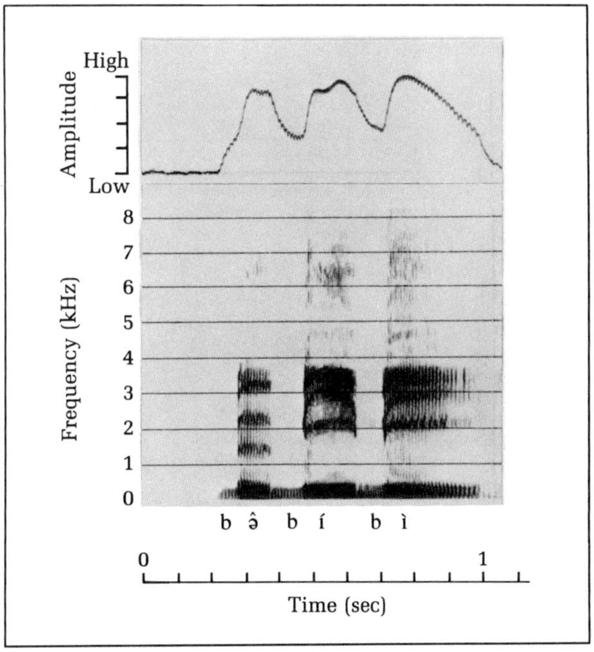

Figure 10-42. Stress and amplitude. As in Figure 10-41, the higher frequencies have been replaced by a measure of amplitude. The nonsense word *beebeebee* was pronounced with the stress pattern of *pimento* [bə̂bíbì].

easy to hold and to reflect on the practical implications of the mechanisms of speech perception.

A commonly held view among those who have not made a study of speech perception is that there are relatively invariant acoustic cues in speech: that while [æ], for example, has *some* acoustic variability, it retains unique characteristics and occupies a unique acoustic territory. From this point of view, speech is something like the tone-dialing used in the telephone system. In telephone dialing, there are ten "phonemes"[9] in use: the numerals 1 through 9 plus 0. In a tone-dialing system, each numeral has a distinct tone corresponding to it; one "talks" to the telephone exchange switching equipment by pressing the buttons that create the tones corresponding to the numerals one wishes to "say." While a small variation in frequency might be permitted to each numeral, essentially each has a discrete, nonoverlapping frequency or tone. Applying this analogy to speech, one might believe that each tone might have quite a bit of variability, but that there would be discrete ranges for each phoneme.

Indeed, this is an exceedingly naïve view of speech. *There is no unique correspondence between acoustic features and phonemes of the language.* The tone-dialing analogy is completely inadequate. What we have, to extend the analogy, is a tone-dialing system in which "3" sometimes sounds like "2," sometimes like "4," and sometimes is not heard at all, coupled with an extremely brainy exchange switching mechanism which, when it "hears" a number dialed that could be any of three different telephone numbers, says to itself, "Well, that could be Mrs. Jones' number that was dialed, or Dr. Smith's, or Mr. Doe's, but since the call is originating at Mrs. Black's and she doesn't know Mr. Doe, that leaves the likelihood that Mrs. Black is trying to reach either Jones or Smith; but since she's been ill lately, and it's not the time of day she usually calls her friends to chat, it's probably Dr. Smith she's

[9]Let us ignore for the moment the eleventh and twelfth buttons, the pound sign (#) and asterisk (*), used in some systems, although not for dialing numbers.

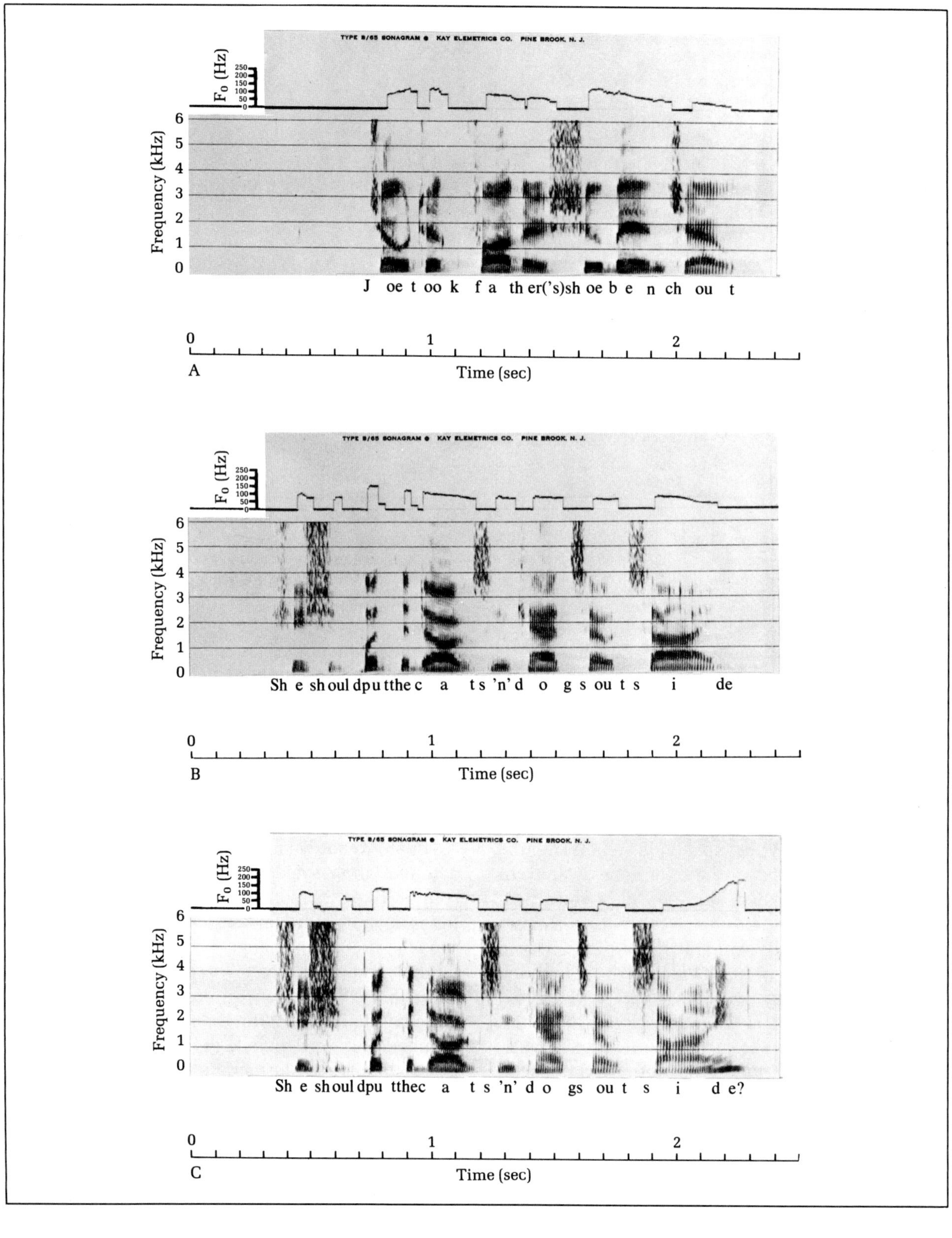
TYPE B/65 SONAGRAM ● KAY ELEMETRICS CO. PINE BROOK, N. J.
F_0 (Hz)
250
200
150
100
50
0
Frequency (kHz)
6
5
4
3
2
1
0
J oe t oo k f a th er('s)sh oe b e n ch ou t
0
1
2
A
Time (sec)
TYPE B/65 SONAGRAM ● KAY ELEMETRICS CO. PINE BROOK, N. J.
F_0 (Hz)
250
200
150
100
50
0
Frequency (kHz)
6
5
4
3
2
1
0
Sh e sh oul dpu tthe c a t s 'n' d o g s ou t s i de
0
1
2
B
Time (sec)
TYPE B/65 SONAGRAM ● KAY ELEMETRICS CO. PINE BROOK, N. J.
F_0 (Hz)
250
200
150
100
50
0
Frequency (kHz)
6
5
4
3
2
1
0
Sh e sh oul dpu tthec a t s 'n' d o gs ou t s i d e?
0
1
2
C
Time (sec)

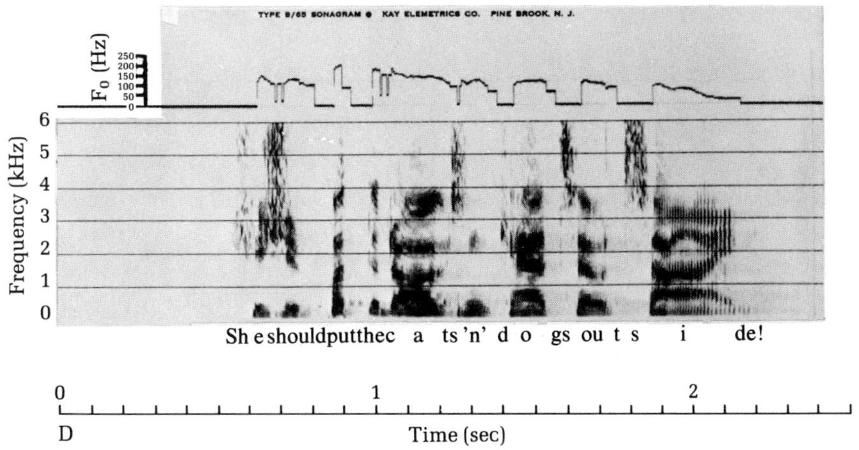

Figure 10-43. Spectrograms and instrumental graphs of intonation patterns. A. The sentence "Joe took father's shoe-bench out." This is the same token (i.e., the identical speech event) shown in Figure 10-39, but with a graphic representation of intonation added at the top of the spectrogram.

Note that the graphic intonation line drops to the baseline (0 Hz) during voiceless segments and silence. Note also the intonation *pattern* (briefly mentioned in Section 10-10.6): there is a rise through "Joe took," a fall through "father's," a peak on "shoe" (the start of a new breath-group), and a steady fall throughout "shoe-bench out," reflecting the declarative nature of the sentence. B–D. The sentence "She should put the dogs and cats outside" said three different ways. Note the many voiceless segments, which require an instantaneous cessation of voicing, and an instantaneous reinitiation of voicing afterwards, at the correct frequency. Notice as well the effects of accommodation; for example, the word "and" is pronounced in its *weak form* (see p. 164). B. "She should put the dogs and cats outside," said as a statement. Note the decline in F_0 toward the end, reflecting the declarative nature of the sentence. C. "She should put the dogs and cats outside?" said as a question with a slightly incredulous tone. Note the rise in F_0 at the end and the prolongation of the word "outside." D. "She should put the dogs and cats outside!" said in an angry, authoritarian manner. Note the faster rate (i.e, a shorter overall length), the higher frequency overall (heightened subglottal air pressure raises the amplitude, but also the F_0), and the falling F_0 at the end (a declarative/imperative pattern). The intonation analyses in these spectrograms were made with the Kay Elemetrics Visi-Pitch fundamental frequency extractor, recorded on the second channel of the Kay Digital Sona-Graph 7800.

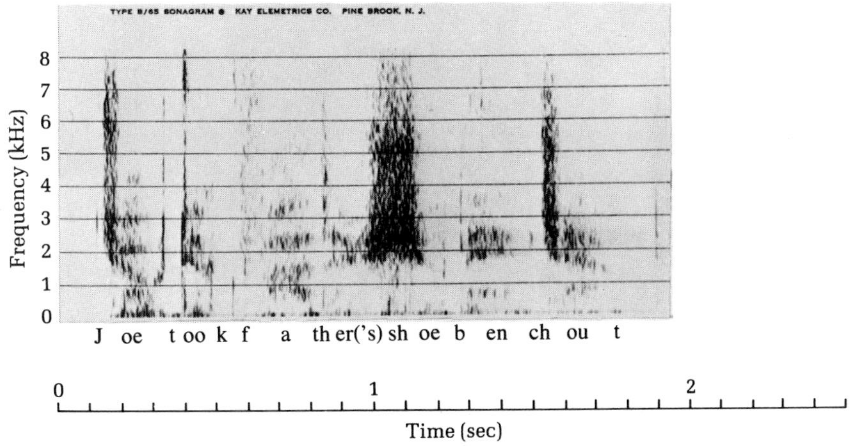

Figure 10-44. Spectrogram of whispered speech. Again the sentence is "Joe took father's shoe-bench out." In the case of whispering, it is not the quasi-periodic vocal fold vibration that excites resonance (i.e., sets up standing waves) but the random matching of components of the aperiodic frictional noise of the air passing through the narrowed glottis. The formants are still visible; Figure 10-39 shows formants excited by harmonics of the F_0, but this spectrogram shows **noise-excited** formants.

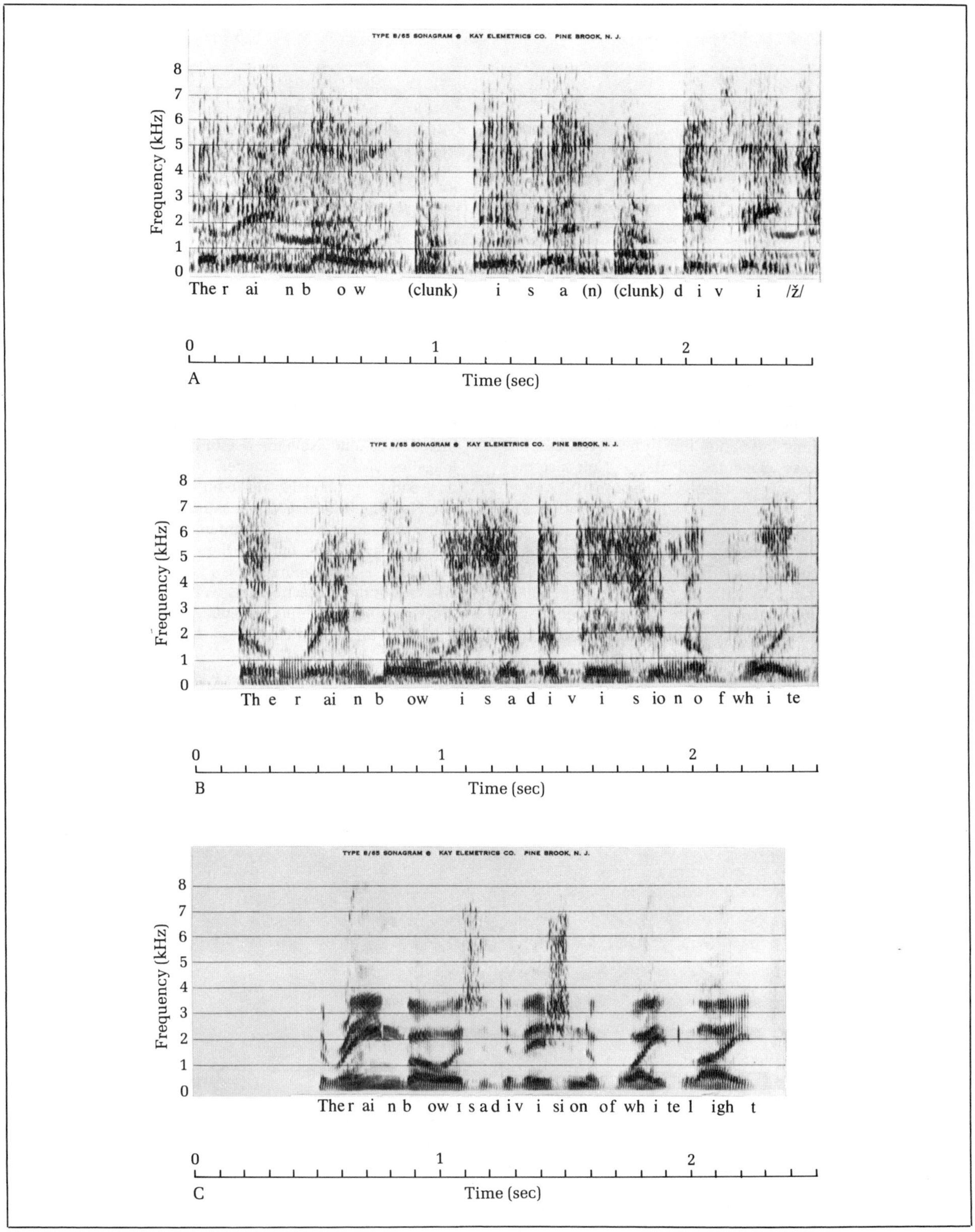
TYPE B/65 SONAGRAM ● KAY ELEMETRICS CO. PINE BROOK, N. J.
Frequency (kHz)
0 1 2 3 4 5 6 7 8
The r ai n b o w (clunk) i s a (n) (clunk) d i v i /ž/
0 1 2
A
Time (sec)
TYPE B/65 SONAGRAM ● KAY ELEMETRICS CO. PINE BROOK, N. J.
Frequency (kHz)
0 1 2 3 4 5 6 7 8
Th e r ai n b ow i s a d i v i s io n o f wh i te
0 1 2
B
Time (sec)
TYPE B/65 SONAGRAM ● KAY ELEMETRICS CO. PINE BROOK, N. J.
Frequency (kHz)
0 1 2 3 4 5 6 7 8
The r ai n b ow ɪ s a d i v i si on of wh i te l igh t
0 1 2
C
Time (sec)

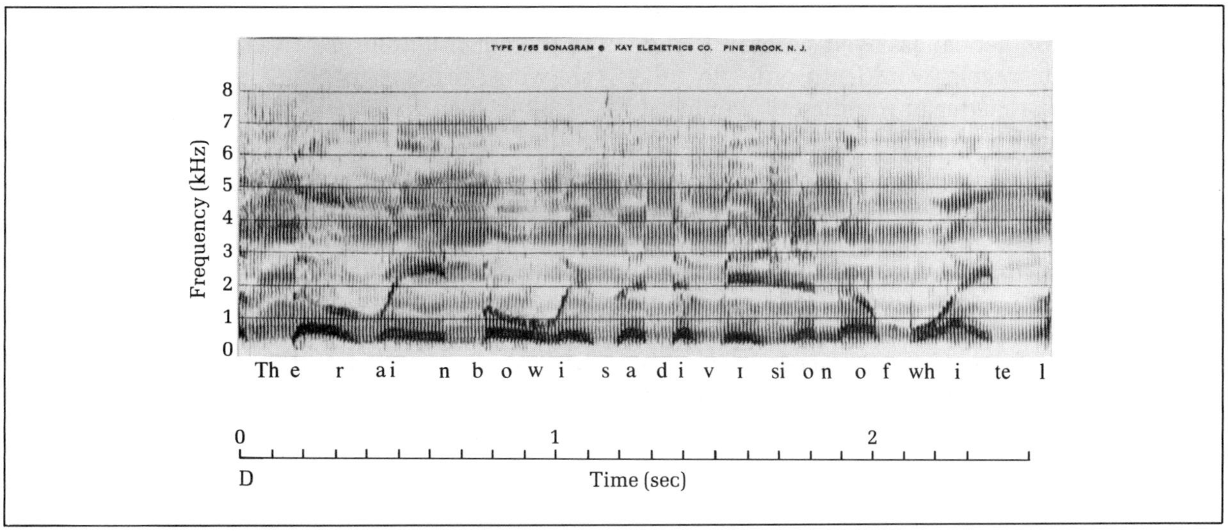

Figure 10-45. Esophageal speech and speech with an electrolarynx. The sentence spoken in each case is "The rainbow is a division of white light into many colors" (only the first part is shown). A. A not-very-accomplished male esophageal speaker. Note the noises ("clunking") while he injects a new supply of air into his esophagus, the small number of syllables he utters with each air supply, and the overall slow rate of his speech. B. An accomplished, very natural-sounding female esophageal speaker. Note the lack of pauses and the faster rate of speech as compared to speaker A. C. For comparison, a normal male speaker using (normal) laryngeal voice. Compare the rate of speech, which is a typical conversational rate, with speakers A and B. D. A normal female speaker using an electrolarynx. Note the extremely regular, dominant, constant "voicing" of the artificial larynx.

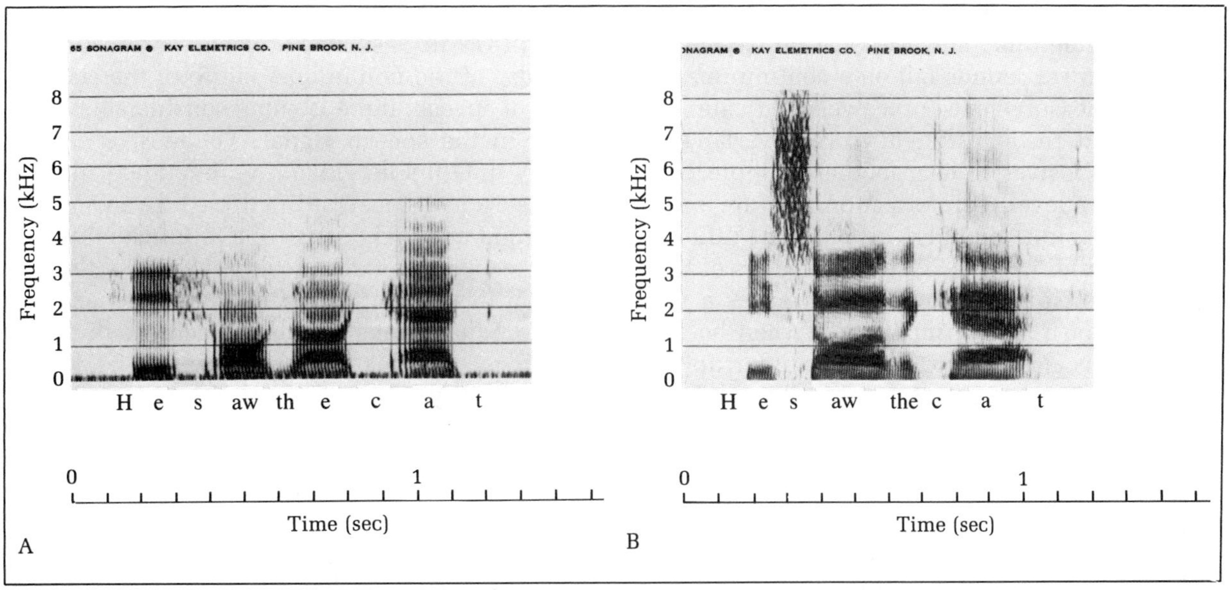

Figure 10-46. A. Spectrogram of synthesized speech. The sentence spoken is "He saw the cat." It comes from a demonstration recording published by Bell Telephone Laboratories and represents no-longer-current synthesis technology. Notice the unnatural regularity of all elements. B. A human speaker for comparison. Note how the stressed syllables are longer than the unstressed ones and how the frequency changes during the sentence.

trying to reach, so I'll connect her to Smith." This completely hypothetical (as well as brainy and nosy) exchange system would not only do this sort of thing as a matter of routine but would be right 99.9 percent of the time.

10-11.2 Redundancy and Ambiguity at the Same Time

One of the puzzling characteristics of speech is that it is both redundant and ambiguous. It is redundant in that there is more information provided, much of the time, than is needed for comprehension. Indeed, whole words often can be left out with little effect on the message. If, after doing a favor for someone, you "heard" him/her say "..... ..... very much," where the dots represent words you saw spoken but did not hear because of background noise, you would have little trouble interpolating the words "Thank you." In this example, you would be benefiting from social form to help you disambiguate the message. Redundancy is also brought about by grammatical rules (see example in Section 10-11.4) and by coarticulation. In the latter case, because of coarticulatory effects, a given segment contains some acoustic information about the surrounding segments and may therefore provide a clue to perception of a segment that is not heard directly.

At the same time, however, speech is ambiguous. The vowel sounds fall on a continuum, and acoustic measurements of vowels indicate that formant patterns for different vowels overlap considerably. Plosives, to take another example, have quite a low level of information and are easily mistaken for one another. In addition, different speakers differ in the acoustic parameters of their vocal tracts, so that an adult man makes a very different noise from a small child when he says [æ]. There is also background noise, interruption, the interference of several people talking at once, and the like to contend with.

10-11.3 Intelligibility and the Confusion Matrix

It appears that individual segments have greater or lesser degrees of **intelligibility,** that is, inherent properties that render them more or less intelligible. We have alluded to this in Section 10-10, in noting the weak spectral pattern shown by [f] and [θ], for example. Studies of intelligibility have led to the construction of *confusion matrices,* tables showing the degree of confusability between pairs of phonemes. A classic study done in 1955 by Miller and Nicely shows confusions between pairs of sixteen consonant phonemes in English. Sample results are given in Table 10-1. On the vertical axis is shown the segment spoken (in a syllable), and on the horizontal axis is shown the segment that the hearer thought he/she heard. It can be seen how likely a particular segment is to be heard for another and that some segments are far more likely than others to be misheard. For example, Table 10-1A indicates that a spoken /p/ was heard as a /p/ 14 times, as a /t/ 27 times, as a /k/ 22 times, as a /f/ 23 times, and so on. Table 10-1A shows results under extremely difficult listening conditions (signal-to-noise ratio, −18 dB; frequency response, 200 to 6500 Hz). Table 10-1B shows far better performance, because test conditions were more favorable (signal-to-noise ratio, 0 dB; frequency response, 200 to 6500 Hz). Even under the more favorable listening conditions, certain confusions are more likely than others. For example, /p/ is much more likely to be mistakenly heard as /k/ than as /s/.

10-11.4 Disambiguation of Ambiguity in Speech

Because of the nonunique nature of the acoustic form of speech, there is some considerable ambiguity in the speech signal. Yet most speech is highly intelligible. Like the hypothetical telephone exchange just outlined, we take an ambiguous input and make sense of it, although this normally occurs at an unconscious level, not through the linear reasoning in the telephone exchange example. What means are used to achieve this end?

In most speech situations there is considerable predictability as to what will be said. Not every word contains new information; the same thing tends to be said more than once in different ways. Indeed, one way in which spoken and written language differ is that the latter tends to be compact, whereas the former tends to be diffuse. This diffuseness gives more than a single opportunity to a listener to understand what was said.

As in the example in a preceding section, social rules of interaction help us to disambiguate verbal

Table 10-1. Confusion matrices

A. RESULTS UNDER DIFFICULT LISTENING CONDITIONS (SIGNAL-TO-NOISE RATIO, −18 dB; FREQUENCY RESPONSE, 200–6500 Hz)

Consonant Spoken	Consonant Heard															
	p	t	k	f	θ	s	š	b	d	g	v	ð	z	ž	m	n
p	14	27	22	23	25	22	14	15	16	7	17	11	12	11	16	12
t	16	26	21	15	15	18	14	7	10	6	17	9	13	11	9	13
k	20	22	24	15	14	29	12	4	11	9	12	10	16	11	17	14
f	27	22	27	23	13	12	10	19	20	14	16	16	15	3	13	18
θ	17	18	18	13	15	21	12	14	20	14	23	6	14	9	12	14
s	18	17	23	11	18	21	17	11	24	15	15	16	11	13	17	5
š	16	20	27	17	13	37	14	10	21	7	20	18	9	8	16	15
b	12	11	24	15	19	15	12	24	20	19	24	12	15	11	18	17
d	16	24	18	13	15	15	14	22	25	21	25	17	18	13	15	25
g	11	20	29	9	18	18	15	26	30	14	18	14	16	20	24	22
v	9	17	18	11	7	12	9	25	14	13	15	15	19	11	12	17
ð	16	11	10	7	6	14	10	20	17	18	15	7	17	12	18	18
z	18	18	15	9	13	19	7	22	14	9	21	12	23	10	22	12
ž	8	16	17	14	12	15	7	22	18	8	15	11	15	11	18	13
m	19	24	15	14	14	14	8	14	15	12	13	8	11	6	25	28
n	11	18	20	6	9	18	9	14	14	13	9	8	10	12	33	32

B. RESULTS UNDER MORE FAVORABLE LISTENING CONDITIONS (SIGNAL-TO-NOISE RATIO, 0 dB; FREQUENCY RESPONSE, 200–6500 Hz)

Consonant Spoken	Consonant Heard															
	p	t	k	f	θ	s	š	b	d	g	v	ð	z	ž	m	n
p	150	38	88	7	13											
t	30	193	28	1												
k	86	45	138	4	1		1									1
f	4	3	5	199	46	4		1				1			1	
θ	11	6	4	85	114	10					2					
s		2	1	5	38	170	10			2						
š		3	3			3	267									
b				7	4			235	4		34	27	1			
d									189	48		4	8	11		
g									74	161		4	8	25		
v				3	1			19		2	177	29	4	1		
ð								7		10	64	105	18			
z									17	23	4	22	132	26		
ž									2	3	1	1	9	191		1
m								1							201	6
n												3		1	8	240

Source: Reproduced with permission from the classic study by G. A. Miller and P. E. Nicely, An analysis of perceptual confusions among some English consonants. *Journal of the Acoustical Society of America* 27:2, March 1955.

input. Certain things are said in certain situations, and when the acoustic input is not clear, the situation rules out certain possibilities. A number of years ago a friend performed the "experiment" of saying "Fink you very much" where "Thank you very much" would be appropriate (*fink* was a mildly insulting word in the slang of the time). Usually the actual wording passed unnoticed by the listener (particularly in noisy environments), to the childish amusement of the "experimenter." [f] and [θ] have great acoustic similarity and low intelligibility (thus great possibility for confusion); the vowels, although not greatly similar, are far from maximally different. The two expressions thus sound very much alike, particularly when said in a conversational context rather than in a citation form. Thus social rules come into play in disambiguating (in this example, disambiguation leads more often to the unsaid message being understood).

Lexical knowledge plays a role in disambiguating speech as well. The segments [t] and [k] are highly confusable, but the sentence "He went to school and taught his students" is highly intelligible, because we know that the meaning of the sentence "He went to school and caught his students" is an unlikely one.

Contextual information helps as well. The two sentences "The hunter shot the moose" and "The hunters shot the moose" are identical in most speakers. However, if we heard a story about two hunters, and the final sentence was one of the two preceding ones, we would "hear" the [z] on *hunters*. If the story was about a single hunter, we would not "hear" the [z]. *The [z] was never there to be heard, but whether one "hears" it or not is a product of what one knows,* in this case what one knows about the number of hunters.

Grammatical knowledge helps disambiguate speech as well. Let us look again at an example used in Chapter 6. The first parts of these two sentences sound alike, due to accommodation: "*I'd do it* if I could" and "*I do it* when I can." Nevertheless, if you heard the two sentences, you would "hear" the [d] in the first sentence and "hear" its absence in the second. Why? Simply because you know the grammar of English and know that there must be a *would* in the first sentence because the (phonetically unambiguous) second clause in the sentence is in the conditional. In this context, remember what was said in Chapter 2 about grammar. Even if you never formally studied a subject called grammar in school, if you can speak the language natively (and if your dialect is standard on this point), then you will "know" you "heard" a [d] for *would* in the former sentence.

There are phonetic disambiguators as well. Coarticulation (see Chapter 6) serves this end, as the acoustic information about a particular segment is not encoded uniquely into that segment; surrounding segments are modified by the sound in question and so give cues to its decoding. We have noted, for example, ways in which vowels are modified in the environment of rhotic sounds and nasal consonants; acoustic information about the *consonant* is thus encoded in the *vowel*.

Aspects of intonation, stress, and emphasis (see Chapter 9) help to disambiguate as well. Grammatical rules cause old information to be treated differently from new; new information tends to be given syntactic structures and/or suprasegmental treatment that reduces ambiguity (see Section 7-3.4). Also, speakers are aware of ambiguity and provide additional stress or slow down when danger of misunderstanding exists. This slowing down or contrastive stress results in a reduction of accommodation and a greater level of redundancy in the message.

10-11.5 Practical Effects of Ambiguity

This high level of ambiguity has implications for the way we talk to each other and interact. For example, in a country with a highly mixed ethnic makeup, people's names do not fit into a limited set of familiar words as they do in ethnically homogeneous countries, but rather are often unique in the hearer's experience and may be made up of strange sequences, breaking spelling, if not phonotactic, restrictions. The result? We often don't "understand" when names are given orally, particularly on the telephone. (By limiting frequencies and by removing visual cues, the telephone causes a heightened level of ambiguity.) People are forever asking for names to be repeated, spelled, and pronounced carefully in contexts in which other words are heard clearly: there is virtually no redundancy in an unfamiliar name.

Another example: when naming letters of the alphabet out loud, we generally include a word to disambiguate it: "⟨B⟩ as in 'Bob' ". Many letters of the alphabet are named with a single consonant followed by the vowel [i]; they are therefore similar acoustically. Generally when we spell a word, it is because the letters convey new information (otherwise they would not be given); and there is usually no disambiguating factor to come to the rescue. But, as noted, letters named out loud are highly ambiguous. In military and aviation circles, a standard set of words is used to label the letters of the alphabet; this is disambiguating in two ways: a larger number of segments in these words than the two in the names of most letters affords more chance of recognition; and the fact that the word labels are standard (rather than the civilian practice of choosing any word that starts with the appropriate letter) gives a higher recognition factor to each letter. This alphabet starts "alfa, bravo, charlie . . . ."[10]

Numbers, too, are ambiguous, although not as much so as letters. The words "nine" and "five" are particularly susceptible to confusion, since they have the same vowel, the same number of consonants before and after that vowel, and consonants of low intelligibility. In areas such as air traffic control, where understanding numbers is critical, *nine* is not called "nine," but "niner." This differentiates "five" and "nine" in two ways: they now have a different number of syllables, and the second [n] of "nine" is now intervocalic; intervocalic consonants have more acoustic cues, and therefore greater intelligibility, than word-final ones.

An unfamiliar dialect possesses a number of parameters that, according to what was said in the preceding section, renders it less intelligible to a listener than familiar speech. Speakers of the dialect are likely to have different vocabulary, may have different social conventions, have different rules of coarticulation and different suprasegmental features, etc., etc. Thus, communication is impeded.

The foreign language learner has even greater reason to have difficulty. He may well be unaware of the social conventions, lexical restrictions, and finer grammatical rules that help the native speaker. For example, a native speaker of Canadian French told of being in England at a time when he spoke little English. Going into a restaurant for breakfast, he was very surprised when the first thing the waitress did was to offer him flowers! Strange customs, indeed. In fact, she did no such thing; what she said was, "Would you like some [ro͜uz]?" In this particular English dialect, /l/'s in postvocalic (particularly word-final) position are realized as [u]. The student thought he was being offered *roses* when in fact it was *rolls* (breakfast pastries) that he was being offered. It is very unlikely that the North American speaker of English, even if he had never before heard this British dialect feature of substituting [u] for /l/, would have concluded he was being offered flowers. Why? The word "rose" ends in a /z/, one of the segments which, in word-final position, takes the form of the plural morpheme whose phonetic shape is /əz/ (rather than the form whose shape is simply /s/ or /z/). We would conclude (rapidly and unconsciously), therefore, that [ro͜uz] could not be the plural of a word ending in /z/ but would have to be either the singular of a collective noun or the plural of the count noun [ro͜u].[11] Since [ro͜u] is nonexistent in standard North American, we would "translate," probably trying and rejecting *row* and settling on *roll*, since it would make sense. However, this French-speaking student did not have enough knowledge of English to know that the plural of "rose" would have to have two syllables. French speakers of English often do not acquire the plural marker in English until late in their learning. Thus, lack of knowledge of a standard pluralization rule led to misunderstanding in this case; conversely, knowledge of such gram-

[10] This alphabet is called the "phonetic alphabet" by those in the field of radio telephony. Obviously, it is "phonetic" in a very different sense from the International Phonetic Alphabet. The complete alphabet is as follows: alfa, bravo, charlie, delta, echo, foxtrot, golf, hotel, india, juliet, kilo, lima, mike, november, oscar, papa, quebec, romeo, sierra, tango, uniform, victor, whiskey, x-ray, yankee, zulu.

[11] After *some* there could be either a collective singular, as in "Would you like some butter," ". . . some sugar," ". . . some coffee," etc., or the plural of a count noun, as in "Would you like some eggs," ". . . some muffins," etc. But the word *rose*, being a count noun, and one ending in /z/, would have to be plural, and that plural form would take the clear full-syllable ending /əz/.

mar rules aids in decoding the phonetic code of speech.

Phonotactic restrictions also aid in speech decoding. Certain combinations are not permitted as a result of phonotactic restrictions, so those can be eliminated from consideration in the decoding process.

The fact that the acoustic makeup of speech differs so much among individuals presents interesting problems. It has been suggested that, in fact, in speaking to a new interlocutor, we make an estimate of his/her vocal tract dimensions and determine the consequences of those dimensions in terms of expected formant frequencies and other acoustic features. So in the first few seconds of speaking to a new interlocutor, we are struggling to zero in on hypotheses that will lead to successful comprehension. It is further suggested that the role of the standard greeting ("Hello," "How do you do?," "Hi there," and so on) is to say something familiar that the listener can use to home in on the speaker's acoustic properties.

Everyday experience tends to confirm this. On the telephone, as noted, there is less acoustic information. There are also no visual cues as to the size, sex, and age of the interlocutor. If the person answers "Hello," one has no difficulty understanding. But if the person answers in some other way, such as the name of the company (without an accompanying "hello" or "good morning"), we often have difficulty in understanding (unless, of course, we are primed to expect that company name; we are not so primed if we reach a wrong number). The reason is that we have been given no stock phrase with which to form and test hypotheses about that person's vocal tract.

All of this goes a long way toward explaining why automatic speech recognition (ASR) is as yet a long way off. ASR is the comprehension of speech by computer, usually considered to be in the form of an automatic dictation machine: you speak, and it writes down what you said. Some minimal applications of this exist already. Computer-interactive devices exist that allow a person, usually either a quadraplegic, a jet fighter pilot, or an industrial worker both of whose hands are occupied, to give a verbal command to a machine. However, these devices at present always employ a very limited vocabulary of phonetically maximally distinct words; they usually require the "training" of both the computer program and the operator; they require single words to be pronounced in isolation, without background interference, and always in the same manner; and they are hopeless at decoding connected speech.

Because of the incredible utility of ASR, many highly skilled individuals are working on the problem. Interestingly, they are generally engineers and computer scientists; very few speech scientists or phoneticians are working in this area. It should be clear to you by now that any successful ASR program will not rely solely on phonetic input to decode speech. That computer program will have to "know" rules of grammar, rules governing accommodation, rules of social interaction, real-world facts about what is probable and what is not probable, grammatical co-occurrence restrictions, and so on. It is clearly a formidable task. However, breakthroughs may come, and perhaps by the time you read this, I will be writing, not by typing at a computer terminal, but by speaking into a microphone.

10-11.6 Models of Speech Perception

A model of speech perception like that of Fant [1967] is essentially one of filtering and decoding the incoming speech signal directly, generally without reference to the speaker's knowledge of speech production. Speech perception is thus essentially passive.

By contrast, the motor theory of speech perception (Liberman et al. [1967]; Liberman [1970]) posits that knowledge of the mechanism of speech production is essential to perceiving speech and is directly brought to bear in the perception process. This theory is most compelling in explaining why discontinuous acoustic signals are perceived in a common way. Looking, for example, at Figure 10-30, you will note that the F_2 locus for [g] changes with the vowel: there appears to be one F_2 locus for]gi], [ge], [gɛ], and [gɑ] and another one, lower in frequency, for [gɔ], [go], and [gu]. Why, then, should we perceive [gi] and [gu] as having any commonality? Why should they *sound* like the same consonant, when there is nothing the same acoustically? The motor theory points to the speaker's knowledge of the articulatory positions of his own speech apparatus and the acoustic consequences of articulatory gestures.

The analysis by synthesis model of speech perception (Stevens and Halle [1967]) is similar to the motor theory, except that it relies on the speaker's making reference more to acoustic than to articulatory patterns.

One factor in perception that must be taken into account is the observed phenomenon of categorical perception. Essentially, categorical perception is the phenomenon by which speakers tend to perceive speech segments as discrete entities, even though the acoustic reality may fall on a continuum. For example, if an experimenter uses a computer to produce synthesized syllables that fall in small increments along a continuum from, say, English /pɑ/ to /bɑ/, he would find that listeners do not hear them as a continuum. Listeners report that they hear each syllable as either /pɑ/ or /bɑ/, but rarely as an intermediate value.

Phenomena such as categorical perception and experimental data showing that human neonates are sensitive to such acoustic markers as voice onset time have led some researchers to posit the existence of **feature detectors,** "hardwired" devices in the neurological mechanism that are specifically sensitive to linguistically relevant acoustic cues in speech. These are taken as evidence for the specific evolution of human neurology (as well as physiology: see Chapter 9) for speech.

Summary

Sound is a form of energy, namely **acoustic energy;** work must be expended to produce it, and it has the potential to do work (such as vibrating the eardrums).

Sound waves have a number of dimensions. The **amplitude** refers to the amount of energy in the wave, shown graphically by the height of the **crests** and the depth of the **troughs.** The **wavelength** is the distance between crests (or between troughs, etc.). The **frequency** of a wave is the number of cycles completed per second and is expressed in **hertz (Hz).** The **period** is the time taken to complete each cycle. The **speed of propagation** is the speed at which the wave advances in a given medium. The crests represent a heightened air pressure or a compression of air molecules. The troughs represent a lowered air pressure, or a rarefaction of air molecules.

A **periodic** wave has a regular cycle; an **aperiodic** wave has individual cycles that are different from one another.

Periodicity relates to tonal quality; **frequency** relates primarily to **pitch;** and **amplitude** relates primarily to **loudness.**

Phase refers to the point at which a cycle starts, relative to another wave.

In a given medium (where speed of propagation is constant), the **wavelength** depends on the frequency.

Harmonics are whole-number multiples of the **fundamental frequency** present in an acoustic signal whenever the vibration causing the sound is undulating in nature. The sound generated by the supple vocal folds is rich in harmonics.

According to **Fourier's theorem,** any periodic wave is the sum of a number of **simple sinusoidal waves;** such a wave is a **complex wave.**

The **standing wave** phenomenon occurs when special conditions are met, namely, when the distance between a source and a reflector, or between two reflectors, is a multiple of the half wavelength (or the quarter wavelength in the case of an open-ended resonator). The multiple reflections increase the amplitude of waves whose wavelengths meet the criterion, making such **resonators** selective in reinforcing certain frequencies and not others.

In speech, the glottal source and its harmonics provide a series of frequencies throughout the spectrum. In speaking, one is adjusting the vocal tract so that its resonant characteristics (i.e., the frequencies it emphasizes) match those of the particular resonant sounds one wants to say. Such resonant sounds generally have three characteristic frequencies, called **formants.** Each vowel and resonant consonant (e.g., [i], [r]) has its own set of formant frequencies, and while the precise frequencies vary among individuals according to age, sex, and individual characteristics, their *relative* values remain stable.

Plosives are characterized by extremely rapid

formant transitions. Fricatives are characterized by frictional noise.

The acoustic speech signal contains considerable ambiguity. It is clear that the listener uses his/her knowledge of grammar, the lexicon, and other factors in perceiving speech.

Some segments are inherently more intelligible than others; certain pairs of segments are more easily confused than others.

Several theories of speech perception are held by speech scientists; these differ in the degree to which, and the way in which, the hearer is active in the decoding process.

Vocabulary

acoustic energy
amplitude
aperiodic
aspiration
complex wave
compress, compression
crest
cycle
cycles per second
degrees (of phase)
dynamic range
excite
F_0
feature detectors
formant
formant transitions
Fourier's theorem
frequency
frequency scale
fundamental frequency (F_0)
glottal source
harmonics
hertz (Hz)
Hz
in phase
intelligibility
intonation
locus, loci
loudness
modes of vibration
node
out of phase
overtones
period, periodic, periodicity
phase
pitch
pole
propagate
rarefy, rarefaction
resonator
sharply tuned
simple (wave)
sine, sinusoidal
sonagram
sound
sound waves
source-filter theory of speech production
spectrogram
speed of propagation
standing wave
surface wave
trough
voice murmur
volume
wavelength
zero

Readings

Textbooks in speech acoustics include Denes and Pinson's [1973] *The Speech Chain*, Ladefoged's [1962] *Elements of Acoustic Phonetics*, and Fry's [1979] *The Physics of Speech*. A number of seminal articles in acoustic phonetics have been brought together in Lehiste's [1967] *Readings in Acoustic Phonetics*. A classic work in this area, recounting early work in speech spectroscopy, is Joos' [1948] "Acoustic Phonetics."

References in neonate perception, acoustic feature detectors, and categorical perception include "Speech Perception in Early Infancy" (Eimas [1975]), "Infant Speech Perception: A Preliminary Model and Review of the Literature" (Morse [1974]); "An Investigation of Categorical Speech Discrimination by Rhesus Monkeys" (Morse and Snowdon [1975]); "Selective Adaptation of Linguistic Feature Detectors" (Eimas and Corbit [1973]); "The Role of Auditory Feature Detectors in the Perception of Speech" (Tartter and Eimas [1975]); and "Feature Detectors for Speech: A Critical Reappraisal" (Diehl [1981]).

References in theories of speech perception include "Auditory Patterns of Speech" (Fant [1967]); "The Grammars of Speech and Language" (Liberman [1970]); "Perception of the Speech Code" (Liberman et al. [1967]); "Remarks on Analysis by Synthesis and Distinctive Features" (Stevens and Halle [1967]); "Toward a Theory of Speech Perception" (Cole and Scott [1974]); "Adaptation of Phonetic Feature Analyzers for Place of Articulation" (Cooper [1974]); "The Motor Theory of Speech Perception: A Critical Review" (Lane [1965]); "Motor Theory of Speech Perception: A Reply to Lane's Critical Review" (Studdert-Kennedy et al. [1970]); "The Quantal Nature of Speech: Evidence from Articulatory-Acoustic Data" (Stevens [1972]); "Some Stages of Processing in Speech Perception" (Pisoni and Sawusch [1975]); "Passive *versus* Active Recognition Models, or Is Your Homunculus Really Necessary?" (Morton and Broadbent [1967]).

References

Abercrombie, David. 1967. *Elements of General Phonetics*. Chicago: Aldine.

Abramson, Arthur S., and Lisker, L. 1970. "Discriminability along the Voicing Continuum: Cross-Language Tests." *Proceedings of the Sixth International Congress of Phonetic Sciences, Prague, 1967*, pp. 569–573. Prague: Academia.

Aitchison, Jean. 1983. *The Articulate Mammal: An Introduction to Psycholinguistics*. 2d ed. London: Hutchison.

Algeo, John. 1982. *Problems in the Origins and Developments of the English Language*. 3d ed. New York: Harcourt Brace Jovanovich.

Allen, Harold B. and Gary N. Underwood. 1971. *Readings in American Dialectology*. New York: Appleton-Century-Crofts.

Baggs, Terry Wayne, and Shirley J. Pine. 1983. "Acoustic Characteristics: Tracheoesophageal Speech." *Journal of Communication Disorders* 16:299–307.

Baugh, Albert, and Thomas Cable. 1978. *A History of the English Language*. 3d ed. Englewood Cliffs, N.J.: Prentice-Hall.

Bloomfield, Leonard. 1961. *Language*. 2d ed. New York: Holt, Rinehart & Winston.

Brosnahan, L. F., and Bertil Malmberg. 1970. *Introduction to Phonetics*. Cambridge, England: W. Heffer & Sons.

Chomsky, Noam, and Morris Halle. 1968. *The Sound Pattern of English*. New York: Harper & Row.

Christensen, John, and Bernd Weinberg. 1976. "Vowel Duration Characteristics of Esophageal Speech." *Journal of Speech and Hearing Research* 19:678–689.

Clark, Virginia P., Paul A. Escholtz, and Alfred F. Rosa (Eds.). 1985. *Language: Introductory Readings*. 4th ed. New York: St. Martin's Press.

Cohen, A., and S. G. Nooteboom (Eds.). 1975. *Structure and Process in Speech Perception*. Berlin: Springer-Verlag.

Cohen, Leslie B., and Philip Salapatek (Eds.). 1975. *Infant Perception*. New York: Academic Press.

Cole, Ronald A., and Brian Scott. 1974. "Toward a Theory of Speech Perception." *Psychological Review* 81:348–374.

Cooper, William E. 1974. "Adaptation of Phonetic Feature Analyzers for Place of Articulation." *Journal of the Acoustical Society of America* 56:617–627.

David, Edward E., Jr., and Peter B. Denes (Eds.). 1972. *Human Communication: A Unified View*. New York: McGraw-Hill.

Denes, Peter B., and Elliot N. Pinson. 1973. *The Speech Chain*. Bell Telephone Laboratories, 1963, 1967. Garden City, N.Y.: Anchor Books.

Dickson, David Ross, and Wilma Maue-Dickson. 1982. *Anatomical and Physiological Bases of Speech*. Boston: Little, Brown.

Diehl, Randy L. 1981. "Feature Detectors for Speech: A Critical Reappraisal." *Psychological Bulletin* 89:1–18.

Drills and Exercises in English Pronunciation: Stress and Intonation. 1967. Prepared by English Language Services. New York: Macmillan.

Eimas, Peter D. 1975. "Speech Perception in Early Infancy." In Cohen and Salapatek [1975], pp. 193–231.

Eimas, Peter D., and John D. Corbit. 1973. "Selective Adaptation of Linguistic Feature Detectors." *Cognitive Psychology* 4:99–109.

Fant, Gunnar. 1967. "Auditory Patterns of Speech." In Wathen-Dunn [1967], pp. 11–125.

Farb, Peter. 1974. *Word Play.* New York: Knopf.

Finocchiaro, M., and C. Brumfit. 1983. *The Functional-Notional Approach.* New York: Oxford University Press.

Frith, Uta. 1980a. *Cognitive Processes in Spelling.* London: Academic Press.

Frith, Uta. 1980b. "Unexpected Spelling Problems." In Frith [1980a].

Fromkin, Victoria. 1971. "The Non-Anomalous Nature of Anomalous Utterances." *Language* 47:27–52.

Fromkin, Victoria (Ed.). 1973. *Speech Errors as Linguistic Evidence.* The Hague: Mouton.

Fromkin, Victoria (Ed.). 1980. *Slips of the Tongue, Ear, Pen, and Hand.* New York: Academic Press.

Fromkin, Victoria, and Robert Rodman. 1983. *An Introduction to Language.* 3d ed. New York: Holt, Rinehart & Winston.

Fry, Dennis. 1977. *Homo Loquens: Man as a Talking Animal.* London: Cambridge University Press.

Fry, Dennis. 1979. *The Physics of Speech.* Cambridge: Cambridge University Press.

Gilhooly, William B. 1973. "The Influence of Writing-System Characteristics on Learning to Read." *Reading Research Quarterly* 8(2):167–199.

Gleason, Henry Allan, Jr. 1955. *Workbook in Descriptive Linguistics.* New York: Holt, Rinehart & Winston.

Gordon, Morton J. 1974. *Speech Improvement.* Englewood Cliffs, N.J.: Prentice-Hall.

Henderson, Leslie (Ed.). 1984. *Orthographies and Reading: Perspectives from Cognitive Psychology, Neuropsychology, and Linguistics.* London & Hillsdale, N.J.: Lawrence Erlbaum Associates.

Hill, Archibald Anderson. 1958. *Introduction to Linguistic Structures.* New York: Harcourt, Brace & World.

Hoard, James E. 1966. "Juncture and Syllable Structure in English." *Phonetica* 15:96–109.

Howell, Richard W., and Harold J. Vetter. 1976. *Language in Behavior.* New York: Human Sciences Press.

Ishizaka, K., and M. Matsudaira. 1972. "Fluid Mechanical Considerations of Vocal Cord Vibration." *Speech Communications Research Laboratory Monograph No. 8.* Santa Barbara: Speech Communications Research Laboratory.

Jespersen, Otto. 1949. *A Modern English Grammar on Historical Principles.* 7 vols. Phototyped ed. Copenhagen: Munksgaard.

Jones, Daniel. 1967. *The Phoneme: Its Nature and Use.* 3d ed. Cambridge, England: W. Heffer & Sons.

Jones, Daniel. 1972. *An Outline of English Phonetics.* 9th ed. New York: Dutton.

Joos, Martin. 1948. "Acoustic Phonetics." Language Monograph No. 23. *Language* 24 (2).

Joos, Martin. 1967. *The Five Clocks.* New York: Harcourt, Brace & World.

Kahn, Daniel. 1976. "Syllable-Based Generalizations in English Phonology." Doctoral dissertation. Bloomington, Indiana: Indiana University Linguistics Club.

Kaplan, Harold M. 1971. *Anatomy and Physiology of Speech.* New York: McGraw-Hill.

Katz, Leonard, and Laurie B. Feldman. 1983. "Relationship between Pronunciation and Recognition of Printed Words in Deep and Shallow Orthography." *Journal of Experimental Psychology: Learning, Memory and Cognition* 9(1):157–166.

Kavanagh, James F., and Richard L. Venezky (Eds.). 1980. *Orthography, Reading and Dyslexia.* Baltimore: University Park Press.

Kyöstiö, O. K. 1980. "Is Learning to Read Easy in a Language in Which the Grapheme-Phoneme Correspondences Are Regular?" In Kavanagh and Venezky [1980].

Ladefoged, Peter. 1962. *Elements of Acoustic Phonetics.* Chicago: University of Chicago Press.

Ladefoged, Peter. 1967. *Three Areas of Experimental Phonetics.* London: Oxford University Press.

Ladefoged, Peter. 1968a. *A Phonetic Study of West African Languages.* 2d ed. London: Cambridge University Press.

Ladefoged, Peter. 1968b. "The Nature of General Phonetic Theories." In O'Brien [1968], pp. 283–298.

Ladefoged, Peter. 1975. *A Course in Phonetics.* New York: Harcourt Brace Jovanovich.

Lado, Robert, and Charles C. Fries. 1954. *English Pronunciation: Exercises in Sound Segments, Intonation, and Rhythm.* Ann Arbor: University of Michigan Press.

Laird, Charlton Grant. 1970. *Language in America.* New York: World.

Lane, Harlan L. 1965. "The Motor Theory of Speech Perception: A Critical Review." *Psychological Review* 72:275–309.

Lehiste, Ilse (Ed.). 1967. *Readings in Acoustic Phonetics.* Cambridge, Mass.: MIT Press.

Lehiste, Ilse. 1970. *Suprasegmentals.* Cambridge, Mass.: MIT Press.

Liberman, Alvin M. 1970. "The Grammars of Speech and Language." *Cognitive Psychology* 1:301–323.

Liberman, Alvin M., F. S. Cooper, D. S. Shankweiler, and M. Studdert-Kennedy. 1967. "Perception of the Speech Code." *Psychological Review* 74:431–461.

Liberman, Mark Y. 1978. *The Intonational System of English*. Bloomington: Indiana University Linguistics Club.

Lieberman, Philip. 1967. *Intonation, Perception, and Language*. Research Monograph No. 23. Cambridge, Mass.: MIT Press.

Lieberman, Philip. 1975. *On the Origins of Language: An Introduction to the Evolution of Human Speech*. New York: Macmillan.

Lisker, Leigh, and Arthur S. Abramson. 1964. "A Cross-Language Study of Voicing in Initial Stops: Acoustical Measurements." *Word* 20:384–422.

Lisker, Leigh, and Arthur S. Abramson. 1967. "Some Effects of Context on Voice Onset Time in English Stops." *Language and Speech* 10:1–28.

Lisker, Leigh, and Arthur S. Abramson. 1971. "Distinctive Features and Laryngeal Control." *Language* 47 (4).

Lowenstamm, Jean. 1979. "Topics in Syllabic Phonology." Doctoral dissertation. Ann Arbor: University Microfilms International.

Lyons, John. 1968. *Introduction to Theoretical Linguistics*. London: Cambridge University Press.

MacKay, Ian R. A. 1977. "Tenseness in Vowels: An Ultrasonic Study." *Phonetica* 34(5):325–351.

MacKay, Ian R. A. 1978. *Introducing Practical Phonetics*. Boston: Little, Brown.

MacKinnon, G. E., and T. G. Waller (Eds.). 1981. *Reading Research: Advances in Theory and Practice*. New York: Academic Press.

MacNeilage, Peter F. 1983. *The Production of Speech*. New York: Springer-Verlag.

Marckwardt, Albert. 1958. *American English*. New York: Oxford University Press.

Mathews, Mitford M. 1966. *Americanisms: A Dictionary of Selected Americanisms on Historical Principles*. Chicago: University of Chicago Press.

Mencken, H. L. 1936. *The American Language*. 4th ed. New York: Knopf.

Mikoś, Michael J., Patricia A. Keating, and Barbara J. Moslin. 1978. "The Perception of Voice Onset Time in Polish." *Journal of the Acoustical Society of America* 63(S1), S19(A).

Miller, George A. (Ed.). 1973. *Communication, Language, and Meaning: Psychological Perspectives*. New York: Basic Books.

Miller, George A., and Patricia E. Nicely. 1955. "An Analysis of Perceptual Confusions Among Some English Consonants." *Journal of the Acoustical Society of America* 27:2.

Moorhouse, A. C. 1953. *The Triumph of the Alphabet: A History of Writing*. New York: Henry Schuman.

Morse, P. A. 1974. "Infant Speech Perception: A Preliminary Model and Review of the Literature." In Schiefelbusch and Lloyd [1974], pp. 19–53.

Morse, P. A., and C. T. Snowdon. 1975. "An Investigation of Categorical Speech Discrimination by Rhesus Monkeys." *Perception and Psychophysics* 17:9–16.

Morton, John, and Donald E. Broadbent. 1967. "Passive versus Active Recognition Models, or, Is Your Homunculus Really Necessary?" In Wathen-Dunn [1967].

Morton, John, and S. Sasanuma. 1984. "Lexical Access in Japanese." In Henderson [1984].

Nash, Walter. 1971. *Our Experience of Language*. London: B. T. Batsford.

O'Brien, Richard J. (Ed.). 1968. *Georgetown University Round Table Selected Papers on Linguistics, 1961–1968*. Washington, D.C.: Georgetown University Press.

O'Connor, J. D. 1973. *Phonetics*. Baltimore: Penguin Books.

Orkin, Mark. 1970. *Speaking Canadian English: An Informal Account of the English Language in Canada*. Toronto: General Publishing.

Oller, D. Kimbrough, and Peter F. MacNeilage. 1983. "Development of Speech Production: Perspectives from Natural and Perturbed Speech." In MacNeilage [1983].

Palmer, John M. 1972. *Anatomy for Speech and Hearing*. 2d ed. New York: Harper & Row.

Pedersen, Helga. 1967. *The Discovery of Language: Linguistic Science in the Nineteenth Century*. Translated by John Webster Spargo. Bloomington: Indiana University Press.

Pike, Kenneth L. 1945. *The Intonation of American English*. Ann Arbor: University of Michigan Press.

Pike, Kenneth L. 1947. *Phonemics: A Technique for Reducing Languages to Writing*. Ann Arbor: University of Michigan Press.

Pisoni, D. B., and J. R. Sawusch. 1975. "Some Stages of Processing in Speech Perception." In Cohen and Nooteboom [1975].

Prator, C. H., Jr. 1957. *Manual of American English Pronunciation*. Rev. ed. New York: Holt, Rinehart & Winston.

Pulgram, Ernest. 1970. "Homo Loquens: An Ethological View." *Lingua* 24:309–342.

Pyles, Thomas, and John Algeo. 1982. *The Origins and Development of the English Language*. 3d ed. New York: Harcourt Brace Jovanovich.

Robbins, Joanne, Hilda Fisher, Eric Blom, and Mark Singer. 1984. "A Comparative Acoustic Study of Normal, Esophageal and Tracheoesophageal Speech." *Journal of Speech and Hearing Disorders* 49:202–210.

Rozin, P., S. Poritsky, and R. Sotsky. 1971. "American

Children with Reading Problems Can Easily Learn to Read English Represented by Chinese Characters." *Science* 171:1264–1267.

Sapir, Edward. 1949. *Language: an Introduction to the Study of Speech*. New York: Harcourt, Brace & World.

Schiefelbusch, Richard L., and Lyle L. Lloyd (Eds.). 1974. *Language Perspectives: Acquisition, Retardation, and Intervention*. Baltimore: University Park Press.

Scholes, Robert J. 1966. *Phonotactic Grammaticality*. The Hague: Mouton.

Schumsky, Donald A. 1977. Personal communication.

Selkirk, Elisabeth O. 1982. "The Syllable." In van der Hulst and Smith [1982].

Shaw, George Bernard. 1963. *On Language*. Edited by Abraham Tauber. New York: Philosophical Library.

Shearer, William M. 1979. *Illustrated Speech Anatomy*. 3d ed. Springfield, Ill.: Thomas.

Shipp, Thomas. 1967. "Frequency, Duration and Perceptual Measures in Relation to Judgements of Alaryngeal Speech Acceptability." *Journal of Speech and Hearing Research* 10:417–427.

Singer, Mark I., and Eric D. Blom. 1980. "An Endoscopic Technique for Restoration of Voice after Laryngectomy." *Annals of Otology, Rhinology and Laryngology* 89(6):529–533.

Singer, Mark I., and Eric D. Blom. 1981. "Selective Myotomy for Voice Restoration after Total Laryngectomy." *Archives of Otolaryngology* 107:670–673.

Singh, Roderick P. 1980. *Anatomy of Hearing and Speech*. New York: Oxford University Press.

Smith, Bonnie E., Bernd Weinberg, Lawrence L. Feth, and Yoshiyuki Horii. 1978. "Vocal Roughness and Jitter Characteristics of Vowels Produced by Esophageal Speakers." *Journal of Speech and Hearing Research* 21(2):240–249.

Stemberger, Joseph P. 1983. *Speech Errors and Theoretical Phonology: A Review*. Bloomington: Indiana University Linguistics Club.

Stetson, Raymond Herbert. 1951. *Motor Phonetics: A Study of Speech Movements in Action*. Amsterdam: North-Holland.

Stevens, Kenneth N. 1972. "The Quantal Nature of Speech: Evidence from Articulatory-Acoustic Data." In David and Denes [1972], pp. 51–66.

Stevens, Kenneth N., and Morris Halle. 1967. "Remarks on Analysis by Synthesis and Distinctive Features." In Wathen-Dunn [1967].

Stewart, John M. 1967. "Tongue Root Position in Akan Vowel Harmony." *Phonetica* 16:185–204.

Studdert-Kennedy, Michael, Alvin M. Liberman, Katherine S. Harris, and Franklin S. Cooper. 1970. "Motor Theory of Speech Perception: A Reply to Lane's Critical Review." *Psychological Review* 77:234–249.

Swisher, Wayne. 1980. "Oral Pressures, Vowel Duration and Acceptability Ratings of Esophageal Speakers." *Journal of Communication Disorders* 13:171–181.

Tartter, V. C., and P. D. Eimas. 1975. "The Role of Auditory Feature Detectors in the Perception of Speech." *Perception and Psychophysics* 18:289–297.

Taylor, Insup, and M. Martin Taylor. 1983. *The Psychology of Reading*. New York: Academic Press.

Twaddell, William Freeman. 1966. *On Defining the Phoneme*. Language Monograph No. 16, March 1935, Linguistic Society of America. Reprint. New York: Kraus Reprint.

Vähäpassi, A. 1977. "The Level of Reading and Writing in Grade 6 of the Comprehensive School Year." Jyväskylä, Institute for Educational Research, Series 88, 1977. Cited by Kyöstiö [1980].

Van den Berg, Janwillem. 1958. "Myoelastic-Aerodynamic Theory of Voice Production." *Journal of Speech and Hearing Research* 1(3):227–243.

van der Hulst, Harry, and Norval Smith. 1982. *The Structure of Phonological Representations*. Part II. Dordrecht, Holland; Cinnaminson, N.J.: Foris.

Van Riper, Charles. 1972. *Speech Correction: Principles and Methods*. 5th ed. Englewood Cliffs, N.J.: Prentice-Hall.

Vennard, William. 1967. *Singing: the Mechanism and the Technic*. Rev. ed. New York: Carl Fischer.

Wang, William S.-Y., and Charles J. Fillmore. 1961. "Intrinsic Cues and Consonant Perception." *Journal of Speech and Hearing Research* 4(2):130–136.

Wathen-Dunn, Weiant (Ed.). 1967. *Models for the Perception of Speech and Visual Form*. Cambridge, Mass.: MIT Press.

Weinberg, Bernd, and Suzanne Bennett. 1971. "A Study of Talker Sex Recognition of Esophageal Voices." *Journal of Speech and Hearing Research* 14:391–395.

Weismer, Gary. 1979. "Sensitivity of Voice-Onset Time (VOT) Measures to Certain Segmental Features in Speech Production." *Journal of Phonetics* 7(2):197–204.

Wise, Claude Merton. 1957. *Applied Phonetics*. Englewood Cliffs, N.J.: Prentice-Hall.

Whorf, Benjamin Lee. 1956. *Language, Thought, and Reality*. Edited by John B. Carroll. Cambridge, Mass.: MIT Press.

Zemlin, Willard R. 1968. *Speech and Hearing Science: Anatomy and Physiology*. Englewood Cliffs, N.J.: Prentice-Hall.

Zlatin, Marsha A. 1974. "Voicing Contrast: Perceptual and Productive Voice Onset Time Characteristics of Adults." *Journal of the Acoustical Society of America* 56:981–994.

Appendix

Phonetic Transcription Exercises

The following exercises are designed to give you practice in phonetic transcription. They may be supplemented with other materials or a laboratory manual.

Phonetic transcription provides the best method, outside of audio recording, of making a record of a speech event. Practice in using the phonetic alphabet will give you an opportunity to learn the conventions that are in use. Further, it will help you to get away from spelling and concentrate on the *sounds* of speech.

Transcription is by no means an exact science. The transcription of speech is based of mutual agreement that two sounds are sufficiently similar in auditory impression that they can be represented with the same symbol. This is a matter of human judgment, which is subject to variation and certainly is tempered by the system of contrasts (phonemics) of one's own native language. Since this judgment is influenced by various factors, and since there is frequently ambiguity in the speech signal, requiring interpretation using nonphonetic information (e.g., meaning), transcription is not something that—with present technology—could be accomplished by machine. It is based in large part on nonmeasurable phenomena.

In a practical sense, what this means is that you may sometimes record what does not exist acoustically and ignore acoustic information that is present. You will make errors based on what you know about English spelling and on what you know about correctness (see Chapter 2). You will find that words spoken out of context have a low degree of intelligibility. Practice is the only method of reducing the errors one makes in transcription.

Since there is considerable diversity in the transcription systems in use, no answer key is given for these exercises (reasons for this diversity are discussed in Chapter 3). The instructor will indicate the appropriate transcriptions. The exercises have been roughly grouped according to sounds, but note that, as a result of dialect differences, these groupings may not always be appropriate.

Exercise 1

THE FRONT VOWELS: /i, ɪ, e, ɛ, æ/

Text reference: Chapter 4.

Transcribe the following words; that is, write them using phonetic symbols. The vowel symbols are listed above; the consonants in these words are all transcribed with symbols that will look familiar to you: /p/ as in pin; /t/ as in top; /k/ as in cough; /b/ as in bad; /d/ as in dog; /g/ as in good; /f/ as in food; /s/ as in sip; /v/ as in vat; /z/ as in zip; /r/ as in run; /l/ as in low; /m/ as in man; /n/ as in no; /h/ as in hat; and /w/ as in wave.

1. heat ____________
2. stack ____________
3. feast ____________
4. hate ____________
5. face ____________
6. sap ____________
7. help ____________
8. hit ____________
9. steak ____________
10. fist ____________
11. trap ____________
12. kept ____________
13. trade ____________
14. bend ____________
15. fast ____________
16. lip ____________
17. fade ____________
18. treat ____________
19. mill ____________
20. pals ____________
21. weep ____________
22. wept ____________
23. sin ____________
24. fat ____________
25. creep ____________
26. left ____________
27. crate ____________
28. hilt ____________
29. feed ____________
30. west ____________
31. weeds ____________
32. still ____________
33. went ____________
34. fame ____________
35. mate ____________
36. fake ____________
37. fits ____________
38. men ____________
39. fell ____________
40. pin ____________

Exercise 2
This exercise is a continuation of Exercise 1.

1. table ______________________
2. tap ______________________
3. kilt ______________________
4. met ______________________
5. beat ______________________
6. grits ______________________
7. mat ______________________
8. mitt ______________________
9. pelt ______________________
10. knell ______________________
11. sane ______________________
12. twit ______________________
13. hail ______________________
14. rim ______________________
15. ham ______________________
16. fin ______________________
17. meet ______________________
18. kindle ______________________
19. candle ______________________
20. kettle ______________________
21. meant ______________________
22. brat ______________________
23. break ______________________
24. smell ______________________
25. faint ______________________
26. safe ______________________
27. end ______________________
28. twin ______________________
29. spat ______________________
30. spit ______________________
31. spent ______________________
32. speak ______________________
33. cats ______________________
34. get ______________________
35. keen ______________________
36. wilt ______________________
37. sand ______________________
38. send ______________________
39. sealed ______________________
40. guild ______________________

Exercise 3

The Back and Central Vowels: /u, ʊ, o, ʌ, ɔ, ɑ, ə, ɚ/
Text reference: Chapter 4.
These exercises continue to use only familiar consonants; some words contain front vowels as well.

1. puts	__________	21. epic	__________
2. bought	__________	22. could	__________
3. foster	__________	23. rude	__________
4. bus	__________	24. faster	__________
5. love	__________	25. lovers	__________
6. mull	__________	26. water	__________
7. hopes	__________	27. cut	__________
8. caught	__________	28. bird	__________
9. float	__________	29. noon	__________
10. cook	__________	30. burn	__________
11. putts	__________	31. boater	__________
12. sew	__________	32. would	__________
13. mood	__________	33. upper	__________
14. kook	__________	34. boots	__________
15. cot	__________	35. haughty	__________
16. fool	__________	36. skipper	__________
17. foot	__________	37. crude	__________
18. fasten	__________	38. fuzz	__________
19. mutter	__________	39. winter	__________
20. pots	__________	40. curse	__________

Exercise 4

This exercise is a continuation of Exercise 3.

1.	hog	________	21.	flaw	________
2.	gruel	________	22.	total	________
3.	swat	________	23.	glow	________
4.	model	________	24.	follow	________
5.	bunt	________	25.	woolen	________
6.	wooden	________	26.	truck	________
7.	solve	________	27.	tunnel	________
8.	socks	________	28.	wrote	________
9.	loose	________	29.	hug	________
10.	crust	________	30.	fault	________
11.	photo	________	31.	stone	________
12.	loan	________	32.	luck	________
13.	Monday	________	33.	boon	________
14.	uncle	________	34.	books	________
15.	flaunt	________	35.	solvent	________
16.	won't	________	36.	mould	________
17.	wonder	________	37.	full	________
18.	vote	________	38.	toll	________
19.	tuck	________	39.	some	________
20.	slower	________	40.	gone	________

Exercise 5

The Diphthongs and /ju/: /a͜i, a͜u, ɔ͜i, ju/
Text reference: Section 4-6

/ju/ is not a diphthong,* but it is often grouped with the diphthongs. This sequence of sounds is so common that we often mistake it for one sound. There is a great deal of variation in the sound of the diphthongs depending on the dialect area and the surrounding consonants; rather than arguing each case, we accept a standard phonemic representation. Also, there is a great variation in the representation of diphthongs; your instructor may prefer a different form. Here are some common transcriptions:

a͜i	aɪ	ay	aj	a^i
a͜u	aʊ	æw	aw	a^u
ɔ͜i	ɔɪ	ɔy	ɔj	$ɔ^i$

While it is common practice to omit the ligature in writing diphthongs (for example, /ai/ rather than /a͜i/), its use is recommended. For example, compare the word "naïve" with the word "knives." The first word has a sequence of vowels in two syllables (/nɑiv/), whereas the latter has a diphthong in one syllable (/na͜ivz/). Consistent use of the ligature thus makes the transcriptions clearer.

1. hives ______
2. foils ______
3. buyer ______
4. fountain ______
5. house ______
6. miners ______
7. foist ______
8. fighter ______
9. bounty ______
10. about ______
11. island ______
12. height ______
13. oust ______
14. glides ______
15. sounder ______
16. mount ______
17. bauxite ______
18. crisis ______
19. precise ______
20. quite ______
21. ewe ______
22. mighty ______
23. eyes ______
24. trounce ______
25. write ______
26. boiler ______
27. dune ______
28. fryer ______
29. friar ______
30. bind ______
31. use ______ or ______
32. indict ______
33. guide ______
34. boys ______
35. joyful ______
36. Cuba ______
37. dyes ______
38. pound ______
39. few ______
40. counter ______

* Or, in the terminology of some, it is a **falling diphthong** rather than a **rising diphthong;** unmodified, the term **diphthong** usually refers only to *rising* diphthongs. See also Section 5-6.1.1.

Exercise 6

This exercise is a continuation of Exercise 5.

1. mighty	______	21. loud	______
2. loyal	______	22. hour	______
3. noisy	______	23. fly	______
4. announce	______	24. impune	______
5. annoy	______	25. turquoise	______
6. tower	______	26. grind	______
7. decoy	______	27. guile	______
8. my	______	28. lined	______
9. royal	______	29. router	______
10. surround	______	30. enjoy	______
11. cue	______	31. purloin	______
12. stymy	______	32. soil	______
13. goiter	______	33. wry	______
14. proud	______	34. howl	______
15. recoil	______	35. coin	______
16. gout	______	36. trousers	______
17. implied	______	37. pointer	______
18. toil	______	38. rely	______
19. scout	______	39. loin	______
20. usual	______	40. blouse	______

Exercise 7
This exercise is a continuation of Exercise 6 but also includes rhotic diphthongs.
Text reference: Section 4-6.1.

1. bard ______
2. bared ______
3. sordid ______
4. pure ______
5. pardon ______
6. wart ______
7. fury ______
8. arid ______
9. boredom ______
10. wear ______
11. word ______
12. weary ______
13. martyr ______
14. sour ______
15. tartan ______
16. beard ______
17. mire ______
18. mayor ______
19. Mary ______
20. hairy ______
21. warden ______
22. lurid ______
23. ardent ______
24. flower ______
25. garter ______
26. scour ______
27. bird ______
28. weird ______
29. purée ______
30. lawyer ______
31. garden ______
32. dreary ______
33. fire ______
34. hard ______
35. hoard ______
36. merry ______
37. rare ______
38. Harry ______
39. iron ______
40. marry ______

Exercise 8

THE CONSONANTS (AND VOWEL REVIEW)

Text reference: Chapter 5.

In the previous exercises, we have used only those consonants whose phonetic symbols look familiar to us: /p, t, k, b, d, g, f, s, v, z, r[1], l, m, n, h, w/. In this exercise, you will have practice in using those consonants whose symbols at first appear unfamiliar. These additional sounds and symbols are:

/θ/ as in thin, thought, ether, Beth
/ð/ as in the, though, either, bathe
/š/ as in ship, issue, sugar, nation (also written /ʃ/)
/ž/ as in vision, leisure (also written /ʒ/)
/ŋ/ as in sing, finger, think
/j/ as in yes, Europe
/ʍ/ as in which, when (only for those dialects that maintain this sound)[2]
/č/ as in church, chip, batch (also written /tʃ/ or /tš/)
/ǰ/ as in judge, jam (also written /dʒ/ or /dž/)

1. judging ____________
2. issue ____________
3. yellow ____________
4. thin ____________
5. ether ____________
6. batches ____________
7. charging ____________
8. push ____________
9. jamb ____________
10. yes ____________
11. shipper ____________
12. lane ____________
13. hutch ____________
14. think ____________
15. badger ____________
16. whine ____________
17. weather ____________
18. whether ____________
19. watch ____________
20. Beth ____________
21. vision ____________
22. chopper ____________
23. charger ____________
24. chamber ____________
25. garage ____________
26. away ____________
27. pleasure ____________
28. thought ____________
29. bashing ____________
30. leisure ____________
31. virgin ____________
32. finger ____________
33. thorough ____________
34. rasping ____________
35. hatchet ____________
36. sinker ____________
37. runner ____________
38. trade ____________
39. mashing ____________
40. manning ____________

[1] See text Section 5-6.2.2 concerning the use of this symbol.

[2] Note: In handwritten work, the symbol /hw/, or the combination /hw/, is less open to misinterpretation than the symbol /ʍ/, which can be mistaken for an ⟨m⟩.

Exercise 9

Practice with Vowels and Consonants

This is a continuation of Exercise 8, giving you practice transcribing English speech sounds.

1. shoving ______
2. zany ______
3. sinned ______
4. sang ______
5. fiend ______
6. bother ______
7. tough ______
8. colonel ______
9. hiccough ______
10. posh ______
11. jaguar ______
12. feather ______
13. bath ______
14. chomps ______
15. ethyl ______
16. hanger ______
17. dizzy ______
18. flutter ______
19. languid ______
20. plumber ______
21. witches ______
22. pneumatic ______
23. wither ______
24. only ______
25. jelly ______
26. chafing ______
27. lanky ______
28. cherries ______
29. perception ______
30. chalet ______
31. lathe ______
32. Cairo ______
33. George ______
34. omission ______
35. shuffle ______
36. raging ______
37. shroud ______
38. warfare ______
39. lithe ______
40. wanted ______

Exercise 10

This is a continuation of Exercise 9.

1. jaunty __________
2. cling __________
3. thunder __________
4. channel __________
5. change __________
6. soldier __________
7. shallow __________
8. whip __________
9. lesion __________
10. thither __________
11. trough __________
12. vivacious __________
13. thatches __________
14. jaundice __________
15. shallop __________
16. fallacious __________
17. inkling __________
18. churches __________
19. witch __________
20. jaw __________
21. judicious __________
22. hitches __________
23. mingle __________
24. when __________
25. awash __________
26. lodge __________
27. chauvinist __________
28. itchy __________
29. vicious __________
30. clutches __________
31. wither __________
32. then __________
33. shingles __________
34. thrive __________
35. worship __________
36. fishing __________
37. vexacious __________
38. jungle __________
39. chalice __________
40. though __________

Exercise 11

ACCOMMODATION AND REGISTER

Transcribe these words, paying attention to accommodation. In many cases, it would be useful to transcribe them twice, once in the citation form and once in the colloquial pronunciation. Depending upon dialect, there may or may not be a difference.

Text reference: Chapter 6.

WORD	CITATION FORM	COLLOQUIAL PRONUNCIATION
1. phone booth	______	______
2. nuclear	______	______
3. iron	______	______
4. menstruate	______	______
5. athlete	______	______
6. film	______	______
7. manufacture	______	______
8. environment	______	______
9. Wednesday	______	______
10. February	______	______
11. something	______	______
12. warmth	______	______
13. duel	______	______
14. arduous	______	______
15. usually	______	______
16. apron	______	______
17. violent	______	______
18. finger	______	______
19. broadcasting	______	______
20. comfort	______	______
21. schedule	______	______
22. symphony	______	______
23. violet	______	______

24. incomplete ______ ______
25. broccoli ______ ______
26. picture ______ ______
27. mature ______ ______
28. interest ______ ______
29. interesting ______ ______
30. diaper ______ ______
31. angry ______ ______
32. anxious ______ ______
33. diamond ______ ______
34. bury ______ ______
35. temperature ______ ______
36. library ______ ______
37. unconstitutional ______ ______
38. probably ______ ______
39. pneumonia ______ ______
40. unconscious ______ ______
41. garage ______ ______
42. turquoise ______ ______
43. police ______ ______
44. nutcracker ______ ______
45. want to ______ ______
46. should have ______ ______
47. united ______ ______
48. button ______ ______
49. cotton ______ ______
50. grandma ______ ______

Exercise 12
Transcribe these words as you pronounce them. Then look them up in an etymological dictionary to see what changes they have undergone. (The process may depend upon the dialect, so for some words you may come up empty-handed.) Indicate the process where applicable. For example, under no. 12, *decal*, you would transcribe your pronunciation, which for most Americans has the stress on the first syllable, with the first-syllable vowel being /i/. Looking the word up, you will discover it is a clipped (abbreviated) form of the word *decalcomania*, having the stress on the second syllable and a schwa (/ə/) in the first syllable. So the clipped word has undergone a stress shift from the second to the first syllable, with a resultant change in vowel quality.
Text reference: Chapter 6.

WORD	PRONUNCIATION	EARLIER PRONUNCIATION, PROCESS, ETC.
1. ask	______	______
2. breakfast	______	______
3. apron	______	______
4. illogical	______	______
5. Hallowe'en	______	______
6. halfpenny	______	______
7. lord	______	______
8. gunwale	______	______
9. forecastle	______	______
10. starboard	______	______
11. cupboard	______	______
12. decal	______	______
13. handkerchief	______	______
14. irrelevant	______	______
15. colonel	______	______
16. Greenwich	______	______
17. assimilation	______	______
18. staffs	______	______
19. brother	______	______
20. purple	______	______

21. father ____________________ ____________________
22. burn ____________________ ____________________
23. thunder ____________________ ____________________
24. impotent ____________________ ____________________
25. heaven ____________________ ____________________
26. knife ____________________ ____________________
27. vehicle ____________________ ____________________
28. article ____________________ ____________________
29. orangutan ____________________ ____________________
30. glamor ____________________ ____________________
31. gnat ____________________ ____________________
32. island ____________________ ____________________
33. debt ____________________ ____________________
34. through ____________________ ____________________
35. of ____________________ ____________________
36. skunk ____________________ ____________________
37. ago ____________________ ____________________
38. male ____________________ ____________________
39. single ____________________ ____________________
40. marble ____________________ ____________________

Exercise 13

STRESS

Transcribe these words; and mark the stress as indicated in Section 7-2.

1. omission __________
2. deception __________
3. perforate __________
4. perimeter __________
5. periscope __________
6. heyday __________
7. watchdog __________
8. renegade __________
9. windshield __________
10. Olympic __________
11. Iceland __________
12. Icelandic __________
13. mobile home __________
14. Roman __________
15. romantic __________
16. thirty __________
17. thirteen __________
18. engineer __________
19. redundant __________
20. transpose __________
21. obscene __________
22. obscenity __________
23. oceanography __________
24. trajectory __________
25. photoelectric __________
26. personnel __________
27. repetition __________
28. repetitive __________
29. scarecrow __________
30. festivity __________

Exercise 14
Transcribe, marking stress, as in Exercise 13.

1. corollary ____________
2. worship ____________
3. warship ____________
4. engine ____________
5. regime ____________
6. regiment ____________
7. important ____________
8. impotent ____________
9. personal ____________
10. personality ____________
11. idol ____________
12. idolatry ____________
13. solution ____________
14. revolve ____________
15. revolution ____________
16. dissolve ____________
17. dissolution ____________
18. household ____________
19. doghouse ____________
20. remind ____________
21. reminiscent ____________
22. forty ____________
23. fourteen ____________
24. populace ____________
25. population ____________
26. fingernail ____________
27. nail file ____________
28. refrigerator ____________
29. caprice ____________
30. model ____________
31. module ____________
32. modulation ____________
33. sacrosanct ____________
34. sanctimonious ____________
35. parsimony ____________
36. infantile ____________
37. eavesdrop ____________
38. sidestep ____________
39. backside ____________
40. underdog ____________

Exercise 15

BROAD AND NARROW TRANSCRIPTION
Text reference: Chapter 8.
After studying Chapters 6 and 8, particularly Section 8-9, transcribe each of the following words twice. First, make a **broad**, or **phonemic**, transcription of each word (including stress), as has been done in the previous exercises. Then make a **narrow** transcription of the same words, including as much phonetic detail as possible. There is no *one* correct answer to the narrow transcriptions, since more or less detail could be included, and there is much dialect variation in the pronunciation of these words:

Samples:

pool	/pul/	[pʰuəɫ]
biting	/báɪ̯tìŋ/	[bɑ́ɪ̯əɾìŋ], [bə́ɪ̯tìŋ], etc. (many varieties of diphthong, intervocalic /t/, and word-final -ing, depending on dialect)
heard	/hərd/	[hɚd̚]
1. phonetics	______	______
2. button	______	______
3. knots	______	______
4. trader	______	______
5. loudness	______	______
6. dress shop	______	______
7. interesting	______	______
8. whatnot	______	______
9. battleground	______	______
10. police	______	______
11. supposing	______	______
12. vulture	______	______
13. discus	______	______
14. cows	______	______
15. house	______	______
16. training	______	______
17. united	______	______
18. lowly	______	______

19. soldier ______ ______
20. kept ______ ______
21. coped ______ ______
22. incapable ______ ______
23. children ______ ______
24. renting ______ ______
25. svelte ______ ______
26. company ______ ______
27. electrician ______ ______
28. hinting ______ ______
29. parade ______ ______
30. during ______ ______

Exercise 16

Transcribe once in broad transcription and once in narrow transcription, as in Exercise 15.

1. curtain ____________ ____________
2. cutlery ____________ ____________
3. total ____________ ____________
4. usual ____________ ____________
5. kill ____________ ____________
6. coal ____________ ____________
7. lots ____________ ____________
8. list ____________ ____________
9. pleased ____________ ____________
10. bottle ____________ ____________
11. simple ____________ ____________
12. tasks ____________ ____________
13. tags ____________ ____________
14. culprit ____________ ____________
15. catalogue ____________ ____________
16. tickle ____________ ____________
17. toggle ____________ ____________
18. barter ____________ ____________
19. puddle ____________ ____________
20. potato ____________ ____________
21. dual ____________ ____________
22. king ____________ ____________
23. collar ____________ ____________
24. winter ____________ ____________
25. flatter ____________ ____________

26. spangle ______ ______
27. tingle ______ ______
28. adamant ______ ______
29. residual ______ ______
30. roofs ______ ______
31. biting ______ ______
32. biding ______ ______
33. writer ______ ______
34. rider ______ ______
35. picture ______ ______

Glossary

Most of the important terms used in this book, including some words outside phonetic science, are given brief definitions here. Many of these terms are defined more fully in the text; you may use the index to find such definitions as well as to locate explanations of words not listed in the glossary.

abduct (vb): To separate, move apart; said of the vocal folds. N: **abduction.** Ant: **adduct.**

accessory respiratory muscles: Muscles (other than the *diaphragm* and intercostals) that are said to have a role or potential role in respiration.

accommodation (n): The process of modifying the *articulation* of *segments* as a function of the other segments in the phonetic environment.

adduct (vb): To bring together, approximate; said of the vocal folds. N: **adduction.** Ant: **abduct.**

affricate (n): A single sound phonemically, analyzable phonetically as the sequence of a plosive followed immediately by a *homorganic fricative*.

airstream mechanisms (n): The various mechanisms by which a moving column of air, or a static pressure of air, is created to power speech.

allophone (n): A variant of a *phoneme;* a *conditioned variant*.

alphabetic writing: (n): In the pure form, writing in which there is a one-to-one correspondence between **phonemes** and letters.

alveolar (adj): Referring to the *alveolar ridge* as a *place of articulation*. Combining form: **alveo-.** (Also, referring to the **alveoli** of the lungs, the place where gas exchange takes place, as in **alveolar duct** and **alveolar sac.**)

alveolar ridge (n): The ridge just behind the upper front teeth, in front of the *palate*.

ambisyllabic (adj): Belonging to two syllables, as the [n] of "running."

amplitude (n): With respect to sound waves, the amount of energy present; perceived essentially as loudness, although complex interactions complicate perception. Illustrated graphically by the extent of deflection from the baseline.

anticipatory (adj): Of *accommodation*, an effect modifying a sound in anticipation of a following sound; right-to-left.

aperiodic (adj): Not *periodic;* that is, not having a regular cycle.

apex (n): The tip of the tongue. Adj: **apical.** Combining form: **apico-.**

aphasia (n): Loss of the ability to use (spoken) language. Adj: **aphasic.**

approximant (n): A class of speech sounds characterized by close proximity, but not contact, of the *articulators.*

arresting (adj): Of a consonant or *cluster,* that which finishes a syllable or word.

articulation (n): The movement of the speech organs in the production of speech; the production of speech. Vb: **articulate:** to move or position the speech organs so as to produce a speech sound.

articulator (n): An *organ of speech,* usually supraglottal, that is moved or approximated in speech.

arytenoid cartilages (n): The cartilages to which the posterior ends of the vocal folds are attached. They are mobile like levers, and they position and tense the vocal folds.

aspiration (n): The *egressive* puff of air that may accompany plosive *release.* Adj: **aspirated.**

assimilation (n): *Accommodation* marked by a crossing of *phoneme* boundaries. Also, *accommodation* in general.

ballistic movement (n): A rapid, loose movement of an *articulator,* generally the tongue *blade,* as in *flap articulation.*

bar-d (n): The name of the symbol [ð].

Bernoulli principle (n): The physical law by which there is a pressure drop when a fluid (gas or liquid) flows through a constriction.

bilabial (adj): Involving both lips.

blade (n): That part of the tongue, between the *apex* and the front, that lies below the *alveolar ridge* at rest. Adj: **laminal.**

bound (adj): Of a *morpheme,* one that must be attached to another morpheme to form a word. For example, *-ty* as in *fifty, sixty,* etc.

brackets (n): The symbols [ ] that enclose a *narrow* or *phonetic transcription.*

breathy voice (n): Phonation that is accompanied by a constant flow of air through the *glottis* due to the constantly open state of the glottis.

broad (adj): Of a transcription, one that records only *phonemic* distinctions; not detailed.

bunched (adj): Of the tongue, retracted and knotted, causing constriction in the pharynx and at the *velar* and/or *palatal* regions; *rhotic.*

cardinal (adj): Of vowels, those at the extremities of the vowel quadrangle that are used as reference points in classifying other vowels; usually /i, e, ɛ, æ, u, o, ɔ, ɑ/, but more extreme in their articulation than their English counterparts.

citation form (n): The self-conscious pronunciation of a word in isolation; often hypercorrect and unnatural.

cleft lip (n): A congenital cleft or split in the upper lip; harelip.

cleft palate (n): A congenital cleft or split in the palate.

click (n): A plosive-type speech sound made with the *ingressive* velaric *airstream mechanism.*

close (adj): Of a vowel, high.

closed (adj): Of a syllable, having a consonant or consonant *cluster* in final position.

closing phase (n): That phase of plosive *articulation* during which the *articulators* are moving toward *occlusion.*

closure phase (n): That phase of plosive *articulation* during which the *articulators* are blocking air movement; *occlusion.*

cluster (n): A group of consonants in the same syllable without intervening vowels.

coarticulation (n): The process or action of articulating more than one *segment* or features of more than one segment at one time, usually as a result of *accommodation.* It may also refer to the production of segments having two primary places of *articulation.* Vb: **coarticulate.**

coda (n): Those *segments* following the *nucleus* of a syllable.

codification (n): The process of writing down in authoritative sources aspects of the *grammar* of a language. Codification is often mistaken for the (existence of) grammar itself. Vb: **codify.**

complementary distribution (n): Sounds are in complementary distribution if they do not occupy the same *environment;* normally the mark of *allophones.*

conditioned variant (n): A variant or *allophone* whose characteristics are a product of the environment.

cycle (n): A dimensionless unit indicating one full sound wave.

dental (adj): Referring to an *articulation* involving the teeth, notably the upper incisors. N: a *segment* whose *articulation* involves the upper front teeth.

descriptive grammar (n): *Grammar,* in the sense of a written treatise about grammar, which attempts to describe, rather than prescribe, grammatical forms as they are used.

diachronic (adj): Historical in perspective; used with respect to language change or historical language study.

diacritic (n): A written mark used in conjunction with a letter or syllabic character to indicate the *quality* of the sound represented; an "accent." Adj: **diacritical.**

dialect (n): An identifiable regional or social variant form of language, characterized by its vocabulary, pronunciation, morphology, and syntax. *All* forms of language are dialects; some have prestige, whereas others do not.

diaphragm (n): The muscular band separating the chest cavity from the abdominal cavity; it plays a role in respiration and therefore in speech.

digraph (n): A combination of two letters used to represent one sound, e.g., ⟨sh⟩ in English.

dilation (n): Distant vowel *accommodation.*

diphthong (n): A single vowel *nucleus* that changes *quality* or *timbre* within a syllable.

dorsum (n): The back and front of the tongue; the surface of the main body of the tongue. Adj: **dorsal.**

doublet (n): A pair of words that are different in the contemporary language but that have the same etymological source; these are often cited as examples of historical sound change. English examples include *ditch* and *dike, poison* and *potion, fragile* and *frail, shirt* and *skirt.*

dynamic range (n): The range of intensity of sound.

egressive (adj): Outgoing.

elision (n): The loss, either historically or as a contemporary variation, of a *segment* or segments. Vb: **elide.**

environment (n): The *segments* and *suprasegmentals* in the vicinity of the segment under discussion.

epenthesis (n): The insertion of a sound into a word, either *diachronically* or as a *synchronic* variation.

epiglottis (n): A structure in the larynx that covers the entrance to the trachea during swallowing; it has no role in speech.

etymology (n): The study of the history of individual words.

$\mathbf{F_0}$ (n): Read "F-zero"; an abbreviation for *fundamental frequency.*

flap (n): A consonant produced with a very brief *occlusion,* normally *apicoalveolar.* May have an /r/-like *quality,* as in [ř], or not, as in [ɾ]. Note: In the IPA, the symbol [r] represents a *flap,* but since this symbol is often used to represent standard American /ɹ/, the symbol [ř] is used to represent the flapped r-sound unambiguously.

formant (n): A band of resonant energy that, in combination with several others, acoustically characterizes a particular vowel sound.

Fourier's theorem (n): A theorem—*not* a theory—that states that any complex wave is the sum of simple sinusoids.

free (adj): Of a *morpheme,* free to stand on its own as a word.

free variation (n): The situation in which *allophones* are not determined by phonological rule but may be selected by the speaker.

frequency (n): The number of times per second a sound wave is repeated; measured in *hertz* (*Hz*).

fricative (n): A class of consonants in which air is forced through a constriction, producing a noisy turbulence.

fundamental frequency (F_0) (n): In speech, the frequency of vocal fold vibration (as opposed to the resonant frequencies); also, the basic frequency of a vibrating object or sound, as opposed to its *harmonics*.

glide (n): A class of speech sounds that are vowel-like in nature but must precede or follow a vowel to make a syllable; characterized by approximation of the *articulators* as for high vowels and rapid movement of the articulators to or from that position.

glossal (adj): Having to do with the tongue.

glossectomee (n): An individual who has undergone *glossectomy*.

glossectomy (n): Surgical removal of the tongue.

glottal (adj): Having to do with the *glottis* or with the *larynx* (as in **supraglottal,** 'above the larynx,' and **subglottal,** 'below the larynx').

glottal stop (n): The sound [ʔ], produced with an abrupt closure of the *glottis*.

glottalized (adj): Produced with the glottalic *airstream mechanism*.

glottis (n): The space between the vocal folds.

grammar (n): The *rules* and *lexicon* of a language taken together; the knowledge of them possessed by a speaker of that language. Also, an attempt to represent that knowledge, as in a book.

grooved (adj): Of a *fricative*, produced with the tongue *blade* cupped.

hachek (n): The *diacritic* [ˇ], used to represent *alveopalatals*.

haplology (n): The process, either *diachronic* or *synchronic*, of dropping one of two identical or similar syllables in sequence.

harmonics (n): Multiples of the *fundamental frequency;* called *overtones* in music.

hertz (Hz) (n): Unit of frequency; 1 Hz is one cycle per second.

hesitation noise (n): A noise produced as a speaker hesitates in speaking; English hesitation noises are often written as "er," "um," "uh," etc.

homophone (n): A word whose pronunciation is coincidentally like another's; not dependent upon spelling. Such words are said to be **homophonous;** the phenomenon is called **homophony.**

homorganic (adj): Of two speech sounds, having the same *place of articulation*.

hypernasality (n): Condition in which speech is produced with too much nasality; for functional or organic reasons the *velum* is lowered (or there is a cleft in the *palate*).

hyponasality (n): Condition in which speech is produced with too little nasality.

ingressive (adj): Ingoing.

intelligibility (n): The degree to which speech is understood by the listener; a lack of intelligibility may be due to factors of *dialect*, speech dysfunction, foreign accent, background noise, quality of transmission, etc. *Segments* differ in the degree to which they are inherently intelligible.

interdental (adj): Between the teeth; said of the tongue in *articulation*.

intonation (n): Patterns of changes in the *fundamental frequency* of the voice, related to the syntactic structure of the sentence or discourse, that convey meaning.

intonation language (n): A language that uses *intonation* to convey meaning, as opposed to a *tone language*.

intraoral air pressure (n): The air pressure within the oral cavity.

labial (adj): Having to do with the lips. Combining form: **labio-**. Vb: **labialize.** Adj: **labialized.**

laminal (adj): Having to do with the *blade* of the tongue. Combining form: **lamino-**.

laryngectomee (n): A person who has undergone *laryngectomy*.

laryngectomy (n): Surgical removal of the *larynx* and associated structures.

laryngopharynx (n): The lower part of the pharynx, just above the *larynx*.

larynx (n): A cartilaginous structure at the top of the *trachea*, below the pharynx, that contains the vocal folds.

length (n): Said of a speech sound; a description of its duration, not its *timbre*.

lexicon (n): The vocabulary or dictionary that a speaker has in his head.

liaison (n): A type of *sandhi* occurring in French in which word-final consonants are pronounced only when the following word begins with a vowel and is part of the same phrase. The term is applied to similar sandhi phenomena in other languages, such as occur in some English r-less dialects.

lingual (adj): Of the tongue.

linguistic (adj): Of language.

liquid (n and adj): A class of speech sounds, including [l] and [ɹ], that are characterized by approximation of the *articulators* and a vowel-like quality.

locus (n): The hypothetical starting point of the *formant* transitions that acoustically characterize plosive consonants. Pl: **loci.**

long (adj): Said of a speech sound; a description of its duration, not its *timbre*.

minimal pair (n): A pair of words differing phonetically by one *segment* only (although their spelling may be different in more ways); the presence of such a pair confirms the phonemic status of the segments in question. Examples pat/bat, pare/bear.

morpheme (n): The minimal linguistic unit to have meaning; *unhelpfully* contains four morphemes; *cats* contains two morphemes. Some morphemes, such as *cat*, can stand alone as words and are thus *free*. Other morphemes, such as -s and *un-*, must be attached to words and are thus *bound* morphemes.

morphophonemic (adj): Referring to a *morpheme* whose pronunciation may vary to the extent of crossing phonemic boundaries. For example, *reduce* and *reduction* contain the same stem *reduc-*, although its pronunciation is different in the two words as a result of a morphophonemic alternation.

narrow (adj): Said of transcription; one that is very detailed; one that records subphonemic differences.

nasalized vowel (n): A vowel produced with a lowered or partially lowered velum.

natural frequency, pitch (n): The normal or relaxed frequency of vocal fold vibration.

neutralization (n): The phonological process by which a phonemic contrast is eliminated, either in a particular environment or as a historical change. Vb: **neutralize.**

noncontiguous accommodation (n): *Accommodation* in which the influenced *segment* is separated by at least one segment from the influencing segment. Usually the effect can be seen as present but not significant in the intervening segment(s).

non-nasal stop (n): Plosive. (See **stop.**)

nucleus (n): Of a syllable, either the vowel or, if there is no vowel, the most sonorant segment in the syllable.

occlusion (n): The phase of plosive production during which the airstream is completely blocked.

off-glide (n): A *transitional articulation* at the end of a given *segment;* for example, vowels before [l] in English generally have off-glides, as in "pool."

organs of speech (n): The organs and anatomical structures used in speech production, all of which have non-speech functions.

palatal (adj): Of the *palate*. N: A speech sound articulated with the tongue arched in the region of the palate.

palate (n): The bony part of the roof of the mouth between the *alveolar ridge* and the *velum*.

period (n): The time taken to complete one cycle; said of wave phenomena such as sound waves. Adj: **periodic:** Having a constant or regular period.

phone (n): *Segment.*

phoneme (n): Contrastive unit of sound, whose precise phonetic shape may vary.

phonemic transcription (n): A *broad* transcription.

phonetic transcription (n): A *narrow* (detailed) transcription.

phonology (n): The branch of linguistic science that deals with the systematic *rule-governed* nature of sound systems.

phonotactics (n): The study of the groupings of *segments* permitted within the syllable or word.

place of articulation (n): In the classification of consonants, the position of the primary *articulator;* for example, if the tongue touches or approximates the *palate,* the place of articulation is *palatal.*

prescriptive grammar (n): Grammar in the traditional sense; that is, a set of statements of what is considered right or wrong in linguistic usage; contrasted with *descriptive grammar.*

prestige dialect (n): The *dialect* having the greatest prestige or social acceptance; in *prescriptive grammar,* the one dialect that is "correct."

pretonic (adj): Before the *stress* or at the beginning of the stressed syllable.

prominence (n): All the phonetic phenomena together that serve to make some *segments* or groups of segments (syllables or words) stand out from others. If it occurs at the level of the word, it is called **stress;** if it occurs at the level of the phrase, it is called **phrasal stress;** if it occurs at the level of the sentence, it is called **emphasis.**

propagate (vb): Of waves, to travel or advance through a medium. N: **propagation.**

pulmonic (adj): With respect to the lungs.

pure (adj): Of vowels, another term for monophthong, in contrast to *diphthong.*

quality (n): Of vowels, the *timbre.*

quasi-periodic (adj): Nearly *periodic.*

r-colored (adj): Of vowels, having a *rhotic* or r-like quality.

reduced (adj): Of a vowel, having a realization that is nearer a neutral vowel (schwa). Vb: **reduce.** N: **reduction.**

regressive (adj): Of *accommodation,* affecting a preceding sound.

release (n): Of a plosive, the phase during which the *articulators* open again after *occlusion.*

releasing (adj): Of a consonant or *cluster,* that which begins a syllable or word.

retroflexion (n): *Articulation* in which the tongue is bent back on itself so that the tip contacts the *palate;* an *apicopalatal* articulation.

rhotic (adj): Having an r-like *timbre.*

romanize (vb): To transliterate from another script to the Roman alphabet (i.e., the alphabet as used in English and other Western European languages).

rounded (adj): Of a speech *segment, articulated* with the lips rounded (perhaps protruded as well).

rule (n): An explicit statement of the operation of some aspect of language. NOT a statement of what is "correct" in the opinion of some person, but a statement of the linguistic knowledge of an individual or of a speech community. Rules taken all together form the *grammar* of a language.

rule-governed (adj): Said of language; a statement of the fact that language is not a random collection of words but follows rigid structure. Even language that is considered substandard is *rule-governed,* in that it has structure (as opposed to randomness).

sandhi (n): Literally, juncture phenomena; *accommodation* or other combinatory phenomena that cross word boundaries.

segment (n): Any individual speech sound without a judgment as to its phonemic status; a *phone.*

semivowel (n): *Voiced glide.*

slash (n): The marks / /, more properly called *virgules,* that enclose a *broad* or *phonemic transcription.*

source-filter theory of speech production (n): A theory of speech production that emphasizes the *glottal* source of sound and the filtering function of the supraglottal cavities.

spectrograph (n): A device that analyzes a complex sound into its component frequencies and displays them graphically as a function of time; such a display is called a **spectrogram.**

speech (n): The spoken manifestation of language.

speech community (n): A group of people speaking the same language and interacting verbally with one another.

speech error (n): An error or "slip of the tongue" in speech: a difference between the speaker's intention and his linguistic performance. Speech errors at the phonetic or phonological level (as opposed to those on a morphological or semantic level) are studied for what they reveal about the speech planning process and about the psychological reality of phonological units.

speech organs. See *organs of speech.*

speed of propagation (n): Of a wave, the speed at which the wave front *propagates* (advances) through a medium.

spelling pronunciation (n): A pronunciation influenced by the spelling, such as the North American pronunciation of "ate."

spread (adj): Of a *segment,* pronounced with the lips spread at the corners, as opposed to *rounded.*

standard dialect (n): The *prestige dialect.*

standing wave (n): A situation in which multiple reflections of a wave are self-reinforcing; a special case situation that results in resonance.

stoma (n): A surgically produced opening in the body; *laryngectomees* breathe through a stoma in the front of the neck connected directly to the *trachea.*

stop (n): An older term for any speech sound produced with complete oral blockage; in this terminology, an *oral stop* is what we have called a **plosive;** a *nasal stop* is what we have called a **nasal.**

stress (n): Prominence given to a syllable or word, manifested as increased loudness or distinctiveness and reduced *accommodation.*

suprasegmental (n): Those aspects of the phonetic quality of speech that are not divided into segments, such as *intonation* and *stress.*

syllabary (n): A group of symbols representing syllables of a spoken language and used to write that language, e.g., the Japanese katakana and hiragana.

synchronic (adj): Literally, without reference to time; contemporary. A synchronic analysis of language looks at the contemporary language and is not concerned with historical development. Ant: **diachronic.**

timbre (n): The *quality* of sound of a *segment;* pronounced "tamber."

tone (n): Phonemic use of the fundamental frequency of the voice to distinguish words; not to be confused with *intonation.* A language that uses tone is called a *tone language.*

trachea (n): The windpipe; the tube connecting the *larynx* with the bronchi and ultimately with the lungs.

tracheoesophageal puncture (n): A surgical puncture connecting the trachea and esophagus. It is sometimes made in *laryngectomees.* Usually in conjunction with a prosthetic device, it permits exhaled lung air to enter the esophagus for the production of esophageal speech.

transitional (adj): Said of a speech sound that is not considered a *phoneme* but that is produced as the *articulators* move from one phoneme to the next; an intrusive sound.

trill (n): A *segment* produced by making an *articulator* vibrate aerodynamically.

umlaut (n): *1.* A form of vowel *accommodation* peculiar to the Germanic family of languages, including English. *2.* A *diacritic* used in the phonetic alphabet (and in German) to indicate vowel *timbre*.

utterance (n): Something said, a meaningful realization of *linguistic* competence; a neutral term implying no *prescriptive* judgment as to whether what was said is a "correct" sentence or word.

uvula (n): The small pendulous fold of tissue attached to the back of the *velum*. Adj: **uvular.**

velum (n): The muscular part of the roof of the mouth, behind the *palate*, that acts as a valve between the pharynx and the nasal passages. Adj: **velar** (in reference to the tongue position in relation to the velum); **velic** (in reference to the movement or position of the velum).

Venturi effect (n): Same as the Bernoulli principle.

virgule (n): The *slash* mark: /.

vocalic (adj): Of vowels. Not to be confused with **vocal.**

voice (n): The sound produced by the vocal folds; a *voice disorder* is a disorder of the vocal folds.

voice onset time (VOT) (n): The difference in time between the release of a plosive and the onset (start) of voicing.

voiced (adj): Of a *segment*, produced with vocal fold vibration.

voiceless (adj): Of a *segment*, produced without vocal fold vibration.

Subject index

Note: "F" following a page number indicates a figure or figure legend, "N" indicates a footnote. Issues relating to disorders of speech, hearing, and language have been grouped under the heading *Communication disorders.*

Index of languages and dialects

Dialects of English can be found under the heading *English*, but *English* has not been indexed, as references to it can be found on most pages of the book. For the same reason, not all references to *American English* have been indexed, although you will find entries for specific dialects of American English.